The Charities of Rural England
1480–1660

by the same author

THE DEVELOPMENT OF RELIGIOUS TOLERATION
IN ENGLAND

1 *From the beginning of the English Reformation
   to the death of Queen Elizabeth I*

2 *From the Accession of James I to the Convention
   of the Long Parliament, 1603–1640*

3 *From the Convention of the Long Parliament
   to the Reformation, 1640–1660*

4 *Attainment of the Theory and Accommodations
   in Thought and Institutions, 1640–1660*

PHILANTHROPY IN ENGLAND, 1480–1660
THE CHARITIES OF LONDON, 1480–1660

The Charities of Rural England
1480–1660

THE ASPIRATIONS AND THE ACHIEVEMENTS
OF THE RURAL SOCIETY

BY

W. K. JORDAN
Professor of History, Harvard University

GREENWOOD PRESS, PUBLISHERS
WESTPORT, CONNECTICUT

Library of Congress Cataloging in Publication Data

Jordon, Wilbur Kitchener, 1902-
    The charities of rural England, 1480-1660.

    Reprint of the 1961 ed. published by G. Allen &
Unwin, London.
    Bibliography: p.
    Includes index.
    1. Charities--Great Britain--History. 2. Great
Britain--Rural conditions. I. Title.
[HV245.J58 1978]   360'.941   78-1390
ISBN 0-313-20304-0

Reprinted with the permission of George Allen & Unwin, Ltd.

Reprinted in 1978 by Greenwood Press, Inc.
51 Riverside Avenue, Westport, CT. 06880

Printed in the United States of America

10 9 8 7 6 5 4 3 2 1

For E. J. G.

PREFACE

This volume concludes a study published in three volumes. The investigation on which this work rests was confined to a representative group of ten English counties: Bristol, Buckinghamshire, Hampshire, Kent, Lancashire, Middlesex (London), Norfolk, Somerset, Worcestershire, and Yorkshire. An effort was made to record all the living gifts and the bequests to charity made in these counties in the course of the long interval extending from the close of the Middle Ages to the restoration of the monarchy in 1660. The ten counties selected comprised something like a third of the land mass, a third of the population, and certainly as much as half the wealth of the realm in our period. We have been especially concerned with tracing out the shifting pattern of men's aspirations in the long period under study, in describing the process by which the largely religious interests of mankind yielded to the mounting requirements of a society which had become secular even when it spoke in terms of older symbols.

The speed, the momentum, of this process of change varied greatly from region to region, from class to class, and, above all, as between rural men and their urban counterparts. But a great social revolution was under way, which this study seeks to document, at least in certain of its larger outlines. We are dealing with an age in which the intervention of the state in the process of social change was at once restrained and almost invariably conservative when its power or its funds were applied in any area of the society. But we are also dealing with an age when men came to possess a vision of their society as they wished it to be, when with a swift and a disciplined outpouring of charitable funds they undertook to create and to order the institutions of a new society with their own substance. Never, it seems safe to say, have new and bold social conceptions been attained quite so quickly or quite so completely by private men. The new and the socially formidable legal device which is the charitable trust was the principal instrumentality with which dedicated and generous men were to build a society which conformed with their aspirations for their own age and for ages still to come.

The first volume of this study, published in 1959 under the title *Philanthropy in England, 1480–1660*, was an essay setting out the conclusions of the entire work and presenting rather elaborate statistical evidence drawn from the ten counties on which it is based. In this olume, too, may be found an extended discussion of the method employed, of the numerous conventions adopted for the entire work, of the statistical assumptions which had on occasion to be taken, and an account of the conclusions which is national rather than regional in its treatment.

The second volume, published in 1960 under the title *The Charities of London, 1480–1660*, was concerned with the immensely important—it is quite accurate to say the dominant—role of London in bringing about a great metamorphosis of social institutions in the England of the early modern era. Not only was London merchant wealth vast, it was also liquid, it was extremely generous, and it was effectively disciplined to ends which her donors held steadily in view. Equally important is the fact that London's concern with social progress and with the enlargement of the ambit of opportunity was in no sense parochial. Her generosity encompassed the needs of the whole of the realm and was in most regions to make decisively important contributions to the process of social change.

This volume deals with the charitable contributions of three predominantly rural counties, Buckinghamshire, Norfolk, and Yorkshire, selected principally because of the historical and geographical diversity which they exhibit and because they yielded to the process of social change in our age with quite differing rates of momentum. Taken together, it may well be held that they represent a fair cross-section of the rural England of the Tudor and Stuart periods.

It is not proposed to deal at full length with all the remaining six counties. Certain of the counties are, however, especially interesting or important, and these will be treated in separate monographs. Thus Bristol and Somerset together offer a most revealing contrast between a lively and aggressive urban complex seated next a prosperous but conservative rural region. These counties have been dealt with in a volume entitled, *The Forming of the Charitable Institutions of the West of England* published in 1960 under the auspices of the American Philosophical Society. The rich and mature county of Kent, greatly influenced by London wealth and aspirations, has been treated in a monograph entitled, *Social Institutions in Kent, 1480–1660*, published by the Kent Archaeological Society in 1961 as Volume 75 of *Archaeologia Cantiana*. Lancashire stands quite apart from all the counties examined in several important respects, and our study of its social and cultural development will be published shortly under the imprint of the Chetham Society.

We should conclude these prefatory comments with brief notes on certain of the conventions employed in the whole study of which this volume is part, though the interested reader may wish to refer to the fuller treatment of these matters to be found in the first volume.[1]

[1] Jordan, W. K., *Philanthropy in England, 1480–1660* (L., 1959), 22–53.

Most important, perhaps, is the fact that our data have not been adjusted to the price changes which occurred over a long historical era. In the first volume of this work we have dealt at some length with this matter, explaining that no reliable price index exists and suggesting that for a number of reasons it is unlikely that one can ever be assembled. To this whole interesting and important question we hope at a future time to lend some attention, particularly since in the research on which this study is based we have collected a considerable store of regional price data. In general, it may be said that we are dealing with an era in which there was a fairly steady erosion of purchasing power under way, though there seems reason to doubt that the rise in prices was so dramatic as has sometimes been supposed. This is particularly true for purposes of our study, since we are principally concerned with what might be described as 'the curve of subsistence' over our period. Though there were pronounced regional differences, donors establishing endowments for household relief between 1480 and 1560 assumed (in average terms) that about £1 11s 3d p.a. was sufficient to keep an unemployed or unemployable human being alive, while over the next century this average figure had risen to about £2 12s 9d p.a. This is to say that responsible and humane men of the age thought it took somewhat less than twice as much in the second half of our period to discharge the social conscience as in the first, and this may well be the particular element in the rising price curve with which we are principally concerned. The standards of survival for this age were very low, and informed opinion thought that they should be kept low because of strongly held views about the nature of poverty and the nature of mankind, though we must always remember that the charitable actions of these donors were freighted with great moral merit. And these men were within the terms of their understanding of the social problems of their age extremely generous. If we concern ourselves with the amount (for the whole group of ten counties) dedicated to poor relief and the social rehabilitation of the poor and assign to the average per decade rate of giving for the period 1480 to 1540 a value of 1, the per decade rate of giving for the two generations following (1541–1600) had risen to about 4·6, and for the last two generations (1601–1660) to approximately 12·4. There was an inflationary process at work, but it was far overmatched by the generosity of private men, buttressed in the last two generations of our era by the taxing authority of the state.

In the key tables on which this study rests we have been obliged for statistical reasons to follow quite arbitrary conventions which do some violence not only to the usual chronological divisions but also to historical fact. The period covered extends from 1480 through 1660, beginning some years before the triumph of Henry Tudor and including as well some months of the period after the restoration of the monarchy.

This was regarded as essential for statistical and comparative purposes, since thereby the accumulation of benefactions and their analysis could be made in decade intervals for the whole of the long era under review.

Useful as are the decade intervals in which we have assembled our data, they are relatively unimportant as compared with the more generally recognized historical periods of our era into which our material has also been aggregated and among which useful and most revealing comparisons and changes may be observed. But since the decade intervals must be kept intact, we have necessarily in this basic scheme of organization done considerable violence not only to convention but to fact. The period 1480–1540 has been called with reasonable chronological accuracy 'The Pre-Reformation Era' and, with the other periods, will ordinarily be so mentioned without repeated and certainly tiresome reference to the dates with which it is defined. The years 1541–1560 have been described somewhat inexactly as 'The Age of the Reformation', while 'The Age of Elizabeth' has been foreshortened to the four decades, 1561–1600. The period 1601–1640 has been regarded as 'The Early Stuart Period', while the two remaining decades have been described as 'The Revolutionary Era'. These divisions, in addition to being methodologically desirable, have the further merit, for purposes of statistical convenience, of establishing successive chronological units of sixty, twenty, forty, forty, and twenty years, which may, of course, be easily and accurately compared in various ways.

The bibliographical citations in this volume are necessarily heavy. Hence no formal bibliography will be presented, but a full reference will be supplied in the first instance of the citation of a printed or manuscript source.

It has been our intention to render all quotations exactly as written or printed, save that capitalization has in all cases been modernized.

When a memoir is to be found in the *Dictionary of National Biography*, no biographical particulars are ordinarily given for a donor unless corrections are suggested or additional facts have been found.

1960   W.K.J.

ABBREVIATIONS

The following abbreviations are used in the footnotes:

Alum. cantab.	Venn, John, ed., *Alumni cantabrigienses* (Cambridge, 1922–1954, 10 vols.).
Alum. oxon.	Foster, Joseph, ed., *Alumni oxonienses* (Oxford, 1891–1892, 4 vols.).
Archd. Bucks.	Archdeaconry Registers, Buckingham.
ARY	Registers of the Archbishops at York.
Berks, Bucks, & Oxon Arch.	*The Berks, Bucks, and Oxon Archaeological Journal.*
Cal. Comm. for Compounding	Green, M. A. E., ed., *Calendar of the Committee for Compounding* (L., 1889–1892, 5 vols.).
CCN	Consistory Court of Norwich.
CCY	Consistory Court of York.
DNB	*Dictionary of National Biography.*
Norf. Arch.	*Norfolk Archaeology.*
PCC	Prerogative Court of Canterbury.
PCY	Prerogative Court of York.
PP	*Parliamentary Papers, Charity Commissioners' Reports.*
S.P.Dom.	*State Papers, Domestic.*
Surtees Soc. Pub.	*The Publications of the Surtees Society.*
VCH	*The Victoria County History.*
Waters-Withington MSS.	Waters-Withington Collection, Essex Institute, Salem, Massachusetts, U.S.A.
Yorks. Arch. Journal	*The Yorkshire Archaeological and Topographical Journal.*
Yorks. Arch. Soc. Rec.	*Yorkshire Archaeological Association, Record Series.*

CONTENTS

PREFACE   *page* 9

ABBREVIATIONS   13

I INTRODUCTION   17

II BUCKINGHAMSHIRE   23
  A THE COUNTY   23
  B GENERAL COMMENTS ON THE DATA   24
  C THE ACHIEVEMENT   33
    1 *The poor*   33
    2 *Social rehabilitation*   49
    3 *Municipal betterments*   50
    4 *Education*   52
    5 *Religion*   60
  D THE STRUCTURE OF CHARITY IN THE PARISHES   71
  E THE IMPACT OF LONDON ON THE COUNTY   77
  F THE IMPACT OF THE COUNTY ON THE NATION   80
  G THE STRUCTURE OF CLASS ASPIRATIONS   81

III NORFOLK   89
  A THE COUNTY   89
  B GENERAL COMMENTS ON THE DATA   91
  C THE ACHIEVEMENT   98
    1 *The relief of the poor*   98
      (a) *Household relief*   98
      (b) *The founding of almshouses*   114
    2 *Social rehabilitation*   130
    3 *Municipal betterments*   143
    4 *Education*   150
      (a) *The founding of grammar schools*   150
      (b) *Support of the universities*   166
    5 *Religion*   172
      (a) *General comment*   172
      (b) *The general uses of the church*   174
      (c) *Prayers for the dead*   176
      (d) *Support of monasticism*   180
      (e) *Maintenance of the clergy*   180
      (f) *Care of the fabric*   182
      (g) *Church building*   185

D THE STRUCTURE OF CHARITIES IN THE PARISHES 191

E THE IMPACT OF LONDON ON THE COUNTY 196

F THE IMPACT OF THE COUNTY ON THE NATION 200

G THE STRUCTURE OF CLASS ASPIRATIONS 201

IV YORKSHIRE 214

A THE COUNTY 214

B GENERAL COMMENTS ON THE DATA 217

C THE ACHIEVEMENT 225

1 The relief of the poor 225

   (a) Household relief 225

   (b) The founding of almshouses 252

2 Social rehabilitation 282

3 Municipal betterments 294

4 Education 299

   (a) The founding of grammar schools 299

   (b) Scholarships and fellowships 350

   (c) Support of the universities 357

5 Religion 360

   (a) General comment 360

   (b) The general uses of the church 363

   (c) Prayers for the dead 365

   (d) Support of monasticism 373

   (e) Maintenance of the clergy 375

   (f) Endowment of lectureships 383

   (g) Care of the fabric 385

   (h) Church building 387

D THE STRUCTURE OF CHARITIES IN THE PARISHES 402

E THE IMPACT OF LONDON ON THE COUNTY 411

F THE IMPACT OF THE COUNTY ON THE NATION 415

G THE STRUCTURE OF CLASS ASPIRATIONS 418

APPENDIX 437

INDEX 452

I

Introduction

England remained a preponderantly rural nation through the whole of the early modern era. It was a rural society only beginning to experience the first strong thrusts of commercial and industrial progress, a society which in broad stretches of the realm remained quite unaffected by the few rich and powerful urban complexes within the national community. It seems probable that in 1600 at least eight of every ten Englishmen were rural dwellers, part of the agrarian community, if we may include, as we should, those living in some scores of small market towns which belonged to the countryside on which they had grown and whose needs they served. There was the single urban colossus, London, which as we have seen in an earlier volume of this study, exercised a powerful influence upon the aspirations and the institutions of all England because of its great and pervasive generosity. There were as well three other urban complexes, Bristol, Norwich, and York, which though almost incomparably smaller exhibited throughout our period characteristics which mark them as cities rather than as towns. More difficult to classify were upwards of twenty provincial and cathedral towns, communities like Gloucester and Taunton, or burgeoning market towns such as Manchester, Aylesbury, or Coventry, ranging in population from something like 5,000 to 15,000 inhabitants and possessing distinct mercantile and sometimes industrial classes, which may perhaps be best described as large towns, some in process of becoming cities, but most of which were to relapse quietly and comfortably into the rural England which had evoked them for a variety of reasons and purposes. All the rest of the realm may with reasonable accuracy be described as rural and was certainly so regarded throughout the long course of our period.

We have examined the development of charitable institutions in eight of the predominantly rural counties of England, having sought to secure a grouping of counties which would represent a fair sampling of the rural society for the whole of the realm.[1] We wish now to discuss rather fully the charitable contributions made by three of these counties and to comment on profoundly important shifts which occurred, even

[1] *Vide* Jordan, *Philanthropy in England*, 25–26 for a discussion of the selection of these counties.

in these essentially rural and conservative regions, in the structure of men's aspirations for themselves and their society. In choosing the counties to be considered we have been persuaded more by their dis-similarities than by their likenesses and have felt it desirable to choose regions in quite different parts of the realm.

We have chosen Buckinghamshire as a southern county because its basic political and parochial structure was mature at the outset of our period and because it remained one of the most classically rural counties in the whole of England. Though geographically almost within the shadow of London, it stood singularly free of the economic and cultural influences of the capital, with a society and an economy which were at once stable and conservative. With no cathedral town, few industries, and no considerable monastic establishments, the county offers a remarkably uncomplicated yet interesting structure of institutions for our study. None the less, Buckinghamshire was prosperous during almost the whole of our era, was relatively heavily populated, and was in the process of steady and significant cultural change.

Norfolk, well to the north and east, is our second county. Through much of our period it remained one of the richest agricultural areas in the entire realm and was never to lose its essentially rural quality. Yet it possessed in Norwich a true city, ranking second or third among the urban communities of the realm, during our whole era. Norwich was the capital city of the county quite as truly as London was the capital city of the realm, exercising a powerful and a forward-looking influence on the life and institutions of the entire shire and serving as the centre of its administrative, financial, and economic activities. Norfolk is interesting, too, because it possessed so much of self-sufficiency, because it progressed and remained great despite a sturdy and occasionally truculent spirit of insularity setting it apart from the realm at large. It was, in truth, the almost perfect microcosm of England, with a rich and variegated culture and economy bestowing on it those capabilities with which its remarkable self-sufficiency could be sustained.

We have chosen Yorkshire as our third county. Lying far to the north, remote, suspect, and badgered by the early Tudors, this last shire was to make rapid and solid cultural and institutional gains during the course of the seventeenth century. It is particularly interesting and important for our purposes since the county was thinly populated, poor, and back-ward as our period opened, with one of the most completely agrarian cultures in the whole of England and certainly one of the most mar-ginal. Yet during the years under study it was to undergo an economic revolution which spawned new and thriving towns in the West Riding and which was to lift much of the shire in wealth, population, and national prestige. Yorkshire was to witness, too, a translation of political and social power to a new gentry, fattening on monastic spoils, on grazing, and even on manufactures, which gave intelligent and dedicated direction to the economy and polity of the county and which was to lend powerful assistance in lifting it level with the nation at large in the course of almost a century. We shall be concerned, too, with the great fracture which ran through the life and spirit of the county as it was engulfed by the Reformation and as its rich and still fruitful monastic institutions were absorbed by the process of secular change, destroying one culture and laying the basis for another. Yorkshire yielded grudgingly and most reluctantly to the forces of historical change, but was itself to be transformed by these new, these confident, and these wholly secular forces of modernity.

Among the counties of England the three which we are taking in view ranked first, fourth, and thirty-third in size, a very large proportion of the 8,853 square miles contained in these shires being accounted for by the great area (6,066 square miles) found in Yorkshire. Our three counties were together slightly more than a half as large as the entire area of the ten counties comprehended in our whole study and encompassed slightly more than a sixth of the total land mass of England proper. We are dealing, then, with a considerable rural region, so selected, we believe, as to include most of the significant elements of diversity which marked the rural economy and society of England even during this relatively early and uncomplicated era.

It is our best estimate that these three counties together possessed in 1600 a population of about 535,000 persons, or perhaps an eighth of the whole of the population of England at the outset of the seventeenth century. These counties at the same date contained 1,261 parishes, or organized places of worship, or not quite a seventh of the whole number in England.[1] Even more significantly, this whole great area was overwhelmingly rural in its aspirations, no more than 6 per cent to 7 per cent of its inhabitants residing in the two truly urban complexes (Norwich and York) within its boundaries and no more than 15 per cent to 17 per cent being urban even if the larger market and manufacturing towns in the three counties be somewhat arbitrarily included and regarded as wholly urban in their complexion and attitudes.

In our study of this extensive and populous rural area we shall be concerned with analyzing the social and historical impact made by the charitable contributions of 13,068 identified donors who sought to secure the perpetuation and enlargement of their aspirations for their society. This is of course a goodly number of benefactors, though many were men and women of most modest means, and it includes well over a third (37·38 per cent) of the whole number for the sampling of ten counties on which the study rests. At the same time, it must be pointed out that the mass of numbers of donors far exceeded in proportionate

[1] *Vide* Jordan, *Philanthropy in England*, 26–29.

terms the weight of total charitable contribution, the whole of the charitable wealth accumulated in these three counties amounting to £509,686 11s. This aggregate of charitable capital amounted to hardly a sixth (16·43 per cent) of the great total given in our ten counties for the various charitable uses, with Yorkshire having contributed 7·85 per cent of that total, Norfolk 5·73 per cent, and Buckinghamshire a scant 2·84 per cent. Useful and stimulating as this wealth was, decisive as it was in founding and ordering the basic social institutions in these rural counties, it seems but slight indeed when compared with the vast total of £1,889,211 12s given by London benefactors for the social and cultural needs of the capital and, since this great wealth knew no parochial boundaries, of the realm at large. This great rural area, then, whose population in 1600 was approximately double that of London, gave for charitable uses only slightly more than a fourth of the immense aggregate built up by the steady and evangelical benefactions of the capital.

Though it would be difficult to suggest three more representative rural counties than those we have chosen, it remains true that even within them the social responsibility assumed by the rural classes was far less dominant than we should suppose. First of all, a tiny group of 284 London donors, numbering no more than 2·17 per cent of all the benefactors noted in these counties, gave the staggering total of £67,983 14s to their needs, this constituting almost a seventh of the aggregate of the charitable wealth of these regions. The proportion of benefactors who were members of the rural classes ranged from 57 per cent in Norfolk to 84·67 per cent in Buckinghamshire, being almost exactly three-fourths (75·20 per cent) of all donors for the three counties as a group; this was, of course, not significantly below the estimate (83 per cent to 85 per cent) we have made of the proportion of rural dwellers to be found in this great area. But, most importantly, the rural classes in these three counties contributed no more than 52·59 per cent (£268,037 1s) of the whole of their charitable wealth. Even in the indubitably rural regions of England, a relatively very small group of urban donors, with powerful assistance from London, bore quantitatively almost an equal burden of social responsibility. And, as we shall later point out, these urban gifts possessed considerably greater qualitative strength and were in fact often decisive in determining the slope of life and development within the counties.[1]

We should likewise emphasize the fact that, predominantly rural though these three counties were, they were in quite different stages of cultural and institutional development throughout our period, just as

---

[1] The proportion of charitable benefactions made by rural dwellers ranges from 38·57 per cent for Norfolk to 71·45 per cent for Buckinghamshire. It should be said that in each county the gifts of unidentified donors known to be rural or village dwellers are reckoned as rural contributions.

their economies show most pronounced differences. Thus, it may be suggested that in Buckinghamshire the parochial organization of the county was mature and the required church building nearly completed as early as the opening of our era, which may account in part at least for the pronounced and certainly pertinacious secularism of the county throughout the long age with which we are concerned. Norfolk was even in 1480 'over-churched', with many of its small parishes already in decay, while in 1600 the 581 parishes in the county exceeded the number in any other county in the realm. In Yorkshire, on the other hand, the parochial structure was still in process of formation as late as 1600, when we have counted 314 legally constituted parishes and 470 settled places of worship, with numerous huge parishes that served ineffectively the needs of a greatly increased population, particularly in the new industrial towns of the West Riding.

So, too, the wealth of the several classes of men, and more particularly the fluid, the viable wealth, differed most markedly from county to county.[1] Thus our data for the average wealth of certain social groups would suggest that a member of the upper gentry of Buckinghamshire during this period disposed wealth well over twice as great as that left by a confrere in Yorkshire, while members of the same class in Norfolk possessed wealth about twice as great as that for members of the upper gentry in Buckinghamshire. Even more startling is the fact that a member of the lesser gentry of Buckinghamshire possessed disposable resources somewhat greater than those of an average member of the upper gentry in Yorkshire, while a typical yeoman of Norfolk possessed wealth amounting to almost two-thirds of that disposed by a typical gentleman of Yorkshire. These were, of course, immensely significant differences which go far to explain the interesting and important variations not only in the amounts afforded for charitable uses in the three counties but also the differences in their composition and social dedication.

But different as these three rural counties may have been, they shared with all of rural England a profound weakness in the essential social institutions required by the modern society if endemic and paralyzing poverty were to be checked and if opportunities for betterment and progress were to be widely extended. These are matters of the utmost significance which could be illustrated in a variety of ways, but perhaps the most important may be documented by the number of almshouses and schools available in the great areas comprehended by the three counties at the outset of our period. There were in 1480 only thirty-six almshouses still functioning and offering those healing services in the care of derelict men and women which the sixteenth century came

[1] This important matter is fully discussed for the whole group of ten counties in Jordan, *Philanthropy in England*, 330–342.

to regard as the prime purpose of a hospital or almshouse. Of this inconsiderable number, only six possessed any endowment, as many as fourteen were so far decayed as to require re-foundation in the course of the sixteenth century, and certainly four, possibly as many as six, had fallen into disrepair or disuse well before the Reformation. Some measure of the greatness of the achievement of private donors of our period may be suggested in the fact that men and women of these rural counties founded and endowed 112 almshouses in less than two centuries, not to mention a considerable number which carried on useful and beneficent work even though the age did not contrive to secure their endowment.

Even more revealing are the facts relating to schools in this great region. The care of the hopelessly poor in any age is an act of mercy, a confession of the failure of a society. But the provision which men make for free education, for emancipation from the toils of the ignorance in which poverty is bred, betokens at once a large measure of hope and a resolution to build a society in which poverty is prevented. In these three counties there were in 1480 not more than twelve schools freely open to lay children, and of these only five possessed either endowments or sufficiency of constitution to guarantee their permanence. In the age with which we are concerned private donors were to found and endow 140 schools in these rural reaches as an act of faith and a pledge that the circumference of opportunity was to be enormously and certainly fruitfully extended. This betokens an immense cultural achievement which men and women of the early modern era were to attain with their own substance and for the fulfilment of their own aspirations. To this annal we may now turn in the three counties which we believe serve as exemplars of the whole realm of England.

II

Buckinghamshire

A. THE COUNTY

Thomas Fuller described Buckinghamshire as 'a long narrow county . . . stretching forty four miles from North to South, whilst the breadth is content with fourteen at the most'.[1] In size it ranks thirty-third among the counties of England, being 743 square miles in area, slightly smaller than Worcestershire, slightly larger than Berkshire. It is divided roughly between the basins of the Thames and of the Ouse. The Thames valley was a fertile and a most prosperous agricultural area during our period, particularly valuable meadow lands being found in the Vale of Aylesbury. But much of the rolling hill land enclosing the valleys was flinty and of marginal fertility. Perhaps most of the land of the county was unenclosed at the beginning of our period, though enclosures for grazing made steady progress during the sixteenth century and provided the basis for a more balanced agricultural economy despite the widespread social protest which accompanied this inevitable development.

The county remained throughout the sixteenth and seventeenth centuries one of the most completely agricultural of all the southern and Midland counties. Fuller very aptly tells us that it lived by its lands rather than by its hands, there being 'no handicrafts of note'.[2] Husbandry dominated the entire county, there being no town of any considerable consequence and the few industries being principally connected with the products of the soil. No borough in the county possessed a royal charter before the sixteenth century. Buckingham, Wendover, Amersham, Colnbrook, and Great Marlow, all principal towns, were no more than small market towns chiefly dependent on the rural areas they served. Aylesbury, perhaps the largest town in 1660, was as late as 1520 so inextricably rural that the lord of the manor still held his court there.

The few industries, save for those supplying local agricultural needs, developed late in the sixteenth century. The cloth trade seems to have been unimportant except for that centring around High Wycombe. In

[1] Fuller, Thomas (P. A. Nuttall, ed.), *The history of the worthies of England* (L. 1840, 3 vols.), I, 192.   [2] *Ibid.*, I, 194.

the early seventeenth century small but prosperous lace-making shops were established at Olney, Newport Pagnell, Aylesbury, and High Wycombe, giving considerable employment, especially to women. Brick-making for local needs was well and widely established in several parts of the county, though Sir Ralph Verney's large works at Claydon, dating from the mid-seventeenth century, seems to have been the first to develop a considerable market outside the county. Paper-making was begun in several towns in the Thames valley very late in the seventeenth century, there being as many as twelve small mills employed in this trade in 1636.

No accurate estimate of the population of the county seems possible. It is evident, however, that despite its almost complete agrarian economy, Buckinghamshire was surprisingly heavily populated, with very few areas of really low density of population. There is also evidence that the growing population of the county bore heavily on its somewhat limited economic resources, with the result that there was throughout our period a steady migration into other agricultural counties as well as to London. Usher's interesting calculations would place most of the county at or slightly above the areas of mean density of population for England in 1570 and 1600 and would suggest a population of between 50,000 and 60,000 at the latter date.[1]

The county was relatively more prosperous than its size or its economy would suggest. Its wealth was certainly enhanced by a considerable speculative rise in land values which seems to have begun in the mid-sixteenth century and which was furthered by heavy purchases of land in the county by London capital towards the end of the Elizabethan period and during the first two decades of the seventeenth century. The calculations of Rogers and of Buckatzsch, based on the subsidy rolls, would seem to give the county a rank in terms of average wealth during the whole of our period very near the top of the second quarter of all English counties, though our own evidence would place it among those at the top of the third quarter of counties.

B. GENERAL COMMENTS ON THE DATA

In this relatively small, but prosperous, rural county, the considerable sum of £88,152 6s was given or bequeathed for charitable uses during our period. This amount was given by 1722 identified donors as well as by a considerable number of additional donors who cannot be identified by name or whose share in known benefactions cannot be exactly stated. The whole of this latter group are to be found among the benefactors

---

[1] This estimate compares interestingly with W. H. Summers' estimate of 68,618 for 1676, which is based on Archbishop Sheldon's census of that year (*Records of Buckinghamshire*, VIII [1903], 146–152).

responsible for church building in the county during this period, and the total of their benefactions was £5630. The average benefaction for each donor in this county was, accordingly, £51 3s 10d, placing Buckinghamshire roughly in the middle range in this respect for the eight rural counties comprehended in this study.

The rapidly shifting pattern of philanthropic interest in the county may be observed by an examination of the master table of benefactions.[1] During the first six decades of Tudor rule, when institutions as well as habits of thought and action retained much that was medieval, men's interests were principally religious. The total of charitable giving for this long interval amounted to only £8904 18s, or not more than 10 per cent of the whole of the benefactions of the county for the entire period under examination. Of this amount well over half (61 per cent) was given in these years for the various religious uses and activities of the age. The needs of the poor were assisted by benefactions totalling about £2000 and amounting to almost 23 per cent of the charities of the period, though it should be noted that one very large benefaction, comprising about half the total, somewhat distorts the pattern of gifts for poor relief. The other great heads of social rehabilitation, municipal improvements, and education received not more than 16 per cent of the whole, the needs of education being almost completely unattended.

The era of the Reformation, and the social and cultural dislocation attending it, witnessed a revolutionary change in the structure of charitable interests, with no considerable increase in the amount of benefactions. During these twenty years, 1541–1560, a total of £5141 7s was provided for the various charitable causes, or somewhat less than 6 per cent of the total for our entire period. But the amount given for religious purposes, it should be noted, fell by more than half to 27 per cent of the total, while the amounts provided for the poor doubled in percentage terms. Moreover, the structure of giving to the poor was significantly changed, since almost half the whole amount was designated for the erection and endowment of almshouses rather than for doles or direct relief of the poor, the prime concern in earlier years. Quite as interesting was the substantial increase, in both relative and absolute terms, of gifts for educational purposes.

The next interval, 1561–1600, which one is tempted to describe as the 'age of secularism', witnessed a considerable increase in the total of all benefactions, which amount to 16·8 per cent of the entire sum for the county, and was marked by an even more revolutionary change in the structure of charitable interests. Gifts for religious purposes fell dramatically and most steeply to about 8·5 per cent of the total, and if the £790 devoted to church building in these years be deducted from the total of £1260 11s, one can only wonder whether the whole fabric

[1] *Vide* Table I, Appendix.

of traditional parish religious activity was not in these years most seriously impaired. Clearly the central preoccupation had become not the state of faith, but the plight of the poor, since the total of gifts to the poor rose to £10,511 17s for the period, representing upwards of 71 per cent of the whole. It is evident that the revolutionary triumph of the secular interest was all but completed during these years when 92 per cent of men's charitable dispositions were made for wholly secular purposes.

During the next era, in Buckinghamshire as in England, we observe a great outpouring of charities of a most amazing diversity and fruitfulness. In this period of four decades (1601–1640) somewhat more than half of the total for the county was provided. The whole amount of £46,991 18s was so large and the gifts so evenly spread among the parishes of the county that very substantial changes occurred not only in the institutions but in the culture and economy of the county. The generous total of £14,525 2s, representing almost one-third of all gifts, was designated for educational purposes, with the result that the educational opportunities of the county were notably expanded and bettered. In fact, in this period about 77 per cent of the whole educational endowment of our entire age was provided. The amounts disposed for the poor during these forty years were almost two and one half times as great as in the preceding period, though, significantly, the relative interest in direct outright relief declined sharply as compared with the Elizabethan era. A startling increase in concern with the various agencies of social rehabilitation should also be noted, the total devoted to this purpose rising from £2 7s in the preceding period to £3342 13s during these years. The benefactions for religious purposes sank to an insignificant 6 per cent of the whole.

Only relatively minor changes occurred in the structure of charitable interests in the county during the revolutionary decades, 1641–1660, save for a sharp rise in gifts and bequests for various municipal betterments and a considerable decline in the proportion of benefactions for educational purposes. But the toll of revolutionary dislocation was none the less evident, when it is observed that the annual average of charitable gifts in these years is slightly less than half that of the preceding forty years, though it remained almost twice that of the Elizabethan period.

Taking in view our whole period, it is evident that men's preoccupations with religion and its needs declined rapidly and all but catastrophically, while a flood of charitable interests, wholly or principally secular in nature, were developing. Thus almost as much was given for religious uses in the years before 1540 (£5461 1s) as during the whole of the remaining years from 1541 to the restoration of the Stuarts (£6399 9s), with the result that, while almost two-thirds of the total of charitable contributions was for religious purposes in the first interval, only a little more than an eighth of the whole was for that purpose during the entire period of our study. This great shift in men's interests and preoccupations is the symbol of the secularization which was in part the cause, in part the consequence, of the Reformation.

Before proceeding to a more detailed examination of the materials for Buckinghamshire, it will be well to deal with certain data that illuminate the structure of charities in the county and elucidate to a degree some of the institutional and economic problems of the era.

In the very nature of the case, rich and well-advised men tend to give or bequeath their property in carefully ordered ways. But most benefactors in this and other rural counties were relatively poor men whose charities were outright sums meant to be disbursed at once for some immediate need. The large benefactors, on the other hand, tended to place their gifts in some type of trusteeship with more or less elaborate provisions for administration of the trusts and the expenditure of the income in perpetuity. Most testators and givers, then, made outright income gifts, with the result that for the county as a whole 76 per cent of all the known donors left outright charitable gifts which, however, amount in sum to only £15,520 9s, or 17·6 per cent of the whole. A relatively small group of donors, on the other hand, provided the impressive total of £72,631 17s of capital gifts, this amounting to 82·4 per cent of the total of charities of the county.

A study of the charitable history of Buckinghamshire in this period likewise reveals a great deal of pertinent information regarding the legal and economic position of women in a rural county and perhaps even more importantly the quite remarkably different complexion of their interests and aspirations. Of the 1722 known donors for the county, 233 were women, or 13·50 per cent of the whole number, and these women gave £11,466 7s, or 13·01 per cent of the total for the county. In other other words, the average benefaction made by women as a group was £49 8s 6d, or almost exactly the same as the average of all benefactions (£51 3s 10d) for the county at large. Somewhat surprisingly, since this was a most conservative rural county, the proportion of the total charities contributed by women donors was the highest for all the counties comprised in this study,[1] and very possibly for all of England. It should also be observed that all gifts and bequests treated as from women are gifts *solus*, joint benefactions of husband and wife having been credited to the husband in the few cases where they occur. These women were of all types of marital status—widowed, married, and spinsters—and their gifts involve all types of property, including land, in proportions not significantly dissimilar from those of men donors. The facts suggest that women were legally and socially in a

---

[1] The proportions range from 3·92 per cent for Hampshire to the 13·01 per cent for Buckinghamshire.

position to dispose much more of property than has sometimes been supposed and that they did in fact possess legally a not inconsiderable fraction of the disposable wealth of the age even in the rural shires.

Unfortunately, it is difficult to determine the social status of a woman donor in this period unless she was married or very recently widowed, with the result that it was possible to establish the status of only about half (114) of the total number. But it is clear from the social distribution of the women whose status is known that the pattern is very similar indeed to that for benefactors for the county in general, save for a somewhat heavier incidence of women among the upper gentry.[1] It is, however, clear that women did not in most cases slavishly follow the philanthropic precedents set by their fathers and husbands, that their charitable interests were on balance quite different from those of men, and that they were, somewhat surprisingly, even more secular in their aspirations than the men of the county.

Their predominant interest was in the relief of the poor, to which they gave about 86 per cent (£9,809 12s) of all their benefactions. These gifts, it may be remarked, were principally for the outright relief of poverty rather than the institutionalization of that relief in almshouse foundations. The devotion of women donors to the needs of the poor stands in quite amazing contrast to the county at large, which dedicated only slightly more than half its charitable funds to this purpose. In fact, the women of Buckinghamshire gave in all rather more than one-fifth of the total of the benefactions for the poor made in the whole of the county. So complete was their dedication to the needs of the poor that they contributed relatively little to the other great heads under which charities have been tabulated. Only small totals were bequeathed for social rehabilitation, even less (2 per cent) for municipal betterments, while the whole of the gifts for education totalled only £648. But most surprisingly of all, only 4 per cent of their total charitable benefactions were for religious causes as compared with 13·5 per cent for the county as a whole.

The variety and solidity of feminine social aspirations in the period may perhaps be better exhibited if in addition to these bare analyses of their charities at least a sampling of the particular benefactions are noted, including some of the larger as well as several of the smaller and more typical of the gifts and bequests made by women in or to the county.

One of the largest of the charitable foundations of the period was that made by Anne, Countess of Warwick, who in 1603 by deed established an almshouse or hospital in Chenies for 'ten poor folks, viz. four men

---

[1] The distribution is: nobility 4; upper gentry 28; lower gentry 30; yeomanry 32; husbandmen 6; lower clergy 2; merchants 6; tradesmen 2; artisans 2; and professions 2.

and six women', who should be sixty years of age or more and who must
be residents of Chenies, Northall, or Wotton-under-Edge, Gloucestershire. The almshouse was completed near the village in 1605, its continued service being secured by an endowment of two rent-charges, the
one of £30 p.a. from lands in Gloucestershire and the other of £20 p.a.
from property in Hertfordshire.[1]

A generation later, another member of the nobility, Lady Elizabeth
Hatton, a granddaughter of Lord Burghley and a daughter of Thomas,
Earl of Exeter, bequeathed £100 to the endowment of the almshouse at
Stoke Poges, founded by Lord Hastings of Loughborough, for the uses
of the poor of that hospital. Her will likewise created a trust of £100,
the income of which was to be employed for the relief of sick, aged, and
impotent poor not of the hospital.[2] The prime concern of women with
the outright and the institutional care of the poor is likewise exemplified
in the bequest by Lady Elizabeth Dormer, the widow of Robert, Lord
Dormer, in 1631, of £10 to the endowment of an almshouse in Wing
and an equal amount in alms for the poor of that parish.[3] Lady Dormer's
will, it might be noted, disposed upwards of £2000 of personal bequests
in addition to her charities.

We have suggested that women of the upper gentry in Buckinghamshire were particularly important in assuming charitable responsibilities
in the period, and among this class an interesting pattern of giving may
be observed. Thus in 1540 Dame Isabel Denton, a member of a prolific
and rich gentle family, by will established a stipend of four marks
annually for a priest who should undertake the instruction of children
in the borough of Buckingham, her annuity to serve as an augmentation
to his income. The grammar school and its tiny endowment survived
the expropriation of the chantries, and it seems probable that Edward
VI meant to add to it the properties of the chantry of St Thomas of
Acon, though there is no certain evidence of a payment from the
Exchequer until 1592 when an annuity of £10 8s was assigned to what
came most improperly to be regarded as another of Edward VI's
foundations.[4]

An even more sophisticated interest in education was exhibited by
Lady Elizabeth Periam, a much-married sister of Lord Bacon, whose

[1] *VCH, Bucks.*, III, 203; *PP* 1833, XVIII, 51–53; *Berks, Bucks, & Oxon Archaeological Journal*, n.s., XII (1906), 59; Sheahan, J. J., *History of Bucking-hamshire* (L., 1862), 837. At the beginning of this century, the endowment was valued at £2269 13s 1d.
[2] PCC 89 Fines 1647; *PP* 1833, XVIII, 118, 121–122; *VCH, Bucks.*, III, 313. *Vide post*, 43.
[3] PCC 51 St. John 1631.
[4] *PP* 1834, XXI, 59–61; Lipscomb, George, *The history and antiquities of the county of Buckingham* (L., 1831–47, 4 vols.), II, 584; *VCH, Bucks.*, II, 208. *Vide post*, 53.

last husband was Chief Baron of the Exchequer. This benefactor in 1621 bequeathed a farm valued at approximately £300 in Hambleden to Archbishop Laud on trust for educational purposes. The Archbishop was to bestow the endowment for scholarships upon any college in Oxford as he saw fit, preference being given to scholars from a grammar school already founded by Lady Periam in Henley, Oxfordshire, or to natives of the county of Buckinghamshire.[1] This benefaction was not specifically for the parish of Hambleden, but it is interesting to note that women were the principal donors of the early charities of that community. In 1562 Agnes Lewen, a native of the town residing in London at the time of her death, bequeathed £40, which in 1577 was used by trustees to purchase a rent-charge of £2 p.a. for the relief of the poor.[2] Lady Philadelphia Scrope, the mother of the first Earl of Sunderland, in 1628 left by will the same capital amount, which was likewise invested by the trustees to yield £2 p.a. for the benefit of the poor.[3]

Almost half a century earlier another widow of a Chief Baron of the Exchequer, Dame Joan Bradshaw, had made an even larger benefaction to Buckinghamshire, not to mention considerable charities in Oxfordshire and Essex. This woman, who must have been very old indeed when she died in 1598, was the daughter of John Hunt of Kingston-upon-Thames, Surrey. Her first husband, who died in 1529, was William Mainwaring of East Ham, Essex. Her second husband was Henry Bradshaw, whose family held extensive properties in Halton parish, Buckinghamshire. Bradshaw, who died in 1553 while Chief Baron of the Exchequer, left his wife well provided for and during her more than forty years of widowhood she proved to be not only 'very chariable to the poore', but sagacious in her charitable dispositions. She built a chapel at Noke, Oxfordshire, and provided for the poor there, but her principal benefactions were to Halton and Wendover parishes in Buckinghamshire. There in 1578 she established a trust with a stipend of £20 p.a. which she vested in the churchwardens and overseers of the two parishes as trustees with the provision that the income should be employed for the relief of the poorest inhabitants of the two parishes.[4]

---

[1] PCC 34 Dale 1621, sentences and codicil 1 Hele 1626; Ingram, James, *Memorials of Oxford* (Oxford, 1837, 3 vols.), I, "Balliol", 7; Sheahan, *Buckinghamshire*, 885; Langley, Thomas, *History of the hundred of Desborough* (L., 1797), 241. Balliol College was vested by Laud with this endowment, it being used to support a fellowship and two scholarships.

[2] PCC 33 Streat 1562; *VCH, Bucks.*, III, 53; *PP* 1833, XIX, 124–125.

[3] *PP* 1833, XIX, 127; Cokayne, G. E., ed., *The complete peerage* (L., 1887–1898, 8 vols.), VII, 88.

[4] Lipscomb, *Buckingham*, II, 225–226; *The Gentleman's Magazine*, LIX (1789), ii, 1011; *PP* 1833, XIX, 112; Sheahan, *Buckinghamshire*, 139; *VCH, Bucks.*, III, 30.

Another member of the upper gentry, Lady Jane Boys, was a considerable benefactor to the town of Great Missenden, having founded by her will in 1636 a charity with a capital of £100 for the 'apprenticing of poor children of this parish'. Her executors, John Hampden and Richard Camden, added £35 of capital in order to purchase a messuage with gardens and a close of land of about five acres, the whole endowment yielding £6 p.a. in 1640.[1]

Numerous charities were endowed by women of the lower gentry, although their gifts were less substantial. Thus in 1574 Dorothy Dayrell established by deed of gift six small almshouses in Buckingham borough, which she endowed with an annual income of £5 4s for the sole benefit of the 'six poore women resident' in the appointed houses. Mrs Dayrell vested the trust in twelve feoffees named in her will, with the prudent provision that when the members should be reduced to nine by death or other causes, additional trustees should be named by the bailiff and burgesses of the town in order to restore the number.[2] This charity was subsequently augmented by a bequest from another woman, Katherine Agard,[3] and having enjoyed careful administration was in 1905 yielding £91 16s p.a. from the original endowments.

A far larger, though possibly less well considered benefaction, was provided in 1649 by Joan Chibnall of Princes Risborough, who by will in that year charged her manor farm, Tring, with an annual stipend of £32 for various charitable purposes. Eight poor widows 'or ancient maids' of the parish were each year to be given one cloth gown each, worth at least 18s, and one ell of cloth worth 2s the ell. In addition, £4 was each year to be distributed to needy persons in the parish in amounts ranging from one to two shillings each and on the occasion of that distribution the clergyman was to be given an honorarium of 10s. These distributions for Princes Risborough, it was reckoned, would require annually an outlay of £12 10s, the remainder to be disbursed in a similar fashion in four other Buckinghamshire and Oxfordshire parishes.[4]

Women of the yeomanry slightly outnumber those of any other social group among the women donors of the county, though their charities were for the most part, like those of their husbands and fathers, relatively small. Typical in amount and in the expressed aspirations of the testators are such bequests as those of Ellen Brockhouse, a widow of Beaconsfield, of 8s for the poor of her parish and 1s for the use of its church;[5] of

[1] PCC 10 Pile 1636; Sheahan, *Buckinghamshire*, 179; *PP* 1833, XIX, 85–86.
[2] Lipscomb, *Buckingham*, II, 584; *VCH, Bucks.*, III, 488–489; *PP* 1834, XXI, 64; Sheahan, *Buckinghamshire*, 240. Vide post, 44.
[3] *Vide post*, 35.
[4] PCC 137 Fairfax 1649; *PP* 1816, XVI, i, 64–65; *PP* 1823, VIII, 503–504; *PP* 1833, XIX, 92–93.
[5] PCC 46 Alen 1547.

Agnes Baldwin, widow in a prolific family of yeomen, of 6s in alms to the poor of Aston Clinton and 6s 8d to the poor of nearby parishes;[1] of Elizabeth Beke, widow, with a bequest of 6d for the use of Lincoln Cathedral in 1606;[2] of Agnes Fryar of Little Marlow, whose will bequeathed to the churchwardens and overseers of the parish £1 p.a. to be distributed to twenty of the poorest women dwelling in Great Marlow;[3] of Margaret Disley who in 1627 left £3 to be disbursed outright to the poor of Aylesbury;[4] of Agnes Hawes whose will provided 13s 4d for the poor of Stewkley;[5] and Anne Deane whose will in 1632 required her executors to distribute 10s to the needy of the parish of Wolverton.[6]

But, typical though these are, there were rich yeomen's widows whose charities rivalled those of many gentle ladies in amount as well as in the care with which the governing provisions were drafted. One of the largest of all benefactions made by a woman of the county was that of Alice Carter, the widow of George Carter, Sr., a yeoman of Brill. This donor set out in her deed of gift dated May 27, 1590, that her late husband had wished to establish an almshouse in the parish. She accordingly nominated trustees who together with the curate of Brill were vested with five houses, with adjoining gardens and grounds, which the donor endowed with properties valued at approximately £30 p.a. Five impotent and needy widows were to be lodged and maintained in these houses, 'uppon theire honeste and good behavyour to remayne and dwell, in pure francke almse, and rent free, during their wydowhoodd and naturall lyves'. Any surplus income after these obligations were discharged and the building placed in repair was annually to be divided among the five almswomen before the communion table in Brill church, they rendering 'unto Almighty God thankes, by saying the lorde's prayer, for his mercifull and greate benyfytte bestowed uppon them'.[7]

Enough examples have perhaps been given to suggest that these women were animated by the same aspirations that moved their husbands in the outpouring of philanthropic wealth that was so effectively to mould the institutions and the mores of a new England. They were especially interested in the plight of the poor, and while they tended to leave their bequests and make their gifts for the immediate, if temporary, relief of the poor they saw about them in the hedges and in the market-places, a not inconsiderable number of them sought to shelter

[1] Baldwin, E. B., *Baldwin family* (Washington, D.C., 1925), 47.
[2] PCC 45 Stafford 1606.
[3] *Records of Buckinghamshire*, VIII (1903), 196; *PP* 1833, XIX, 139.
[4] PCC 87 Skynner 1627.
[5] Archd. Bucks., 1632.
[6] PCC 1 Audley 1632.
[7] *VCH, Bucks.*, IV, 18; *PP* 1834, XXI, 12; Lipscomb, *Buckingham*, I, 114. *Vide post*, 44.

and maintain the helpless and the social bankrupts in the new almshouses which constituted the first concerted attack of the modern era on the ancient problem of poverty. These women were secular in their basic interests, they disposed considerable wealth, and their charities are in most instances quite independent of those of their spouses. We are dealing with an era in which women as a social group were making very considerable strides towards cultural as well as personal independence.

C. THE ACHIEVEMENT

1. *The Poor*

We should now turn to a detailed examination of the structure of charities during the entire period under study, with special attention to the shifting pattern of men's social and cultural aspirations. We have already observed that in Buckinghamshire, as in England as a whole, the harassing problem of poverty came deeply to engage men's minds and consciences and that a number of plans of attack on the problem were fully developed and richly endowed during our era. As we have stated, during the whole period, 1480–1660, rather more than half (52·04 per cent) of all gifts and bequests were made in an almost infinite number of plans, both simple and complex, to alleviate the suffering occasioned by poverty. It is notable that in this agricultural county, possessing no considerable urban complexes, a substantially larger proportion of charitable wealth was devoted to the succour of the poor than in any other of the ten counties included in this study, or, for that matter, there is reason to believe, any other county in England.[1] It was only gradually, however, even in Buckinghamshire, that the social curse and the political danger of poverty and unemployment were fully borne in on the sixteenth-century mind; that concerted, continuous, and effective measures were taken to deal with it, if not to cure it, by means of private charity. During the first eighty years of our period not much more than 9 per cent of the total amount to be given for the relief of poverty had been disposed in this great effort to resolve a problem as old as mankind, and this had on the whole been given sporadically and without pattern. This does not mean that there was not great distress and considerable unemployment in England prior to 1560. It means rather that the conscience of the nation had not been rallied to deal with the evils of poverty and that men's aspirations were not yet sufficiently secular to divert their generosity from ecclesiastical and religious causes to the problems of this world.

It should likewise be observed that during the whole of our period the

---

[1] The proportion of total charitable wealth dedicated to poor relief ranges from 22·01 per cent (Lancashire) to 45·96 per cent (Bristol) for the other counties studied.

prime concern was with the household relief of the poor by alms, distribution of food and clothing, the provision of shelter, direct assistance for the aged, and a myriad of other forms of outright alleviation. We have noted that this important form of relief tended as our period wore on to become endowed, with the result that about 77 per cent of the whole amount provided for poor relief was in capital sums. Moreover, as the period progressed an ever-increasing proportion of benefactions for the assistance of the poor came to be devoted to such institutional devices as almshouses, where the impotent and derelict might be separated from the society as incurably charitable charges.

During our first interval, a total of £1890 8s was given or bequeathed for outright poor relief. This represents principally an accumulation of many small bequests for doles. One considerable benefaction was, however, made for outright poor relief during these years by John Bedford, a member of the lower gentry and a resident of Aylesbury. Bedford in 1493 bequeathed a number of houses and 107 acres of land to the parish of Aylesbury upon trust. The income, it was provided, should be used for the perpetual care of the roads of the parish and in alms for the poorest persons of the community. The capital value of the estate was of the order of £1400, not the huge sum which would be implied in the £600 p.a. occasionally reported, of which approximately half was devoted to alms for the poor. In the course of the sixteenth century, the charity suffered from serious mismanagement on the part of the nine feoffees who seem to have let the property on long leases to friends and relations at wholly uneconomic rentals. The charity was investigated and reorganized by Act of Parliament in 1593, thereby securing a full restoration of the property and the application of the economic income to the appointed purposes.[1]

During the two decades marked by the dislocation of the Reformation, the relative importance of bequests for poor relief approximately doubled and a considerable number of endowments, ranging from £20 to £210, were established in all parts of the county. The total provided during these years for this purpose was £1188 12s. But it was in the Elizabethan period that a most significant and ever-growing movement got under way for dealing with the problem of poverty. More than 71 per cent of all benefactions of the period were designated for household relief, almshouses, or general charitable purposes in which the poor were uppermost in the minds of the donors. More specifically, £3866 14s was given or bequeathed for household relief by upwards of 200 donors, several of whom may be briefly mentioned.

One of the most considerable of these donors was Thomas Pigott of

[1] VCH, Bucks., III, 18; Gibbs, Robert, A history of Aylesbury (Aylesbury, 1885), 460–462; PP 1816, XVI, i, 62–63; PP 1833, XIX, 45–49. Vide post, 51. The income of the charity in 1911 was £540 p.a.

Doddershall. Pigott was a son of a serjeant-at-law of the same name who had by his will in 1520 established an endowment of £100 to secure the repair of bridges in and near the town of Stony Stratford, where he held property and probably resided.[1] The younger Pigott established his charity by a deed of trust dated March 25, 1573, endowing it with considerable land and other real property then possessing a capital worth of £800. The income was to be devoted to the relief and general assistance of the poor of Simpson village.[2] In the next year Katherine Agard, a widow of Ambrosden, Oxfordshire, gave or bequeathed various properties in the town of Buckingham on trust for the relief of the poor of that community. The estate was valued at £314 capital and the income was to be devoted to the relief of the twelve poorest inhabitants of the borough of Buckingham with 1s in money and 6d in bread each Sunday.[3]

Almost invariably one substantial benefaction given by a member of a well-placed family resulted in the setting of a tradition of responsibility and in habits of charity which not infrequently continued in a family, usually with the same general interests, for two or three generations. We have noticed this tradition in the Pigott family, and it was to be even more markedly the case in the Duncombe family, members of the lower gentry settled in the parish of Ivinghoe in Cottesloe hundred. William Duncombe, Esq., of Aston, in Ivinghoe, in 1576 bequeathed certain lands of the value of £10 p.a. to trustees with the stipulation that the whole of the rents and profits should be distributed to the poor of the parish at the discretion of the vicar and six of the most substantial men in the community.[4] A few years later his wife, Alice, added to the trust by conveying lands with a then value of £2 15s p.a. for this same purpose.[5] A generation later, another William Duncombe, probably a son, then of Battlesden, Bedfordshire, settled an even larger endowment, totalling £35 p.a., to be distributed each year in various amounts to poor widows of Ivinghoe and other parishes and hamlets in Buckinghamshire and elsewhere.[6] A later descendant of William Duncombe, a London merchant of the same name, in 1631 founded by

---

[1] PCC 26 Ayloffe 1520; Ratcliff, Oliver, *History of the Newport Pagnell hundreds* (Olney, Buckinghamshire, 1900), 368; *VCH, Bucks.*, IV, 481.

[2] *VCH, Bucks.*, IV, 461; Sheahan, *Buckinghamshire*, 605; Ratcliff, *Newport hundreds*, 443; *PP* 1834, XXI, 196–198. The original property comprised 44 acres of arable land, rather more than 6 acres of meadow, 3 cottages, a forge, a shop, and additional scattered tracts of land. The subsequent income has been remarkably stable, having been £41 17s. 10½d. in 1786; £50 in 1843; £82 3s. in 1862; and £90 in 1927.

[3] Lipscomb, *Buckingham*, II, 584; Willis, Browne, *History of Buckingham* (L., 1755), 83; *PP* 1834, XXI, 56–59; *VCH, Bucks.*, III, 488–489. *Vide ante*, 31.

[4] PCC 30 Carew 1576; *PP* 1834, XXI, 89.

[5] *PP* 1816, XVI, i, 70–71.   [6] *VCH, Bucks.*, III, 386.

indenture an endowment for the relief of the poor of another Buckinghamshire community, Great Brickhill.[1] In sum, this family over a period
of fifty-five years gave a total of £1115 of capital, most prudently vested
in trusteeships, for the outright relief of the poor of Ivinghoe and other
Buckinghamshire communities in which they had strong personal or
property ties.

A more considerable family, again with London connections, were the
Cheyneys of Drayton Beauchamp and, in its earlier branches, of Burnham. This was an old family, one of whose number had as early as 1488
left £33 11s for religious causes.[2] The family gained eminence and opu-
lence from the career of Sir John Cheyney, a lord mayor and merchant of
London, who died, however, in 1585 as lord of the manor of Drayton
Beauchamp. During his lifetime, Cheyney had purchased lands in
several parishes which, with other properties, were charged, under
trusteeship, with substantial charities, including £7 p.a. to Trinity
College, Cambridge, and £16 p.a. to be distributed 'in brotherly charity
towards the pious poor professing the gospel' who 'should be good
and godly in living, and had most need of relief'. The parish of Drayton
Beauchamp was to receive £2 p.a., Chesham, Burnham, and Bukenfield a similar amount, Chesham Bois and Cholesbury somewhat lesser
annuities, and Aylesbury a total of £8 p.a. Cheyney, who was a staunch
Puritan, devoted the greater part of his charities, which totalled £1260
of capital value, to the advancement of the Gospel which he insisted his
poor must most piously profess. He endowed a lectureship in the parish
of Tring, Hertfordshire, with the munificent stipend of £40 p.a. which
he thought sufficient to secure an excellently educated and able preacher
of the reformed faith who should disseminate there the true doctrines
of the Reformation.[3] Cheyney's daughter, who died in 1595, left a small
bequest for alms to Little Missenden,[4] and his nephew, Thomas
Cheyney, by deed in 1598 established under trusteeship rent-charges
totalling £5 p.a. for the relief of the poor of the parishes of Chesham,
Drayton Beauchamp, and Amersham.[5] Sir John's heir, Sir Francis
Cheyney, following the example of 'his good ffather', created an
endowment of £20 as a stock for the poor of Amersham, while by his

[1] *VCH, Bucks.*, IV, 298; *PP* 1834, XXI, 121; Ratcliff, *Newport hundreds*, 493.
[2] Lady Agnes Cheyney, of Chenies, Burnham (PCC 15 Milles 1488). *Vide
post*, 64.
[3] PCC 16 Windsor 1585; *Records of Buckinghamshire*, I (1858), 132, II (1863),
134–135, III (1870), 74, VI (1887), 199; *VCH, Bucks.*, III, 217, 221, 345;
Lipscomb, *Buckingham*, III, 265; and *vide post*, 59. In addition to his charities,
Cheyney left four farms in Buckinghamshire, as well as 200 acres of land in
scattered tracts, a valuable leasehold, a rich parsonage in Hertfordshire, and
upwards of £900 to his children.
[4] PCC 43 Scott 1595.
[5] Lipscomb, *Buckingham*, III, 159; *PP* 1833, XVIII, 22–23, 61.

will, proved in 1620, he bound his heirs to pay £3 p.a. in perpetuity to the poor of Drayton Beauchamp and Chesham. These stipends were to be limited to the most godly and impotent of the poor and, in accordance with the principle of local responsibility, should include 'no newe comers to ye towne, nor [those] dwelling in newe created cottages'.[1]

The great outpouring of benefactions for the poor occurred in the period 1601–1640, when well over half (57·61 per cent) the amount provided for household relief during our entire period was concentrated. These amounts rose from £1618 7s in the first decade of the period of £2049 13s in the second, to the really huge total, for a small rural county, of £7571 13s in the third decade, falling away in the fourth troubled interval of the century to the still considerable total of £3457 3s.

Only a few of the principal or more interesting of the bequests for poor relief in this crowded period can be noticed in detail. Among them was the gift of Sir John Dormer, made in 1603 and augmented by deeds of trust in 1620. Dormer was a member of a family, long settled in Buckinghamshire, which had risen during the preceding century from the ranks of the lower gentry to a prominent place among the upper gentry. Sir Robert Dormer of West Wycombe, who served as Sheriff of Buckinghamshire, had in 1552 left £40 of capital for the use of the poor, while an ancestor, William Dormer, had in 1506 left a larger sum, £120, to be equally disposed for the poor, the church, and the roads of West Wycombe.[2] Sir John Dormer, by his seventeenth-century deeds, charged lands in Buckinghamshire and Oxfordshire with annuities totalling £30, of which £4 p.a. was to be employed for the maintenance of the south aisle of Crendon church and his own monument, while the remainder was to be disbursed by his trustees for the relief of ten poor inhabitants of the parish.[3] His son, Sir Robert Dormer, who was reputed to have purchased a peerage in 1615 for the handsome sum of £10,000,[4] was more strait in his will when he died in the following year leaving no more than £20 of charitable capital, the income to be employed for the relief of the poor of High Wycombe and Aylesbury, and augmenting sums earlier given for this purpose by his mother.[5]

The great family of Tudor lawyers, the Crokes, who remained seated in Buckinghamshire, were likewise deeply and continuously interested in the relief of the poor of their county. John Croke of Chilton, successively a Clerk in Chancery, a serjeant-at-law, and

---

[1] PCC 4 Soame 1620; *Records of Buckinghamshire*, I (1858), 132.

[2] Nicolas, N. H., *Testamenta vetusta* (L., 1826, 2 vols.), II, 474; *Records of Buckinghamshire*, V (1878), 181; Langley, *Desborough*, 403. Other relations had in the course of the sixteenth century left varying sums to the poor, the church, and to Oxford scholars.

[3] *VCH, Bucks.*, IV, 45; Lipscomb, *Buckingham*, I, 218; *PP* 1833, XIX, 14–15.

[4] *The court and times of James I* (L., 1848, 2 vols.), I, 365.

[5] *VCH, Bucks.*, III, 18; *PP* 1833, XIX, 162.

Master of Chancery, had in 1555 bequeathed £19 to the poor of several Buckinghamshire and Oxfordshire parishes.[1] His son and heir, Sir John (1530–1608), bequeathed or gave during his lifetime £14 outright to the poor of Chilton and other parishes and established a trust valued at £20 p.a. for the assistance of worthy poor in those parishes in which he held property, as well as £20 p.a. to augment the living of the parish of Chilton.[2] His son, also Sir John Croke (1553–1620), Justice of King's Bench and Recorder of London, left small amounts to the poor of Chilton, Easington, Studley, and Horton, not to mention valuable books to the Bodleian library.[3] One of his several distinguished grandsons, Sir George Croke (1560–1642), the judge of Ship Money fame, left £23 to the poor of Chilton and certain London and Oxfordshire parishes, as well as the richly endowed almshouse to which we shall refer in later pages.[4]

Another donor of the period, of very different social status, left capital sums for the relief of the poor of Wingrave and other parishes in Buckinghamshire and Bedfordshire. Thomas Pratt was a shepherd. In 1614 he founded by deed of gift a charity for the poor of Wingrave, Cheddington, Mentmore, and Wing parishes with a capital worth of approximately £160, to which he added by will in the next year £20 to remain as a stock for the poor of Leighton Buzzard, Bedfordshire, £15 of capital for the poor of Aylesbury and certain other parishes in Buckinghamshire, as well as £4 for the repair of highways.[5]

Very little has been learned concerning Nicholas Almond of Thame, Oxfordshire, who by deeds and indentures established numerous charities in Buckinghamshire between 1628 and his death in 1653. Almond was apparently a member of the lower gentry and certainly held extensive landed properties in Buckinghamshire and a considerable estate in Thame. His successive gifts for the poor of Brill, Chilton, Easington, Aylesbury, Cuddington, and Wendover totalled £330 of capital value. In addition, he vested in trustees capital of £480 (£24 p.a.) with which the clergymen of Cuddington and Great Missenden

---

[1] Lipscomb, *Buckingham*, I, 130; Croke, Alexander, *The genealogical history of the Croke family* (Oxford, 1823, 2 vols.), I, 405–407.

[2] PCC 50 Dorset 1609. Croke left a personal estate of £1,334, rents in Berkshire and Oxfordshire, and land in Buckinghamshire and Oxfordshire.

[3] Lipscomb, *Buckingham*, I, 130–131; Croke, *Croke family*, I, 483.

[4] PCC 58 Cambell 1642. *Vide post*, 48. Croke left a personal estate of £2000 plus a considerable residue. All his English books were left to his wife, save for the *Book of Martyrs*, which his son was to have, reserving the use of it to his mother for her lifetime. Croke's widow augmented his almshouse endowment at Studley, Oxfordshire, by a capital bequest of £205 (PCC 669 Wootton 1658).

[5] PCC 51 Rudd 1615; *VCH, Bucks.*, III, 333, 401, 464; Sheahan, *Buckinghamshire*, 791; *PP* 1834, XXI, 106–107. These charities were in 1909 yielding a total of £50 4s 4d p.a. Pratt left, in addition to the charities mentioned, a personal estate of £114 6s 8d.

were annually to be paid 6s 8d for preaching their Easter sermons, while the remainder of funds in hand by the trustees was 'immediately after the said sermon' either to be distributed among the poor, or part to be laid out 'towards the provision of a stock to set the poor . . . on work, or to place out a child to be kept or youth to be bound out apprentice' as the trustees might think most advantageous for the benefit of the poor.[1] In 1630, William Cavendish, Earl of Devonshire, redeemed an earlier promise to endow the poor of Chesham by the gift, upon trust, of thirty-nine acres of land, the income of which was to be distributed to seven poor and impotent persons of Chesham Woburn and Chesham Leicester.[2] The capital value of the gift was about £200.

The most generous of all Buckinghamshire benefactors, Sir Simon Bennett of Beachampton Hall, by a will dated August 15, 1631, provided very large endowments for university scholarships, marriage portions, and various municipal uses which will be noted later.[3] His charities were to total £9390, and all were principally or wholly for the benefit of his county and university. Bennett set aside properties then worth £44 10s p.a. to provide clothing, consisting of blue jerkins, breeches, and stockings for poor and honest workmen who were beyond the age of labour. Recipients of these stipends must have resided within the parish for at least seven years, must not live in a house containing more than one family, and must have a personal record clear of hedge-breaking and other such depredations. Persons eligible under these restrictions, which reflect the preoccupations of a seventeenth-century justice of the peace, in the parishes of Beachampton, Calverton, the west side of Stony Stratford, and the town of Buckingham were to be benefited by the charity, which was endowed with the tithes of Bourton, Buckinghamshire.[4] A relative of Sir Simon's, Ambrose Bennett of London, likewise remembered the poor of Calverton in his will (1630), in which he charged his manor of Rotherhithe, Surrey, with a perpetual annuity of £1 to assist in conveying the poor to the local almshouse and providing them with proper boots.

These instances will perhaps suffice to illustrate the variety as well as the extent of the many charities established for poor relief during the early decades of the seventeenth century. It is clear that the problem of poverty was foremost in the minds of responsible and charitable men and that even in these endowments for direct, or household, relief, the medieval system of alms, of alleviation, was giving way to more con-

[1] Lipscomb, *Buckingham*, I, 116, 149, II, 133; *VCH, Bucks.*, II, 347, 353, IV, 27; *PP* 1833, XIX, 12–13, 72, 84–85, 113–114; Sheahan, *Buckinghamshire*, 179.
[2] *PP* 1833, XVIII, 57–59; *Records of Buckinghamshire*, III (1870), 73–74.
[3] *Vide post*, 51, 59.
[4] PCC 100 St John 1631; Lipscomb, *Buckingham*, II, 529; Willis, *Buckingham*, 139–140; *VCH, Bucks.*, III, 488, IV, 153, 310–311, 481; *PP* 1834, XXI, 46–49, 67, 191; Ratcliff, *Newport hundreds*, 390.

sidered and certainly better administered plans. In something more than two score parishes in Buckinghamshire in these forty years endowments were established yielding upwards of £20 p.a. each, which, all evidence suggests, somewhat exceeded the normal outlays for the poor provided from all sources, whether by taxation or voluntary gifts, in most rural parishes in this period. Very great gains had been made, traditions of generosity as well as responsibility had been well established, and a solid structure of locally administered charities had been well founded for the relief of poverty somewhat before the advent of the troubled years of civil war.

The great outpouring of charitable wealth of these four decades simply could not be maintained. None the less, during the next twenty years of political dislocation, the proportion of benefactions given for the benefit of the poor remained almost exactly the same as in the early Stuart period, while it may be noted that the total so provided in each decade, £1969 14s in the first and £1900 9s in the second, was higher than in any decade prior to 1601 save for one. There was, in fact, far less disruption of normal life and of local institutions during these years than has sometimes been supposed.

One of the largest donors in the Cromwellian period was a rich yeoman of Beachampton, William Elmer. In various documents Elmer is described as 'gentleman' and 'yeoman' indifferently, but he firmly called himself a yeoman in his will. Elmer's benefactions in Buckinghamshire, by gift and bequest, totalled £1621 and were notable for the wisdom as well as the discretion with which they were drawn. Rather more than half the total was employed for the foundation of a grammar school,[1] a fund of £5 p.a. was provided for apprenticing poor and deserving boys from Beachampton, and an income of £3 16s p.a. was established for the repair and maintenance of bridges and roads within that parish. By indenture and bequest Elmer likewise provided an endowment of £745, the income of which was to be employed for the relief of the poor of Beachampton, Whaddon (with Nash), and Calverton parishes. Each man selected was to be aged, honest, and 'worn out' by labour and should have £2 p.a. The women chosen should be widows, aged and of quiet temper, and they were to have £1 each annually. Every third year each recipient was to have a black gown of 15s value and during that year should receive only half the normal monetary stipend.[2]

One other example will possibly suggest the continuing and substan-

---

[1] *Vide post*, 57 for a discussion of this foundation.
[2] PCC 62 Brent 1653; Lipscomb, *Buckingham*, II, 534–536, III, 503; PP 1834, XXI, 50–54; *VCH, Bucks.*, III, 442. Elmer left to charity all his landed property, subject to a life estate for his widow. His personal estate cannot be accurately calculated, but certainly considerably exceeded the £150 of personal bequests made in his will.

tial interest in the welfare of the poor that characterized the Cromwellian era, though it may be observed that, not inappropriately, it is drawn from the middle class. In 1657 Thomas Pitt, a mercer of Colnbrook, conveyed to twenty trustees three cottages, lands, and buildings of an estimated value of £300 capital for the relief of the poor of Horton and Langley Marish. Rather elaborate provisions were set out for the administration of the trust and the usual wishes were expressed regarding the selection of worthy pensioners.

These are but examples of the wealth which England ranged against poverty in the sixteenth and seventeenth centuries. We have seen that the total was substantial and since it was principally in capital funds, its use remained curative and applicable from generation to generation. Yet in one sense these men and women whose benefactions have been noted are not exemplars, for we have chosen either large or especially interesting instances. The web of charity was woven not only from these large benefactions, but from hundreds of small bequests and gifts to the poor, almost wholly in the form of direct alms. Of these, to choose at random, Sir William Anne's bequest of £1 13s to the poor of Aylesbury and nearby parishes, or James Annesley's of £3 7s for the poor of Newport Pagnell, or Edmund Ardys' of 10s to the poor of Sherington, or John Baker's £2 to the poor of Buckland, or William Baldwin's £3 to the poor of Amersham, or John Ball's bequest of 3s to the poor of Boarstall are typical. This short list, chosen quite at random, includes members of the upper gentry, the lower gentry, the yeomanry, the husbandmen, and the shopkeepers of the county. All classes of men had come by 1560 to look upon the relief of the impotent poor as a responsibility to be shared by all.

The care of the poor passed through several stages during our period. The medieval tradition of occasional and indiscriminate alms persisted in Buckinghamshire benefactions until about 1540 when it began to give way to endowments established under the supervision of trustees who were responsible for the exercise of some measure of selection, regularity of distribution, and a considerable degree of charitable discretion. This may be said to have begun the institutionalizing of poor relief, the ultimate form of which was the almshouse intended to withdraw from the community those persons unemployable because of age, disease, or incompetence. This notable and important experiment in the relief of poverty began to yield in its turn, in Buckinghamshire in approximately 1600, to a great variety of schemes of social rehabilitation contemplating the abolition or mitigation of poverty by an attack on its roots. The development of these plans of rehabilitation, with which even the foundation of the grammar schools was so clearly connected, was, as we shall see, less advanced in Buckinghamshire than in several other counties. In Buckinghamshire, almost completely rural and relatively prosperous through the whole of our period, the principal attention was rather paid to the foundation of almshouses; to the sealing off of the unemployable under conditions which promised at least decent care, clothing, and shelter for the remainder of life.

During the whole period under examination the impressive total of £16,287 6s was given or bequeathed to almshouses, all save £24 6s having been given for the building or endowment of these institutions rather than as gifts for income. This amounts to 18·48 per cent of the whole of the charities of the county and represents well over a third of all gifts and bequests disposed for the relief of the poor.

It is important to note that almost all these foundations, as well as gifts or bequests to existing almshouses, occurred after 1551, or more precisely, after 1557. The dividing line is clear and sharp: £13 3s was given for this purpose before 1557; the large total of £16,274 3s in the next century, and, indeed, most of this (£9927) was concentrated in the years 1601–1640. During the whole of the Middle Ages, Miss Clay's valuable study would suggest, something like twenty hospitals and almshouses were founded in Buckinghamshire.[1] Of this number it would appear that eight, possibly nine, at some time exercised those functions which the sixteenth century came to associate with almshouses. Though no really thorough study of the question has been undertaken, it may at least be said that only four of these earlier foundations, most of which were small or poorly endowed, survived in the sense that they were attracting even small gifts and bequests in the years 1480–1547 or fulfilling their functions by affording lodging and maintenance to the poor. In contrast, a total of twenty-two almshouses were founded and endowed in Buckinghamshire in the relatively short period 1557–1644, one other very small house having been established in 1494. This suggests at once the over-emphasis that has been placed on medieval alms and the remarkable surge of the secular spirit in its effort to deal with the problem of abject poverty during the first century of the Reformation in England.

We should now examine at least certain of these foundations in some detail. They are of all kinds, large and small, well and poorly constituted, in towns and in rural parishes, but they all exhibit a resolute interest in the cure of at least the worst of the evils of poverty and a recognition that society must undertake, in some institutionalized sense, the care of the unfit and the unemployable.

The earliest of these foundations in Buckinghamshire was also the weakest. In or somewhat before 1494, one Thomas Elliott gave two tenements in Aylesbury for perpetual use as almshouses with, it seems probable, a modest endowment. The churchwardens were constituted the trustees of this small foundation, which survived until the houses

[1] Clay, R. M., *The mediaeval hospitals of England* (L., 1909), Appendix.

were burned in 1631, at which time the income came to be used for general poor relief.[1]

Rather more than a half century later, in 1557–1558, Edward, Lord Hastings, began the erection at Stoke Poges, his seat, of the first of the considerable number of well-endowed and more carefully administered almshouses that characterize this period. Hastings, an ardent Roman Catholic and a member of Mary's Privy Council, found himself out of favour and, indeed, for a short time in prison, with the accession of Elizabeth. He retired to Stoke Poges where he built a chapel and began the erection of his almshouses, which were completed and endowed by the terms of his will in 1573. His hospital, which cost an unknown amount to build, was designed for a master, four poor men and two women, with a chimney in each room and four loads of firewood for each almsperson. The master was to be a chantry priest with £10 p.a., and £20 p.a. was to be distributed amongst the almspeople in the hospital, as well as every second year a 'blue gown of broad cloth, of four yards, and a bull's head on the sleeve'. Lord Hastings had intended to augment the endowment with additional revenues from rents on the manor of Creech St Michael, Somerset, and other properties with a total value of £66 13s 4d p.a., but it seems clear that the original value of the whole endowment was not more than £53 10s p.a. which, be it said, represents a very substantial capital worth.[2]

An equally ambitious plan was in the mind of Edward, Lord Windsor, of Bradenham parish who in his will dated December 20, 1572, instructed his executors to erect an almshouse there with room and chambers sufficient for the accommodation of a master, who should be the parish parson, and six poor men. His executors were further instructed to purchase lands for charitable uses to the value of £40 p.a., of which one-third was to be employed for the augmentation of the living of the parish and the remaining £26 13s 4d p.a. placed in trust for the endowment of the almshouse. Windsor's estate seemed sufficient for the execution of the instructions, but there is no certain evidence that the almshouse was ever built or endowed in the parish and the benefaction has consequently not been tabulated.[3] Not infrequently, indeed,

---

[1] *PP* 1833, XIX, 55–56; Gibbs, *Aylesbury*, 465–466.

[2] Nicolas, *Testamenta vetusta*, II, 740–742; Lipscomb, *Buckingham*, IV, 561; *PP* 1833, XVIII, 111–120. Hastings' will provided, as well, outright alms amounting to £38 13s for the poor of Stoke Poges, £20 for road repairs, £45 for London prisons, £40 for poor scholars in Oxford and Cambridge, and £27 for the maintenance of the clergy.

His brother, Sir Thomas Hastings, who died in 1558, left £1 each to the six almspeople in his brother's foundation, as well as small gifts to prisons, the poor, and the friars of Greenwich and St Bartholomew (Nicolas, *Testamenta vetusta*, II, 750–752).

[3] Lipscomb, *Buckingham*, III, 558n.; Langley, *Desborough*, 163.

the aspirations of a donor either exceeded his property or failed to take fully into account the tenacious property instincts of his heirs or the charges of his lawyers.

Dorothy Dayrell, a member of the lesser gentry of the county, who in 1574 had established a fund for poor relief in the borough of Buckingham, by her will gave to trustees six small almshouses which she had built, at an uncertain cost, with an endowment of £5 4s to secure, somewhat meagrely, the care of the six poor persons already resident in them, under trust provisions on which we have commented in earlier pages.[1] We have noted, as well, the unusually generous and well-considered foundation of an almshouse for five poor widows of Brill made by Alice Carter, a yeoman's widow, by a deed of gift in 1590.[2] At about the same time another almshouse, for five or six almsmen, was provided for Aylesbury by William Cockman, Esq., these poor men to be nominated by the churchwardens and overseers. It seems doubtful if any considerable endowment was given by the donor, though the building was used as an almshouse until the early nineteenth century when it was sold to assist with the erection of a workhouse for the parish.[3]

Another of the Elizabethan almshouses in the county was that founded in Wing by Dame Dorothy Pelham in 1596. A daughter of Anthony Catesby of Northamptonshire, this woman had first married Sir William Dormer, lord of the manor of Wing, who had died in 1575. Her second husband, Sir William Pelham, Lord Chief Justice of Ireland, having died in 1587 Lady Pelham retired to Wing where she built Dormer's Hospital, 'of the foundation of Dame Dorothy Pelham', for eight poor persons. This brick structure was built at a cost of upwards of £200 and was endowed with property sufficient to provide an income of £4 p.a. for each of the eight almsmen. Lady Pelham, who died in 1613, left £100 to be distributed in clothing at her funeral, as well as capital sums for the benefit of the poor, the lame, and the impotent of Aylesbury, Great Wycombe, and Wing in Buckinghamshire, and £53 for road repairs in Buckinghamshire and Bedfordshire. Her charities totalled £1070 13s.[4]

The great Queen has herself sometimes been regarded as the founder of Queen Elizabeth's Hospital, or Christ's Hospital, in the borough of Buckingham, where the almshouse was legally established in 1597 for the care of seven poor almswomen. The endowment seems, however, to date from about 1590, when Robert Harris, a miller, created by deed of gift a fund yielding £12 10s p.a. from rents, the profits of the wool

---

[1] *Vide ante*, 31.   [2] *Vide ante*, 32.   [3] *PP* 1833, XIX, 62.
[4] PCC 104 Capell 1613; *VCH, Bucks.*, III, 458; Lipscomb, *Buckingham*, II, 48, III, 525, 652; *PP* 1833, XIX, 56, 162; Langley, *Desborough*, 64. The almshouse endowment, as reported in the *VCH* (1914-1925), was valued at £105 4s p.a. Lady Pelham was rich in her own right, having in addition to her charity disposed £2360 in personal bequests in her will.

market and of two annual fairs in Buckingham, for the support of the hospital. Some years later this donor, or possibly another of the same name, willed to the hospital £1 p.a. of income out of a public-house in the town as additional income. The capital of the foundation was further increased by the bequest of three houses in Stony Stratford, worth approximately £100, by Michael Hipwell in 1598.[1] Small additional bequests totalling £110 were from time to time left to the hospital prior to 1660, the Bishop of Lincoln reporting its annual income as £14 in 1666.[2]

In the year of the Queen's death, Anne, Countess of Warwick, founded a large almshouse at Chenies, which she endowed with rent charges of £30 p.a. from lands in Gloucestershire and £20 p.a. from Hertfordshire properties.[3] The almshouse, which was erected in 1605 at an unknown cost, was designed to house four poor men and six women, each inmate to receive £5 p.a. for his sustenance. During the seventeenth century the value of the endowments increased and the income beyond the prescribed £50 p.a. came to be assigned to aged pensioners in Chenies and two nearby parishes. At about the same date another parish in Burnham hundred, Amersham, was given an almshouse to accommodate four paupers by John and Agnes Bennett. The building continued to be used for its original purpose for upwards of three hundred years, but we have found no particulars concerning the deed of gift or the value of the property or its endowment.[4]

John Brinkhurst, a tradesman or merchant of Great Marlow, by deed of gift founded an almshouse for that town with room and support for four poor widows. The endowment comprised real property in Buckinghamshire and Oxfordshire of considerable value, since the instruction was that each almswoman should receive £1 p.a. in addition to her maintenance, that £1 p.a. be used for a dinner for the trustees and for maintenance, and additional rents were provided for the repair of the building. The very small stipends were increased later in the century and the steadily mounting income was employed in the nineteenth century to enlarge the structure and likewise for further increases in the annual stipends.[5]

In all, twelve almshouses were founded in Buckinghamshire in the short period 1615–1640, not to mention two other possible or, perhaps

[1] Vide post, 55.
[2] PP 1834, XXI, 54–55; VCH, Bucks., III, 488, IV, 165; Lipscomb, Buckingham, II, 583, 585; Willis, Buckingham, 83–84; S.P. Dom., 1598, CCLXVI, 30. The benefaction of the Rev. Robert Higginson to the hospital, which has been listed as having been given in 1629, was possibly a bequest dated beyond our period, in 1689.
[3] PP 1833, XVIII, 51–53; VCH, Bucks., III, 203; Sheahan, Buckinghamshire, 837; Berks, Bucks, & Oxon Arch., XII (1906), 59. Vide ante, 28–29.
[4] PP 1833, XVIII, 33; Lipscomb, Buckingham, III, 159.
[5] PP 1833, XIX, 136–139; Langley, Desborough, 112; VCH, Bucks., III, 77. (The income in 1907 was £128 9s 8d p.a.)

more accurately, abortive plans for such establishments. In this quarter century more true almshouses were established in the county than during the whole of the Middle Ages. We shall deal briefly with at least the principal of these charitable undertakings. Thus in 1615 a derelict hospital was reorganized and endowed by various donors in Newport Pagnell as Queen Anne's Hospital. Four trustees were appointed, with the provision that they were to choose their successors from the 'honestest men' of the parish, who were to administer an endowment then of approximately £500 capital value in the interests of three poor men and three poor women, each of whom was to receive in addition to his sustenance an allowance for clothing in every second year.[1] Somewhat earlier (1607), Thomas Stafford, gentleman, of Tattenhoe, founded and generously endowed an almshouse for four men and two women. By his will he empowered his trustees, including his son, to choose the town to be assisted and endowed the foundation with land then worth £30 p.a. Each pensioner should have a room and a garden plot and should annually receive sustenance at the rate of 3d a day (2d for the two almswomen), as well as a gown having a red cross on the left sleeve. The trustees settled the endowment in Shenley parish (Newport hundred), where the almshouse was erected in 1615 at an estimated cost of £210.[2] At about the same time, 1617, Sir William Drake built and endowed an almshouse in Amersham with capital of approximately £500. This brick structure, facing on three sides of an open court, was dedicated to the 'glory of God, and for the relief of six poor widows well reputed' in the parish and was to be administered by self-perpetuating and substantial trustees.[3]

Another of the numerous almshouses in Buckinghamshire provided by natives of the county who had made their fortune in trade in London was established in 1624 by Thomas Wedon [Weedon], a London draper of St Clement Danes parish. Wedon by will left outright £20 to the poor of Chesham and £500 in mortgages, which was to be employed by his feoffees to build an almshouse for four poor persons of the parish and to purchase lands as an endowment which he hoped might yield £30 p.a. for its support.[4]

---

[1] PP 1834, XXI, 148–158; VCH, Bucks., IV, 420–421. The aggregate income, according to VCH, was in the early twentieth century £300 p.a.

[2] PCC 47 Hudleston 1607; VCH, Bucks., IV, 445, 451; PP 1834, XXI, 113–115; Ratcliff, Newport hundreds, 419–420.

[3] Records of Buckinghamshire, II (1863), 346; Lipscomb, Buckingham, III, 159; PP 1833, XVIII, 16–22; VCH, Bucks., III, 155. The Charity Commissioners' Reports would suggest that the almshouse was built in 1617, having been supported by gifts from Drake during his lifetime and not having been endowed until 1669, the year of his death.

[4] PCC 82 and 114 Bryde 1624. Wedon was not a rich man. His charities consumed all his estate, save for £30 of personal property and lands and tenements

A somewhat different kind of foundation was provided by David [Daniel] Salter of Colnbrook, who in 1625 built a hospital in the town for the lodging and care of four poor cripples who might be succoured while passing through the town towards their homes or other points of destination.[1] This gift and these services were 'to remain forever', but there is no indication that the establishment was ever endowed. The Reverend Thomas Knyghton by will in 1629 likewise provided for Slapton parish an almshouse foundation with unusual trust provisions. He devised lands in Leighton Buzzard, Bedfordshire, with a capital value of approximately £384, in trust for the repair of four dwellings occupied by paupers. The surplus income was to be employed for paying the funeral expenses of labourers and their families resident in the parish and to relieve the married poor of the town.[2]

Sir John Kiderminster, of Langley Marish, was a substantial benefactor of his parish. During his lifetime he had provided a library for the community, had begun the erection of two organs in his parish church and the building of an almshouse for four poor men and women. His will provided that the library and the books he had appointed for it should be open to the clergy of the town and such other persons as might desire to use it, but with the careful provision that no book might be taken from the building. Moreover, £20 of endowment was provided for the purchase of additional books from time to time. His almshouse was to be finished by his widow at the charge of his estate and an endowment of £15 p.a. was established for the support of his almspeople.[3]

Only scant mention can be made of Sir Ralph Verney's almshouse for six poor residents of Middle Claydon, which he endowed with deeds of gift providing an income of £2 12s p.a. for the support of each almsman;[4] or of William Tipping's gift of £300 to secure the erection of a bridewell and almshouse in Shabbington parish in 1640;[5] or of Arthur Goodwin's provision in 1644 for the erection and endowment of almshouses for the support of six poor widows of Waddesdon parish.[6]

in Hertfordshire of unspecified value. He was the grandson of Thomas Wedon, gentleman, of Chesham, who had left £1 3s to the poor of Chesham and Great Missenden (Archd. Bucks. 1561, f. 124), and the son of Richard Wedon, gentleman, who by will (PCC 6 Scott 1595) gave £3 17s to the poor of the same parishes, as well as 6s 8d for the repair of Chesham church.

[1] Gyll, G. W. J., *History of Wraysbury* (L., 1862), 288.

[2] *VCH, Bucks.*, III, 414; Sheahan, *Buckinghamshire*, 743; *PP* 1834, XXI, 94. The endowment yielded about £80 p.a. gross in 1914.

[3] PCC 57 St John 1631; Lipscomb, *Buckingham*, IV, 543n.; *PP* 1833, XVIII, 95-99.

[4] Lipscomb, *Buckingham*, I, 197.

[5] *Ibid.*, I, 452. Tipping was the vicar of the parish. He was the author of a number of tracts and took the Covenant during the Civil War.

[6] PCC 1 Rivers 1644; *VCH, Bucks.*, IV, 117; *PP* 1834, XXI, 32-33; Moreton, C.O., *Waddesdon and Over Winchendon* (L., 1929), 155-156; Brunton, D., and

Our discussion of these numerous foundations may be closed with a brief description of the almshouse founded in 1639 by Sir George Croke, Justice of the King's Bench. The buildings were erected across the Oxfordshire border at Studley, but the almspeople were to be chosen from named parishes in both Buckinghamshire and Oxfordshire. Croke provided an endowment of £60 p.a. from the manor of Easington for the support of eight almspeople, four men and four women, each of whom should receive 2s weekly, who should enjoy separate apartments and a garden plot, as well as coals and a clothing allowance. The men were to be upwards of sixty years of age and the women more than fifty, unless they were lame or blind persons. If the preferred parishes did not have a sufficient number of qualified persons, choice was to be made by the governors from neighbouring parishes in Buckinghamshire or Oxfordshire within a radius of six miles of the institution. The terms of the deed of gift further provided that those elected for relief should be well reputed for religion and should not include 'cursers nor common swearers, nor idle persons, noe drunkards, none having committed fornication or adultery, noe haunters of ale houses, noe gadders or wanderers abroad, noe tale-bearers, noe busie bodies', but only such as live quietly and peaceably who are natives or who have for ten years been residents of the favoured parishes. Croke's widow, by her will proved in 1658, further supplemented the funds of this well-endowed almshouse by an outright gift of £5 and an endowment of £10 p.a.[1]

We have discussed in somewhat summary fashion at least the principal of the twenty-three almshouses certainly built and endowed in Buckinghamshire during the period under review. A considerable number of other capital gifts were made to similar foundations in other counties or for establishments which were apparently either never built or which lasted for only a short time. In fourteen cases we have reliable particulars regarding the allowances for support in the endowed almshouses, yielding an average of £4 8s 7d p.a. for each almsperson, the median being £5. The annuities ranged widely from an almost impossible minimum of £1 p.a. each to the generous provision of Croke and Wedon of £7 10s for each pensioner. On the whole, since lodging, a garden plot, and some clothing were also normally furnished, the

D. H. Pennington, *Members of the Long Parliament* (Cambridge, Mass., 1954), Appendix, 232. Goodwin, who sat for Buckinghamshire in the Long Parliament, recited his instructions in his will, requiring his trustees to erect the almshouse as soon as the civil distractions of the times permitted and to endow it with an annuity of £30, to be distributed equally among the six widows. Each almswoman was to have two rooms and a garden plot, in addition to her annuity. Goodwin's father (?), Sir Francis, had left an annuity of £20 to the poor in 1630.

[1] PCC 58 Cambell 1642; DNB; Lipscomb, *Buckingham*, I, 149; Croke, *Croke family*, I, 600, 602; VCH, Bucks., IV, 27. *Vide ante*, 38.

average stipend was sufficient to provide a maintenance probably not much less straitened than that of an agricultural labourer with a family in this period.

In twenty-two instances the deed of gift or the will sets forth the number of almspeople to be sheltered, with a certain total of 126 almsmen for whom full maintenance was provided. This is a not inconsiderable number for a relatively small and not particularly populous county, but the total of the capital given for almshouses during the period suggests that it represents not quite the whole of the achievement. Reasonably reliable data on the ordering of eight almshouses permit the deduction that it required a capital outlay of about £24 to provide shelter for an almsperson in this county, while something like £92 of endowment was required to produce the average allowance for maintenance. Since £16,263 of capital was contributed during the years under discussion, we may infer that sufficient endowments were established for the complete relief of 140 impotent persons in the almshouses of Buckinghamshire founded in our period.

It will likewise be recalled that a capital total of £23,872 was given to secure the household relief of the poor and for general charitable purposes which recognized poor relief as the first of the obligations of the trustees. Payments from these trusts were normally much smaller than the average stipend for the completely impotent almsperson and if they may be calculated, without really reliable statistical evidence, at £2 p.a. for each recipient, enough charitable capital had been accumulated by charitable gifts by the end of our period for the support of another 600 persons, or more accurately, families, in temporary straits. To this must of course be added the outright gifts to the poor, common especially in the earlier decades, which relieved an unknown but considerable number of persons. It is clear that private charity was lending continuous and possibly sufficient support to as many as 740 of the poor of the county, and we may be sure that it was carrying throughout these years a far larger share of the burden of poverty than was taxation or semi-voluntary rating.

2. *Social rehabilitation*

The principal charitable concern of this rural county was for the relief of poverty. Only a relatively small amount, £3920 2s, was left or given for the numerous and important ventures in social rehabilitation with which urban communities were beginning to experiment in a search for the cure and prevention of poverty. Nothing was provided in Buckinghamshire for loans to the poor or to assist young tradesmen who were seeking to establish themselves in business. Only very small amounts were given for the relief or redemption of prisoners (£73 2s), and not much more was provided for the care of the sick who were not at the same time paupers. Only a few bequests have been noted for the establishment of workhouses or work schemes for the poor, and relatively small endowments were available for the assistance of poor boys who desired to enter into apprenticeship undertakings. In only one particular, the provision of marriage subsidies for poor girls, for which capital was given totalling £2014, was the county notable in its giving to a group of charities which represented the best and perhaps the most effective of all possible assistance to the needy. Significantly, all save £69 9s of the total for social rehabilitation was provided after 1601 and reference to the master table for the county makes it clear that gifts and bequests for these experimental purposes were increasing very rapidly during the decades before the dislocation of civil strife intervened.[1]

3. *Municipal Betterments*

A much larger proportion (8·80 per cent) of benefactions were designated for various schemes of municipal betterment, these totalling £7757 19s for the whole period. This is a surprisingly large amount, since benefactions of this type are more characteristic of urban communities than of a predominantly rural society. Rather more than a third of the total was given for a variety of municipal purposes such as tax relief, improvement of public buildings, the building or repair of markets, or to local authorities for unspecified uses. The whole of the amounts given, it might be observed, came to hand after 1571, with benefactions of this type remaining quite unimportant until after 1591. The remainder of gifts for general purposes, totalling £5015 19s, was designated for the maintenance or improvement of the roads and bridges of the county. These amounts were spread rather evenly over the whole of our period and this need attracted gifts from every class of society and from urban as well as rural donors. It might also be noted that a very high proportion (99·2 per cent) of the gifts for municipal uses were capital sums and that an amazingly high percentage (93·2 per cent) of gifts for roads and bridges were in the form of endowments.

The benefactions for various municipal purposes were attempts by the responsible elements of the community to secure local betterments which were in time to be assumed as part of the social and civic burden of taxation. In the Tudor and Stuart periods, however, great areas of administration as well as of improvement were left, with little governmental support or direction, to local ingenuity or to private charity.[2]

[1] *Vide* Table I, Appendix.
[2] The central government could on occasion intervene in the interests of a particularly important undertaking. Thus in 1605 the King wrote to Sir Robert Dormer and Sir Francis Fortescue to inform them that 'various gentlemen have

A few examples will suffice, though it should be said that the bulk of gifts of this type, and particularly for the maintenance of roads and bridges, were quite small amounts given by relatively humble persons.

In the late fifteenth century John Bedford, a gentleman of Aylesbury, whose benefactions for the poor have already been noted,[1] stipulated in his will that the first charge on his charitable estate should be the amendment, in perpetuity, of the roads in and about Aylesbury. It seems probable that an income of something like £35 p.a. was immediately available for this purpose from the estate.[2] Some years later, William Bates of Grendon Underwood left slightly more than five acres of land in his parish as an endowment to secure the 'maintenance, sustentation, and reparation' of Grendon Bridge, which spanned an arm of the Ray.[3]

We have previously spoken of the notable charities of Sir Simon Bennett of Beachampton, who in his carefully drafted will in 1631 left £20 p.a. for the repair and maintenance of the highways in the parishes of Beachampton, Calverton, and the western side of Stony Stratford.[4] The village of Datchet, lying on the Thames near Windsor, benefited in 1644 by a substantial trust created by Robert Barker, who conveyed to seven trustees a house and garden and about five acres of valuable land. The rents and profits of the trust were to be employed for the erection of a bridge in the middle of the town over waters that lay stagnant there 'to the great annoyance of the inhabitants', while any surplus was to be used for other municipal purposes.[5] A similar trust was established by Thomas Drew for his native town of Great Marlow, he in 1651 bequeathing an annuity of £4 towards the maintenance of Great Marlow Bridge across the Thames, as well as £5 p.a. towards church repairs.[6]

Perhaps two other instances of municipal betterments in the town of Great Marlow will suffice to illustrate the great variety of the benefactions being considered. One John Seymour, who died in 1565, left to

---

been repairing the highways between London and Watford', a considerable portion of which lay in Buckinghamshire. The King continued, 'As there is great resort from many places of that county of Buckingham to and from the citye by that way we thincke there is none whome it concerneth but wilbe willing to affoord their healp toward so good a worke.' Accordingly, Dormer and Fortescue were requested to arrange to receive contributions, freely given, for the purpose. (*S.P. Dom.*, 1605., XVII, 78, 79.)

[1] *Vide ante*, 34.

[2] *VCH, Bucks.*, III, 18; Gibbs, *Aylesbury*, 460–462; *PP* 1833, XIX, 45–49.

[3] *Ibid.*, XIX, 16. This trust was lost during the course of the eighteenth century.

[4] *Vide ante*, 39 and *post*, 59.

[5] *PP* 1833, XVIII, 68–70; *VCH, Bucks.*, III, 254.

[6] PCC 237 Grey 1651; *Records of Buckinghamshire*, VIII (1903), 200; *VCH, Bucks.*, III, 76–77; *PP* 1833, XIX, 140.

the bridge 'one convenient oak' each year for a period of sixty years, together with an annuity of £1 for the same period of time in order to assist with the proper maintenance of the structure. The wardens or bridge masters were to bear the cost of felling and carrying the timber.[1] A generation later John Rotherham, Esq., left £40 for the purpose of securing a charter and purchasing a market for the benefit of the town and £60 of capital for the proposed corporation, with the provision that the benefaction was to revert to the uses of the poor if his intentions could not be carried forward.[2]

4. *Education*

Interesting and important as are the gifts for public improvements, they amount in total and doubtless in effectiveness to no more than a fraction of the benefactions made during our period for the advancement and dissemination of education. A total of £18,741 2s, this being 21·26 per cent of the whole, was given for various educational purposes during the years under study.[3] These substantial endowments, for all save £10 15s of the total were capital gifts, were created almost wholly in the post-Reformation era, and the curve of giving for these purposes mounts steadily and fruitfully until the political disturbances of the seventeenth century damped somewhat men's certainty that wider and better educational opportunities afforded not only a more godly life but served as well as a preventive of poverty and social malaise.[4]

In the course of our period a total of £6789 2s was given for the foundation of new grammar schools or for the augmentation of the resources of the existing schools. Only about 3 per cent of this amount was given prior to 1541; only slightly more than 12 per cent before 1601. The great outpouring of wealth for educational purposes occurred in this rural county in the two decades just prior to the Civil War, when almost two-thirds of the whole amount for grammar-school foundations was given. Furthermore, in these same years, Buckinghamshire benefactors gave £9777 to other educational needs—almost the whole of their gifts to universities, everything given in the county for the foundation of non-university libraries, and almost two-thirds of the £5003 provided for scholarships. In fact, during the years 1601–1640 about three-

---

[1] *The Home Counties Magazine*, I (1899), 30.

[2] PCC 4 Woodhall 1601; Langley, *Desborough*, 109 n.; *PP* 1833, XIX, 144. The terms of the will were not fulfilled, and, after an inquisition held in 1618, the £100 was ordered paid out for poor relief.

[3] It should be remarked that Buckinghamshire lagged well behind other counties in the proportion of charitable resources designated for education. The proportion for the other counties ranges from 21·33 per cent for Bristol to 41·79 per cent for Lancashire.

[4] *Vide* Table I, Appendix.

fourths of the whole amount given for general educational purposes was provided by Buckinghamshire donors.

In none of the other charitable heads is such a heavy preponderance of the benefactions concentrated in so short and rich a period. The evidence suggests that this was an era of excited interest in education; a period in which the vision of a new and better society enhanced by wide educational opportunities gripped men's minds. These were all secular foundations which had by 1660 established throughout the county new and reasonably well dispersed opportunities for able boys to proceed not only through grammar school but on to the university, if their parents possessed at least modest means to support the ambition of their sons. These were foundations which were to assist powerfully in the creation of the liberal society not only in Buckinghamshire, but in England as well.

There were relatively few schools functioning as foundations principally concerned with the instruction of the young in 1480 and none was founded in the long interval 1481–1540. Though no certain list can be presented, it seems probable that there was in 1480 some instruction at Buckingham; Eton College had been founded some forty years earlier; and some systematic instruction was afforded by the Hospital of St John in High Wycombe. From these small beginnings it will now be well to trace at least the principal of the foundations for education created by private charity during our period.

We have commented elsewhere on the bequest of Isabel Denton which in 1540 established an endowment in Buckingham ensuring ordered instruction by one priest in the school there which, as we have observed, was probably in existence in some form in 1480.[1] This foundation was left undisturbed when the chantries and hospitals were confiscated and was greatly strengthened in 1592 by a crown grant establishing it as the Royal Latin School.

The Free School at Aylesbury was founded in about 1590 by the Elizabethan soldier and courtier, Sir Henry Lee, who had represented Buckinghamshire in Parliament in 1558 and again in 1572 and whose seat was nearby in Oxfordshire.[2] Lee, who was also to renovate the chapel at Quarrendon, near Aylesbury, where he was buried,[3] apparently erected a school building at Aylesbury and endowed it with two mes-

---

[1] *Vide ante*, 29.

[2] Lee (1530–1610) was a native of Kent, but his father, Sir Anthony, had his principal seat at Borston, Buckinghamshire. Lee entered the royal service in 1545, was knighted in 1553, and was well regarded by Queen Elizabeth. A great landowner, Lee was well known as an enclosing landlord and sheep farmer. He was appointed Master of the Ordnance in 1590 and in 1592 entertained the Queen at Quarrendon, Buckinghamshire. He was continued in his office by James I. On his death his property passed to a cousin, Henry Lee.

[3] Lipscomb, *Buckingham*, II, 400–409.

suages then worth £8 p.a. He made further gifts of uncertain value in 1598 and 1603, while on his death in 1610 he left endowments valued at £10 p.a. from properties which were subsequently lost by the trustees.[1]

Some instruction had been offered at the Hospital of St John in High Wycombe prior to 1480, though it is clear that it was at once irregular and relatively slight. In 1548 the then master of the hospital, Christopher Chalfount, a priest, disposed of the property, valued at the time of the Dissolution at £7 15s 3½d p.a., to nominees who in turn conveyed it to the mayor, bailiff, and burgesses of High Wycombe with the intent that it should be employed to support a grammar school to be erected within two years. Funds were provided by various local donors and neighbouring gentry, including Sir Edward Pelham, for the construction of the school, the corporation in 1552 ordering that the endowments should be let and that the stipend of £8 p.a. should be paid to the schoolmaster with five loads of wood and the right to pasture a cow or two. The new school stood in some danger under Queen Mary, who granted the properties to Sir Thomas Throckmorton. But the trustees hastened, on the accession of Elizabeth, to secure a firmer legal basis for the foundation by conveying the property to the Crown, it being re-granted to the mayor and burgesses and their successors as a hospital for the support of four poor persons and for the maintenance of a schoolmaster and the instruction of children and youths.[2]

At about the same time a grammar school was founded in Lathbury by Anthony Cave, a gentleman whose seat was near by in Chicheley. Cave established the foundation with the tithes and parsonage of Lathbury, which had been vested in him by the Dean and Chapter of Christ Church in 1553 (or 1554) for a period of ninety-four years, and with other properties which secured a then substantial income of £12 p.a. for the schoolmaster. The school was to be kept in a chapel in the churchyard and the schoolmaster was to be nominated by the Dean and Chapter of Christ Church with the consent of Cave and his heirs. Cave's great interest in education was further manifested by his creation of two scholarships, for students of Lathbury School, to study divinity at Oxford, one being at Christ Church, to be endowed with a rent-charge on his estate in the amount of £12 p.a.[3]

[1] PCC 41 Wood 1611; *PP* 1833, XIX, 36; Gibbs, *Aylesbury*, 476–477. It seems probable that the 1610 (1611) gift came from Sir *Henry*, whose will was proved in that year, rather than from Sir *Richard* Lee as is stated in the *PP*.

[2] *PP* 1833, XIX, 150–159; Carlisle, Nicholas, *A concise description of the endowed grammar schools in England and Wales* (L., 1818, 2 vols.), I, 94; *VCH, Bucks.*, II, 210; Lipscomb, *Buckingham*, III, 647.

[3] PCC 7 Welles 1558; decree, 37 Mellershe 1560; Waters, R.E.C., *Genealogical memoirs of the extinct family of Chester of Chicheley* (L., 1878, 2 vols.), I, 82–86; Lipscomb, *Buckingham*, IV, 207. Cave, who apparently had extensive

Another grammar school was founded in Newport Hundred in 1609. This was an humble foundation in Stony Stratford, quite typical of scores of earnest local efforts in England in this period to secure education for the children of many communities. One Michael Hipwell, of unknown social status, of Stony Stratford, by will conveyed to trustees a tavern belonging to him called the 'Rose and Crown', with all the barns, stables, and houses belonging to the property, for the creation and endowment of a free grammar school. The school was to be kept in a barn behind the inn and lodgings were appointed for the schoolmaster in a convenient loft. The income of the property, apparently then valued at about £10 p.a., was to be employed for the payment of the schoolmaster who must accept all students of the town, or the towns next adjoining, who desired to learn to write and cipher and who were also to be instructed in grammar and the principles of religion.[1]

A much more substantial foundation was created by the bequest of Robert Chaloner, Rector of Amersham and Canon of Windsor, on his death in 1621. Chaloner had some years earlier (1616) founded a grammar school at Knaresborough, Yorkshire, with an endowment of £20 p.a.[2] He likewise required his executors and trustees to found a free grammar school in Amersham with temporary quarters in the church until the school could be built. The statutes for the school were to be drawn from 'the best ordered schoole' in England, and Latin and, if need be, Greek were to be taught by the master. The school was endowed with £20 p.a. out of lands in Wavendon and with properties at Waddesdon which have been, perhaps too generously, estimated to have been worth £90 p.a. Chaloner likewise established an endowment of £20 p.a. to be employed for the maintenance of a divinity lecturer at Christ Church, Oxford, or, as was done, to create scholarships for three poor boys drawn from Amersham or from Knaresborough or Goldsborough in Yorkshire.[3]

It would seem that a school was either contemplated or being built in Walton at about the same time, since the will of Jeffrey Bampton of that parish in 1619 bequeathed 5s to the schoolhouse. There is, however, no other available evidence of a school there in this period, and one must

properties in Buckinghamshire, Northamptonshire, and London, also left bequests to the poor in scattered parishes in Buckinghamshire, Bedfordshire, and Northamptonshire.

[1] *VCH, Bucks.*, II, 212–213, IV, 478, 481; Ratcliff, *Newport hundreds*, 390–392. Hipwell also left three houses in Stony Stratford as endowment for an almshouse (Christ's Hospital) in Buckingham (*vide ante*, 45).

[2] *Vide post*, 331.

[3] PCC 69 Dale 1621; Carlisle, *Endowed grammar schools*, I, 44; *VCH, Bucks.*, II, 213–214; Petty Bag Inq., 22 Jas. I, no. 7; Lipscomb, *Buckingham*, III, 159–161; *Home Counties Mag.*, IV (1902), 55; *PP* 1833, XVIII, 8–14. In 1862 the income of the trust was £190 p.a., of which £10 10s was disbursed to the poor and £20 p.a. to the school at Knaresborough.

conclude that Bampton, like so many other small benefactors, was reflecting in his bequest a community interest in a school which was not to be immediately built or endowed.

A few years later a school was founded in Great Marlow by Sir William Borlase, of Medmenham, who at the time of his death endowed it richly and laid down most interesting and detailed instructions regarding the constitution and functioning of the institution. Borlase had built the schoolhouse in 1624 and for the four remaining years of his life supported it and immersed himself in its work. By gift and bequest he endowed the trust with lands in Great Marlow then worth more than £14 p.a., with lands and houses in Bix, Oxfordshire, worth about £24 p.a., and with funds suffcient for the purchase of lands to yield an additional £20 p.a. The total income of £58 p.a., a most substantial amount, was to be employed by governors chosen from Great and Little Marlow and one from Medmenham for the operation of the school and related charitable purposes. The master, who was to receive £12 p.a., was to teach twenty-four poor boys to read, write, and do sums, the enrolment being limited to boys between the age of ten and fourteen whose parents or friends were not able to defray their school expenses. After the students were competent in the studies to be taught, 'which I conceave in 2 years they will bee ready to doe', the six ablest were to be chosen by the governors and to be awarded £2 p.a. each to secure their apprenticeship in some appropriate trade. The vacancies thus created were to be filled by the governors in such manner that the enrolment of the institution would always stand at the statutory number. The trustees were also to provide a free house for the schoolmaster and to furnish each student with two reams of paper each year in addition to the books and other materials required.

This trust was likewise to support an unusual school for twenty 'weomen children' from Great Marlow, who were to be housed in a dwelling place given by Borlase and there taught spinning, knitting, and lace-making. The girls were to be nominated by the churchwardens and overseers, but chosen by the governors for their tuition. Moreover, the endowment was to support a workhouse for Great and Little Marlow, with Medmenham, the man in charge to receive £6 to £8 p.a. in salary at the discretion of the governor. Not only were the poor to be rehabilitated and set at work, but wanderers and rogues apprehended in these parishes were to be held for four days and then punished and whipped in accordance with the laws of the realm. Should any surplus remain after these trusts had been discharged, the governors were to employ it at their own discretion for the benefit of the poor of the three favoured parishes.[1]

[1] PCC 95 Ridley 1629; *Records of Buckinghamshire*, X (1916), 238–242; *VCH, Bucks.*, II, 214; *PP* 1833, XIX, 133–136; Sheahan, *Buckinghamshire*, 896;

Great interest in education was also exhibited by Charles Parrett, a London draper, but a native of Bow Brickhill. Parrett bequeathed £10 to the support of the school at Hampstead, Middlesex. His will also provided that a Bible should be given by his executors to every cottage in Bow Brickhill, at a cost of 6s 8d for each volume, after the death of his sister, in whom he vested a life estate. An endowment of £5 p.a. was to be employed to teach poor children of the parish and an additional £5 p.a. was to be used by his trustees for securing apprenticeships for worthy and needy boys. Parrett's will suggests that a school of some sort was already established in Bow Brickhill in 1634, when his testament was first drawn, and that his bequests may well represent its first endowment.[1]

Three years later, in 1637, John Pym, the great parliamentary leader, by deed of gift established a school for Brill parish. Pym laid a charge of £10 p.a. on 120 acres of land as a stipend for a schoolmaster who should teach ten poor children of the town. In the next century (1710), arrears had accumulated on the annuity to the extent of £300, which was employed for the purchase of land sufficient to increase the annual stipend of Pym's Free School to £32 p.a.[2]

The political disturbances of the next decade had the inevitable effect of discouraging the substantial endowments required for the foundation of grammar schools, but with the restoration of political stability under the Protectorate the progress was at once resumed. The keen interest of all classes in education was shown by the foundation, with a liberal endowment, of a school at Beachampton by a yeoman, William Elmer, whose large gifts for other charitable uses in the county have already been noted.[3] By the terms of his will, proved in 1653, Elmer's estate was conveyed to trustees who were to erect a schoolhouse and to provide a sufficient endowment for the proper administration of the school. The building, which cost upwards of £100, was to be constructed of stone and timber, was to be lofted, and was to bear two chimneys. An endowment of £30 p.a. was provided from the estate, after the other charities were established, for the employment of a schoolmaster, unmarried, and a sufficient scholar who could write a 'legeble hand', to teach all children

Petty Bag Inq. 1631, no. 21. Borlase left money and rents with a capital value of £886 in addition to his charities, as well as houses and lands in his own and in five nearby parishes. It should be noted that there was also a school at Little Marlow as early as 1629, since Borlase left the schoolmaster there a bequest.

[1] PCC 17 Sadler 1635; *VCH, Bucks.*, IV, 293; Ratcliff, *Newport hundreds*, 469; *PP* 1834, XXI, 119–120. Parrett, in addition to bequests to London and Kentish charities, also left £5 p.a. for the poor and aged of Bow Brickhill, £1 p.a. for a lectureship in that parish, as well as annuities of £2 for the poor of Loughton and Walton, and £1 p.a. for the poor of Wandon [Wavendon].

[2] *VCH, Bucks.*, IV, 18–19; Sheahan, *Buckinghamshire*, 346; *PP* 1834, XXI, 12–14.

[3] *Vide ante*, 40.

who should resort to him. A house was likewise provided for the master, who was enjoined to teach children both English and Latin, as well as to write and to cast accounts. The master was forbidden to take any tuition or gratuities, save for an entrance fee of 2d which he might exact. This charity, like all founded by Elmer, was to benefit both sexes equally, with the result that boys and girls were both accepted for admission.[1]

We should mention, finally, the foundation of a school at Steeple Claydon in 1656 upon open land then known as 'the Lord's Waste'. It is not certain that the donor, Thomas Chaloner, a member of the lesser gentry, paid for the costs of the building, but he certainly settled on the school an endowment to yield £12 p.a. for the support of the master.[2]

In summary, during our period twelve schools were founded in Buckinghamshire, one (at Buckingham) was re-founded and more suitably endowed, and one (Eton College) was greatly strengthened by benefactions drawn, however, almost wholly from outside the county. There were by the close of our period, then, at least fourteen endowed schools in the county, not to mention an uncertain number of village schools which were precariously but bravely attempting to provide at least rudimentary instruction. These schools were reasonably well spread over the whole of the county, and it seems probable that any able boy in the region could without considerable hardship to himself or his family have gained a grammar-school education at any time after 1640. The endowments are accurately known for twelve of the foundations and average £14 5s p.a., an amount adequate for the stipend of a well-qualified schoolmaster in the early seventeenth century. The total income we have noted, when translated into a capital amount, yields £3426, leaving a slightly lesser amount (£3363 2d) not commented on, which represents costs of construction, bequests to Eton College, grammar-school endowments outside the county, and the augmentation of existing endowments.

The notable gains made in grammar-school education in the county were supported by an almost equally generous provision for scholarships in the universities, normally with a preference or restriction to students from the county. In all, the considerable capital amount of £5003, which was sufficient to support perhaps twenty-five students in the universities, was given during our period. We have already mentioned Anthony Cave's provision for two scholarships from Lathbury School (1554) and Robert Chaloner's foundation (1621) for three scholars from Buckinghamshire or Yorkshire in connection with the grammar schools which they had founded, as well as Lady Periam's foundation of two scholarships at Oxford with a preference for natives of Buckinghamshire,

[1] PCC 62 Brent 1653; *VCH, Bucks.*, II, 218, IV, 153; Lipscomb, *Buckingham*, II, 534–536; Willis, *Buckingham*, 141–142; *PP* 1834, XXI, 50–54.
[2] *Ibid.*, XXI, 69–70.

or for graduates of her school at Henley. Of the considerable number of other foundations or small capital augmentations, perhaps two more could be briefly noted to suggest the range of the benefactions and the interest in scholarship endowments in all classes of society.

In 1632 a not particularly prosperous yeoman of Little Marlow left £3 to the poor and the same amount to poor scholars, in this case doubtless for the school which we know existed in that parish.[1] The redoubtable Puritan parliamentarian, Francis Rous, who became Provost of Eton College in 1644, by will bequeathed in 1659 a total of £60 p.a. to maintain three students at Pembroke College, Oxford, from the tithes of Bookham Magna, Surrey, and from certain properties in Devon and Cornwall.[2]

Closely linked with the scholarship endowments, which were normally vested in the universities, were the substantial gifts and bequests made to the endowment or buildings of the universities by residents of Buckinghamshire during our period. These benefactions totalled £6886, or slightly more than the gifts to schools, though most of the amount is accounted for by one great gift.

The earlier gifts, all before 1545, were in small outright bequests by priests to their own colleges, normally conjoined with some provision for prayers, or the gift of objects such as plate, vestments, or missals. In 1585, however, John Cheyney, whose large charities have already been discussed, by will gave properties worth £7 p.a. to the endowment of Trinity College, Cambridge.[3] A decade later (1596) Thomas Bickley gave a capital amount of £100 to Merton College, which he had served as warden for nearly two decades, as well as £40 to the grammar school adjoining Magdalen College, Oxford.[4]

The largest of the gifts to the universities was that of Sir Simon Bennett, whose great charities for the county have been noted.[5] Bennett, who had inherited great wealth from his father, Sir Thomas Bennett, a mercer and Lord Mayor of London, spent his life at Beachampton. Some years before his death, he purchased properties in Whittlebury Forest and in 1629 bought for £6000 the estate of Hanley Park, comprising 863 acres, which were on his death in 1631 left to University

---

[1] PCC 68 Audley 1632. *Vide ante*, 56 for the reference to this school.

[2] PCC 51 Pell 1659; Macleane, Douglas, *A history of Pembroke College* (Oxford, 1897), 295–296.

[3] PCC 16 Windsor 1585. *Vide ante*, 36.

[4] Henderson, B. W., *Merton College* (L., 1899), 91–93; Wood, Anthony (Philip Bliss, ed.), *Athenae oxonienses* (L., 1813–1820, 4 vols.), II, 839; DNB. Bickley, a native of Stone, Buckinghamshire, was educated at Oxford, where he served as Greek lecturer from 1542 to 1557. He was a chaplain to Edward VI, was appointed Chancellor of Lichfield in 1560, and served as Bishop of Chichester from 1585 until his death in 1596.

[5] *Vide ante*, 39, 51.

College, Oxford. The profits from the great estate were to be employed for the rebuilding of the college and for the creation of four fellowships with a stipend of £20 p.a. each and as many scholarships with an annual stipend of £10 each.[1]

5. Religion

We commented at the outset of our consideration of Buckinghamshire charities on the steadily declining curve of gifts and bequests for religious uses as the period wore on. For the entire span of almost two centuries, £11,860 10s was given for religious purposes, amounting to only slightly more than 13 per cent (13·45 per cent) of the total of benefactions for the county. Somewhat surprisingly, this proportion establishes Buckinghamshire as decidedly the most completely secular of all the agricultural counties we have studied and almost as stoutly secular in its aspirations as the city of Bristol.[2] Almost half the whole sum (£5630) provided for religion is to be found in the estimated total of gifts made for church building, leaving only relatively very small sums for the various other religious uses. The dominantly secular aspirations of the period as a whole are suggested by the fact that almost four times as much was given for the needs of the poor as for all religious purposes and almost twice as much was provided for education. Rather more was given for the establishment of workhouses than for the general uses of the church; more was bequeathed for apprenticeship schemes than for prayers; almost as much was left for municipal betterments as was donated for the augmentation and the preservation of the church fabric in this county.

It should be stressed that the decline of giving for religious causes, which shrank from about 61 per cent of all charities in the period 1480–1540 to an incredibly low proportion of 6 per cent during the early Stuart period—the era, incidentally, of Laud's stern but unavailing efforts to halt the rising tide of secularism—was in an important sense relative. It is true that approximately half the total of all religious benefactions were made during the earliest of our periods, but thereafter the actual amounts held relatively steady.[3] These gifts and bequests, which tended to come from a great number of small testators, were rather dwindling into relative insignificance when compared with the flood of benefactions for secular causes that mark the later intervals of our period.

[1] PCC 100 St John 1631; Carr, William, University College (L., 1902), 104–105; Lipscomb, Buckingham, II, 529.

[2] The proportions of total charitable resources designated for religious uses range from 13·18 per cent for Bristol to 31·94 per cent for Lancashire.

[3] In 1541–1560, £1387 5s; 1561–1600, £1260 11s; 1601–1640, £2836 11s; 1641–1660, £915 2s.

Of the benefactors to religion, by far the largest number in any rural county left some amount for the general purposes of the church. In many parishes these bequests, usually of very small value, were customary until about 1540 and then continued to be common among the husbandmen and yeomanry, the most conservative of all the social classes, for another twenty to thirty years when, quite suddenly, in an almost dramatic break with the past, these small sums were left as outright amounts to the poor rather than for religious uses.

In Buckinghamshire, there was no large bequest for the general uses of the church during our entire period, the total of £534 13s having been contributed by some hundreds of men and women in bequests and gifts ranging from 2d to £62. The nature and variety of such gifts will be illustrated by dealing briefly with certain of them noted in those parishes of the hundred of Ashendon which range alphabetically from Kingsey to Waddesdon, mentioning at the same time the other charitable bequests of this sampling of donors.

Richard Lee of Quarrendon in 1499 left 6s 8d to the general uses of his parish church and another shilling to Lincoln Cathedral, as well as 6s 8d to the vicar of a nearby parish.[1] Joan Ingram in 1519 bequeathed an estimated 18s in wax for the six lights of her church of North Marston and £3 6s 8d for repairs to the highways of her parish.[2] A husbandman of Pitchcott, John Perrott, who died in 1524, left grain to the value of 5s to the several altars of his church, as well as providing an estimated 2s for the repair of the fabric and bells.[3] A member of the gentry of the region, Joan Brudenell, wife of the lord of the manor of Quainton, left, in addition to £7 10s for prayers and £1 for road repairs, 3s 4d to Quainton church for tithes forgotten, and 4d to Lincoln Cathedral. She provided, as well, 3s 4d for lights and as much for bells at Quainton and the same amount for torches at Lincoln. She likewise left 6s 8d to the monks at Aylesbury for an obit there and the usual noncharitable funeral outlays.[4] In 1532, Thomas Boller, who had until 1517 held the lease of Kingsey rectory, left wax and barley to the value of 8s to that church for general uses, as well as an estimated £3 for church repairs and renovations.[5] A member of the lower gentry, John Dynham of Waddesdon, left £1 for general purposes to his parish church and a total of £21 15s for prayers.[6] Sir Robert Lee of Quarrendon and Burston left 3s 4d to Lincoln and total of £5 to Quarrendon church and other churches within a radius of three miles of his home, as well as ten marks

[1] PCC 4 Moone 1500.
[2] Lipscomb, *Buckingham*, I, 348–349; *VCH, Bucks.*, IV, 80.
[3] Sheahan, *Buckinghamshire*, 414.
[4] *Records of Buckinghamshire*, XIII (1934–1940), 427–431.
[5] Shorter, Clement, *Highways and byways in Buckinghamshire* (L., 1910), 36; *VCH, Bucks.*, IV, 68.
[6] PCC 28 Hogen 1535.

to the friars at Aylesbury for an obit and nine marks annually for twenty years for other prayers.[1] A yeoman of Waddesdon, William Delafield, whose personal estate may be valued at £30 4s 6d, exhibited much the same interests in his will proved in 1544. He left 2d to the mother church of Lincoln and contributions totalling 6s to the altar and rood light of Waddesdon church and 6s 8d to buy a mass book, as well as half a quarter of malt to the poor to pray for his soul and 6s 8d for the repair of roads in Westcott.[2] Roger Gyfford, Esq., of Middle Claydon, who died in the same year, left 10s to the general uses of his parish church.[3]

The pattern of bequests in these rural parishes changed markedly during the decade 1545–1555, the proportion of gifts to the poor rising very rapidly and those for religious purposes holding barely steady before beginning to decline absolutely as well as relatively about two decades later.

Small bequests for a great variety of general church uses had during the later Middle Ages been not only an important expression of charitable aspiration but a substantial source of parochial revenues. It is clear that in many parishes, one would suppose where there was an able and vigorous resident priest, they had become so traditional as to be almost obligatory for those leaving wills. They were in almost all cases outright gifts for immediate use, only £88 (16·46 per cent) of the total for our whole period having been left as endowments. These small testamentary offerings bespoke the piety as they did the insularity of parish life in early sixteenth-century England, and it is with a probably sentimental regret that one observes the structure of aspirations change so dramatically and completely even in the remote parishes of a rural county. This change, occurring so very swiftly, offers clear and decisive evidence of the great revolution of the mind which not only accompanied but which helped to cause the Reformation in England.

The solvent of change is also strongly suggested when one examines the structure of gifts and bequests to the monastic foundations during our period. It is true that Buckinghamshire had few monastic establishments, the net income of its houses having been no more than £1061 16s at the time of the Dissolution. These foundations, it should be noted, reported only £7 7s in alms disbursed under trusts.[4] But even so the evidence is clear indeed that the monasteries enjoyed neither much favour nor confidence in the county during the half-century preceding their dissolution. In all, only £182 was given by

[1] PCC 27 Dyngeley 1539.
[2] Archd. Bucks, 1540–1544, f. 173.
[3] PCC 2 Pynnyng 1543.
[4] Savine, A., *English monasteries on the eve of the Dissolution* (Oxford, 1909), 235, 270.

donors of the county to the monasteries, whether in Buckinghamshire or elsewhere, during the years 1480–1540, and of this pitiful amount £133 was given for prayers as early as 1491. The total of these monastic benefactions constitutes only 3·3 per cent of all gifts and bequests for religious purposes and only about 2 per cent of the total of all charities for the period prior to the Reformation. But even more relevantly, during this period of two full generations the men and women of Buckinghamshire increased the capital resources of the monasteries of the county, whose capital worth may be reckoned at about £21,236, by something less than 1 per cent (0·86 per cent), an almost savagely eloquent testimony to the nearly complete disinterest in these once noble and respected institutions. The loss of substance by fire, decay, and mismanagement in any single year must surely have exceeded the whole amount bequeathed to the monasteries of Buckinghamshire in the course of these six decades. The only possible conclusion that can be drawn from these data is that monasticism had lost the support of pious and charitable men and women in Buckinghamshire and that its claims and its endowments no longer fitted into the aspirations of the society. The ease with which Henry VIII laid waste an ancient and well-entrenched institution is better understood when it is realized that the springs of popular support and confidence had run dry long before his visitors set out on their somewhat perfunctory mission. The monasteries of England were doomed as early as 1480.

The withering of the medieval system of piety is also suggested by the relatively small amounts left or given for chantries and the humbler gifts made to secure obits or other forms of prayers for the dead. Such gifts were perhaps not normally charitable at all, but the larger usually carried some expressed charitable provision and all of them helped to maintain the structure and services of what had for so long been the one great institution commanding the loyalty of mankind. The curve of benefactions for prayers did not decline dramatically during the period 1480–1540, but very few large chantries were being established at any time in this interval and the meagre sums provided bespeak either the loss of confidence in the efficacy of such prayers or some measure of suspicion regarding the performance of the trusts. From the late Middle Ages onwards, indeed, this suspicion is clearly manifest in the carefully explicit instructions normally provided for chantry endowments, in the almost universal tendency to secure the oversight of lay trustees, and in the not infrequent reversionary clauses with which such trusts were safeguarded.

In all, £708 3s was left between 1480 and 1590 for prayers, or about 9 per cent of the total given for all religious purposes during these years and, one should observe, only 0·80 per cent of the charitable funds in the county. The meagre provision for a religious observance deeply rooted for centuries past in England was in relative, as well as absolute, terms decidedly the lowest in any county we have studied, and we may with some certainty suggest in the whole of the realm.[1] Possessing no see of its own, with no strong monastic leadership, and served by a particularly incompetent clergy, Buckinghamshire had moved far towards a repudiation of an ancient system of practice, if not of belief, even as our period began. It should also be remembered that though the foundation of chantries was forbidden by law after the Reformation, there was no specific prohibition in law against prayers for the dead and that in every county the custom of leaving at least small bequests for this purpose died out relatively slowly in the rural areas of England. But this was not to be the case in this amazing county: endowments for prayers had ceased to be an important part of the religious traditions of Buckinghamshire even before our period opened.

In number, almost all the bequests for prayers were small gifts for an obit or for a group of masses to be sung relatively soon after the death of the donor. Hence it is not surprising that only 30·65 per cent of the total of the legacies for prayers were left as endowments for chantries or other perpetual arrangements. To mention a few of the more important foundations is, therefore, to distort the factual and statistical structure of these gifts, yet the larger bequests have greater individual interest.

The largest of the chantry endowments in Buckinghamshire during our period was created in 1491, when under the will of Roger Dynham, a brother to Lord Dynham, Eythrope Chapel, then being built, was consecrated as a chantry and an endowment of £6 13s 4d p.a. was appointed to secure the services of a priest from Fotheringhay College.[2] Lady Agnes Cheyney of Chenies, dying in 1488, in addition to bequests for general church purposes and a stipend of 10s p.a. for a priory, left £20 outright for the celebration of a thousand masses for the safety of her soul.[3] Richard Halley, Vicar of Stowe, some years later (1520), among other bequests left £3 6s 2d outright to secure prayers (at Oxford) for the health of his soul, for inclusion in the rolls of Osney fraternity and a mass, and 6s 8d to each of two monastic houses for similar prayers.[4] A priest at Soulbury, Percival Duvall, by his will in 1528 prudently required his executors to arrange three masses each year, at which they should be present, when three priests and four

---

[1] Here again we have an example of the stout secularism of this remarkable county. For 'All England', 4·82 per cent of all charitable wealth was disposed for prayers; for the other counties examined the range is from 1·17 per cent for Hampshire to 10·49 per cent for Yorkshire.

[2] *VCH, Bucks.*, IV, 117.

[3] PCC 15 Milles 1488; *The Archaeological Journal*, X (1853), 51; *Records of Buckinghamshire*, XI (1926), 339. *Vide ante*, 36.

[4] Browne, A. L., 'Wills of Buckinghamshire Clergy in the Sixteenth Century', in *Records of Buckinghamshire*, XIII (1936), 195–204.

clerks should participate and for which a total of 2s 2d should be given to the participating clergy.[1] William Hampden of Dodington, a member of a rich gentle family, in 1521 left, among other religious bequests, an estimated £18 to secure prayers during the lifetime of his wife. Much the same limit of time, in this case doubtless inspired by the religious uncertainty of the period, may be seen in the bequest, among others, of £1 p.a. for twenty-one years by Sir John Baldwin, a lawyer, for an obit in Aylesbury church.[2] More typical, particularly of the earlier decades of the century, was the bequest of William Lewin of Medmenham, who in 1556 gave a cow to his parish church for its stock on condition that 'I maye have a yerely mynde perpetually'.[3]

While gifts to monasteries, bequests for prayers, and benefactions for the general uses of the church were either withering or markedly declining, a considerable percentage increase was occurring in gifts to secure a more adequate maintenance for the clergy of the county. The Reformation legislation and the purposeful might of Elizabeth had the effect of seriously diminishing clerical income in most rural counties, and increasing concern was manifested in the plight of the parochial clergy, always so ill-provided for in this county. In the whole of our period, £1625 10s, or almost 14 per cent of all gifts for religious purposes, was left for the augmentation of clerical revenues. Most of these benefactions were in small legacies for the use of named clergymen, only £517 being constituted in endowments, in seven parishes, to secure some measure of augmentation in the income of the incumbent. To these totals should be added £404 in capital left in the county for the creation of lectureships by Puritans who were seeking to reconstitute the clergy on a more learned and godly basis.[4]

Even more suggestive of the decline of the religious preoccupation during our period was the comparatively slight attention paid to the repair of the church fabric, the installation of bells, the purchase of vestments and other articles connected with the service, gifts for renovation and decoration, and the host of other items of this kind which are included under the head of church repairs. Gothic architecture is subject to inherent frailties demanding constant outlays if buildings are not to decay and collapse. Though most of the charges for repairs were normally borne by parish funds and assessments that cannot be regarded as voluntary or charitable, it is none the less remarkable how sorely neglected was the fabric of the county during our period. The religious dislocations of the era may account in part at least for the drying up of

---

[1] *Ibid.*, XIII, 202–203.　　　　[2] PCC 39 Pynnyng 1545.

[3] Plaisted, A. H., *The manor and parish records of Medmenham* (L., 1925), 333.

[4] The very large endowment of £40 p.a. for a lectureship at Tring, Hertfordshire, made by Sir John Cheyney in 1585 lies outside the county and is hence not included in this summary. *Vide ante*, 36.

benefactions to the monks, to prayers, and even to the general uses of the church, but the parish church stood as the one capacious and beautiful edifice in most rural parishes and it had for generations past commanded the steady and loyal affection of the community in the arrangements for its preservation. It may certainly be said that during our period as a whole the church fabric of Buckinghamshire was constantly neglected and that during two generations (1541–1600) it was almost completely ignored by the charity of the county. This suggests, and there is abundant additional evidence to sustain the view, that Laud and his supporters were guilty of no exaggeration when they spoke of the ruin of churches throughout the realm. It suggests, as well, in a most emphatic and conclusive fashion, the growing and hardening secularism of the sixteenth century, obsessed as that period may have been with theological brawling.[1]

More specifically, a total of £2958 4s was given or bequeathed from 1480 to 1660 for church repairs and furnishings. This is a relatively large amount, being 3·35 per cent of all charities in the county and approximately one-fourth of all the religious benefactions, but it dealt most inadequately with a heavy and continuous liability for the lovely and numerous churches inherited from earlier centuries. This liability was possibly just adequately met during the first period, when the substantial total of £1538 17s was given for this purpose. But during the 'high Tudor period', 1541–1600, the incredibly small total of £114 13s was given for this need, and in one decade of that interval only £1 11s is counted, that being comprised of nine tiny bequests. This means that for two generations somewhat less than £2 p.a. on the average was being voluntarily given for the repair of fabric. An immediate and a considerable revival of interest in this by then pressing need began with the accession of James I, while Laud's efforts were rewarded by the relatively substantial total of £424 19s given during the decade of his great power and most earnest efforts.

Of the total of £2958 4s given for church repair, the quite surprising amount of £1855, this being 62·71 per cent of the whole, was left as capital sums to aid with repairs in perpetuity. These capital benefactions were, however, left by relatively few donors, the great bulk of these benefactions, especially during the earlier decades, having been small gifts or bequests for immediate use. A few examples will suffice to illustrate both types of bequest. In 1505 Nicholas Aston of the borough of Buckingham left £2 towards the new aisle being built in Buckingham church and 6s 8d for the bells.[2] Two years later Richard Levynder left

---

[1] For a more extended comment on this matter, and with a particular consideration of the decay of the church fabric of Buckinghamshire, *vide* Jordan, *Philanthropy in England*, 314–316.

[2] Lipscomb, *Buckingham*, II, 584.

£2 towards the repair of Lincoln Cathedral and a flock of 100 sheep, whose value we have estimated at £25, towards the completion of an aisle at Lincoln.[1] Richard Cook of Olney gave £6 6s 8d in 1520 towards the cost of a pair of organs being built in his church.[2] The largest of the bequests for repairs was that of Thomas Plaistowe, Esq., who in 1508 (?) placed in trust a large estate then valued at £945, the income of which was to be employed for the maintenance and repair of Aston Clinton church.[3] Far more representative was the bequest of a yeoman of Aylesbury, Edmond Bradbury, in 1537, of a modest 3s for the repair of the fabric of his parish church.[4] The inconsiderable benefactions of the decade 1571–1580 include that of John Ball, a husbandman of Boarstall, who left 3s 4d for church repairs,[5] and the upsurge of donations in the Laudian decade is represented by the bequest of Cecilia Rools [or Rooks] who in 1630 gave £40 for the repair of Turville church.[6]

There was, it would appear, serious neglect of the fabric of Buckinghamshire churches throughout our period, and there was what can only be described as almost complete neglect for two generations. Our discussion of benefactions for church repairs has thus far been limited to the chronic minor repairs and renovations required by Gothic structures and the normal wear and tear on edifices and furnishings which throughout the years under survey was simply not being met. The suspicion arises that, for the county as a whole, the decay of the fabric, the spoiling of medieval paintings and decorations, and the slow decline in the splendour and dignity of services was far less due to the reformers than to the want of interest and neglect inspired by the increasing secularism of English life. This neglect can be documented and all but plotted from parish accounts and from the wills of the period.

When, however, we turn to another aspect of this question, major renovations and enlargements of existing structures and the building of new churches, our evidence is somewhat less certain. Such major undertakings were normally financed by gifts and voluntary subscriptions rather than by bequests, and though we can determine with fair exactness what construction took place, and though we know that the financing of such building was normally by gifts, all too few accounts remain either of those who gave or of the total costs of such construction.

Fallible though our evidence is, it is quite sufficient to warrant the

[1] Willis, *Buckingham*, 59.
[2] Lipscomb, *Buckingham*, IV, 310.
[3] *PP* 1833, XIX, 33–35; *VCH, Bucks.*, II, 319. The income on this fund in the early years of this century was £344 p.a.
[4] PCC 10 Dyngeley 1537.
[5] PCC 2 Peter 1573.
[6] Sheahan, *Buckinghamshire*, 912; Langley, *Desborough*, 395; *Home Counties Magazine*, I (1899), 335.

statement that the neglect of building and of major renovations was quite as pronounced as had been the neglect of fabric and furnishings. Buckinghamshire had in the early seventeenth century about 210 parish churches and a relatively small number of chapels of ease. The population of the county increased substantially during our period and, what is even more important, there were considerable shifts of population within the county. A number of churches were destroyed during the long period under examination by the twin ills of fire and decay, and a larger number were brought to the point of disuse by the steady neglect of the fabric. Yet it appears that only four churches were built or rebuilt during the whole of the period and that substantial repairs or improvements were undertaken on only fifty-eight edifices, most of which were already old at the beginning of our period. Moreover, almost all that was done was accomplished in the earlier decades of our period. This remarkable annal of neglect is borne out by the estimated amounts given by Buckinghamshire donors for church building. In the late fifteenth century £1490 was given for this purpose and in the early decades of the sixteenth century somewhat more (£1650) was provided. Indeed, during these early years, 1480-1540, almost 56 per cent of the total for the entire period was given for what may be described as the completion of Gothic architecture in the county. The very small sum of £630 was provided during the mid-sixteenth century, a period, it will be recalled, likewise of almost complete neglect for the repair of church buildings, while during the later Elizabethan era (1571-1600) only £510 was donated, or not much more than an average of £2 8s 6d for each church in the county. The closing period, 1601-1660, witnessed a mild revival of interest in the church fabric when a total of £1350 was given for building or major renovation. Any detailed discussion of church building during our period would necessitate a lengthy digression, but at least a brief summary of the evidence may be presented in support of the conclusions just stated.

The building during the first period (1480-1500) was limited to two relatively small churches. St Giles' church at Stony Stratford was built as a chantry chapel during these years, with a nave, north and south aisles, vestries, and a tower, at an estimated cost of £400.[1] In the last decade of the century the church of Hillesden was rebuilt, save for the tower, at a charge of about £380.[2] This represents the whole of church building or rebuilding by voluntary funds, so far as available evidence indicates, for the first two decades of our period. Towers during these years were added to churches at Little Missenden, where a north aisle was rebuilt; and at Chicheley, where a new chancel was also built to the

[1] VCH, Bucks., IV, 479-480.
[2] Berks, Bucks, & Oxon Arch., n.s., XV (1909), 23; Records of Buckinghamshire, XII (1933), 93; VCH, Bucks., IV, 176.

east of the new tower; and towers were restored at Addington and at Shenley. At Stewkley (St Michael) extensive work was also done on an apparently existing tower.[1] Clerestories were added to the nave at Hardmead and at Great Linford in this same period,[2] while clerestories were added with extensive additional remodelling at Hanslope, Lavendon, and Sherington.[3] In 1490 a chapel was rebuilt at Waddesdon by Roger Dormer,[4] and at about the same time the south chapel and aisle were built at Loughton, where a porch and tower were also added and the nave re-roofed.[5] At Langley Marish new windows were inserted in the nave and other renovations were undertaken, while at Bletchley a new roof was put on the chancel and chapel.[6]

During the next interval, 1501–1540, the church at Tattenhoe was rebuilt from the shattered fabric of Snelshall Priory in adjoining Whaddon at an estimated cost of £300, but the work was done so badly or subsequent neglect was so complete that it could not be used during the early seventeenth century until heroic repairs were undertaken in 1636.[7] The fashion of adding towers to existing churches continued strong in this era, they having been constructed or rebuilt at Bradwell, Turville, Aston Abbots, and at Swanbourne, where some work was done as well on the north wall.[8] A tower was also built at Dorney at a cost of approximately £40 from the bequest of John Scott for a 'new steeple for Dorney', and at Grandborough, where the walls of the nave were tightened at the same time.[9] Clerestories continued to be added in this period: at Stoke Goldington, where an aisle was also shortened; at Newport Pagnell, where the chancel and part of the north wall were rebuilt at the same time and the church re-roofed; probably at Whaddon; at Soulbury, where the nave arcades were also rebuilt, an aisle extended, and a tower added; at Drayton Beauchamp, where a porch was also built; at Chicheley, where a porch was likewise built and an aisle re-roofed; at Bletchley, where extensive additional improvements were made at about the same time; and at Mentmore, where the arcades were also rebuilt and a tower added.[10] During the same period chapels were built at Stoke Poges; at Bradenham (by Lord Windsor); at Stowe; and at Hulcott, where at the same time a second bay was added to the south arcade.[11] Porches were added at Wexham; at Little Hampden; and at

[1] VCH, Bucks., II, 358; IV, 315, 139, 450; III, 424.   [2] Ibid., IV, 365, 390.
[3] Ibid., IV, 357, 385, 457.   [4] Moreton, Waddesdon, 77.
[5] VCH, Bucks., IV, 400.   [6] Ibid., III, 298; IV, 279.
[7] Berks, Bucks, & Oxon Arch., n.s., XIV (1908), 10; Sheahan, Buckinghamshire, 760.
[8] VCH, Bucks., IV, 287; III, 104, 330, 431.
[9] PCC 38 Holgrave 1505; VCH, Bucks., IV, 49.
[10] VCH, Bucks., IV, 469, 418–419; III, 440, 418, 343; IV, 315, 279; III, 400.
[11] Ibid., III, 311; Sheahan, Buckinghamshire, 881; VCH, Bucks., IV, 236; II, 343.

Stokenchurch, where the north transept was also rebuilt.[1] The walls of the chancel at Radnage were raised and a new roof added, and the chancel of Middle Claydon was built at the charge of Roger Gyfford and his wife.[2] At Burnham, the rector, Richard Capel, left £40 for the construction of a new rectory, and at High Wycombe (All Saints) new arcades were built, two chapels reconstituted, extensive work done on the chancel, and a new tower built to replace one that had been demolished in 1509-1510.[3]

As we have indicated, little was undertaken in the way of major repairs or improvements during the mid-sixteenth century, even less during the great Elizabethan decades. During the period 1541-1570, a tower was added at Hitcham and the tower at Great Missenden (St Peter and St Paul) was enlarged, possibly to make room for the bell from a nearby abbey that had just been suppressed.[4] The Bedford Chapel was built at Chenies,[5] and extensive renovations were undertaken in 1562 on the church at Newton Blossomville.[6] A note from the visitation of the diocese of Lincoln in 1556 would suggest that the chancel and other parts of the church at Olney may have been restored, since it was reported: 'Gardiani presentant cancellum fere collapsum esse, ac vix centum marcas sufficere ad reperationem ejusdem.'[7] In the later Elizabethan period (1571-1600) a tower was rebuilt at Horton and a tower built at Little Horwood, where minor repairs were made at the same time.[8] At St Mary's, in Amersham, a clerestory was added and fairly extensive general repairs undertaken when a tower, a porch, and a chapel were constructed.[9] A chapel was also added at Grendon Underwood by the terms of the will of Thomas Pigott,[10] while at the very close of the period a new arcade and a roof were provided for Pitstone church.[11]

We have noted that during the years 1601-1660 there was considerably more given for church building and major repairs than during the preceding sixty years. During this period, the church at Fulmer was entirely rebuilt in 1610 at the charge of Sir Marmaduke Darrell at an estimated cost of £400.[12] Relatively minor improvements were also undertaken at Stewkley and at Langley Marish.[13] But all the remainder given during this period was, probably of necessity, devoted not to

---

[1] VCH, Bucks., III, 319-320; II, 292; III, 99.

[2] Ibid., III, 91; IV, 34. Vide ante, 62.

[3] Sheahan, Buckinghamshire, 921; VCH, Bucks., III, 129-130; Records of Buckinghamshire, IX (1909), 13 ff., 312.

[4] VCH, Bucks., III, 234; II, 351.   [5] Ibid., III, 201.

[6] Ratcliff, Newport hundreds, 20.   [7] VCH, Bucks., IV, 436, n. 97.

[8] Ibid., III, 284-285, 377.   [9] Ibid., III, 153.

[10] PCC 15 Stevenson 1564.

[11] Records of Buckinghamshire, XIII (1940), 246-247.

[12] VCH, Bucks., III, 277.   [13] Ibid, III, 424, 298.

improvements or major renovations but to basic repairs on at least a few of the church fabrics that had decayed so woefully during the past sixty years or more. Thus the chancel and nave at Hedsor church were considerably repaired in 1600 or thereabouts;[1] badly needed repairs on the chancel of Great Brickhill church were undertaken in 1602;[2] the interior of Chesham church had to be rebuilt in 1606 by the voluntary contributions of the parishioners at a cost of £137 12s 8d';[3] extensive repairs and decorations were carried out at Colnbrook in 1628–1630;[4] the nave of Bow Brickhill was roofed in 1630, and the south wall of the nave of Swanbourne church was rebuilt two years later;[5] ambitious repairs and roofing were effected at Bierton in 1636;[6] and all the roofs, save for the chancel, were renewed at Lillingstone Lovell in 1639.[7]

The evidence regarding church building and church repair during our period, when considered in conjunction with the steady and immense broadening of secular charities, suggests the dramatic and decisive nature of the cultural and social revolution that took place even in a rural county during the course of these years. What we have been documenting is the translation of men's aspirations, a process which had begun well before Bosworth Field and which quite as much occasioned as it was occasioned by the Reformation. The neglect of the church fabric, a great and noble monument to past generosity and piety, was not the result of poverty in rural Buckinghamshire, but rather was caused by the welling up of new interests and new preoccupations. The village church and the neighbouring abbey were symbols of a past itself in process of repudiation. This is why a community could look with equanimity on the slow decay of the fabric of its church and with surprisingly little evidence of regret or protest on the quarrying of the abbey by the new squire building his manor house on abbey lands or his enclosures to enfold the sheep that now grazed these acres.

D. THE STRUCTURE OF CHARITY IN THE PARISHES

We should now turn from our consideration of the county as a whole to at least a brief discussion of the structure of the charities that were created in the parishes during the long period under examination. For it is important to note that the really substantial social and economic

---

[1] VCH, Bucks., III, 56.   [2] Ibid., IV, 297.
[3] Records of Buckinghamshire, IX (1909), 329–348, 393–414; X (1916), 1–18. The contributions ran from 6s to £7. The contribution of James Birch, who had given three pieces of cherry wainscotting worth 2s 4d a yard, was disallowed as not voluntary, since he 'made the churchwarden to sell him a peece of a long rope at 13/4 price and so agreed, and when he had the rope he kept back the mony for the weinscott wch was a cunning and subtle pt'.
[4] Gyll, Wraysbury, 289.   [5] VCH, Bucks., IV, 292; III, 431.
[6] Ibid., II, 325.   [7] Ibid., IV, 196.

resources that were accumulated in the course of two centuries of generosity and social responsibility were not evenly or well distributed at the close of our period. In a considerable number of parishes for a variety of reasons—the most common being a rich and responsible family, a local son who had made a fortune in London, or a succession of able and forceful clergymen—large endowments were created which altered the whole structure of parish life by the relief of poverty, the widening of educational opportunities, or the provision of effective agencies of social rehabilitation. These parishes are extremely interesting and would be worth detailed study, since charities once well begun tended to attract a steady stream of later supporting augmentations and to create new and bolder charitable experiments. It is not too much to say that these parishes had become in the course of our period 'areas of opportunity' within the county, which tended to produce men of high ability and responsibility and which fed London with the steady flow of talent on which the capital, always a devourer of men, subsisted. But there were, at the same time, 'blighted areas' within the county, where what might be called the process of social investment never got under way. These were principally small and isolated rural parishes, often badly served by their clergy and either without gentry or owned by absentee landlords. Such parishes were in process of decline during our period and not infrequently became festering areas of poverty and wretchedness for which no one, save as the Elizabethan poor laws were effective, was quite responsible in the Tudor and Stuart societies.

The presentation of the parochial evidence is considerably complicated by the fact that it is not possible at any given date to be completely certain how many parishes there were in the county or what were their precise boundaries. Though the parish is one of the most stable of English institutions, it remains true that this is far less the case at the beginning of our period than at its close and that throughout these almost two hundred years parishes were being consolidated, were otherwise losing their identity, or, much more rarely, were being constituted. We must, however, for statistical purposes make some assumption and that is that in 1600 there were approximately 210 parishes in the county and that this represents a fair average number for the entire period. This assumption, it must be repeated, imposes static limitations on a structure of life and of institutions that was in point of fact fluid.

Certain other fallibilities of method and presentation should be noted. Benefactors did not make their gifts or bequests tidily and exclusively within the parish of their residence. We have for purposes of the parish analysis endeavoured to assign each benefaction to the parish which it was to serve. This is normally not difficult, but not infrequently a donor would leave amounts to all surrounding parishes, neighbouring parishes, or to all parishes in which he held land, with no clear indication of the parishes that were meant. The consequence is that all such gifts cannot be assigned to a particular parish and hence that the parish totals are necessarily somewhat less than those for the county. Moreover, a fair number of benefactions, such as scholarships, grammar schools, and sometimes almshouses or apprenticeship schemes, were on occasion vested in trustees for the benefit of all or most of the county. These gifts have been assigned to the parish in which they were made or, in a few instances, where the endowing properties were situated, with a consequent distortion of the charitable totals for such parishes.

The £78,581 10s of charitable gifts which may with certainty be credited to particular parishes was distributed amongst 178 parishes, this being 84·8 per cent of the total number, with the rule applying that a parish will be listed only if the total of its charities during our period exceeded the nominal sum of 10s. In addition, tiny amounts, usually for some religious purpose, have been noted in twenty-seven other parishes, with the result that some charity has been credited to 205, or 97·6 per cent of all the parishes.

Many of these parishes possessing some endowed charities had so small an amount that they could not have been a considerable solvent in the life of the community or have done more than relieve an inconsequential fraction of distress, augment the vicar's income by a few shillings a year, or provide an occasional dinner for the vestry. It has been assumed, therefore, that endowed charities of at least £100, yielding on the average the not inconsiderable total of £5 p.a. were required before the structure of community life could really be substantially changed and that endowments of at least £400 were required to lift parishes into the 'area of opportunity'.

Thus forty-one, or 19·5 per cent of the parishes of the county, they being well distributed geographically, were by the end of our period to possess endowments sufficient to serve as social catalysts and powerfully to stimulate the life and structure of the society within these communities.[1] Only three of these parishes, Aylesbury, Buckingham, and High Wycombe, were more than small country towns in size, and even these were not more than large towns with small commercial communities within a still predominantly rural structure of society. These forty-one parishes were the foci of social and cultural change in the county, approximately 78 per cent (£68,954 2s) of the total charities of the county being in fact concentrated in them. Hence, though there is no reason to believe that these parishes included much more than their due proportion of the population of the county, private munificence had vested in them a preponderant fraction of the total endowments of the county and had thereby constituted them, as it were, laboratories of social and cultural change.

[1] *Vide* Table A, Appendix, for the particulars.

We have also suggested that endowments of from £100 to £400 were sufficient in the England of this period, and more especially in the rural parishes typical of this county, to affect importantly, if not decisively, the life and institutions of the community. It would be tedious to list these parishes in detail, but it may be said in summary that forty of the Buckinghamshire parishes were thus endowed by the close of our period. These parishes were possessed of a total of £7837 12s of charitable funds, or a substantial average of £195 18s 9d for each community. But the 'more favoured' communities possessed on the average almost £1682 of such funds, an average distorted it is true by the remarkable charities vested for or in Beachampton. Moreover, there is a most substantial and telling difference in the quality and structure of the charities of the more favoured group as contrasted with those only moderately well endowed. The charities of the former included a total of £6731 15s for the various religious causes, amounting to not quite 10 per cent of the whole as compared with 13·45 per cent for the county. But the charities of the latter group included £2767 6s for religious uses, or 35·31 per cent of the whole, suggesting in most evident fashion the more conservative character of these parishes which do not reflect the extraordinary secularism of the well-endowed communities or, for that matter, of the county as a whole.

We have seen that eighty-one of the 210 parishes of the county possessed a total of £76,791 14s, or almost 98 per cent of the whole amount that may be certainly ascribed to a particular parish, though these parishes constituted only 38·6 per cent of the total number in the county. Of the remaining 129 parishes, 99 possessed charities ranging from 10s to £100, 25 held wholly nominal endowments, and there is no record of a charitable contribution of any amount in the remaining five parishes. Moreover, of the small total of £1789 16s belonging to these ill-favoured parishes, a very high proportion (almost 60 per cent) was given for religious purposes which did not reflect either the temper of the age or the dominant structure of charities in the county as a whole. These were the communities in which change occurred only very slowly, in which distress was greater and more completely unattended, and in which the opportunities for youth were more circumscribed and thwarted. A rural county, itself remarkably homogeneous in its economy, was none the less a most complex and diverse area in terms of change, opportunity, and progress.

These conclusions may be more fully documented by a short discussion of the amounts given or bequeathed to the poor in the several parishes of the county during the period under study. There is considerable evidence to suggest that save for the industrial and heavily populated urban parishes of the realm, of which Buckinghamshire had none, a parish did not normally expend more than about £20 p.a. on poor relief, whether from taxation or charity, even in periods of dearth or unemployment. In other words, a parish possessing upwards of £400 of endowed funds for the relief of poverty, in whatever form, may be said fully to have met the normal early modern standards of poor relief by the medium of its private charities. Such communities possessed wealth which set them apart as exemplary in terms of the conscience and social resources of the age. Similarly, any rural parish endowed with £200 of such funds, it may be suggested, had by existing standards substantially met its social obligations for the poor, while any parish with such capital in the range of £10 to £200 had made far more than a nominal contribution to the care of the distressed poor.

In our discussion of the structure and geographical spread of these endowments for the poor, it should be noted that of the total of £45,872 13s given or bequeathed in the county for outright relief, almshouses, general charitable purposes, and the care of the aged, slightly more than 12 per cent (£5752 13s) was in fact not endowment, but rather immediate gifts for alms. But since these gifts cannot readily or accurately be separated for purposes of this analysis, the totals given represent in certain cases a slight overstatement of the amount of endowed funds accumulated during our period. Moreover, it will be recalled from our earlier discussion of certain of the larger charities, not infrequently an endowment for the poor or the creation of an almshouse opened benefits to nearby parishes or occasionally to the whole county, with the result that the dispersion of benefits was considerably more widespread than the categories about to be presented suggest.

In all, there were twenty-six parishes in Buckinghamshire which by 1660 possessed upwards of £400 of endowment for the care of the poor, an amount quite sufficient by seventeenth-century standards for the sustenance of the distressed and the care of the unemployed.[1] These favoured parishes were evenly distributed over the county, and they

[1] The parishes or towns with endowments of upwards of £400:

	£	s		£	s
Aylesbury	1,652	6	Hanslope	604	1
Beachampton	2,877	10	Ivinghoe	507	12
Bradenham	653	0	Langley Marish	773	15
Brickhill	625	0	Newport Pagnell	551	1
Brill	1,533	3	Quainton	556	0
Buckingham	1,085	10	Shenley	604	0
Burnham	603	3	Simpson	800	13
Chenies	1,101	5	Stoke Poges	1,614	10
Chesham	1,030	19	Waddesdon	1,048	5
Chilton	1,578	2	Wendover	649	10
Colnbrook	575	0	Wing	1,000	0
Great Marlow	1,928	15	Wooburn	464	0
Halton	421	0	High Wycombe	3,950	12

were truly favoured since they possessed a disproportionate share of the total of endowments for the poor in the county, the median parish of Simpson having endowments of £800. These funds range from £421 for Halton, of which £400 was a London benefaction, to £3950 12s for High Wycombe, including Great and West Wycombe, of which, it should be noted, £3067 was London capital. This group of parishes, including the three principal towns of Buckinghamshire, but otherwise representative, possessed endowments totalling £28,788 12s, or almost two-thirds (62·76 per cent) of all the funds for the poor in the entire county. In point of fact, some of them, as for example richly favoured Beachampton, Chilton, and Brill, must in relation to their size and responsibilities have had resources so large as to have attracted paupers and vagrants from other regions. The somewhat eccentric nature of private charity has always had this effect, and the outpouring of philanthropy in the seventeenth century, especially by the great London merchants, produced it to a remarkable degree.

The heavy weight of London gifts in fourteen of the twenty-six favoured parishes doubtless explains the curious fact that there were almost twice as many parishes with upwards of £400 of endowments for the poor as there were parishes with the more modest, but none the less substantial, capital of £200 to £400. In all, there were fourteen of these parishes with endowments ranging from the £209 3s for Denham to the £397 16s for Slapton, with Mentmore (£283 7s) being the median parish of the group. These parishes were likewise distributed through the county in a reasonably even fashion, and a considerable number of them had as well been the beneficiaries of the London philanthropy which was rapidly moulding the institutions of England in this period. The endowments for the poor held by this second group of parishes totalled £4084 5s.

The third group of parishes being considered are those possessing endowments for the poor within the range of £10 to £200, a capital amount in this period capable in a rural parish of substantially relieving the distress of the poor and, as important, of attracting further gifts of endowments by the philanthropic contagion so frequently induced in a parish by even a small capital gift. There were forty-nine of these parishes in Buckinghamshire, again well distributed geographically over the county, with the median parish in the group being Medmenham with funds for the poor totalling £61.

In all, then, eighty-nine of the 210 parishes of the county possessed endowments of more than £10 for the support of the poor. Another group of ninety-one parishes had smaller amounts which could not have constituted more than token sums towards discharging the responsibility which bore so heavily on England during this era. Taking into account the fact that most of the larger funds were not specifically limited to the parish in which they were vested, it would seem that rather more than half the parishes of the county were able to assume their responsibilities wholly or principally as a consequence of the remarkable private generosity of our period. This was a splendid accomplishment, indeed, one which must be counted among the great achievements of the early modern era.

E. THE IMPACT OF LONDON ON THE COUNTY

We have had occasion to refer in our discussion of endowments for the relief of the poor to the decisive effect in many parishes of large benefactions made by residents of London for their benefit. Gifts from London loom large in the whole structure of Buckinghamshire's charities and institutions. Since the remarkable role that London played in reshaping the institutions of early modern society has been considered in detail in our treatment of the city, we shall not deal with individual benefactions but seek rather to analyse the spread of London's gifts over the county.[1] These London benefactors were of three types: the native of Buckinghamshire who, having made his fortune in the city, remembered his home parish with a gift or bequest towards the close of his life; Londoners who held land in the county or who had settled there on retirement from active trade, not infrequently as new members of the lesser gentry; and the Londoner with no demonstrable connection with Buckinghamshire who apparently determined on the establishment of a charity in a particular parish on the objective evidence of great need.

Buckinghamshire is of course relatively close to London, an arc with a radius of twenty miles from St Paul's falling beyond the nearest county border and a similar arc with a radius of sixty miles enclosing the whole of the county. None the less, in our period there is little evidence that any part of Buckinghamshire lay within the dominant orbit of London in the way that portions of Kent, Surrey, Hertfordshire, and Essex did or that there were any closer ties than those that bound London with the interests and institutions of other and even more distant counties in the south of England. London's intervention in the life and institutions of the county was rather an instance, and a quite typical one, of the pervasive and dominant leadership of the capital and its remarkable group of merchants in our period.

In all, the amazing total of £15,019 17s of Buckinghamshire's charitable endowments were vested by Londoners, this representing 17·04 per cent of the whole for our period. The structure of these gifts and bequests is extremely interesting as compared with that of the county as a whole, revealing the intensely secular and progressive quality

[1] *Vide*, Jordan, W. K., *The Charities of London*, 1480–1660 (London, 1960).

of London thinking on the great social and economic problems of the age:

	Poor	Social rehabilitation	Municipal betterments	Education	Religion
London	£7,590 11s (50·54%)	£1,535 0s (10·22%)	£4,256 0s (28·33%)	£510 0s (3·40%)	£1,128 6s (7·51%)
County	£45,872 13s (52·04%)	£3,920 2s (4·45%)	£7,757 19s (8·80%)	£18,741 2s (21·26%)	£11,860 10s (13·45%)

It will be observed that the proportion of London gifts for the benefit of the poor is approximately level with that for the county as a whole, but a closer examination of the individual gifts reveals that a much higher proportion of them were endowments for almshouses and carefully devised funds for general charity, while correspondingly a much smaller proportion was for the outright relief of the poor. A surprisingly lesser percentage of London gifts was devoted to the foundation of grammar schools in the county, particularly since during this period London merchants were literally endowing the schools of England. But in the varied experiments for the social rehabilitation of the poor and under-privileged and in endowments within the parishes for the lifting up of the whole community to a better standard of life, the influence of London on the county was not only important but very evidently decisive. Thus almost 40 per cent of all the plans for social rehabilitation were financed with London money and well over half of the funds devoted to municipal improvements were so endowed. The intensely secular nature of London aspirations in this period is further documented by the fact that its benefactors gave only a little more than half as much proportionately to the needs of the church as did the county as a whole, even though this was the most starkly secular county in England.

These London benefactions were relatively very large, the whole of the total of £15,019 17s having been given by seventy-one donors, or an average of £211 10s 11d per benefactor. Needless to say, these substantial gifts tended to affect directly the structure of life and of institutions in the parishes in which they were vested. These were carefully concentrated gifts, always well devised, normally effectively administered, and frequently dominant in their effect in a rural parish. The quality of London benefactions may be at least roughly appraised by a brief analysis of them in relation to specific parishes. For these gifts, as for the county as a whole, a proportion cannot be sensibly assigned to a particular parish, with the result that the total by parishes is £14,092 11s.

These great London gifts were spread across the face of the county in a most eccentric fashion, since the donors were ordinarily interested in enlarging the areas of opportunity in their native parish or region. There were, in fact, twenty-five principal communities of the county, all with charitable resources in excess of £400, none of which owed any considerable proportion of its charitable wealth to London generosity. These parishes as a group possessed 57 per cent of all the charitable wealth of Buckinghamshire, yet the London contribution amounted to only 3·8 per cent of the total and affected only slightly either the charities or the institutions of the parishes. In these communities local leadership was strong and responsible and the structure of life was determined principally by local aspirations.

But a dramatically different situation is revealed by a study of fourteen other communities in which the London intervention was not only strong but clearly decisive:

Parishes with substantial charities decisively affected by London gifts

	Charities from county sources		Charities from London sources		Total	
	£	s	£	s	£	s
Brickhill (Great, Bow, and Little)	219	2	700	0	919	2
Brill	1,492	3	242	0	1,734	3
Chenies	234	16	1,000	0	1,234	16
Chesham	1,173	7	814	10	1,987	17
Chilton	314	19	1,610	0	1,924	19
Colnbrook	475	0	1,010	0	1,485	0
Cuddington	69	0	320	0	389	0
Drayton Beauchamp	251	0	300	0	551	0
Fulmer	0	5	725	0	725	5
Great Missenden	421	3	256	0	677	3
Halton	22	8	400	0	422	8
Ivinghoe	308	8	200	0	508	8
Shabbington	47	13	300	0	347	13
Wycombe (High, Great, and West)	1,406	17	3,705	0	5,111	17
	6,436	1	11,582	10	18,018	11

Hence, in these fourteen parishes, possessing about one-fifth of all the charities of the county, a total of £11,582 10s was given by London philanthropists, this amounting to 64·3 per cent of all the charitable endowments of these parishes. These endowments comprehend about 82 per cent of all the London gifts to Buckinghamshire that may certainly be assigned to specific parishes; they were benefactions concentrated very heavily in favoured communities in which the donors had familial or personal interests and which were singled out for the always interesting and normally sophisticated charitable experimentation so typical of London giving. Great as was the economic power of London in our period, of even greater historical significance was the quality and strength of leadership afforded by the rich and articulate merchant aristocracy of the great city.

F. THE IMPACT OF THE COUNTY ON THE NATION

The vigour and decisiveness of London benefactions in Buckingham-shire suggest that there was far less of economic and cultural insularity in the England of our period than has sometimes been supposed. Even the most casual examination of the wills of the period evidences, since the place of birth is normally given, a quite amazing geographical mobility even in a rural county like Buckinghamshire, while a complex pattern of land ownership extending across county lines amongst the yeomanry as well as the gentle classes attests to the same fact. Excluding all gifts for university endowments and scholarships, which belonged to the nation rather than to the charitable uses of a particular county, Buckinghamshire donors gave a total of £4275 16s for charities in other counties. This considerable sum, amounting to 4·85 per cent of the whole of the county's charities, was given by forty-five separate donors drawn from all classes of society in proportions not greatly dissimilar to that of the county at large. Of this number, two were of the nobility, thirteen of the gentry, and, surprisingly, fifteen of the yeomanry. Two of these donors were lawyers, four were members of the lower clergy, two were tradesmen, and the social status of the remaining seven is uncertain.

As we should expect, most of the counties benefiting from Bucking-hamshire charity were either bordering or nearby, though a total of seventeen English counties receiving some benefaction has been counted, as the following table will suggest:

County	Number of donors	Total of benefactions
		£
Middlesex	8	144 0
Oxfordshire	7	1,225 5
Northamptonshire	6	20 13
Hertfordshire	5	1,092 2
Suffolk	3	48 0
Bedfordshire	2	50 10
Essex	2	10 0
Wiltshire	2	0 11
Yorkshire	2	520 0
Berkshire	1	1,134 0
Cheshire	1	0 5
Devon	1	2 0
Kent	1	11 0
Norfolk	1	0 10
Shropshire	1	10 0
Surrey	1	2 0
Warwickshire	1	5 0
	45	4,275 16

The structure of the charitable gifts of these donors is likewise little different from that of the county as a whole, a total of about half having been given for the relief of the poor, mostly in quite small amounts. But the benefactions do include a grammar school for Yorkshire, a heavily endowed Puritan lectureship for Hertfordshire, an almshouse with a large endowment for Oxfordshire, and a substantial capital sum for the benefit of the poor of Berkshire. These gifts were part of the warp and woof of the fabric of charities being woven by many thousands of benefactors, large and small, of this period, whose interests and aspirations cut cleanly across county lines to include the whole of England. These men were creating a new England in the image of their own ideals and their own intensely secular aspirations.

G. THE STRUCTURE OF CLASS ASPIRATIONS

It has been possible to determine the social status of 1222 (71 per cent) of the 1722 known donors for this county. In many of the 500 remaining cases the family name in its parish setting carries a strong implication of a particular status, but in a socially fluid age it would be unwise and certainly statistically hazardous to assign a status when the will itself or some other contemporary document does not provide certain proof.

The structure of the charities of the county in terms of the social status of the donors may be presented in tabular form:

Number of Donors	Class	Percentage of all donors	Total of benefactions £ s	Percentage of county total
2	Crown	0·11	3,808 0	4·32
20	Nobility	1·16	2,740 0	3·11
130	Upper gentry	7·55	25,294 1	28·69
326	Lower gentry	18·93	13,362 9	15·16
358	Yeomen	20·79	3,877 5	4·40
104	Husbandmen	6·04	154 2	0·17
26	Agricultural labourers and poor	1·51	8 13	0·001
6	Upper clergy	0·35	3,710 0	4·21
78	Lower clergy	4·53	2,329 10	2·64
20	Merchants	1·16	4,931 18	5·59
54	Tradesmen	3·14	1,875 14	2·13
22	Burghers	1·28	1,105 0	1·25
42	Artisans	2·44	73 6	0·08
34	Professional	1·97	1,918 1	2·18
500	Uncertain status	29·04	17,334 7	19·66
	Church building		5,630 0	6·39

Buckinghamshire was almost classically a county dominated by a rich and vigorous gentry. Rather more than a third (37·3 per cent) of all known donors in the county were members of this numerically small class and, as we shall point out, their gifts in terms of quantity as well as quality were to determine the structure of charities in the county. This is, of course, a reflection of the predominantly rural character of the shire in the early modern period, which is further attested, if one may include the parochial clergy, by the fact that 85 per cent of all identified donors were members of the rural society of the county. The relative weakness of the urban groups is suggested when we consider that of the twenty merchants leaving bequests to the county, eighteen were Londoners, as were nineteen of the fifty-four tradesmen and eighteen of the 'additional burghers' noted. The dominance of the rural groups within the county is further demonstrated when we reflect that they gave 54·17 per cent of all its charities, to which may be added nearly the whole of the substantial gifts (19·66 per cent) made by unidentified donors, who were with very few exceptions residents of rural parishes.

It will be observed that the gentry contributed almost 44 per cent of all charitable benefactions in the county, with the quite conservative estimate that this proportion would exceed half if precise assignment could be made for the whole group of donors of uncertain social status in the county. This was indeed a proud and a significant record of achievement and provides ample demonstration of the steady sense of social and cultural responsibility which animated this group during the period under review.

The nobility, strongly represented in Buckinghamshire in terms of birth, residence, and landholding, made only a slight and relatively unimportant contribution to the charities of the county, quite failing to assume those responsibilities which had in earlier ages, at least supposedly, marked the traditions of this class. The twenty of the nobility who gave or left benefactions totalling £2740, or an average of £137 per donor, made a contribution considerably less than the merchant group of the same number, less than the yeomanry of the county, and not much more than the tradesmen or the quite impoverished lower clergy. Their interest was principally in the poor to whom they left £2068 of all their benefactions, either in the form of outright relief or for the endowment of almshouses. One member of the class left £400 for university scholarships and another £267 for the augmentation of clerical incomes, which almost completes the inconsiderable charities of a class which was 'famed for its charity'. In Buckinghamshire, as in England, it is abundantly clear that Tudor policy, failure to adjust standards of living and the management of estates to the stern realities of an inflationary era, and an all too evident decline in a sense of social responsibility had conspired to make this class of insignificant consequence in the process by which a new England was being created in this period by vigorous, articulate, and clear-visioned men.

Such a class in Buckinghamshire were the upper gentry, who gave rather more than nine times as much to the institutions of the county as did the nobility and whose benefactions account for well over a quarter of the total charitable endowments of the county. In all, £25,294 1s was given by the 130 members of this class, or an average of £194 11s 5d per donor, an amount substantially exceeding that for the average nobleman and less only than the average for the upper clergy and the merchant class. These gifts were well distributed over the whole spectrum of charitable interests in the county, bulking so large in fact that they went far towards defining and establishing these interests. Slightly more than 35 per cent of their gifts were made to the poor, as compared with 52 per cent for the county; even more (42·6 per cent) was left by them for various educational purposes, as compared with 21 per cent for the county; their interest in schemes for social rehabilitation was considerably greater than that of the county; while their concern with undertakings for municipal improvement was slightly less. It is particularly important to note that their interests were overwhelmingly secular in nature, really inconsequential amounts being left by them to the various religious needs of the period for a total of only 8·43 per cent of all their gifts.

This class undertook steady and heavy social responsibility from the very beginning of our period, though the total of its benefactions from 1480 to 1600 (£5618 13s) was slightly exceeded by that (£6082 17s) of the lower gentry. During the first period, 1480–1540, when they left £1779 19s to charities, somewhat more than half (53·45 per cent) of their benefactions were for religious purposes, which, however, gave way with remarkable rapidity and certainly with remarkable completeness to the intensely secular aspirations which marked the temper of this class thereafter. The heyday of the upper gentry occurred in the early Stuart period when they gave a staggering total of £19,545 8s to charity, this constituting 77·27 per cent of the amount given by them during the whole of almost two centuries and being nearly 42 per cent of the totals given by all classes during these four remarkable decades. This would persuasively suggest not only the great prosperity of the upper gentry in this age but likewise the powerful and dominant position of the class in the affairs and institutions of the county. But their great role in this period was to give way most dramatically and almost completely during the cataclysm of the Civil War, which all but destroyed them, at least temporarily, as a socially responsible group in the county. We have observed that the revolutionary period resulted in no more than a slackening of the great outpouring of benefactions that had set in about 1600, but it ended it for the great gentry. During these twenty years members of this class left or gave only £130 to charities, an amount constituting only 0·52 per cent of the total charities of the class and almost exactly 1 per cent of the amount (£12,329 5s) contributed by all classes of men during this interval. Indeed, so precipitous and complete was the decline of their fortunes that the upper gentry gave not only a tiny fraction as compared with the lesser gentry and yeomanry of the county, but an amount considerably less than that provided by such groups as the lower clergy, the tradesmen, and the burghers.

Any of several possible explanations for the catastrophic decline in the fortunes and charitable impulses of the upper gentry ought also to involve the lesser gentry who were in any case separated from the great landholders by a not wholly clear and an occasionally arguable line of status. But it so happens that the period of the Civil War witnessed the climax in the giving of the lower gentry, who in these twenty years gave to charities in the county £5489 7s or 41·08 per cent of the whole for their class and very nearly 45 per cent of the total contributions of all classes for this period. It should likewise be noted that this substantial and aggressive social group exhibited a spectrum of charitable interests almost precisely that of the county as a whole, save for the fact that they were more decidedly secular in their aspirations. Thus they gave 55·56 per cent of their charities to the poor (as compared with 52·04 per cent for the county); 4·69 per cent to the several schemes of social rehabilitation (4·45 per cent for the county); 14 per cent to municipal improvements (8·80 per cent for the county); 18·86 per cent for education (21·26 per cent for the county); and only 6·91 per cent for religious purposes as compared with 13·45 per cent for the county at large. The 326 members of this social group gave a total of £13,362 9s during our whole period to the charitable needs of the county, this providing the substantial average of £40 19s 9d per donor and constituting almost a sixth of all benefactions made in Buckinghamshire. Their share in the social responsibilities of the county was heavy from the beginning of our period and was maintained with remarkable consistency through the whole of the era, with, as has been noted, a great outpouring of charitable wealth in the difficult revolutionary years.

The yeomanry, closely linked with the lower gentry in interests, and not infrequently as prosperous as their manorial neighbours, also played a notable role in the institutional and charitable life of the county. The class is scarcely recognizable in the early decades of our period, but began to gain rapidly in numbers, wealth, and status at about 1560, after which date almost 98 per cent of its charitable contributions were to be made. The 358 testators certainly identified as yeomen gave a total of £3877 5s during our period, an average of £10 16s 7d each for the class. The charitable interests of this rural group were after 1560 increasingly secular, the amazingly small proportion of 2·61 per cent of their total benefactions having been left to church uses. No other social group in Buckinghamshire was quite as vehemently secular as was the yeomanry. These were men who as small landowners and as wardens and overseers grappled daily with the problems of poverty in their parishes. Hence they displayed an almost obsessive interest in and responsibility for the care of the poor, leaving as a class £2752 18s, or 71 per cent of all their benefactions, for one or another form of poor relief. It is interesting to note that a very large proportion of this amount was left in the form of endowments, usually relatively small and almost invariably for the benefit of a specified parish.

The preoccupation with the problem of poverty in the parish was quite as strongly exhibited by the husbandmen who, with two exceptions, left their contributions as outright doles for poor relief in an amount constituting in percentage terms almost exactly (70·51 per cent) that of the yeomanry. The total given by 104 husbandmen during our period was very small, the sum being £154 2s, or an average of £1 9s 8d per donor, and constituting only 0·17 per cent of the whole of the charitable funds of the county. The structure of the giving of these poor men was simple, reflecting the immediate problems and interests that lay about them. Rather more than 12 per cent of their bequests were for the repair of their parish churches or for general church use, while almost as much (10·35 per cent) was left for the maintenance and improvement of parish highways and bridges.

The role of the clergy in the charities of the county was inconsiderable in relation to the wealth and social traditions of this group. Buckinghamshire possessed no cathedral church of its own and boasted no great abbey, with the result that only six members of the upper clergy, men who had been born in the county or who had held benefices there, made contributions to its charities. It so happens that these six bishops all made their bequests after 1621, and consequently these benefactions reflect quite strikingly the secular sentiments of that period. These men left nothing to church uses. They gave in all the generous total of £3710, or an average of £618 6s 8d each, an amount far exceeding the average for any other social group in the county. Of this sum, £3000 (80·86 per cent) was designated for educational purposes and the remainder was bequeathed for the benefit of the poor.

The lower clergy of the county gave considerably less, a total of £2329 10s having been left by them for the various charitable causes. The average benefaction for the seventy-eight members of the clergy who gave to charity was £29 17s 4d and in all their contributions amounted to 2·64 per cent of the total for the county. Their charitable interest was not markedly different from that of the county as a whole, upwards of half (54·32 per cent) of their gifts having been made to the poor, roughly a tenth for municipal uses (10·88 per cent), and for education (9·63 per cent) and, rather surprisingly, nothing at all for schemes of social rehabilitation. But contrary to the inclinations of their episcopal colleagues, these clergymen were deeply interested in the affairs of the parish. They gave a quarter (25·17 per cent) of all their benefactions for one or another religious purpose, a proportion roughly twice as substantial as for the county as a whole and much higher than that of any other group. Their great preoccupation was with the repair of the fabric of their church, which, as we have observed, was in a state of decay through most of two centuries, to which they gave well over half of their religious contribution. The Buckinghamshire clergy, as their wills testify, were on the whole reasonably prosperous before the Reformation, though only a relatively small proportion of them left charitable benefactions. In the period prior to the Reformation they gave to charities £564 11s, or something like a fourth (24·23 per cent) of the total contribution of their class. Their gifts during the period of the Reformation show a considerable percentage decline, but in the Elizabethan era their wills make it clear that they were at once in severe financial straits and without serious charitable inclination. During these four decades the clergy of Buckinghamshire gave only £21 13s to all charitable purposes, this amounting to less than 1 per cent of the total of charities of their class over our entire period and in percentage terms to be compared only with the husbandmen, who in the Elizabethan age gave about 6 per cent of their own total contributions to charitable uses. This suggests most persuasively the uncertainty and perhaps the discouragement of the clerical group of the county during this age of 'high secularism'. There was a marked revival in the charitable giving of the clergy in the early Stuart age when they gave almost half (43·66 per cent) of their total benefactions for the entire period, despite the fact that their wills do not suggest any considerable improvement in the relative prosperity of the class.

We have pointed out that Buckinghamshire was in this period an almost completely rural county. There were small and relatively unimportant mercantile and commercial groups in not more than three or four communities in the county and there was no substantial industrial activity in any part of the region in this age. Almost the whole of the benefactions made to the county by urban groups came consequently from London which, as we have seen, was to have a profoundly important impact on the social and charitable institutions of Buckinghamshire. A fair number of these London gifts came from men who had in later life retired to country estates in Buckinghamshire or elsewhere and who for purposes of this analysis have been classified as members of the class in which they died, the gentry. Accordingly, not quite 50 per cent of the total of London capital that was poured into Buckinghamshire by the benefactions of these men (£15,019 19s) is regarded as 'urban wealth' in the following analysis of the structure of charitable aspirations as a function of social status.

The various urban groups, the professions being included, gave a total of £9903 19s to charities of the county, only slightly more than

11 per cent of the whole. The charitable aspirations of these groups differed markedly from those of the older rural classes and tended to be concentrated in relatively large endowments for quite specific charitable purposes under excellently devised trusteeships. Thus the merchants, only twenty in number, of whom eighteen were Londoners, gave almost two-thirds of their benefactions to various endowed almshouses or schemes for the relief of the poor in their own households. They also gave substantially for the repair of roads in the county and one of their number left £200 for an apprenticeship plan, while another left, as an endowment, £400 for church repair, and still another gave an endowment of £400 for a Puritan lectureship. The total given by these merchants was £4931 18s, or 5·59 per cent of the whole for the county, their average benefaction of £246 12s being exceeded only by that of the bishops.

The fifty-four tradesmen, of whom a larger proportion were residents of the county, gave £1875 14s to the charities of Buckinghamshire, or 2·13 per cent of the total for the county. These men left an even larger proportion (79·1 per cent) of their benefactions to the needs of the poor. Though the average charity of members of this class reached the substantial sum of £34 14s 8d, so relatively weak were the religious interests of the group that on the average only £1 13s of this amount was given to religious needs. The remaining burghers, who cannot be more precisely identified, left the amazing proportion of 97 per cent (96·97 per cent), or £1071 10s, of their charities to poor relief, a proportion scarcely approached by any other social class in the county. The forty-two artisans and urban poor left a very small total of £73 6s to charities, which, it may be observed, was more traditionally distributed. About 78 per cent of this small sum was left in outright doles for the poor, while not quite 14 per cent, this being almost exactly the proportion for the whole of the county, was given for religious causes.

The professions are represented by only thirty-four donors, of whom twenty-four were lawyers, principally, it may be said, of or from London, four were teachers, two were stationers, two were scriveners, and two were physicians. This group gave in all £1918 1s, or an average of £56 8s 3d per donor. An extremely high proportion of their benefactions (88·67 per cent) was for the relief of the poor and a surprisingly low proportion (3·5 per cent) for education. The secularism of the group is most pronounced, their total contribution to religious causes being no more than £25 7s, or 1·32 per cent of the whole of the charitable funds given by this class. It should be remarked that this represents by far the smallest proportion of charitable benefactions given for religious purposes by any social group in the county; in fact, the contribution of the professional men to all religious causes after 1545 came to exactly £4.

In concluding our analysis of the structure of class interests and aspirations, brief comment is required on the spread of the benefactions of the 500 donors whose class cannot be exactly ascertained. This number includes an undue proportion of widows, whose social status is very difficult to determine, and probably includes as well a substantial number of yeomen. Otherwise, it is believed the group is spread in fairly even proportions over all the social categories just considered, an assumption supported by the fact that their charities, save for an amazingly large amount left for roads and bridges (14·1 per cent), follows fairly evenly the proportions for the county at large. These donors gave a total of £17,334 7s to the various charitable needs of the county, or an average of £34 13s 3d as compared with the county average of £51 3s 10d from each benefactor.

The benefactors of Buckinghamshire had accomplished much during the course of our period, in their own way and principally with their own substance. Though the county remained almost wholly rural even as late as 1660, it had made fair provision for its poor, had greatly extended the range of opportunities open to its needy, and had greatly strengthened, had, in fact, founded, the educational institutions of a sprawling and rather thinly populated rural region. Buckinghamshire was throughout this age of almost two centuries one of the most stubbornly secular of all English counties, an attitude shared by all classes and well sustained as the society built institutions which were in the end consonant with its own aspirations.

We turn now to Norfolk for a study of this same process of historical change and accomplishment. Norfolk lay not far to the north and east, but it was in our period a quite different world, richer in its resources, more complex in its economy and institutions, and moving out to meet and resolve social problems at once more intricate and pressing.

III

Norfolk

A. THE COUNTY

Norfolk was during the whole of our period an old, a mature, and a richly favoured county. The fourth county in the realm in area, it rested on a bed of chalk, outcropping in the west, and offered a greater variety of soil than any other shire. It was for the most part fertile, well deserving Camden's praise as being 'fat, luscious and moist', though this perceptive observer did not fail to note the 'lean and sandy' stretches along its western borders. In the west, too, there were still great areas of undrained fen lands, very lightly inhabited and in many ways isolated from the life and culture of a notably closely knit shire. In the north and west the soil was generally chalky, while in the southeast a very light sand was found, giving way in the centre and east to a light and easily worked loam. Almost four-fifths of the soil may be regarded as naturally arable, while during the period under study probably as much as two-thirds of the available land was so employed. Norden tells us that almost the whole of the county was open champion, with corn to be found in great abundance. It was in point of fact the premier grain county in the realm, with, however, far more rye than wheat grown through most of our age.

The county, it is important to stress, was predominantly agricultural throughout the sixteenth and seventeenth centuries, though it was experiencing an interesting and an important economic change. For one thing, its geographical position, its many small, though somewhat unreliable, ports, and its long coast-line helped to make it a leading maritime county. Its vessels engaged not only in a lucrative coastwise trade, but many hundreds of families were dependent on the fisheries well established in numerous coastal towns. A return of 1582 suggests that its 145 vessels, employing as they did 232 masters and 1438 seamen, placed it immediately after London in its importance as a shipping centre, while its persistent and close commercial connections with the Low Countries were to have not only important economic consequences for the life of the county but significant cultural consequences as well.

Norfolk was likewise one of the most important of all the areas in the realm for the manufacture of woollen cloth. The industry had been introduced in the time of Edward III, principally by Flemings settling in Norwich and Worstead. The golden age of this lucrative trade came in the first half of the fifteenth century, when Norfolk very possibly ranked next after Middlesex in wealth and when its principal towns, and especially Norwich, were thriving indeed. This late medieval industry was highly decentralized, the wool being put out to cottages in and around the numerous wool towns. Norwich was the financial and entrepreneurial centre for the industry which employed a long-staple wool then procured principally from Lincolnshire and Leicestershire. The cloth was sold either directly to the Continent through Great Yarmouth or by coastwise traffic to London middlemen. Later in the fifteenth century much of the raw wool came to be supplied from Norfolk itself, but by this date the whole industry was in rapid decline as it failed to meet rising competition in other parts of England. It was not until the mid-sixteenth century that the trade experienced a notable revival when great numbers of Dutch and Walloon weavers and other experienced artisans, many of whom were quite as much economic as religious refugees, settled in the county and introduced new methods for the manufacture of fine woollens which quite restored the industry. These settlers, who were to have a profoundly important effect on the cultural as well as the economic life of the county, were particularly heavily concentrated in Norwich, where in 1572 it was reported that about 4000 of them were residing. Their steady migration into Norwich restored the city, which had for many decades past been in slow decline and which in 1579–1580 was to suffer from a particularly devastating scourge of plague.

Norfolk was a relatively populous county throughout our period, with, it would seem, a not significantly denser population in 1600 than it had supported a century earlier. The parochial structure of the county was nearly complete at the opening of our period, while there is early evidence of comparatively dense population groupings in most rural parishes blessed with reasonably fertile soil. The total population of the county may be estimated at from 170,000 to 185,000 in 1600, with some bias towards the larger figure. In relative wealth the county also ranked high, Buckatzsch and Rogers, using somewhat different methods, appearing to agree on an average ranking for our whole period near the top of the second quartile of counties. Our own evidence would suggest a somewhat higher average ranking not far from the middle of the first quartile of counties for the period as a whole, somewhat higher in the early decades of our interval, considerably lower towards its middle, and with a notable recovery in the first half of the seventeenth century.

Norfolk is particularly renowned for its economic and cultural self-sufficiency throughout our long period. We shall have repeated occasions to refer to the remarkable cultural independence of the county during the course of our discussion, though it may be noted here that Norfolk was in many ways the almost perfect English microcosm. With an old, a prosperous, and a proud provincial city as its centre, the county provided rich and sufficient resources to create good and adequate institutions for itself. If we may regard Gonville and Caius College as a kind of cultural appanage, then it stood self-sufficient indeed. There was little of parochialism in this self-sufficiency, but it did have the flavour of difference and occasionally of somewhat obdurate singularity. Thus heresy became seated at an early date in Norfolk, when Bishop Nix, the firm and able Bishop of Norwich (1501–1536), complained with reason in 1530 that the infection was already deeply rooted among the merchants and those who lived in the coastal towns, though he regarded Gonville Hall as its true centre. Nix was unable to stamp heresy out in Norfolk, just as his successors found it impossible to root out Puritanism and later the nonconformity which so early gained a firm footing in this prosperous, articulate, and proud county. Blessed with great resources, centring on an old and a great county city, versatile and stalwart in its cultural heritage, and invincibly independent, Norfolk is one of the most interesting of all the English counties as we observe working within its life and institutions the process of rapid, indeed revolutionary, historical change.

B. GENERAL COMMENTS ON THE DATA

The county of Norfolk, rich in agricultural wealth throughout our period, provided for charitable uses in the age under examination the substantial sum of £177,883 11s, which places the county well beyond Lancashire and Somerset among the middling counties of the group under study.[1] The large total of benefactions was given by 2714 identified individual donors, the average charitable gift of £65 10s 10d being relatively high. The charities of the county were well supported by all classes in the society, with, however, a considerable proportion (18·63 per cent) having been given by men and women of unknown social status.

The structure of charitable aspirations in Norfolk differed significantly from that in other rural counties. Thus the £60,075 6s provided for the care of the poor, while a large sum, amounted to only slightly more than a third of the whole, whereas in most agricultural counties the proportion of funds given for this purpose was markedly higher. At the same time, the donors of the county maintained a remarkably persistent and advanced interest in various schemes for the rehabilitation of the poor and the cure of poverty, nearly 10 per cent of all benefactions

[1] *Vide* Table II (Appendix) for the detailed data on which this discussion rests.

having been made for this purpose. The steadily increasing importance of these experiments in the minds of benefactors of the county is suggested by the fact that in the final interval of our period almost a quarter of all gifts were designated for one or another of these rehabilitating uses. Moreover, the county was remarkable in its steady devotion to the various schemes of municipal betterment, such as the repair of roads, the building of bridges, the protection of harbours, or the erection of public buildings. To the various charities comprised within this very broad category, a total of £18,820 15s was given, amounting to about a tenth of the whole. If we may regard benefactions for schemes of social rehabilitation and municipal improvement together as a kind of venture capital invested by a community of men feeling its way towards new institutions and a richer common life, Norfolk must be ranked very high indeed among the counties of England. To these two great charitable heads combined slightly more than a fifth of all charitable benefactions were made, a proportion considerably exceeding that to be found in any other predominantly rural county.

The proportion given for the enlargement of educational opportunities amounted to not quite a quarter (23 per cent) of the whole, and compared very closely with that found in other rural counties, with the always notable exception of Lancashire. The money total was most substantial, being £40,920 4s, and, as we shall have occasion to observe, was sufficient to go far towards founding in the county a well-endowed and a fairly evenly distributed group of schools as well as impressive scholarship endowments.

The county was, after our first time interval, only moderately interested in religious causes and was to suffer the magnificent legacy of its parochial churches to fall into serious decay. Almost precisely the same amount was given to religious uses as to education, the 23·01 per cent of all charities given for this purpose not distinguishing the county markedly from most other rural counties, once more with the exception of Lancashire.

During the six decades prior to the Reformation, nearly a quarter (24·56 per cent) of the whole of the charitable benefactions of the county were made, when the impressive total of £43,685 1s was given for the several charitable purposes. As we should suppose, the religious interests of donors in this early period were paramount, slightly more than 60 per cent of all gifts having been given for this purpose, though there was already an unusual, in fact almost a precocious, interest in the other charitable aspirations which were to become predominant in all of England later in our period. The relatively large sum of £5348 9s was given for the relief of the poor, principally, it is true, in the form of the funeral doles and outright alms so characteristic of medieval charity. This amount represented 12·24 per cent of all charities of the era, but it was exceeded by the amazing proportion of 15·04 per cent (£6568 17s) provided for various plans for municipal betterment. The interest of the county in education in this early period was demonstrated by gifts totalling £4792 5s for this purpose, or not quite 11 per cent of the whole, while a by no means trivial sum of £600 9s, or 1·37 per cent of the total, was given for experiments in social rehabilitation.

A momentous, and, as time was to show, a permanent shift in the structure of men's social and charitable aspirations was to occur during the period of the Reformation. In that brief interval slightly less than 7 per cent of the total of the charities of the county was given by Norfolk donors. The benefactions for religious purposes, so overwhelming in amount in the preceding generation, all but withered away, the small total of £1528 14s representing but 12·38 per cent of charities of the period. The contributions to poor relief rose in a quite astounding fashion, constituting well over a third (38·56 per cent) of the whole sum given in the interval. About 30 per cent of all benefactions were for needed but also non-controversial municipal betterments, the £3666 16s provided for this purpose alone being well over twice the sum given for religious uses. The needs of education absorbed a slightly increased proportion (11·76 per cent) of the whole, while the amount given for the several plans of social rehabilitation rose sharply to £940 11s, or 7·62 per cent of the total.

During the Elizabethan period the secularization of men's aspirations was all but completed. The large total of £31,803 9s was given by men of the county to its social needs during these years, or 17·88 per cent of the whole for our period. Concern with the problem of poverty was in this generation dominant in men's minds, £13,975 18s being provided for one or another form of poor relief, or almost 44 per cent of the whole amount given for charitable uses during the age. Well over a quarter (28·95 per cent) of the benefactions of this generation were designated for educational purposes, the total of £9206 6s adding significantly indeed to the educational resources which Norfolk was accumulating against the requirements of modernity. Almost £4000 was given for municipal enterprises, amounting to 12·54 per cent of the whole, while not quite 7 per cent was given for the implementation of the decidedly secular experiments being undertaken by laymen in social rehabilitation. The almost complete secularization of aspirations during these culturally revolutionary years is suggested by the fact that the relatively insignificant total of £2499 15s, accounting for not more than 7·86 per cent of all benefactions, was disposed for the needs of religion, rendered all the more pressing because of the steadily Erastian policies of the Crown.

The pattern of aspirations so firmly established under the great

Tudor monarch prevailed with relatively little change during the first four decades of the seventeenth century. Norfolk was at once rich and generous in the early Stuart period, the very large total of £63,769 10s, or 35·85 per cent of the whole of the county's benefactions, having been given during this brief interval. But the county was generous only in terms of its now firmly defined secular interests. Despite the friendly attitude of the Crown and the mounting pressure of the Laudian bishops, only £9265 1s, or 14·53 per cent, of charitable resources was provided for the now almost desperate needs of the church and its fabric. Roughly twice as much (£18,471 13s) was given for the needs of education in the county, and in the nation, since substantial gifts were made from Norfolk to the universities during these years. The requirements of the poor absorbed not quite 40 per cent of all charities, the generous total of £24,940 10s, of which almost the entire amount was in the form of capital gifts, sufficing to lay solid foundations for institutions and mechanisms which were with some success to attack this chronic social evil. A relatively large sum of £7260 5s was risked on experimentation in social rehabilitation, while about 6 per cent, or £3832 1s, was given for various municipal undertakings of worth to the whole community.

The political disturbances which marked the whole of our last and brief period had amazingly little effect on the outpouring of charitable funds in this generous county. A total of £26,276 1s was given during these two decades, or 14·77 per cent of the whole, for a pattern of interests even more completely secular than that found in the Elizabethan age. Of all the charities given in these years, the high proportion of 42·05 per cent was designated for the relief of poor men and women, to which may reasonably be added almost 24 per cent provided for many and helpful efforts in the social rehabilitation of the poor. In other words, nearly two-thirds of all the benefactions of these decades were provided by donors determined to find a cure for the age-old problem of economic distress. A generous proportion of somewhat more than a fourth of all benefactions was likewise given for the insatiable requirements of education. But gifts for religious purposes had dried up in this traditionally pious county. The tiny sum of £1270 19s, amounting to no more than 4·84 per cent of the whole, was given for the various religious needs, and of this pitiful amount almost half was designated for the care of the church fabric, often quite as much a civic as a spiritual interest on the part of donors.

Before undertaking a detailed study of the structure of charitable giving in Norfolk, we may well present certain statistical comments which throw some light on the origin of charitable resources and the means of their accumulation. Thus, we have differentiated the capital gifts, the endowments, from the outright gifts designated for immediate charitable uses. The former possessed an impressive effectiveness since they created charitable institutions: social apparatus permanently dedicated to the attack on problems of concern to the age and to posterity. Such a benefaction enlisted the interest and in an amazing number of instances the imitation of substantial men of a parish who served as executors or trustees. The outright gifts were far more typically medieval in origin. They were normally alms or doles distributed haphazardly by executors to the poor of a parish, while many hundreds of them were very small and customary bequests for some religious purpose, especially during the earlier decades of our period.

In all, the large sum of £144,019 2s was given as endowments in Norfolk, which represents 80·96 per cent of the total of charitable benefactions in the county and sets it in this respect well within the extraordinarily tight range of the proportions for the other counties comprehended in this study.[1] The great institutional mechanisms—the almshouses, apprenticeship programs, the schools, the universities, and scholarship resources—received almost none save capital gifts or bequests through the whole course of our period. Quite surprisingly, almost the whole (97·26 per cent) of the large total left to municipal uses was likewise in this form of benefaction. Of £36,055 given for direct relief of the poor in our period, something over 80 per cent was provided as endowments by enlightened men and women of the county to ensure permanent care of the poor in their own homes. It is interesting to note that prior to 1560 considerably more than half of the total for this important use was in the form of outright doles or funeral alms, whereas thereafter such bequests became insignificant in amount, though not in number. In Norfolk, as in most counties, legacies and gifts for the improvement of roads and bridges, for church repairs, church building, and the general uses of the church tended to be outright bequests for immediate use. The capital gifts, not only because of the huge total so constituted but because of the admirable care which society from the sixteenth century forward has given to charitable endowments, were decisive in creating and ordering the social and cultural institutions of the county. Yet it must be remarked that of the 2714 donors in the county, something over three-quarters (76·79 per cent) left their benefactions, obviously on the average very small in amount, for immediate use in bettering life within their communities.

We tend to speak in this study of all charitable benefactions as being bequests, when in point of fact a considerable proportion of the total was in every county derived from gifts made during a donor's lifetime. The search for these gifts, particularly the small ones, is a tantalizing and a time-consuming process of combing local and parish records with

[1] The proportion of capital gifts ranges from 76·83 per cent (Lancashire) to 91 per cent (Bristol).

the inevitably discouraging consequence that the more thorough the search the more certain the student becomes that only a tithe has been found and that most of the casual charity of this or any other period never finds its way into historical records. This is, however, by no means true of all small gifts, and it was certainly rarely true of the large benefactions. In almost every instance the large gifts made during a donor's lifetime were vested in a trust instrumentality of some sort which ensured not only the perpetuity but the record of his action. A fairly extensive random sampling of the donor cards for Norfolk suggests that something over a third (35·6 per cent) of the total of the charitable funds of the county were disposed as gifts made prior to the death of the donor, a proportion established as reasonably accurate as well by certain other evidence.[1]

Despite its insularity, Norfolk was not only one of the richest but also one of the most advanced socially and culturally among the counties of England. This fact may well explain the relatively significant role of women in the social development of the county and the considerable amount of wealth which they disposed.[2] There were 352 women donors in Norfolk, who gave a total of £16,849 5s to its charitable institutions. This means that women donors comprised almost 13 per cent of all benefactors and that they gave 9·47 per cent of the whole of the county's charitable funds. Moreover, their average gift reached the relatively very high figure of £47 17s 4d, which compares not too badly with the average of £65 10s 10d given by all the donors of the county. These facts suggest that women of the county were in a social and economic position much more favourable than that of women in most rural counties.

It is also important to observe that women of the county gave in a

---

[1] *Vide* Jordan, *Philanthropy in England*, 109–125, for a detailed study of the history of charitable trusts, including those established in Norfolk during the period under study.

[2] The following table sets out the proportions given by women in the several counties:

	Percentage of women donors	Percentage of total gifts made by women
Bristol	15.44	7·58
Buckinghamshire	13·50	13·01
Hampshire	12·17	3·92
Kent	12·56	5·49
Lancashire	11·28	6·34
London	14·88	9·14
Norfolk	12·97	9·47
Somerset	14·63	6·03
Worcestershire	12·71	5·31
Yorkshire	12·99	12·55

significantly different pattern from their spouses and fathers, though it must be said that these differences are in part accounted for by the fact that a quite disproportionate share of their philanthropy dates from the beginning of the Elizabethan era when the cultural process of secularization had been well established. Women benefactors of the county gave a third (33·03 per cent) of their bequests for the relief of the poor, a proportion almost precisely that for the county as a whole (33·77 per cent). The somewhat hazardous experiments in social rehabilitation commanded no more than 3·66 per cent of all their gifts, as compared with almost 10 per cent provided for these purposes by the county at large, while the extraordinarily generous support of the county for various municipal enterprises (10·58 per cent) found but scant favour among women donors, who gave only 1·55 per cent of all their benefactions for such purposes. But Norfolk women were persistently and certainly importantly interested in the educational needs of their county. They provided a total of £4690 7s for various university purposes, the large sum of £2272 6s for the endowment or aid of grammar schools, and £696 6s for scholarship endowments. In all, their generous benefactions for educational purposes commanded rather more than 45 per cent of all their charities, as compared with 23 per cent for the county at large. Their interests were, then, remarkably secular: while the county as a whole gave about 23 per cent of all its funds for the support of the several religious needs, its women gave only slightly more than 16 per cent of their charitable wealth for this use.

We have on several earlier occasions complained of the great difficulty in ascertaining precisely the social status of unmarried women, whether widows or spinsters, in legal and historical sources. One can in most instances be almost certain because of family name or other internal evidence in a deed or will, but these inferences are too unreliable to permit of statistical use. We have, however, been more fortunate in Norfolk than in several other counties, since we have been able to identify positively 138 of the women donors, or not quite 40 per cent of the total number.

Somewhat more than half, seventy-six, of these identified women donors were members of the rural society, while place of residence at death would indicate that a large proportion of those of unknown social status were likewise rural dwellers. Three of these women were of the nobility, their combined charities reaching the unimpressive total of £335 3s, of which almost 80 per cent was given for religious uses. Far more significant were the charities of twenty-five women of the upper gentry, whose gifts are spread through the whole of our period and who were particularly notable for their support of education and poor relief. While eight of these women left charitable bequests of £10 or less, their average benefaction was high, there being among them three donors who left charitable bequests, principally for education, of £600 or more.

There were as well thirty-four members of the lower gentry, whose benefactions ranged from one modest bequest of 8s for the poor to a large benefaction of £856 5s, of which £533 6s was provided for university scholarships. We have certain records of only nine gifts from women of yeoman status, ranging in amount from 1s to £17 12s, and of only five of the husbandman class, though the place of residence and nature of the bequest makes it quite certain that many of our unidentified women donors were members of these two agrarian groups.

There were nineteen women donors, mostly of Norwich, who were members of the substantial and numerous mercantile aristocracy of the county. These women gave in a range from £6 8s to £400, the median benefaction for the class being £69 1s, an amount considerably greater than that of the women of the lower gentry of the county. There were fourteen women who were the wives or widows of tradesmen and eleven who were of that somewhat amorphous urban group which we have been able to identify no more precisely than as 'additional burghers'. The social and economic health of Norfolk during most of our period is suggested by the fact that there were as well fifteen women donors drawn from the artisan group, whose benefactions ranged from a customary legacy of 6d for the general uses of the Church to two bequests of £10 each. The remaining three identified women donors were also urban dwellers, two being widows of Norwich lawyers and one the widow of a bishop.

C. THE ACHIEVEMENT

1. *The Relief of the Poor*

(a) *Household Relief.* As we have noted, approximately a third (33·77 per cent) of all Norfolk charitable funds was given for the relief of poverty. This large total of £60,075 6s was distributed among several uses. By far the largest sum, amounting to £36,055, was given for the care of the poor in their own houses, and of this amount, it is important to observe, more than four-fifths was in the form of capital foundations designed to give relief in perpetuity within the boundaries of particular communities. The impressive total of £18,146 7s was provided for almshouses and their support, all save a tiny proportion having been given as capital amounts. In addition, £4493 9s was left for general, or unspecified, charitable uses, but was employed by executors or trustees for the relief of needy persons, about half of this total having been given in small amounts for immediate use rather than as endowments. Finally, £1380 10s, of which all but 10s was capital, was given with a restriction for the relief of the aged.

The absorption of Norfolk with the problem of poverty was continuous. In only three decades of the long interval under study was less than £1000 provided for the various forms of poor relief, all these being prior to 1541. Norfolk was a rich county, but its principal city was subject during much of the period to a serious industrial depression which likewise involved many of the rural parishes lying about Norwich and caught up within its economic orbit. This fact, to which we shall recur in greater detail, somewhat differentiates Norfolk from the essentially rural counties with which we have been concerned, for Norwich, it must be remembered, was during the whole of our period either the second or the third city in the realm.

During the years prior to the Reformation men of the county gave £5348 9s to one or another form of poor relief. This wealth, amounting to roughly an eighth of all the benefactions of this pious period, was principally given in the form of funeral doles or outright distributions to poor persons by executors entrusted with the responsibility for the selection of needy recipients. In no decade in this interval did the total of benefactions for the poor fall below £521 7s. A fair fraction of the whole, £1331 2s, was provided for the establishment of almshouses for the permanent succour of indigent persons in the several communities thus favoured by rich and forward-looking donors.

The advent of the Reformation in Norfolk, as elsewhere, heralded an immediate and a most significant heightening of interest in the chronic problem of poverty. Almost as much was provided for poor relief in this brief interval as in all the preceding six decades. The £4761 9s given for these uses amounted to 38·56 per cent of all benefactions in the period, and of this amount the impressive sum of £2696 10s was designated for almshouse endowments.

The concern of socially responsible men with the problem of poverty was greatly increased during the Elizabethan era, when Norwich particularly was setting an example for the whole of England in its intelligent and aggressive effort to arrive at some understanding of the problem and then to deal with it adequately. During these four decades a total of £13,975 18s was given for poor relief, amounting in all to more than two-fifths of the whole of the charitable benefactions in the county for the period. It is particularly significant that of this considerable total almost 95 per cent was given as endowments, the custom of funeral doles and casual alms having been all but abandoned as men undertook for the first time in Christian history a really serious attack on the roots of poverty. During these years the substantial sum of £5912 6s was given for the endowment of almshouses, while nearly £7000 was disposed for the support of the poor of the county in their own houses.

The outpouring of charitable moneys for the relief of poverty was greatly increased during the more prosperous years of the early Stuarts, when £24,940 10s was given for the succour of the needy. This amount represented a slight decrease in the proportion of all charities given for this purpose, declining from 43·94 per cent to 39·11 per cent, but it constituted a rich addition to the social resources of the county. The large total of £14,873 5s was given for outright relief, while £7863 19s was settled by Norfolk men and women as almshouse endowments.

Nor was there any real slackening in the generosity and concern of the county with the problem of indigence during the short interval of political upheaval.[1] In these years the large sum of £11,049 was given for the various uses of the poor, of which upwards of £10,000 was provided for the augmentation of the endowments of the parishes of the county for the support of their poor.

Concern with the problems of poor relief in Norfolk became after 1560 widespread among all classes of men. Small and usually outright bequests to the poor of the parish came gradually to replace the customary legacies for religious uses in the wills of poorer men, while men of greater substance began to undertake the foundation of almshouses and the establishment of endowments in their own parishes in order to meet a sense of social obligation which the Tudors had occasionally harshly but none the less effectively engrained in their realm. We should now note at least briefly certain of the larger of these benefactions for the benefit of the poor.

There were, as we have suggested, a number of substantial foundations made for the relief of poverty in Norfolk well before the secularization of life which attended the Reformation Settlement. Thus John Barker, of unknown social status, had in 1486 settled the profits of an estate of approximately forty acres for the care of the poor of South Lopham, for the relief of the parish from taxation, and other charitable causes. It seems clear that the title to the trusteed property was vested in the church of the parish and that in the seventeenth century, when it possessed a capital worth of about £300, it was administered in an informal fashion by responsible men of the community.[2] A few years later, 1492, a wealthy widow of Ormesby died who had been famous for her great generosity during her own lifetime. This woman, Elizabeth Clere, who had, as we shall see, been a great benefactor to education, by her will required her executors to make distributions of grain to her poor tenants each quarter until a total of £133 10s had been expended. She left as well £10 to the monastic clergy, £92 for the celebration of masses, £66 13s 4d for the repair of roads within her lordship, £11 for the making of a steeple for the church at Ormesby, and approximately £10 to hospitals in Norwich and Yarmouth.[3]

---

[1] It must be noted that £507 given for outright relief is included in this period, though actually of uncertain date.

[2] CCN 290, 291 A. Caston 1486; PP 1835, XXI, 733.

[3] CCN 131-135 Wolman 1492; Blomefield, Francis, History of the county of Norfolk (L., 1805-1810, 11 vols.), IV, 35, VI, 351, XI, 236; Norfolk Archaeology,

A well-known Tudor soldier and diplomatist, Sir Thomas Lovell, a native of Barton Bendish, on his death in 1524 left the bulk of his charities, totalling £960 4s, to various uses in or near London, but did not forget his native county. He provided £200 for distribution as funeral doles to the poor, as well as £30 to various monastic establishments in Norfolk.[1] A few years later, Robert Jannys, a rich Norwich grocer, charged his executors to lay out a total of £208 over a period of twenty years on penny doles to eighty poor of Norwich, as well as an estimated £10 immediately for the relief of blind, lame, and bedridden persons within the city. Jannys left as well substantial sums for municipal uses and education,[2] £54 18s for prayers, and £10 for the embellishment of St Andrew's church, and smaller amounts for various other pious purposes.[3]

These are but the largest of a great many bequests for the relief of the poor which were essentially medieval in the sense that they provided for more or less indiscriminate doles and alms. A great and a lasting change was to occur towards the middle of the century as the responsibility for poor relief began to be assumed as a function of state and as men of a more secular temper began to assess closely and thoughtfully the instrumentalities with which poverty might be more surely curbed and relieved, and as they began to embark on bold schemes of social rehabilitation which might cure or prevent the ravages of indigence.

These tendencies are well exhibited in the quite remarkable charitable

III (1852), 383; *The Reliquary*, n.s., I (1887), 143, III (1889), 48; Venn, John, et al., eds., *Biographical history of Gonville and Caius College* (Cambridge, 1897–1912, 4 vols.), III, 13, 21, 214, 279, 285, IV, ii, 30, 90. *Vide post*, 168, for her great educational gifts. Elizabeth Clere left personal bequests totalling £873, a considerable amount in jewels and plate, and an unspecified amount of land.

[1] PCC 27 Jankyn 1528; DNB; *Norf. Arch.*, XVIII (1914), 46–77; Jordan, *Charities of London*, 197, 277, 300, 378, 417. Lovell had supported Henry VII at Bosworth Field and rose rapidly in his favour. He was chosen Speaker of the House of Commons in 1485 and was knighted in 1487. In 1502 he was made Treasurer of the Household and President of the Council. He was fully trusted by Henry VIII during the early years of his reign, but withdrew from public life shortly after Wolsey's rise to power.

[2] *Vide post*, 146, 153.

[3] PCC 1 Thower 1530; Blomefield, *Norfolk*, IV, 228, 234; Cozens-Hardy, Basil, and E. A. Kent, *The mayors of Norwich* (Norwich, 1938), 42; *PP* 1833, XIX, 226–227; *PP* 1834, XXI, 499–500. Jannys was a native of Aylsham, where he endowed a grammar school. He was Mayor of Norwich in 1517 and again in 1524. His portrait in the Guildhall bears this incription:

> For all welth worship and prosperite
> Fierce death ys come and restyd me
> For Jannys prayse god, I pray you all
> Whose actes do remayne a memorial.

dispositions of a Norwich merchant, William Rogers, who died in 1553, and of his widow, Katherine, who survived him for a period of three years. Rogers, a grocer who had represented Norwich in Parliament in 1542 and who had served his city as mayor, left £7 16s outright to the poor in weekly distributions, a marriage favour of a silver spoon weighing one ounce and bearing the injunction, 'Remember Rogers', to each of one hundred maidens during the next five years, and £10 towards the construction of a wall within the city. He bequeathed as well the sum of £300 to be employed for interest-free loans to needy merchants and other inhabitants of the city, the fund to be administered by the mayor and three justices, who were to lend not more than £20 to any one person. And, finally, Rogers purchased, presumably as an executor of the will of Robert Jannys, a manor at Shropham which he charged with £10 p.a., for the discharge of tolls and customs in the markets and fairs held in the city, while assigning a remainder, with an estimated value of £5 p.a., for the relief of indigent persons in a Norwich almshouse. In all, these impressive and carefully devised charities totalled £642 16s, a most substantial sum and one addressed with discernment towards the needs of a city and its people.[1]

William Rogers' widow, Katherine, a native of Great Yarmouth, was if anything more intelligent and prudently helpful in her charities than her merchant spouse. On her death in 1556 she added capital of £100 to the loan fund recently established by her husband in Norwich and created a similar fund with a capital of £100 to provide loans in amounts not to exceed £10 for needy persons of Great Yarmouth. The trust was vested in the bailiffs and justices of the town with the provision that if any loss should occur the remainder should revert to the City of Norwich for identical purposes. She likewise established a fund of £100 to be employed by the city authorities for the purchase and distribution of grain, 'as well to beat down the covetous minds of those greedy cormorants, who never cease to grind the faces of the poor, by inhancing the prices, making a dearth when God sendeth plenty—as to relieve the poor inhabitants' by selling corn in small quantities below the prevailing market price. Katherine Rogers also provided at her own cost three wells at Great Yarmouth for the washing of fishermen's nets and the washing and bleaching of linen manufactured in the town. And, finally, she settled a rent-charge of £1 10s p.a. on the City of Norwich which was to be expended annually at a public ceremony, with sixty poor persons comprising the audience, where the trustees of the loan fund created by her husband and herself should report on the state of the fund, announce the persons who held loans, and engross the accounts; 10s

[1] PCC 12 Tashe 1553; Cozens-Hardy, *Mayors of Norwich*, 51–52; Blomefield, *Norfolk*, IV, 395, 509; *PP* 1834, XXI, 575.

was to be distributed amongst the sixty poor at the conclusion of the ceremony.[1]

But these important changes in the structure and the quality of charitable funds, dramatic and complete as they were in the course of a generation, were first visible among informed urban men of substance, having been much more slowly adopted by the old-fashioned squire-archy. Thus we may contrast the essentially medieval will of Sir William Paston, who died in 1554, with the carefully devised endowment of a Norfolk-born merchant of London, Ralph Greenaway, whose will was proved a few years later.

Sir William Paston, a lawyer and courtier, was a severe landlord and a careful guardian of his family estates. On his death he bequeathed token favours to the clergy, £4 to prisoners in Norwich Castle and Norwich Guildhall, and the large sum of £100 to be distributed to the poor in meat, drink, and money. This was an amount sufficient to endow a modest almshouse or to relieve in a substantial sense the problem of poverty in the parish of Paston for generations to come. But this bequest is all too typical of the lavish funeral doles and subsequent alms, so common in the later Middle Ages, which brought beggars flocking in by the hundreds from half the realm and which effected no real good for living men, whatever repose it may have gained for the soul of the donor.[2]

Time and reason ran rather with the bequest of Ralph Greenaway, a London grocer, who on his death in 1558 left a substantial sum for the relief of the poor of his native parish of Wiveton. This endowment may well be regarded as typical of the new and secular spirit of charity. It was carefully devised capital; it addressed itself with intelligent flexibility to the care and cure of poverty, while providing the pos-sibility of other worthy uses; and it sought to do permanent good for men rather than to expend a very large sum on what could be described

[1] PCC 18 Ketchyn 1556; Blomefield, *Norfolk*, IV, 509; Swinden, Henry, *The history of Great Yarmouth* (Norwich, 1772), 872–873; Manship, Henry (C. J. Palmer, ed.), *The history of Great Yarmouth* (Great Yarmouth, 1854), 124–130; *PP* 1833, XIX, 349; *PP* 1834, XXI, 575. Katherine Rogers was the daughter of John Garton, a Yarmouth merchant.

[2] PCC 15 More 1554; Venn, John, ed., *Alumni cantabrigienses* (Cambridge, 1922–1954, 10 vols.), I, iii, 317; Blomefield, *Norfolk*, VI, 487; DNB. Educated at Cambridge, Paston was bred to the law. Commissioner of array in Norfolk in 1511, he was knighted shortly afterwards. In 1516 he was appointed legal counsel to the Corporation of Yarmouth at the rather staggering fee of £40 p.a., which he apparently retained for almost forty years, since he lived to a great age. He was designated Sheriff of Norfolk in 1517 and of Norfolk and Suffolk in 1528. Paston served Henry VIII in various military capacities, especially on the Scottish border, and assisted in the expropriation of the monastic properties. His heir, Erasmus Paston, died during his lifetime, his grandson, Sir William, the founder of the North Walsham grammar school (*vide post*, 160), succeeding to his estates.

as a classical instance of 'conspicuous waste'. Greenaway's will provided that two hundred marks should be employed by his executors for the purchase of lands or other real property with a clear annual value of £6 13s 4d. This property should in turn be conveyed on trust to the churchwardens of Wiveton and sixteen other 'honest parishioners', with the instruction that they should each Sunday distribute 13d in money and thirteen penny loaves to as many poor men of the parish, the residue, if any, to be employed for the maintenance and repair of the parish church. The executors, themselves men experienced in trade, purchased the rectory and parsonage of Briston, with the advowson, and when they conveyed the property to the trustees in 1560 it possessed a clear value of £7 6s p.a., or slightly more than the prudent Greenaway had contemplated. This capital amount, not greatly larger than Paston's pyrotechnic bequest, was sufficient to soften the sharp edges of poverty for thirteen families in this rural parish immediately and, because it was well founded and well conceived, it grew in social utility as the generations passed. By 1679 the clear annual worth of the property was £11 19s, while in 1796 the advowson alone was sold for £850. The remaining properties, with other investments, were in 1843 yielding annually £264 5s and in 1864 the large sum of £538 5s, of which £400 was expended for poor relief, £38 5s on the church, and £25 on the educational needs of the parish.[1] Greenaway, like the merchant class of which he was a member, sensed the true currents of need and of opportunity for his own and future times, whereas Paston reflected in equally generous charitable impulse a seignorial splendour no longer relevant to the requirements of a new and complex age.

The poor of Norwich, as well as the city itself, were remembered under the terms of the will of Peter Rede, Esq., the son of a merchant who had been Mayor of Norwich in 1496. An adventurer and soldier, Rede had retired to his native city in his later years. He left two hundred marks to provide annual distributions of £6 13s 4d among the poor 'until the whole summe were runne out' and charged his wife as well to expend £4 p.a. during the next six years in order to supply the weekly diet of twelve poor families. Rede left in addition a salt dish of the value of £20 to adorn the mayor's table and devised land and houses in St Giles' parish, with an estimated annual value of £4, to endow the charges for ringing each morning and evening the great bells of St Peter Mancroft for the aid of those who should travel into Norwich at those seasons of the day.[2]

[1] PCC F. 30 Noodes 1558; Beaven, A. B., *The aldermen of the city of London* (L., 1908, 1913, 2 vols.), II, 35; *PP* 1833, XIX, 294; *PP* 1843, XVII, 68-69; *PP* 1867-68, LII, ii, Norfolk, 100-101. Greenaway was elected an alderman of London in 1556 and master of his company in 1557, the year before his death.

[2] PCC 4 Sheffelde 1568; *PP* 1834, XXI, 594; Blomefield, *Norfolk*, III, 317, IV, 200-201. Rede, who had ranged widely during his lifetime, was evidently

A few years later the social resources of Norwich were further augmented under the will of Roger Mundes, perhaps a tradesman, who left real property with a then (1574) probable value of £200 to be administered on trust by twelve substantial men of his parish. The income was to be distributed each year at Christmas in money, fuel, and clothing to the poor of the parish.[1] At about the same time (ca. 1576) a rural parish, Pulham St Mary Magdalene, took effective steps to pool scattered but valuable properties which had been left for the benefit of the poor or general charitable uses. It seems probable that the churchwardens and vestry served informally as trustees until 1625 when the property, with certain additions, was surrendered to more formally designated feoffees.[2] The poor of Hemsby were assisted in 1583 by the will of Edmund Drake, who left real property of a probable worth of £100, the income to be given to poor families of the parish who declined to take relief from the collections then being made for the indigent.[3] Just two years later, Edmund Bedingfield, a member of the gentry, left £10 for the repair of Oxborough church and property with a capital value of £180 for the succour of the worthy poor of that parish.[4]

The number and size of bequests for the poor of this general kind, creating endowments and providing a mechanism for the sensible distribution of income, increased steadily and fruitfully during the closing years of the Elizabethan era. But perhaps these additional examples, two being drawn from King's Lynn and one from a rural parish, will suffice. A local merchant of King's Lynn, William Garratt, in 1586 left numerous small bequests totalling £24 to church repairs, the clergy, the care of highways, the local almshouse, and the poor, and likewise provided that a fraction of his estate with an estimated value of £150 should on the death of two relations be vested in the municipality as capital for the maintenance of a stock of coal for distribution to the needy.[5] Just three years later, another merchant and alderman of the town, Thomas

not wholly accepted by the staid governing group of his city. He had been knighted by Charles V in 1538 for 'valiaunt dedes' in the Emperor's service in Barbary and at the siege of Tunis. In the church of St Peter Mancroft, says Blomefield, 'lies buried Sir Peter Rede, Knt., though that honour being conferred on him by the *Emperor*, he was acknowledged here as an *esquire* only'.

[1] *PP* 1834, XXI, 643; Blomefield, *Norfolk*, IV, 316. The property was valued at £12 p.a. in 1695.

[2] *PP* 1835, XXI, 592–593.

[3] Clark, Zachary, *An account of the charities of Norfolk* (L., 1811), 104; *PP* 1833, XIX, 268.

[4] PCC 12 Windsor 1585; Blomefield, *Norfolk*, VI, 178–179; *Alum. cantab.*, I, i, 124. Bedingfield was the son and heir of Sir Henry Bedingfield, governor of the Tower of London under Mary and for some time the officer responsible for the 'security' of the Princess Elizabeth. The son, educated at Cambridge and probably at Lincoln's Inn, was an inconspicuous country squire.

[5] PCC 20 Windsor 1586.

Grave, left on trust to the mayor and burgesses the substantial sum of £200 to be lent at the rate of 6·67 per cent to responsible merchants and artificers of the town, with the provision that half the annual income be employed for the purchase of coal for the poor and the remainder distributed in cash for their support.[1] Towards the close of the Elizabethan era, a London merchant, William Cutting, probably a native of East Dereham, left that parish an endowment of £200 for the maintenance of its poor householders, as well as £37 in outright alms, while establishing in Cambridge a scholarship fund to maintain 'foure poore schollers there . . . as shall be thought meet, and . . . schollers borne within the Countie of Norfolk shall be relieved therewith before any others.'[2]

As we have already observed, the great outpouring of endowments for the poor of the county came during the early years of the seventeenth century (1601–1640), when a total of £24,940 10s was so devised. Almost the whole of this large sum was in the form of endowments. We are here particularly concerned with funds left for the direct relief of poor men and women in their own homes (£14,873 5s) and for general charitable purposes (£1183 6s). There were scores of these endowments with a capital value of upwards of £60, but we must be content with commenting on only a few of the larger or more interesting of them.

[1] PCC 44 Leicester 1589; PP 1834, XXII, 47; Blomefield, Norfolk, VII, 193–194. The will further provided that if these stipulations should prove to be illegal, the trustees might purchase lands as endowment for the same purpose. In 1614, 352 bushels of coal were distributed from half the income. This donor had been thrice mayor and in 1574 had purchased the manor of Pinkeny.

[2] PCC 14, 15 Wallop 1600; Blomefield, Norfolk, X, 213; Venn, Caius College, III, 230; Nichols, John, ed., Bibliotheca topographica britannica (L., 1780–1790, 8 vols.), II, No. 5, App., 7. Cutting's executor, a London goldsmith, placed the following inscription in the church at East Dereham and in St Katherine's by the Tower, London:

> Here dead in part whose best part never dyeth,
> A benefactor William Cutting lyeth,
> Not dead, if good deeds could keep men alive,
> Nor all dead, since good deeds do men survive.
> Gonville and Kaies may his good deeds record,
> And will no doubt him praize therefore afford,
> Saint Katrin's near London, can it tell,
> Goldsmithes and Merchant Taylors knowe it well;
> Two country towns his civil bounty blest,
> East Derham, and Norton Fitz-Warren West,
> More did he than this table can unfold,
> The world his fame, this earth his earth doth hold.

Cutting left large additional benefactions in London, including an endowment of £200 to an almshouse in his parish (St Katherine's by the Tower), £40 to London hospitals, £200 for the charitable uses of the Goldsmiths' Company, and £500 as a loan fund for tradesmen with the Merchant Taylors as trustees.

In 1601 Joan Smith, of London, a merchant's widow, left £200 to the Corporation of Norwich under agreement that the fund be so invested as to afford £13 6s 8d p.a. for the sustenance of the poor of this her native city.[1] Two years later, Peter Peterson, a Norwich goldsmith, in addition to small bequests totalling £10 for church repairs, loans to the poor, the relief of prisoners, the sick, and the poor Dutch inhabitants of the city, by will provided four tenements and lands worth roughly £200, to provide 5s for herbage for the minister of his parish church and the substantial remainder for stocks of fuel for the poor of his parish.[2] In the next year, 1604, a London tradesman, Thomas Cressy, a native of Aylsham, devised to feoffees extensive property, including twelve houses in that town with a then capital worth of £380, with the instruction that the whole of the income, after necessary maintenance of the property, be employed by the churchwardens of the parish for the care of the poor.[3] Approximately a decade later William Mowting of East Dereham provided still another endowment for the care of the poor of that parish, as well as other parishes in the hundred of Mitford, by laying a rent-charge of £14 on certain of his properties, this to be disbursed annually to worthy poor under the advice of the minister and churchwardens.[4]

The Reverend Thomas Hopes, of the parish of Gayton, by his will proved in 1616, left substantial benefits for the poor of that parish and certain other livings which he held in Norfolk. Lands were conveyed on trust to Trinity College, Cambridge, with the provision that £3 8s 8d p.a. of the income should be employed for the maintenance there of a poor scholar to be chosen by the vice-master of the college and the Mayor of Lynn from among the graduates of the Lynn Grammar School. The remaining income of £8 3s p.a. should be paid by the trustee annually in amounts ranging from 3s 4d p.a. to £3 8s 8d p.a. to the churchwardens of Didlington, Colveston, East Walton, Middleton, East Winch, Gayton, and North Runcton for distribution by these officers to church-going poor persons.[5] Several parishes likewise shared

---

[1] PP 1834, XXI, 578–579; Blomefield, Norfolk, III, 358, IV, 165. In 1603 an estate in East Smithfield (London) was settled on the Corporation to provide the required stipend. In the early nineteenth century the property was taken by the City for street improvements, capital of £500 being settled on the charity as damages.

[2] Norwich Archdeaconry Wills, 1603, fol. 190; Norf. Arch., XI (1892), 259–302; Blomefield, Norfolk, IV, 98; PP 1834, XXI, 698–699; PP 1843, XVII, 18; PP 1867–68, LII, ii, Norfolk, 118–119. The property was yielding £11 p.a. in 1667, £35 p.a. in 1831, and £50 p.a. in 1864.

[3] PCC 81 Harte 1604; PP 1833, XIX, 227–228.

[4] PP 1835, XXI, 792. The will was dated August 20, 1613 and proved at Norwich.

[5] PP 1834, XXII, 69; Blomefield, Norfolk, II, 231, IX, 66–67, 148; Alum. cantab., I, ii, 405. Hopes was graduated from Cambridge in 1587 and received

in the generous bequest of Jane, Lady Berkeley, in 1618, who left in perpetuity £20 p.a. to be divided among five rural parishes in Gallow Hundred where her first husband, Sir Roger Townshend, had held estates. Lady Jane devised sufficient property to her grandson, Sir Roger Townshend, to secure the specified payments to the clergyman, the churchwardens, and the overseers of the poor, who were enjoined to distribute the whole of the annual revenue to the most aged and impotent of the poor of the several favoured parishes.[1]

One of the greatest of the benefactors in the county during our period was a Norwich woollen merchant and alderman named Henry Fawcett, who died in 1619 leaving a personal estate of about £3000, as well as extensive landholdings in Yorkshire and valuable properties in Norwich and Great Yarmouth. Fawcett had made large charitable benefactions in Norwich in the later years of his life, to which he added most generous bequests by his will. His contributions to the social needs of his city and county by gift and bequest totalled £1394 13s 4d, a very large amount indeed for a provincial merchant to have provided in this period. We shall later comment on Fawcett's interest in the almshouse being established in Norwich and on his support of education, but we should at this point deal with his complicated and large contribution to the poor and to their social rehabilitation. Fawcett's will left £94 6s 8d outright to the poor of Norwich, as well as £40 as a stock for the poor of the Dutch and the French communions in the city. He provided £45 6s 8d as a stock to be laid out annually by the churchwardens and overseers of six parishes for the purchase during slack seasons of coal to be sold at cost to the poor in the course of the winter. The sum of £40 was left as a stock to be lent, or rather advanced, each winter by the mayor to some entrepreneur who would undertake to quarry stone in order to make work for poor masons during their season of unemployment. The large stipend of £10 p.a. was provided by Fawcett before his death for the relief of poor weavers in the city, while his will established loan funds of £300 to be made available to as many as thirty poor worsted weavers, £30 to six dornix (Dornick) weavers, £20 to shoemakers, and £10 to poor smiths. Fawcett gave £60 to be expended in dowries for

his M.A. degree in 1590. He was Rector of West Winch (1588–1590), of Colveston (1592–1616), of North Runcton and Setchey (1592–1616), Vicar of East Walton (1590), and Vicar of Didlington.

[1] PCC 24 Meade 1618; *Complete peerage*, I, 333–334; *PP* 1835, XXI, 654; DNB. Lady Jane was the daughter of Sir Michael Stanhope, a strong supporter and brother-in-law of the Protector Somerset. He fell with Somerset, beheaded for alleged conspiracy against Northumberland. Lady Jane's first husband had his seat at East Raynham, Norfolk, and was a well-known Elizabethan courtier. The parishes to receive the stipends were: East Raynham, £5 p.a.; West Raynham, £3 6s 8d p.a.; South Raynham, £3 6s 8d p.a.; East Rudham, £5 p.a.; Helhoughton, £3 6s 8d p.a.

poor and deserving young women, set aside in a particularly complicated clause of a complex will £10 15s p.a. for sermons 'at the common
place and the Green-yard' and to the minister of St Michael's for an
annual sermon, and left smaller sums totalling approximately £35 for
the relief of prisoners and the repair of a bridge.[1] These diffuse gifts and
bequests fall into a very precise pattern; Fawcett was evidently deeply
concerned with the industrial and seasonal unemployment which Norwich had suffered for many years, and these measures, supplemented by
his generous support of unemployable persons in the almshouses of the
city, were designed to afford substantial alleviation to this situation.
This view was shared by some scores of lesser merchants of the city
who by 1640 had greatly strengthened the social and charitable mechanisms for dealing effectively with the complex problems confronting the
new, the modern, economic society.

Nor were these sentiments confined to the mercantile aristocracy;
the gentry of the county, closely linked by blood and marriage with the
merchants of Norwich and Yarmouth, shared their aspirations and
sought in their simpler communities to raise up bulwarks against the
social erosion of poverty and the social disease which was its inevitable
handmaiden. Thus in 1625 a staunchly Calvinistic gentleman of
Oxborough, Thomas Hewar, left to trustees a large dwelling and

---

[1] PCC 72 Parker 1619; Blomefield, *Norfolk*, III, 368–370, IV, 395, 498–499;
PP 1834, XXI, 501, 513–515, 532, 575, 590, 614, 652. *Vide post*, 118, 132, 161–
162, 332. Fawcett, who was an alderman of Norwich and sheriff in 1608, was
buried in St Michael Coslany, his tomb bearing this inscription:

> Stay reader here, and e're a foot thou pass,
> See what thou are, and what once Fawcit was,
> Whose body resteth in the earthly bed,
> But heavenly soule, to heaven it's home, is fled:
> What in his life he did, behold! the root,
> Body, branches, and afterward the fruit,
> Of him that lived by his godly care,
> Of him that died with a heavenly fear,
> For look, how many branches here you see,
> So many hands imagine, hath this tree,
> Not dealing pence, unto the poor around,
> But royally imparting, by the pound,
> Oh! England, might in every city be,
> So brave a vine, so beautifull a tree,
> To check the base, and viler shrubs below,
> Who now on earth, unprofitable grow,
> But Fawcit, now thou art in lasting fame,
> Let rich admire thee, poor will bless thy name,
> In earth thy body sleep, thy soul above,
> With angels rest, in charity and love,
> And Norwich mourn thy loss, not like to see,
> Hereafter, such another, like to thee.

approximately eighty-six acres of land, of which eighty-two were arable, from the income of which he directed that £12 p.a. be disbursed, on the advice of the churchwardens and overseers, to the most needy of the poor of the parish. Hewar's will likewise provided that £6 p.a. should be made available towards the repairing and beautifying of the church at Oxborough, while if in the future any improvement should be made in the rental of the property comprising the trusts, distribution should be made to the two uses in the proportions originally prescribed.[1]

A few years later, in 1628, another rural parish coordinated and properly vested such of its charitable funds as might be employed for the relief of the poor. The rich agricultural parish of Outwell, lying partly in Norfolk and partly in Cambridgeshire, had at intervals between 1562 and 1626 been the beneficiary of charitable donors who had left property on trust to the community for general charitable uses. The property, comprising thirty-three acres of land and at least five houses, was valued at approximately £370 and had been designated by the donors to be employed either for the whole parish or that portion in one or the other county. In 1628 a most sensible arrangement was effected by which the properties were consolidated for administrative purposes, two parish officers from Norfolk and two from Cambridgeshire being vested with full control of the trust and with the division of the income for the care of the poor and for general parochial needs.[2] In this same year two Norfolk parishes received considerable assistance under the terms of the great charitable trust established by the London merchant, Henry Smith. The rural parish of East Dereham, already beneficiary of a number of local endowments for poor relief, was provided with £4 p.a. for its general charitable needs under Smith's deed of gift, while Thetford was to receive the substantial sum of £10 p.a.[3] Just a year later (1629) William Allee, of East Lexham, of uncertain social status, devised valuable lands on trust to a nephew of the same name for the payment of amounts ranging from £1 p.a. to £2 p.a. to East Lexham and six neighbouring parishes for the better maintenance of their worthy poor. The income specified amounted in all to £13 p.a., suggesting a capital value of approximately £260 for this substantial charity.[4] Finally, the rural parish of East Raynham benefited in 1637 by a bequest of £100 for its poor under the will of Sir Roger Townshend,

---

[1] *PP* 1835, XXI, 695–696; Blomefield, *Norfolk*, VI, 183–184. A monumental inscription in Oxborough commemorates the charity and records the donor's faith.

[2] *VCH, Cambs.*, IV, 218–219; *PP* 1835, XXI, 518–519.

[3] *Vide* Jordan, *Charities of London*, 35, 113, 114, 117–122, 182, 283, 309–310, 343.

[4] *PP* 1835, XXI, 761.

who had recently completed the building of Raynham Hall as his seat in that parish.[1]

Meanwhile, Norwich continued to build up its already large endowments for the relief of the poor by the legacies of its citizens, though such endowments during the early Stuart period tended to be vested in the almshouses of the city. In 1627 Sir John Suckling, a member of one of the old merchant families of the city and the son of Robert Suckling, an Elizabethan mayor, left a legacy of £6 p.a. to be distributed to the poor of certain parishes by the city authorities.[2] A decade later, to cite a more substantial example, Luke Fisher by will conveyed agricultural property at Elm, Cambridgeshire, probably valued at £480, on trust to fourteen feoffees, the income of which was to be distributed £10 p.a. for providing woollen clothing to four poor men and as many poor women of Berstreet, Norwich, £10 p.a. for fuel for the poor of the parish, and the residue for the general relief of the poor.[3]

We have previously observed that the great flow of funds into endowments for the relief of the poor continued almost without abatement during the years of political and constitutional upheaval. During this short interval, nearly £10,000 was given by Norfolk donors for the household relief of the poor alone, while upwards of £11,000 was provided for all the various uses of the poor. We should at least mention a few of the more interesting and important of these great legacies of men who were endeavouring with their own efforts to improve the whole social climate of their county.

We might well speak first of a quite small bequest of £4 to the poor made by a gentleman of Norwich, Charles Green, who died in 1641 in not particularly affluent circumstances. Green's testamentary injunctions to his wife reveal clearly indeed the social and cultural aspirations of his age. His wife was to pay his bequests and his debts and to bring up her children under God's care. He prayed his wife to be 'allwayes zealous of His glory and careful of her own and her childrens good welfare . . . that they may grow up in godliness and goodness'. Green desired, if God should bless his eldest son 'with the grace of learning fitt for the university, then my wife should strain her selfe to maintaine

---

[1] PCC 104 Goare 1637. Townshend was the grandson of Lady Jane Berkeley (*vide ante*, 108). He was the son and heir of Sir John Townshend by Anne, daughter of Sir Nathaniel Bacon. He served in Parliament in 1621 and in 1628 and was sheriff of his county in 1629.

[2] PCC 55 Skynner 1627; DNB; Blomefield, *Norfolk*, IV, 309–311; *PP* 1834, XXI, 590–591. Suckling also left endowments of £220 for the maintenance of the clergy.

[3] PCC 125 Lee 1638; *PP* 1834, XXI, 671–673; Blomefield, *Norfolk*, IV, 139. The connections of Fisher, who was residing at Elm at the time of his death, are quite as uncertain as is his social status. His name does not appear in Norwich records and there is no suggestion that he was a merchant or a tradesman.

him there; if of an inferior ranke and quallity otherwise to bind him forth as an apprentice to some honest man that lives in the feare of God', while he enjoined his wife as well to be careful with the portions accorded his younger children 'that their souls may bless her'.[1] Green, his will makes clear, was a man of charitable disposition who dared not hazard more for other men because of the responsibilities that lay on him for the uncertain future of his own family.

In 1643 a member of the upper gentry of the county, Sir Edmund Moundeford of Feltwell, established a substantial charity with unusual provisions. He conveyed to trustees a large tract of 840 acres of marsh-land lying to the west of Feltwell village, called the 'ten-foot ground' and 'Wannage', in the apparent conviction that what was then scarcely better than waste land could be drained and made extremely valuable. The land was to be held in trust until this should be accomplished and its value had in consequence risen to at least £60 p.a. At such time, the poor of the parish were to receive £20 p.a. in clothing, £40 p.a. was to be employed for the endowment of a free school for the parish, and any surplus remaining after these uses had been met was to be retained by the trustees until they could build and endow an almshouse for the poor of the parish. Moundeford's confidence in the future value of the land and in the security of the trust was well founded, since this area, lying on the southeastern edge of the Great Fen, benefited by the seventeenth-century drainage efforts and became steadily more valuable as the drains were improved during the eighteenth century.[2]

More immediately useful was the bequest of Henry Bonfellow in 1650, who left lands to the use of his son and grand-daughter with the provision that if they should die without issue, as did occur, the pıoperties, valued at approximately £400, should be employed for the support of the poor of Kirby Cane and Ellingham.[3] A decade later, a Norwich alderman, Edward Heyward, placed on trust urban property which he charged with £12 p.a. for the poor of four Norwich parishes, the distribution to be made by the churchwardens and overseers to

---

[1] Reg. 1641, Norwich, 100.

[2] PCC 45 Rivers 1645; PP 1835, XXI, 707–710; PP 1843, XVII, 32–33; PP 1867–1868, LII, ii, Norfolk, 30–31; Blomefield, Norfolk, II, 191–199. Drainage taxes were a heavy burden on the income and it was not until the nineteenth century that surpluses could be accumulated for the support of the almshouse contemplated by Moundeford's will. In 1868 the income of the trust was £486 12s p.a. before large but unspecified drainage assessments. The charity was ultimately almost exhausted by drainage assessments and possibly mis-management. Moundeford was the last of a long line of his name who had held manors in Feltwell from the days of Richard II. His estates descended to Simon Smith of Winston, Norfolk, who had married Moundeford's sister. For the Feltwell school, vide post, 164.

[3] PP 1835, XXI, 547; PP 1867–1868, LII, ii, Norfolk, 48–49.

poor widows, orphans, and 'laborious poore people'.[1] In 1657 a member
of the lower gentry of the county, Robert Annison of Bromholm, by will
bequeathed outright £3 to the poor of two parishes while devising on
trust twenty acres of marsh-land and certain tenements with an estimated total capital value of £200 for the perpetual relief of the poor of
Witton.[2] Sir Thomas Woodhouse, an eminent supporter of the Parliamentary cause in the county, who in 1634 had by deed poll placed on
trust property charged with £3 p.a. for the benefit of the poor of Litcham, further charged his estate by his will, proved in 1658, with
£26 13s as a stock for the poor and established an annuity of £9 for the
relief of the poor of Kimberley.[3] In the same year (1658) Edward
Bulwer drew his will, creating a rent-charge of £6 10s p.a. for the relief
of the poor of Wood Dalling, where his family had long been resident, it
being stipulated that none should be eligible for benefits who was on
poor rates.[4] Still another member of the gentry of the county, Richmond
Girling, of Old Buckenham, by his will proved in 1659 provided an
annual income of £7 11s by a charge on certain property in Suffolk, for
the relief of 'the most honest poor people' of Diss and Old Buckenham
parishes as well as two parishes in Suffolk, one in Cambridgeshire, and
one in Yorkshire.[5]

We have mentioned but a few of the many scores of endowments
created during our period in order to provide relief for poor families
in their own households. These funds were under accumulation over
the whole course of our period, but began to grow with an ever-
gathering momentum after the accession of Queen Elizabeth. In all, the
generous total of £40,548 9s was given for the household relief of the
poor and the closely connected use which we have designated as 'charity
general'. As we have pointed out, a considerable proportion of this total
was given outright for immediate use, particularly in the earlier decades
of our period, in the form of alms and almost casual doles. But there
remained the very large sum of £32,316 4s of endowments with which
the county had vested itself for the care of poverty by the close of the

---

[1] *PP* 1834, XXI, 650; Blomefield, *Norfolk*, IV, 260, 271.

[2] PCC 30 Ruthen 1657; *PP* 1833, XIX, 328.

[3] PCC 354 Wootton 1658; *PP* 1835, XXI, 763–764; Blomefield, *Norfolk*, II,
555; Cokayne, G. E., ed., *Complete baronetage* (Exeter, 1900–1906, 5 vols.), I,
52; *Alum. cantab.*, I, iv, 459. Woodhouse, like so many of the Norfolk gentry,
was a Caius man. He studied at Lincoln's Inn, was knighted in 1603, and
succeeded as baronet in 1623. He was appointed Sheriff of Norfolk in 1624. He
was M.P. for Thetford in 1640 and in the Long Parliament. He married a daughter
of John, Baron Hunsdon.

[4] *PP* 1835, XXI, 623; Blomefield, *Norfolk*, II, 345, III, 401, VIII, 322.
Bulwer, an ancestor of Edward Bulwer-Lytton, first Earl Lytton, was the son
and heir of Roger Bulwer, Esq., lord of the manor of Gestwick and Mendham.

[5] PCC 373, 423 Pell 1659; Blomefield, *Norfolk*, I, 37; *PP* 1835, XXI, 574;
Bryant, T. H., *The churches of Norfolk, hundred of Diss* (Norwich, 1915), 80.

Cromwellian period. If we may assume a yield of 5 per cent on trusteed capital of this sort, something like the substantial annual sum of £1615 was available in the parishes of the county for the relief of at least the worst aspects of poverty and unemployment. Norfolk donors of the seventeeenth century seemed to believe that £2 10s p.a. was quite sufficient to provide complete maintenance for a poor family in its own house; so this probably means that as many as 646 families, or well over 3000 individuals, were being held above the level of stark privation by the resources which several generations of pious concern and social responsibility had accumulated. We are, then, recording in the cold and always barren outline of statistics an immense and a most fruitful accomplishment.

(b) *The Founding of Almshouses.* These great endowments were supplemented and strengthened by the foundation of numerous almshouses in many parts of the county. During the entire course of our period, £18,146 7s was provided for this essentially experimental purpose by many scores of benefactors, practically the whole (99·45 per cent) of the amount being in the form of capital gifts. The interest in this form of institutional attack on indigence was relatively slight in the interval prior to the Reformation, when only £1331 2s was given for the founding of new and secular establishments or the strengthening of older religious institutions. Somewhat more than double this amount (£2696 10s) was given during the brief period of the Reformation, when in Norfolk as in all of England there was a quickening of interest in a trial of secular institutions for the relief of a poverty which, while not new, was now more acutely and likewise more sensitively regarded by the social conscience of responsible men. The Elizabethan era witnessed a steady and a growing concern for the problem of poverty, nearly £6000 being provided during these forty years for the creation of new establishments in every part of the county. The watershed of this interest, as it were, was attained between 1591 and 1610, since in these two decades £8547 16s was given for almshouse endowments, amounting to almost half (47 per cent) of the total dedicated for this use in the whole of our long period. In the early Stuart interval a total of £7863 19s was provided, while there was a sharp decline in such endowments during the last two decades, when the interest of donors was, for reasons not wholly clear, principally confined to the further creation of endowments for the household relief of poverty.

Of all the ten counties comprised in this study, Norfolk was relatively by far the richest in almshouse (hospital) resources at the beginning of our period. During the course of the Middle Ages as many as forty-nine almshouses, hospitals, and other similar institutions had been founded, possibly a greater number than in any other county in the realm save Yorkshire. It is uncertain how many of these may be regarded even in an approximate sense as almshouses. It should also be noted that most of these establishments were not endowed; many vanished after a short period of service; and others underwent successive changes of function as the Middle Ages wore on. But we are on firmer and more relevant ground when we say that there survived in 1480 as many as nine, possibly ten, religious or quasi-religious establishments which were at that time carrying on the work and function of almshouses. These foundations were in 1480 providing shelter and at least partial maintenance for something like 105 almsmen. These were very considerable social resources, and it was upon this base that the secular almshouses of our period were built.

The earliest of the almshouses founded in our period was endowed in 1489 under the will of Simon Blake, a gentleman of Swaffham. Blake's principal legacy was for the founding of a chantry, to which we shall recur,[1] but he gave as well £40 for the repair of Swaffham church, where the steeple had fallen with considerable resulting damage to the fabric, £5 as a loan fund, to be kept in the church chest, from which any poor person of the town might borrow as much as 5s on pledge, and smaller bequests to the clergy and to monastic establishments. He and his wife, Joan, had some years earlier provided an almshouse for the succour of four poor persons, to which property was assigned for support by the bequest with an estimated capital value of £80.[2]

Late in the following decade James Goldwell, Bishop of Norwich, while leaving the bulk of his charitable bequests to chantries and other religious uses,[3] gave £2 outright to St Giles' Hospital, Norwich, and settled the residue of his fortune on that medieval institution, whose history we should now briefly trace. St Giles'[4] was founded in 1249 by Walter Suffield, Bishop of Norwich, as a parochial church (St Helen), an almshouse, and a chantry served by four stipendiary priests. The founder vested as endowment the tithes of six Norfolk parishes and in the deed specified that thirteen poor were to receive a meal within the hospital each day, as were seven poor scholars in the grammar school who might be nominated by the schoolmaster. He further provided that thirty beds were to be maintained for the relief and care of poor, aged, and infirm persons who might apply for succour. In 1430 the hospital was providing food for thirteen poor persons and caring for eight bed patients, as well as supplying food and lodging to poor chaplains of the diocese and poor strangers passing through the city. The hospital was well regarded by the townspeople during the whole course

[1] *Vide post*, 147, 177.
[2] CCN 20–22 Typpes 1489; Blomefield, *Norfolk*, VI, 202–203; Rix, W. B., *Swaffham* (Norwich, [1931]), 55–56; *PP* 1835, XXI, 701–702.
[3] *Vide post*, 178.
[4] It was variously known during the course of our period as St Giles', God's House, and as the Great Hospital.

of the fifteenth century and was evidently carefully administered. The foundation received a substantial number of small outright bequests during these years, while, after the settlement of Bishop Goldwell's estate, endowments with a capital value of £307 were added to its funds.[1]

The hospital, then possessing endowments worth approximately £1800, or £90 p.a., was confiscated by the Crown in 1535 upon the exchange of the bishops' lands and revenues. Henry VIII intended to convey to the city the institution and its endowments, free of all charges to the Crown, but died before this intention could be honoured. The conveyance was, however, made by Edward VI in his first regnal year, when properties worth £142 19s 2d p.a. were vested on the foundation, which was henceforward to be known as 'the House of God' or 'the House of the Poor'.[2] The church of St Helen was declared to be parochial and was appropriated to the city with the provision that its minister should be chaplain to the almshouse, while a second priest, with a stipend of £6 p.a., should visit these poor as well as prisoners in the Guildhall. The almshouse was to provide accommodations for the complete care and maintenance of forty poor persons and was licensed to acquire endowments not to exceed £200 p.a. in value. This careful reorganization of the hospital, amounting to a re-foundation, added from royal funds income of approximately £53 p.a. and also provided that an annual stipend of £16 13s 4d be employed from its resources for the re-founding of a grammar school to instruct boys in the art of grammar under a learned master and a competent usher.[3]

St Giles', as we shall persist in calling it despite the royal injunction, benefited just a year after its re-founding by the legacy (or gift) of Edmund Wood of two tenements and a garden in St Botolph's, with an estimated capital value of £80, for the general uses and needs of the almshouse, this donor leaving as well one hundred marks for cleaning the streets of filth after the manner of London, £40 for the provision of wheat, £20 for exhibitions for poor scholars at Cambridge, and £20 to teach the children of poor men in Norwich.[4] There was evidently great

---

[1] PCC 35 Horne 1499; DNB; Robertson, C. G., All Souls College (L., 1899), 34–35; Blomefield, Norfolk, III, 539–542, IV, 178, 389. Goldwell was also a benefactor to All Souls College, rebuilt Chart church in Kent, founded several chantries, and spent a large sum on the completion of Norwich Cathedral.

[2] A governmental review of the hospital's affairs made late in the Elizabethan reign suggests that Henry VIII gave the grant 'by will and Edward VI confirmed it'. The revenues were to be used for the maintenance of fifty-two aged, lame, and impotent people, 'with holsome meate, drinke, and lodging', as well as the appointment of the necessary officers and servitors. S.P. Dom., 1603 [?], V, 57.

[3] PP 1834, XXI, 492–498; Blomefield, Norfolk, IV, 390–394.

[4] PCC F.19 Populwell 1548; Blomefield, Norfolk, III, 294–295; Kirkpatrick John (Dawson Turner, ed.), History of the religious orders of Norwich (L., 1845),

interest in the foundation and its work, for there were numerous small bequests from 4s to £20 made to its capital during the next twenty years. For example, Sir Richard Southwell in 1561 left £10 to buy beds for the almspeople,[1] and in 1570 Thomas Parker, a former mayor, left £2 to purchase sheets, as well as 2d outright to each poor person in the hospital.[2] Two substantial bequests were also made to the almshouse in these years. In 1559 Thomas Codd, a beer brewer and the Mayor of Norwich during Kett's Rebellion, left considerable property for charitable uses, including £10 p.a. to the curate of St Peter's parish, other property to the hospital subject to the payment of £1 6s 8d p.a. for the relief of taxation in the ward of North Conisford, £100, or thereabouts, to the city as an endowment for poor relief, and other real property worth upwards of £2 6s 8d p.a. to St Giles' subject to certain religious uses.[3] In 1570 Augustine Steward, an alderman of the city and three times its mayor, bequeathed to St Giles' five tenements and lands with a probable value of £180 on condition that the houses be made 'wind and water tight' and then be made freely available as dwelling places for five poor widows.[4]

In 1572 still another royal augmentation of the endowment was provided by Queen Elizabeth, who vested in the city property with a clear annual value of £11 16s which had escheated to the Crown by the attainder of George Redman.[5] This endowment was to be used for the better maintenance of the almspeople in St Giles' as well as towards the support of four scholars from Norwich holding exhibitions at Cambridge.[6] Numerous small gifts and bequests, mostly for immediate use, have been noted during the next generation, of which that of a cottage and orchard valued at perhaps £30 made by Thomas Cory in 1578 and

93; Cozens-Hardy, *Mayors of Norwich*, 53; PP 1834, XXI, 505. Wood, a grocer, had been sheriff in 1536 and mayor in 1548. His son, Sir Robert, was twice mayor.

[1] PCC 19 Stevenson 1564; DNB; Blomefield, *Norfolk*, III, 279; Kirkpatrick, *Religious orders of Norwich*, 220. Southwell was of a Suffolk family and was a privy councillor under Edward VI. He left £120 to the poor of Norwich, to be laid out at the rate of £10 p.a., save that the first payment must be made to St Giles'. *Vide post*, 120 note 2.

[2] PCC 13 Lyon 1570; Cozens-Hardy, *Mayors of Norwich*, 59.

[3] CCN 431 Colman 1559; Cozens-Hardy, *Mayors of Norwich*, 54; PP 1834, XXI, 498; Blomefield, *Norfolk*, III, 225, 227, 263, 271, 276, IV, 97–98; Kirkpatrick, *Religious orders of Norwich*, 93. Codd at first signed Kett's petition of grievances, but at the moment of decision denied passage into the city to the rebel leader.

[4] PCC 43 Holney 1571; PP 1834, XXI, 706; Cozens-Hardy, *Mayors of Norwich*, 48.

[5] Blomefield, *Norfolk*, III, 284. Redman, a gentleman of Cringleford, was one of those executed for a conspiracy in 1570 to raise armed men and to expel strangers from Norwich and the realm.

[6] PP 1834, XXI, 498–499.

that of 3s 4d by a mercer, Christopher Barrett, Sr., in 1598 may be regarded as typical.[1] In 1608 the hospital was further endowed by a former mayor, Francis Rugge, a mercer, who gave property worth £8 p.a. (in 1728) on an undertaking that support should be given to two additional almspeople 'in such manner as other poor people were there maintained'.[2] Henry Fawcett, the great merchant benefactor of Norwich, among many other bequests, left three tenements and a close, of a capital value of £120, to the hospital in 1619 on condition that two poor and old worsted weavers, to be chosen out of the ward of Fyebridge, be maintained there by his nephew during his lifetime and then by the mayor and aldermen.[3] And, finally, we should mention the substantial benefaction of a worsted weaver, Augustine Blomefield, who in 1645 bequeathed valuable properties in East Winch to the hospital as an augmentation of endowment, on condition that as many additional aged men and women unable 'to get their living' be maintained as the funds would permit. After a legal altercation with the copyholder of the land, a settlement was reached in 1650 which established a rent-charge of £18 p.a. as the value of this worthy bequest.[4]

The history of St Giles' during our period is particularly interesting because it enjoyed such steady and enlightened support from the citizenry of Norwich. The hospital was one of the few in England that had been continuously well administered by clerical hands during the Middle Ages, and it was respected and generously sustained even as our period began. In 1480 it probably possessed capital resources of something like £1460, which had been increased by various bequests to £1800 at the time of the Reformation seizure. Its work and good repute were in no wise injured during the Henrician period, and it was given an excellent and well-considered secular reorganization by Edward VI, who likewise greatly enhanced its endowments. From this date forward to the close of our study it was a notable and respected local institution, receiving the steady support of benefactors and rendering humane and essential services to the city of which it was a principal institutional adornment. During the years 1547–1660 we have recorded £1271 in additional capital sums given for the augmentation of its endowments,

---

[1] (Cory) PP 1834, XXI, 501; (Barrett) CCN 89 Adams 1598; Eastern Counties Collectanea (Norwich, 1873), 269.

[2] PP 1834, XXI, 504; Cozens-Hardy, Mayors of Norwich, 52, 64; Blomefield, Norfolk, IV, 307, 394. Rugge, the son of Robert Rugge, mayor in 1545 and 1550, married the daughter of another mayor of the city. A substantial merchant, he was sheriff in 1572, represented Norwich in Parliament, and was himself thrice mayor.

[3] Vide ante, 109, and post 132, 161–162, 332.

[4] PCC 103 Rivers 1645; Blomefield, Norfolk, IV, 165, 394, 410–412; PP 1834, 503, 519, 535, 542. Blomefield also left £3 outright to the poor and property with an estimated capital worth of £100 to the Children's Hospital in Norwich (vide post, 135).

not to mention the £74 7s 2d left in the form of small outright bequests by men and women of all classes of society. In 1480 the institution probably sheltered thirty almspeople, a number steadily increased as its endowments and facilities were enlarged until in 1645 there were, so to speak, endowed beds for fifty-seven indigent persons.

St Giles' was the almshouse normally favoured by the mercantile aristocracy of the city when the time came to fix their social aspirations and to order their bequests. But an even older hospital in Norwich tended to enjoy the favour of lesser men of the city, as its work and functions were transformed under secular guidance. This was Norman's Hospital, founded with its church in the very early twelfth century (*ca.* 1118). The hospital was the recipient of a number of substantial bequests from pious benefactors in the thirteenth century, though it seems to have languished during the fourteenth. In 1429 it was substantially re-organized, it being determined thereafter to admit only aged and infirm almswomen, of whom seven should have their lodging on the premises, while the same number should be maintained in their own quarters. The work of the hospital once more began to enlist the support of benefactors of the county in the late fifteenth century, eighteen small bequests having been noted for the period 1480–1540 that range in amount from 2s to £5 10s and which total £27 0s 8d.[1] Norman's, for all its meritorious work and the customary support of the citizenry, was not well endowed and seems to have survived on small legacies and gifts made less formally to its poor box. The hospital was left wholly unmolested by the Reformation settlement, its relatively poor estate as an endowed almshouse being suggested when in 1548 its property was leased at £3 6s 8d p.a. by the Dean and Chapter, in whom the legal title was lodged. In 1558 Thomas Salter, a London priest who was evidently a native of Norwich, created an endowment of £1 6s p.a. to be paid to the churchwardens of St Paul's parish to ensure a halfpenny loaf of 'wheaten loffe new bake' every Sunday for the sisters in the

---

[1] Typical of these small outright legacies were the bequest of John Caster, an alderman, in 1494 of 8d to the needs of the hospital and 4d to each of the sisters (CCN 185 Wolman); of Joan Williamson, widow, who in 1502 left 3s 4d to the sisters, as well as bedding (CCN 229, 230 Popy); of Dame Joan Blakeney, who in 1503 provided 5s 10d for the almswomen (CCN 315–317 Popy); of Thomas Wymer of Aylsham, who left 7s to the sisters (CCN 5, 6 Spyltymber 1507); of the widow of Sir Henry Heydon (*et vide post*, 179-180), who in 1510 left 15s to the almswomen as one of a long list of charitable bequests totalling £290 6s (Gurney, Daniel, *Supplement to the record of the house of Gournay*, King's Lynn, 1858, 823); of John Harmer, a tailor, who in 1515 bequeathed 2d to the almswomen (Kirkpatrick, *Religious orders of Norwich*, 212); of William Elsy, who in the next year left 6s 8d to buy linen sheeting for the hospital (CCN 19–21 Briggs 1516); and of Dame Margery, widow of Sir James Hobart, who bequeathed £2 outright for the better support of the inmates (CCN 49, 50 Briggs 1517).

institution.[1] But no substantial endowments were received, and in 1565 the Dean and Chapter surrendered the almshouse to the city with the understanding that it be employed as formerly for the 'lodging, comfort, and relief of poor strangers, vagrants, sick, and impotent persons'.[2] A rather heated altercation then broke out between the city and the Dean regarding the power of nomination for the living of St Paul's, which led to the revocation of the undertaking to maintain the institution as an almshouse. In 1571, accordingly, this ancient almshouse was transformed into a house of correction for idle and lusty beggars. Some years later, in 1585, a new bridewell was provided for the city and the rental on the old premises of Norman's, amounting to £5 5s p.a., was applied to its maintenance.[3]

There had been an almshouse in the churchyard at Hingham, probably of fifteenth-century foundation, which by the beginning of our period had fallen into serious, if not complete decay. In 1513 Richard Heyhow, of that town, left by will a tract of three and a half acres to endow a yearly obit and church repairs and a close valued at approximately £20 to St Peter's Guild of Hingham, on condition that the guild brethren maintain the alms table and put the almshouse into proper repair.[4] A few years later, in 1518, Alice Crome, the widow of a Norwich merchant, Nicholas Crome, by will provided a foundation of seven almshouses for poor widows of the parish of St George Colegate, who were to be designated by the churchwardens. This will further stipulated that the property be maintained by the rental of one of the houses, though no endowment was provided by the donor for the support of her almswomen.[5]

---

[1] PCC F.13 Welles 1558; Kirkpatrick, *Religious orders of Norwich*, 216–218. Salter in his will tells us that he was establishing this bequest 'bycause that a verie good devowte syster of the said howse . . . was the first . . . that tawght me to knowe the lettres in my booke when I was skoller seventy-two yeres ago . . . in the sayde parrysh'.

[2] Blomefield, *Norfolk*, IV, 433. The hospital was never able to gain substantial endowments, though it continued to attract relatively small outright bequests. Thus from 1550 to 1571 there were sixteen bequests recorded, all being outright gifts, ranging in amount from 5s to £20, and totalling £62 17s. Among them we may mention Sir Richard Southwell's bequest of £10 (PCC 19 Stevenson 1564); the legacy of a worsted weaver of 5s in 1562 (Kirkpatrick, *Religious orders of Norwich*, 212); the legacy of £3 6s 8d provided in 1567 by Henry Bacon, a former mayor (*ibid.*, 220); a mercer's annuity of £4 given in 1568, to be paid during his wife's lifetime, from which £12 was received (PCC 6 Sheffelde); a small legacy of 5s received from the estate of John Elwyn, a clergyman, in 1569 (CCN 228 Ponder); and that of Thomas Parker, mayor in 1568, who provided 10s for the repair of the premises (PCC 13 Lyon 1570).

[3] Blomefield, *Norfolk*, IV, 434.

[4] CCN 239, 420 Johnson 1513; Blomefield, *Norfolk*, II, 426.

[5] CCN 94, 95 Gylys 1518; Blomefield, *Norfolk*, IV, 472; *PP* 1834, XXI, 657–658.

The earliest post-Reformation foundation of an almshouse was made at East Bradenham very fittingly by a substantial and successful speculator in monastic lands, Robert Hogan, Esq., who in a decade purchased and resold a score or more of monastic tracts. Hogan died in 1547 seised of five manors in Norfolk and other extensive landholdings in the county. By will he left £58 outright for the relief of the poor and £1 p.a. for the succour of prisoners in Norwich gaols, as well as three houses and gardens with an approximate capital value of £90 and a rent-charge of £1 p.a. for the support of three poor men of the parish who were to have their dwelling places without charge.[1] Shortly afterwards, in 1553, a yeoman of Emneth, Thomas Spurlynge, in addition to modest bequests for the poor and the general uses of his parish church, left a house and two small tracts of land, with an estimated capital worth of £50, for the founding of an almshouse in his community.[2] Another rural parish, Mattishall, benefited substantially in 1558 under the will of a gentleman, Thomas Harleston, of Mattishall Burgh. Harleston left £10 outright to the poor of his own and nearby parishes, and devised as well two houses, lands, and sheep, with a total value of approximately £180, one of the houses to be an almshouse, and the other house and the lands to be let, the profits to be used for poor relief and the lightening of taxation.[3]

The movement for the founding of almshouses rapidly gained in momentum with the accession of Queen Elizabeth, though most of the establishments were small and modestly endowed, evidently offering succour for only the most depressed and helpless of the poor in the rural parishes in which most of them were situated. Sir Richard Fulmerston, who had obtained rich and extensive landholdings in Thetford from the Duke of Somerset and the Duke of Norfolk, founded an almshouse for this community by his will proved in 1567. Fulmerston, much devoted to the 'modern persuasion' regarding charity, sternly enjoined his executors that he wished 'no common doll [dole] to be made at the daye of my buriall'. He did, however, leave £5 outright to the poor of Thetford and £3 to be distributed to the poor of seven neighbouring villages. He devised as well £1 p.a. for the relief of Norfolk and Suffolk prisoners and £2 p.a. for the augmentation of the stipends of the clergy of his parish. Fulmerston also provided premises, with an estimated capital value of £100, to be employed by trustees as an almshouse for the maintenance of two poor men and two poor women, and an endow-

[1] PCC 42 Alen 1547; *PP* 1835, XXI, 682; Blomefield, *Norfolk*, II, 354, VI, 16, 38, 48, 136, 236, VII, 177, 371, X, 88.

[2] PCC 13 Tashe 1553; *PP* 1834, XXII, 86. At an uncertain but later date the premises were converted into a workhouse.

[3] CCN 219 Ingold 1558; *PP* 1835, XXI, 808; Blomefield, *Norfolk*, X, 197, 235. Harleston's grand-daughter, Margaret, married Matthew Parker, Archbishop of Canterbury.

ment of £10 8s p.a. for their complete support, as well as £2 p.a. so that each almsperson might have a new gown every year.[1]

A bequest of a shilling to each of the three poor women in the alms-house at Wiggenhall St Mary in 1572 certainly suggests the existence of what was evidently an unendowed almshouse in that village by this date.[2] A much more surely based foundation was arranged in Costessey under the will of Sir Henry Jernegan, who had received this great manor by royal gift for his devoted services to Queen Mary. Jernegan stipu-lated that the old priory of St Olave's should be converted into an alms-house for the relief of five poor men, who were each to have £2 12s for their maintenance, 3s 4d for their fuel, and a gown, the establishment to be endowed by a charge of £38 10s p.a. on the rich revenues of the old priory lands, which even his ardent Romanism did not persuade him to restore. His will further provided that St Olave's church was to be kept in repair by his heirs 'as they will answer before the terrible throne of God', though he failed to arm this injunction by the more prosaic but, as time was to prove, effective, means of a charitable bequest for the purpose.[3] A few year later, in about 1585, the almshouse at Walsingham was renovated and its finances strengthened. This alms-house had been first endowed, if not founded, in 1491 under the will of Robert Pygott, who left messuages for the use of two poor and leprous men, as well as small bequests to the friars of Walsingham and Yar-mouth.[4] There were a number of small outright bequests made to the establishment in the early Elizabethan period, while in 1585 Thomas Sidney, Esq., bequeathed it £3 8s.[5] There is no record of further endowment of the almshouse until 1639(?) when Philip Brown provided an endowment of £100 for the charitable needs of Walsingham, the income to be divided £2 for an annual commemorative service, £2 10s

[1] PCC 33 Stonard 1567; Blomefield, *Norfolk*, II, 57–58, 66, 70–77, 86–88, 93–94, 128–130, 136, 145; *PP* 1835, XXI, 866–871. This charity was, on petition from the municipal authorities of Thetford, regulated by Act of Parlia-ment in 1610. The poor almspeople had from the beginning received but 1s each week. The Act increased this stipend to 2s a week and also provided for the proper maintenance of the premises. *Vide post*, 157, for comment on Ful-merston's school foundation.

[2] Walter Palmer (Reg. Busby, 359). The establishment may possibly have had some connection with Crabhouse Nunnery in this town (*PP* 1834, XXII, 102; Blomefield, *Norfolk*, IX, 173).

[3] PCC 18 Peter 1573; Blomefield, *Norfolk*, II, 411; DNB. Jernegan was the first important supporter of Queen Mary. He was made Master of the Horse in 1557, was a privy councillor and the captain of the guard. He routed Wyatt in 1554. The manor of Costessey was worth £118 6s 8d p.a. in 1571 and the priory lands an additional £37 6s 8d p.a. Jernegan also had three lesser Norfolk manors and certain scattered lands.

[4] Norwich Archdeaconry Wills, 1491, reg. Fuller, fol. 204; *Norf. Arch.*, I (1847), 255–257; *Reliquary*, n.s., I (1887), 143; Blomefield, *Norfolk*, IX, 281–282.

[5] PCC 17 Brudenell 1585; Blomefield, *Norfolk*, IX, 280.

for the maintenance of the almshouse, and the residue for the relief of the poor.[1]

A London goldsmith, William Feke, in *ca.* 1590 built an almshouse in his native parish of Wighton, at an approximate charge of £120, to provide lodging and shelter for six poor women of the community. It seems probable that Feke supported his almshouse from his own purse until his death in 1595, when his will conveyed an estate of eighteen acres, of at least £80 capital value, for its support and for the distribution each Sunday in the parish church of 6d for bread among the poor of the parish.[2] Some years earlier Richard Manseur, a member of the lower gentry, whose family had resided in North Creake since the days of Edward IV, had built appropriate almshouses for four poor widows of the parish. Manseur's will, declaring that he had heretofore supported his almspeople from his own purse, endowed his almshouses with fifteen acres of land, to ensure £4 3s each year for the support and clothing of the poor and the repair of the premises.[3]

Robert Smith of Brancaster recited in his will, drawn in 1593, that he had for some time past maintained four almsmen in as many cottages prepared for this purpose. He undertook to assign 100 acres of land and certain tenements in the parish, together with his copyhold lands, for the endowment of a free school,[4] as well as to provide fuel, clothing, and support for his almshouse establishment. The will was defective, but in 1596 his sister and heir, Elizabeth Simpson, honoured his intention by vesting in trustees land in Brancaster and Burnham Deepdale, from the income of which approximately £5 p.a. was designated for the support of the almspeople.[5]

The almshouse at King's Lynn had a long but most disordered history. Founded in the twelfth century as St Mary's Hospital, it survived many vicissitudes and really accomplished mismanagement until the period of the Reformation. The hospital was seized under the statute of Edward VI dissolving chantries, presumably to be vested with a secular consitution, but was taken and all but razed by Kett's forces, who also

[1] *PP* 1835, XXI, 673–674.
[2] PCC 34 Scott 1595; *PP* 1835, XXI, 681. The bread charity may include certain of the funds left in 1597 to the poor of Wighton and Hindringham by Gregory Smith, a merchant tailor of London who was a native of Wighton (PCC 89 Cobham 1597).
[3] PCC 6 Nevell 1592; Bryant, T. H., *The churches of Norfolk, hundred of Brothercross* (Norwich, 1914), 121; Blomefield, *Norfolk*, VII, 25, 69, 73; *PP* 1835, XXI, 501–502. Manseur had purchased the lordship of North Creake from Sir Thomas Knevet in 1591, the year before his death, for £1,300. He had earlier come into possession of the lands of the former Peterston Priory in Burnham Overy.
[4] *Vide post*, 158.
[5] *PP* 1835, XXI, 838–841; *Norf. Arch.*, XI (1892), 199–200; Blomefield, *Norfolk*, X, 301.

destroyed or carried away its movable property. A few indigents were maintained on the premises by the city from time to time, but the effective and legal existence of the hospital had come to an end. The premises and the lands comprising its endowment fell into private hands and ultimately into the possession of one of the shrewdest of all Elizabethan speculators, Theophilus Adams; part ownership devolved upon Thomas Butler, also of London, a frequent associate of Adams in large-scale land speculations and jobbing. Adams conveyed the property to the city in 1593, and renovations on the almshouse were begun. But the local authorities were unable to quiet counter-claims on the property, which was then valued at £26 2s 6d p.a. Proceedings were begun in Chancery in 1612 to establish title. The decree vested the endowment in local trustees who should in perpetuity apply the income for the maintenance in the almshouse of from five to ten poor men and women under the care of a *custos*. However, the hospital seemed ill fated. It was burned during the Parliamentary siege of Lynn in 1643, but was rebuilt by the city in 1649.[1]

Two more almshouse foundations were made in Norfolk in the last decade of the Elizabethan reign. Clement Paston by his will proved in 1598, but drawn in 1594, directed his executors to build six convenient houses in Oxnead which should forever remain as almshouses for the relief of six poor aged men who had served the family. Each almsman should have 1s a week for his subsistence, a frieze gown and necessary fuel each year, while being provided with Sunday dinner and supper at the donor's house. A sufficient charge to meet the stipend of £15 12s was laid upon the estate to give effect to the trust.[2] A few years later, in 1601, a rich yeoman of Diss, Richard Fisher, drew his will, instructing his son and heir to purchase a half-acre of freehold land in the parish and to build a suitable house for the lodging and maintenance of from two to four old and indigent persons, while conveying to trustees, they being principal inhabitants of the town, sufficient land to constitute a proper endowment for his almshouse.[3]

Great as was the interest of substantial and responsible Elizabethan

---

[1] *PP* 1834, XXII, 28–29; Blomefield, *Norfolk*, VIII, 519; *VCH*, *Norfolk*, II, 441–442; Taylor, Richard, *Index monasticus* (L., 1821), 54–55; Mackerell, B., *King's-Lynn* (L., 1738), 194–198; Richards, William, *Lynn* (Lynn, 1812, 2 vols.), I, 530–552.

[2] PCC 27, 28 Lewyn 1598; *PP* 1833, XIX, 252–253; Blomefield, *Norfolk*, VI, 487–489; Fuller, *Worthies*, II, 456; DNB. Paston also left £1 for the repair of Oxnead church, £2 to each lazar house in Norwich, £1 8s to Norwich prisoners, and instructed his executors to heighten the steeple of Oxnead church and to provide a new and larger bell than any that hung there. Paston, the son of Sir William Paston, served four sovereigns as soldier, sailor, courtier, and magistrate. He left his wife £200 of plate, £1,000 in money, and the lease of his London house as well as a life estate.

[3] PCC 23 Hayes 1605; *PP* 1835, XXI, 572; Blomefield, *Norfolk*, I, 36.

men of Norfolk in the endowment of almshouses in all parts of the county, their benefactions were quite overshadowed by the establishments made during the early Stuart period. The very large sum of £7863 19s was provided during this generation for the founding of new almshouses in the county or for the endowment of existing institutions. Thus Sir Miles Corbett of Sprowston in 1607 gave lands to the value of £20 p.a. as an endowment for an almshouse which he appears to have built for six poor men of the parish.[1] In the next year one of the greatest of all the almshouse foundations in Norfolk was arranged by Henry Howard, Earl of Northampton, whose family had deep roots and large landholdings in the county. Northampton erected (*ca.* 1608) an almshouse at Castle Rising, at a cost of £451 14s 2d, for the lodging and support of twelve poor women and a governess, which he maintained until his death in 1614 from his private funds. In accordance with the terms of his will, letters patent were secured in 13 James I for the legal vesting of the foundation, and rentals of £100 p.a. were assigned for its maintenance from lands in Norfolk. Northampton had likewise founded a great hospital at Greenwich[2] and a well-endowed almshouse at Clun, Shropshire, during his lifetime.[3] Shortly afterwards (*ca.* 1610) Thomas Damett, formerly a bailiff of Great Yarmouth, bequeathed four dwellings to be held by the corporation of that city on trust as almshouses for four poor seamen's widows, whose husbands had left them with children and no place of abode, where they might dwell without charge for the remainder of their days. Damett provided no endowment for his establishment.[4]

Four substantial almshouse endowments were made in Norfolk in a period of two years, 1611–1612, of which two were in Norwich and two in rural parishes. Ann Johnson, an alderman's widow, in 1611 gave an almshouse and a garden in St Etheldred parish for the lodging of five poor widows which possessed a capital worth of about £110. She retained an intelligent interest in the needs of the city, in 1615 giving an endowment of £50 as a loan fund for the community and by her will in 1626

[1] PCC 95 Hudleston 1607; Blomefield, *Norfolk*, X, 458–463, 475; *Complete baronetage*, I, 219. Corbett was the son of John Corbett, a successful Elizabethan lawyer. Sir Miles established his family with extensive estates in Norfolk, based on the manor of Wroxham which he purchased in 1605. His heir was Sir Thomas Corbett, and his grandson, John Corbett, was created a baronet in 1623. A younger grandson, Miles Corbett, was a regicide judge. There is no certain indication that the gift was fully carried out; in any case the almshouse did not apparently survive until Blomefield's day.

[2] This foundation will be treated in our discussion of Kent.

[3] PCC 55 Lawe 1614; DNB; *Complete peerage*, VI, 70–71; *PP* 1834, XXII, 63–67; Blomefield, *Norfolk*, IX, 55–56; Fuller, *Worthies*, II, 467–468; Bradfer-Lawrence, H. L., *Castle Rising* (King's Lynn, 1932), 60–81, 132–134.

[4] Palmer, C. J. .*Great Yarmouth* (Great Yarmouth, 1856), 302.

leaving £10 outright in alms for the poor of Norwich.[1] Still another almshouse was provided in Norwich in 1612 when Thomas Pye, a grocer and a former mayor, with his wife, Anne, built six cottages for as many poor people, to be chosen from three parishes of the city. The six almsmen should, according to the terms of the indenture drawn in 1614, be above fifty years of age and should be chosen by three of the 'most ancient justices of Norwich'.[2] Edward Goffe of Threxton in 1612 established two almshouse foundations in the adjoining parishes of Watton and Saham Toney. Late in his life this member of the lower gentry had built dwellings for four poor and aged couples in each of these two rural parishes, with gardens and grounds adjacent, at a probable charge of £200. His will, which likewise provided for the endowment of a grammar school which he had founded in Saham Toney,[3] vested in the parsons of Caston and Saham Toney, the vicar of Watton, and the chief constables of the hundred of Wayland, as trustees, the almshouses and an annuity of £10 from certain of his lands. The almspeople in both institutions were to receive this stipend, at the rate of £1 5s p.a. for the maintenance of each couple, save during each tenth year when their stipend should be halved and £5 devoted to the repair of the premises.[4]

A carpenter of King's Lynn, John Peirson, in 1623 left to the mayor and burgesses of that town a messuage with a wharf and yards to be sold on the death of his wife (1625) and the proceeds applied, after certain bequests, for indicated charitable purposes. The property yielded £183 6s 8d, which was sufficient to add £2 p.a. to the revenues of the existing almshouses in King's Lynn, while the residue secured a payment of £2 p.a. for the relief of the poor of Stonegate Ward and a scholarship of £2 p.a 'upon some poor scholar, yearly, who should go out of the grammar school of Lynn and live in any college in Cambridge'.[5] Generous provision was made by Sir Ralph Hare, of Stow Bardolph, for the poor whom he had since 1603 maintained in com-

---

[1] PCC 148 Hele 1626; Norwich Court Book; *PP* 1834, XXI, 654; Blomefield, *Norfolk*, III, 366, IV, 73, 75; Cozens-Hardy, *Mayors of Norwich*, 61–62.

[2] *PP* 1834, XXI, 563; Cozens-Hardy, *Mayors of Norwich*, 66; Blomefield, *Norfolk*, IV, 222, 245. Pye was appointed sheriff in 1581 and served as mayor in 1597.

[3] *Vide post*, 160–161.

[4] Blomefield, *Norfolk*, II, 317–318, 322–323; *PP* 1835, XXI, 859–861, 864. Blomefield cites the following epitaph from a brass in Saham church: 'Here lieth the bodye of Edwarde Goffe late of Threxton, who departed this lieff the 20 of Maye 1612, and before his death to the glorye of God and advancemente of learninge, erected a ffre-schole and 4 almesse houses in the towne of Saham Toneye, and also 4 almesse houses in the town of Watton, and gave unto everye of the same for ever, a reasonable and convenient meyntenance.'

[5] (John Peirson) PCC 112 Swann 1623; (Elizabeth Peirson) PCC 28 Clarke 1625; *PP* 1834, XXII, 27.

modious quarters, consisting of two rooms for each of six almsmen chosen from his parish. Sir Ralph, who by his will proved in 1625 also left £30 outright to the poor of Clackclose and £20 to the needy of Snetterton, provided an endowment of £15 12s p.a., or more if it could be gained from the land vested in his trustees, for the maintenance of the almspeople, each of whom should have 1s weekly, to be paid on every Sunday at the parish church. None was to be nominated to his foundation who was not a native of the parish or a resident there for at least ten years, while all must be aged and impotent poor.[1] An even more generous foundation was made for another rural parish, Walpole St Peter, in 1630 by Robert Butler, Esq. Before his death, Butler had built an almshouse which he by indenture conveyed to trustees together with an endowment of thirty-six acres of rich land which was to be let at the best possible rental. The property evidently possessed a worth of at least £300 at that date, in view of charges laid on it for the support of four poor widows who were to be maintained on the foundation. Each almswoman was to have 1s a week from May 1 to November 1, and 1s 4d weekly during the remainder of the year, for her complete maintenance, while 3s 4d each was to be provided each winter for the purchase of a chaldron of good sea coal. The income beyond these prescribed amounts was to be employed by the trustees for the repair of the house, then for the clothing of the inmates, and then for the augmentation of the basic stipends.[2]

A most complicated foundation was made in 1634 by Christian Gooch, under the will of her late husband, Thomas, for the benefit of the poor of East Dereham and Hoe, with lesser aid for the poor of three nearby rural parishes. Gooch, who also left £200 to the Children's Hospital in Norwich, had instructed his widow, as executrix, to convey to twenty named trustees valuable lands and buildings with the intent

---

[1] PCC 78 Clarke 1625; *PP* 1835, XXI, 523–524; Blomefield, *Norfolk*, VII, 383, 441–442, 448; Howard, H. F., *Finances of the college of St John the Evangelist* (Cambridge, 1935), 61, 75, *et passim*. Hare was the grandson of John Hare, a London mercer, and married the daughter of a London alderman. At the coronation of James I, he was created Knight of the Bath. In addition to his charities for the poor, Hare gave during his lifetime (1623) the impropriate rectory of Marham to St John's College, Cambridge, the income for the first three years to be spent on the library, then under construction, and thereafter towards the maintenance of poor scholars.

[2] PCC 93 Scroope 1630; *PP* 1834, XXII, 93–95; Blomefield, *Norfolk*, IX, 116. The inscription on Butler's monument in the parish church at Walpole:

En pius ornator templi, benefactor egenis,
Solamen pariae consorti fidus amicus.

Robertus Butler, obiit primo die Aug. an. 1630, aetat. sua 59, ej. monumentum hoc, Gulielmus Coney, generosus, statuit a. Dom. 1632. Abi viator, et ad tuos reversus narra te vidisse locum in quo pater patriae jacet.

that the income, of approximately £25 p.a., should be distributed in
annual stipends of 5s each to thirty-six of the poor of East Dereham,
seven of Hoe, one of Worthing, three of North Elmham, and three of
Beeston-next-Mileham. These benefactions to poor living in their own
houses totalled £12 10s, but the surplus income, after £1 p.a. for
sermons at East Dereham and Hoe, was to be disbursed to the poor
of Hoe by the trustees, arrangements presumably being made that
certain of them should reside in Gooch's house in Hoe after the death
of his wife.[1] In the same year a Norwich widow, Prudence Bloss, by
will devised to the municipal government three houses in the parish of
St Saviour worth approximately £100, to secure an almshouse for as
many widows of that parish, though no endowment was settled. She
likewise gave £100 to the Children's Hospital, an annuity of 13s 4d to
the poor of St Saviour to be added to the 6s 8d p.a. given under the
will of her first husband, Edward Nutting, £10 to be disbursed to the
poor of the parish over a period of ten years, and a Spanish Bible which
had cost £25 to the city library.[2] And, finally, in our summary of the
many almshouse foundations made in the early Stuart era, we should
mention that built at Wilby in 1637 by Richard Wilton, a gentleman
of Topcroft, which was likewise left for the use of the parish, but with
no endowment.[3]

The great movement for the establishment of almshouses in Norfolk
was all but concluded by 1640. As has been mentioned, there was no
diminution of the interest of benefactors of the county in the needs of
the poor during the revolutionary era, but the principal concern shown
in this period was with the creation of endowments, normally vested
for the benefit of specified parishes or towns, for the support of the
worthy poor in their own households. The great sum of £10,306 10s
was provided for this purpose alone during the last two decades of our
period, as contrasted with the relatively very small capital of £342 10s
given for almshouse endowments. Only two of these need be mentioned.
In 1657 William Brereton, who lived just outside Norwich, by will
provided an almshouse for two of the aged and infirm poor of Brooke
and stipulated that his estate should be charged with the annual sum of
£2 12s for their support.[4] Finally, Thomas Jermyn, of West Tofts, of
a substantial gentle family of that parish, who somewhat plaintively
requested his vicar to bury him 'the old way if it may not be preiudi-
ciall to him', in 1658 bequeathed £5 p.a. for the support of an alms-

---

[1] *PP* 1834, XXI, 539; *PP* 1835, XXI, 793; Blomefield, *Norfolk*, IX, 50, X,
218.
[2] PCC 34 Sadler 1635; *PP* 1834, XXI, 539, 701; Blomefield, *Norfolk*, III,
377, IV, 445, 447. *Vide post*, 134.
[3] PCC 107 Goare 1637; Blomefield, *Norfolk*, I, 364-365.
[4] PCC 28 Ruthen 1657; *PP* 1835, XXI, 540; Blomefield, *Norfolk*, V, 429.

house in his parish, as well as 10s p.a. for the poor and outright bequests to the poor of nineteen other Norfolk parishes, this last legacy totalling about £25 10s.[1]

We have dealt at considerable length with the great movement which so plentifully supplied Norfolk with almshouse foundations. We have discussed briefly at least thirty-two of these foundations made during our period as well as the substantial augmentations, amounting to reconstitution, made by benefactors of this age to the earlier foundations of St Giles' and Norman's in Norwich. In total, £11,285 2s was provided for the permanent endowment of these institutions during our period and by the end of our era at least 219 almspeople were receiving shelter and maintenance in these well-devised and on the whole well-administered places of social refuge. In addition, a total of £4710 1s had been provided either for the augmentation of the surviving medieval almshouses, which we number somewhat uncertainly as ten, or for the support of a considerable number of simple and unincorporated almshouses, which were lending effective if transitory assistance to the distressed folk of the county. It seems fair to assume, since Norfolk benefactors regarded £2 12s p.a. as adequate maintenance for one almsperson who had his lodging supplied, that an additional ninety-one persons may well have been supported in these lesser establishments. Further, the considerable sum of £2151 4s was given by Norfolk donors for the construction of almshouses or for the repair or enlargement of existing premises. In all, then, it seems certain that men and women of our period had provided a capital structure sufficient for the complete care of at least 310 of the most helpless of the poor of the county. We have noted that the accumulations of capital during our period had as well provided an income sufficient for the care of something like 646 families, or possibly 3000 individuals, in their own houses—men, women, and children not quite as hopelessly stricken by the dread infection of poverty. This means that a vastly significant social contribution had been made by the benefactors of our period, that the sharpest edges of poverty had at least been blunted, and that an experiment in communal responsibility of almost revolutionary proportions had been successfully accomplished. Most of these almshouses were small, several were inadequately endowed, and a few were not to survive the chilling blasts of eighteenth-century social indifference. But they were well dispersed across the county, only certain villages in Erpingham Hundred to the north lying more than ten miles from the nearest almshouse. They stood as the magnificent accomplishment of men who were not the less charitable because their social aspirations were so stubbornly and aggressively secular.

[1] PCC 172 Wootton 1658.

2. Social Rehabilitation

Norfolk's great generosity in seeking to establish institutions and endowments for the relief of its poor was displayed as well in the leadership taken by the county, and more particularly by Norwich, in the development of experimental undertakings for the prevention of poverty and the rehabilitation of the poor and underprivileged. During the whole of our period the impressive sum of £17,127 16s was dedicated by benefactors of the county to the various charitable uses which we have grouped under the head of *Social Rehabilitation*. It is significant that the proportion of charitable gifts devoted to these bold and hopeful undertakings rose steadily during the years under study, from slightly more than 1 per cent during the pre-Reformation decades to almost a quarter during the Cromwellian era. Hence, of the impressive total of funds given for purposes of rehabilitation, somewhat more than nine-tenths was provided during the last century of our period. In all, nearly 10 per cent (9·63 per cent) of the total of charitable funds for the county were given for experiments in social rehabilitation, a proportion far higher than we have noted in any other rural county in the realm, and rivalling that observed in the two great urban communities considered.[1] This remarkable accomplishment was due almost wholly to the vigorous and enlightened leadership of Norwich and of its singularly cohesive merchant aristocracy which was not only capable of bold conceptions but possessed the means and the sense of continuing social responsibility required for carrying out large-scale community undertakings principally dependent on private philanthropy.

The Norfolk contribution to experimentation with the agencies of social rehabilitation was especially significant and fruitful in the building up of endowments for apprenticing poor boys and providing destitute children with at least the basic skills required if they were to compete successfully in an increasingly complex economic order. Here Norwich led the way, the success of the institutions which its philanthropy created being closely watched by all of England. Most beneficent consequences ensued as other cities sought to emulate the agencies devised by this provincial mercantile aristocracy. This particular form of social experimentation attracted only trifling support until 1611, but thereafter a flood of gifts and bequests was received, with the result that for the whole of our period almost £5000, or 2·80 per cent of the whole of Norfolk's charities, was poured into apprenticeship programs. Further, it should be noted that almost the whole (99·12 per cent) of this large

---

[1] The proportion of charitable wealth devoted to this purpose ranges from 2·66 per cent in Somerset to 5·94 per cent in Worcestershire, among the predominantly rural counties, and is 10·42 per cent and 13·32 per cent respectively for Bristol and London.

sum was provided in the form of endowments, so that permanently effective institutions were established for the prevention of poverty by arming youth with requisite skills and confidence.

The notable achievement of Norwich in the training of youth was largely the consequence of the generosity and the sensitive understanding of the nature of the problem of poverty displayed by a mercer and mayor of that city, Thomas Anguish. At his death in 1617, at the age of seventy-nine, Anguish left to the city as trustee a house and grounds, 'being large, spacious, & new built, and many rooms therein', for the reception and proper training of underprivileged children of the city. His will likewise provided an endowment comprising urban real property then renting for £14 p.a. for the support of the institution, shortly to be called the Children's Hospital, 'untill it shall please God to putt in the harte of some able & godlye minded men, or by the general charge of the citty' the better financing and enlargement of the social opportunities which he hoped to create. Anguish suggested in his will that such an institution had been 'for many years wished & desired' by the merchant community of which he was such a notable leader. He declared his 'compassion and great pitye' for the young and poor children, 'borne & brought up in this city . . . and specially suche as for wante, lye in the streetes . . . whereby many of them fall into great and grievous diseases and lamenesses, as that they are fitt for no profession, ever after'. He therefore proposed to gather in as many as forty such children, boys and girls, who should be lodged in his hospital under the tuition of a master and dame, as well as other teachers. They were to be admitted from the age of five to seven years and kept until they were about fifteen. During the years of their upbringing, they were to be fitted for service and prepared to maintain themselves by their own work.[1]

Anguish had left certain uses in the property devised for the foundation of his hospital to his sons for a period of ten years, but they renounced their legal rights, with the result that the hospital was established in 1618, the fitting out being undertaken with city funds. It is evident that Anguish bespoke the sentiments and the progressive aspirations of the class of which he was so distinguished a member, for the hearts of 'able & godlye minded men' were moved to make substantial and continuous bequests for the endowment of the Children's

[1] *PP* 1834, XXI, 531–554; Blomefield, *Norfolk*, IV, 407–414; Cozens-Hardy, *Mayors of Norwich*, 70; Neville, Alexander (Richard Woods, trans.), *Norfolk furies* (L., 1623), sig. P, 2–3; *S.P. Dom.*, 1628, CXXI, 45. Thomas Anguish was a member of a family long settled in Walsingham; he married a daughter of the lesser gentry, by whom he had nine sons and three daughters. He was sheriff in 1596, mayor in 1611. His portrait, now in Norwich City Hall, depicts a handsome man of seventy-three, with a firm face relieved by sensitive, if searching, eyes.

Hospital until the conception which the founder had so persuasively laid out was fully realized. Not long after Anguish's death a goldsmith, Emanuel Garrett, left £100 of endowment with the indicated wish that the work of the hospital might be begun at a date earlier than that assured by the founder's will,[1] while in the same year Henry Fawcett, the rich cloth merchant whose generous bequests to the poor have already been noticed, left the same amount to the foundation.[2] Also in 1619 a grocer, Hammond Thurston, by will provided £10 for the purchase of eight beds for the hospital, then being prepared for use.[3]

The hospital was inaugurated in 1620 when a modest beginning was made by opening one wing of the house provided by Anguish for the reception of ten boys and two girls. A master and dame, as well as a master to teach the children to read English, were appointed and an appropriation of £70 p.a. from endowments in the city chest, not included in the charitable computations that follow shortly, was made to supplement the slender endowments then in hand. Thus well established and certainly well administered, the hospital enjoyed the warm and continuing support of the burghers of Norwich, substantial bequests to its endowment being almost traditional during the next generation until its resources were assured. In 1621 William Rugge, son or grandson of a former alderman of Norwich, bequeathed £40 to the uses of the hospital.[4] John and Edmund Anguish, sons of the founder, in 1623 settled an estate valued at £200 on the hospital, subject to the payment of £1 6s 8d p.a. for certain other charitable uses, while the other sons of the founder, William and Thomas, gave £100 and £20 respectively at later dates.[5] In 1625 a prosperous worsted weaver, Matthew Peckover, added £20 to the endowment by will,[6] while a baker, Andrew Martin, gave £5 in 1628.[7] A substantial addition to the *corpus* of the hospital's funds was received in 1626 under the will of Thomas Tesmond, of Norwich, who left an estate situated in Bixley, just to the south of the city, possessing a capital worth some years later of approximately £600, subject only to a payment of £1 p.a. for sermons on the days commemorating Kett's rising, Gowrie's conspiracy, the Gunpowder Treason, and Coronation Day. Tesmond likewise devised lands and

---

[1] PCC 25 Parker 1619; *PP* 1834, XXI, 532.
[2] *Vide ante*, 109, 118, and *post*, 161–162, 332.   [3] PCC 21 Parker 1619.
[4] Norwich Court Book; Blomefield, *Norfolk*, XI, 35.
[5] *PP* 1834, XXI, 539; Blomefield, *Norfolk*, IV, 408–409, V, 17; Cozens-Hardy, *Mayors of Norwich*, 79. John Anguish, a mercer, was sheriff in 1618 and mayor in 1635. Like most members of his family, he was long lived, dying in 1643 at the age of eighty-three. Edmund became a member of the county gentry; he was lord of a manor in Great Melton and died in 1657, aged eighty-four.
[6] CCN 171 Belward 1625; Millican, Percy, ed., *Register of the freemen of Norwich* (Norwich, 1934), 156.
[7] Blomefield, *Norfolk*, IV, 409.

tenements, also principally in Bixley, for the augmentation of the endowments of St Giles' Hospital, with a then probable value of £660.[1] Shortly afterwards, in 1629, a Norwich merchant, Thomas Herring, gave £100 to the city for the purchase of additional lands for the support of the Children's Hospital.[2] A considerable sum was received in 1630 when John Tolye, a dornix weaver and merchant, who was later to become mayor, paid in £525 which he held as executor of the estate of Nicholas Reeve, a London scrivener and his brother-in-law, and of Mirabell Bennett, also a Londoner, the widow of a prosperous merchant. This amount represented residues from the two estates which, according to the wills of the testators, were to be disposed for general charitable purposes, being now granted to the Children's Hospital in order that the number maintained and trained there might be substantially increased.[3]

Tolye's important augmentation of the endowments was invested by the governors as part of a sum of £1100 of capital accumulations in hand. In all, about £2150 of capital had been provided during the brief interval 1619–1630 by Norwich donors for the implementation of Anguish's noble undertaking. This must have meant that the hospital by that date enjoyed an income from these funds in excess of £100 a year quite beyond the subvention of £70 p.a. originally provided from the charity chest of the city, which was in part still continued. But the work of endowing this notable institution, which had no great single benefaction, was not then completed, as the next generation of benefactors, principally drawn from the merchants and tradesmen of Norwich, pertinaciously continued the worthy work. Thus in 1631 a rich Norwich hosier, Nathaniel Remington, left £20 to the endowment of the hospital among other thoughtfully considered charitable bequests.[4] In the same year another merchant, Thomas Gooch, bequeathed £200 to the

[1] PCC 108 Hele 1626; PP 1834, XXI, 501–502, 532, 710; Blomefield, Norfolk, IV, 409; S.P. Dom., 1628, 45. The city, as trustee, apparently merged the estates in the course of the seventeenth century, dividing the revenues in such wise that one-third was paid to the account of St Giles' and two-thirds for the support of the Children's Hospital. The income (combined) in 1834 was £181 p.a.

[2] PCC 73 Goare 1637; Blomefield, Norfolk, IV, 409; PP 1834, XXI, 539.

[3] Ibid., XXI, 533–534; Blomefield, Norfolk, IV, 409; (Reeve) PCC 43 Hele 1626; (Bennett) PCC 32 Barrington 1628; Cozens-Hardy, Mayors of Norwich, 74; Millican, Freemen of Norwich, 55. Vide Jordan, Charities of London, 148, 358, for a discussion of the London charity of Mirabell Bennett. For Tolye, vide post, 134.

[4] PCC 52 St. John 1631; Blomefield, Norfolk, III, 371; Millican, Freemen of Norwich, 86. Remington, the son of a hosier, left an estate of more than £5,000. In addition to the above-mentioned charity, he left £50 15s for the poor of Norwich and Wymondham, £20 for various municipal uses, £53 13s for loans to young hosiers, £7 for a gilt cup for St Andrew's church, and £1 14s to the clergy.

endowment,[1] while Daniel Collins, of uncertain social status, added
£100 by his will.[2] Prudence Bloss, whose almshouse foundation has
already been mentioned,[3] gave £100 to the hospital's endowment in
1634, and a grocer, Robert Smith, bequeathed the same amount in 1636
for the support of an additional boy to be chosen from Trowse Milgate.[4]
In the same year another grocer, and a former mayor, Francis Smallpece, gave £100 towards the augmentation of the endowment,[5] while
in 1637 a valuable property came to the hospital under the will of
Tobias Dehem, a citizen of Dutch descent, who died in 1629.[6] The
widow of a grocer donor, Robert Smith, gave £100 in 1637,[7] while two
years later Robert Craske, a grocer and a former mayor, added houses
in St Martin at Oak then worth, we have estimated, £110 of capital
value to the endowments, as well as providing £75 for loans to needy
grocers and property of approximately £40 capital value for the maintenance of three sermons and the relief of the poor.[8] Craske's brother-
in-law, John Tolye, also a merchant and also Mayor of Norwich, gave
to the governors in 1638 certain property then worth about £60 on
condition that he might appoint two children to the institution during
the remainder of his life.[9] Another member of the closely-knit and
certainly well-disciplined mercantile society, Robert Debney, an alderman and mayor and the son of a former mayor, gave £10 to the hospital's
endowment in 1638,[10] and two years later Ann Craske, daughter of one
mayor and the widow of another, Robert Craske, whose benefaction has
just been noted, bequeathed £40 for the same purpose, as well as leaving

---

[1] *Vide ante*, 127.   [2] *PP* 1834, XXI, 539.   [3] *Vide ante*, 128.

[4] Blomefield, *Norfolk*, IV, 410; Millican, *Freemen of Norwich*, 76; *PP* 1834,
XXI, 539.

[5] PCC 69 Russell 1633; Cozens-Hardy, *Mayors of Norwich*, 75; *PP* 1834,
XXI, 539. Smallpece was sheriff in 1605 and mayor in 1622. One of his daughters
first married a son of Thomas Anguish and then Sir John Dethick, Lord Mayor
of London.

[6] PCC 75 Ridley 1629; *PP* 1834, XXI, 534, 540; Millican, *Freemen of Norwich*, 219–220; Blomefield, *Norfolk*, III, 372, 374. Dehem was of the second
generation of a refugee family which had been assimilated into the burgher
aristocracy of the city. He had given £3 to the endowment for the poor of his
parish, £10 outright to the city poor, and £27 for sundry municipal uses.

[7] *PP* 1834, XXI, 539; Blomefield, *Norfolk*, IV, 410.

[8] PCC 165 Harvey 1639; Cozens-Hardy, *Mayors of Norwich*, 75; Blomefield,
Norfolk, III, 38; *PP* 1834, XXI, 534. Craske married a daughter of a former
mayor of the city. He hoped that two children might be added to the then
number by his bequest and that they could be bound out for their apprenticeships as a charge on the city.

[9] PCC 191 Aylett 1655; *PP* 1834, XXI, 534; Cozens-Hardy, *Mayors of Norwich*, 80. Tolye was sheriff in 1630, served as mayor in 1638 and again in 1644,
and also was a burgess in Parliament. His father, Richard, had also been mayor.
He was involved in Royalist riots in 1648, declared a delinquent, fined £1000,
and imprisoned for three months.

[10] PCC 83 Lee 1638; Blomefield, *Norfolk*, IV, 410; Norwich Court Book.

£10 outright to the poor of Norwich and £40 for loans to needy and trustworthy brewers.[1]

The political and economic disturbances of the era of revolution by no means halted the great charity on which the merchants of Norwich had been for so long and so notably engaged. In 1641 a merchant, John Gilbert, added £100 of endowment to the hospital's funds on condition that two additional children be admitted,[2] while in 1642 a Norwich draper, Nicholas Pipe, gave £120 in cash and real property which three years later was leased at a rental suggesting a capital worth somewhat in excess of £400.[3] A merchant, Augustine Blomefield, whom we have noted as a principal benefactor of St Giles' Hospital, left houses, tenements, and a malthouse, in East Dereham, which we have uncertainly reckoned as worth £5 p.a., to the hospital in 1645 for the maintenance of as many additional children as possible,[4] while two years later Richard Harman, a rich skinner and a former mayor, left the modest sum of £20 to the endowments, as well as £21 10s for immediate use for poor relief and £4 for church repairs.[5] Alexander Peckover, who died in 1649 while sheriff, added £50 by his will proved in 1650,[6] while at the close of our period William Barnham, a hosier who had served Norwich as sheriff, mayor, and as a parliamentary burgess, vested in the governors of the hospital a rent-charge of £4 p.a. for the maintenance there of a poor boy to be chosen from the town of Thetford.[7]

Thus during the second interval of accumulation of endowments for the Children's Hospital (1631–1660), substantial capital had been added to its funds. In 1660 these endowments stood at about £4260, an

---

[1] PP 1834, XXI, 574; Blomefield, *Norfolk*, IV, 410; Norwich Court Book; Cozens-Hardy, *Mayors of Norwich*, 74.

[2] Blomefield, *Norfolk*, IV, 410; PP 1834, XXI, 539.

[3] PCC 70 Rivers 1645; Millican, *Freemen of Norwich*, 3; PP 1834, XXI, 534, 541; Blomefield, *Norfolk*, III, 391, IV, 165, 411, 412. Pipe also left £12 to the poor and a silver chalice to St Stephen's church. He was the son of a Norwich baker and made a considerable fortune as a draper.

[4] *Vide ante*, 118.

[5] PCC 49 Fines 1647; Blomefield, *Norfolk*, III, 381, 397–398; Cozens-Hardy, *Mayors of Norwich*, 80. Harman had been sheriff in 1626 and mayor in 1639. He sat for Norwich in the early sessions of the Long Parliament. His father was a worsted weaver; his first wife was a member of the foreign colony of the city. His will disposed £5600 in personal property and extensive real property worth by estimate £3710.

[6] Blomefield, *Norfolk*, III, 402, IV, 411; Millican, *Freemen of Norwich*, 1.

[7] PP 1834, XXI, 536; Clark, *Norfolk charities*, 241; Cozens-Hardy, *Mayors of Norwich*, 87. This interesting attempt to extend the benefits of the hospital beyond Norwich failed. Well after our period, in 1674, it is evident that the terms of the gift had not been met. Barnham enjoined his executors to secure a commitment to pay the £4 p.a. to Thetford for apprenticeships, and, if this were done, to pay £100 to the endowment of the Girls' Hospital, as well as any residues accumulating to the chest of the Children's (Boys') Hospital.

amount sufficient to provide complete maintenance and training for about fifty-three children, since £4 p.a. had for many years been regarded as the true charge for such tuition. It is particularly note-worthy that this great institution had been built and endowed by a class rather than by individual men, only three of the many capital gifts received having been more than £500 in amount, while the customary gift, almost a prescribed amount for a former mayor, had been £100. A most significant contribution had been made by these men and women of Norwich, for the great benefits derived by the whole com-munity and its citizenry were universally recognized within the city and with envy by every other city in the realm. Norwich had learned how to move out alone in a new and most difficult economic and social terrain.

The success of the Children's Hospital had been so notable and it had grown so large that there was considerable discussion during the era of the Civil War regarding the possibility of opening a second institution in which girls might be more appropriately lodged and where more specific attention given to their training for later life. This aspira-tion was realized when in 1649 the staunch Parliamentarian mayor, Robert Baron, died leaving £250 for the building of a separate hospital, which came at once to be called the Girls' Hospital, while the older establishment came somewhat later to be known as the Boys' Hospital. Baron's bequest stipulated that the sum provided should be employed 'for the training up of women children, from the age of seaven, untill the age of fifteen years, in spinning, knitting, and dressing of wooll' under the guidance of a discreet and religious woman to be appointed by the magistrates. The bequest was to become effective only if the city appointed quarters for the reception of girls, which Baron held would 'become a means of great benefit to the city, and comfort to the poor'.[1] The terms were met by the city, new quarters being erected for the Girls' Hospital in 1651 or 1652.

The new venture attracted substantial bequests despite the political uncertainties of the period. Robert Whittingham, a merchant, be-queathed the foundation £200 in 1652,[2] while a widow, Alice Bishop, left it £100 by her will proved in 1659.[3] A Norwich grocer, William Brooke, vested property then worth £12 p.a. in the city government, as

[1] PCC 195 Pembroke 1650; Cozens-Hardy, *Mayors of Norwich*, 84; Millican, *Freemen of Norwich*, 86; *PP* 1834, XXI, 546; Blomefield, *Norfolk*, III, 402, IV, 450. The son of a local apothecary, Baron made a comfortable fortune as a hosier. He was sheriff in 1641 and mayor in 1649. He subscribed to the Solemn League and Covenant in 1649 and was known as a zealous Parliamentarian. One of his sons (Robert, 1630–1658) was a minor poet and dramatist, while a daughter married a future mayor of Norwich (John Mann).

[2] Blomefield, *Norfolk*, IV, 451; *PP* 1834, XXI, 549.

[3] PCC 358 Pell 1659; Blomefield, *Norfolk*, IV, 451; *PP* 1834, XXI, 549.

trustee, by deed in this same year 'towards the education and bringing up of poor girls . . . who should be destitute of maintenance'.[1] In a period of less than a decade a total of £790 of endowments had been gathered, wholly from the remarkably cohesive and responsible merchant class of the city, for a second and certainly a hopeful experiment in social rehabilitation and the prevention of poverty by the dissemination of useful knowledge under discipline.

Norfolk likewise was regarded by contemporaries as pioneering in various experiments for the rehabilitation of the poor by the establishment of stocks of goods on which they might be put at work, by the building and endowment of workhouses where useful trades might be taught, and by the founding of houses of correction in which, it was much too hopefully assumed, rootless men might by a judicious mixture of fear and tuition be won from the habits of vagrancy and beggary. Much of the interesting development of these undertakings in Norfolk, as in other counties, flowed from the taxation enjoined by statute, but there was likewise a substantial amount provided by private benefactors for the vigorous prosecution of these schemes. In all, a total of £3927 16s, amounting to 2·21 per cent of all the charitable funds of the county, was hypothecated as capital for these highly experimental attempts to deal with poverty at its sources. These undertakings were begun at a very early date in Norfolk, the first house of correction given by private charity having been erected in 1543, while interest in them was continuous, at least some endowment having been provided for these uses in every decade thereafter. The significance of this development in Norfolk is suggested by the fact that none other of the counties included in our study even rivals it in the proportion of capital funds dedicated to this use.[2] We should now comment on at least a few of these foundations.

In 1543 Robert and Joan Marsham, members of a family long seated at Marsham, to the south of Aylsham, built a house of correction in the latter town at an estimated charge of £60.[3] Tentative efforts to deal with the problems of vagrancy and unemployment were also undertaken in Norwich and Great Yarmouth in the next decade, while, as we have noted, Norman's Hospital in Norwich was in 1565 granted to the city for the establishment of a house of correction for the 'lodging, comfort, and relief of poor strangers, vagrants, sick, and impotent persons'.[4] There was serious unemployment in Norwich in this period, with the result that in 1571 the city authorities took an elaborate census of the condition of the poor. It was found (though the total seems improbably high) that there were 2300 men, women, and children not

[1] PCC 529 Pell 1659; *PP* 1834, XXI, 546; Blomefield, *Norfolk*, IV, 451.
[2] The proportions range from 0·69 per cent (Somerset) to 1·68 per cent (Bristol).
[3] Blomefield, *Norfolk*, VI, 281.   [4] *Vide ante*, 119–120.

engaged in useful work within the city, including a verminous swarm of beggars who alone were costing Norwich £200 p.a. for their support. Therefore orders were taken, by purely local initiative and authority, for the absolute prohibition of begging under pain of six lashes, with a fine of 4d to be laid against any person guilty of giving individual alms. Vagabonds were to be bound to work for a period of twenty-one days, the city government assuming direct responsibility and supervision of the house of correction. Food, fuel, and work stocks were to be provided and Norman's put in a state of repair for the reception of those assigned there by order. At the same time, the genuinely unemployable poor were to be given weekly sums for their support, children of sufficient age in indigent households were to be bound out, and poor persons who had not resided in Norwich for at least three years were to be sent away. These regulations were earnestly enforced with results which the local authorities, reporting to the Archbishop of Canterbury with visible pride, regarded as eminently successful. Hundreds of idle children had been placed in work, more than sixty men 'which dayelie did begge and lyved ydelye' were earning about a shilling a week, 180 women had been placed in employment, while beggars had fled the city. In all, the city authorities reported to the Archbishop, the municipality had been saved at least £2118 1s 4d in charges each year, 'besydes greatly and ofte trowblynge the maiestrates wt the ponishment of vacabondes of wch they are nott nowe trowbled wt the tenth parte for the feare of the terrour of the house of Bridwell'.[1]

The 'Norwich system', as it might well be called, was of great importance not only because it was the first but because it was also the best administered and the most successful of the many municipal attempts during the Elizabethan period to deal with the problems of poverty, beggary, and vagabondage.[2] It was so remarkably successful because these communal efforts were supported by large endowments for the relief of the unemployable poor, because the city already possessed substantial almshouse resources, and because its merchant aristocracy, who likewise constituted the city government, laboured so persistently and intelligently with the stern problems imposed by a new age. Thus, as an example of this steady and almost formidable ingenuity, when in 1581 the chancel of St Giles' church was so decayed that it had to be abandoned, 'all the lead, timber, iron, and stone' were taken over by the parish trustees as a stock to be put out for the relief and employment of the poor of the parish.[3] The Norwich system was, then, an intelligent

[1] Hudson, William, and J. C. Tingey, eds., *The records of the City of Norwich* (Norwich, 1906, 1910, 2 vols.), II, 339–358.

[2] *Vide* Jordan, *Philanthropy in England,* 77–103, for a fuller discussion of this topic.

[3] Eade, Peter, *Parish of St Giles, Norwich* (Norwich, 1886), 103; Blomefield, *Norfolk,* IV, 238.

mixture of private endowments and enterprises financed wholly or principally from city funds raised largely by taxation. Experimentation was
thus carried forward with a system of relief which was a generation later
to become nation-wide. But we must not confine our attention to
Norwich's brilliant contribution in this respect.

Thus, in 1580 a hospital for the relief and rehabilitation of poor
children was founded in King's Lynn, which was shortly afterwards
endowed by the generosity of a London goldsmith who was a native of
this Norfolk town. The town officials appropriated £600 to defray the
cost of converting the derelict church of St James for this worthy purpose. John Lonyson two years later bequeathed £200 to the local
authorities for the endowment of the hospital, to be known as the 'New
House for the Poor'. Lonyson's endowment was invested in lands yielding £10 p.a., which was used to provide stocks for the poor to work at
the manufacture of baize, the dressing of hemp, and the twisting of
tows for fishermen of the town.[1] At a somewhat later date (1588) a considerable local benefactor, John Titley, whose scholarship foundation
will be discussed later, added £100 to the stock in hand for providing
work for the needy poor.[2]

Another Londoner, a clothworker named Richard Bond, in 1640
provided a stock for the poor of Little Walsingham, his native town, in
addition to settling a most generous foundation of a grammar school for
the community.[3] His will gave the sum of £100 wherewith to set the
employable poor at useful work as well as another £100 to provide fuel
and clothing for the aged poor who were no longer capable of labour,
amounts which his executors seemingly doubled from the residue of
Bond's substantial estate.[4]

The social institutions of Great Yarmouth were literally remade by
a remarkable and most aggressive merchant of that town during the
period of the Commonwealth and Protectorate. This man, Edward
Owner, who was born in 1576, was very rich and of decidedly strong
opinions. He represented Great Yarmouth in Parliament on four occasions. A resolute and successful defender of a local clergyman against
the Bishop of Norwich in 1628, Owner was a stout opponent, in and out
of Parliament, of Ship Money, and almost literally drove his native
town into the Parliamentary camp in 1641. Some years earlier, in 1634,
he defended with threat of physical violence and legal action the independence of Great Yarmouth against the claim of the bailiffs of the

[1] PCC 45 Tirwhite 1582; *PP* 1834, XXII, 41–42; Hillen, H. J., *King's Lynn*
(Norwich, [1907], 2 vols.), I, 289–290. Lonyson was the son of a Lynn goldsmith.
[2] PCC 20 Leicester 1588, sentence 8 Drake 1596; *PP* 1834, XXII, 26, 56;
Hillen, *King's Lynn*, I, 290. *Vide post*, 169.
[3] *Vide post*, 163–164.
[4] PCC 40 Coventry 1640; Goodrich, P. J., *Walsingham* (Norwich, 1937), 38;
Blomefield, *Norfolk*, IX, 281; *PP* 1835, XXI, 670–672.

Cinque Ports that they should be represented at the town's annual fishing fair. In 1636 Owner fitted up a yard for the exercise of his artillery company and in 1641 subscribed £600 on behalf of his town for putting down the Irish rebellion, which incidentally had the later effect of giving the town an Irish estate from the forfeited lands of the Earl of Ormonde. Owner became a republican and a Presbyterian during the course of the Civil War and despite his advanced age remained the principal citizen of Yarmouth and certainly its most lively inhabitant.

Owner proposed in 1646 that a public library be founded by the Corporation. He indicated his own willingness to subscribe to this worthy purpose, suggesting that other substantial inhabitants simply be required to contribute. This scheme was abandoned, but, as we shall see later, Owner was the prime mover in the reorganization of the local grammar school, to which he left a large endowment.[1] Shortly before his death in 1650 he founded, or more accurately bludgeoned the Corporation into founding, a workhouse, or hospital, for the employment and maintenance of the poor children of the town. Owner had given sums, of which no certain record exists, which may have totalled as much as £1500 to the school and workhouse during his lifetime, while entering into a contract with the Corporation under which at his death £950 of cash should be paid in as endowment, as well as £30 p.a. from a corn stock kept for the benefit of the borough and an additional £30 p.a. of income. It was further agreed that every future alderman should on election add £5 to the stock and every common councillor £2 10s until the annual income of the foundation should attain the enormous total of £500 p.a. Owner's will added still another £100 of endowment, while his shrewd intervention in the Irish rebellion, on behalf of Great Yarmouth, resulted in the settlement on the charity of a great estate of 2159 acres in Ireland which in 1714 was leased at £100 p.a. Our best reckoning, excluding Owner's gifts to the workhouse (hospital) during the years before its full constitution, is that he provided from his own estate not less than £1125 for the workhouse and probably as much for the grammar school. In addition, an amount fairly exactly reckoned at £1231 had been added to the endowments of the two institutions by 1660, in small part by the payments made by incoming aldermen and councillors, but probably for the most part from Owner's unrecorded benefactions and from the Irish estates acquired through him.[2]

[1] Vide post, 155.
[2] PCC 193 Grey 1651; PP 1833, XIX, 334–336; Manship, Great Yarmouth, 131, 232, 348, 378, 424; Palmer, Great Yarmouth, 307; Swinden, Great Yarmouth, 873. We have not been able to explain fully the remarkable and very rapid growth of this endowment. In 1676 it was officially valued at £9001 13s 6d, yielding £337 9s p.a. We have accounted for only slightly more than half (£4712) of this huge sum, not counting Owner's probable unrecorded gifts of £1500.

There were still other important experiments in Norfolk in plans for social rehabilitation and the care of the distressed. Thus in the course of our period £457 was given for the relief of prisoners, particularly in Norwich Gaol, and the redemption of men held for fines and debts. A somewhat surprising proportion, 58·34 per cent, of this total was in the form of capital, with the result that by the close of our era perhaps £13 p.a. was available for this purpose. There was likewise a steady concern with providing care for the sick, principally in lazar and pest houses in several communities in the county. Though no notable hospital was founded during these years, the not inconsiderable total of £740 4s was given for the care of the diseased, of which £538 9s was in the form of permanent endowments. Further, £185 15s was given for marriage subsidies for poor young women, an old-fashioned form of charity which tended to die out in Norfolk by the beginning of the Elizabethan era. And finally there was great and persistent interest in the establishment of loan funds for the benefit of young tradesmen or for the relief of poor men who could provide some surety, a very important and socially fruitful form of charity which had an especially early and mature development in Norfolk.

More capital was accumulated in these loan funds, normally vested in the municipalities, than for any of the several experiments in social rehabilitation which we have thus far considered. During the course of our period these accumulations reached the impressive total of £6833 1s, amounting to 3·84 per cent of the whole of the charitable funds of the county. The significance of the development of this noteworthy experiment in Norfolk is suggested by the fact that the total of this fruitful capital was nearly quadruple the combined amount provided for this purpose in the four counties of Buckinghamshire, Hampshire, Lancashire, and Somerset, and considerably more than the sum made available for this use in the flourishing commerical city of Bristol. These loan endowments were of many types and were organized in almost as many different schemes of administration as there were trusts, but they possessed certain common characteristics. They were designed either to provide starting working capital for poor young men who had completed their apprenticeships or to make available to temporarily distressed men small amounts, at low or no interest, sufficient to tide them over periods of emergency or to save them from utter ruin. They were practically all designed to be perpetual revolving funds, though in the very nature of the charity these capital amounts were subject to an inevitable and often quick erosion.

By 1660 such endowments had been settled in ten Norfolk communities, but we shall content ourselves with describing a few of several types in Norwich, where, quite naturally, they tended to be concentrated. In 1524 John Terry, a mercer and former mayor of the city, established a loan endowment of £200 to be lent in sums not to exceed £40 and for not longer than three years to needy merchants, artificers, and others 'to easse ther nede and payne'.[1] A full generation later Richard Head, a haberdasher, by his will proved in 1568, in addition to £22 5s left outright to the poor, £4 2s given to the support of an almshouse, £10 for municipal uses, and other small charitable bequests, left £100 to be lent in small sums not to exceed £10 to poor and needy men without interest but on proper and sufficient surety. The aldermen and two other principal men of the two parishes so favoured were to approve the loans and the security.[2] Thomas Pettus, a leading draper of Norwich, and its mayor in 1590, in 1598 left £20 as a stock to set the poor at work in the bridewell, about £86 to general charitable purposes, and £100 for a loan fund. The loan capital was to be put out in amounts of from £5 to £10 on proper security, half among poor worsted weavers and half among needy dornix weavers, no recipient to hold the loan for a period of more than two years.[3] A few years later (1611) a local trades-

[1] PCC 29 Bodfelde 1524; *PP* 1834, XXI, 565, 575; Blomefield, *Norfolk*, III, 199, IV, 291; Cozens-Hardy, *Mayors of Norwich*, 45. *Vide post*, 145. The fund was well administered by the city authorities in whom it was vested, only £50 having been lost at the time of the parliamentary report in 1830. Terry's monumental inscription celebrates his charity in these terms:

> Devote crystene peple desioruse to knowe,
> Whose body resteth under thys stone so lowe,
> Of John Terry marchant, the tyme hys lyf ledde
> Mayr et alderman of thys cyte in dede,
> Vertuose in lyvynge, to the commonwelth profyghetable,
> And to ryght and conscyence ever conformable,
> The same to preserve, ande also to ayde
> And eyke to be mayntenede, CC l. have payd:
> Among the cytizens, in love for ey to remayne,
> Therewyth for a tyme to easse ther nede and payne.
> And over that, CC l. to purchase lande or fee,
> To comfort and releve por fowks at necessyte,
> When herafter yt chauncyth the kyngs tasks to be layde,
> The rentts of the same for them to be payde . . .

[2] CCN 54 Ponder 1568; *PP* 1834, XXI, 576; Blomefield, *Norfolk*, III, 358, IV, 164; Millican, *Freemen of Norwich*, 82.

[3] PCC 15, 16 Lewyn 1598; Cozens-Hardy, *Mayors of Norwich*, 64; Millican, *Freemen of Norwich*, 58; Blomefield, *Norfolk*, III, 362; *PP* 1834, XXI, 574. Two loans of £20 each, both, it may be noted, exceeding the prescribed maximum, had been lost by 1786. Pettus was the son of John Pettus, a local cloth merchant. He was a trusted merchant and served his city in many offices. His monumental inscription gives us some flavour of the man:

> . . . Conditur hic, celebris civis, celeberrimus urbis
> Norwici civis, grande simulque decus;
> Nomen ei sacro baptismi fonte dabatur
> Thomas, cognomen cum patre, Pettus erat
> Inter et ille notos, hoc nomine clarus,
> Inter et ignotos, nomine clarus erat;

man, Augustine Wood, established a loan fund with a capital of
£133 6s 8d, as well as leaving £40 for the relief of prisoners in Norwich Castle. The capital was to be lent on proper security to poor but
reliable tradesmen in amounts not to exceed £6 13s 4d and at no
interest.[1] Similar provisions governed the loan fund created in a will
dated 1612 by a staunchly Puritan draper, Thomas Doughty, who left
£100 for loans to ten worsted weavers for terms of not more than seven
years.[2] These are but fair examples of the many loan endowments
created during our period, which served not only to relieve men im-
perilled by economic emergencies but likewise as sources of ready
and free capital for young men who were setting themselves up in a
craft or trade.

3. Municipal Betterments

Norfolk is likewise remarkable for what can most accurately be described as its civic sense. We may well believe that few counties in
England during our period devoted so large a proportion of their charitable funds to various schemes for municipal betterment and the
general well-being as did Norfolk; certain it is that no essentially rural
county dedicated so large an absolute amount to these purposes. In all,
the substantial total of £18,820 15s, constituting 10·58 per cent of all
the charitable funds of the county, was provided for these uses, of which
a large proportion was in the form of capital gifts. Aside from the
relatively small sum of £504 4s left to companies for the public benefit,
these funds were concentrated heavily under two uses: general municipal purposes, to which £15,032 18s was given, and public works
(roads, bridges, and harbours), £3283 13s.

The amount vested by benefactors in general municipal betterments
was relatively very large indeed, constituting 8·45 per cent of all the
charities of the county, and exceeding, for example, the total given for
any specific religious use and approaching in amount the total provided for grammar-school foundations. Moreover, it was distributed
with extraordinary evenness throughout the county, only 17·4 per cent
(£2616 4s) of these endowments having been settled on Norwich.
There is another interesting and unusual aspect to be noted regarding
these benefactions for general municipal uses: a major fraction of them
were specifically given in order to provide relief for poor men or for

> Namque suos inter, gradibus perfunctus honorum
> Omnibus, ad summum praemia summa tulit.
> Percrebuit fama totius gentis, atque decorum,
> Tum fidei plenum, tum probitatis erat. . . .
>   Qui Thomas obiit septimo die Jan. 1597, ao. aet. sue 78.

[1] Blomefield, *Norfolk*, III, 363.
[2] PCC 55 Weldon 1617; *PP* 1834, XXI, 676; Blomefield, *Norfolk*, III, 364.

whole communities from the burden of royal taxation or, in far fewer cases, some measure of relief from local rates. We know of no other county in which this was a really major concern of donors, or of any in which this form of charitable interest continued through the whole period under study.[1] The amount given for this purpose, the whole being capital, had by the close of our period reached the impressive total of £4358, a sum sufficient to yield about £218 p.a. and to provide substantial relief indeed from the irregular subsidies imposed by Parliament. We should now note at least a few of these particularly interesting endowments.

The benefactors who provided such endowments seem principally to have been concerned with the burden imposed on their communities by parliamentary taxation, light though this was in fact until the Stuart period. Thus Jeffrey Ellingham of Fersfield by will in 1493, after certain pious bequests, left his house with various scattered tracts of land then having a capital value of about £160, the income to be employed for the relief of the inhabitants of the parish from the payment of fifteenths when they should be imposed; in other years for the repair of the parish church or any other public use to which the inhabitants might agree.[2] In the same year William Lynster of Tibenham, in

[1]

	General municipal purposes		Tax relief		Total	
	£	s	£	s	£	s
1480–1490	420	0			420	0
1491–1500	428	0	790	0	1,218	0
1501–1510	691	13	652	0	1,343	13
1511–1520	357	13			357	13
1521–1530	60	5	310	0	370	5
1531–1540	1,036	0	770	0	1,806	0
1541–1550	6	0	30	0	36	0
1551–1560	1,209	13	455	0	1,664	13
1561–1570	430	0	200	0	630	0
1571–1580	138	14	265	0	403	14
1581–1590	95	0	180	0	275	0
1591–1600	2,192	0			2,192	0
1601–1610	87	10			87	10
1611–1620	1,505	5	126	0	1,631	5
1621–1630	752	5	300	0	1,052	5
1631–1640	653	5	280	0	933	5
1641–1650	71	15			71	15
1651–1660	540	0			540	0
	10,674	18	4,358	0	15,032	18

[2] CCN 141, 142 Aubry 1493; PP 1835, XXI, 577; Blomefield, Norfolk, I, 96, 102. Vide post, 187. Ellingham also left a cross of £2 value to his parish church, a good carpet to lie before the altar, four marks to build a church porch, and funds for a new bell sollar, similar to that at East Harling. He further provided five marks towards building a new bell sollar at Kenninghall, 1s 8d towards a

addition to lands worth possibly £200 left as capital for church repairs, provided an endowment of nine acres of freehold, not many years later possessing a capital value of about £80, the income of which was to be employed for the relief of poor men from the king's taxes when levied, and in other years for the repair and adornment of his parish church.[1] In the year of Henry VIII's accession to the throne a gentleman of Hillington settled on twelve trustees a messuage and a considerable tract of land of about thirty-three acres, the income to be used to discharge all inhabitants of East Walton and Hillington of any parliamentary taxes that might be imposed, while the residue was to be employed for the relief of the most needy inhabitants of the two favoured parishes.[2] The Norwich merchant, John Terry, whose loan charity has already been noted, in 1524 left £200 on trust to the city of Norwich to relieve the poor of local and royal taxes,[3] while in 1559 Robert Rickman of Ellough, Suffolk, and Robert Smith of Hedenham, Norfolk provided lands worth £205 for the relief of the inhabitants of the latter parish from the payment of such tenths and fifteenths as might be imposed.[4] These are but typical of many such legacies for more than twenty Norfolk communities, all left primarily to provide relief from the detested weight of national taxation, throughout our period regarded as an intolerable kind of local calamity, with provisions making the income available for general charitable or municipal uses during those years when such levies were not imposed.

A much larger sum, amounting to £10,674 18s, almost the whole of which was endowment, was provided for a considerable variety of uses which may be fairly described under the heading of general municipal uses and betterments. Thus as early as 1490 Thomas Bole, a member of a gentle family long seated in Garboldisham, left lands in thirty-six tracts, worth by estimate £300, for the general use of 'the whole town and inhabitants' of the parish. This considerable charitable estate was constituted as a town trust, the income normally being employed for church repairs and poor relief, to which additions were made, of £75 capital value, by three seventeenth century donors.[5] A decade later

new bell at Rushworth College, and 4d each to the monks at that place. The parish was authorized to sell the lands constituting the trust, but none to any gentlemen or any man then having 'any lands or tenements in the world'.

[1] CCN 136 Aubry 1493; Bryant, *Norfolk churches, Diss*, 306; Blomefield, *Norfolk*, V, 277–278. *Vide post*, 183.

[2] (Francis Calybut) PCC 21 Holder 1516; *PP* 1834, XXII, 77; Blomefield, *Norfolk*, VIII, 361.

[3] *Vide ante*, 142.

[4] *PP* 1835, XXI, 782; Blomefield, *Norfolk*, X, 143; Clark, *Norfolk charities*, 102.

[5] *PP* 1835, XXI, 726–729; *PP* 1867–68, LII, ii, Norfolk, 32–33; Blomefield, *Norfolk*, I, 274. In Blomefield's day (*ca.* 1734) the town estate yielded £22p.a.; in 1868, £70 7s 2d p.a.

John Peyrs, a mercer of Great Yarmouth, vested in the township of Northwold extensive lands and grazing rights, worth upwards of £450, for an obit and the general uses of the parish. Each householder was to receive a penny loaf of bread on the donor's death day, while the bulk of the income was to be employed for discharging the 'King's tasks', the repair of the church, the maintenance of roads, and general municipal purposes.[1] A rich Thetford merchant, Robert Love, who had been mayor of the town in 1506, in 1511 left substantial charitable bequests for church purposes and for municipal betterments. He bequeathed sums totalling £31 7s for church repairs and £43 to the regular clergy in the monastery at Thetford, as well as 6s p.a. for prayers. He stipulated, in addition, that eight acres of his land should be enfeoffed in order to yield 1s 6d p.a. for the repair of the guildhall of his town and 5s p.a. for the repair of designated bridges, while he devised £6 13s 4d outright towards the repair of Melford Bridge. His will further provided £20 to purchase the freedom of the customs for Thetford, if the town could 'find means to purchase of the King's grace' within a period of five years.[2]

The parish of East Tuddenham gained a considerable charitable estate in 1526 when John Proo of that community settled on six trustees four plots of land comprising about eleven acres and, a somewhat later terrier would suggest, a small tract of town land with five cottages, for the general uses of the inhabitants and to bear any common charges which might be levied on the parish. This endowment, which we have quite uncertainly estimated as having a capital worth of £120, was employed to defray the taxes laid on the parish and for general municipal purposes.[3] A leading Norwich merchant of the same period, Robert Jannys, whose generous benefactions to the poor of his city have already been noted,[4] in 1527 settled property with a capital value of about £150 on the city, the income of which was 'yeerly and holly to be expended, upon, aboute, and towardys, the charges of a comon cart or carts, for the carriage awey of the filthy mater comyng of the makyng clene . . . and swepyng of the stretys and cisternys of the city'. His will, proved in 1530, provided £20 for the repair of the roof of the guildhall, while he also charged his estate with an annual payment of £8 that all persons coming to Norwich 'to buy or sell at any gate or port', whether at fair time or ordinarily, might be wholly discharged of tolls and customs.

[1] CCN 253, 254 Ryxe 1505; Blomefield, *Norfolk*, II, 215; *PP* 1835, XXI, 720–721.

[2] CCN 108–110 Johnson 1511; Blomefield, *Norfolk*, II, 62, 65, 69, 71, 74, 75, 82, 91, 100, 126. The freedom of the customs was not gained by Thetford until Elizabethan times; so the bequest was paid over for the repair of the monastery at Thetford.

[3] *PP* 1835, XXI, 820. At a later date the five cottages were used as almshouses.

[4] *Vide ante*, 101.

This notable bequest did much to free the economy of Norwich from the remaining medieval restrictions on commerce and laid the basis for the strong and almost fanatically loyal community spirit of the city so evident throughout the next century.[1]

The town of Swaffham gained a valuable estate for general municipal uses in 1550 when through the persistent efforts of two of its citizens, John Wright and William Walter, it purchased from the Crown the chantry of Simon Blake, established by his will in 1489. Blake, the lord of Aspall's manor in Swaffham, conveyed it on trust for the establishment of his chantry in the church of Swaffham, the property possessing at the Expropriation a probably understated value of about eight marks p.a. The manor, comprising ninety-eight acres of farm lands and grazing rights over several hundred acres of heath, was purchased for the benefit of the parish, presumably by private subscriptions, for £126 2s 1d, with the covenant to pay annually £2 16s to nine poor people of the parish, for the general relief of the poor, for the maintenance of roads, for the making and maintaining of common wells, and for all other appropriate municipal uses. The title to and the administration of this fund was vested in twelve trustees to be elected annually by the inhabitants of the parish.[2]

During the Elizabethan era the considerable total of £3500 14s was provided for general municipal uses in numerous parishes of the county, some being substantial amounts. Thus Thomas Malby, an alderman of Norwich, by his will in 1558 extended the freedom from custom tolls which Jannys had secured by his bequest a generation earlier. Malby left £100 to the city for the purchase and redemption of the remaining tolls levied on persons trading in Norwich by means of the river Wensum and using either of the two wharfs there provided.[3] The parish of Winfarthing gradually built up an estate, employed for the relief of the poor and general municipal purposes, given by several donors between 1545 and 1621, almost certainly including some released chantry properties, and totalling twenty-three acres and two or three houses.[4] In 1596 Edward Everard, lord of the manor of Gillingham, conveyed to trustees lands worth perhaps £200 for the benefit of the parish of Gillingham St Mary with uses designated for certain other parishes. The income of about £10 p.a. was to be allocated so that £1 p.a. should be paid for the relief of his own parish, with similar stipends in three adjoining communities; £2 p.a. was to be available to

---

[1] Vide post, 153, for Jannys' grammar-school endowment at Aylsham.

[2] Vide ante, 115, and post, 177. The holding was not as substantial as it might sound, being but one-fortieth of a knight's fee.

[3] PCC F. 11 Welles 1558; PP 1834, XXI, 593; Blomefield, Norfolk, III, 272; Millican, Freemen of Norwich, 63.

[4] PP 1835, XXI, 582; Blomefield, Norfolk, I, 190; Bryant, Norfolk churches, Diss, 306.

the surveyors and constable of Gillingham St Mary and Gillingham All
Saints for the maintenance of a foot-path much used by the inhabitants;
and the remainder should be expended for the general uses and needs
of the parish.[1] The parish of Bergh Apton gained its estate in 1599 by a
deed of trust established by Christopher Tenwinter, a yeoman of that
community, who gave about sixty acres of land with appropriate buildings, worth upwards of £400, to the town for its general uses but subject
to a stipulated payment of £1 p.a. to the churchwardens for the poor
and certain annual payments to nearby parishes for their poor during
the next thirty years.[2]

A considerable number of similar endowments were constituted
during the early Stuart period, while a larger number of existing
municipal charitable estates were either consolidated or agumented by
private benefactors during these years. In all, £3704 5s was given in
this generation for general municipal uses, including tax relief, while
gifts for this purpose fell away drastically during the last two decades of
our period, when the total provided declined to £611 15s. But a notable
accomplishment had been attained by men and women of Norfolk.
Upwards of fifty of its parishes by 1660 enjoyed the benefits of parish
estates, dedicated to the general well-being of these communities and
providing a firm and certain basis on which local institutions could be
built and preserved.

We should note, finally, that £3282 13s was provided by donors of
our period for the repair of roads and streets, the maintenance of harbours and wharfs, and other public works of this kind. A large proportion (77·18 per cent) of this amount was of course for immediate use,
though by the close of our era there were endowments providing
£37 10s p.a. for the permanent maintenance or improvement of these
facilities in various parts of the county. Although there were many
of these benefactions, no two quite alike, we shall content ourselves
with discussing only the principal of the earliest of them.

Sir James Hobart, the great and trusted Norfolk lawyer of the early
Tudor period, during his lifetime was a noted benefactor. He had
rebuilt Loddon parish church in 1495, subscribed to the fund for the
repair of the roof of Norwich Cathedral, and in 1511 gave £26 13s 4d
towards the rebuilding of Norwich Guildhall, while some years earlier
he with his wife had built a bridge and causeway over the Waveney
River, connecting Norfolk and Suffolk, at a charge of upwards of £200.[3]

[1] CCN 174 Force 1600; PP 1835, XXI, 543–544; Blomefield, Norfolk, I, 10, 175.
[2] CCN 149 Pecke 1599; PP 1835, XXI, 540.
[3] PCC 33 Ayloffe 1517; Blomefield, Norfolk, IV, 228, VI, 296–297, X, 160–161;
Fuller, Worthies, II, 464. Vide post, 189. Hobart's will reflects other interests.
He left £30 for prayers, £19 to monasteries, £123 7s for church repairs and
furnishings, and smaller amounts to clergy, the general uses of the church, and
to Norwich lazar houses. Hobart, a younger son, was born in Suffolk. After

Robert Segrave, who had served as mayor of Lynn in 1534, on his death in 1537 provided for the building of a dike to protect a considerable marshland area in that community from periodic inundations.[1]

Such municipal betterments could on occasion constitute a heavy and a continuing charge not only on the private charity of a community, but on the county and the realm at large. A perhaps unusual instance is provided by the struggle of Great Yarmouth to keep open its constantly silting harbour, on which its great fishing trade and general prosperity were so completely dependent. From the mid-fourteenth century the town had appealed repeatedly to the Crown as haven after haven silted in. For this engineering work which lay far beyond the resources of the community, Henry VII in 1502 remitted fifty marks out of the customs and the fee-farm rents for a period of five years, continued on petition in 1508 for a term of twenty-five years. In 1528 the town laid its problem before Henry VIII, who continued the rebate for a period of thirty years and assigned the tenths and fifteenths levied in the town for the work, on which £1500 was expended. But the haven was once more clogged in 1548 and really heroic measures were undertaken. The property and the ornaments of the discontinued church of St Nicholas and the Charnel, worth in all £1169 17s 11d, were assigned by the Crown to the freeing of the harbour. The City of Norwich contributed £133 7s 8d towards the venture, the Dean and Chapter £20, while an impressive number of the citizens of Great Yarmouth, principally tradesmen, merchants, and fishermen, gave the not inconsiderable sum of £449. In all, something over £1800 was raised, which, with the amounts available because of the continued remission of taxes, was sufficient to carry forward work from 1549 to 1557 on what proved to be a wholly unsuccessful effort to cut a new and permanently clear haven for the trade of the town. The town became deeply committed to this great project, never fully carried out, and during the remainder of our period scores of bequests were made, almost as customary legacies, for this ambitious work which so intimately involved the well-being of all the inhabitants of the town. Thus in the interval 1558–1640 we have recorded some sixty of these benefactions, totalling £417 6s, and

being trained in the law at Lincoln's Inn, he settled in Norwich, where he practised for many years. As early as 1472 Walter Lyhert, Bishop of Norwich, made him his executor and from that time forward he was legal adviser to the principal families of the county. In 1496 he was made Recorder of Norwich and represented the city in Parliament. He was knighted in 1503. He maintained a country house at Loddon and town houses at London and Norwich. His will mentions twenty-one manors which he held in Norfolk and Suffolk, as well as scattered lands in four parishes, a salthouse in Yarmouth, and real property in Norwich.

[1] PCC 10 Dyngeley 1537; Blomefield, *Norfolk*, VIII, 533. Segrave left as well 10s for general church uses, £17 7s for prayers, £1 10s for church repairs, and an estimated £20 to the poor of Lynn and other communities.

ranging from 2s to £50 in amount. The whole of the community was engaged in this heroic, if bootless, undertaking which enlisted the support and the generosity of men of all classes. Men of Great Yarmouth, still without a silt-free harbour, had at least learned how to live and work together and that seems to constitute the essence of civilized living in the modern world.

4. Education

(a) *The Founding of Grammar Schools*. Somewhat less than a fourth of all the charitable benefactions in Norfolk were made for the betterment of the educational institutions of the county and for the enhancement of opportunity for poor boys. Very nearly all the substantial total of £40,920 4s provided for this use was in the form of capital gifts, the sum given for the founding or strengthening of grammar schools, for example, being 99·96 per cent in capital. The endowments provided for educational purposes in Norfolk, amounting as they do to 23 per cent of all charitable wealth, compare only relatively favourably with the other counties in our sample when measured in percentage terms.[1] The educational interests of men and women of the county were comparatively slight during the first two periods comprised in our study, when not much more than a tenth of all benefactions were made for that purpose. But in the Elizabethan era there was a sharp and certainly most substantial increase in interest in such foundations, with £9206 6s provided for various educational uses, this amounting to well over a fourth (28·95 per cent) of the total of charitable benefactions for the interval. During the early Stuart period, when the great outpouring for all secular charities occurred, the impressive total of £18,471 13s was given for education, this being almost 29 per cent of the whole of charitable amounts provided during these decades.

By far the largest sum was provided for the foundation of grammar schools. The generous total of £20,865, or 11·73 per cent of all county charities, was vested in these institutions, no other single charitable use save endowments for the care of the poor eliciting so large a contribution. The concentration of interest in the enlargement and strengthening of school foundations came relatively late in Norfolk. During the long period from 1480 to 1560, only £1758 was provided for school endowments, this being not much more than 8 per cent of the sum given for this purpose during the whole of our era. The growth of these foundations was also relatively slow during the Elizabethan decades, when £2775 was given for the founding of a number of schools. But the crescendo of interest was attained during the early Stuart era, when the impressive sum of £10,124 was dedicated to the almost violent expan-

---

[1] The proportions range from 21·26 per cent for Buckinghamshire to 41·79 per cent for Lancashire.

sion of the educational facilities of the county. This momentum was maintained and more during the unsettled final interval of our study when the £6208 given for this use represents an average annual rate of giving considerably in excess of that achieved even in the early Stuart period.

For all its relative wealth and medieval renown, Norfolk was ill endowed with schools in 1480. The very fact that it possessed so many and such rich monastic establishments had led to the comparative neglect of educational foundations. Education in grammar was provided within several monastic precincts, but, save for two or possibly three cases, there is no certain evidence that this tuition was available to boys outside the walls, and hence these schools did not continue past the Expropriation. Nor did the chantry foundations of Norfolk render so important an educational service as we have noted in some counties, with the result that few of them were sufficiently rooted to survive despite the disposition of the Edwardian commissioners to secure this diversion of funds whenever possible.

With few and in every case probably arguable exceptions, which will be noted as re-foundations, then, we may say that Norfolk's task as the early modern period opened was the creation *de novo* of the facilities for secondary education. The earliest of these foundations was that constituted at Rushworth by a rich and remarkable woman, Lady Anne Scrope, whose ancestor, Edmund Gonville, had founded the college of priests there before making his more famous foundation of Gonville Hall at Cambridge. In 1482, after the death of her second husband, Sir Robert Wingfield, she built a substantial chapel and established a chantry at Rushworth College, conveying the manor of Brettenham to the college in 1485. Then, by an indenture in 1490, rather plaintively reciting the fact that she was old, a widow, and childless, she provided for the maintenance of five poor children out of the diocese of Norwich in the grammar school kept by Rushworth College, to be called 'Dame Anny's childeryn', with eight others to have free tuition, all to be taught by one of the two priests, or fellows, to be added to the college by her foundation. Sometime thereafter, Dame Anne married John, Lord Scrope de Bolton; both died in 1498, she a few weeks after him. A fellowship at Gonville Hall was also founded by this lady, her intention being carried out in 1503 by her executors in a deed directing that 'oon wele dysposed priest or oon goode yong man disposyd to lerne, borne in the diocis of Norwych . . . to be callyd Dame Annys priest' should have £8 p.a., the college to keep an obit for the donor. The number of children to be maintained at Rushworth was increased to seven by Dame Anne's executors in 1501, but the school there, organically linked as it was to Rushworth College, was not to survive after 1541. In all, the charitable gifts of this remarkable woman may be reckoned at just under

£1000, there having been as well substantial gifts for religious uses ordered in her will.[1]

A few years later, in 1505, a very different kind of foundation was made at Cromer by a rich London merchant, Sir Bartholomew Rede. Lady Scrope's will and her dispositions, generous as they were, were in a true sense medieval, whereas in Rede's more modest bequest we have a glimmering of the social order and of the aspirations that were shortly to prevail. Rede, a native of Cromer, who in 1502 had served as Lord Mayor of London, made his company, the Goldsmiths, his trustee, carefully arranging the completely secular control of his foundation. Valuable properties in London were vested in the company on condition that they pay annually £10 'to a virtuous priest, cunning in grammar', who should keep a school in Cromer for gentlemen's sons, the sons of substantial men of the community, and more especially for such poor children of Cromer and adjoining parishes as might benefit from such instruction.[2]

A rich provincial merchant, Thomas Thoresby, of King's Lynn, was far less successful in his aspirations for that town in 1510 because he bound the school inextricably with the great chantry which he also devised. Thoresby had some years before his death begun the building of a college, to whose completion he assigned an additional five hundred marks by his will. His will likewise arranged for an endowment of £16 p.a. for the foundation within the college of a grammar and song school for six children who should be given instruction without charge to their parents. A careful stipulation provided that his son and heir might lay claim to a reversion of the endowment if such instruction were not maintained. A new master was appointed as late as 1534, but in 1543 Thoresby's son, Thomas, seized the property until a new master was

---

[1] PCC 26 Horne 1498; *Norf. Arch.*, X (1888), 277–382; Blomefield, *Norfolk*, I, 284–292, 321; *Complete peerage*, VII, 86; *Surtees Society Publications*, LIII (1868), 94–97, 149–154; Venn, *Caius College*, III, 21, 215, 285, IV, ii, 24, 115; DNB. Lady Anne was the daughter and heiress of Sir Robert Harling, her mother having been Joanna, sole heiress of the Gonville line, which had founded the college in 1342. She inherited nineteen manors and five advowsons in Norfolk alone. Her first husband was Sir William Chamberlain, K.G., of Gedding (Suffolk). The executor of her will was her nephew by marriage, whom she had brought up from the age of three, who served as a privy councillor to Henry VIII and on several occasions on diplomatic missions abroad. *Vide post*, 166, for further notes on Lady Anne.

[2] PCC 40, 41 Holgrave 1505; *PP* 1823, VIII, 323–324; *PP* 1833, XIX, 211; Beaven, *Aldermen of London*, II, 19. Rede, who served as an alderman from 1498 to 1505, was knighted in 1503 during his mayoralty. He was Master of the Mint (1482–1497) and prime warden of his company (1492–1493). Rede was a very substantial benefactor to London, his charities totalling £1,102 8s (*vide* Jordan, *Charities of London*, 221, 276, 327, 388). In addition to the school foundation, Rede left £12 for general church uses at Cromer and at Shipden Chapel in Norfolk, 7s for church repairs and £10 for pier repairs at Cromer.

appointed by the corporation of the town. The substantial endowments and other property of the chantry, on which Thoresby had expended by gift and bequest probably as much as £1003, were confiscated during the reign of Henry VIII, but the school was continued in the same building. The master received £13 6s 8d p.a. and the usher £10 p.a. in the early Elizabethan period, though it seems certain that by 1594 the original endowment had been eroded by the double attrition of Reformation confiscations and an imperfectly arranged trusteeship, for in that year the corporation undertook from its own funds to maintain the school for the children of poor men in the community.[1]

The school at Aylsham was founded in 1530 under the will of that remarkable Norwich merchant and mayor, Robert Jannys, whose other substantial benefactions for his city and county have been recited. Jannys, a native of Aylsham, in his will directed that his executors should purchase lands providing £10 p.a. for the founding of a school in that town and for the support of a competent schoolmaster who should offer free instruction to all qualified pupils. In 1554 the City of Norwich, as trustee under Jannys' will, assigned a portion of the income of Pakenham Manor for this purpose, with a clear indication that the school had been carrying on its work for some time past.[2] The Vicar of Aylsham, John Bury, seemed still sceptical of the new school's strength when in 1558 he bequeathed the foundation £2 if it should be continued.[3] Still another Norwich merchant and mayor, Nicholas Norgate, who was probably born in Aylsham, secured the better future of the school when in 1568 he bequeathed lands in Aylsham and Blickling valued at £10 p.a. for the augmentation of the endowment subject to certain rights of succession.[4]

[1] PCC 34 Bennett 1510; Hillen, *King's Lynn*, I, 222–231; Eller, George, *West Winch manors* (King's Lynn, 1861), 123, 133–139; *PP* 1834, XXII, 25; Blomefield, *Norfolk*, VIII, 512. Thoresby, in addition to his chantry and school endowments, gave or bequeathed £66 13s 4d for municipal uses; £215 3s for church repairs and ornaments; £10 for the repair of Stoke Ferry Bridge; an estimated £10 in 2d doles; and £60 to the papacy to secure remission of sins for those who might come on certain feast days to attend St Margaret's church in Lynn. Thoresby was the son of a former mayor of King's Lynn, Henry Thoresby. He himself was mayor in 1477, 1482, and 1502. He owned lands in seven parishes in Norfolk and held extensive lands in Northamptonshire. He owned many flocks of sheep and also held valuable, though scattered, property in King's Lynn. *Vide post*, 190.   [2] *Vide ante*, 101, 146.

[3] CCN 132 Ingold 1558; Michell, A. T., ed., *Parish register of Marsham* (Norwich, 1889), xiii–xiv.

[4] PCC 6 Sheffelde 1568; Cozens-Hardy, *Mayors of Norwich*, 58; *PP* 1833, XIX, 227; Blomefield, *Norfolk*, III, 295, IV, 436; Kirkpatrick, *Religious orders of Norwich*, 220. Norgate was a mercer. In addition to this bequest, he left £20 to the poor of Norwich, £4 p.a. during his wife's lifetime to Norman's Hospital (£12); and a rood of land outside one of the city gates on which the citizens might lay their compost.

The grammar school at Norwich was of medieval origin, having developed under episcopal direction and control. Though there is a possibility that a school open to boys of the community was kept at an earlier date, the first certain evidence of its institutional existence is to be found towards the middle of the thirteenth century. The school flourished for something more than two centuries, but it is clear that it had ceased to be a significant local institution after about 1497, when its records come to an end, and that it was all but moribund by the time of its Edwardian reconstitution in 1548. It possessed no endowments, and the language of the letters patent most strongly suggests that it had offered no instruction whatsoever for some years past. The foundation was made by the Crown as part of the action taken in vesting squarely in the municipal government the great almshouse of St Giles.[1] The stipend of the master was set at £10 p.a. and that of the usher at £6 13s 4d p.a., while two houses probably valued at £5 p.a. were to be set aside for their residence. This action had the effect of placing responsibility for the governance and maintenance of the school solely in civic hands and of providing revenues of £21 13s 4d p.a. from the Court of Augmentations for the support of the institution.[2]

This grammar school flourished throughout the remainder of our period, with an enrolment of from sixty to one hundred students. In 1562 the stipend of the master was increased to £20, while in 1570 that of the usher was raised to £13 6s 8d; a half-century later the master was receiving £40 and the usher £16, very high salaries indeed for the England of that day.[3] Further, it is clear that the extraordinarily competent and bold government of the city had in the early Elizabethan period undertaken what came close to a program of required public education for both boys and girls in at least the rudiments of learning. The census of 1571–1572 reveals that in every ward 'select' women teachers had been appointed to teach poor children 'to worke or learne letters . . . whose parentes are not hable to pay for theyr learinge' and that an amazing proportion of young children of the indigent listed in the census were then at school.[4] This system of what amounted to compulsory education supported by the public chest had as its objective the cure of poverty by reclaiming the poor from the grip of ignorance, and it was designed principally to afford to very young boys and girls some training in the crafts and the simpler technical processes. But it likewise taught them to read and to write and evidently created a pool of talent from which the Norwich Grammar School drew many of its

[1] *Vide ante*, 116.

[2] *PP* 1834, XXI, 492–493; Saunders, H. W., *History of the Norwich Grammar School* (Norwich, 1932), *passim*.

[3] Saunders, *Norwich Grammar School*, 247.

[4] Hudson and Tingey, *Records of Norwich*, II, 339–343, 352.

students. A tradition of broad civic responsibility for education had enjoyed an interesting, an almost unique, development in Norwich, which doubtless accounts for the fact that the grammar school was somewhat neglected by the rich and generous benefactors of the city during the remainder of our period, save as substantial provision was made for exhibitions for the ablest of its graduates.[1]

The grammar school at Great Yarmouth was even more clearly of royal foundation. Upon petition from the civic authorities, the buildings of St Mary's Hospital, recently confiscated, were granted by the Crown to the inhabitants for their uses. At an assembly held in 1551, a large hall in the hospital chapel was set aside as a grammar school and orders were adopted for the building of a suitable dwelling for a schoolmaster. A Mr Hall, of Norwich, was persuaded to 'resort unto the town, and to be the school-master' at a salary of £10 p.a., which was increased in 1554 by a rate levied on the community. In 1612 the master's salary was further increased to £20 p.a. and shortly afterwards the space allocated for the school premises had to be substantially enlarged. The support of the grammar school had, then, been assumed by the burghers of the town as a direct civic responsibility and so it continued until its affairs became complicated by the formidable will and charities of Edward Owner, whose role in remaking the institutions of Great Yarmouth has already been fully discussed.[2] Owner poured his great benefactions into the Children's Hospital, which he designed for the maintenance and education of poor children in the community. At least £1125 of his bequests and gifts to that institution were disposed for the support of free education within the town. The affairs of the hospital, which, as a consequence of Owner's benefactions and shrewd management, had become very rich indeed, were organically mixed with those of the school, the hospital 'custos' undertaking to pay the generous salary of £40 p.a. to the schoolmaster.[3]

The first great London foundation in Norfolk was made at Holt by Sir John Gresham in 1554. Gresham, a member of the greatest merchant family of his age, was born in Holt, being admitted to the Mercers' Company in 1517.[4] He was chosen Lord Mayor of London in 1547 and at about the same time purchased from his brother, William, the family manor at Holt with the expressed intention of converting it into a free

---

[1] The bequest of £20 left by Edmund Wood, a grocer who was mayor in 1548, is the largest addition to the endowment we have noted (Cozens-Hardy, *Mayors of Norwich*, 53). *Vide post*, 166–172, for some mention of the more important of the scholarship foundations.

[2] *Vide ante*, 140.

[3] Manship, *Great Yarmouth*, 44, 232; Palmer, *Great Yarmouth*, 368–369; PP 1833, XIX, 334.

[4] *Vide* Jordan, *Charities of London*, 95, 225, 327, 329, 331, for a full discussion of his other charities.

grammar school for his native community. The school was founded by letters patent in 1554 as 'The Free Grammar School of Sir John Gresham, knight, citizen, and alderman of London' for the education of boys and youths in grammar. The constitution provided for a master and an usher, while designating the Fishmongers' Company as trustees and as the governors. Shortly afterwards Gresham conveyed to the trustees extensive properties, with an approximate capital value of £2620, including the manor of Holt Pereers, the manor of Holt Hales, all his property formerly held by the priory of Beeston, ten acres in Holt with all the messuages and other buildings belonging to the manors, and other lands which he had lately purchased in ten Norfolk parishes, as well as three messuages in London, these diverse properties forming the endowment of the school. The number of full scholars on the foundation was set at thirty, and a rigorously classical program of education, excellently supported and ordered, was established for this rural community.[1]

By the beginning of Queen Elizabeth's era there were six endowed grammar schools in widely scattered parishes of the county. During the course of her reign another six schools, all carefully constituted, were founded for the further encouragement of learning and the relief of the ignorance which was now so patently connected with indigence. The first of these foundations was made at Wymondham in the second year of the Queen's reign. On petition from the principal inhabitants, certain properties formerly belonging to the dissolved monastery of Wymondham and the guild and fraternity of Corpus Christi of that town were settled on feoffees for the maintenance of a free school, to be kept in a chapel which was likewise part of the expropriated property. These lands, remnants of the Dissolution spoils still in royal hands, possessed a then value of £40 p.a., an amount quite sufficient for the endowment of a large and strong grammar school. The trustees were, however, negligent and an enquiry was made in 1570, after complaint to the Privy Council, as a consequence of which the feoffees were ordered to institute the school immediately and to pay a 'sufficient schoolmaster' a proper salary for teaching all youths who might qualify for admission. In 1604 the value of the endowment had risen to £50 p.a., while by 1639 further surrenders of property originally belonging to the monastery or the guild increased the already substantial endowment to a worth not less than £1500.[2]

[1] PCC 28 Ketchyn 1556; PP 1825, X, 103–108; PP 1884, XXXIX, iv, 229–245; Beaven, Aldermen of London, II, 30; Leveson Gower, W. G., Family of Gresham (L., 1883), 30–35; Fox Bourne, H. R., English merchants (L., 1866, 2 vols.), I, 172–174; DNB.

[2] PP 1835, XXI, 639–640; PP 1843, XVIII, 81; Carlisle, Endowed grammar schools, II, 199; Blomefield, Norfolk, II, 523–524, 534; Armstrong, M. J., History and antiquities of Norfolk (Norwich, 1781, 10 vols.), IV, 201.

Sir Richard Fulmerston, of Thetford, who had enriched his family by the acquisition on most favourable terms of choice and extensive monastic lands in Norfolk, provided for a substantial grammar-school foundation under his will proved in 1567. There had been a school kept in Thetford from the early fourteenth century (*ca.* 1328) until shortly after the beginning of our period (1496), but it possessed no endowment and apparently was discontinued until Fulmerston built a school at a cost of upwards of £100 and paid a master from his own purse in the later years of his life. His will provided that his executors, who included the Duke of Norfolk and three others, should within seven years secure a royal licence for the foundation of an endowed school at the charge of his estate. Three tenements were settled for the residence of the master and the usher, while another was to be converted into an almshouse as part of the foundation.[1] Lands were designated for the endowment of the school, subject only to a charge of £2 p.a. as an augmentation of the stipend of the local clergyman. It was conservatively assumed that the clear value of the properties constituting the endowment was of the order of £30 p.a., but they in fact possessed a capital worth of approximately £1200. It appears that the terms of the bequest were not fully carried out, since the mayor and commonalty of Thetford lodged a complaint with the Crown in *ca.* 1608 asserting that for twenty years after Fulmerston's death the payment had been limited to £13 6s 8d for the master and £5 p.a. for the usher, while more recently the master had received £20 p.a. and the usher £5 p.a. The enquiry disclosed that the endowment was at that date worth £100 p.a., or a capital value of £2000, and that no increase had been made for the clergyman or for the poor, who were provided with no more than the original alms of 1s each week. Orders were thereupon taken by Act of Parliament in 1610 incorporating the trust as the 'Master and Fellows of the School and Hospital of Thetford' and providing more adequate maintenance for the master (forty marks) and the usher (£20 p.a.), setting the clerical augmentation at £30 p.a., and disbursing 2s weekly to each of the four poor lodged in Fulmerston's almshouse.[2]

---

[1] *Vide ante*, 121–122.

[2] Fulmerston acquired the manor of Thetford by deed from the Duke of Somerset in 1548 and shortly afterwards the toll of the bridges in Thetford and three other parishes as well as the profits of Thetford market. He gained Halwick Manor, formerly belonging to Thetford Priory, from Somerset, and the church of St Mary, which he re-edified, from the Duke of Norfolk. Six other priory churches and their tithes also fell into his hands, of which two were demolished and two others consolidated. He gained, as well, most of the lands of the hospital of St Mary Magdalen, after a division was effected with the town of Thetford, which also laid claim to the property. Fulmerston also gained such tid-bits as the house and site of the Austin Friars in Thetford, the church and hospital of the Black Friars, the house of the Benedictine nuns of St George in

An interesting effort to provide some instruction to poor children in
a rural parish may be seen in the gift made by Robert Harleston, a
yeoman of Mattishall, in 1570. Harleston, the father-in-law of Archbishop Parker, settled on trustees property charged with payments of
£1 10s annually to the thirty poorest persons of the parish, 5s to poor
of his name, and 15s to the vicar, parish clerk, or curate who 'ever will
take paynes to teach children'.[1] A more ambitious foundation was made
a few years later (1577) at Tilney by a local gentleman, Richard Nicholls,
who vested property with a capital value of perhaps £200 for the
stipend of a schoolmaster who should offer free instruction to the youth
of the parish.[2] This school, if ever properly constituted, had disappeared
by the middle of the eighteenth century.

A far better endowed and ordered school was founded at Brancaster
in 1596 under the directions of the will of Robert Smith of that place.
Smith had before his death founded an almshouse in the parish.[3] He
had earlier built and intended to endow a free school with one hundred
acres of freehold lands and other properties which he owned in Brancaster, possessing a total capital worth of £900. The master was to
teach twenty-two poor scholars to be chosen from Brancaster, Titchwell, Thornham, and Burnham Deepdale, while each student was to
have two yards of blanket cloth each year, any surplus of income being
employed to maintain the school and the almshouse.[4] Smith failed to
perfect the legal details before his death in 1596, but his sister and heir,
Elizabeth Simpson, carried out her brother's intention by conveying
the intended endowment on trust to Richard Stubb, Esq., and two
other trustees. Stubb, on his death in 1620, left on his own account
£2 p.a. and £10 outright towards the augmentation of the almshouse
endowment, £10 p.a. for a period of twelve years for the enhancement

Thetford and all the lands belonging to it. He became the lay owner or proprietor of most of the monastic lands in and around Thetford and a powerful
local figure. With his son-in-law, Edward Clere, he represented the borough
in Parliament in 1563.

[1] PCC 10 Pyckering 1574; PP 1835, XXI, 808; Blomefield, *Norfolk*, III, 306,
313.

[2] PCC 19 Martyn 1574. *Vide post*, 187.

[3] *Vide ante*, 123.

[4] Smith's memorial brass bears the following inscription:

Here lyethe for all that please to see
Robarte Smithe disposed to great charitie
A free schoole he built and two almes houses of fame,
Who entended to geve lands to mayntayne the same,
But sodaynlie he dyed in this towne of Brancaster,
So the right of all was in Elizabethe his sister,
Which buildinges for ever this godly matron did assure,
W[th] foure score & twelve acres land, for ye pvrpose to endvre
To the bringinge vpp of youthe, and relief of the poore.

of the schoolmaster's salary, as well as an estimated £100 for the general uses of the Dean and Chapter of Norwich Cathedral, not to mention £4 for the poor of Sedgeford and Edgefield.[1]

Towards the close of the Elizabethan period an adequately financed school was founded at Burnham Thorpe by a gentleman of that region, Richard Bunting. The donor by an indenture of feoffment dated September 24, 1599, conveyed to trustees a manor and certain other lands for the use of his wife, but subject in perpetuity to a charge of £12 p.a. for the payment of a schoolmaster for the parish. Other premises were conveyed for the use of a niece and her heirs, save that a chamber over a malthouse was to be used and kept in repair as a schoolroom for the teaching of children in the community.[2]

As we have observed, the great outpouring for the grammar schools of Norfolk came in the later decades of our period. Beginning with the last decade of the Elizabethan era (1591–1600) and continuing without interruption until the close of the Cromwellian period, these endowments were made in a steady and ordered succession as schools were founded in all parts of the county. During these seventy years a total of £17, 432 was provided for new establishments or for the augmentation of existing endowments, which means that slightly more than 83 per cent of all benefactions for this purpose were concentrated in this relatively brief interval. At least the more important or interesting of these foundations should be mentioned.

In 1604 a gentleman of Old Buckenham, dying at an advanced age, left £100 on trust to the churchwardens and 'twelve other chiefest inhabitants of the parish' for the purpose of founding a school and paying a schoolmaster to teach the children of the community.[3] In the same year, William Secker, a yeoman of Scarning, who left outright £10 for the repair of Scarning church and £10 as a stock for the poor, left on trust for his wife approximately sixty-nine acres of land with appropriate buildings, possessing two decades later a capital value of about £600, for the endowment of a free school when her death should occur. He appointed, as well, a house in Scarning for his wife's use and then for employment as a 'free school to be kepte forever in the said house while the world endure'.[4]

---

[1] PCC 3 Soame 1620.

[2] PCC 20 Montague 1602; *PP* 1835, XXI, 497–500; Bryant, *Norfolk churches, Brothercross*, 66. The trustees were negligent in carrying out the terms of the deed of gift. In 1704 they were required to discharge the trust and to pay £100, to be invested as endowment, of arrears of income, then amounting to £118 4s.

[3] PCC 48 Hayes 1605; *PP* 1835, XXI, 833; Blomefield, *Norfolk*, I, 392. This donor, Matthew Sturdivant, also left £20 towards three new bells for his parish church. The school bequest was well invested in land which in 1821 was yielding £23 5s 6d p.a.

[4] PCC 95 Harte 1604; *PP* 1835, XXI, 768–771; Blomefield, *Norfolk*, X, 47.

One of the richest men in Norfolk and one of its principal benefactors, Sir William Paston, of Oxnead, gave much attention during the closing years of his life to the foundation of a well-endowed and carefully vested grammar school at North Walsham for the benefit of that and nearby parishes. Paston's charitable gifts and bequests reached the very large total of £2280. During his lifetime he had provided £200 for the repair of the cathedral churches in Norwich and in Bath and £100 for the rebuilding of his college, Gonville and Caius. He likewise granted on trust certain properties formerly belonging to the chapel and chantry of Caister to secure the payment of £8 p.a. to the poor of Great Yarmouth, £2 p.a. to be distributed to the poor of Caister by the minister, and the residue, of approximately £2 10s annual value, to the incumbent of Caister for a weekly sermon demonstrating 'the godly exercise of preaching and expounding the holy word of God'. But his absorbing interest was in his grammar-school foundation. In 1602 he had purchased the site on which the school was built during the next two years. The statutes being drafted in 1604, a master and usher were appointed, though the deeds of gift establishing the trust were not sealed until 1606. Endowments to yield at least £42 10s p.a. were settled on the trustees, who were to pay the master £20 p.a. and the usher £10 p.a. Free instruction was to be provided in the rules of grammar and the Latin language for forty scholars from any of the parishes comprised in the hundreds of North Erpingham, Tunstead, Happing, East Flegg, and West Flegg, an extensive area incorporating some scores of parishes. A weekly lecture with a stipend of £10 p.a. was likewise endowed, the lecturer to be appointed by the Bishop of Norwich, who, with a number of the leading gentry of the county, was among the twelve governors of this important foundation.[1]

An humbler gentleman of the county, Edward Goffe, of Threxton, whose almshouse foundations have already been noted,[2] founded a free

---

[1] PCC 98 Wingfield 1610, sentence 46 Fenner 1612; DNB; Venn, *Caius College*, III, 280; Forder, C. R., *A history of the Paston Grammar School* (North Walsham, Norfolk, 1934), *passim*; Blomefield, *Norfolk*, VI, 490, XI, 215; *PP* 1833, XIX, 259–260, 318–324; *PP* 1867–68, LII, ii, Norfolk, 94–95. In 1867 the property constituting the endowment yielded £303 17s p.a.

Paston (1528–1610) was the son of Erasmus Paston and the grandson of the more famous Sir William Paston. He succeeded to the estates of his grandfather in 1544, his father having died in 1540, and to those of his uncle, Clement (*vide ante*, 103), in 1597. In the latter year he removed to the great house recently built at Oxnead. Paston took no part in national affairs but was a careful and reliable country magistrate. He was an extremely rich man, the value of his estates at the time of his death amounting to £3,376 13s p.a. of clear rental. He maintained elaborate and old-fashioned hospitality which he ordered to be continued for twenty years after his death. His property included at least twenty-three Norfolk manors, with almost as many advowsons.

[2] *Vide ante*, 126.

school at Saham Toney by bequest in 1612. Goffe, who had purchased property at a probable cost of £80 for a schoolhouse prior to his death, by will settled on his trustees lands then worth £5 10s p.a. for the payment of the wages of the schoolmaster and 10s to 'be bestowed upon a drinking to make good cheer withal' when the trustees should meet to examine the scholars or to appoint the master. The students admitted to the free school were to be chosen without limit of number from Saham Toney, six from Watton, and one from Threxton. The school was greatly strengthened some years later by a gift (1622) and a bequest (1626) from the then rector of Saham Toney, Richard Terry. Terry left his furniture and other household possessions with a value of perhaps £200 to his successor, gave lands with a value of £3 p.a. to reward the parish clerk for ringing the church bell daily at eight o'clock, and vested an additional endowment of £10 p.a. for the better support of the school on condition that no charge should be imposed on students drawn from the parish.[1]

We should mention, as well, the large foundation created in 1615 by Stephen Perse, a native of Norfolk with large property holdings there, though the benefit of his grammar-school foundation and his other charities was for the adjoining county of Cambridgeshire. Perse was born at Great Massingham and had been educated at Norwich Grammar School before entering Gonville and Caius as a pensioner, where he was graduated B.A. in 1569. Perse, who prospered as a practising physician and as a shrewd speculator in lands, was a fellow of his college from 1571 until his death in 1615. His will vested the great sum of £5000 in the corporations of Norwich, Cambridge, Bury St Edmunds, and Lynn, to establish loan funds at 5 per cent interest, the income to be paid to Gonville and Caius College for certain charitable purposes. The bequest being declined by all the named communities, the executors purchased lands instead, the capital value being principally dedicated, in accordance with the donor's intention, to the founding of a grammar school in Cambridge, the endowment of an almshouse there, and the establishment of six fellowships and six scholarships at Caius. Norfolk benefited at least to some degree from this latter bequest because of the old and very strong connections of the county with Perse's own college.[2] Two other Norfolk foundations of grammar schools for the benefit of other counties may be mentioned. The munificent charities of Henry Fawcett, the Norwich merchant whose philanthropy for that city has

---

[1] PCC 136 Hele 1626; Blomefield, *Norfolk*, II, 312–322; *PP* 1835, XXI, 860–861.

[2] PCC 96 Rudd 1615, sentence 69 Cope 1616; Blomefield, *Norfolk*, III, 302; Cooper, C. H., *Annals of Cambridge* (Cambridge, 1842–1853, 4 vols.), III, 93; Venn, *Caius College*, I, 57, III, 73, 83. We have dealt in summary fashion with this great charity, since the benefits to Norfolk were indirect.

been described in earlier pages, provided an endowment of £200 (£10 p.a.) for the support and maintenance of a grammar school at Halton Gill, Yorkshire,[1] while in 1630 Margaret Higginson, a spinister of King's Lynn, left £50 for the endowment of a school recently instituted at Norton in Hales, Shropshire.[2]

We have far too little information concerning a small school foundation established in or about 1619 at Mileham. The benefactor was apparently Allan Elwyn, a London leatherseller, who conveyed a house and approximately three and one-half acres of land, with an uncertainly estimated value of £80, for the support of a free school for this his native parish.[3] A few years later, in 1623, Lady Anne Townshend, a granddaughter of the Elizabethan councillor, Sir Nicholas Bacon, gave on trust £500 for the purchase of lands wherewith a school for the children of the poorest inhabitants of Heydon, Stiffkey, Sall, Little Ryburgh, and Stanhoe should be educated and then apprenticed in the same fashion as her aunt, the late Lady Periam, had arranged in her school and hospital at Henley, Oxfordshire.[4] In the same year a school was founded in the rural parish of Martham by the bequest of a yeoman of that community, Christopher Amies, and the persistent efforts of other humble men of the parish. Amies, who also left £120 to the poor of his own and three nearby parishes, bequeathed £100 to the churchwardens of Martham, as trustees, for the foundation of a free English school. Within the next six years Robert Amies, probably a brother, left £10 for the same purpose and another legacy of £2 was likewise received by the minister and churchwardens as trustees. A voluntary collection yielded another £1 and by 1629 there was £113 in hand. The trustees purchased a house for £30 and converted it into a schoolhouse at a cost of £20, investing the remainder as the school's stock. The school was then instituted to 'teach and inform children of the knowledge of the English letters and perfection of reading', admission being limited to students drawn from the parish.[5] Still another school was founded in 1623 by the efforts of a community, though in this instance the endowment was not to be garnered until somewhat after the close of our period. A chapel in the parish church at Attleborough was con-

---

[1] *Vide ante*, 109, 118, 132. For the school, *vide post*, 332.

[2] PCC 82 Scroope 1630; *PP* 1831, XI, 320.

[3] PCC 21 Montague 1602; *PP* 1835, XXI, 765; Blomefield, *Norfolk*, X, 24.

[4] PCC 15 Swann 1623; *Complete baronetage*, I, 110; Blomefield, *Norfolk*, VII, 134, IX, 250; *PP* 1833, XIX, 247–248. Lady Townshend also left an estimated £60 to the poor and £20 for church repairs. This school, if founded, was not continued later than the early eighteenth century. The parliamentary commissioners (1833) confessed that they had found no certain evidence of the trust. Lady Anne Townshend had married Sir John Townshend, who died of wounds received in a duel in 1603. She was coheir of her father, the manor of Stiffkey coming into the Townshend family by her marriage.

[5] Waters-Withington MSS.; *PP* 1833, XIX, 269–270.

verted into a schoolroom, the Earl of Sussex providing the timber for the seats and the clergyman of Morley providing a lectern for the shelving of the dictionaries. Thomas Heath, who had been graduated from Trinity College, Cambridge, in 1611, was engaged as the first master at the unbelievably low salary of £4 p.a., which was supplied by instituting a charge on the income of certain charitable funds already in the possession of the parish.[1] It seems probable, too, that a school was founded in East Dereham at about this date. A schoolhouse was provided and a graduate of Caius appointed schoolmaster in 1633, his stipend being paid from the charity chest of the parish. But the school attracted no endowments and was abandoned in 1662.[2]

A free school was founded at Grimston in or about 1632, when an outright bequest for its maintenance in the amount of £2 was left to it by Robert Bullock, a yeoman of that parish.[3] This school, too, possessed no endowment, being supported by a mixture of annual subscriptions and fees laid against the parents of its students. In 1640 the trustees of a medieval charity, founded in 1394 by John Talman, who had given forty-four acres of land with a number of houses, the income of which was to be employed for relieving the inhabitants of Grimston from half of all royal taxes that might be levied, determined upon a partial diversion of the trust. An indenture recites that the original value of the fund was £4 14s 4d p.a., which was quite sufficient to carry out the intention of the donor. Many improvements had been made on the properties of the trust, which was then yielding £24 p.a. and had for many years past been partly employed to relieve the poor of the parish. The trustees had consequently determined to reserve £9 p.a. for the payment of half such taxes as might be levied and to use the remainder to support a schoolmaster to teach all the children of the community in grammar, writing, and ciphering and then to bind out as apprentices such poor children as might require assistance.[4] There is a suggestion that the school was not well or legally founded as late as 1647 when William Allen of London, a native of the town, left £20 towards the endowment of the institution provided it be 'really and legally' established within two years after his death as a free school offering instruction to poor children of the parish in 'religion and learning'.[5]

Under the terms of the will of Richard Bond, a London clothworker, a large grammar-school foundation was created in 1640 at Little Wal-

---

[1] Blomefield, *Norfolk*, I, 534; *PP* 1835, XXI, 826; *Alum. cantab.*, I, ii, 348. The endowment was supplied in 1678 under the will of the Rev. Henry Nerford.
[2] *Ibid.*, I, iii, 311; Blomefield, *Norfolk*, X, 218.
[3] PCC 35 Audley 1632.   [4] *PP* 1834, XXII, 72–75.
[5] PCC 63 Essex 1648; *New-England Historical and Genealogical Register*, XLVI (1892), 331–332.

singham, where there is some evidence that a school was kept as early as 1612.[1] This benefactor, a native of the parish, bequeathed £500 outright towards erecting and endowing a free school, the legacy to be settled on feoffees comprising the principal inhabitants of the parish, and also provided that a further settlement of endowments should be made from the residue of his estate. Some years later an additional £540 was paid over from the residue by the executors, thus providing in all £1040 for the stock of the school. Under the terms of incorporation a master and an usher were to be employed to offer instruction to as many as thirty scholars chosen from 'the meaner sort of inhabitants' of the town. The trustees, with two learned preachers chosen by them, were each year to visit the school and to examine the scholars. Tuition was to be given in the Greek and Latin authors, as well as in arithmetic and in writing. If possible, instruction was also to be offered in navigation and the use of 'the sea cards', it being of great importance that the youth of the region should enjoy an advanced understanding of 'sea affairs'.[2]

Shortly afterwards, just as the Civil War was wracking the life and economy of the county, Sir Edmund Moundeford of Feltwell settled on trustees a large area of fen lands under quite unusual conditions. As we have noted, these lands were to be held by the trustees until better drainage enhanced their value to the point that at least £60 p.a. of income was in hand. At that time £20 p.a. was to be employed for the relief of the poor of the parish and £40 p.a. for the maintenance of a free school for the youth of what was at this time a backward and most isolated region, while any surplus income was to be devoted to the building and maintenance of an almshouse.[3] A short while later, in 1646, William Juby of New Buckenham conveyed to trustees several houses, brewhouses, and a shop, apparently worth somewhat more than £200 of capital value, half the income of which was to be devoted to the maintenance of a preaching minister in the parish and half for the employment of a schoolmaster.[4] Finally, we should mention the foundation of William Small, a member of the Suffolk gentry, who owned the manor at Swanton Morley in Norfolk. Small in 1654 conveyed by will a rent-charge of £21 p.a. to trustees who were instructed to pay £1 p.a. to the Mayor of Norwich for the relief of the poor of that city and £10 p.a. to the churchwardens and ten principal inhabitants of Swanton Morley for the education, maintenance, and apprenticing of the poorest boys of the parish until they should have reached the age of sixteen.

---

[1] Sir Henry Sidney left £5 in 1612 (PCC 103 Fenner) for the repair of the schoolhouse in the town. But there is no evidence of any endowment prior to 1640.

[2] *Vide ante*, 139.   [3] *Vide ante*, 112.

[4] *PP* 1835, XXI, 830–831.

Identical provision was made for the parish of Eye, just across the Suffolk border.[1]

We have dealt most briefly with the foundation of thirty schools by Norfolk benefactors, of which three were instituted in other counties. These twenty-seven foundations within the borders of the county represent a most notable achievement by men and women who were endeavouring by their own efforts to create and endow a network of grammar and elementary schools which would provide instruction and useful knowledge for the youth of the entire county. Two of these schools possessed no endowment at the close of our era. A few of them gained no substantial support from benefactors of our period but had rather been constituted from earlier charities diverted to these new purposes, while twenty of the institutions had by 1660 been vested with probably sufficient endowments of £200 or more. In all, the donors of the county had poured £19,030 of funds into these new foundations, which by the close of our era represented a far greater extension of secondary education than Norfolk had ever known before or was ever to know again until deep into the nineteenth century. In addition, the sum of £1835 had been given to other schools, for the building or repair of schoolhouses, for equipment, or as outright gifts to local schools possessing no endowment. We have noted as well nine schools, in addition to the twenty-seven we have discussed, which gained some measure of testamentary support, all insecurely founded and deriving their resources principally from local rates or from the fees paid by parents for the education of their children.

The immensity of this achievement is all the more arresting when we bear in mind that at the beginning of our period Norfolk possessed almost no school resources. But by the close of the remarkable era under survey there was an endowed school for every seventy-six square miles of the countryside. No famous school was the consequence of Norfolk generosity during these years, but far more important was the fact that a widespread and well-endowed system of education had been created within the reach of any poor and able boy who thirsted for knowledge and who aspired to escape the grip of poverty. No family in Norfolk in 1660 lived more than twelve miles from an endowed school of some sort, and, save for two rural regions of the county, none was more than nine miles distant.

In the main, this great work had been carried out in the course of a century (1554–1654) by a variety of men and of classes. There were three royal foundations, or refoundations, in the county during our period, at Norwich, Great Yarmouth, and Wymondham. Five were established by the upper gentry of the county, and six by the lower gentry. Some-

[1] PCC 228 Alchin 1654; *PP* 1830, XII, 144; *PP* 1834, XXI, 577; *PP* 1835, XXI, 772; Blomefield, *Norfolk*, X, 56.

what surprisingly, six were founded by the yeomanry, and these were by no means small or inadequately constituted. In all, then, seventeen were instituted in the rural regions of the county by members of the rural classes, or rather more than 60 per cent of the total number. Five were founded or greatly augmented by the provincial merchants of Norwich, Great Yarmouth, and King's Lynn, while three of the greatest, Cromer, Holt, and Little Walsingham, were the creation of the ubiquitous London merchants who were in this period reshaping the social and cultural life of all England. These men had built well, they had built solidly, and they had built for all time.

(b) *Support of the Universities*. But these foundations, serving the county so fruitfully, by no means represent the full extent of the support lent by Norfolk men and women to education. Norfolk donors likewise provided the considerable total of £9408 18s for the needs of the universities, not counting, it should be stressed, the great refoundation of Gonville Hall, Cambridge, by Dr John Caius, a native of Norwich who received his early education in its grammar school.[1] Almost the whole of this sum was given for the strengthening of the University of Cambridge, to which Norfolk was bound so intimately by cultural and geographical ties, while Gonville, almost a Norfolk college in this period, was most generously and persistently favoured.

We have already mentioned the earliest of these benefactions in connection with Lady Anne Scrope's foundation of a grammar school and chantry at Rushworth in 1490.[2] Her ancestors had founded Gonville Hall in the fourteenth century and she vested in the college the basic endowments which it had heretofore enjoyed only by leasehold. She provided as well £8 p.a. for two additional fellowships in the tenure of the college, the income being assured by the manor of Newnham, then leased at £13 6s 8d p.a., which her executors conveyed to the college. In 1520 Geoffrey Knight, a Norwich priest who likewise held two livings in the county, bequeathed estates then valued at £12 13s 4d p.a. to Gonville as a fellowship stipend for two priests on the foundation who should 'keep their study in art and divinity' and pray for the soul of the donor.[3] Some years later, in 1539, John Whitacre, presumably a graduate of the college and a priest in Norwich, 'moved with great zeal and godly devotion to further and maintain . . . the study of holy letters', gave one hundred and forty-seven acres of arable lands and a messuage with five acres of pasture to Gonville. It is not possible to

[1] *Vide* Jordan, *Charities of London*, 262–263, where this great benefaction is discussed.
[2] *Vide ante*, 151–152.
[3] PCC 3 Maynwaryng 1520; Venn, *Caius College*, III, 249–250, IV, ii, 72; Blomefield, *Norfolk*, IX, 253.

arrive at any fair estimate of the worth of this endowment, the lands having been sold in 1799 for £1485, save to point out that Whitacre was allowed a life annuity of £3 13s 4d as a consequence of his gift.[1]

Gonville, refounded in 1557 by Caius, was further benefited under the will of his successor as master, Thomas Legge, also a native of Norwich. Legge, a layman and an antiquarian of considerable repute, left to the college his unexpired leasehold of the manor of Newnham and other properties on his death in 1607, the £786 10s 5d realized from the legacy having been employed for the construction of a new hall, which came to be called the Legge Building.[2] Still another master of Caius, the rich and renowned physician, John Gostlin, a native of Norwich and a graduate of its grammar school, for unexplained and probably perverse reasons left a considerable endowment to St Catharine's College, as well as £73 outright to Caius, £4 to the poor of the city of Cambridge, £3 to the poor of Norwich, and £3 to the poor of Drayton, Norfolk. To Caius, Gostlin bequeathed as well an inn in Cambridge for which he had paid £280, and a rent-charge of £30 p.a. from his manor and other lands in Milton, which was to be accumulated for seven years, after which £40 p.a. was to be vested for four new scholarships of £5 p.a. each for poor scholars selected from Norwich and the remainder to augment the existing stipends of the fellows and scholars on the foundation. In addition, Gostlin left to St Catharine's the Bull Inn in Cambridge, then valued at £24 p.a., for the founding of six new scholarships, each of which was to have an annual value of £4. In all, therefore, Gostlin's bequests to his university possessed a capital worth of something like £1433.[3]

[1] CCN 46–48 Wymer 1547; Venn, *Caius College*, III, 249–250, IV, ii, 65; Blomefield, *Norfolk*, III, 301. We have entered the gift with the probably nominal value of the annuity, as £73 of capital.

[2] PCC 81 Hudleston 1607; Venn, *Caius College*, I, 73, III, 64–69, IV, ii, 25–26; Blomefield, *Norfolk*, III, 301; Fuller, *Worthies*, II, 491; DNB. Legge was in his earlier years a member of Trinity. He was one of the masters in Chancery and a professor of civil law when Caius resigned his mastership to him in 1573. Archbishop Sandys protested against the appointment because of Legge's alleged popish sympathies. Legge was also well known as a dramatist, having written two tragedies, *The destruction of Jerusalem* and *Richard III*.

[3] PCC 150 Hele 1626; Venn, *Caius College*, I, 116, III, 74, 231, IV, ii, 22; Blomefield, *Norfolk*, III, 303–304; Browne, G. F., *St. Catharine's College* (L., 1902), 94; Jones, W. H. S., *St. Catharine's College* (Cambridge, 1936), 237. Gostlin was the son of a Norwich merchant, Robert Gostlin, sheriff in 1570. He was admitted as a scholar in Caius in 1582 and was graduated B.A. in 1587, M.A. in 1590, M.D. in 1602. He remained a fellow of Caius for many years, holding most of the college offices open to a layman. He was in 1607 chosen master by the fellows, but the choice was set aside by the Chancellor because of his reputed Catholic sympathies. Gostlin then retired for some years to Exeter, where he carried on a very successful medical practice. He was Regius Professor of Physic at Cambridge from 1595 to 1625. In 1619 he was again, and this time

Norfolk donors were even more generous in the contributions which they made for the founding of university and school fellowships and scholarships, the whole amount of their commitment to this need being £10,576 6s. Many of these foundations lent substantial support to the grammar schools of the county as well as greatly strengthening the resources of the universities. Norfolk benefactors gave almost 6 per cent (5·95 per cent) of all their charities for these uses, a proportion somewhat higher than that found in any other county in our group.[1] We have in passing noted a fair number of these gifts and bequests during our discussion of the gifts made for grammar schools and the universities, but there remain several which should be at least briefly mentioned.

Even before Lady Scrope's foundation for Gonville Hall, another woman benefactor of the institution, Elizabeth Clere, of Ormesby, left the college very substantial legacies. The widow of a member of the gentry of the county, Elizabeth Clere, named by Caius 'the nurse and almost the mother' of his college, had during her lifetime completed the fourth side of the court of Gonville Hall at a charge of two hundred marks. In 1487 she had settled two estates valued at about £400 on the foundation for the support of additional fellowships, while by her will she left £40 for the further augmentation of the endowment. In all, therefore, this remarkable woman must have given directly or by bequest not less than £573 towards this foundation in which Norfolk maintained such a constant and certainly generous interest.[2]

Most of the endowments given for scholarships and fellowships prior to the Reformation were subject to an obligation on the part of the favoured college to provide prayers for the repose of the soul of the donor. Thus a Norfolk priest, Edmund Stubb, who was likewise Master of Gonville (1504–1513), in 1503 gave to the university two balances for weighing jewels and plate, while by his will he left his books and his vestments, as well as land valued at £200 to provide exhibitions in the university for the education of three intended priests.[3] The last of the

successfully, chosen as Master of Caius. His own financial accounting compiled in 1619 lists houses in Norwich and Exeter, cash in the amount of £475, lands and annuities worth £1,082 7s 2d, as well as personal property and household effects.

[1] The proportions range from 0·51 per cent (Bristol) to 5·78 per cent (Yorkshire) in the remaining counties.   [2] *Vide ante*, 100.

[3] PCC 31 Fetiplace 1514(?); Venn, *Caius College*, I, 12, III, 23, 285; *Alum. cantab.*, I, iv, 178; Cooper, C. H., *et al.*, eds., *Athenae cantabrigienses* (Cambridge, 1858–1913, 3 vols.), I, 16, 525. Stubb was a native of Scottow, Norfolk. He was gaduated from Cambridge, B.A. in 1474 and B.D. in 1507. He was a fellow of Gonville from 1480 to 1504, thereafter master. For the support of the clergy, he left £18 outright, as well as two Norwich tenements valued at an estimated £50 for the maintenance of the priests of St Michael Coslany, Norwich, where he was rector. He wished to be buried there, 'pauperime et sine pompa', at a cost not to exceed 13s 4d.

pre-Reformation foundations was provided by Richard Nix, the stubbornly orthodox and most unpopular Bishop of Norwich for a full and troubled generation. Nix established in Trinity College, Cambridge, three fellowships and a scholarship with an endowment valued at about £400, as well as founding an obit there with an annual revenue of £1.[1]

The Elizabethan period in Norfolk, as in most other counties, was one in which relatively small foundations were made for fellowships and scholarships. The clergy found themselves poor, the great princes of the church were no more, and lay benefactors were as yet unprepared to assume an educational responsibility which had for many generations been principally borne by the clergy, the upper gentry, and the nobility. During this interval a total of £1281 was given for such endowments, of which the larger may be noticed.

In 1568 Archbishop Parker, a native of Norwich, whose brother, Thomas, was mayor of that city, vested the sum of £200 on the municipal authorities and the fellows of Corpus Christi, Cambridge, to which he added £320 in the following year. The then income from the property purchased for the endowment was £18 p.a. and was designated for several purposes. Five scholars were to be nominated from Norwich, Wymondham, or Aylsham, who were to be granted a stipend of 1s weekly for their commons at Corpus Christi, as well as their lodging, while the two thought most learned should be designated the Norwich fellows, with stipends of £6 each. In addition, £2 p.a. from the endowment was to be employed for sermons in several Norfolk churches, not to mention a small honorarium to the civic authorities of Norwich.[2]

Parker's generosity had substantially strengthened the exhibitions available for the support of boys from the ever-increasing number of grammar schools in the county. In 1596, Mrs John Titley of King's Lynn recited in her will the fact that her husband, whose endowment of a workhouse foundation for his town has already been mentioned,[3]

---

[1] Malden, H. E., *Trinity Hall* (L., 1902), 94; Blomefield, *Norfolk*, III, 543-547; DNB.

[2] PCC 39 Pyckering 1575; Stokes, H. P., *Corpus Christi* (L., 1898), 50-62; Masters, Robert, *Corpus Christi College* (Cambridge, 1753, 2 vols.), I, 85-95; Blomefield, *Norfolk*, III, 306-317; PP 1834, XXI, 527. Parker's great benefactions, save as they affect Norfolk, should not be recounted here, since they are not, except the scholarship foundation, included in the Norfolk totals. His foundation of Rochdale Grammar School is discussed in another place. He augmented the foundation of Corpus Christi by two fellowships and eight scholarships. He endowed a medical scholarship at Gonville with a stipend of £3 0s 8d p.a., as well as a scholarship in Trinity Hall for a student of civil law. He left a valuable library to the University. Parker likewise founded three exhibitions, to be called the Canterbury scholars, one of whom must be chosen from Canterbury School, one from Wymondham, Norfolk, and the third from Aylsham.

[3] *Vide ante*, 139.

had wished to vest £130 in the municipal authorities of King's Lynn for the purpose of founding two scholarships in Emmanuel College, Cambridge, for the benefit of two Lynn students. The town authorities a few years later (1603) agreed to waive a small legacy left to the mayor under Mrs Titley's will and to add £1 5s from the town revenues in order to endow the two scholars, who were to be appointed for terms of seven years with £4 p.a. each, an additional £3 p.a. being paid for the general uses of the master and fellows.[1] Another Norfolk burgher, William Roberts, of Great Yarmouth, at about the same time (1591) by gift established three scholarships in Magdalene College, Cambridge, with an endowment of approximately £360, he having earlier devised the Staple House for Wool to the Corporation of Great Yarmouth for general municipal uses.[2]

The bulk of scholarship endowments in Norfolk was furnished during the years 1601–1660, when a total of £7489 was given for this charitable use, or slightly more than 70 per cent of the amount so vested during the whole of our period. Most of these benefactions were relatively small in amount; almost the whole was for the benefit of local grammar schools or the University of Cambridge; and most of the donors were members of the gentry. No more than a sampling of these foundations can be mentioned.[3]

Among these benefactions was still another left by a Norwich master of Caius, William Branthwaite, who died in 1618. Branthwaite bequeathed to his college his private library, valued at £230, as well as lands, to be purchased by his executor, worth £26 13s 4d p.a., 'for the founding and establishing of four scholarships of my foundation in Gonville and Caius College, and two at Emmanuel'.[4] Yet another Nor-

---

[1] PCC 68 Drake 1596, sentence 53 Cobham 1597; *PP* 1834, XXII, 26, 56. Mrs Titley likewise left the city £40, the income of which was to be employed for the augmentation of clerical incomes.

[2] Cooper, *Memorials of Cambridge*, II, 170; Blomefield, *Norfolk*, VI, 325, VIII, 68; Manship, *Great Yarmouth*, 58, 202; Palmer, *Great Yarmouth*, 337; *Students admitted to the Inner Temple* (L., 1877), 5. Roberts, who had prospered in the law, was for some years Steward and later Town Clerk of Great Yarmouth. He was a native of Beccles, Suffolk.

[3] What was meant to be the largest of the scholarship and fellowship foundations of the period apparently failed for want of funds in the estate. Sir Edward Clere, High Sheriff of Norfolk in 1580, in 1606 bequeathed £66 13s 4d p.a. for fellowships and scholarships in St John's College, Cambridge. It seems certain that Clere's huge debts, which had compelled him to sell much of his estate shortly before his death, consumed the intended legacy. Clere had lived much abroad, always on a grand scale and attended by a great retinue. His funeral in London was a notable event of the year, but he died a poor man. (PCC 99 Stafford 1606; Blomefield, *Norfolk*, VI, 395.)

[4] PCC 39 Parker 1619; Venn, *Caius College*, I, 196, III, 70–73, IV, ii, 97; *Alum. cantab.*, I, i, 207; Blomefield, *Norfolk*, III, 302; DNB. Branthwaite matriculated at Clare from Norwich in 1579. He was graduated B.A. in 1583,

wich fellow of Gonville and Caius, Matthew Stokes, created an even richer endowment for fellowships and scholarships in his college by his will proved in 1635. Stokes, the son of a Norwich merchant and a graduate of the grammar school there, left £4 p.a. for an annual feast on his commemoration date, as well as creating a new fellowship at Caius with an income of £16 p.a. and three scholarships with a total value of £16 10s p.a. Thus the whole of his endowments must have possessed a capital worth of £730, with Norfolk benefiting quite directly since two of the scholars were to be appointed from that county, with an expressed preference for Norwich.[1]

A member of the gentry of the county, John Borage, of North Barsham, in 1636 provided an endowment of £15 p.a., to be paid by a rent-charge levied on his extensive estates, for a fellowship in Clare College, Cambridge, which might not be held for more than five years after the fellow had received his M.A. degree. Borage likewise endowed a scholarship with a value of £5 p.a. in Corpus Christi College, Cambridge, the deeds of gift for both foundations limiting the appointments to natives of Norfolk.[2] Finally, we should mention the foundation under the will of Edward Coleman, of Norwich, at the close of our period, of four scholarships in Corpus Christi College, Cambridge. Coleman charged his estate with an annuity of £20 for the maintenance of this foundation, providing that youths of his own name were to be preferred, but otherwise opening the exhibitions to youths from Norwich and Norfolk.[3]

We have dealt all too briefly with a great cultural achievement. Upwards of £10,000 had been vested in a relatively short period to strengthen the whole fabric of university education by the creation of new and well-endowed fellowships and scholarships, almost exclusively in Cambridge and with a heavy bias indeed for Gonville and Caius. This contribution from one county, itself by no means the richest in

B.D. in 1593, and D.D. in 1598. He was a fellow of Emmanuel from 1585 to 1607 and was appointed Master of Caius in 1607 by royal mandate when Gostlin's election was overruled. An excellent Hebrew scholar, Branthwaite was one of the translators of the revised version of the Bible.

[1] PCC 80 Sadler 1635; Venn, *Caius College*, I, 124, III, 218, 232, IV, ii, 40; *Alum. cantab.*, I, iv, 167. Stokes (1569–1635) was admitted to Caius as a pensioner in 1585. He was graduated B.A. in 1589 and was a fellow of his college from 1592 to 1635, serving as dean for a brief period in 1600–1603.

[2] *Ibid.*, I, i, 261; Blomefield, *Norfolk*, VII, 51; Wardale, J. R., *Clare College* (L., 1899), 125; Cooper, *Memorials of Cambridge*, I, 37. I find no supporting evidence for Blomefield's statement that the Clare foundation was worth £35 p.a. Borage was born at Lackford, Suffolk, and was educated in the grammar school at Bury St Edmunds, at Clare, and at the Middle Temple.

[3] *Alum. cantab.*, I, i, 369; Saunders, *Norwich Grammar School*, 173; Bryant, T. H., *Norfolk churches, hundred of Forehoe* (Norwich, 1905), 217; Cooper, *Memorials of Cambridge*, I, 149.

the realm, was a most notable accomplishment of very great consequence in the history of education and, for that matter, of England. Not
only had the universities been greatly strengthened by this persistent
generosity of Norfolk men, but the whole system of secondary education
in the county, likewise the fruit of private generosity, had been greatly
assisted and matured. We have counted thirty-six fellowships and
scholarships limited to or with a preference for youths from Norfolk
and the schools there so recently constituted and endowed. To this
number should be added the two fellowships and the twelve scholarships
at Caius, endowed by the founder with an expressed limitation to Norwich and the diocese of Norwich, which we have treated as a benefaction
from another county.[1] In all, then, there were something like fifty
places in the universities to which poor boys of the county might
reasonably aspire, at a time when the total enrolment of both universities was not much in excess of 3000. The county of Norfolk had
created cultural institutions which ensured its own great future and
which constituted a noble and an enduring contribution to the history
of the realm.

5. Religion

(a) *General Comment.* Norfolk was by tradition a pious county with great
and esteemed religious foundations which during the Middle Ages had
enjoyed the steady and generous support of its citizens. It was likewise
an old, a populous, and a settled county in which the parochial institutions had on the whole been completed well before the beginning of
our period. Towards the close of the sixteenth century it was organized
into 581 parishes, and, as Fuller reminds us, it possessed a half-century
later 660 churches (and chapels), far more than were to be found in any
other county in the realm.[2] It was also the seat of a great bishopric,
administered during much of our era by men of fine devotion and
ability who afforded a direct and dedicated leadership in the ecclesiastical life of the region. But it also faced the North Sea, and the chill
winds of heresy blew early across its shores. Heresy and a determined
nonconformity gained roots in the commercial and industrial towns of
Norfolk at a very early date—which could not be extirpated despite the
heroic efforts of the bishop and the frightened authorities in Westminster. The traditions of the county and the inclinations of the strong
and articulate commercial aristocracy of Norwich likewise made it an
early and an important centre of Puritan strength in England, resulting
in an almost chronic religious turmoil which had fruitful consequences
in stimulating the intellectual life of the community, however grimly
the central authorities might view the unsettlement of this rich and

---

[1] *Vide* Jordan, *Charities of London*, 262–263.
[2] Fuller, *Worthies*, II, 444.

powerful shire. There remained, as well, scattered among the rural parishes and closely interrelated by blood and marriage, old gentle families who maintained a stubborn devotion to the ancient faith; men and women whose lives and fortunes have been recorded in the quiet and beautiful prose of the saintly Jessopp.

Norfolk was, then, a county of mixed traditions, directly and immediately affected by the great process of religious change that swept England again and again during the course of our period. During the age under study, Norfolk men and women gave for the various religious uses the large sum of £40,939 10s, amounting to 23·01 per cent of the whole of the charitable funds of the county. This proportion, which was almost exactly that provided for educational purposes, was rather less than we should expect when the traditions of the county and the maturity of its religious institutions are taken into account.[1] Furthermore, it is important to observe that of this total, £26,375 1s, or almost two-thirds, was given by pious benefactors during the first interval of our period, in the sixty years prior to the Reformation. During these six decades, to state the facts somewhat differently, approximately 60 per cent of all charitable benefactions made were for one or another of the several religious uses The deep devotion of certain substantial classes of men to the doctrines and the institutions of Catholicism is suggested by the fact that during this interval the very considerable sum of £10,934 6s, or about 41 per cent of all gifts and bequests for religious purposes, was provided for chantries and other forms of prayers for the repose of the souls of the dead, which should have been sufficient for the support of very nearly eighty stipendiary priests had the whole amount been vested in chantry endowments.

In no county in England were the effects of the Reformation more immediate or decisive than in Norfolk. During the twenty years which we have quite arbitrarily defined as the era of the Reformation, the amount provided for all religious purposes fell abruptly to the pitifully small total of £1528 14s, or only 12·38 per cent of the whole amount given for all charitable purposes. The significance of this decline may be indicated when we say that this amount was less than a third as great as that given for the relief of the poor and considerably less than half that given for the various schemes of municipal betterment during these same years. The secularization of life and of aspirations was nearly completed in the Elizabethan period that followed. In the course of this long interval the relatively tiny total of £2499 15s, amounting to only 7·86 per cent of all charitable benefactions, was given for religious needs in this large and populous county. This was an amount representing

---

[1] Norfolk occupied a 'middling' position in the proportion of its charitable funds devoted to religious purposes. These proportions range from 13·18 per cent (Bristol) to 31·94 per cent (Lancashire).

only a small fraction of the huge totals given to the poor and for educational needs, and exceeded only slightly the total provided for various
experiments in social rehabilitation. Further, a large proportion
(42 per cent) of this almost insignificant sum was given for the semi-
civic purpose of repairing the fabric of Norfolk's many churches,
leaving only about £2 10s on the average for clearly religious purposes
in each parish of the county during this generation.

The early Stuart period witnessed a considerable revival of interest
in the then really desperate needs of the church. A total of £9265 1s
was given for all religious purposes, but since this was the generation
when the great outpouring of philanthropy came in Norfolk, the total
represents only slightly more than 14 per cent of all charities. Considerably more than a third (£3459 18s) of the total was given for the repair
of church fabric, in many parishes now in a state of utter dilapidation,
while a somewhat larger sum (£4214 2s) was provided for the augmentation of clerical stipends or for the foundation of Puritan lectureships.
But an almost complete relapse into secularism accompanied the Puritan
Revolution in Norfolk. Though, as we have frequently observed, there
was but slight diminution in the rate of charitable giving during this
short interval, the needs of religion commanded no more than the
insignificant total of £1270 19s, or not quite 5 per cent of the great sum
provided for the charities of the county during these turbulent years.[1]

(b) *The General Uses of the Church.* As we have earlier suggested, the
most reliable measure of the devotion of a county to the needs of the
church may probably be gained by an examination of the charitable
head which we have described as *Church General.* These gifts and
bequests, usually small in amount, were of many kinds: for lights, for
various altars, for the maintenance of the services, and undesignated
gifts for a particular parish church, but they were all meant to lend
support to the direct ministrations of the church and the enrichment of
its services. Until about 1530 such bequests were customary in Norwich, and they remained common in the rural parishes of the county
for still another generation. The church, which had enjoyed a steady
flow of such gifts from the thirteenth century, counted them as an
important part of its parochial revenues, particularly as parochial
tithes came so generally to be diverted into monastic or lay hands. In
the course of our whole period the sum of £4801 8s was given for this
religious use, amounting to 2·70 per cent of the total of the charities of
the county and comparable in significance to such secular concerns as

---

[1] This is a slight statistical overstatement, since various religious gifts which
cannot be exactly dated have for convenience been grouped within this closing
period. These amounts total £278 1s, including £40 for prayers, and hence
somewhat distort our percentages.

apprenticeship endowments and workhouses. In Norfolk, a rather high proportion (63·44 per cent) of these benefactions were in the form of endowments, though most of them were relatively very small and many were in the certainly hazardous capital form of sheep or cattle given in the forlorn hope that a permanent stock for the parish might be created.

The curve of gifts for these parochial purposes is revealing. In the decades prior to the Reformation the large and possibly sufficient sum of £2819 15s was provided by a host of small donors, amounting, it will be observed, to nearly 60 per cent of the total given for this intensely spiritual use during the whole of our period. But in the two decades of reformation the number of these donations fell away in a most precipitous manner, with the result that only £349 4s was so given. The restoration of ecclesiastical stability did not, however, revive men's interest in this basic and continuous need of the church in the Elizabethan age. Quite the contrary. During these forty years the incredibly small total of £383 14s was given for the general uses of the church, the amount sinking to under £30 in two decades of the reign. This means that during this unbelievably secular generation not more than 14s was provided for the support of the religious services of the church in the average Norfolk parish. This is secularism with a vengeance! There was an immediate lifting of the rate of giving for this purpose with the beginning of the Stuart period, though statistically the improvement was decidedly unimpressive. In the course of the early Stuart period a total of £986 1s was given for the general uses of the church, or about 1·5 per cent of all charitable benefactions, as compared with about 1·2 per cent during the Elizabethan era. In the closing interval of our long period these gifts fell away once more to approximately the significance they enjoyed under Elizabeth, a total of £262 14s having been given for this important religious use.

A brief analysis of the structure of these benefactions in a few decades will suggest not only the rapid secularization of English life but the loss by the church of a wide base of popular support. In the first decade of our study, one marked by serious political and social instability, there were sixty-one gifts or bequests noted for the general uses of the church, in amounts ranging from 1d to a capital bequest of £40, the total given being £563 9s. In the decade in which Henry VIII came to the throne, there were 210 separate benefactions for this purpose, in amounts ranging from 1d to a capital gift of £64. The total given during this most pious of all our decades was the considerable sum of £873 6s. The number of such donors fell during the decade of the Henrician Reformation to eighty-eight, though the total of these benefactions reached the relatively large sum of £340 16s. In contrast, the number for the Elizabethan decade 1571–1580, by which time the church settlement was reasonably secure, had further declined to forty-eight, while the

range of gifts had narrowed from 6d to £10, and the total of all gifts for
the general uses of the church had declined to the incredibly low sum
of £21 8s. The charitable interests not only of the forward-looking, the
substantial, and the aggressive groups within the society, but of the
mass of men as well, had by this date shifted dramatically and almost
completely to secular concerns.

(c) *Prayers for the Dead.* The all but complete secularization of the
aspirations of the county after the Reformation is the more remarkable
because of the intense religious commitment of men of wealth in Norfolk who prior to 1540 poured great sums into the endowment of prayers
for the dead. There is abundant evidence that these foundations were
already in disrepute in much of England by the beginning of our period,
not because of any doctrinal doubts or perhaps any question regarding
efficacy, but because of the wretched record of misappropriation and
neglect which had marked the administration of chantries during the
later Middle Ages. It must be said that most large donors of chantry
foundations were cautious, making monasteries, universities, or laymen
trustees for the performance of the terms of the deeds of gift, very frequently with the added protection of reversionary clauses. But they did
none the less give most liberally to this perhaps dubiously charitable use.

Norfolk donors gave in all the large total of £11,328 14s for the
endowment of chantries or for the support of prayers. This represents
the amazing proportion of 6·37 per cent of all the charitable benefactions
provided during our entire period, a proportion placing the county
high in the group to which we are lending attention.[1] Of this sum,
£10,934 6s was given prior to 1540, representing for that period almost
exactly 25 per cent of the whole amount given to charitable causes.
Moreover, a considerable fraction (86·65 per cent) of the total provided
for prayers was in the form of capital endowments, suggesting of
course that these gifts were principally for founding chantries or for
securing lesser stipends for perpetual prayers in a favourite and trusted
monastery or in the donor's parish church. This means that something
like £480 p.a. had been vested for the services of stipendiary priests,
as well as to secure in perpetuity the occasional services of regular and
parochial clergy. This was an amount, as we have pointed out, almost
sufficient to endow eighty stipendiary priests had the whole of this
large sum been settled as chantry endowments. One cannot escape the
reflection, too, that it would have been sufficient for an augmentation
of nearly £1 p.a. for every parish priest in Norfolk in this period. We
should comment at least briefly on a few of the many of these interesting
endowments.

[1] The proportions of charitable funds devoted to prayers range widely from
0·80 per cent for Buckinghamshire to 10·49 per cent for Yorkshire.

An old and pious knight, Sir John Jermy of Metfield, just across the Suffolk border, who had rebuilt the parochial chapel of St John in Metfield before the beginning of our period, on his death in 1487 bequeathed £66 13s 4d to be distributed in alms to the poor, a small legacy for church repairs, and £133 6s 8d to the Abbot of St Bennet's, in Ludham, an executor of his will, for a perpetual chantry, the income to be paid to a stipendiary priest.[1] We have already had occasion to note briefly the ambitious foundation of another gentleman of the county, Simon Blake of Swaffham, on his death in 1489. Blake, who was the founder of an almshouse, vested the manor of Aspall's, in Swaffham, on feoffees under instruction to employ the income to secure the services of a chantry priest who was to have a stipend of eight marks, to say prayers in the chantry chapel which he had recently built in Swaffham church, as well as 7s 4d p.a. for an obit which he desired to be said yearly on his commemoration day.[2] Similar provisions were made under the will of a Norwich merchant, Thomas Bokenham, in 1492, creating an endowment of perhaps £140 for the maintenance of a chantry, the priest who served it to have in perpetuity a stipend of eight marks annually.[3]

Thomas Briggs, of Sall, a friend of John Paston and a member of an old gentle family, by his will proved in 1494 made a number of bequests for religious uses. He left £10 for general church needs in Sall and legacies totalling £25 for the repair of three Norfolk churches, but his principal interest was in the endowment of prayers for the repose of his soul. During his lifetime he had built a chapel in Sall church at an uncertain cost, and for the service of this chantry he provided approximately £60 to ensure the singing of masses for a period of ten years. Briggs likewise settled £66 13s 4d on the priory of Binham to ensure perpetual prayers there, while an equal amount for the same use was bequeathed to the Grey Friars of Norwich, in whose monastic precincts he was buried before the high altar.[4] Briggs' chantry endowments were typical of the legacies of the pious gentry of the county. Another and similar instance might be cited. In 1505 Walter Hough, a gentleman of Worstead, left a total of £271 to various charities. His concerns were by no means exclusively spiritual, for £20 was given for marriage portions, £10 (partly estimated) for the repair of roads, £4 for the relief

---

[1] CCN 332–333 A. Caston 1487; Blomefield, *Norfolk*, V, 386, VII, 213. Jermy was lord of four Norfolk manors.

[2] *Vide ante*, 115, 147.

[3] PCC 17 Dogett 1492; Cozens-Hardy, *Mayors of Norwich*, 33. Bokenham was a raffman or chandler by trade. A wealthy merchant, he was sheriff in 1469, represented Norwich in Parliament in 1472, and served as mayor for two terms. Bokenham also left £6 to monasteries, £4 to church repairs, 6s to church general, 7s to Norman's Hospital, and £2 for the repair of the city gates.

[4] CCN 202–205 Wolman 1494; Blomefield, *Norfolk*, IV, 111, 216, VIII, 270.

of prisoners, and a small legacy to Norman's Hospital in Norwich. But the will likewise provided capital sums totalling £166 for four series of endowed masses to be sung at Cambridge, £4 to the general uses of the church in the four parishes in which he held lands, £4 outright for church repairs, and an estimated £60 for building a vestry at Worstead.[1]

We have already dealt with the substantial bequests left by Bishop James Goldwell to the poor of Norwich, where he was bishop from 1472 until his death in 1499. But the bulk of his fortune was left for religious purposes. He bequeathed various vestments and antiphonaries to five churches, as well as £50 to All Souls College for the ornamentation of the high altar of its chapel. Scattered bequests to the monastic clergy of Norwich and elsewhere totalled £18. There were likewise outright bequests of about £38 to various monastic churches for prayers. He settled 6s 8d each Sunday on twenty poor men who should pray for him for a period of three years and thereafter £4 6s 8d p.a. for such meritorious supplications of the poor. Goldwell left as well £146 for the foundation of a chantry in All Souls College, while, following the injunctions of his will, his executors founded in Norwich a perpetual chantry with an endowment of about £400, to support three stipendiary priests. In all, therefore, something like £636 of Goldwell's private fortune was devoted to the endowment of prayers.[2] Similar charitable dispositions were made in 1503 by John Norris, the priest at South Lynn. Norris left £1 to the poor, a total of £3 7s for the repair of his own and four nearby churches, and 3s 4d to the friars in Lynn and South Lynn. Scattered legacies totalling £1 10s were left to nunneries and to an anchorite for immediate prayers, while land with an indicated capital value of about £120 was vested in his executors, the church reeves and a local guild, to provide an endowment for a stipendiary priest, as well as 1s 9d p.a. for certain connected observances.[3]

The mercantile aristocracy of Norfolk was much more prudent in its outlays for prayers than were the clergy and gentry of the county, being especially distrustful of endowed chantries. In most instances, in fact, the amounts left for prayers by merchants and tradesmen were nominal, though there were exceptions in addition to those previously cited. Thus in 1501 Richard Ferrour, a Norwich dyer and metal merchant, among charitable bequests totalling £133 8s, left £9 outright for prayers by the regular clergy as well as making provision for prayers during a period of ten years at a charge of £53 7s.[4] A former mayor of Lynn, William Awnflys, in 1507 left £133 6s 8d for masses to be spread over

[1] PCC 42 Holgrave 1505.   [2] Vide ante, 115.
[3] CCN 448–450 Popy 1504; Blomefield, Norfolk, VIII, 547; Chadwick, J. N., Memorials of South Lynn (Lynn, 1851), 15–20.
[4] PCC 7 Blamyr 1501; Cozens-Hardy, Mayors of Norwich, 31–32. Ferrour also left £28 11s (partly estimated) for church repairs, £37 15s to the poor, £2 5s to hospitals, and £2 10s for the repair of the city walls.

a period of twenty years, as well as bequeathing £30 for general charitable purposes, £4 to the monastic clergy, £3 for church repairs, and £2 13s for general church purposes.[1] To conclude, a Norwich draper, William Potter, in the same year provided £110 6s of capital to ensure prayers and £1 7s for immediate masses, these being the principal among charitable benefactions totalling £124 11s.[2]

But the gentry of the county remained the most important and certainly the most persistent founders of chantries. Perhaps instances chosen from the class during the brief interval 1505–1510 will suffice to suggest their conservative temper. In 1505 Sir William Boleyn, the grandfather of Anne Boleyn, left £20 7s for church repairs and an estimated £5 for the poor of Blickling. He likewise instructed his executor to provide forty marks a year to secure prayers by four secular priests, three in Norwich Cathedral and one in Cambridge, during a period of twenty years, as well as monastic prayers, laying an ultimate charge of nearly £550 on his estate.[3] A year later (1506), Robert Smith of Cockley Cley, left funds for paving his parish church and setting up a stone cross on the 'hill between Lyn and Cley' and another 'in the ling at South Pickenham gate', as well as bequeathing lands worth approximately £60 to the priory of Ingham to secure prayers there during a term of a hundred years, after which the land, comprising thirteen acres, was to be sold and the funds invested in plate for the priory.[4] In the same year, one of the most substantial of the gentry of the county, Sir Roger Le Strange, left large charitable bequests to widely scattered churches and parishes where he held lands, which, when reduced to capital amounts, total £1176 5s. The sum of £80 was provided for university scholarships, £100 over a period of twenty years was to be spent on alms, while £15 was to be disbursed immediately as doles for the poor of twelve Norfolk parishes. His will left, as well, a total of £184 5s for the repair and ornamentation of numerous parish churches, £70 principally for the monastic clergy, £20 for general church uses, and approximately £707 for prayers.[5] The widow of Sir Henry Heydon, Dame Anne, left a particularly complicated will on her

[1] PCC 31 Adeane 1507; Blomefield, *Norfolk*, VIII, 533.

[2] PCC 26 Adeane 1507.

[3] PCC 40 Holgrave 1505; Blomefield, *Norfolk*, IV, 33–35; *Norf. Arch.*, XXV (1934), 399–400; DNB. William Boleyn was the son of Sir Geoffrey, a rich London merchant who was mayor in 1457. His wife was a daughter and coheir of Thomas Butler, Earl of Ormonde; his daughters married men of great wealth and good status; his son, Thomas, was his heir.

[4] CCN 368–369 Ryxe 1506; Blomefield, *Norfolk*, VI, 44.

[5] PCC 2 Adeane 1506; *Norf. Arch.*, IX (1884), 226–239; Blomefield, *Norfolk*, X, 318; Burke, John and J. B., eds., *Extinct and dormant baronetcies* (L., 1844), 311. Sir Roger was the son and heir of Sir Henry Le Strange of Hunstanton. He succeeded in 1485 and was appointed High Sheriff of Norfolk in 1495. His brother, Sir Robert (d. 1511) was his heir.

death in 1510, with widely scattered bequests to monastic houses and for other charitable uses. She was generous in her dispositions for the relief of Norwich prisoners and provided £11 10s for doles to the poor in various parishes, £1 in alms, and 10s for the sick. But her principal concerns were religious, since she left £18 for church repairs, £8 to the regular clergy, and bequests of £176 6s, in part estimated, for prayers.[1]

(d) *Support of Monasticism.* The pronounced and persistent religious conservatism of Norfolk during the earliest of our periods is likewise demonstrated by the relatively generous support given, particularly by the gentry, to the many monastic foundations that dotted the county. In all, donors during this interval gave £2008 1s for various monastic uses, an amount markedly greater than that provided in most of the rural counties examined. This sum was given almost wholly, it should be noted, to monasteries within the county boundaries. But this amount is placed in a far more meaningful light when we reflect that it was not more than 7·61 per cent of the large total given for religious purposes of all kinds during this interval of remarkable pious generosity. This was true despite the fact that Norfolk possessed a number of famous and very old monasteries which were by no means reticent in making known their claims on the piety of testators. The monasteries of the county enjoyed annual revenues of £5180 5s 6d at the time of the Dissolution, or a capital worth of perhaps £103,605, Norfolk ranking ninth among the counties of England in the wealth of its many houses. But this great legacy of the past was by no means enhanced by the piety of the two generations of men immediately prior to the Reformation. The bequests and gifts we have recorded represent an increase of not quite 2 per cent in the value of these assets, a rate of growth far less than would be required simply to keep pace with the inevitable inroads of time, fire, flood, and mismanagement. The plain fact is that the monasteries had outlived their social usefulness and very possibly their spiritual usefulness as well. Of the great wealth vested in them just before the Expropriation, only £136 5s p.a. was being disbursed under trusts in alms in Norfolk. This is approximately 2·6 per cent of their income and represents a capital worth of only £2725, an amount within the attainment of many private donors of Norfolk in, say, 1540. The social returns, as reckoned by this ultimate measure, were simply too scant and marginal.

(e) *Maintenance of the Clergy.* Prior to the Reformation, most gifts and bequests made to the clergy of Norfolk, whether regular or secular, were small in amount, but they were very numerous indeed. In this period, too, they were normally outright gifts for immediate use, which

[1] PCC 28 Bennett 1510; Gurney, *House of Gournay*, 823–829. *Vide ante,* 119.

must have augmented clerical income to a considerable degree, that of the parochial clergy in particular. During this first interval the not insubstantial total of £724 17s was given for the better support of the clergy of the county, while even during the next two decades of ecclesiastical unsettlement these gifts were continued at approximately the same decade rate, the sum of £234 19s having been provided.

As we have frequently observed, the Reformation on balance brought no real financial relief for an already hard-pressed parochial clergy in England. The quality of the clergy was markedly improved by the skilful and steady attention of the Elizabethan bishops and, quite as importantly, by the insistence of a better informed laity, but the financial plight of the parochial clergy and of their churches became steadily more critical as this long and intensely secular reign wore on. At least scattered efforts were accordingly made by private donors to augment clerical livings by endowments. In the Elizabethan era in Norfolk a total of £630 12s was supplied for this purpose, almost the whole of which was in the form of capital gifts. These augmentations were notably increased under the early Stuarts, when £2570 2s was provided, or substantially more than half the total of £4279 15s given for the better maintenance of the clergy during the whole of the long period under survey.

Simultaneously, modest efforts were being made in Norfolk, after 1581, by Puritan benefactors to secure a godly and a soundly Calvinistic clergy by the endowment of lectureships. In all, £1820 was provided for this purpose during the critical years 1581–1620, of which at least a few typical bequests may be noted. Thus in 1586 Edmond Gresham of Thorpe Market, the third son of the great London merchant, Sir John, 'hoping to be onely saved by the merittes of my savyor and redemer Jesus Christ . . . by whose death and passion I hope to haue remission and forgivenes of all my sinnes', founded a lectureship in the village of Southrepps, a short distance to the east of Thorpe Market. He charged his estate with an annual payment of £8 as a stipend to some learned clergyman, to be chosen by his heirs with the advice of three godly preachers, who should weekly read a divinity lecture 'for the godly instruction of suche as be desyrous to knowe and learne the waye of salvac'on'.[1] Gresham's discreet and careful endowment was typical of the methods used by Puritan gentlemen who, all over England, were endeavouring to reform the church from within by building a clergy which would more faithfully reflect their own stalwart views. Some years later, in 1619, Henry Peart, a gentleman of Norwich, left

[1] PCC 64 Windsor 1586; Blomefield, *Norfolk*, VIII, 152; Leveson Gower, *Family of Gresham*, 7–8, 17, 32, 88–92. Edmond Gresham married a daughter of Augustine Hinde, a rich London merchant. He retired to Norfolk, long the seat of his family, settling there as a member of the gentry. He inherited manors in Norfolk and Surrey from his father, as well as the reversion of two more manors on the death of his mother.

the income from a farm in Essex, with a capital value of approximately £500, for the maintenance of a preaching minister at Mountnessing, Essex, and a lecturer in London.[1] In all, seven such lectureships were appointed in Norfolk by donors of the county, while four were provided by them in other parts of England, since these were men animated by a zeal and a vision of truth which knew no parochial or, for that matter, national bounds.

(f) *Care of the Fabric*. The neglect of the clergy in Norfolk was far more serious than the decay of the church fabric. During our whole period the considerable total of £13,004 13s was given for the ordinary repair and maintenance of the possibly 600 church structures of the county, the cathedral church, save for the small total provided by private benefactions, being excluded from our accounts. This impressive amount constituted almost a third of the whole given for religious uses during our period and comprised 7·31 per cent of all the charitable benefactions of the county, being a much larger proportion than has been found in any other county save Kent.[2] This means that about £21 13s was on the average provided for the many churches of this large and certainly heavily 'churched' county. But the average is most deceptive, since this sum was not evenly spread over the whole period. Far more than half the total (£7356 3s) was given during the six decades prior to the Reformation; this we may well believe represented the contribution required for the normal care of the immense investment made by medieval piety in the church fabric of the county. There was a sharp diminution of giving for the purpose during the era of the Reformation, when only £590 3s was disposed for these routine repairs and for the embellishment of churches. In the next, and the most coldly secular of all our periods, Elizabethan benefactors gave no more than £1049 9s for this purpose during the long span of forty years. This means, in average terms, that not quite £1 15s was given for the care of the fabric of each church in the county, thus documenting the widespread complaints that churches were being permitted to decay for want of interest and assistance on the part of parishioners. The early Stuart period witnessed at least a modest revival of private responsibility for the repair and maintenance of parish churches, but the £3459 18s provided during these years was wholly inadequate for the now pressing need for the repair of Elizabethan dilapidations. And even this support all but disappeared during the era of political and religious disturbances, when the incredibly scant total of £549 was given for church repairs and decoration.

---

[1] PCC 80 Parker 1619. The bequest was subject to the life enjoyment of the profits of the farm by his widow.

[2] In Kent 7·60 per cent of all charitable funds were given for this use.

These dramatic and profoundly important shifts in men's aspirations during the course of our period may be documented by at least a summary presentation of a portion of the detailed evidence from two of our time intervals. Thus, during the years prior to the Reformation, there were hundreds of small bequests or gifts for the repair of the fabric, the maintenance of interiors, or for the embellishment of the service, as well as a number of substantial sums given for such purposes. At Aylsham a chapel was refitted in 1489 by the generosity of local benefactors; a church porch was added at about the same date at the charge of Richard Howard of Norwich; and a few years later (1507) the roof was repaired by several inhabitants of the town.[1] In 1493 William Lynster of Tibenham gave lands with a capital worth of £200, the income of which was to be used for the repair and adornment of the parish church.[2] At about the same date Thomas Amys of Barton Turf left bequests totalling £11 7s for a cope, the repair of bells, and the amendment of the fabric of his local church.[3] A member of the upper gentry, Sir Edmond Bedingfield, in 1496 provided £10 in his will for the leading of the church of Caldecote,[4] while a similar bequest of £20 to his parish church was made for this purpose in 1500 by a Norwich burgher, John Jowell, a parishioner of St Lawrence.[5] Another Norwich tradesman, James Cootes, in 1502 provided two copes for his parish church at a charge of £25 and repaired and refurbished a chapel at an estimated cost of £40.[6] Agnes Parker, a Norwich widow, left £6 8s for the repair of St Michael Coslany in 1505, as well as a modest rent-charge for maintaining a lamp before the rood.[7] In the same year a Norwich priest, Thomas Daywell, left an estimated £8 10s for glazing two windows and providing a new lectern for the choir in St Martin's church,[8] while in 1507 a Norwich draper, Henry Wilton, gave £5 to buy needed lead for the steeple of St Peter Mancroft.[9] Minor repairs were undertaken at Swaffham in 1507–1511 at a total cost of £5 10s, though not quite certainly by public subscription,[10] while Alexander

[1] Blomefield, *Norfolk*, VI, 277–278.
[2] The property was let for £28 p.a. in 1652. Lynster also left lands with approximately £80 capital value for general municipal uses (*vide ante*, 144).
[3] PCC 28 Vox 1496; Waters-Withington MSS.; Rye, Walter, *Early English inscriptions in Norfolk* (L., n.d.), 37. *Vide post*, 189.
[4] PCC 7 Horne 1496; *Norf. Arch.*, XXVII (1941), 336.
[5] PCC 2 Moone 1500; *Norf. Arch.*, XXVII (1941), 336; Blomefield, *Norfolk*, III, 192. Jowell also left £20, paid by his executors in 1509, to rebuild the local wool-houses.
[6] Blomefield, *Norfolk*, IV, 141.
[7] CCN 226–227 Ryxe 1505; Rye MSS., No. 33, Norwich; Blomefield, *Norfolk*, IV, 497.
[8] CCN 193–194 Ryxe 1505; Blomefield, *Norfolk*, IV, 369.
[9] CCN 42–46 Spyltymber 1507; Blomefield, *Norfolk*, IV, 214.
[10] Rix, *Swaffham*, 45–46.

Pynnes of East Dereham gave 6s 8d towards the purchase of a new bell for his church in 1508.[1] These few examples will perhaps suffice to illustrate the quality and the great variety of the gifts made for church repairs, which amounted in all for the decade 1501–1510 to £2195 16s, considerably more than was given for any other single charitable purpose with the exception of chantry endowments.

To pass to a briefer interval, 1516–1518, it is clear that concern for and pride in the church fabric of the county remained widespread in the early Henrician period. In a will drawn in 1516 Richard Duplake of Hilborough left twenty marks for repairs on the aisle of his parish church and towards making a new porch,[2] while John Hamelyn, Rector of Barnham Broom, gave forty marks for the leading of the chancel of his church.[3] William Smyth of Knapton in 1517 provided £7 for the purchase of a chasuble and other religious objects for his church;[4] in the following year Ralph Goodwyn of North Burlingham left a total of £4 3s for repairs on three churches, or chapels, and towards the building of steeples in two other churches of the county.[5] William Bisby, a Norwich draper, in 1518 left £12 19s for the repair of the roof of St Simon and St Jude, a new vestment for the church, and £2 for a cope for a Lincolnshire church.[6] In addition, some sixteen bequests of less than £1 each have been recorded during this brief period for the fabric of other Norfolk churches.

In the next decade, 1521–1530, though the Reformation was at hand, there was no immediate slackening of the interest of Norfolk benefactors in the church structures of the county. During these years a total of £1235 1s was provided for these purposes, from benefactors of all social classes and in amounts ranging from 2d to an estimated sum of £321. Among these contributions was the bequest of William Fuller, a gentleman of Castle Acre, who in 1523 provided £6 for the repair of a monastic fabric and £120 for repairing the aisle of his church, the buttresses, and the end of a church wall.[7] A merchant of King's Lynn, Thomas Mason, in the next year, after making modest dispositions for an obit to 'continue as long as God's law and the King's will suffer it', bequeathed the residue of certain properties, with an approximate capital value of £321, for the repair of St Margaret's church in his

---

[1] PCC 7 Bennett 1508; *Norf. Arch.*, XXVII (1941), 337.

[2] CCN 67–68 Briggs 1518; Blomefield, *Norfolk*, VI, 113.

[3] CCN 19–21 Gylys 1516; Blomefield, *Norfolk*, II, 378.

[4] CCN 17–18 Gylys 1517; Hoare, C. M., *History of an East Anglian soke* (Bedford, 1918), 460.

[5] CCN 50–59 Gylys 1518; *Norf. Arch.*, I (1847), 262; Blomefield, *Norfolk*, VII, 226, XI, 92, 96, 142.

[6] CCN 76 Gylys 1518; Blomefield, *Norfolk*, IV, 363; Waters-Withington MSS.

[7] PCC 14 Bodfelde 1523.

native city.[1] Thomas Strutte of Burgh (near Aylsham) left ten marks towards the repair of the roof of his church in 1524,[2] while Henry Palmer of Moulton shortly afterwards provided £16 13s 4d and timber of unspecified value towards the repair of the roof of his parish church and the building of a rood loft.[3]

These are at least fragmentary instances of the interest and the persistent responsibility borne by men and women of all classes of society for the maintenance and embellishment of the church fabric in the 'age of piety' in Norfolk. In dramatic contrast stands the indifference of the Elizabethan era, when the whole of the immense investment in the parochial churches of the county was almost completely neglected, for, as we have noted, only slightly more than £1000 was spent on these edifices during this long, prosperous, but sternly secular age. Such repairs as were ordered by private charity were for the cure or the prevention of collapse. Hence James Calthorp, a gentleman of Cockthorpe, in 1559 repaired the roof and provided lead for the south aisle of his church at an estimated charge of £40.[4] A yeoman of Upton, Richard Taylor, in 1588 contributed £1 to the repair of his church and £4 towards the rebuilding of its steeple, which had been permitted to collapse.[5] Badly needed, if minor, work was done on the spire of St Gregory's, Norwich, in 1597, though more extensive repairs and adornments had to wait until 1626 when £110 was laid out on repairs, half being raised by rates and the remainder by gifts from Norwich merchants and the county gentry. These are among the relatively few outlays undertaken during the Elizabethan period by private means in order to secure the preservation of the magnificent Gothic and Norman inheritance with which the Middle Ages had endowed the county. Nor, as we have already indicated, was there any really substantial increase in the amounts provided for the care of the ecclesiastical fabric of Norfolk during the early Stuart age, despite the more favourable attitude of the central authorities. It is true that in the decade when Laud's somewhat frantic ministrations were at their height (1631–1640), gifts for this use rose to £1805 10s, but, this one brief and bitter interval aside, it is all too clear that from 1531 to the end of our period the church fabric of Norfolk was almost completely neglected.

(g) *Church Building.* The evidence for the increasingly secular preoccupations of Norfolk donors and the incredible neglect of the ecclesiastical needs of the county is even more dramatically suggested when

[1] PCC F. 27 Bodfelde 1524; *PP* 1835, XXI, 700; Blomefield, *Norfolk*, VI, 217, 221. *Vide post*, 190.
[2] CCN 228–229 Alblaster 1524; Blomefield, *Norfolk*, VI, 429.
[3] CCN 3–6 Palgrave 1526; Blomefield, *Norfolk*, XI, 110.
[4] PCC 28 Chaynay 1559; Blomefield, *Norfolk*, IX, 217.
[5] Hill, P. O., *A history of Upton, Norfolk* (Norwich, 1891), 58, 124.

we examine the record of church building, including major renovations or enlargements of structures. In all, only £5605 was provided for this purpose by donors during the whole of our period, amounting to a scant 3 per cent (3·15 per cent) of all charitable gifts and roughly comparable to the sums given for apprenticeships or loan funds for tradesmen. Even more significantly, almost the whole of this relatively very small sum was given during the decades prior to the Reformation, the substantial total of £4540 (or 81 per cent) having been provided in this one brief interval. The tiny total of £260 was given for this use during the whole of the next interval of the same length, 1541–1600, when it is evident that in Norfolk, as in most of England, interest in church building or the major alteration of existing churches simply disappeared. There was a slight enhancement of interest during the early Stuart age, when £605 was given for church building, and then an almost total eclipse of interest during the two decades of civil war and political unsettlement.

In Norfolk private donors spent more than twice as much on church repairs as on church building; this is unusual, a relationship quite exceptional in our study of repairs and building. In part, this withering of interest in church building might have been due to the fact that no other county in the realm in 1480 possessed so many completed parish churches; even taking in view size and population, no other county probably had so many. But the almost complete ending of such building in 1540 is too dramatic for this to rest as a wholly sufficient explanation, particularly when we have quite incidental evidence that upwards of thirty of the more than six hundred churches of the county were destroyed during our period by fire, wind, or dilapidations so complete as to make the buildings unfit for use. These churches were simply not replaced during our period, save in the few instances which we shall record. In Norfolk, as in the whole of England, other aspirations and other social and cultural concerns had come to engage men's minds and to command the ultimate sanction of their resources.

In the course of our period we have noted the construction of thirteen chapels in existing churches at a total charge to the donors which we have very roughly estimated at £520. Among the more important of these were the lady chapel in a Norwich church built by John Le Grice in 1494;[1] that provided by a wool merchant, Robert Foster, at Mattishall in 1507 at a charge of £26 13s;[2] a chapel built in Norwich before 1518 by Thomas Large, a leading merchant of his day, for approximately £40;[3] the more elaborate chapel built by Sir Thomas Windham in Norwich Cathedral at a cost of perhaps £200 some time before 1522;[4]

[1] CCN 82–84 Cage 1500; Blomefield, Norfolk, IV, 127.
[2] CCN 487 Ryxe 1507; Blomefield, Norfolk, X, 239.
[3] CCN 95–96 Gylys 1518; Blomefield, Norfolk, IV, 67.
[4] PCC 3 Bodfelde 1522; Blomefield, Norfolk, IV, 7, VIII, 112; DNB.

and, to pass to the Elizabethan period, the chapel provided by Richard Nicholls of Tilney at a cost of £60 in 1574,[1] and the side chapel built at Stow Bardolph in 1589 by Nicholas Hare.[2]

Norfolk donors were far less affected than those of most counties we have examined by the general enthusiasm of the early sixteenth century for building church towers and vexing the fabric with porches. In all, we believe we can estimate with reasonable accuracy, something like £410 was expended by private benefactors during the course of our period for such conspicuous, if not needed, improvements on existing churches. Among them may be mentioned the building of the church tower at Ingham in *ca.* 1491, to which the Rector of Sutton, Roger King, had bequeathed 6s 8d two years earlier;[3] the construction of the south porch and belfry at Fersfield in 1494, aided by a bequest of four marks from Jeffrey Ellingham;[4] the new tower built at South Walsham under the urging of the priest, Miles Walker, who in 1495 left £3 6s 8d for the purpose;[5] the porch built at St Peter Hungate (Norwich) about 1497 by Nicholas Ingham, a mercer, at a cost of about £20;[6] and the relatively large bequest of £26 13s made by Walter Cooper of Terrington towards the building of a new steeple at that place in 1499.[7]

During the first decade of the sixteenth century, building of this type reached considerable proportions in many parts of the county. Thus at East Dereham something like £40 was given and spent on the construction of a large tower to support the bells to which the community aspired, though the work was never completed.[8] A similar tower was finished at Carleton-Rode in about 1502,[9] while a new porch may have been started at Tottington in the next year.[10] William Taylor of Bunwell left £1 13s 4d towards the building of a steeple in that parish in 1505, to be paid out at the rate of 6s 8d each year while the masons were engaged on the construction,[11] and the bequest of a 'bondsman' of the same parish, John Hirnynge, for this purpose in the next year suggests that the work was well begun.[12] The steeple of St Lawrence church

[1] *Vide ante,* 158.
[2] Messent, C. J. W., *The parish churches of Norfolk* (Norwich, 1936), 228.
[3] CCN 31 Wolman 1489; *Norf. Arch.,* VIII (1879), 206.
[4] *Vide ante,* 144.
[5] PCC 30 Vox 1495; *Norf. Arch.,* XXVII (1941), 337.
[6] CCN 2 Wight 1499; Royal Archaeological Institute, *Memoirs of Norfolk* (L., 1851), 171.
[7] PCC 7 Moone 1499; *Norf. Arch.,* XXVII (1941), 337.
[8] Messent, *Parish churches of Norfolk,* 71; Blomefield, *Norfolk,* X, 212.
[9] Blomefield, *Norfolk,* V, 125.
[10] CCN 256–258 Popy 1503; *The East Anglian,* I (1864), 158.
[11] CCN 241 Ryxe 1505; Blomefield, *Norfolk,* V, 133. The tower was finished *ca.* 1520.
[12] Davenport, F. G., *The economic development of a Norfolk manor* (Cambridge, 1906), App., lxxx.

(Norwich) was being built by private subscription in 1508,[1] as was a porch for another church in the same city.[2]

Most construction of this kind had been completed in Norfolk before 1520; there was little of it indeed after 1540. Extensive repairs were undertaken on the steeple and bells of the church at Redenhall in 1585 and in 1623.[3] The steeple at Stanfield was heightened and roofed with lead in 1607 at a charge of £9 13 11d,[4] while the north porch at Rockland St Peter was built in 1619 at an estimated cost of £20.[5] These, so far as our records disclose, comprise the principal private outlays for building of this sort in the years 1541-1620.

An almost identical curve of interest is to be observed in the expenditure of the sum of £4675 which we have estimated was provided by Norfolk benefactors for the building of new churches and chapels of ease during our long period or, more commonly, for the rebuilding of old churches which had decayed or had been destroyed. In all there appear to have been twenty-one churches built or rebuilt during the course of our period, with one other (Alderford) regarding which we have little information save that it was completed at the charge of one Richard Angos in 1523.[6] Though there was more new construction in Norfolk than in many other counties during our period, it represented an addition of not more than 4 per cent to the churches and chapels already completed in 1480 and fell far short of replacing the many architectural casualties that were to occur during this span of almost two centuries. Further, as we shall now note, almost the whole of this building was concentrated with a kind of late medieval fervour in the relatively short interval just prior to the Reformation.

The parish church at New Buckenham has not been counted in the group under discussion, since it had been built in stages and appears to have been completed about 1480, when Sir John Knevet built the south aisle, porch, and tower.[7] The chapel at Shotesham was built in 1486 by Bartholomew White, who died a few years later.[8] Sir William Calthorp, a rich member of the upper gentry of the county, rebuilt the church of St Mary in North Creake in about 1494, as well as providing £74 6s for the completion of work already begun on the choir and presbytery

---

[1] Blomefield, *Norfolk*, IV, 270.   [2] *Ibid.*, IV, 105.

[3] Candler, Charles, *Notes on the parish of Redenhall* (L., 1896), 63-64; L'Estrange, John, *The church bells of Norfolk* (Norwich, 1874), 195-196. Outlays totalling £21 10s were undertaken on the bells and the general repair of this church in 1623. *Vide* Candler, 143-145, for very interesting and detailed expense accounts.

[4] Carthew, G. A., *The hundred of Launditch* (Norwich, 1877-1879, 3 vols.), II, 477.

[5] Blomefield, *Norfolk*, I, 477.

[6] CCN 212-213 Alblaster 1524; Wortley, J. D., *Alderford church* (Norwich, 1928), 10; Blomefield, *Norfolk*, VIII, 184.

[7] *Ibid.*, I, 397.   [8] *Ibid.*, V, 505.

of Creake Abbey.[1] Just a year later, Sir James Hobart, the great Norfolk lawyer whose secular benefactions have already been discussed, rebuilt the church at Loddon at something like the same cost.[2] In the same year, 1496, Thomas Amys, who had made a considerable fortune in the wool trade, died leaving generous and widely dispersed bequests for religious purposes, having somewhat earlier provided a chapel at Barton Turf, presumably his birthplace.[3] Many legacies and outright gifts were provided for the rebuilding of the church at Tacolneston at a charge of upwards of £300 during the first decade of the sixteenth century.[4]

During the decades just prior to the Reformation there was likewise considerable church building in Norwich, principally financed by members of the prosperous burgher aristocracy of the city. St Michael Coslany was all but rebuilt between 1479 and 1511, when the work engaged the interest and support of many citizens, including John and Stephen Stalon, both of whom were sheriffs, and William Ramsey, a mayor of the city.[5] Similarly, building was in progress almost continuously on St Andrew's from about 1500, when the old chancel was pulled down and rebuilding and enlargement begun, until 1506, when the work seems to have been completed. Gifts and legacies totalling £220 have been noted for this substantial undertaking, whose total cost we are unable to appraise. Among these benefactions were bequests from Robert Gardiner, thrice Mayor of Norwich, in 1508 of £10 for glazing the windows of the north aisle as well as an unspecified amount to provide the stools for the church; from a widow, Agnes East, who gave £20 towards the rebuilding; from another woman, Clare Withnale, who left £6 13s 4d for the same purpose in 1503, not to mention the bequest of £13 6s 8d provided by her husband in the same year; and the legacy of Nicholas Colich, a grocer who had been mayor in 1497, who gave £33 6s 8d towards the rebuilding, £6 13s 4d for a new vestment, £7 for a new legend, and a silver vessel valued at £17.[6] The church of St Stephen, also in Norwich, was likewise in a decayed state at the close of the fifteenth century. Extensive repairs, amounting to a rebuilding, of the nave and steeple were undertaken in 1501 and carried forward for more than a generation. In this instance, however, it appears that most of the charges were borne by the convent and the

[1] CCN 206–207 Wolman 1494; Bryant, *Norfolk churches, Brothercross*, 78, 137–138, 151; *East Anglian*, II (1866), 210–212.

[2] *Vide ante*, 148.

[3] *Vide ante*, 183.

[4] Blomefield, *Norfolk*, V, 168; Messent, *Parish churches of Norfolk*, 235.

[5] Blomefield, *Norfolk*, IV, 496–497.

[6] Blomefield, *Norfolk*, IV, 303–305, 312; Messent, *Parish churches of Norfolk*, 154; *Norf. Arch.*, III (1852), 192–193; Cozens-Hardy *Mayors of Norwich*, 35–38.

vicar, private benefactions for the rebuilding of no more than £56 having been noted for the long period 1501-1550.[1]

The church at Knapton was built about 1504 at an estimated charge of £200, principally by the generosity of John Smith, the clergyman, and Thomas Franke, of this parish.[2] A member of the lower gentry, Thomas Hoot, provided a chapel at Yelverton at a charge of approximately £120 in 1505.[3] At about the same time extensive building was under way on St Margaret's in King's Lynn. The north aisle was added in 1502-1510 with the help of gifts, amounting to upwards of £80, from the great local merchant and benefactor, Thomas Thoresby, whose will provided that the battlement should be completed by his executors and who added £5 outright towards the cost of construction, as well as £40 for vestments for the re-edified and enlarged church.[4] That the work lagged following Thoresby's death is suggested by a bequest from another local merchant, Thomas Mason, made in 1524 for its further and more vigorous prosecution.[5] The handsome tower at Redenhall, begun in the fifteenth century, was at last completed in *ca.* 1520 by the efforts of local donors, but had later to be extensively repaired when it was damaged by storms in 1585 and 1616.[6] The church at North Lopham was rebuilt during a period of about a half-century by many small local donors, the last gift for this purpose being in the amount of £1 towards the construction of the steeple in 1526.[7] Sir Roger Pilkington began the rebuilding of the church at Bressingham about the time of the accession of Henry VII, the work having been completed at a cost of perhaps £350 in 1527, some years after Pilkington's death.[8] A full generation was also required for the construction of the church at Saxthorpe (*ca.* 1482-1536), which was principally financed by the contributions of the lord of the manor, successive vicars, and the local tenantry.[9] A vain effort was made to rebuild the church at Hackford, which had burned in *ca.* 1542, when Anthony Sugate left £13 7s for that purpose,[10] while in the next year the church at Middle Harling was razed.[11]

In all, our evidence would suggest that nineteen churches were built or rebuilt during the six decades just prior to the Reformation. This was a relatively high figure if one takes in view the great number of churches

[1] Blomefield, *Norfolk*, IV, 146.

[2] *Ibid.*, VIII, 134; *Norf. Arch.*, XXVI (1938), 95. Franke (*alias* Tanner) gave £26 13s towards the construction costs.

[3] CCN 190-191 Ryxe 1505; Blomefield, *Norfolk*, V, 494.

[4] *Vide ante*, 152-153.   [5] *Vide ante*, 184.

[6] Candler, *Redenhall*, 26-29; Blomefield, *Norfolk*, V, 361-362. *Vide ante*, 188.

[7] Blomefield, *Norfolk*, I, 232-233.

[8] *Ibid.*, I, 66; Messent, *Parish churches of Norfolk*, 42.

[9] Blomefield, *Norfolk*, VI, 499.   [10] *Ibid.*, VIII, 225-226, 295.

[11] *Ibid.*, I, 315.

already completed prior to 1480 and probably roughly equalled the number destroyed or abandoned because of the dilapidations to which Gothic architecture is peculiarly subject. But with the year 1540, in church building as in so many other forms of religious need, the support of the county and the interest of donors were abruptly withdrawn. We have no record of any church building begun by private donors until 1624 when the church at Hoveton St Peter was entirely rebuilt at a charge of approximately £300[1] and the ruined church at Santon completely re-edified by Thomas Bancroft, Esq., in *ca.* 1628 at a cost of perhaps £200.[2] The preoccupation with religious needs and concerns was manifestly at an end in Norfolk, as in most counties of the realm, even before Elizabeth came to the throne. Her own secular tastes and policies reflected clearly and accurately the momentous shift in men's aspirations that had now taken place, of which the Reformation was perhaps more the consequence than the cause. The age of faith was at an end in England.

D. THE STRUCTURE OF CHARITIES IN THE PARISHES

We must bear steadily in mind that the parish was the most important of all the units of social and cultural organization in the England of our period. We have necessarily proceeded with our analysis in the larger and more convenient framework of the county, despite the fact that the lives and fortunes of most men of our era were shaped and fixed by forces more immediately about them. The flow of charitable funds and the creation of new and socially effective institutions did not proceed evenly across the length and breadth of this large and very complex county. Norwich and several smaller communities in Norfolk became during the period under study among the most enlightened and advanced in the whole of England as they made the necessary adaptation to the requirements of the modern society. At the same time, as we shall observe, many isolated and poor rural parishes gradually sank deeper into an all but hopeless quagmire of poverty and ignorance when the means of regeneration did not come to hand. Much depended on local leadership by responsible men, whether they were of the gentry, the clergy, or the yeomanry, or on the local youth who had made his fortune in trade in Norwich or in commerce in London. It is particularly clear in Norfolk, too, that the tradition of giving to a local parish chest, to an endowment for the relief of poverty, or to the stock of a local grammar school once established could in time, without the almost eccentric intervention of a great local philanthropist, build solid and effective institutions which created even in very poor parishes opportunity, hope,

[1] Messent, *Parish churches of Norfolk*, 121.
[2] *Norf. Arch.*, XXIII (1929), 354; Blomefield, *Norfolk*, II, 157.

and a fair climate of social and cultural life. But in some parishes these traditions simply never got themselves established.

We have likewise observed that the parochial structure of Norfolk was nearly mature at the beginning of our period, though new parish units came into being quite steadily until about 1600. Our count as of that date is 581 parishes for the whole of the county, a considerable number being in over-churched Norwich, though the formal parochial structure of perhaps nine of the counted parishes in rural parts of the county is certainly debatable. We are consequently concerned with the manner in which the very large total of £177,883 11s was spread amongst these 581 units of local life and activity during the course of our long period and with the quickening and leavening effects which this fruitful sum had on local life and institutions.

The whole of the charitable funds given in the county was not, however, designated for the benefit of specific parishes. Large amounts were given for charitable uses in other parts of England and considerable sums were provided for purposes which had the whole of the county rather than local units of organization in view. We may, however, assign the benefits of the large total of £167,689 6s to particular parishes in which the donor had a specific interest and to which he wished the favour of his charity to flow. This sum was spread amongst 533 of the parishes of the county, or 91·7 per cent of all the local entities comprising it in our period. In the almost meaningless terms of averages, this provided £314 12s 3d for each parish possessing charitable funds, but, as we shall notice, charitable endowments were in point of fact distributed most unevenly. No charitable benefactions have been found in forty-eight thinly populated parishes, in several of which church services had long since been abandoned for want of communicants. Further, there were another forty parishes, some lying very near Norwich or King's Lynn, in which the total of charitable gifts amounted to the really nominal sum of £1 or less during the whole course of our period. Thus, in all, there were eighty-eight parishes, or 15 per cent of the total number, scattered over the whole of the county, in which the tradition of charitable giving never got established and which failed to attract the generous instincts of outside benefactors.

We have concluded from abundant evidence that any parish enjoying charitable endowments of as much as £400 was highly favoured and possessed resources adequate to create the institutions essential if opportunity and hope for a release from poverty and ignorance were to be afforded men and women of this age. This was an amount quite sufficient in all save urban centres for the establishment of an almshouse, the endowment of an apprenticeship plan, or the founding of an excellent grammar school. The assured income of perhaps £20 p.a. was a social and cultural solvent, for whatever purposes designated, which in a remarkably short time raised the level of life and of hope in such a favoured community. Such parishes we have described as 'areas of opportunity' in our period, and they are clearly and cleanly separated from their less fortunate neighbours by the better climate of life which they afforded and the talent which they provided for the county and the nation. We should now note in some detail the distribution and the assets of these parishes in which the great bulk of all charitable endowments came for a variety of reasons to be so heavily concentrated.[1]

These 113 favoured parishes include thirty-eight in the city of Norwich, four in King's Lynn, and seven in the small town of Thetford, the latter being left by medieval piety with an almost embarrassing wealth of parish churches. It should be observed that a heavy proportion, amounting to exactly 81 per cent, of the whole of the charitable wealth of the county was vested in these highly favoured parishes. All the principal towns of Norfolk in this age were included among them, though at least sixty of the total number were completely rural communities with no urban centre larger than a small village. Considerably more than half the funds of these favoured communities were settled in the three principal urban communities of the county, Norwich, King's Lynn, and Great Yarmouth, they by the close of our period being blessed with a total of £75,738 12s of charitable funds, or rather more than 42 per cent of the whole of the charitable wealth of the county. It is likewise important to observe that the 113 favoured parishes, spread over the county in an interesting and on the whole well-distributed fashion, had been endowed with institutions which gave them relatively an even greater qualitative strength than the large proportion of the charitable wealth of the county which they held might suggest. Thus, somewhat more than 96 per cent of all the amounts given for the many experiments in social rehabilitation were provided for these communities; they held more than 85 per cent of the educational endowments of the entire county; and they disposed 80 per cent of all the funds which troubled men of the county had given for its poor. In contrast, less than three-fourths (73·73 per cent) of all the amounts given for the various religious uses were to be found in these parishes. In other words, these favoured parishes possessed almost the whole of the socially effective endowments of the county; all save a few of the grammar schools, the scholarship endowments, the apprenticeship schemes, and the almshouses of the county were to be found in the parishes which had in the course of our period gained from private sources those institutions required by modernity.

At least some special comment should be made on the impressive charitable endowments accumulated by Norwich during the course of our period, though the particulars relating to the principal of these trusts

---

[1] The parishes are listed with details in Appendix, Table B.

have been fully discussed in earlier pages. The second or third city in the realm during the years under study, this rich provincial capital enjoyed the continuous and the intelligent charitable support of a prosperous, responsible mercantile aristocracy which, as we have already seen, literally built its institutions with its own wealth and in accordance with its own aspirations. The total of the charitable wealth provided during our period reached the impressive sum of £53,018 5s, or almost 30 per cent of the whole for the county. Though a tiny sum when compared with the immense philanthropic outpouring in London and surprisingly far less than that provided by the benefactors of Bristol, it none the less placed Norwich third among the cities of England.[1] It is likewise important to note that only £1727 of the charities of Norwich were the gift of London benefactors, or only 3·26 per cent of the whole of its charitable wealth, though London wealth supplied more than 13 per cent of the total of the charitable endowments of the county at large. This sturdy provincial independence was unmatched among the other principal cities examined in this study and quite confirms the reputation of the city for an almost truculent independence during the Tudor and Stuart eras. Norwich built its charities to accord with its sense of the needs of the present and the requirements of the future. Nor was that all, for the city was intensely parochial in its own range of interests and bore only a narrow view of its social responsibility. During the long period under examination it gave but £3187 4s to the charitable needs of country parishes outside its own walls. This parochialism is all the more startling when we reflect that Norwich provided for the charitable needs of the county at large less than one-seventh of the amount given by London benefactors.

We have had frequent occasion to observe that Norwich from the very beginning of our period was building sound and certainly impressive traditions of charitable giving. The curve of benefactions in the city differed markedly from that of the county as a whole, a considerably lesser proportion having been provided during the decades prior to the Reformation and a substantially larger proportion during the years of the Reformation and in the Elizabethan era. It is evident, too, that the economy and confidence of the burgher aristocracy were severely

[1] The order among the principal cities in the counties comprehended in this study is as follows:

	£	s		£	s
London	1,889,211	12	Manchester	23,028	0
Bristol	92,042	6	Winchester	17,393	2
Norwich	53,018	5	Taunton	16,046	11
Canterbury	48,605	2	Worcester	15,149	1
York	26,067	9	Rochester	14,803	7

Moreover, fairly careful estimates lead us to conclude that Norwich was certainly third among all the cities in the realm in its charitable endowments.

damaged by the unsettlement of the revolutionary era, since the proportion of funds given during the last of our intervals was only 7·90 per cent of the whole as compared with 14·77 per cent for the county at large. Even more significantly, the pattern, the structure, of charitable interests in Norwich differed markedly from that of the county. The dominant concern of the burgher aristocracy of the county town was the plight of the poor. Very nearly half of the total of all benefactions (46·46 per cent) was provided, principally in capital sums, for their relief and sustenance, as contrasted with a third (33·77 per cent) for the whole of the county. Similarly, 14·62 per cent of all charitable capital was given for the various experiments in the rehabilitation of the poor, as compared with rather less than 10 per cent for all of Norfolk. Much less, proportionately, was given for municipal uses, particularly tax-relief endowments, and for education, while slightly less was provided for religious uses. This ordered giving reflects a pattern of interests widely and persistently held by many men over a long period of time. In all, there were 839 Norwich donors who made charitable gifts for the needs of their city in amounts exceeding 2s. A surprising number of these (217) were artisans whose pattern of interests differed little, particularly after 1541, from that of the merchant aristocracy which contributed almost two-thirds (61·17 per cent) of the total. The large sum amassed for Norwich charities stands as the proud heritage of men who with a kind of prescience had accurately sensed the needs of their own and of future ages.[1]

There were in addition eighty-eight parishes, all rural and with no larger centre than a village, with charitable endowments which by the end of our period stood between £100 and £400. These endowments ranged in amount from £100 6s for East Lexham, of which almost the whole was for poor relief, to £376 18s for Mattishall, with a total of £331 6s for poor relief, £30 8s which had been given as outright sums for various religious purposes, and smaller amounts for education and social rehabilitation. It might also be observed that a considerable proportion of Mattishall's endowments for the poor had come from two native sons who had made comfortable fortunes in trade in Norwich and in London. In total, the parishes of this group possessed charitable wealth at the close of our period amounting to £17,623 2s, or a surprisingly high average of almost precisely £200 each. It seems probable that, when the simple and stable agricultural economy which typified this large and scattered group of parishes is taken into account, they possessed

---

[1] This brief treatment of the social institutions of Norwich owes much to the important, though as yet unpublished, doctoral dissertation of my former student, B. H. Allen, *The administrative and social structure of the Norwich merchant class, 1485–1660*. Mr. Allen, while pursuing his work in Norwich, also supplied me with considerable and valuable information regarding the charities of the city and with biographical particulars regarding many of its donors.

sufficient resources to care for their poor in at least all save periods of severe and general agricultural depression and that the roughly £10 p.a. accruing to them on the average was quite enough to make of them 'areas of opportunity' in terms of the needs of the age.

There were, then, in all 201 parishes in the county which we may regard as especially favoured. These were parishes, principally rural, with charitable endowments of more than £100, which had gained sufficient resources from private benefactors to sustain the institutions that the modern age required; they stood as exemplars for the whole of the county. They comprised a considerable proportion (34·59 per cent) of all the parochial units of the county, yet it must be said that they arrogated an almost staggering proportion of the total charitable wealth of Norfolk. In all, they were vested with £161,705 18s of funds, or slightly more than 90 per cent of the whole. This means, of course, that the remaining 380 parishes of Norfolk disposed only £16,177 13s. As we have already noted, there were forty-eight parishes in poor and thinly settled reaches of the county in which no charitable benefactions have been recorded and still another group of forty in which the total of contributions did not during the course of our period exceed the nominal sum of £1. There remain, therefore, 292 parishes in the county among which a total of £16,169 2s was distributed. This works out to the really amazingly high average of £55 7s 6d of charitable endowments, which for these small and wholly rural parishes was no mean sum and which may well have been sufficient to relieve at least the most abject suffering or to lighten the density of ignorance. We may truly say that in Norfolk no more than eighty-eight of its many parishes, or a scant 15 per cent of the whole number, principally lying in the fen lands or along barren coastal stretches, were at the close of our period areas of social blight.

E. THE IMPACT OF LONDON ON THE COUNTY

Norfolk lay somewhat more than seventy miles to the north and east of London, relatively closely connected with the capital by sea and by reasonably good road communication. Moreover, it was intimately and importantly connected with London because of its export of food staples and its cloth trade. But, none the less, Norfolk remained throughout our period not so much an economically and culturally isolated county as one notably self-sufficient, self-contained, and certainly somewhat self-satisfied. Significantly, in relation to its population few of its sons entering trade or commerce went to London for their apprenticeships and hence relatively few of the great merchants of the capital, almost wholly drawn though they were from shires other than Middlesex, were Norfolk born. The county was proud of its own institutions and content with its own resources, with the result that aspiring young men from all over the county, as well as from northern Suffolk, tended to seek and to find their fortunes in Norwich or in one of the lesser local centres of trade. The county possessed a strong, an indigenous, and a most interesting culture of its own, and roots once struck there were not easily removed—Norfolk was not lightly to be shed. Thus even a family like the Greshams seem to have regarded themselves as temporary sojourners from Norfolk for a half-century after they had settled in London, and they often managed, with, one would suppose, considerable difficulty, to get their children properly born in that proud county.

These facts, partly cultural and partly economic, explain the most interesting further fact that, Yorkshire aside, Norfolk was far less dependent on London than any other county in the whole of the realm for the creation and support of its social and charitable institutions. London merchants were effectively creating these institutions over the whole face of England in accordance with their own vision of the present and future. But hardly so in Norfolk. In all, London benefactors supplied the certainly large total of £23,506 3s towards the needs of what was in most cases their native county. But this amount, impressive and useful as it was, accounts for little more than a seventh of the whole of the charitable funds of the shire and is significantly lower than that for any other county in our group save remote Yorkshire.[1] It should, however, be noted that almost the whole (94·70 per cent) of these London benefactions were in the form of capital sums and that they were with few exceptions well and carefully vested and administered to accomplish with a predictable efficiency the designs of the donors.

This large total of charitable benefactions was provided for the county by a relatively small group of forty-two donors, of whom only six made their gifts or bequests prior to the accession of Queen Elizabeth. Hence they were on balance extremely large gifts, averaging nearly £560 each, which, it must be said, lent to them a peculiar significance. The scale of giving of this small group of Londoners is suggested by the fact that, though they comprised only 1·5 per cent of all donors in the county, they gave something over 13 per cent of all its charitable benefactions. Almost half, twenty, of these benefactors were London merchants, whose gifts ranged from £80 to Gresham's great grammar-school

[1] These proportions of total charitable funds derived from London gifts vary widely and should perhaps be set down in detail:

	per cent		per cent
Bristol	19·73	Norfolk	13·21
Buckinghamshire	17·04	Somerset	26·05
Hampshire	29·23	Worcestershire	23·01
Kent	40·74	Yorkshire	12·09
Lancashire	28·03		

foundation of £2500, and who as a group gave the generous total of £17,609 to the institutions of what was in all save one case their native county. There were as well six Londoners whose social identification is somewhat uncertain, though the size of their gifts, £3344 6s for the group, would suggest most persuasively that they too were members of the mercantile aristocracy of the capital. Of the remainder, eleven were tradesmen, two were artisans, and three were members of the professional classes. The ties of this whole group with Norfolk were strong and direct. We are certain that thirty-four of the London donors were Norfolk born, four were connected with the county because a parent or a wife had been born there, while the birthplaces of the remaining four are uncertain.

It is likewise significant that the interests and aspirations of these great London donors differed most markedly from those of the county as a whole.[1] The London benefactors were almost wholly moved by secular interests, only the tiny proportion of 2·32 per cent of all their benefactions having been given for religious uses, as compared with almost a quarter (23·01 per cent) for the county as a whole. Their interest was heavily, almost exclusively, concentrated on the relief of the poor of the county, particularly by the founding of almshouses and the enlargement of the educational opportunities available for able and aspiring youths in their native towns. To these two great heads they poured in nearly 90 per cent of all their great gifts; Norfolk donors gave not much more than 56 per cent for these uses. These men knew exactly what they wanted and they possessed the means and the skill for gaining it.

In Norfolk, as in all other counties, the London benefactions because of their size and the care with which these trusts were fashioned possessed a qualitative strength and significance far exceeding their total in pounds sterling. These endowments were not spread thinly over the county, but were rather concentrated as grammar schools, almshouses, or lectureships in favoured communities in which they quickly and permanently altered the whole life and tone of concentrated areas of the county. This fact was to have the most important consequences not only for particular communities thus singled out, but because there is abundant evidence that these carefully vested institutions served as models and as inspiration for later provincial donors who not infre-

[1] The evidence may best be presented in a brief table setting out the proportions provided for the several charitable heads by the county at large as contrasted with the gifts of these London merchants and tradesmen:

	Poor	Social rehabilitation	Municipal betterments	Education	Religion
Norfolk at large	£60,075 6s (33·77%)	£17,127 16s (9·63%)	£18,820 15s (10·58%)	£40,920 4s (23%)	£40,939 10s (23·01%)
London gifts to Norfolk	£10,075 18s (42·86%)	£1,249 11s (5·32%)	£979 (4·16%)	£10,656 (45·33%)	£545 14s (2·32%)

quently acknowledged their indebtedness in their deeds of gift or the 'orders' for their own foundations. Hence we should examine the disposition of these London benefactions in the individual parishes, noting first a group of parishes with generous charitable endowments of £400 or more which were quite unaffected by London's generosity and then a second group in which it is evident that the architecture of local institutions was conceived and financed by London wealth.[1]

There were fifty-four of these unaffected communities, comprising ninety-nine parishes, including all save one of Norfolk's principal towns and in the aggregate possessing at the close of our period almost two-thirds of the whole of the charitable wealth of the shire. Yet these sturdily self-reliant parishes, all with substantial charitable endowments were almost completely independent of London in the building and in the maintenance of their local institutions. These were the areas in Norfolk in which the local gentry or the burgher aristocracy tended to be dominant, with, as we have observed, somewhat different aspirations and interests from those which animated the London benefactors of the age. It is this deep sense of local responsibility which gives to the history of Norfolk institutions in our period its peculiar and certainly its significant interest.

But we should note, as well, that even in Norfolk there is a second group of parishes, including one large market town, in which London generosity played a far more important role in the formation of the social and charitable institutions of the community.[2] These were in

[1] *Vide* Appendix, Table C, for the listing of these parishes.

[2] Norfolk parishes with substantial charities, decisively affected by London benefactions:

	Charities from local or county sources		Charities from London sources		Totals	
	£	s	£	s	£	s
Aylsham	1,181	11	380	0	1,561	11
Castle Rising	2	0	2,551	14	2,553	14
Cromer	50	4	205	0	255	4
Dereham, East	419	2	1,138	0	1,557	2
Harpley	38	17	4,520	0	4,558	17
Hedenham	536	12	200	0	736	12
Holt	12	5	2,560	0	2,572	5
King's Lynn	9,147	18	3,433	0	12,580	18
Mattishall	276	18	100	0	376	18
Raynham, East	113	0	100	0	213	0
Rushford	1,040	12	922	0	1,962	12
Shotesham	200	0	154	0	354	0
Southrepps	7	16	160	0	167	16
Swannington	70	1	100	0	170	1
Wighton	1	1	420	0	421	1
Wiveton	5	11	133	7	138	18
Wymondham	865	12	1,500	0	2,365	12
	13,969	0	18,577	1	32,546	1

most instances rural parishes or villages which had the good fortune to send to London a native son who never quite severed the sentimental ties with his place of birth as his fortune was being made and who remembered it liberally and often decisively when he came to put his affairs in order for this world and the next.

It will be observed that the London benefactions were heavily concentrated in these seventeen communities, almost 80 per cent of all funds given from the capital having been vested in these parishes. These communities were for the most part rural parishes in which the London endowment of the grammar school, the almshouse, or the fund to provide household relief for the indigent was the decisive and the culturally moulding institution for the entire community and very often for neighbouring parishes as well. These parishes, reasonably well spread over the entire county, possessed not quite a fifth (18·30 per cent) of all its charitable funds, but they as a group derived substantially more than half of all their charitable resources from the generosity of a relatively small group of London benefactors. While London endowments in Norfolk lacked the dominating quality which we have found in most counties, they can by no means be regarded as without importance even in this proud county.

F. THE IMPACT OF THE COUNTY ON THE NATION

Norfolk was amazingly self-sufficient in other respects as well. If we exclude its substantial endowments for Cambridge University, during the whole course of our period Norfolk donors gave the relatively small sum of £4277 19s to the charitable needs of other counties of the realm. This total, provided by eighty donors, amounts to 2·40 per cent of the whole of the charitable wealth given in the county and compares quite unfavourably with certain of the counties we have examined in which cultural and economic ties with the England beyond the shire borders were much stronger.[1] It will be observed, in the table that follows, that a large proportion (38·17 per cent) of these extra-county benefactions were concentrated in London, to which Norfolk returned something like 7 per cent of the great and fruitful wealth it had received, and in Cambridgeshire, a county in which Norfolk took an almost proprietary interest, quite beyond the university and its insatiable needs.

These gifts outside Norfolk were relatively large in average amount and were, as contrasted with most counties, made principally by members of three rather clearly defined social groups: the gentry, the upper clergy, and the burgher aristocracy. They were neither large nor numerous in the interval before 1540, when they were mostly given for

[1] The proportion of total charities provided for other counties ranges from 0·79 per cent (Bristol) to 8·54 per cent (Hampshire), London being excluded.

County	Number of donors	Total £	s.
Bedfordshire	1	40	0
Buckinghamshire	1		10
Cambridgeshire	6	1328	0
Derbyshire	1	1	0
Devon	1	1	0
Essex	5	353	10
Gloucestershire	2	4	13
Herefordshire	1		13
Hertfordshire	2	16	0
Leicestershire	1	5	0
Lincolnshire	6	18	8
London (Middlesex)	18	1633	0
Northamptonshire	1	20	0
Shropshire	2	105	0
Somerset	2	101	0
Suffolk	20	346	4
Surrey	3	35	0
Westmorland	1	2	0
Wiltshire	1	1	0
Yorkshire	3	206	0
Rome	2	60	1
	80	4277	19

the support of monasteries or other religious purposes. In the later period, especially after 1590, they were at once more numerous and larger in amount and include the endowment of two schools, three almshouses, and two Puritan lectureships. The gifts of the humbler classes, yeomen particularly, were almost wholly for the relief of the poor in the adjoining counties of Suffolk, Lincolnshire, and Cambridgeshire, but they do not comprise a significant proportion of the total of Norfolk gifts for the charitable needs of the remainder of the realm.

G. THE STRUCTURE OF CLASS ASPIRATIONS

Norfolk differs from the other counties in our group in the fact that it was not during our period overwhelmingly rural either in terms of its total population or in the sources of its wealth and culture. Though it is doubtful whether the combined population of Norwich, King's Lynn, and Great Yarmouth comprised more than an eighth or a ninth of the total population of the county at any given time, none the less their relative importance and the great and fruitful wealth of Norwich gave to Norfolk a balanced character quite wanting in the other counties examined. But it remained as well a densely populated and a rich agricultural county with a wealthy and long-established gentry. Moreover, it possessed a rising body of substantial yeomanry, very difficult to differentiate from the lower fringes of the gentry in terms of wealth, social responsibility, and even status. It should be mentioned as well that the merchant aristocracy of Norwich, which was marked throughout our period by an amazing insularity of interest, was recruited principally from the rural stretches of the county and in turn merged with its gentry by marriage and by that ultimately effective means, the purchase of manors for themselves or their elder sons. It may be said, then, that Norfolk was a microcosm of England, with Norwich in this narrower ambit assuming for the county the vastly significant role which London played in the life, the institutions, and the aspirations of the whole of the realm.

There were in total 2714 identifiable individual donors to the charities of Norfolk. As has been observed, these benefactors gave in all the large total of £177,883 11s to the charitable needs of the county, or a relatively low average of £65 10s 10d for each donor.[1] It has been possible to establish the social status of 2023 of these men and women who provided the charitable institutions of the county, or not quite three-quarters of the whole number. There remain 691 individual donors, of which number 119 were widows of uncertain social status. The place of death and the nature of the bequest identify 407 of these persons as rural or village dwellers, while the average of their benefactions would suggest a social and economic status somewhat lower than that of the lower gentry and substantially higher than that of the yeomanry. The remaining 284 of these persons of uncertain status were urban dwellers, principally in Norwich and King's Lynn, the average of whose gifts would indicate, as it were, a composite status approximately that of the tradesman class.

The quite unusual social balance of Norfolk is demonstrated by the fact that a total of 1546 of all the donors in the county were rural, if we may include the 407 benefactors known to be rural, but not further identified, as well as the whole of the 200 members of the lower clergy who made charitable gifts during our period. This rural group constituted about 57 per cent of all the donors of the county, and it gave 38·57 per cent of the whole of the charitable funds. On the other hand, the number of urban donors, including eighteen members of the upper clergy, was 1164, while the benefactions of this much smaller group amounted to 38·85 per cent of the charities of the county, the remainder having been given by the Crown or by the donors not certainly identified as to social status.

The closely knit structure of responsibility borne throughout our period by the gentry and their urban counterparts, the merchants and

[1] The average benefaction per donor ranges from £28 4s 6d in Yorkshire to £255 12s 2d in London.

tradesmen, is most impressively substantiated by an examination of the evidence.[1] In all, these two groups numbered rather more than a third (37·47 per cent) of all the donors of the county, while they gave substantially more than half (54·46 per cent) of its charitable funds. Thus the gentry, probably numbering not more than 2·6 per cent of the population of the county, as a social group constituted 16·17 per cent of its donors and were responsible for more than a fourth of all its charitable endowments.[2] It may in this connection be appropriately observed that there were 342 identified donors who were members of the lower gentry, constituting the largest single social group among the county's benefactors with the single exception of its yeomanry. At the same time, the burgher classes comprised 21·3 per cent of all Norfolk's charitable donors and gave well over a fourth (28·72 per cent) of its charities. Moreover, conclusive as this evidence may be of the extraordinary responsibilities assumed by these two classes of men, it considerably underestimates their role in the life of the county since many, if not most, of the unidentified donors who contributed 18·63 per cent of the benefactions were undoubtedly members of one or other of these two aggressive and most generous classes.

We should now comment on the social contribution made by the several classes of men in Norfolk.[3] Among these contributions the

[1] Analysis of the social status of Norfolk donors:

No. of donors in the class	Social status	Per cent of all county gifts	Per cent of county donors	Amounts given	
4	Crown	3·95	0·15	7,035	0
10	Nobility	6·27	0·37	11,158	7
97	Upper gentry	14·58	3·57	25,930	7
342	Lower gentry	11·16	12·60	19,846	17
353	Yeomen	3·23	13·01	5,749	10
99	Husbandmen	0·07	3·65	131	1
38	Agricultural labourers and poor	0·03	1·40	51	5
18	Upper clergy	1·50	0·66	2,661	7
200	Lower clergy	3·23	7·37	5,743	18
181	Merchants	19·10	6·67	33,976	5
210	Tradesmen	4·65	7·74	8,265	8
187	Burghers	4·97	6·89	8,832	19
234	Artisans	1·18	8·62	2,102	4
50	Professions	7·45	1·84	13,247	9
691	Unidentified	18·63	25·46	33,151	14

2,714

[2] We here follow Tawney's calculation for the class structure of Gloucestershire in this period (*Econ. Hist. Rev.*, V [1934], 47), somewhat amended by local evidence for this county.

[3] *Vide* Jordan, *Philanthropy in England*, 330–365, for comments on the relative wealth and generosity of the several classes of men in the counties under examination.

direct charitable grants of the Crown to Norfolk were not without importance. There were four of these benefactions, totalling £7035, or 3·95 per cent of the whole of the charitable funds of the county. The Crown gave more to Norfolk than to any other rural county in our study, though its gifts to Buckinghamshire accounted for a slightly higher percentage of the total charitable gifts in that small county. These benefactions, as we have earlier noted, were given for abidingly useful purposes, somewhat more than 40 per cent of the whole having been directed to the educational needs of Norfolk, almost as much (37·84 per cent) having been given for almshouse endowments, and most of the remainder for municipal uses.

The nobility of the county, of whom ten made charitable benefactions of consequence during the course of our period, were likewise to make contribution to establishing its charities. Men, and more particularly women, of this class gave a total of £11,158 7s to various charitable uses, or 6·27 per cent of all Norfolk's philanthropic funds, an amount somewhat less than was provided by the professional classes and some-what more than was given by the tradesmen. They contributed quite heavily to the educational resources of the county and likewise disposed almshouse endowments with a substantial capital of £2851 14s. They gave, as well, generous gifts for poor relief and general charitable uses. The religious interests of the nobility of the county were less marked than in most other counties, somewhat under a fourth (22·36 per cent) of all the gifts of the class having been made for such use.

The upper gentry of Norfolk, rich, numerous, and socially responsible, were by far the most important of the rural classes in ordering and in defining the charitable aspirations of the county. The substantial total of £25,930 7s was provided for charitable purposes by ninety-seven members of this class, or an average of £267 6s 6d for each donor. This amounts to 14·58 per cent of the whole of the charitable funds of Norfolk and represents a contribution in percentage terms exceeded only by the gifts made in Buckinghamshire and Yorkshire by members of the class. Donors of this group gave in roughly equal proportions to the three great charitable heads—the relief of the poor, the endowment of educational opportunities, and the needs of religion—only a small proportion of their gifts having been made for the experiments in social rehabilitation and the schemes of municipal improvement which enjoyed the warm support of urban dwellers. They vested somewhat more than a third (34·49 per cent) of all their benefactions in the various plans for the relief of the poor, a proportion only slightly higher than that (33·77 per cent) of the county at large, with a much greater interest in the endowment of household relief plans than in the founding of alms-houses. Donors of this class gave about 30 per cent of all their benefactions for educational needs, as compared with 23 per cent for the county as a whole, these contributions reaching the substantial sum of £7982, an amount unmatched in this particular by the gifts of any other class of men in the county. Men of this class likewise displayed a greater interest in the religious needs of their parishes than did most other social groups, with very nearly a third (31·59 per cent) of all their benefactions as compared with 23·01 per cent for Norfolk at large. Their bequests for the endowment of chantries, totalling £3204 13s, were unmatched by those of any other social group, as were their gifts for church repairs, the latter amounting to somewhat more than 10 per cent of all their charitable benefactions.

This sturdy and certainly self-confident class exhibits a most interesting shift in its aspirations as our period progresses. It was clearly moving towards an all but complete secularization of interests, though a little more slowly and reluctantly than the county at large. In the long period prior to the Reformation members of this class gave the large total of £8747 11s to various charitable purposes, approximately a third of the whole benefactions of the class and an amount quite unrivalled by the benefactions of any other social group.[1] The overwhelming interest of the class in this era was in the several religious needs of their parishes and of their own souls, well over two-thirds (68·43 per cent) of all their benefactions having been made for these uses. Thus members of this class gave more for prayers in this period, their largest single interest, than to all secular purposes. The needs of education commanded the respectable proportion of 18·22 per cent of all their gifts, but poor relief was supported by no more than 7·84 per cent of their benefactions, mostly in the form of doles. But their preoccupation with religion withered during the period of the Reformation, though it seems clear that they were very uncertain about the course of history and their own interests, since they gave only £172 3s, or less than 1 per cent of their total benefactions during these two troubled decades. The confidence of the class revived during the Elizabethan age, when a total of £3166 4s was given to charity by its members, though it should be noted that this amounts to no more than 12·21 per cent of the whole of the benefactions of the class. The secular interests of the upper gentry were now clearly and most confidently expressed. The needs of the poor now commanded 44·75 per cent of all their benefactions, with almost as much (41·06 per cent) being provided for the grammar schools of the county. The pressing requirements of the church were met with scarcely more than token gifts, which in all account for a scant 10·4 per cent of the whole of the benefactions of the upper

[1] The amounts given in this period by other important social groups were:

Merchants	£6,014	1s
Lower gentry	£5,655	4s
Lower clergy	£3,674	1s

gentry in this most secular of all periods. During the early Stuart era, when £8019 14s, representing 30·93 per cent of all the charities of the class, was given, there was a substantial revival of interest in religious needs, somewhat more than a fifth of the whole being designated for these purposes, though the predominant interest of the class was in education, to which more than half (53·47 per cent) was dedicated. Quite inexplicably, interest in the requirements of the poor fell away sharply during these years, something less than a quarter (23·61 per cent) of the whole being vested in the endowment of almshouses or plans for household relief. In our final period, the upper gentry of the county evidently remained at once prosperous and confident, for the large total of £5824 15s given during this brief interval represents a rate of giving per decade far in advance of that in any earlier decade interval. The gifts of this era were concentrated on poor relief, to which 85·21 per cent of the whole was given, the incredibly small total of £15 2s, or 0·26 per cent of the whole, being the measure of the then interest of the class in religious needs.

The much larger body of donors drawn from the lower gentry of the county may almost be described as average benefactors. The 342 donors of this class, who comprised 12·60 per cent of all donors in the county, gave £19,846 17s to the charitable funds of Norfolk, or 11·16 per cent of the whole. And the lower gentry were average donors in yet another sense, the structure of their charitable aspirations being remarkably similar to that of the county at large, while the rapid shift in their charitable interests to the secular needs of their communities closely paralleled that of the county as a whole.

In the earliest of our periods, the lower gentry committed about two-thirds (64·89 per cent) of all their charitable gifts to religious needs. In this period they gave the large total of £5655 4s to charitable uses, amounting to 28·49 per cent of the whole of the benefactions of the class. Of this amount, it seems difficult to explain, slightly more than 44 per cent (44·04 per cent) was provided for prayers alone. In contrast, the needs of the poor were met with not more than 13·41 per cent of all their gifts, while £599 19s, or 10·61 per cent of the whole, was designated for scholarship endowments. But in the Elizabethan age the aspirations of the class underwent a violent and, as time was to show, a permanent metamorphosis. During this period alone, members of the class gave £3057 12s, or 15·41 per cent of the total of their benefactions, and of this amount nearly half was provided for one or another form of poor relief. The needs of education commanded rather more than a quarter (26·61 per cent) of their contributions, while 7 per cent was given for various schemes of municipal improvement. The requirements of the church absorbed no more than 15·49 per cent of the benefactions of the class, and almost the whole of this slender proportion was given for the semi-civic purpose of church repairs or for the endowment of lectureships, sceptically regarded as they were by the ecclesiastical authorities. In the course of the next interval, 1601–1640, the lower gentry of Norfolk gave the large total of £6096 17s to the charitable needs of their county, or 30·72 per cent of the whole of the benefactions made by the class. Substantially more than half (56·70 per cent) of this amount was provided for endowments for the care of the poor, while about a fifth was given to education (20·17 per cent) and a little less (19·98 per cent) to the various religious needs, with the founding of lectureships and the repair of the fabric of parochial churches still the predominant religious interests of the class. As in the case of the upper gentry, the charitable benefactions of these men were actually considerably increased during the next two decades of revolution, when a total of £4213 5s was given, of which, be it noted, less than 1 per cent was designated for church uses. In this final period almost half of the whole was provided for grammar schools, rather more than a quarter for poor relief, and the relatively very high proportion of 17·08 per cent for the several schemes of social rehabilitation.

The yeomanry of Norfolk were a numerous and a prosperous social group, particularly in the period following the accession of Elizabeth, when approximately 85 per cent of the whole of their benefactions were made. There were 353 of these donors who contributed £5749 10s to the social needs of the county, or 3·23 per cent of the total. The average benefaction for members of the class was the rather high sum of £16 5s 9d, while their relative social significance is suggested by the fact that their benefactions almost exactly equalled those of the lower clergy and were something more than twice as great as those of the upper clergy. Since the class became numerous and prosperous late in our period, its stalwart secularism is somewhat exaggerated, but it was none the less very real. Almost half (49·17 per cent) of the charitable benefactions of the class were made for poor relief, as compared with approximately a third (33·77 per cent) for the county at large. It is interesting to note that almost a fifth (19·56 per cent) of all their gifts were for various municipal improvements, a proportion considerably larger than that dedicated to religion (14·59 per cent) or to education (16·14 per cent). The hey-day of the class is to be observed in the early Stuart period when £2668 15s, or 46·42 per cent of the total given by the group, was provided for the several charities of the county. In this prosperous period, it may be observed, rather less than 7 per cent of all their gifts were made for the various religious uses which laid claim on men's interests and generosity.

We have recorded benefactions from ninety-nine husbandmen of the county, who gave in all the tiny total of £131 1s, or only 0·07 per cent of Norfolk's charitable funds. This poor and backward class in Norfolk, as in other counties, remained relatively unaffected by the currents of historical change. Over our whole period the class gave almost half (47·08 per cent) of all its benefactions for religious uses, a proportion exceeded only slightly by the 52·34 per cent provided for the outright relief of their even poorer neighbours. It is interesting to observe, however, that men of this class in about 1580 began to shed the habit of leaving small and customary bequests for church uses and instead to give tiny outright sums for doles for poor men. Thus in the Elizabethan period nearly 90 per cent of the small total of £31 5s given by them to charity was in the form of doles, a proportion very nearly maintained during the remainder of the period under study.

Though Norfolk was the seat of a great bishopric and, until the Reformation, possessed several rich monasteries, it must be observed that the upper clergy of the county were of only slight consequence in building the charitable endowments of the shire. In all, eighteen members of this class made benefactions totalling £2661 7s, or only 1·5 per cent of the whole of the charitable funds of the county, this being rather less than half as much as was provided by the yeomen and not much more than the sum given by the artisans of Norwich and King's Lynn. About 40 per cent of all the gifts of this class were for religious purposes, with the endowment of prayers and the repair of churches absorbing almost the whole of these funds. Almost as much (35·04 per cent) was provided for educational purposes, though the whole of these gifts were for the universities or for scholarships, the grammar schools of the county being completely neglected. The needs of the poor were scantily regarded, since only 22·82 per cent of the benefactions of the great churchmen were designated for this purpose, as contrasted with 33·77 per cent for the county as a whole. One is favourably impressed neither by the generosity of these churchmen nor by the quality of their charity.

Rather surprisingly, the same stricture must be laid against the lower clergy of the county. Gifts have been noted from 200 of these parish priests who in all gave £5743 18s to various charitable purposes. This means that the average benefaction for members of the class was £28 14s 5d and that this group, constituting 7·37 per cent of all known donors in the county, gave 3·23 per cent of the total of its charities. Our evidence abundantly suggests that the clergy of Norfolk were hard pressed financially after the Reformation, since almost two-thirds of the total of the benefactions of the class was provided prior to 1540. Taking the whole of our long period in view, somewhat more than half (55·42 per cent) of the benefactions of the clergy were for religious purposes, though the interests of the class were almost as secular as those of the population at large after 1600. The needs of the poor, in terms of our whole period, commanded the incredibly small proportion of 18·62 per cent of the funds given by these men, while educational interests and municipal uses absorbed 13·06 per cent and 11·66 per cent respectively of their total of charitable gifts.

The charitable contributions of the relatively small merchant class were by far the largest of any social group in the county and were in every respect the most interesting. The great total of £33,976 5s was given by 181 members of this class during the course of our period, or an average of £187 14s 4d for the group. These men, comprising only 6·67 per cent of all the donors of the county, gave in all 19·10 per cent of the whole of the charitable funds of Norfolk, a substantially larger total than that provided by the next most important social group, the upper gentry, who gave 14·58 per cent of the whole. It must, however, be pointed out that this was by no means all Norfolk wealth. This group included twenty London merchants, all Norfolk born, who together gave £17, 609 of the total, or almost 52 per cent of the whole contribution of their class. This very large *corpus* of gifts from a handful of London merchants was in fact a larger amount than that provided by any other class in the county save the upper gentry and the lower gentry. The remainder of the merchant total was provided by 161 humbler merchants of Norwich, King's Lynn, and Great Yarmouth. But whether the benefactions came from London or from Norwich, they were derived from a class with remarkably coherent and decisive aspirations which was building modern England in terms of its own apprehension of the needs of the society and its own ideals for the future of the nation.

Taking in view the whole span of our period, this merchant aristocracy was unbelievably secular in its interests and concerns. In all, only 8·83 per cent of its charitable funds were given for the several religious uses as compared with the 23 per cent provided by the county at large. In fact, considerably more was given for loan funds alone than for all the religious needs to which men might lend their support. Something over 18 per cent (18·04 per cent) was vested for the support of education, the founding of grammar schools being the particular interest of this group of donors, while the astonishing proportion of 29·69 per cent of all their gifts were made for the many experiments in social rehabilitation which appealed so strongly to the pragmatic and evangelical minds of merchants throughout England. At the same time, these men were deeply interested in the needs of the poor, to which they gave nearly 40 per cent of all their funds over the length of our long period. These proportions differ markedly from those of the county as a whole and they possessed the sanctions of impressive bulk and of excellent implementation under well-drawn and well-administered trusts. They possessed, in other words, a powerful leverage which was to affect the whole thinking of the county most profoundly and to form many of its most important institutions.

The merchants very evidently possessed differing and pertinaciously held aspirations which marked them as apart from the society of the county even in the years prior to the Reformation. It is remarkable that in this era, in which they gave £6014 1s to various charities, only about 37 per cent of their benefactions were made for religious purposes, while roughly a quarter was devoted to education. Even in these early years they gave almost 10 per cent (9·11 per cent) of their funds for purposes of social rehabilitation and slightly more (10·87 per cent) for various municipal undertakings. During the two decades of the Reformation their contributions for religious purposes fell to less than 2 per cent (1·72 per cent) of their considerable benefactions, to rise slightly to 4·21 per cent during the Elizabethan era when the total of the benefactions of the class was £5447 16s. During this latter period the merchant aristocracy was principally concerned with the needs of the poor, to which they gave more than 80 per cent (82·63 per cent) of the whole of their endowments, principally, it should be noted, for the establishment of almshouses. But the great outpouring of merchant benefactions came in the early Stuart period when the group gave £11,115 3s for the charitable uses of the county, or about a third of the total given by the class. In this remarkable period almost the whole (91·13 per cent) of all merchant gifts were concentrated in an impressive and certainly telling fashion on the problem of poverty: approximately half (47·34 per cent) of these gifts were made for the direct relief of the poor and aged and nearly 44 per cent (43·79 per cent) was poured into fruitful and hopeful experiments in social rehabilitation. Nor was there any slackening of merchant generosity or confidence in the final short period of our study when the annual rate of merchant giving was almost doubled even over the early Stuart period. The great total of £10,146 2s was given during this tumultuous interval, or nearly 30 per cent of the total for the class. Not more than the insignificant sum of £59, or 0·58 per cent of the whole, was provided for religious purposes during these years when the always pronounced secularism of the class became all but complete. The interests of the class were shifting from the needs of the poor, to which not quite a fifth (19·10 per cent) of the total was given, to the expansion of the educational system of the county, to which merchants of the period gave £4175, or 41·15 per cent of the whole for the class. At the same time, the now settled interest of these men in plans for social rehabilitation remained about constant, since upwards of a third (37·2 per cent) of their charities were directed towards one or another of these various undertakings.

The tradesmen, drawn principally from the same cities as the merchant donors, were animated by far more modest and certainly more conventional aspirations than were their merchant *confrères*. In fact, the difference in the structure of interests of these two groups in Norfolk is quite startling, and it is a true difference in no sense accounted for by the heavy weight of London benefactions in the merchant group. There were 210 tradesmen donors, who gave in all £8265 8s to the charities of the county, or 4·65 per cent of the whole. These were pious men, and, save inevitably for the Elizabethan period when the proportion given by them for religious purposes fell to 2·84 per cent, they remained, for an urban class, remarkably devoted to the needs of the church during the whole course of our period. In all, they designated 27·46 per cent of their gifts for religious purposes, as compared with 23 per cent for the county as a whole, the needs of the fabric appealing especially to their apparently tidy minds. They gave rather more than a third (35·37 per cent) of all their benefactions for the relief of the poor and shared with the merchants an active interest in schemes for social rehabilitation, to which they gave about a fifth (22·82 per cent) of all their funds. They were also civic minded, giving 11·19 per cent of their charities for various plans of municipal improvement, and were inexplicably uninterested in education, which commanded no more than 3·14 per cent of their contributions.

We are concerned, too, with a group of prosperous urban dwellers, numbering 187, who can be no more exactly identified than as 'additional burghers'. These men had all held minor civic offices during their lifetime and one would suppose from the structure of their charitable interests that most of them were tradesmen, probably with a liberal admixture of small merchants. These burghers, comprising 6·89 per cent of the donors of the county, gave £8832 19s to its charities, or 4·97 per cent of the charitable resources of Norfolk. The structure of their charitable aspirations suggests that they stood midway between the bold interests of the merchant class and the remarkable social and cultural conservatism of the tradesmen of the county. The class was principally interested in the needs of the poor, to whom they gave approximately 30 per cent (29·45 per cent) of all their funds, and in the process of social rehabilitation, with a special interest in workhouses and stocks for the poor, which commanded nearly a fourth (22·73 per cent) of their charities. Schemes of municipal improvement received not quite 10 per cent (9·63 per cent) of their gifts, while they did not share the strange neglect of the tradesmen for the needs of education, having given very nearly 17 per cent (16·95 per cent) of all their funds for this use. They were rather less devoted to the needs of religion than the county as a whole, having given 21·22 per cent of all their benefactions for the various and certainly the compelling needs of the church in Norfolk.

There remains another large group of urban donors, the 234 artisans, most of whom were skilled or semi-skilled workers in the cloth trade in the several industrial centres of the county. This group gave in all

£2102 4s, or an average of £8 19s 8d, comprising 1·18 per cent of the total of the charitable resources of the county and comparing not unfavourably with the benefactions of the upper clergy. It possessed from the very beginning of our period, especially in Norwich, a continuous tradition of charitable giving which was at once discriminating and sophisticated when compared with the artisans in most counties or with the humbler rural classes in Norfolk, or, for that matter, with the vastly more prosperous Norfolk tradesmen. Save for the period prior to the Reformation, the artisans' interest in the needs of religion was restrained. Their concern with the betterment of educational opportunities, though developing relatively late, was for our whole period only slightly less proportionately than that of the county at large, being, however, chiefly limited to gifts for scholarship purposes. The artisans were especially interested in building up loan funds for needy persons, to which they gave £255 of capital, while all the various plans for social rehabilitation attracted 12·76 per cent of their gifts as compared with 9·63 per cent for the county as a whole. One is especially interested in the fact that their concern with the problems of the poor was limited, since these men apparently were doubtful about the merits of outright relief, not quite a third (33·15 per cent) of all their benefactions having been given to the several heads which we have grouped together under poor relief. The record not only of the generosity but of the social wisdom of this group is remarkable and deserves more intensive study.

There were as well fifty donors to the charities of the county drawn from the several professions. This small group, numbering 1·84 per cent of all donors, gave the large total of £13,247 9s to the charitable institutions of Norfolk, or 7·45 per cent of the whole. Almost all the contributions made by this interesting group were in the form of capital and the class was able to command quite as skilful services in forming its trusts as were the merchant donors. In fact, half the total number were lawyers, while the remainder included eight physicians, five notaries, five scriveners, five teachers, a musician, and an author. The consuming interest of this group was in the advancement of educational opportunities, to which they gave the astonishing proportion of 70·29 per cent of their benefactions. Their gifts were well spread over the various educational uses, the impressive total of £3413 having been given to the universities, £3107 for the endowment of schools, and £2793 for the augmentation of the scholarship resources of the county and of the University of Cambridge. The relatively very slight proportion of 10·91 per cent of their gifts were designated for the relief of the poor and only a modest 7·11 per cent for the advancement of the schemes for social rehabilitation so beloved by the urban classes. Men of this class were starkly secular in their aspirations throughout our long period, the group giving no more than the tiny proportion of 5·55 per cent of their benefactions for religious uses, a proportion slightly less than that provided even by the Norfolk merchants.

There remains an unfortunately large group of 691 donors, almost exactly a fourth (25·46 per cent) of all known donors, whose social status has not been ascertained. This group, comprised, as we have noted,[1] of both rural and town dwellers, gave £33,151 14s to the various charitable needs of the county, or 18·63 per cent of the whole for Norfolk. We have suggested that both the amount and structure of their giving strongly argues that in a composite sense those who were country-men possessed a status somewhat lower than that of the gentry and that those who were townsmen must in average terms have been very close indeed to the status of tradesmen. The structure of charitable interests displayed by the group was remarkably similar to the pattern of giving in the county as a whole, save for a slightly larger proportion of bene-factions for religious purposes (29 per cent) and a markedly lesser con-cern with the educational opportunities and needs which were such a compelling interest to the dominant social groups in the county. This group, clothed in social anonymity, does, however, very accurately represent the sentiments and the aspirations of the rank and file of men of this great and extraordinarily interesting county.

Men and women of Norfolk had with their own energies and sub-stance built a fairer and a better society during the age with which we have been concerned. They took proper pride in the achievement which they had wrought, with relatively little help even from London, and many of the institutions which they had founded served as models for troubled or aspiring men in distant counties. Few counties in England in 1660 possessed as generous or as useful social institutions as did Norfolk, fewer still were animated by as sturdy and as steadfast a deter-mination to master the twin scourges of poverty and ignorance. Norfolk's donors had built well and they had built for all time.

But Norfolk was even at the outset of our era a relatively rich and a mature county, properly and generally regarded as one of the 'pillars' of the realm. We turn now to Yorkshire, lying not so very far to the north even by fifteenth century criteria of distance, but culturally and economically remote, backward, and depressed during the first three generations of our long period.

[1] *Vide ante,* 202.

IV

Yorkshire

Yorkshire far surpassed in size, though hardly in complexity, any of the other counties comprised in this study. It extended to 6066 square miles in area and was by far the largest in the kingdom, being somewhat more than double the size of Lincolnshire, the next largest. The historic division of the county into Ridings possessed in our period considerable administrative and cultural significance and will be respected in our discussion of the parochial structure of charities within the county. The Ridings varied markedly in size, the West Riding including very nearly half of the total area, the North Riding somewhat more than a third, and the East Riding slightly less than a fifth.

The diversified topography of the county was of great significance in an age when the region was overwhelmingly agricultural. The centre of the county is a plain, which in our period was heavily populated and which included the best farming land, while the hills of the Pennine chain cover almost the whole of the West Riding and the northwestern stretches of the North Riding. The hills to the east of this central plain and in the northern quarter of the North Riding comprise the range of the Cleveland Hills. Most of the county is drained by the Ouse, which also dominated the communications of the region, though the extreme western reaches drained to the Irish Sea. The East Riding was well populated during our period, almost the whole of the area being arable and capable of supporting a quite advanced agricultural economy. The West Riding, too, was predominantly rural, though the parochial structure would suggest that about half the region was thinly populated in the hilly stretches and that the older agricultural economy of the area was beginning to give way before a remarkable industrial development. The North Riding was at once remote, poor, and sparsely populated, not much more than half the entire expanse being suitable for farming of any kind.

Yorkshire was throughout our period, and most particularly during the age of the Tudors, a remote region quite imperfectly fitted into the structure of order and administration which the great Tudor sovereigns had devised. It lay far from Westminster and far from London as well, for the economy of the region was in the sixteenth century backward as compared with the precocious economic and industrial developments spreading out into the southern and midland counties from the three great centres of London, Bristol, and Norwich. In sixteenth century terms Yorkshire was an historical anachronism, whose greatness lay in the already misty past of the Middle Ages and whose present posed chronic and occasionally critical administrative, political, and religious problems. It was a county in which local landed magnates wielded a considerable personal power at the outset of our era, though their power and their wealth were to suffer a steady and rapid erosion during the course of these two centuries. It was a region in which monasticism was firmly and powerfully seated, there being at the time of the Dissolution 120 religious establishments in the county, or something like one to every 50 square miles of its vast area.[1] The endowments of these great foundations were unmatched in all of England, and it is clear that they still played a significant and responsible role, when compared with the other counties we have examined, in the culture and life of this great area; that they yet fulfilled an essentially medieval function in an essentially medieval society. The whole structure of charitable giving and the very evident confusion of aspirations suggest that Yorkshire, unlike most of the rest of the realm, was not ready for the overwhelming revolution which was the Reformation and that the county was severely injured by its impact and by the grave political disturbances which followed, leaving the region suspect by the unrelenting Tudors for two full generations.

The economic and cultural recovery of Yorkshire, beginning in the mid-Elizabethan period, came about as a strong yeoman and entre-preneurial system of agriculture tended to replace the traditional farm-ing methods on the estates of the local magnates and monasteries, and as a powerful and pervasive industrial expansion, centring in the West Riding, began to create new stores of capital, to found urban institutions, and to link the entire region more intimately and fruitfully with the rest of the realm's economy. This swift development may in a sense be best estimated against the background of the decline of the City of York, whose medieval glory, wealth, and population was outmatched in the whole realm only by London. As early as 1377 York possessed a population of possibly 12,000, being almost one-third the size of London, but from the beginning of our period onwards it was in process of slow decline. Its cloth industry collapsed during the course of the sixteenth century, though the city was given a monopoly in the making of certain materials in an effort to bolster its economy. It came quickly to be surpassed in population by both Bristol and Norwich. The popula-

---

[1] There were 28 abbeys, 26 priories, 23 nunneries, 30 friaries, and 13 cells.

tion of the city was actually declining, there being perhaps not more than 10,000 inhabitants in 1660, while fifteen of its forty churches were simply pulled down and the parishes merged as the medieval greatness and strength of York slowly but majestically declined.[1]

But simultaneously the county as a whole was experiencing the stimulating effect of a remarkable and persistent industrial expansion through the whole of the second half of our period. This new prosperity, which engendered a considerable increase in the population of the West Riding, was based principally on the cloth industry. The great centres of this development were Halifax, Leeds, and Wakefield, where the manufacture of broadcloths and kerseys reached a high level of efficiency, with most serious consequences to many older centres of cloth manufacturing in several parts of the realm. These products required long-staple wool and water power, both of which were easily available in the West Riding, and the form of industrial organization developed was to have direct and certainly beneficent effects on a huge area comprising possibly a fourth of the entire county. The industry, and its financing and administration, became established in a score of towns, of which Halifax, Leeds, and Wakefield were only the chief, spreading far out into the surrounding countryside to cottage clothiers and to yeomen in the quest for cheap labour, while stimulating as well an insistent demand for wool from all parts of the county. Halifax grew in a half-century from a country village to a thriving and populous manufacturing and commercial centre, by the close of our period rivalling York itself in population and in wealth.

At the same time, a significant expansion was under way in the extractive industries, financed for the most part by London capital. Limestone was quarried at Hazlewood and was burned for fertilizer at Tadcaster and nearby villages. Alum was mined in the North Riding near Whitby. Sheffield, famous for its cutlery and other iron wares even in medieval times, experienced a great expansion of its traditional industries and doubled its population in the space of about two generations. But the great development occurred in coal mining, beginning in southern Yorkshire in the late Elizabethan period. By 1603 there were scores of small mines, clustered principally about Sheffield and Rotherham, while during the remainder of our period pits were opened in a kind of frontier movement of mining to the north of the original field, roughly in an area extending from Marsden in the west to Pontefract in the east and beyond the Aire as far north as Barwick in Elmet.[2]

This great expansion undoubtedly was accompanied by a sharp and sustained increase in population, setting in about the middle of the

[1] Darby, H. C., ed., *An historical geography of England before A.D. 1800* (Cambridge, 1951), 441; Rowse, A. L., *The England of Elizabeth* (L., 1951), 162.
[2] Nef, J. U., *The rise of the British coal industry* (L., 1932, 2 vols.), I, 57–60.

Elizabethan period and continuing to the close of our era. There is considerable evidence in our parochial materials that the population of the county had been roughly stationary for the preceding century but that a rapid increase then began, stimulated by the more extensive opportunities for employment and fed quite as much by migration into Yorkshire from other northern and midland counties as by natural increase. The most careful estimates of the population of the county in about 1600 would suggest that it lay within a range of from 300,000 to 350,000 inhabitants, though our own study of various parochial materials would on the whole persuade us that even the lesser estimate may be slightly too high.[1]

Whatever may be the facts regarding the gains in population in Yorkshire during the course of our period, it seems evident that the wealth of the county, both relatively and absolutely, has been much underestimated. Both Rogers and Buckatzsch, using subsidy rolls as the basis for their estimates, would on the average for our period seem to rank the county as thirty-second or thirty-third in the entire realm, or well within the fourth quartile of the English counties. Our own evidence from the flow of charitable funds, as well as the relative worth of the various classes of society, would suggest a Yorkshire which, particularly after 1558, was much richer than the central government thought it to be. The great total of Yorkshire's charitable contributions, London always aside, placed the county just after Kent in wealth, and these two were quite unrivalled in this respect. When this wealth is translated into terms of the relative area and probable population of the county, it would seem that Yorkshire, taking our whole period into account, ranked high in the second quarter of English counties in the fluid wealth which possessed such effectiveness in laying the foundations of the modern society.

B. GENERAL COMMENTS ON THE DATA

Yorkshire benefactors contributed £243,650 14s to the charitable needs of their county in the course of the period under examination. This great sum was exceeded among the counties comprehended in our study only in Kent by the slightly larger total of £251,766 12s, the incomparable generosity of London's donors of course always excepted. This accumulation of charitable funds was made possible by a widely dispersed tradition of social responsibility in many classes of society; by a host of

[1] *Yorkshire Archaeological Journal*, XXXVII (1951), 24–33; Usher, A.P., *An introduction to the industrial history of England* (Boston, 1920), 98, *et passim*; Dickens, A. G., *Lollards and Protestants in the diocese of York*, 1509–1558 (Oxford, 1959), 2. It is difficult to interpret Usher's map of density of population with any accuracy for this county. Professor Dickens believes that Yorkshire and Nottinghamshire together had a population of more than 300,000 in 1603.

small donors as well as a relatively small group of very large benefactors. There were in all 8632 recorded donors in the county, a number exceeding that for London by something over a thousand and more than a third as many as gave of their substance in Kent. Thus the average benefaction for the county was not more than £28 4s 6d, somewhat lower than that for any other county included in our study.[1]

Almost exactly a third (33·46 per cent) of the whole of Yorkshire's charitable funds were given for one or another form of poor relief. In all, the considerable total of £81,513 13s was given for these uses, an amount exceeded only by Kent among the rural counties of the realm. Of this amount, approximately half (£40,261 19s) was provided for household relief, while £2414 17s was designated for general charitable purposes, which in effect meant the care of the poor. In every decade of our long period, at least one substantial gift was made for the founding or further endowment of almshouses, the flow of funds for this purpose rising to a flood with the beginning of the seventeenth century and continuing unabated for two generations.

Yorkshire donors were old-fashioned and conservative in their approach to the problem of poverty. While extremely generous in their provision for the alleviation of poverty, they were relatively cautious in their experimentation with the several schemes for securing the social rehabilitation of the poor which so intrigued the urban classes in the England of our period. In all, Yorkshiremen gave £11,805 17s of capital for these 'trials at social regeneration', this amounting to only 4·85 per cent of the whole of the charitable funds of the county. And these cautious donors were even less disposed to bequeath their substance for municipal betterments, however badly required in this remote shire. The total given for the various uses comprehended under this head was no more than £6121 11s, or only 2·51 per cent of the whole, a proportion markedly less than that found in most counties of the realm.

The intensity and the persistence of Yorkshire's interest in the improvement, or, more accurately, in the formation, of an educational system for a sprawling and a thinly settled county was unmatched in all of England, save always for the fanatical devotion of Lancashire to these ends. In the course of our period the very large total of £75,812 8s was provided for educational needs, amounting to 31·12 per cent of the total of benefactions and considerably exceeding the amount given for any other great charitable purpose except poor relief. Some measure of the greatness of this achievement may be suggested when we reflect that the endowments provided for the education of the youth of the county exceeded the combined totals for the relatively far more prosperous counties of Buckinghamshire, Hampshire, and Somerset.

[1] The average benefactions in the other counties range from £32 2s 3d for Somerset to £255 12s 2d for London.

Yorkshire, as we have already indicated, was a conservative and a pious county. In all, £68,397 5s was given for the various religious needs of the age, this being upwards of a quarter (28·07 per cent) of the total of the charitable wealth of the county, and with a particularly heavy concentration of endowments for chantries and other forms of endowed masses. No other county, Lancashire once more aside, remained so stubbornly devoted to the requirements of the church as did Yorkshire, it having yielded but slowly to the infinitely powerful forces of secularization which were transforming the institutions and the mind of England.

The county was prosperous and its conservative pattern of thought and aspirations remained relatively undisturbed during most of the long and, for Yorkshire, essentially medieval period extending from 1480 to 1540. In this interval donors of the shire gave for various charitable uses the large total of £51,362 5s, which represented more than a fifth of the whole of the accumulation of charitable funds during our entire period.[1] The central preoccupation of benefactors during these two generations was with the needs of the church, on which the enormous total of £35,814 2s was vested, or nearly 70 per cent of all benefactions made during these pre-Reformation decades. Moreover, the stalwart and unwavering piety of this northern county is suggested by the fact that nearly two-thirds (£22,933 5s) of all religious contributions were for prayers. In fact, more was given for prayers alone than for all the non-religious charitable uses combined. There is little evidence that scepticism regarding either the efficacy of prayers for the dead or the good faith of the church in administering them in perpetuity had gained any substantial hold in Yorkshire, though we have observed that these doubts were pervasive in the southern counties.

The interest of next importance to Yorkshiremen in these years prior to the Reformation was in bettering the woefully inadequate school facilities with which their county entered the modern era. The substantial sum of £10,274 2s was given for various educational purposes, the founding of schools and the endowment of scholarships commanding most of these resources. This capital represented exactly a fifth of all charitable benefactions of the interval and was to create in the county a tradition of giving for educational purposes which would bear rich fruit a century later. The needs of the poor, and there were many of them and they were restless in the Yorkshire of this period, were strangely but persistently disregarded, the hopelessly inadequate total of £4209 12s having been provided, while of this a large proportion was in the form of casual alms or funeral doles. The small sum of £814 1s, representing 1·58 per cent of all charitable gifts for the interval, was given for municipal improvements and the tiny total of £250 8s for various experiments in the social rehabilitation of the poor.

[1] For the details of this analysis, *vide* Table III, Appendix

The paralyzing effect of the Reformation and of the accompanying civil disturbances on the aspirations and the economy of the county is most dramatically evident when we review the flow of charitable funds during these critical years. In the decade just prior to the Reformation (1521–1530), £14,060 9s was given for various charitable causes within the county, while the total for the next and violently unsettled decade fell calamitously to £4154 17s, the lowest for any decade interval during our entire period. The county remained doggedly devoted to the ancient ways of faith, giving nearly four-fifths (78·70 per cent) of all its slender charitable resources for religious causes; and two-thirds of that total, be it noted, was for prayers. Recovery in the county was slow and the shift in aspirations was even slower, it being significant that not until the first decade of the Stuart period did the total of charitable funds provided reach approximately the level of giving attained during the years just prior to the Reformation.

The shock of change had its withering effect particularly upon the lower classes of society, which persisted in the period of the Reformation with their customary bequests for religious purposes when they gave, but which within a generation were scarcely giving at all. But even in Yorkshire, in the towns and among the new gentry, doubling their sheep runs as monastic property came ultimately into their competent hands, the change in the structure of aspirations was swift and complete. One has the sense of a great and almost inert mass of mankind bewildered, all but paralyzed, by the revolutionary changes ordained in far-off Westminster and of a perplexed gentry and nobility stubbornly opposed to what had occurred, but not daring, after the terrible vengeance wrought following the Pilgrimage of Grace, to lend political or moral leadership within the bounds of their county. Hence leadership passed, and that quickly, to new hands, to men who had staked their fortunes and their lives on the process of revolution and who even in the short interval of the Reformation began to build a society on the new foundations. In these two decades (1541–1560) the considerable total of £16,935 10s, representing 6·95 per cent of the whole of the county's charitable funds, was given for philanthropic uses. It is especially noteworthy that the £4261 5s given for religious purposes amounted to only a fourth of the whole, contrasting most significantly with the overwhelming proportion of 69·73 per cent given for such uses in the preceding period. A substantially higher proportion (38·79 per cent) was given for the relief of the poor; the £6568 13s provided in these two decades for this grievous need was much larger than the amount given in the two generations prior to the Reformation. The relatively large total of £5142 14s, or 30·37 per cent of the whole, was given for educational betterments, almost all of this amount having been designated for the foundation of new or the strengthening of old grammar schools. The charitable giving during these tumultuous decades was almost wholly concentrated on these three great charitable interests, the relatively small sum of £753 17s, or 4·45 per cent of the whole, having been given for municipal improvements and the trivial total of £209 1s for efforts at social rehabilitation.

The Elizabethan age offers an extremely interesting pattern of change and development in Yorkshire. It was not until the closing years of the reign that economic and, shall we say, moral, recovery was complete in Yorkshire. This was a period when new classes, with new aspirations consonant with those held by similar but more firmly seated classes of men in the southern and midland counties, were establishing their fortunes and translating their values into institutions by the sanctions of their own generosity. In this metamorphosis of aspirations, however, Yorkshire was clearly lagging a full generation behind the dominant regions of England.

During this long interval the sum of Yorkshire's charitable benefactions was only £23,807 14s, or somewhat less than a tenth of the charitable funds given during our entire period. But straitened though the giving may have been, a new and completely dominant pattern of secular aspirations had triumphed in the county. Such men as possessed both the competence and the confidence to give at all gave in a pattern not significantly different from the rest of England. Modernity had triumphed in Yorkshire, if in a modest and restrained form, and was laying the solid foundations for the rapid building of social institutions which was to occur in the next generation. Thus £11,275 11s, or almost half (47·36 per cent) of the whole, was provided, principally in endowments, for the relief of the ubiquitous poor of the county. Moreover, the impressive total of £8925 1s, 37·49 per cent of the whole, was given for the further enlargement of educational opportunities. A considerably increased sum, £1356 1s, was given for experiments in social rehabilitation, this amounting to nearly 6 per cent of all benefactions for the period. The preoccupation of the county with the needs of the church, with the requirements of religion, had all but withered in the cool climate of the Elizabethan administration and definition of national values. The incredibly small total of £1543 9s, or 6·48 per cent of the whole, was given for all religious uses during this long interval. Secularism had at last gained as complete a triumph in Yorkshire as in the rest of the realm.

The great outpouring of Yorkshire's generosity, the process of building the institutions of modernity, began in the last decade of Elizabeth's reign and was to continue unabated to the close of our period. During the early Stuart decades private benefactors gave £89,290 1s for various charitable purposes, this amounting to 36·65 per cent of the sum of the charitable endowments of the county. The principal concern remained with the needs of the poor, the great total of £33,067 3s, or

37·03 per cent of the whole, having been provided for endowments for almshouses or for the care of the poor in their own houses. An almost equally great total of £32,768 5s was given to secure an immense expansion of the educational resources of the shire, a sum far exceeding the amount given for this purpose during the preceding 120 years. Plans for the rehabilitation of the poor commanded £5234 16s, this being 5·86 per cent of the whole, while the various municipal betterments undertaken by private donors were financed with contributions aggregating £2276 19s, or 2·55 per cent of the amount given for charity in these decades. There was likewise a marked increase in gifts for religious uses, encouraged by the more favourable attitude of the central government and the now shrill admonitions of the Laudian episcopate. In all, £15,942 18s was provided for religious purposes during these years, though it will be noted that this substantial sum, given in large part for the maintenance of the clergy, amounted to only 17·86 per cent of the whole of the benefactions of this generation.

The rising curve of charitable giving in Yorkshire was unaffected by the Civil War and the unsettled years which followed on it. Yorkshire, like almost all of England, was deeply divided during this conflict and was itself the scene of important campaigns, but there is much evidence to suggest that the remarkable prosperity which the county had enjoyed for a full half-century continued without more than local interruptions. But even more impressive is the fact that the now securely seated and dominant classes in town and country continued without pause in the task of constituting and endowing the institutions of relief and opportunity which their fathers had so well begun. The great sum of £62,255 4s was dedicated to charitable causes during this brief interval, this amounting to a fourth (25·55 per cent) of the whole of the charitable funds of the county, given at a rate almost 40 per cent greater than that which had prevailed during the generous and peaceful decades of the early Stuart period. The needs of the poor commanded £26,392 14s, or 42·39 per cent of all the benefactions of the revolutionary era, while £4755 11s, or 7·64 per cent of the whole, was given for furthering the efforts to secure the social rehabilitation of the poor. The strengthening of the educational system of the county continued at an accelerated rate, 30·04 per cent (£18,702 6s), having been given for this purpose during this relatively short interval. The needs of religion were met with benefactions totalling £10,835 11s, or 17·41 per cent of the whole, most of which was devoted to augmenting the notoriously inadequate stipends of the clergy of the county. Yorkshire had emerged slowly and somewhat timorously into modernity, but once new and vigorous classes had gained command of its resources and had given definition to its aspirations, the task of overtaking the older and more mature regions to the south was well and most courageously advanced.

We may now turn briefly to a number of statistical comments on the data which have some bearing on the quality and nature of the structure of charitable institutions in the county. Our first comment will deal with the relation of capital creations to gifts or bequests made for immediate use. Benefactions of the latter type tended to be smaller, though more commonly customary, and normally displayed no particular pattern of charitable aspirations. These gifts to income, to immediate use, were in number and in value far more common in the earlier decades of our period, though they not infrequently appear as 'addenda' of distributions in wills establishing large capital trusts.

In Yorkshire, of the total of charitable funds provided during the period under review, the impressive sum of £200,201 15s was vested, whether by gift or bequest, as capital. This means that 82·17 per cent of all the charitable benefactions in the county were established in order to secure perpetual uses and that thereby a powerful sanction was lent to the aspirations of the age. This proportion in Yorkshire differs only slightly from that in the other rural counties included in our study, there having been a remarkable consistency in the pattern in which men of the period vested their gifts.[1] The benefactions creating institutions with which social change and improvements might be secured—the schools, the scholarship funds, the almshouses, the apprenticeship schemes, and Puritan lectureships—were almost wholly established and supported by capital sums designed to secure them for all time. Indeed, even the £40,261 19s given to household relief of the poor was largely settled in the form of endowments, more than three-fourths of the whole amount being thus constituted. It is interesting to note in this connection that while 74 per cent of all individual donors making gifts for poor relief left them for outright uses, as doles, a relatively small group of large donors established the dominant pattern of poor relief and undertook a permanent attack on the dread problem of poverty by the settlement of endowments.

We have likewise sought to ascertain the proportion of benefactions left as bequests in relation to those funds given during the donor's lifetime for charitable uses. In Yorkshire, an extensive sampling suggests, a very high proportion of the whole of charitable giving was in the form of bequests. In fact, no other rural county in England even approaches the 70·87 per cent which was left by will for carrying out the charitable intentions of the donors.[2] We must at the same time note that the great bulk of charitable benefactions made by bequest remain as a matter of

[1] For the eight rural counties studied, the range is from 76·83 per cent for Lancashire to 82·40 per cent for Buckinghamshire.

[2] The range for these counties, Yorkshire excluded, is from 27·60 per cent for Buckinghamshire to 64·40 per cent for Norfolk. In London 70·37 per cent of all benefactions were made by bequest; in Bristol 77·75 per cent.

record in the wills which society has preserved with a quite special pertinacity. Most of these, we are reasonably confident, we have gleaned in our researches. But, while even more effort has been expended in seeking out the benefactions made by gifts, we can be certain only that we have learned of those which were vested as endowments. The acts of casual charity, the spontaneous deeds of mercy, the occasional subscription to renew the roof of a parish church or to rebuild the burned house of a neighbour, have a peculiarly poignant and human quality, but they likewise were normally unrecorded and hence are forever lost.

Though, as we have so frequently said, Yorkshire was a conservative county, it is remarkable for the extent and the quality of the participation of its women in the founding of its social institutions. There were in all 1121 women making charitable benefactions, comprising nearly 13 per cent of all benefactors in the shire. These women as a group gave the large total of £30,589 7s to various charitable uses, or 12·55 per cent of all the benefactions for the county. Moreover, their average charitable contribution was £27 5s 9d, a figure only slightly lower than the average for the county as a whole (£28 4s 6d). In no other county that we have examined, save Buckinghamshire, was the contribution of women as significant or as pervasive through the whole of our period.[1] It seems clear indeed that Yorkshire's women possessed in their own right control of a considerable proportion of the disposable wealth of the county and that they were encouraged by a tradition of social effectiveness to employ that wealth for charitable uses in which they believed.

The women donors of Yorkshire likewise displayed a stalwart independence in supporting charitable needs which fulfilled their own social aspirations, with the consequence that the structure of their giving differs markedly from that for the county as a whole. Their great and abiding preoccupation was with the needs of the poor, towards which they gave nearly half (48·93 per cent) of all their benefactions as compared with a third (33·46 per cent) for the county at large. They exhi

[1] The relative significance of the contributions of Yorkshire women to the charitable needs of the county may be estimated by examining the following table:

	Per cent of all donors	Per cent of all contributions
Bristol	15·44	7·58
Buckinghamshire	13·50	13·01
Hampshire	12·17	3·92
Kent	12·56	5·49
Lancashire	11·28	6·34
London (Middlesex)	14·88	9·14
Norfolk	12·97	9·47
Somerset	14·63	6·03
Worcestershire	12·71	5·31
Yorkshire	12·99	12·55

bited only a cautious interest in the schemes for social rehabilitation, to which they gave 2·64 per cent of their funds as compared with 4·85 per cent for the whole of the county, and a most casual concern for various plans for municipal betterment, which commanded no more than £487 8s (1·59 per cent) of their funds. They gave in all the considerable total of £6237 5s for the educational resources of their county, but this represented only a modest fifth (20·39 per cent) of all their benefactions as compared with almost a third (31·12 per cent) for the shire as a whole. Somewhat surprisingly, their benefactions for religious purposes, amounting to £8089 8s., were proportionately somewhat less than the average for the county, this representing 26·45 per cent of all their contributions as compared with 28·07 per cent for the whole of Yorkshire.[1]

C. THE ACHIEVEMENT

1. The Relief of the Poor

(a) Household Relief. Yorkshire was a large and sprawling county with a relatively dense population which bore heavily upon its marginal resources until an expanding industrial and commercial economy towards the close of the Elizabethan era greatly enlarged the ambit of economic opportunity. Moreover, its somewhat backward agriculture was in the course of the first half of the sixteenth century almost too abruptly revolutionized by new and entrepreneurial landlords. Much of

[1] The social groupings of women donors, and their relative generosity, are exhibited in the following table. Attention should be called to the relatively great contribution made by urban donors in this predominantly rural county:

	Number	Per cent of women donors	Total of contributions	Per cent of all women donors contributing
Crown	I	0·09	1,340 0	4·38
Nobility	7	0·62	4,969 6	16·25
Upper gentry	55	4·91	6,724 2	21·98
Lower gentry	108	9·63	3,486 15	11·40
Yeomen	79	7·05	518 14	1·70
Husbandmen	211	18·82	56 9	0·18
Agricultural labourers	2	0·18	0 2	—
Upper clergy	2	0·18	812 0	2·65
Lower clergy	10	0·89	204 0	0·67
Merchants	36	3·21	9,566 14	31·27
Tradesmen	46	4·10	685 10	2·24
Burghers	51	4·55	539 9	1·76
Artisans	29	2·59	19 12	0·06
Professional	3	0·27	191 7	0·63
Public officials	I	0·09	44 10	0·15
Unidentified	480	42·82	1,430 17	4·68
	1121		30,589 7	

the marginal arable land was put under grazing, and there was a considerable depopulation which resulted in the decay or disappearance of whole village communities.[1] These developments, occurring on a less violent scale in much of England, were unfortunately co-terminous with the expropriation of the vast monastic properties in Yorkshire and combined to provoke the serious and widespread rural poverty and malaise so eloquently, if imperfectly, expressed in the manifestoes of the leaders of the Pilgrimage of Grace.

The problem of poverty, then, always chronic in western Europe throughout the Middle Ages, became critical in Yorkshire early in our period. This social crisis was no doubt immediately and seriously worsened by the dissolution of the monasteries which in this county had continued to bear honourably a considerable burden of alms. The commissioners' reports would suggest that the monastic foundations were annually disposing under trusts about £332 5s for the relief of indigence, an amount spread widely and rather evenly over much of the county. This was a considerable sum and it was disposed by a social mechanism attuned to the needs of a people, to their habits, and to local conditions. The withdrawal of this alleviating sum, representing the income on a capital of perhaps £6645, had an immediate and a most serious consequence, which we have not noticed in any other county examined, precisely because of the persisting social integrity and utility of monasticism in Yorkshire. It is true that the social vacuum was speedily filled and more by private charity, though this could not be accomplished for approximately two decades.

Thus the attack on the problem of poverty had a special significance in Yorkshire. In the course of our entire period the large total of £81,513 13s was provided for the several forms of poor relief, this amounting to a third (33·46 per cent) of all benefactions made in the shire. The largest amount, £40,261 19s, was given for the care of the poor in their own homes, to which in effect may be added £2414 17s provided by donors for general charitable uses in various parishes. Of these combined amounts, the substantial total of £33,148 10s was in the form of endowments designed to afford permanent care of the poor and the unemployed in some hundreds of designated parishes, while the remainder, principally given in the earlier decades, had been left as outright distributions according to the medieval custom of alms. Another very large sum of £38,836 17s, of which 98·98 per cent was capital, was left by a variety of substantial donors for the establishment or the endowment of the scores of almshouses with which the age sought to resolve the problem of irremediable indigence and incapacity. It may be mentioned that these endowments constituted nearly a sixth of the total

[1] This whole subject has been most admirably studied by Maurice Beresford in *The lost villages of England* (L., 1954).

of charitable funds accumulated in Yorkshire during our entire period.

Very possibly because the monasteries bore so considerable a responsibility for the relief of poverty in the county, Yorkshire donors did not address themselves seriously to the problem in the decades just prior to the Reformation. In this interval only £4209 12s, or 8·20 per cent of all charitable gifts, was disposed for poor relief, of which, it may be noted, £1772 8s was in the enduring and socially most effective form of almshouse endowments. With the Reformation, however, there came an immediate and, as time was to show, a permanent concern for the amelioration of the lot of the poor. In twenty years (1541–1560) donors of the county gave the large sum of £6568 13s for the needs of the poor, an amount about equal, it may be observed, to the capitalized value of the monastic alms which had been largely lost. This amount, which, it will be noted, was considerably larger than the sum dedicated to poor relief in the preceding six decades, was principally vested in almshouse foundations, to which £3816 15s was given. In all, it represents nearly 40 per cent of the benefactions, for whatever purposes, made in the course of these two tumultuous decades.

It is significant that from 1551 onwards there was no decade in which less than £2300 of capital funds were vested for the care of the poor in the various parishes of the county. The social conscience of Yorkshire was aroused, as well as the Tudor concern with the problem of social order, and a continuing and dogged attack was to be made by private donors on a problem which had from time immemorial plagued the western society. During the Elizabethan era, a total of £11,275 11s was provided for the alleviation of poverty, this considerable sum amounting to almost half (47·36 per cent) of all benefactions made in this long generation. Of this, £7132 4s was given for the direct relief of the poor in their own houses, and, it should be mentioned, nearly the whole (88·64 per cent) of this sum was in the form of endowments, the customary doles for the poor having largely, and happily, disappeared in this provident age. Something over £4000 was likewise provided for almshouse foundations in the Elizabethan period, these having been well scattered over most of the county.

But considerable as these benefactions were, what may be described as the intensity of concern with the problem of poverty was increased by a factor of about three during the early Stuart period. During these four decades the generous total of £33,067 3s was given to secure the better relief of the indigent, this being 37·03 per cent of all charitable benefactions for the period. In no decade from 1601 forward did capital gifts for poor relief fall under the total of £4000, surely a most impressive and courageous attack on the problem of want. The principal interest of donors of the county during these years was in the further foundation of almshouses, to which they devoted £16,736 2s of capital. The household relief of the poor commanded the large sum of £15,875 16s, almost the whole being capital, while £455 5s was left for the general charitable needs of various parishes.

The momentum of concern for the alleviation of poverty which had been gathering for a full century was too powerful to be stayed by the catastrophe of civil war and economic unsettlement during the two final decades of our period. Actually, the rate of giving for this purpose was most substantially increased, for the generous total of £26,392 14s was provided for the needs of the poor, this being 42·39 per cent of all charitable benefactions of the interval. Some measure of the immensity of this social and humane accomplishment may be suggested when it is considered that a larger sum was given for poor relief in the two revolutionary decades than during the whole long interval extending from 1480 to 1610. Of this great total of contributions, £12,457 18s was devoted to the founding of still more almshouses or the strengthening of older foundations, while about the same amount, £12,591 16s, was vested in endowments for outright relief, and £1343 was left for the general charitable needs of various parishes.

Having sketched in outline the herculean effort made by sensitive and responsible men and women of the county to deal with the social blight which was poverty, we should note at least a limited number of the larger benefactions designed to secure permanent relief for the poor in communities in which the donors were particularly concerned. It will be borne in mind that prior to about 1540 in Yorkshire, as in all English counties, most gifts for the aid of the poor were in the form of casual doles, outright distributions for immediate use, or in the socially injurious custom of funeral alms, which attracted wandering poor men from a whole countryside. But even in this early period a number of substantial endowments were created which lent effective relief in the various parishes and which laid the solid groundwork for later, larger, and more sophisticated trust funds for the relief of poor men and women.

In about 1483 John Moulston conveyed a messuage and twelve acres of land, then valued at approximately £90, to trustees for the use of the inhabitants of Bradfield (W.R.) and for good works within the community. Many years later, in 1616, the Commissioners for Charitable Uses determined that the income from the estate, with later additions, had been employed for the relief of the poor, for the payment of taxes and certain town charges, and for the repair of the chapel of the town.[1] A more typical bequest was made a few years later by John Carre, a

---

[1] *PP* 1828, XI, 561; Eastwood, Jonathan, *History of Ecclesfield* (L., 1862), 474–475; *Surtees Soc. Pub.*, XCII (1893), 401. The Commissioners intervened because the Earl of Shrewsbury had gained possession of the town estate and was withholding income. An order was given to ensure the resumption of the uses originally intended.

merchant and twice mayor of York, whose will provided generously for poor relief, including £13 in gowns, £7 in funeral doles, £33 6s 8d in beds and bedding, and £20 in outright distributions to poor house-holders, as well as £26 in marriage portions.[1] Even more typically medieval, in fact classically so, were the funeral doles and alms dis-tributed on the occasion of the death of the Earl of Northumberland in 1489. This nobleman left £200 for general charitable distributions, as well as very large bequests for the endowment of prayers, while gowns for 160 poor were provided at a cost of £42, doles distributed, it is reported (one hopes apocryphally) at a cost of £123 6s 8d to 13,000 poor on the occasion of his burial. The funeral of the Earl must have given occasion for a riot potentially as dangerous as that in which he had him-self been killed.[2] Similar, though less formidable, distributions of alms were made in 1507 when £72 13s 9d was given in doles at the funeral of the Archbishop of York, Thomas Savage,[3] while £200 was distributed in alms by the executors of John Vavasour, Justice of the Common Pleas and Recorder of York.[4]

The familiar pattern of medieval charity may also be noted in the distributions under the will of Martin Collins, Vicar of Leeds and Treasurer of York Cathedral, who left £66 13s 4d to be distributed in general alms on his death in 1509,[5] and in the most generous will of Sir

[1] PCY 5/327 1488; *Surtees Soc. Pub.*, LIII (1868), 26–30. Carre, a draper, also left £5 for the general uses of the church, £5 to the clergy, £2 to leper houses, £3 to prisoners, £1 to anchorites, an estimated £40 in plate and jewels to monasteries, and £113 7s for prayers.

[2] *Surtees Soc. Pub.* XLIV (1864), 304–310; *Yorks. Arch. Journal*, IX (1886), 243–245; Oliver, George, *The history of Beverley* (Beverley, 1829), 172–174; *Complete peerage* (L., 1887–1898, 8 vols.), VI, 85; *DNB*. Northumberland's will disposed an enormous estate. He came into the title and the estates in 1470 when his father's attainder was reversed. Holding high office under Richard III, he deserted the King at Bosworth, being thereafter held in scant favour in the North where Richard was popular. In 1489 he was called upon to maintain order while an unpopular tax levy was being collected. Alarmed by disaffection near his own seat at Topcliffe, he raised a force of 800 which came into collision with a rebellious commons near Thirsk, where he was killed.

[3] *Surtees Soc. Pub.*, LIII (1868), 322; *DNB*.

[4] PCY 6/181 1507, PCC 16 Adeane 1506; *Surtees Soc. Pub.*, LIII (1868), 89–92; *DNB*. Vavasour also left a large sum for a chantry and prayers (*vide post*, 365, 372). Vavasour was addicted to a frugality that could be miserly: 'There was a justice but late in the reame of England callyd Master Vavesour, a very homely man and rude of condycyons, and lovyd never to spend much money.' *Test. ebor.*, IV, 90, quotes an amusing contemporary tale of how Vavasour's frugality was undone by a Yorkshire housewife.

[5] PCY 2/84 1509; *Surtees Soc. Pub.*, LIII (1868), 277–307; Drake, Francis, *Eboracum* (York, 1736), 568; *VCH, Yorks.*, III, 346; *Alum. cantab.*, I, i, 374. *Vide post*, 351. Collins was a clerical administrator. A Cambridge graduate (1477) he was made Prebend of York in 1494, Treasurer in 1503, and Vicar of Leeds in 1508. His charities totalled £328 6s.

John Gilliot, a merchant and former mayor of York, who died in the same year. Gilliot, in addition to a large bequest for prayers, which will be noted later,[1] left £46 for general church uses, £13 6s 8d for roads and as much for the marriage dowers of poor maids, £16 17s for church repairs, £7 for the relief of prisoners, and £3 for hospitals. His will likewise ordered distributions of a particularly complex nature amounting in all to £203 for the relief of the poor of his city and the surrounding countryside. Thus, for example, thirteen gowns were to be given to the poor bearing torches at his funeral, 100 black gowns and 100 linen sheets to poor and bedridden persons in and about York, £20 was to be laid out in doles, fifty beds were to be given to the poorest men and women of the city, together with bedding, and £10 was to be given to poor householders.[2] Some years later, in 1532, John Rycroft, of Kildwick, left £80 to his parish for the purchase of 120 cattle, the profits from the herd to support a perpetual obit for the repose of his soul and to provide for the relief of the poor of the community.[3] A few years later, at Walkington, in the East Riding, William Sherwood devised property worth an estimated £72, likewise to support an obit, but with the bulk of the profits to be devoted to the relief of the poor of the parish.[4]

We have spoken of the immediate and marked increase in giving for the relief of the poor with the advent of the Reformation. Not only was this the case, but there was a most pronounced change in the quality of bequests. Save for the very humble and for an occasional nobleman, the medieval custom of funeral doles and lavish distribution of alms for outright use gave way, and that quickly, to more carefully considered and on the whole well-devised endowments to secure the permanent relief of poor households. Perhaps a few such instances will suffice. In 1546 Richard Pymond, a cloth merchant of Wakefield, who was

---

[1] *Vide post,* 372.

[2] PCY 8/32 1510; *Surtees Soc. Pub.,* LXXIX (1884), 12–17; Drake, *Eboracum,* 363; *Surtees Soc. Pub.,* XCI (1892), 67. Gilliot was mayor of the city during two terms, in 1490, and 1503. Thrice master of the Merchants Company, he was chosen to represent the burgh in Parliament in 1487. He was created Knight of the Bath in 1501 and in 1503 entertained the Princess Margaret on her way north to Scotland.

[3] *PP* 1825, XI, 635; *PP* 1894, LXIV, Kildwick, 6–9, 16. The stock of cattle had apparently not diminished when Edward VI's commissioners were scheduling chantry foundations. The herd was left with the parish for the support of the poor, though the churchwardens were to pay £70 to the Crown in instalments of £10. This fund, as was so happily often the case, attracted later additions. In 1620 the sum of £66 13s 4d was added by bequest, while in 1653 an addition of £60 was made, to be followed in 1656 by one of £33. The endowment was all invested to secure the relief of the poor of the parish.

[4] Lawton, George, *Collectio rerum ecclesiasticarum* (L. 1842), 368–369; PP 1823, IX, 748–751.

also a merchant tailor of London, left £100 outright to be distributed to the poor of Wakefield in instalments of £5 over a period of twenty years and likewise bequeathed to trustees tithes possessing a capital value of £200 to ensure the payment of £5 annually in perpetuity to the poor of Wakefield and South Kirkby.[1] A strongly Protestant tone began by this date to be evident in wills, such as Pymond's, creating this kind of bequest for the poor, as well as in many wills of more humble testators, such as Edward Hoppay, a yeoman, also of Wakefield, who in 1549 left 7s to the poor of the parish and who testified that he believed in 'but one God and one mediator betwixt God and man whiche is Jesus Christe. So that I accepte non in hevyn neither in erthe to be my mediator . . . but he onlie'.[2] A merchant of Hull, Christopher Scales, in 1557 left to the corporation of that town two houses, one being a tavern, of an approximate capital value of £200, with the provision that the income should be distributed each Christmas Eve to the poorest people of the community,[3] while a year later still another Hull merchant, William Crokehay, in addition to founding a small almshouse,[4] left £60 to the poor of Hull, £5 to the poor of Beverley, and £3 to the needy of other parishes.[5]

The tradition of poor relief through private charity, and more particularly by endowments vested to secure a systematic and controlled distribution, was becoming well established by the close of the period of the Reformation, at least in the larger towns. But the older tradition yielded only slowly in rural Yorkshire. A sample of one hundred small benefactions in the year 1558, the total of each less than £1 for all purposes, the donors, yeomen, husbandmen, or lower gentry, suggests that the needs of the church were still paramount in the interests and aspirations of the great mass of the population. These one hundred small benefactors all left something either to the church or to the poor; in seventy-eight cases the bequest was limited to the uses of the church;

---

[1] PCY 13/185 1546; Sheard, Michael, *Records of Batley* (Worksop, 1894), 79–83, 326–329; *PP* 1826–27, X, 691. Pymond also left £10 outright to the poor of Hornby, 'where I was born'. *Vide post*, 297, for his bequest for municipal betterments.

[2] PCY 13/595 1549.

[3] PCY 15/1/250 1557; Tickell, John, *The history of Kingston upon Hull* (Hull, 1796), 696. The rents in 1690 were £14 p.a.

[4] *Vide post*, 259–260.

[5] PCY 15/3/154 1558; Tickell, *Hull*, 696, 771. Crokehay also provided £6 for the repair of roads and £4 for the common sewer; £6 for marriage subsidies; £1 7s for the general uses of the church; and £1 for the clergy. The affirmation of faith found in his will is particularly eloquent: 'I geve my soull to allmightye God and all the celestiall companye of heaven trusting fyrmely and stedfastely by the onely merites and passion of his sonne Jesus Christ, my savior and redemer to optayne and have the eternall frution and lyfe everlasting and to be partaker of joye everlasting with all sancts.'

in twelve the gift was for the poor only; and in ten cases small bequests were left to both the church and the poor. These were still customary bequests, on the whole not dissimilar from those so common in the late Middle Ages. At the same time, the ferment of change was working in the remotest areas of this interesting and somewhat dour county.

The great revolution in aspirations in Yorkshire occurred during the Elizabethan era, when, as we have already seen, the substantial total of £11,275 11s was left for the various forms of poor relief, this being 47·36 per cent of all the charitable benefactions of the period. In this same amazing interval only £1543 9s was provided for the needs of the church, this constituting only slightly more than 6 per cent of the whole. The bulk of the benefactions given for poor relief in this generation was disposed to secure the care of the needy in their own houses. In all, if a small capital sum for general charitable purposes may be included, £7221 17s was given for this use during these four decades, of which a very large proportion was capital. At least a representative group of the larger of these benefactions may be briefly noted.

Richard Vavasour, a gentleman of Askham Richard, by his will proved in 1563, left £108 for the relief of the poor of four communities, as well as £10 for the support of an almshouse, £20 for the succour of prisoners in York Castle, and £3 7s for church repairs.[1] A decade later Margaret, Lady Gascoigne, by indenture conveyed to trustees lands charged with £10 p.a. for the relief of the poor of Whitkirk parish, to which on her death in 1575 she added £17 in clothing and alms.[2] At about the same time, Richard Bailey of the chapelry of Hook conveyed lands with a then capital value of approximately £180 for the relief of the poor and other public uses as 'the townships of Hook and Goole may think most needfull'.[3] Brian Bayles, a Wakefield merchant who had established himself as a country gentleman, by his will proved in 1579 conveyed £109 to 'the four chief inhabitants' of Wakefield as trustees, the income to be employed for poor relief, the sum of £66 13s 4d to the municipality of Hull under similar conditions, and £83 6s 8d to the poor of Sturton (Nottinghamshire), where he had acquired extensive

---

[1] PCY 17/267 1563. His bequest to the poor was divided into £60 of capital, for the relief of the poor of Whitby and of the Ainstey of York, and £48 in outright alms.

[2] PCC 4 Carew 1575; PP 1826, XIII, 690; Kirk, G. E., *The parish church of St. Mary, Whitkirk, Leeds* (Leeds, 1935), 64–65. The co-heiress of Sir Robert Scargill, she married Sir John Gascoigne of Bedfordshire, who died in 1568. She was buried at Whitkirk.

[3] PP 1825, X, 664; PP 1898, LXVIII, Snaith, 29; Surtees Soc. Pub., XCII (1893), 283–288. Hook was in the parish of Snaith. There is the possibility that these may have been chantry lands and that Bailey may have been the surviving feoffee of an earlier and forgotten vesting for charitable uses.

properties.[1] An estate for the benefit of the poor of Thorganby was created, probably in the next year, when lands with a then capital value of about £140 were conveyed to the principal inhabitants of the parish for the relief of its poor.[2]

A London girdler, Thomas Mowfett, in 1583 left £5 4s p.a. for a term of twenty years for the relief of the poor of Whitby, as well as £40 for sermons in this his native town.[3] In the next year, Thomas Wood, of Kilnwick Percy, a country gentleman who had had a most varied career in the public service, by will charged his estate with an annuity of £10, with the provision that the trustees should annually pay sums ranging from 1s 8d to 10s for the relief of the poor in forty-four parishes and chapelries lying about Kilnwick Percy.[4] Shortly afterwards, Queen Elizabeth made two grants for the benefit of the poor of York and six other communities in the vicinity, ensuring in all annual payments of £59 under carefully regulated provisions.[5] The town of Wakefield was further benefited in the same year (1588) when Anthony Blythe, a landed

[1] PCY 21/397 1579; *Bradford Antiquary*, n.s., V (1933), 93. Bayles made a fortune in trade in Wakefield. Armed with a grant of access, in 1566 he purchased the manor of Cottingley (sold by his daughter in 1590 for £1040), as well as lands in Wakefield and in Durham.

[2] *PP* 1816, XVI, ii, 1430–1431; *PP* 1824, XIII, 674; McCarthy, S. T., *The MacCarthys of Munster* (Dundalk, Eire, 1922), 51–57; *Complete peerage*, II, 250. A return to Parliament in 1786 stated that this property, comprising 23 acres of pasture and arable land, had come into the hands of the parish in about 1580 from a 'Lord Viscount Valentia'. This donor may well have been the son of Sir Donald Maccarty, created Earl of Clancare and Baron of Valentia in 1565. His son and heir, styled Lord Valentia, was brought to England in 1578 in effect as a hostage for the good behaviour of his father. He died, it is believed, before 1588.

[3] PCC 15 Rowe 1583; *Surtees Soc. Pub.*, CXXI (1912), 223.

[4] *Yorks. Arch. Journal*, XVI (1902), 288; *PP* 1824, XIV, 735. Wood's services and honours are fully recited in his epitaph at Kilnwick Percy: he had served in the royal army in the war with Scotland, had been comptroller of Boulogne 'when yt was Englishe', had served as deputy of the Court of Wards for twenty-six years, had been collector of Selby 'with tenne pounde yerelyffe', and had served as 'clerke of the statut in London noble cytye'.

[5] The first grant, in *ca.* 1588, was a payment of £41 7s p.a. of fee-farm rents arising to the Crown in the county of York, and the second, also in 1588, was £17 13s p.a. paid out of the rectories of Hooton Pagnell and Thorp Arch. (*PP* 1825, XI, 607; *PP* 1826, XIII, 716–717.) In 1598 the Queen made another grant, remitting to the City of York £300, part of the tax levy of 1597, 'considering the great rayne and longe decaye of our said citie, wherby a great number of houses . . . are wasted and become void, as also the great chardge and continuall expenses which the same citizens and inhabitants doe susteyne yearly in the upholding and maynteyning of six great stone bridges with other water works belonging to the same citie being sore decayed and in relieving, nourishing instructing and bringing up of orphanes and poore younge children and also in relieving a great number of poore aged and impotent people within the said citie' (Elizabeth to Barons of the Exchequer, *S.P. Dom.*, 1598, CCLXVIII, 120, Nov. ?).

gentleman with extensive properties in the county, left capital of about £140, the income to be employed for the relief of the needy of the parish.[1]

Robert Windle, a clergyman at Chastleton, Oxfordshire, by his will proved in 1592, in addition to providing for the foundation of a school in his native parish of Thornton, left £126 to the poor of that place and certain other communities in which he was interested,[2] while in 1594 James Sedgwick, a gentleman of Sedbergh, left an endowment of £80 for the care of the poor of that parish and an equal amount for the relief of the needy of Dent.[3] Robert Wade, a gentleman of Sowerby in Halifax, in the same year established an endowment of £80 value for the relief of the poor of his community, as well as leaving £20 for outright distributions to the needy of Halifax and £10 to those of Sowerby.[4] The poor of Hull and Howden benefited in 1596 under the will of a merchant and mayor of the former town, John Gregory, who in addition to providing twenty mourning gowns and £6 outright, left £4 p.a. for the relief of the needy of Hull and £2 p.a. for the poor of Howden.[5] Francis Metham, an old man and almost certainly a secret Romanist, sometime before his death in 1596 established a trust with a capital worth of £80 for the relief of the poor of Terrington, as well as leaving £60 to be distributed among the prisoners at York and Durham in semi-annual stipends.[6] A mercer of Stamford, Lincolnshire, Reginald Har-

---

[1] PCY 23/925 1588; *PP* 1826–27, X, 692; Yorkshire Archaeological Association, *Record Series*, VII (1889), 102, 113, 144.

[2] PCC 17 Nevell 1592; *Surtees Soc. Pub.*, CXXI (1912), 231; *Bradford Antiquary*, n.s., VII (1952), 257–275; *PP* 1826–1827, IX, 437. Windle was a member of a gentle family of this parish which acquired considerable monastic property. He was educated at Oxford and was successively rector of Tackley and Chastleton, in Oxfordshire. His will suggests that he had numerous relations surviving in and near Thornton, where he desired to be buried. *Vide post*, 322, 337, for a fuller discussion of his bequests.

[3] PCC 64 Dixy 1594; *Surtees Soc. Pub.*, CXXI (1912), 154–157. Sedgwick also left £80 for scholarships for boys from Sedbergh School (*vide post*, 353), £5 to poor boys in an almshouse, £6 13s 4d each to the general uses of Sedbergh and Dent churches, £8 13s for the repair of roads, £6 13s 4d for bridges, and four bulls valued at £1 7s each, plus £1 7s additional, for each of the four constableships of Sedbergh parish, in order to provide in perpetuity four bulls for the use of the poor.

[4] PCY 26/48 1594; *Halifax Antiquarian Society Papers*, 1914, 176–179; Walker, E. J. and W. J., eds., *Early registers of Halifax parish church* (Halifax, 1885), 127; *PP* 1828, XX, 570. Wade was also a benefactor to Heath Grammar School in Halifax (*vide post*, 324).

[5] PCY 26/262 1596; Gent, Thomas, *Annales regioduni hullini* (Hull, 1735), 122–126. Gregory was sheriff in 1567 and mayor for two terms, in 1579 and 1589. He likewise created a Cambridge scholarship by will (*vide post*, 354).

[6] PCY 26/352 1596; *VCH, Yorks., NR,* I, 523, II, 205–206; *Yorks. Arch. Journal*, VIII (1884), 367–376. Metham spoke bitterly and sadly of the 'long continued undutifulnes, unkyndnes, and unnaturallnes of my owne daughter, and onely child', leaving most of his property not to her, but to her children.

rison, who was evidently a native of Sedbergh, in 1598 left £11 out-right to the poor and £5 p.a. for the succour of the indigent of Sedbergh 'at most needful times where most need is', while also providing £20 10s for the support of Sedbergh School and a substantial bequest for the maintenance of 'Sawrethaite Bridge'.[1] A great London merchant and lord mayor, Sir Richard Saltonstall, on his death in 1601 left £100 as an endowment for the poor of his native town of Halifax, as well as a small sum for the support of Heath Grammar School, 'though, to the discredit of his family, the poor whom he designed to benefit never, enjoyed the fruits of his care'.[2] We may conclude our brief review of the Elizabethan endowments for the care of the poor with mention of the interesting provisions in the will of Thomas Cartwright, a gentleman of Brodsworth, who, in addition to founding a university scholarship,[3] vested £400 on trustees with the intention that the income should be employed to help with the support of thirty of the poorest men and women in twenty-five Yorkshire communities who attended divine services on the two disbursement dates and who might not be 'drun-kards, common swearers, or of other evil demeanour'.[4]

As we have already observed, the great flood of benefactions for the relief of poverty, beginning in the last decades of the sixteenth century, was to continue without diminution through the remaining years of our period. In the course of the early Stuart interval, the very large total of £33,067 3s was provided in endowments for the poor, £16,736 2s being for the support of almshouses and £16,331 1s, if gifts for general charitable uses are included, for the maintenance of poor men and women in their own houses. Since there were many of these benefac-tions, a considerable number being substantial, we shall content our-selves with brief reference to only a few of the more interesting and typical of these funds designed to rid many parishes in the county of the spectre of hopeless poverty.

In 1603 William Gee, a merchant, a speculative builder, and a former mayor of Hull, who had founded an almshouse during his lifetime and also endowed a school by his will, in addition to other considerable charitable bequests left £359 for the care of the poor. A total of £25 was

[1] PCC 14 Lewyn 1598; *Yorks. Arch. Soc. Rec.*, XXXIII (1903), 384; *Northern Genealogist*, I (1895), 165–166; *Yorkshire Genealogist*, II (1890), 102–104. *Vide post*, 297, 309.

[2] PCC 32 Woodhall 1601; *Halifax Antiq. Soc. Papers, 1903*, no folios, *1910*, 257–259; Midgley, Samuel, *Halifax* (Halifax, 1789), 143–144, 487; Cox, Thomas, *The grammar school of Queen Elizabeth at Heath* (Halifax, 1879), 131. The endowment could not be found in an inquisition taken in 1651. For the school benefaction, *vide post*, 324–325.

[3] *Vide post*, 354.

[4] PCY 28/109 1600; Jackson, Charles, *Doncaster charities* (Worksop, 1881), 87–88; Hunter, Joseph, *South Yorkshire* (L. 1828, 1831, 2 vols.), I, 322; *PP* 1826–27, X, 803–804; Gilbert, Richard, *Liber scholasticus* (L., 1829), 466–467.

to be distributed in gowns, food, and money on the occasion of his funeral; £150 was to be invested as a perpetual stock for the aid of the poor of Hull and £160 to be employed as capital by the town government in order to maintain a stock of corn that would ensure equitable prices when sold to the poor; £1 p.a. was to be employed for forty years to pay the taxes of poor men; and £4 was left outright to the poor of Rothley, Leicestershire.[1] A yeoman of Rotherham, Thomas Woodhouse, in 1606 left lands, then possessing a capital value of £100, the income to be distributed by the churchwardens of the parish for the benefit of the poor,[2] while a year later another yeoman, Luke Springell, bequeathed £100 to feoffees, the income to be given, on the nomination of the Vicar of Sandal Magna, by the churchwardens to 'all the indigent poor people' in the parish.[3]

The burden of social responsibility and leadership was passing to the new urban classes and to the second generation of Protestant gentry during the early Stuart period. The vigorous leadership supplied by these groups is most abundantly demonstrated in the will of Brian Crowther, a yeoman clothier of Halifax who died in 1608. Crowther was evidently one of many parishioners deeply influenced by a most remarkable clergyman, John Favour, who was literally creating the social institutions of Halifax.[4] Crowther, in addition to a legacy of £400 which secured the principal endowment of the school which Favour called into being by his own eloquence and insistence, left to 'John Favour, Doctor of Laws, and Vicar of Halifax' and another trustee, a stipend of £10 p.a. to be distributed among the poor by 'six honest and

---

[1] PCY 29/128 1603; VCH, Yorks., I, 451; PP 1823, IX, 804–805; PP 1833, XVIII, 606–607; Yorks. Arch. Journal, XVII (1903), 121–126; Tickell, Hull, 766–769; Gent, Hull, 121–125; Symons, John, Hullinia (Hull, 1872), 81. Gee's total benefactions came to £1068 10s. Vide post, 265, and 306, for his almshouse foundation and his educational charity. An enterprising merchant, Gee greatly enlarged his fortune by speculative building. He was probably a native of Leicestershire. He was mayor of Hull on three occasions, in 1562, 1573, and 1582. In addition to his benefactions for education and almshouses, which will be dealt with later, he left £30 for marriage portions, £1 for church uses, £102 13s for church repairs, £10 to the clergy, and £20 for various municipal uses. Some sense of the vigorous and belligerent quality of the man may be gained from his will which recites that 'whereas in the Scriptures the Great God of heaven and earth willed by the prophet to say to Hazekie the kinge to make his wille and put things in order for that he must die Soe I doe now pray and humbly beseech that great and mightie God to confound and destroy all those men, lawyers and others whatsoever, to the deviles to dwell in the pit of Hell which doth . . . take upon them to alter this my will. Amen Lord, in the name of God, Amen'.

[2] PCY 30/93 1606; PP 1828, XX, 632; PP 1895, LXXV, Rotherham, 51. Woodhouse also left £3 7s outright to the poor. He was variously described as 'yeoman' and 'gentleman'.

[3] PCY 30/333 1607; PP 1826–27, X, 676.

[4] Vide post, 323–326, for a brief account of the ministry of this great man.

sufficient persons', of whom the vicar and churchwardens should be three.[1] A few years later, Richard Royd, a chapman, left £90 to the poor of Halifax and nearby communities as well as smaller sums for the maintenance of the clergy and for church repairs,[2] while in 1611, perhaps the greatest of all capitalist entrepreneurs of the period, Thomas Sutton, of London, bequeathed £300 for the support of the poor of Beverley.[3] Another Londoner, William Weddall, a merchant who was a native of York, in 1617 left £150 of endowment for the care of the poor of that city, £20 outright for the needy of St Nicholas Shambles, and £10 for the relief of prisoners in York Castle.[4] In 1620 a London tradesman, Jeffrey Childe, left £100 of capital for the relief of the poor of 'Northend' (Norland, Halifax) as well as smaller sums of £10 and £5 respectively for the poor of the parishes of Harthill and Wales.[5]

But the rapid establishment of these very substantial endowments for the relief of the indigent was by no means confined to the thrusting burgher aristocracies of the new cloth towns and the sons of Yorkshire who had made their fortunes in trade in London. Members of the landed classes, and most particularly those families whose wealth and local prestige dated from the monastic expropriations, were likewise dedicating large endowments in order to ensure controlled and predictable distributions to the poor of the rural parishes of the shire. Thus in 1616 William Day, of the lower gentry, of Hornsea, left charges on land with which £2 p.a. was ensured for the relief of the poor in each of the parishes of Hornsea, Withernwick, and Hatfield.[6] Dame Troth Mallory,

[1] PCY 30/613 1608; *PP* 1828, XX, 572; *PP* 1899, LXXI, 278; Watson, John, *History of Halifax* (L., 1775), 713; Crossley, E. W., ed., *Monumental inscriptions, Halifax parish church* (Leeds, 1909), 58; *Yorks. Arch. Soc. Rec.*, XXXIV (1904), 44–45; Walker, *Halifax registers*, 39, 122–123, 127; Turner, J. H., *Biographia Halifaxiensis* (Bingley, 1883), 43–44, 351. Crowther's widow and her sister, Ellen Hopkinson, gave an almshouse to the town, and the widow gave, as well, a rent-charge of £8 p.a. for teaching poor children in the almshouse (*vide post*, 267). The inscription on Crowther's tomb read: 'Here under resteth the body of Brian Crowther, clothier, of Halifax, who deceased in the faith of Christ Jesus, full of yeares and good workes . . . benefactor to the free schoole and pore.' *Vide post*, 325.

[2] PCY 33/213 1614; *Halifax Antiq. Soc. Papers*, 1904, 65.

[3] For a notice of Sutton's immense charitable dispositions, the largest in our entire period, *vide* Jordan, *Charities of London*, 35, 151–152, 205, 218, 233, 360, 361.

[4] PCC 34 Weldon 1617; Drake, *Eboracum*, 221, 223; Lawton, *Collectio*, 10. Weddall also left £393 to London charities.

[5] PCC 102 Soame 1620.

[6] PCY 34/92 1616; Poulson, George, *History of Holderness* (Hull, 1840–1841, 2 vols.), I, 331; *Alum. cantab.*, I, i, 24; *PP* 1823, IX, 763. Day was thirty-four when he died. His epitaph:

> If that man's life be likened to a day,
> One here interr'd in youth did lose a day,
> By death, and yet no loss to him at all,

whose second husband, Sir John Mallory, was a member of the Council of the North, had in 1602 given £100 of capital for the support of the poor of Rotherham and eight adjoining townships, to which in 1616 she added £100 for the enlargement of the endowment.[1] At about the same date, Barney Wood of Kilnwick left £10 outright and an endowment of £200 for the care of the poor of that parish and forty-two other nearby towns and hamlets, thereby strengthening the similar dispositions made by his father, Thomas Wood, in 1584.[2] The eighth Earl of Shrewsbury by his will proved in 1618 provided £100 of capital for the relief of the poor people of Rotherham and an identical trust for the needy of Pontefract.[3] Thomas Cutler, of the lesser gentry of the county, in 1622 left £40 capital for the relief of the poor of Silkstone, as well as a large endowment for founding a lectureship in Stainborough chapel,[4] which was augmented by his widow, Ellen, in 1636 with a bequest of property,

> For he a threefold day gain'd by his fall;
> One day of rest in bliss celestial,
> Two days on earth by gifts terrestryall—
> Three pounds at Christmas, three at Easter Day,
> Given to the poure until the world's last day,
> This was no cause to heaven; but, consequent,
> Who thither will, must tread the steps he went.
> For why? Faith, hope, and christian charity,
> Perfect the house framed for eternity.

[1] PCY 34/442 1616; *PP* 1828, XX, 647; *PP* 1895, LXXV, Rawmarsh, 5, Rotherham, 62–64; *Surtees Soc. Pub.*, LXVII (1876), 328; Eastwood, *Ecclesfield*, 307–310. She was the daughter of Sir William Tyrwhitt, of Lincolnshire, and her first husband was Sir Godfrey Foljambe, of Aldwark, Yorkshire, who died in 1585. Lady Mallory explained in her will, 'Foreasmuch as these my worldly goodes were given to me to the end that I should distribute some parte thereof to the necessitie of the poore, lame, blind, and comfortless, and although I have given alreadie some parte thereof and that in reasonable measure, viz., £100 to the poore within the parishes of Rotherham, Raumarsh, Egglesfield, thinkeinge it better in these cases of charitie to worke some goode whilest I lived than to have all done after my death by my xr., I give £100 more to the same. . . . '

[2] PCY 34/350 1616; *Alum. cantab.*, I, v, 451. For Thomas Wood, *vide ante*, 233.

[3] PCC 19 Meade 1618; *PP* 1895, LXXV, Rotherham, 17; *PP* 1898, LXVIII, Pontefract, 25; Holmes, Richard, ed., *The booke of entries of Pontefract* (Pontefract, 1882), 39–40; Drury, Charles, *A sheaf of essays* (Sheffield, 1929), 42; *Complete peerage*, VII, 140–142. The third son of the sixth earl, Talbot was born in 1561, was educated at Oxford, and was M.P. for Northumberland in 1584–87. He succeeded to the peerage in 1616. There was a long delay in the payment of his legacies, the tenth earl making good the bequests in 1632.

[4] PCY 37/182 1622; Hunter, *South Yorkshire*, II, 266; *PP* 1826–27, X, 760; *PP* 1896, LXIII, ii, Silkstone, 1–3, 10–11. The son of John Cutler, a London lawyer who acquired estates in Yorkshire, Cutler was a justice of the peace and an ardent Puritan. His son and administrator was Sir Gervase Cutler. *Vide post*, 384.

worth approximately £100, for the further relief of the poor of Silkstone and £320 for the augmentation of the lectureship.[1] Finally, among the group of benefactions made by members of the landed classes, we may mention the capital bequest of £100 for the relief of the poor of Wakefield made by Dorothy Sproxton of London, a member of the great Savile family of Yorkshire and a sister to the famous Sir Henry and Sir John of Methley.[2]

There is a variety of interesting and substantial benefactions made for the benefit of the poor during the early Stuart period. In 1613 a prosperous yeoman, Richard Somerscales, who had begun life as a poor shepherd and who was for many years a waller, left property then worth £240 and situated in Halifax and Ovenden, to trustees for the benefit of the poor of these communities. In 1894 the Halifax portion of the trust alone was valued at £7906 3s, the land having increased enormously in value before it had been sold, while some years later the Ovenden portion was valued at approximately £500.[3] Elizabeth Craven, the widow of the great London merchant, Sir William, who was a notable benefactor to Burnsall,[4] by her will proved in 1624 established an endowment of £100 for the relief of the poor of that parish as well as augmenting with a bequest of £200 the stock left by her husband for the support of his charities.[5] The Vicar of Northallerton, Francis Kaye, in 1624 left an annuity of £10, of which £8 p.a. was to be paid for the support of two poor widows from that parish and as many from Brompton, while the remaining £2 p.a. should be employed for their clothing.[6] In the same year Henry Swinburne, himself the author of *A brief*

---

[1] PCY March 1636; Jackson, Rowland, *Barnsley* (L., 1858), 224–225. Ellen Cutler was the daughter of Roger Rainey of Wombwell.

[2] PCC 11 Savile 1622; *PP* 1898, LXVIII, Wakefield, 70; Peacock, M. H., *History of the free grammar school at Wakefield* (Wakefield, 1892), 9.

[3] PCY 32/628 1613; *PP* 1828, XX, 571; *PP* 1899, LXXI, 233, 423–426, 438; Crossley, *Monumental inscriptions*, 40; Watson, *Halifax*, 583–585; *Yorks. Arch. Soc. Rec.*, XXXIV (1904), 46; Turner, *Biographia Halifaxiensis*, 47–49. Somerscales likewise left £1 for repairs on Illingworth chapel in Ovenden.

[4] *Vide post*, 298, 328–329, 400.

[5] PCC 61 Byrde 1624; Beaven, *Aldermen of London*, II, 176; *Yorks. Arch. Journal*, XIII (1895), 442; *Complete peerage*, II, 404; *PP* 1825, XI, 621–622. Vide Jordan, *Charities of London*, 237–238. Elizabeth Craven was the daughter of William Whitmore, a very rich London merchant, and of Ann, a daughter of William Bond, a London merchant and alderman. Her son, William, became the first Earl of Craven, and her daughters married Lord Powis and Lord Coventry.

[6] *VCH, Yorks., NR*, I, 433; Ingledew, C. J., *History of North Allerton* (L., 1858), 175, 270; Lawton, *Collectio*, 496; Peile, John, ed., *Biographical register of Christ's College* (Cambridge, 1910, 1913, 2 vols.), I, 129; *Alum. cantab.*, I, iii, 12; *PP* 1823, VIII, 700. A graduate of Cambridge in 1578, Kaye was ordained in 1584. He was headmaster of Durham School (1579–1593), being as well Vicar of Heighington, Durham, until 1593, in which year he was instituted Vicar of Northallerton, serving the parish until his death in 1624.

treatise of testaments and last wills, left property charged with the payment of from £4 to £5 annually for the relief of the poor of York City,[1] who were likewise assisted in 1629 under the terms of the will of Susanna Marshall, widow of a mercer and a former mayor of the city. This staunchly Puritan lady had previously conveyed to trustees real property valued at £100, the income of which was to be employed by the churchwardens of All Hallows parish for the relief of their poor. To this fund she added £100 by will, the income to be distributed in bread to widows or artificers, it being most carefully stipulated that no Papist was to enjoy benefits.[2]

One of the greatest of the many benefactors in this most generous period was Thomas Ferres [Ferries], a merchant of Hull who left a total of £4297 17s for various and carefully considered charitable uses principally in the city where his great fortune had been made.[3] Ferres left £1000 in 1630 as a stock for the Corporation of Hull to be employed for the general good of the city and more specifically for the relief of its poor. He left as well lands worth upwards of £467 capital value to the municipal authorities, from the income of which £3 6s 8d should each year be distributed to the poor of Hull at Christmas time and £20 p.a. for the relief of the poor of Howden, while the remainder of the income should be employed for maintaining a poor scholar of the town at Oxford or Cambridge. Lesser endowments for the care of the poor were likewise provided by will or gift, with the result that the total of this remarkable man's benefactions for the succour of the poor in their own houses was of the order of £1564.[4]

---

[1] PCY 5/248 1624; Drake, *Eboracum*, 377. A native of the city, Swinburne was Proctor of the Ecclesiastical Court of York, subsequently appointed Judge of the Prerogative Court.

[2] PCY 40/355 1629; *Yorks. Arch. Journal*, VII (1882), 101–103; *PP* 1825, X, 607. Mrs Marshall was the daughter of Robert Brooke, a merchant and alderman of York. Her husband, Thomas Marshall, third son of Roger Marshall, of the lower gentry, was admitted a freeman of York in 1586. He was successively chamberlain (1597), sheriff (1607), and mayor (1613), dying in 1622.

[3] *Vide post*, 271, 288, 296, for his other benefactions.

[4] PCY 41/351 1630; Hadley, George, *Kingston-upon-Hull* (Hull, 1788, 2 vols.), 757–758, 781, 812; *Yorks. Arch. Soc. Rec.*, XXXIV (1904), 199; Smith, William, ed., *Old Yorkshire* (L., 1881–1891, 8 vols.), I, 92; *VCH, Yorks., NR*, II, 349; Tickell, *Hull*, 677, 697, 882; Symons, John, *Kingstoniana* (Hull, 1889), 109, *Hullinia*, 76–77; Sheahan, J. J., *Kingston-upon-Hull* (Beverley, 1866), 591–594; Lawton, *Collectio*, 389; *PP* 1823, IX, 788–792. Ferres was born in *ca.* 1568 in the North Riding, probably in Danby parish, his will having provided an annuity for the minister and a sum for the repair of Glaisdale chapel there. He settled in Hull as a very poor boy, if not, as legend has it, as a tramp, and was apprenticed to Thomas Humphrey, a ship owner and wool merchant. He was admitted to the freedom of the city in 1596 and in the same year became master and part owner of a coasting vessel. For some eighteen years his activities were concentrated on shipping; he was admitted as a younger brother of the Trinity

A yeoman of Rotherham, John Shaw, in 1629 left property valued at
£60 for the assistance of the poor of his parish, as well as a house in
Sheffield on which he laid a rent-charge of £4 p.a. for the relief of the
needy in Ecclesfield.[1] Two years later, another yeoman, Arthur Harper
of Sutton, left capital valued at £80 in order to distribute £4 p.a. in
twelve penny loaves each Sunday, with a yearly sermon on November
5 'in remembrance of God's great mercy and deliverance of this whole
land from yt monstrous and horrible treason of those bloudy papists',
to be followed by a dinner for forty poor children. Harper's intricate
will also provided for the distribution of Bibles to the twelve poorest
families of the district, stipulating that there be one person in each
family who 'can distinctly reade the same to the rest', the Bibles to be
passed on to another poor household upon the death or removal of any
favoured family from the parish.[2] Shortly afterwards, John Rainey, a
rich London draper, not only settled an endowed school and lectureship
on his native hamlet of Worsborough, but provided, with the Drapers'
Company as trustees, an endowment with a capital value of £133 for the
relief of the poor of the chapelry.[3]

Towards the close of the early Stuart era there was a pronounced
acceleration in the vesting of endowments for the care of the poor, with
a notable revival of giving for this purpose on the part of the lesser
gentry and the substantial yeomanry of the county. Among these benefactions was the settlement on trustees in 1632 of lands worth £120 by
Margaret Wormeley for the benefit of the poor of Sprotbrough, Arksey,
and Smithley.[4] At about the same date, Samuel Rabanke of Danby,
who had translated himself from trade in London to gentle status in the
North Riding, transferred to trustees lands with a then value of upwards
of £370 with the stipulation that a charitable use to be determined by his

House in 1602 and assistant in 1613. One legend has it that the beginnings of his
great wealth were gained when all on board one of his vessels, fleeing the plague
in London, died, leaving a fortune in gold and jewels unclaimed in his hands.
Ferres became a merchant on shore in 1614 and was chosen sheriff of the city.
He was named warden of the Trinity House in 1617, 1622, and 1627 and served
as Mayor of Hull in 1620. Though twice married, he died childless.

[1] PCY 40/628 1629; PP 1828, XX, 632; PP 1829, VIII, 613; PP 1894, LXIV,
Ecclesfield, 22; Eastwood, Ecclesfield, 314.

[2] Blashill, Thomas, Sutton-in-Holderness (Hull, 1896), 182–184.

[3] PCC 30 Russell 1633; PP 1826–27, X, 789–790; PP 1896, LXIII,ii, Darfield, 24–25, 28–29, 34–35; Hunter, South Yorkshire, II, 121, 294–295; Complete
baronetage, II, 153, 415. Rainey, whose total benefactions for the community
came to £1050, was the son of Roger Rainey of this region. His son, John, was
created a baronet (S.) in 1635, a baronet of England in 1641, and resided at
Wrotham, Kent. Vide post, 336, 384. Vide Jordan, Charities of London, 288, 412,
for Rainey's large London benefactions.

[4] PP 1826–1827, X, 788; Yorks. Arch. Soc. Rec., LVIII (1917), 55. Margaret
Wormeley was probably the widow of Thomas Wormeley, a gentleman of
Sprotbrough, who died in 1627 (vide post, 333).

will should prevail. Rabanke died four years later, in 1635, and his carefully composed will directed the distribution in weekly instalments of £16 4s p.a. to nine poor of the parish of Danby, to be chosen by his principal trustees from eighteen nominated by the curate, the church-wardens, and the overseers. The trust also provided 10s for a sermon to be preached annually by 'some godly and able' clergyman, with a further distribution on that occasion of a peck of rye to each of the poor.[1] Still another of the lesser gentry of the North Riding, William Smithson, of Kirby Misperton, in 1637 charged a farm in that parish with an annuity of £5 to be distributed weekly in bread for the poor of the community and 10s for a special distribution following an anniversary sermon. Smithson, who also founded a school in the parish and who left a substantial endowment for the repair of roads,[2] carefully addressed his charities, which totalled £420 in capital value, to the most pressing needs of his community.[3] In the same year Thomas Thistlethwaite, very possibly a Londoner, conveyed to trustees lands then valued at upwards of £104 to pay £5 4s annually to six poor men and six poor women of Dent chapelry (Sedbergh) 'every Sabbath day weekly, 12 tenpenny loaves of the second sort of bread, and 2d apiece in money.'[4]

In 1638 the parish of Knaresborough was beneficiary under the will of Anthony Acham, a London merchant who had purchased the manor of Asterby (near Horncastle) in Lincolnshire and who on his death bestowed the whole of its capital worth in generous charities in six counties of the realm. The trust provided that £6 p.a. of the income should be payable to the vicar and churchwardens of Knaresborough for distribution in bread to poor persons of the parish chosen at their discretion.[5] In the same year, a London merchant tailor, Robert Gray, left a capital sum of £200 for the benefit of the poor of Howden and Beverley.[6] At the very close of the early Stuart period a yeoman of

[1] PCY December 1636; PP 1822, X, 715; VCH, Yorks., NR, II, 339, 469; Ord, J. W., History of Cleveland (L., 1846), 334; Yorks. Arch. Soc. Rec., LIII (1915), 57, 132, 206. Rabanke had, with Thomas Swinfield, purchased the manor of Kingthorpe in 1627.

[2] Vide post, 298, 337.

[3] VCH, Yorks., NR, II, 449; PP 1822, X, 736; Yorks. Arch. Soc. Rec., LIII (1915), 215. Smithson was a native of Essex who had purchased extensive properties in Yorkshire in 1613.

[4] PP 1825, XI, 662; this may well be Thomas Thistlethwait of St Bride's parish, London, who died in 1638 (PCC 112 Harvey 1639).

[5] PCC 84 Evelyn 1641; PP 1820, IV, 467; PP 1839, XIV, 275, XV, 31. The will was drawn in 1638; indentures were entered into with trustees in 1640; Acham died in 1641. If the bequests are translated into capital values, the poor of London were left £180; the poor of Lincolnshire £640, as well as a school with an endowment of £200; the poor of Nottingham £100; of Northampton-shire £160; and of Leicestershire £180.

[6] PCC 150 Lee 1638; Lawton, Collectio, 345; PP 1824, XIV, 758. Vide Jordan, Charities of London, 157, 363.

Coxwold, Richard [or John] Forster devised to trustees property then worth upwards of £160 which he charged with an annuity of £8 to be distributed to the poor of Coxwold and four adjoining parishes by the churchwardens and overseers.[1] In the same year, Henry Metcalf of Leeds, of a merchant family of that town, but himself a substantial landed proprietor, charged lands in Armley with a rent of £5 p.a. to be distributed by the churchwardens or overseers of Holbeck chapelry in money and clothing to the poor of the community, as well as an annuity of £1 to secure the services of a preaching minister at Holbeck chapel.[2] Finally, in 1640, George Smith, a prosperous yeoman of Aldfield devised to trustees certain tithes, with a capital worth of £120, to be employed at their discretion for the relief of the sufferings of the poor of his community (which was done), or 'some other charitable and pious use'.[3]

We have noted but a few of the host of gifts, made by men and women of all classes and of every region, that were designed to relieve the condition of the poor in Yorkshire. We have inevitably been concerned with the larger and more carefully devised endowments which were in their totality during the early Stuart period to rear high and permanent bulwarks against utter want in the county. There were thirty-five such substantial benefactions of £100 or more made during this interval, while there were another thirty-four, all being capital creations, that ranged in value between £50 and £100. It is significant that the practice of lavish funeral doles had almost completely died out, the largest gift or bequest for immediate distribution in this whole generation being one in the amount of £40. These generous benefactions, which of course account for a very high proportion of the total of gifts and bequests for the poor, somewhat obscure the social significance of the fact that men of all classes were now dedicated to the assault being made on misery and want. In this interval of forty years there were 1201 bequests to the poor of £1 or less, usually in the form of outright distributions. The total of these gifts was not large as compared with the fruitful capital being accumulated by the generosity of the gentry and the burghers, but it none the less betokened a new, a responsible, and a civilized attitude towards poverty on the part of the generality of men.

During our final period, in spite of the serious and pervasive distraction of armed conflict, political unsettlement, and a disturbed economy, the curve of giving for the relief of the poor continued its abrupt rise. In this brief interval of twenty years the huge total of £26,392 14s was

[1] PCY August 1640; *VCH, Yorks., NR*, II, 133; *PP* 1820, V, 391; *PP* 1822, IX, 598.

[2] PCY June 1640; *Thoresby Society Publications*, VII (1897), 134; *Old Leeds charities* (Leeds, 1926), 40; Lawton, *Collectio*, 96; *PP* 1826, XIII, 679.

[3] PCY November 1640; *PP* 1820, IV, 492; *PP* 1898, LXVIII, Ripon, 84.

disposed for the cure of poverty, of which £13,934 16s was for the relief of poor people in their own houses, if bequests for general charitable uses be included. We should review at least a sampling of the large number of substantial capital foundations for poor relief vested in the course of these two decades.

A particularly testy merchant of York, Henry Atkinson, in 1641 left £10 outright to the poor of that city and £100 for general charitable works under the terms of his will.[1] William Dickinson, of the lesser gentry, in the same year left £100 as a stock for the benefit of the poor of Ecclesfield.[2] The parish of Fishlake benefited under the terms of the will of Richard Rands, a native of that place, who was Rector of Hartfield in Sussex. Rands, who likewise founded a school in the parish,[3] left a stipend of £5 p.a. for the perpetual relief of poor people at the discretion of the parish officers.[4] By will drawn in the same year, 1641, Samuel Casson of Leeds, who describes himself as a gentleman but who was more probably a tradesman, left to the town authorities, after the death of his widow, farm lands, the income, then amounting to £6 15s 8d p.a., to be distributed for the relief of poverty in the community.[5] Charles Greenwood of Thornhill, who though a clergyman possessed by inheritance substantial landed estates in Yorkshire, at his death in 1643 bequeathed £100 to the poor of Thornhill and adjoining towns, as well as vesting a large charitable estate totalling £4630, principally for educational purposes.[6] In the same year a Leeds merchant, Josias

[1] PCY September 1641; *Surtees Soc. Pub.*, CII (1899), 9, 32, 49. Atkinson also left £100 as a loan fund to Ripon (*vide post*, 294). He explained that because of 'unkind usage' he had revoked a legacy of £50; for a gold chain for the Mayor of York and £50 as a stock for the poor there. He had also set aside £100 for the purchase and redemption of impropriations, but here he had been 'crossed by high powers' and instead left the amount for general charitable purposes.

[2] PCY July 1641; Eastwood, *Ecclesfield*, 314-315; *PP* 1829, VIII, 613; *PP* 1894, LXIV, Ecclesfield, 23. There was a long delay in the payment of this bequest, feoffees being appointed under a Commission of Pious Uses in 1681. A portion (£40) was used to build a workhouse in 1710, and the remainder was invested.   [3] *Vide post*, 341.

[4] *PP* 1819, X-B, 166; *PP* 1826-1827, X, 790; Foster, Joseph, ed., *Alumni oxonienses* (Oxford, 1891-1892, 4 vols.), III, 1233; Blakiston, H.E.D., *Trinity College* (L., 1898), 110; Wood, Anthony (John Gutch, ed.), *History of the colleges in Oxford* (Oxford, 1786), 530; British Record Society, *Index Library*, XXIV (1901), 231. Rands' will was proved at Lewes in 1640 (Book A27, B7, 113-225). He matriculated at Trinity, Oxford, in 1604, aged 14, and was graduated B.A. in 1608, M.A. in 1612, B.D. in 1619. He founded a grammar school with an income of £20 p.a. at Hartfield, left £5 p.a. to the poor of that parish, and £20 p.a. to his college, as well as twenty-eight volumes from his library.

[5] PCY October 1643; Thoresby, Ralph (T.D. Whitaker, ed.), *Ducatus leodiensis* (Leeds, 1816), 56; Smith, *Old Yorkshire*, I, 99; *Old Leeds charities*, 37-38; *PP* 1899, LXXII, 357-361. *Vide post*, 294.

[6] *Halifax Antiq. Soc. Papers, 1908*, 163, *1917*, 122-147; *VCH, Yorks.*, I, 483; Parsons, Edward, *History of Leeds* (Leeds, 1834, 2 vols.), II, 373-374; *PP*

Jenkinson, who during his lifetime had provided eight almshouses for desitute persons of his city, bequeathed to four trustees a farm then possessing a capital worth of about £200 under instructions to dispose the 'yearly rents and profits thereof, among such poor, impotent, and aged people' of the town as they might determine.[1]

It will be observed that even during the years when the county was torn by actual warfare the accumulation of endowments for the poor continued almost without diminution. Thus Henry Clifford, the last Earl of Cumberland, 'knowing the daly hazards I undergoe by the greate charge and trust that my gracious soveraine hath committed unto me, for the maintenance of the true Protestant relligion, the knowne lawes of the land, the privilege of Parliament, the iust liberty of the subject and his majesties iust prerogative', drew his will in which he bequeathed a stock of £160 for the benefit of the poor of several Yorkshire parishes.[2] An humbler servant of the Crown, Edmund Rogers, of Barnsley, a yeoman who was the collector of the Queen's rents in that community, in 1646 left an estate with a capital worth of £310 for the relief of the poor of the town, £2 6s 8d p.a. being reserved for the poor of Thorpe Audlin and the hamlet of Wentbridge, as well as £50 each to Silkstone and South Kirkby for their poor.[3] By deeds recorded in 1645 and 1648,

---

1826–1827, X, 680; *PP* 1828, XX, 587; Skelton, Joseph, *Pietas oxoniensis* (Oxford, 1828), 11–12. Greenwood was the son of James Greenwood of Greenwood Lea, Heptonstall, a rich country gentleman. Though a second son, Greenwood inherited considerable landed wealth and acquired other lands near Heptonstall at intervals from Sir Arthur Ingram, then lord of the manor. He attended Oxford, where he was a tutor at University College from 1598 to 1604 and Proctor of the University in 1609. He was Strafford's tutor there and accompanied him abroad. In 1612 he was instituted Rector of Thornhill, a community which he so generously remembered in his charities. He founded a grammar school there, and in 1635 he had subscribed £35 to the needs of Halifax Grammar School. Greenwood's charities reached the great total of £4630. One of his executors, Anthony Foxcroft, was imprisoned for non-performance of the will, and his estate was sequestered to secure payment. In the litigation which ensued, University College lost part of a benefaction intended to endow fellowships. *Vide post*, 294, 338, 341, 355.

[1] *PP* 1826, XIII, 667; *PP* 1899, LXXII, 373–374; Parsons, *Leeds*, II, 143; *Thoresby Soc. Pub.*, I (1889), 13n., 238, 273, VII (1897), 193. Jenkinson's daughter and co-heiress, Grace, became a Quaker minister; she married William Sykes (*vide post*, 248). Jenkinson's bequests should not be confused with those of William Jenkinson of Boston, Lincolnshire, who in 1642 devised to trustees lands charged with the payment of £2 p.a. to the poor of Burley (Yorks.), of which he was a native, £2 p.a. to the poor of Otley (Yorks.), £1 p.a. to the poor of Halton (Yorks.), and £5 p.a. to the poor of Boston. For Josias Jenkinson's almshouses, *vide post*, 275.

[2] PCY August 1644; *Yorks. Arch. Journal*, XVIII (1905), 397–400; DNB.

[3] PCY January 1646; Hunter, *South Yorkshire*, II, 254–255; *PP* 1826–1827, X, 767; *PP* 1896, LXIII, ii, Silkstone, 6, 16. A native of Midhope (in Bradfield), Rogers held property in that community, as well as in Thorpe Audlin, Bads-

John Jackson, the Rector of Marske, conveyed certain rents with a capital value estimated at £340 for such charitable uses as the lord of the manor and the parson of Marske might determine, the income to be employed for the relief of the deserving poor.[1]

In 1648 William Shirecliffe, a gentleman of Ecclesfield, left £100 as an endowment for that parish, which was later augmented by a gift of £40 from his sister, Margaret.[2] One of the largest of all benefactions for the relief of the poor was made in this same year under the will of John, Lord Craven, a son of Sir William, who was himself a principal benefactor of the county.[3] Craven, whose various charities totalled £5160, left £2060 of capital for the relief of poverty. Of this amount, £1000 was placed on trust, with £200 provided as a stock for each of the towns of Skipton in Craven, Knaresborough, Ripon, Ripley, and Boroughbridge, the whole of the income to be distributed to the poor at Christmas each year by the parsons and churchwardens. In addition, an endowment of £500 was vested for the relief of distressed cottagers and farmers in Yorkshire and elsewhere, while £20 each was left for two rural parishes. This great charity was completed by an endowment of £400 left for the aid of the poor in specified parishes in Northamptonshire, £100 for similar uses in Binley, Warwickshire, and a small endowment for a London parish.[4]

worth, and Barnsley. He also left £50 for building a schoolhouse, £10 for erecting a clock in the town hall of Barnsley; £50 for building a suitable house for the clergyman at Barnsley, and £20 towards maintaining a minister at Midhope Chapel. *Vide post*, 342.

[1] *VCH, Yorks., NR*, I, 104; *PP* 1822, X, 725; *Alum. cantab.*, I, ii, 455. We have not seen these deeds. The secondary sources quoted would suggest that there were two rent-charges of £100 and £40 respectively, redeemable under prescribed conditions, which would ordinarily suggest that these amounts represented the annual income, or a very large capital value. But the rentals were redeemed later in the century at approximately £340.

Jackson was the son of the rector of Melsonby, Yorkshire. Born in 1600, he was educated at Cambridge, from which he was graduated B.A. in 1617 and M.A. in 1620. Master of Richmond Grammar School from 1618 to 1620, he was ordained priest in 1623 and from that date forward was Rector of Marske. A staunch Puritan, he was a member of the Westminster Assembly. Two of his brothers, Nathaniel and Timothy, were also Yorkshire clergymen.

[2] Eastwood, *Ecclesfield*, 318-320. Shirecliffe was the second son of Thomas Shirecliffe of Whitley Hall. He was graduated M.A. from Cambridge in 1640. He died without issue.

[3] *Vide ante*, 239, and *post*, 298, 328-329.

[4] PCC 20 Essex 1648; *Yorks. Arch. Journal*, XIII (1895), 444-446; Dawson, W. H., *History of Skipton* (L., 1882), 329; Whitaker, T. D. (A. W. Morant, ed.), *Deanery of Craven* (L., 1878), 510; Cooper, *Memorials of Cambridge*, III, 428; *Complete peerage*, II, 407; *Sussex Archaeological Collections*, XIX (1867), 110. *Vide post*, 290, 356, for a discussion of Craven's other charitable dispositions. John Craven was the second son of Sir William, whose great fortune had been made in trade in London. He inherited £5000 outright from his father and some-

The poor of Ripon were further benefited in 1649 under the terms of the will of George Teasdale, a yeoman of that place, who devised to trustees properties then worth £156, the income of which, after the death of his wife, should be employed to afford relief to the deserving poor.[1] At about the same time, 1651, several rural communities in the West Riding were assisted under the bequest of a Royalist member of the lesser gentry, Thomas Stringer of Sharleston. Stringer left on trust a rent-charge of £3 p.a. to be distributed by the churchwardens and overseers to the poor of Sharleston and Foulby, as well as £2 p.a. for the relief of the poor of Kirkthorpe, Warmfield, and Heath.[2] In the following year, Robert Metcalf, a retiring and distinguished Cambridge scholar, left substantial and well-considered legacies for the benefit of Beverley, his birthplace.[3] Among them was the grant to the municipality of lands recently purchased in Cambridgeshire then yielding a rental of £22 10s, of which £20 p.a. was to be distributed to the poorest people of the town each December 20th, while the remainder should be paid to the Corporation for general municipal uses, but to assist in the payment of taxes and rates for the maintenance of the Commonwealth's army so long as that need should continue.[4] A lesser endowment was created in the same year for the relief of the poor of Tankersley and Wortley with the bequest of £150 of capital left by Sir Francis Wortley.[5]

The steady and the rapid accumulation of endowments for the benefit of the poor continued unabated during the whole of the period of the Protectorate. Thus in 1653 a widow, Cicely Tenant of Arncliffe, who

what later (1634) married Elizabeth, daughter of the second Baron Spencer. He was raised to the peerage in 1643 at Oxford with the title Baron Craven of Ryton. Craven died without issue in 1648.

[1] *PP* 1820, IV, 501–502; *PP* 1898, LXVIII, Ripon, 92; *Yorks. Arch. Soc. Rec.*, LVIII (1917), 102.

[2] PCC 97 Grey 1651; *Yorks. Arch. Soc. Rec.*, IX (1890), 30–31; Green, M.A.E., ed., *Calendar of the Committee for Compounding* (L., 1889–1892, 5 vols.), II, 1219; *Alum. cantab.*, I, iv, 175. The son of Francis Stringer, Thomas was educated at Emmanuel College, Cambridge, which he entered in 1603 at the age of 17. He married Barbara Fleming, also of Sharleston. He was in prison in York in 1646 under suspicion of Royalist activity, and his estate was sequestered. He was released in bond, and in 1650 his estate was discharged on payment of a fine of one-sixth, or £485 13s. Stringer died in the next year without issue.

[3] *Vide post*, 302, 360, 385 for Metcalf's educational and religious bequests.

[4] *PP* 1824, XIII, 677; Gilbert, *Liber scholasticus*, 278; Lawton, *Collectio*, 320; Poulson, George, *Beverlac* (L., 1820), 456–458; *VCH, Yorks.*, I, 429; Wilson, B., ed., *Sedbergh School register* (Leeds, 1909), 89; Baker, Thomas (J.E.B. Mayor, ed.), *History of the College of St. John* (Cambridge, 1869, 2 vols.), I, 341; *Alum. cantab.*, I, iii, 179; *Yorks. Arch. Soc. Rec.*, XXVII (1899), liii.

[5] PCC 242 Bowyer 1652; *Yorks. Arch. Soc. Rec.*, IX (1890), 49–50. Wortley, created a baronet in 1611, had served as a colonel of foot under the King during the Civil War. His was a nuncupative will.

in 1649 had given £10 of capital for the poor of Wortley and a matching sum for the poor of Holbeck, bequeathed £200 to be employed by named trustees for the purchase of lands, the rents to be used for the support of the poor of Arncliffe. In addition, she left £20 outright to the poor of Holbeck, £10 to the poor of Abbotside, and £6 13s to the poor of Armley.[1] In the same year, William Sykes, a rich landowner, who, like the rest of his family, had made a fortune as a merchant in Hull, left considerable sums for the outright relief of the poor, particularly those of the Quaker persuasion: £100 for the poor of 'Mr. Luddington's congregation' and £10 to the poor of 'Mr. Marshall's congregation', £6 to the poor of Knottingley, where he was residing at the time of his death, £6 to the poor of Leeds, £6 to York, and £3 to Wakefield. In addition, he left two beefs, valued at £6, for the succour of prisoners in York Castle and £5 for the relief of Elizabeth Hooton and 'her fellow prisoners that came upon the like commission'.[2] Sir Gervase Clifton, lord of the manor of Wakefield, in the same year settled on trustees, under particularly complicated terms, certain properties then valued at £160 with the provision that the income should be employed for the support of the poor of Horbury chapelry (Wakefield) or for the maintenance of a curate there, as the trustees might determine.[3]

In 1655 Thomas Hutchinson, a London merchant, with a residence and lands in Marske, by indenture charged his Yorkshire estate with an annuity of £5 of which £3 p.a. should be paid to the poor of Skelton

[1] PCC 55 Brent 1653; *Old Leeds charities*, 40; *PP* 1826, XIII, 679.

[2] PCC 68 Brent 1653; *S.P.Dom.*, 1647, DXV, 48; *S.P.Dom.*, 1653, XLII, 89; Green, M.A.E., ed., *Calendar of the Committee for Advance of Money* (L., 1888, 3 vols.), II, 941. Sykes was certainly a Quaker in sympathy, his widow, Grace (*vide ante*, 245), having been an early preacher for the sect. He was also an ardent, if a somewhat nervous, Parliamentarian. In a petition to Parliament dated April 22, 1647, he claimed that he had advanced the huge sum of £8463 18s 5d in loans to Fairfax and Hotham, as well as having undertaken a mission for the Parliamentary armies which resulted in his capture and imprisonment by the Royalists. Further, during his imprisonment his father had altered his will, bequeathing £300 p.a. intended for him to his brother. An order was finally secured for the payment of £350 to Sykes, but in late 1649 only a fraction of this amount had been paid, and his widow in 1653 received £85 with an acknowledgement of £428 10s 3d still due her husband's estate. Sykes was not, however, so destitute as he portrayed himself. He owned manors and lands in Yorkshire, Cumberland, and Durham worth £1400 and his will disposed an additional £1650.

[3] *PP* 1826–1827, X, 712; *Cal. Comm. for Compounding*, II, 1318; *Complete baronetage*, I, 19. Clifton was the posthumous son of George Clifton (d. 1587) and of Winifred, a daughter of Sir Anthony Thorold, of Lincolnshire. He succeeded to his large estate when aged four months. He was made a Knight of the Bath in 1603 and created a baronet in 1611. He served in nine parliaments, being a member of the Long Parliament until he was disabled in 1644. A staunch, if quiet, Royalist, he was fined upwards of £7600 before regaining his estates. Clifton was married seven times and died in 1666 at the age of 80.

and the remainder to the needy of Marske.[1] The ardently Royalist gentleman, James Pennyman, of Ormesby, under his will proved in 1656 laid a rent-charge of £10 p.a. on certain of his lands for the perpetual benefit and relief of worthy poor in the parish of Ormesby.[2] Still another Royalist, a London jeweller, Matthew Broadley, in 1651 left £250 to provide bread and other necessaries for the poor of his native village of Hipperholme (Halifax), as well as a most generous foundation for a grammar school in the community.[3]

The Puritan clergyman at Market Weighton in the East Riding, William Hide, by his will proved in 1657 left extensive charities for the parish and nearby communities.[4] His principal concern was with the plight of the poor, to whom he left a rent-charge of £8 p.a. as well as a stock of £100 for household relief and another £100 to be used by trustees for general charitable purposes. In addition, Hide left part of a garth, the house being set aside as a parsonage, to be used in growing carrots, turnips, and parsnips for the poor. He likewise disposed £26 outright for the needy of his parish, as well as £13 for the care of the poor of nearby parishes.[5] A London grocer, William Underwood, in the next year bequeathed property in Ripon with a capital value of £100 to secure the support of ten poor widows 'of good conversation' who should be nominated by the mayor and commonalty, with a further

[1] PCC 339 Berkeley 1656; *VCH, Yorks., NR*, I, 104; *Archaeologia aeliana*, n.s., V (1861), 22, 75; *PP* 1822, X, 724; *Cal. Comm. for Advance of Money*, I, 149.

[2] PCC 10 Berkeley 1656; *VCH, Yorks., NR*, II, 278; *Yorks. Arch. Soc. Rec.*, IX (1890), 89, XV (1893), 187–194; *Alum. oxon.*, III, 1143; *PP* 1822, X, 727. Pennyman and his son, Sir James, were staunch Royalists. Pennyman, who was 66 years of age in 1646, was, together with his son, fined £1835 3s 4d, this being twice the estimated annual income of their landed properties. Sir James, who was created a baronet in 1664, had served as a colonel in the royal army. Another son, Thomas, was a minister at Stokesley, while another, John, was a London merchant.

[3] PCC 139 Grey 1651; *Alum. cantab.*, I, i, 223; *PP* 1828, XX, 574–578; *PP* 1899, LXXI, 235, 475–487; *VCH, Yorks.*, I, 484; Parsons, *Leeds*, II, 374–375; *Halifax Antiq. Soc. Papers*, 1924, 195, 205n.; *Yorks. Arch. Soc. Rec.*, XX (1896), 89. *Vide post*, 344, for his educational foundation. A native of Hipperholme, Broadley became a well-known London jeweller and, during the war, paymaster to the King's army. Broadley, who declined to take the oath or the Covenant, made some composition for his estate before his death, while his executor succeeded in securing a reduction of the remaining fine due, from £252 10s to £176 6s 8d, in part because of the charitable legacies ordered in the will.

[4] *Vide post*, 344, 382, for his support of education and the clergy.

[5] PCC 49 Ruthen 1657; *PP* 1825, X, 645; Shaw, W. A., *History of the English church 1640-1660* (L., 1900, 2 vols.), II, 550; *Alum. cantab.*, I, ii, 445. Educated at St John's, Cambridge, where he was graduated B.A. in 1624, Hide was ordained in 1626. In addition to his endowments for the poor, a school, and the clergy, he also left £20 for loans to the needy and £10 to the sick of his parish. His charities totalled £649.

endowment to secure the education of poor children,[1] while Richard
Benson, a yeoman of Well, bequeathed £6 p.a. for the better maintenance of the poor of that parish and of Snape.[2] Joseph Hillary, a
wealthy clothworker who was twice Mayor of Leeds, in addition to
endowing a school at Calverley and augmenting the clergyman's stipend
there with an annuity of £3, in 1658 left bequests totalling £205 for the
benefit of the poor of Leeds and Calverley, of which £150 was designated for the care of poor clothiers in the two towns.[3] Matthew Francke,
a merchant and former mayor, in 1659 bequeathed £100 as a stock for
the poor of his native town of Pontefract,[4] while a member of the upper
gentry, Sir Richard Hawkesworth, in the same year gave £10 as a stock
to each of seven parishes in which he held property, as well as £20
outright to the needy of six other Yorkshire parishes.[5] In 1660, the parish
of Marske received £100 as an endowment for its poor under the will
of the rich and redoubtable physician John Bathurst, who had found his
wife there some twenty years earlier.[6]

We may conclude with mention of two substantial endowments
vested for the benefit of the poor at the close of our period. John Savile

[1] PCC 147 Wootton 1658; *PP* 1898, LXVIII, Ripon, 51–52; Beaven, *Aldermen of London*, II, 79. A native of Ripon, Underwood made a considerable fortune as a grocer in London. He was a colonel in the trained bands and served as
Sheriff of London in 1652. *Vide post*, 344, for his bequest to education.

[2] PCC 587 Wootton 1658; *PP* 1821, XII, 653; *VCH, Yorks.*, NR, I, 354.

[3] PCC 589, 691 Wootton 1658; *PP* 1826–1827, X, 732; *PP* 1897, LXVII, iv,
Calverley, I, 5–6; Smith, *Old Yorkshire*, I, 100; Lawton, *Collectio*, 117; *Cal.
Comm. for Compounding*, II, 975; *Thoresby Soc. Pub.*, III (1895), 110; *Yorks.
Arch. Soc. Rec.*, XV (1893), 137–139; Margerison, Samuel, ed., *Registers of
parish church of Calverley* (Bradford, 1880), 26. *Vide post*, 345. Hillary was born
at Calverley in 1583. An enterprising cloth merchant, he was chosen Mayor of
Leeds in 1631 and in 1639. He was married to Margaret, a daughter of John
Metcalf. A Royalist supporter, he contributed a horse, a man, and money to the
King, but was too advanced in years to serve himself. He took the Covenant in
1645 and compounded with a fine of £140 to regain his estates. The inventory of
his property made on that occasion estimated his total wealth as £1650.

[4] PCC 237 Pell 1659; *PP* 1826–1827, IX, 428; *PP* 1898, LXVIII, Pontefract,
5–6, 23–24; *Yorks. Arch. Soc. Rec.*, IX (1890), 144–145. *Vide post*, 280, 296. The
son of a merchant and a mayor of Pontefract, Matthew Francke, who died unmarried, was in turn mayor of the town in 1649.

[5] PCC 535 Pell 1659; Baildon, W. P., *Baildon* (L., 1918?–1926, 3 vols.), I,
415; *Yorks. Arch. Soc. Rec.*, IX (1890), 157, XV (1893), 236. Hawkesworth was
born in *ca.* 1594, being the eldest son of Walter Hawkesworth. He first
married Anne, daughter of Thomas Wentworth of Elmsall, and after her death
a daughter of Sir Henry Goodrick. He was knighted in 1621. Hawkesworth
supported Parliament during the Civil Wars.

[6] PCC 237 Nabbs 1660; *VCH, Yorks.*, I, 475, 484; *VCH, Yorks.*, NR, I, 38;
PP 1833, XVIII, 608; Gilbert, *Liber scholasticus*, 299; Clarkson, Christopher,
History of Richmond (Richmond, 1821), 235–236; *Yorkshire Genealogist*, I
(1888), 102; DNB. *Vide post*, 291, 346, 356, for mention of Bathurst's other
substantial charities in Yorkshire.

of Methley at his death in 1659 left outright £20 to the poor of Elland, Stainland, and Barkisland, while creating a trust with a capital worth of £240 to ensure the support, on the nomination of his trustees, of six poor people of the parish of Methley.[1] In the same year, Stephen Watson, a merchant and a mayor of York, in addition to bequests for education and the social rehabilitation of the poor, left a house and grounds worth £160, the income of which should be employed by the mayor and aldermen for the support of six poor men of the city.[2]

We have sketched in some detail the long and certainly impressive effort of private benefactors in Yorkshire to make adequate provision for the poor of their county. In all, as we have noted, the large sum of £42,676 16s had been dedicated towards the amelioration of the lot of the poor in their own households, gifts for general charitable uses being included. A substantial fraction of this amount had, of course, been given in the form of outright alms, but there remained £33,148 10s which had been vested in endowments designed to assist permanently in the cure of at least the worst aspects of poverty in the households of the needy in scores of parishes throughout Yorkshire. Reckoning the interest rate as 5 per cent on trusteed funds, we may assume that by the time of the Restoration trustees and churchwardens of the shire would annually have had in hand something like £1658 to apply to the needs of the indigent. This was a very substantial sum even for so large and populous a county as Yorkshire and, since donors of the era seemed on the average to assume that £2 p.a. was sufficient to keep a household at least on the level of subsistence, we may believe that provision had been made for perhaps 829 households in various parts of this sprawling county. This was not, when compared with richer and more nearly socially mature counties, sufficient for the need, but it is none the less a memorable achievement on the part of hundreds of donors who were determined to keep in rein the socially demoralizing evil of unmitigated

[1] PCC 402 Pell 1659; *Yorks. Arch. Soc. Rec.*, IX (1890), 150–152; *Cal. Comm. for Compounding*, I, 380; Boothroyd, B., *Pontefract* (Pontefract, 1807), 191; Drake, *Eboracum*, 352. John Savile was the son of Sir John, Baron of the Exchequer, by his second wife Elizabeth, daughter of Thomas Wentworth of Elmsall. Born in 1588, he succeeded his half-brother, Sir Henry, as heir in 1632. He married first Mary, daughter of John Robinson of Ryther, and then Margaret, daughter of Sir Henry Garway, a merchant and Lord Mayor of London. Savile supported Parliament, commanding a body of troops in the second siege of Pontefract (1645), serving as high sheriff of the county in 1649, and on the committee for sequestration in 1650. He was an enormously rich gentleman, his fluid wealth being of the order of £10,000 and his landed worth about £600 p.a.

[2] PCC 74 Nabbs 1660; *PP* 1825, X, 637; Drake, *Eboracum*, 171, 222, 366; *Surtees Soc. Pub.*, CXXIX (1917), 289. Watson was a grocer. In 1644, when the Parliamentary authorities were ensuring themselves a well-affected municipal government in York, Watson was appointed an alderman. He was made mayor in 1646. Watson also left £120 for loans and £80 for a scholarship at Cambridge.

poverty. Great endowments had been accumulated, sound traditions had been developed, and the social conscience of this northern county had been fully aroused.

(b) *The founding of almshouses.* But this by no means represents the whole of the achievement of the county in its effort to establish resources for the relief of poverty. Almost as large a total was given by substantial benefactors for the founding of almshouses or for the strengthening of the endowments of already existing institutions. The liberal sum of £38,836 17s was provided for this purpose during our period, representing 15·94 per cent of the whole of charitable funds for the county. It is likewise significant that all, save the inconsequential sum of £395, of this large total was given in the permanently effective form of endowments vested in the rapidly maturing mechanism of the charitable trusteeship.

The interest of private donors in the immensely important role played by almshouses in the relief, in the insulation, of hopeless poverty was evident throughout our period, there being only one decade in which less than £100 of capital was given for this purpose. Even in our first interval a total of £1772 8s was provided, while in the brief period of the Reformation there was an immediate and a most pronounced quickening of interest, £3816 15s having been given. The curve of almshouse giving declined somewhat in the Elizabethan era, when a total of £4053 14s was settled in such endowments. But in the early Stuart generation there was a great outpouring of funds for the founding of new and for the better support of old almshouse establishments. In these four decades the impressive total of £16,736 2s was added to the accumulated almshouse endowments of the county. Nor did the enthusiasm of private donors for these institutions, very properly accounted as one of the most effective of all charitable mechanisms in this period, wane during the troubled decades with which our study concludes, when £12,457 18s was provided for almshouses, reflecting a rate of giving for this purpose substantially higher even than that of the early Stuart interval.

The men of Yorkshire in our period raised these institutions on surviving medieval foundations which were perhaps sounder and deeper than those of any other county in England. This was true in part because medieval institutions seemed to possess a greater survival value in Yorkshire than in other counties of the realm and in part because so many of the foundations in Yorkshire were very late medieval establishments which were under at least partial lay control and which had not had time to decay or undergo an alteration in function. It is extremely difficult from existing records to be certain when a medieval hospital possessed the functions of an almshouse or to make sure that a change in function had not taken place between, shall we say, a late fourteenth-century visitation or inquisition and the beginning of our period. But it seems probable that in the course of the medieval period there were in all forty-six charitable foundations in Yorkshire which at least for a period or at least in part undertook the charitable responsibilities which the sixteenth century regarded as properly belonging to an almshouse: the sheltering and maintenance of the hopelessly indigent. By the beginning of our period twenty of these foundations had disappeared as almshouses and most of them had in fact withered completely as corporate entities, the attrition having been particularly heavy in and around Beverley and York.

There remained, therefore, in 1480 a total of twenty-six foundations, of which three were not at that date fulfilling in any proper sense the functions of an almshouse but two of which were reorganized at the time of the Reformation to undertake this social responsibility. The other, the great medieval foundation of St Leonard's in York, was only imperfectly an almshouse, having been almost wholly diverted from its purposes by the sale of corrodies, and it was suppressed with the Reformation. These numerous establishments were not well distributed across the reaches of the county, rather more than half the number having been concentrated in or near the medieval urban centres of Beverley, Hull, Pontefract, and York. We may, however, say with certainty that in the general period 1480–1540 these foundations gave shelter and maintenance to 162 almspeople, St Leonard's being excluded, and possibly to as many as 42 in addition. Most of these establishments were not endowed; in others practically the whole of the revenues were vested in the master or in priests attached to the foundation; and in few cases were they well administered in the sense that the revenues intended for the maintenance of the helplessly poor were so applied. None the less, it can be said that £190 1s 4d p.a., these values being dated within the pre-Reformation period, was applied for the relief of the poor, suggesting an available capital of something like £3800 for the support of existing almshouses at the outset of our period. It is likewise notable that, save for St Leonard's and for one foundation at Northallerton, none of these establishments was suppressed, while two were restored to a more precise responsibility of function during the time of the Reformation Settlement. It should be noted, however, that four, or possibly five, of these institutions, having no endowments, were so weak that they did not survive for more than a generation or two in the sixteenth century.

Very substantial additions were made to the almshouse resources of the county during the early years of our period. In the decades prior to the Reformation, donors gave or bequeathed a total of £147 15s for the augmentation of the existing endowments of these institutions or as outright gifts for their support. But there were likewise a number of new and most needed foundations, most of which were, it should be said, small, often transitory, and usually the unendowed creations of men who maintained almspeople during their lifetimes, but who failed to make adequate provision from their estates in order to institutionalize their charity. Among these may be noted Dame Alice Nevile's house for two women in Holbeck, built during her lifetime at an estimated charge of £40 and endowed at her death in 1481 with a rent-charge of 13s.[1] Edmund Mauleverer, a gentleman of Bardsey, during his lifetime provided an almshouse at an unknown cost at Bramham, to which at his death in 1494 he gave an annuity of 7s for its future maintenance.[2] In the same year a gentleman with the improbable name of Sir Martin of the Sea, who had built and maintained an almshouse during his later years, enjoined his wife to continue the care of his almspeople but failed to make specific provision for its endowment.[3] Some years later (1511) Thomas St Paul, of the gentry in Badsworth, settled on trustees a cottage and garth near the chapel, valued at £30, for use as an almshouse, but likewise without endowment,[4] while in 1515 a Hull merchant, Richard Doughty, conveyed by will a tenement valued at £20 to the White Friars to be used permanently as a bedehouse.[5] A gentleman of Halifax, John Midgeley, in 1533 ordered a house built for the profit of his parish church, which should include space for an almsperson who should there receive free lodging.[6]

There were, in addition, more substantial and enduring foundations established by donors of the county during this early period. A Doncaster mercer, Edmund Brookhouse, who had earlier been in trade in Barnsley, in 1493 founded and built an almshouse in the latter community at a charge of £26 13s. He further stipulated that a couple should live in the premises rent free in exchange for the supervision of the institution. Brookhouse provided an endowment with a capital worth of £33 to ensure the care of seven old and infirm persons, they being husbands and wives 'past their labour'.[7]

[1] PCY 5/106 1481; *Thoresby Soc. Pub.*, XXIV (1919), 61-62. She was the widow of Sir Thomas Nevile. This donor also left £1 and a vestment for church repairs, £14 for prayers, and £6 13s 4d outright for the poor.

[2] PCY 5/440 1494; *Yorks. Arch. Journal*, XVI (1902), 221-225; *Surtees Soc. Pub.*, LIII (1868), 39-40. Mauleverer also left £11 13s for prayers and 10s for the general uses of the church.

[3] PCY 5/453 1494; *Surtees Soc. Pub.*, LIII (1868), 100. Sir Martin took an active part in opposing Edward IV after he landed at Ravenspur. He was a considerable sheep farmer, his will mentioning 800 animals.

[4] PCY 8/75 1511; *Surtees Soc. Pub.*, LXXIX (1884), 26.

[5] PCY 9/17 1515; *VCH, Yorks.*, III, 269; *Surtees Soc. Pub.*, LXXIX (1884), 47-48.

[6] PCY 11/77 1533; *Halifax Antiq. Soc. Papers*, 1908, 39-41.

[7] *PP* 1826-1827, X, 767; *PP* 1896, LXIII, ii, Silkstone, 5-6, 13; Hunter, *South Yorkshire*, II, 259. There was also a provision that prayers should be offered for the soul of the donor. The endowment may have been regarded as a chantry and was apparently for a time suspect. In 1615, however, an enquiry under the Statute of Charitable Uses restored it.

A great merchant of York, Sir Richard York, active in the affairs of the city for a half-century, on his death in 1498, in addition to substantial benefactions for religious uses, required his executors to build an almshouse for six men and six women at an estimated charge to his estate of £120. York likewise instructed his executors to vest lands sufficient to support his foundation, but we have found no certain evidence that this stipulation was carried out.[1] Just two years later a brewer of Hull, Brand Adryanson, built a hospital, with a pleasant garden and a small oratory, for four old and indigent men of Hull. By the terms of his will, proved in 1503, he vested in his heirs certain properties with a then capital value of £120 for the perpetual support of the foundation.[2] Hull gained still another almshouse in 1518 when a native of that city, John Riplingham, Rector of St Martin Vintry, London, and former fellow of Queens' College, Cambridge, erected at an unknown cost quarters for twenty poor almsmen, which he endowed with property valued at £208, approximately half the income of which was to be employed for the care of his almspeople and the remainder for the support of a chantry which he had established in Trinity Church.[3]

The ill-fated Thomas, Lord Darcy in *ca.* 1520 founded an almshouse, as well as a grammar school, at Whitkirk, near Leeds. The hospital was built and endowed to provide for a master, a hermit, and twelve poor people, each of the almsmen to receive £1 10s 5d annually for maintenance and a gown containing three ells of cloth at Christmas time, while the master, who was to administer both the school and almshouse, was to have £16 13s 4d as his salary, the hermit £1 p.a., and the barber

[1] PCC 36 Horne 1499; *Surtees Soc. Pub.*, LIII (1868), 134–137; *Yorks. Arch. Journal*, XXXVII (1951), 213–230; Drake, *Eboracum*, 278. *Vide post*, 390. York was probably a native of Berwick-upon-Tweed. He purchased his freedom of the City of York and became a prominent merchant there in the mid-fifteenth century. He was chamberlain in 1460, sheriff in 1466, and Mayor of the Staple of Calais the same year. He was chosen to represent the city in Parliament first in 1472 and was elected six more times. He was Master of the Mercers in 1475 and served twice as mayor, in 1469 and 1482. He was knighted in 1487 on the occasion of Henry VII's visit to the city. He left five sons, including Sir John, Mayor of the Staple of Calais, and Thomas, Abbot of Whalley, as well as two bastard sons. York made generous dispositions for prayers, establishing a chantry endowed with £8 15s 4d p.a. and leaving £24 to friars for masses.

[2] PCY 6/64 1503; *Surtees Soc. Pub.*, LIII (1868), 16 n.; Tickell, *Hull*, 190; Hadley, *Hull*, II, 748. Adryanson was a member of a Dutch family which had settled in Hull a generation earlier.

[3] Tickell, *Hull*, 146; *VCH, Yorks.*, III, 313; Cooper, *Athenae cantab.*, I, 20–21; Hadley, *Hull*, I, 71, II, 749, 777; Smith, *Old Yorkshire*, n.s., I, 150; Mayor, J. E. B., ed., *Early statutes of St. John's College* (Cambridge, 1859), 399–400. The son of William Riplingham, a merchant of Hull, Riplingham was a fellow of Queens' College and vice-president after 1484. In addition to the charities mentioned above, he endowed two scholarships in St John's College, Cambridge, and built fish-shambles, at an approximate charge of £50, for the improvement of trade in Hull.

and washerwoman £1 each. Darcy provided as endowment lands then possessing a capital value of £226, if the funds may, as he intended, be equally divided between the almshouse and the school.[1] A few years later, another soldier, Sir William Bulmer, founded a chapel at Wilton in the North Riding, to which was attached an almshouse for five poor men and women; the cost and endowment of the two institutions we have quite uncertainly estimated at £510.[2] Finally, in noting the foundations made prior to the Reformation, we should mention that of Thomas Ryther, a rich gentleman of Ryther parish, who by the terms of his will proved in 1528 provided one thousand marks for the building and endowment of an almshouse for four poor men and one poor woman. His executors were instructed to set aside the revenues of two manors in Lincolnshire until the required capital had been accumulated, while in the meantime they should 'kepe iiij beademen and on beadewoman with mete, drinke, clothe, mansion, and al other things, as they have ben founde in the tymes of my uncle Sir Roberte Rither, and Sr Rauf Rither my fader, and in my tyme'.[3]

There was, then, considerable and persistent interest in the founding of almshouses in Yorkshire well before the advent of the Reformation. In the two generations just reviewed seven endowed institutions and six smaller and unendowed almshouses had been established in various parts of the county, principally, it will have been observed, by the

[1] Kirk, *St. Mary, Whitkirk*, 244–248; Platt, G. M., and J. W. Morkill, *Records of the parish of Whitkirk* (Leeds, 1892), 43; DNB; *Yorks. Arch. Journal*, VII (1882), 38–40. *Vide post*, 308. Lord Darcy (1467–1537) was a faithful and valued servant of the Tudors until the advent of the Reformation, serving especially as a soldier. He surrendered Pontefract Castle to the rebels during the Pilgrimage of Grace but was pardoned by the Crown because of his efforts in the suppression of Sir Francis Bigod's rebellion in 1537. Betrayed by a treasonable letter to Robert Aske in the same year, he was promptly beheaded. It seems probable that much of the endowment of the almshouse and school fell under the attainder, though both survived with reduced incomes.

[2] PCY 10/105 1531; *Surtees Soc. Pub.*, LXXIX (1884), 306–319; Lawton, *Collectio*, 510; *VCH, Yorks.*, III, 90; *VCH, Yorks., NR*, II, 382. *Vide post*, 395. The foundation was made *ca.* 1528. Bulmer, the son of Sir Ralph, was one of the commanders at Flodden. He was a very rich and influential landholder in Yorkshire. His charities also included an annuity of £8 10s for the stipends of priests in his chapel, and by the instruction of his will £16 was given for general church uses, £3 to the clergy, and £63 for prayers. Bulmer's son, Sir John, and his son's wife were executed for complicity in the Pilgrimage of Grace.

[3] PCY 9/405 1528; *Surtees Soc. Pub.*, LXXIX (1884), 225–230; Drake, *Eboracum*, 352. Ryther also provided for a most substantial scholarship endowment in both universities for a term of twenty years, bequeathed £27 outright to the poor, £2 for marriages, £5 for the repair of roads, £5 to the relief of prisoners, £4 10s for general church uses, £40 for church building, and £110 for prayers. The Rythers were retainers of the Percies. Sir Ralph, Ryther's father, was High Sheriff of Yorkshire in 1504. Thomas Ryther died without issue.

landed aristocracy of the shire and normally in conjunction with chapels or chantries. But it was with the Reformation that an immediate and a sustained impulse was given to the creation of almshouse endowments, usually completely secular in their trusteeship and administration. In a brief period of two decades donors of the county, representing a much more impressive cross-section of social classes, contributed the substantial total of £3816 15s, almost the whole being capital, for the creation of institutions designed to offer care and protection for the irremediably poor.

It was not until the tempestuous reign of Henry VIII was at an end and the future course of English religious and social life became somewhat more precisely predictable, however, that the Reformation foundations were to begin. There was, however, one reorganization, or, perhaps more accurately, a refoundation, of considerable moment at the very close of the reign. In 1545 a commission was granted to the Archbishop of York to bring order into the affairs of the Hospital of St John the Baptist at Ripon. Founded in the early twelfth century, the hospital had once been well endowed and had offered support to poor clergy teaching in Ripon School, as well as alms twice weekly to poor persons seeking succour. The hospital was not well administered and in the early fifteenth century found itself unable to maintain its responsibilities. It was apparently again in need of financial aid by the middle of the century, when the then Archbishop of York offered indulgences to those who would contribute to its support. In 1545 the income had shrunk to £12 0s 4d p.a., the foundation evidently being little more than a chantry. The Archbishop joined the hospital with the almost equally decayed Hospital of St Mary Magdalen, which in 1535 was expending no more than £1 13s 4d for the care of five inmates from a total revenue of £27 5s 6d p.a. The two hospitals were merged under one administration as almshouses, their income being rededicated to the pious uses contemplated by earlier donors. The new foundation was greatly strengthened by numerous benefactions in the course of the sixteenth and seventeenth centuries.[1]

In 1546 a small almshouse for two persons was provided at Wakefield by Thomas Knowles, formerly vicar of the parish, who likewise gave a modest endowment of £17 for its support.[2] A much more substantial foundation was made in Hull in 1548 by a merchant of that city, John Harrison, who was mayor in this same year. Harrison built an almshouse, with commodious quarters, for ten almspeople at an estimated charge of

---

[1] *VCH, Yorks.*, III, 323–328, provides the account principally followed here.
[2] *PP* 1898, LXVIII, Wakefield, 70; Walker, J. W., *Wakefield* (Wakefield, 1939, 2 vols.), I, 284. Born at Westgate, Yorkshire, Knowles was educated at Magdalen College, Oxford, was instituted Vicar of Wakefield in 1502, and Sub-Dean of York in 1508. He served as President of Magdalen College, 1527–1535.

£100 and by his will, proved in 1551, endowed the institution with property worth upwards of £520 with which to ensure £2 12s p.a. for the maintenance of each of his almsmen.[1] Still another foundation was made at Kirkby Ravensworth under the will of William Knight, Bishop of Bath and Wells, who died in 1547. Knight, who had long held the rectory, founded both a school[2] and an almshouse in the parish, though it was not until 1556 that his instructions were carried out by his executor, John Dakin, then Rector of Kirkby Ravensworth, who is usually credited with the charity. The almshouse was provided with an endowment representing a capital worth of about £240, from the income of which the five almspeople were to have only 1d daily for their maintenance, the remainder being payable for administrative perquisites.[3] Shortly afterwards, William Walker, a London lawyer who was a native of the region, substantially augmented the income of the almshouse by a bequest of extensive properties then valued at upwards of £300 and subject only to a life income of £10 p.a. to the testator's sister. This endowment was to be employed for increasing the number of poor cared for in the institution and such other necessities as might arise.[4]

The greatest of all the foundations made in the period of the Reformation was that instituted in 1556 under the will of Robert Holgate, Archbishop of York, who had amassed a large private fortune by assisting Henry VIII in the expropriation of the monastic properties in the North. Holgate, who likewise founded three grammar schools in Yorkshire,[5] devised to trustees lands valued at upwards of £1000, with which he established an almshouse at Hemsworth, his birthplace, for the complete support of a master, who should have £20 p.a., and twenty almsmen, each of whom should be given £4 p.a. The master should be a clerk in holy orders and should carefully administer the affairs of the house for the benefit of the almsmen, who must be drawn from Hemsworth and those parishes next adjoining. The almspeople, unless blind or crippled, should be at least sixty years of age and no one might be chosen who had not been resident in the community for at

---

[1] Hadley, *Hull*, I, 89, II, 749; Ingram, M. E., *Our Lady of Hull* (Hull, 1948), 31; Tickell, *Hull*, 212, 769–770; Gent, *Hull*, 117; PP 1823, IX, 804–805. Harrison was sheriff in 1531 and mayor in 1537, serving for a second time in 1548.   [2] *Vide post*, 314–315.
[3] *VCH, Yorks.*, I, 478; *VCH, Yorks., NR*, I, 96; Whitaker, T. D., *Richmondshire* (L., 1823, 2 vols.), I, 118–121; *Yorks. Arch. Journal*, XIX (1907), 98, XXXVIII (1953), 207n.; DNB.
Dakin was involved in the Pilgrimage of Grace but gained his pardon. He was not only Rector of Kirkby Ravensworth, but was appointed the first master of Knight's grammar school as well. He was made Archdeacon of the East Riding in 1551.
[4] PCC 10 Noodes 1557; PP 1822, X, 637; *Alum. oxon.*, IV, 1558; Surtees Soc. Pub., CXVI (1908), 296.   [5] *Vide post*, 311–312.

least two years prior to his admission.[1] Still another great prelate, Owen Oglethorpe, Bishop of Carlisle, in 1555 founded an almshouse and school at Tadcaster, near his birthplace in Newton Kyme. By his will, proved in 1560, he charged his executors to purchase lands worth £40 p.a. for the support of the two institutions. The almshouse was endowed to secure the succour of twelve poor persons and was probably supported with approximately £400 of the capital vested in these two joint establishments. The almspeople were to be chosen from Rawdon, Tadcaster, Newton Kyme, and Bramham upon the nomination of the trustees, each poor person on his entrance to give all his goods to the institution.[2]

In 1558 Othoneus Sagar, himself of uncertain social status, but of a family of husbandmen and yeomen, left an almshouse which he had built during his lifetime, charging his estate with a perpetual annuity of £12 for the care of four of the poor of the parish of Warmfield. The trust and the selection of the almsmen were vested in 'four of the most substantial honest men' of the parish, who from the outset provided £3 p.a. for each almsperson, the building apparently having been maintained by private subscriptions.[3]

These were the principal of the well-endowed and carefully vested almshouses founded during the period of the Reformation. But there were, as well, a number of smaller houses established, many of which were not to serve for long, which betoken the general interest of the county in creating a mechanism for the care of the hopelessly poor. Among these was the almshouse for three poor constituted by John Dixson, a clergyman, for the benefit of Pontefract sometime prior to 1556, which was, however, supplied with no endowment save two closes of land.[4] Robert Thornhill of Woodhall in Holderness, a member of the lesser gentry, by his will proved in 1557 ordered the erection of an almshouse for seven persons at Walkeringham, Nottinghamshire, which he endowed with an annuity of £3 3s in order to provide 9s annually for each almsman.[5] In 1558 John Mawdeslay, a husbandman of Birkin (W. R.), left his house, valued at about £10, for the use of one almsman,[6] while in the same year William Crokehay, a Hull merchant, stipulated

---

[1] PCC 25 Ketchyn 1556; PP 1825, X, 637–640; PP 1826–1827, X, 671–673; PP 1895, LXXV, Hemsworth, 1–23; VCH, Yorks., I, 474–475; Gilbert, Liber scholasticus, 291; Surtees Soc. Pub., CXVI (1908), 232–235; DNB.

[2] PCC 29 Mellershe 1560; PP 1824, XIII, 722–728, 777–784; PP 1898, LXVIII, Tadcaster, 1–16; Yorks. Arch. Journal, XIV (1898), 402; VCH, Yorks., I, 478; DNB. Vide post, 315.

[3] PP 1826–1827, IX, 411–412.

[4] PP 1898, LXVIII, Pontefract, 71–72. The deeds relating to this almshouse were lost during the Civil War.

[5] PCC 10 Noodes 1557; PCY 15/2/71 1557; Surtees Soc. Pub., CXVI (1908), 242–244.   [6] PCY 15/3/85 1558.

in his will that his house, which some years later was valued at £80, should be converted into an almshouse, for which he likewise provided a modest endowment.[1] There was likewise an almshouse at Tickhill (W. R.), founded at an uncertain date, and receiving numerous outright gifts and bequests during the period of the Reformation for the support of its inmates.[2]

The foundation of almshouses in Yorkshire continued steadily during the Elizabethan period, though with a marked slackening in the relative rate of giving for this purpose. During these two generations a total of £4053 14s was provided for new foundations or for the augmentation of the endowment of the now considerable number of existing institutions.

One of the earliest and certainly one of the most generous of these foundations was established in Hull by the 'stiffly papistical' Bishop of Hull, Robert Pursglove. A native of Tideswell, Derbyshire, wherein ca 1560 he founded a grammar school with an endowment of at least £200, Pursglove received letters patent in 1561 to make an even more generous foundation in Guisborough, Yorkshire. The grammar school and almshouse, to be known as the 'Hospital of Jesus in Guisburn', were endowed with capital then valued at £914, each institution sharing in prescribed proportions in the income and being built as adjoining structures.[3] The hospital was to furnish lodging and care for twelve poor men and women, each of whom should receive 1s weekly, with a further £2 p.a. to be divided equally amongst them for apparel and other purposes. This is to say, the almshouse was endowed with £33 4s of the income of the trust, representing a capital of something like £664.[4] The endowment of the institution was strengthened shortly after its foundation by a number of local bequests and gifts, including lands of £47 capital value devised by Roger Tocketts, Esq., and of lands worth

---

[1] *Vide ante,* 231. The house was used as a barracks during the Civil War and was not restored to its intended use, though a rental of £4 p.a. was paid and distributed to the poor of the community.

[2] Thus Christopher Golland, a husbandman, left 2d to each almsman in 1557 (PCY 15/2/137); Edmund Hynd, a gentleman, made an identical bequest in the same year (PCY 15/2/114); and John Ellvis, a husbandman, left the institution £1 in 1559 (PCY 15/3/163).

[3] *Vide post,* 316, for a discussion of the grammar school.

[4] PCC 32 Arundell 1580; Smith, *Old Yorkshire,* V, 151–154, n.s. III, 235; *PP* 1823, VIII, 724–730, 805–806; *PP* 1826–1827, X, 266–276; *Surtees Soc. Pub.,* CXXI (1912), 226; Tickell, *Hull,* 157–158; Graves, John, *History of Cleveland* (Carlisle, 1808), 426–427; *Yorks. Arch. Soc. Rec.,* XXXIII (1903), 194–195; DNB. His monumental inscription in Tideswell church reads:

Two gramer schooles he did ordain with land for to endure
One hospital for to maintain twelve impotent and poor.
O Gisburne, thou with Tiddeswall town, lament and mourne you may,
For this said clerk of great renown lyeth here compast in clay.

£20 by George Conyers, Esq., these men being trustees of the foundation. Some years later Robert Rookby, of Guisborough, gave the hospital an annuity of 7s as further endowment, while Robert Tristram provided lands worth £1 p.a.

The town of Doncaster benefited by the establishment of an almshouse there in 1562 under the terms of the will of Thomas Ellis, a well-to-do local merchant. Ellis had during his lifetime built an unendowed lodging house for poor wayfarers passing through Doncaster and had likewise paid for the erection of a market cross in the town. But his will contemplated a much more ambitious foundation, 'calling to my remembrance the manifold benefits received by the great goodness of Almighty God, and minding to impart some deal of my possessions and inheritance, obtained through grace and sufferance . . . to and for the relief and harbour of the poor'. A substantial house was provided with two rooms and a garden space for each of the six poor and decayed householders of the town who were to be his almspeople. The trust was settled on a self-perpetuating body of eighteen persons, including the then mayor and four former mayors, who were to order the income derived from capital then valued at £208, paying to each inmate at least 6d weekly as well as a load of fuel in the winter.[1] Some years later, probably in 1568, Ellis' brother-in-law, Thomas Fullwood, a merchant and a former mayor, gave three almshouses 'at the west end of the parish church', these being cottages with an estimated value of £40, for the use and occupancy of three poor widows and endowed the institution with an annuity of £6 in order to provide each pensioner with £2 p.a. for her support.[2]

Hull, already generously blessed by its benefactors with provision for the care of its indigent, gained two additional endowed almshouses during the Elizabethan period. In 1572 Robert Ratcliffe, a weaver, bequeathed two tenements to the municipal authorities to serve as an almshouse for four poor persons under the direction of the mayor, providing as well a small endowment for the support of the almspeople.[3] A widow of the city, Elizabeth Brotherick, a few years later gave her

---

[1] PCY 17/133 1562; *PP* 1828, XX, 610–612; *PP* 1894, LXIV, Doncaster, 25–29; Smith, *Old Yorkshire*, I, 92; Jackson, *Doncaster charities*, 53–71, and Appendix; Jackson, J. E., *St. George's church at Doncaster* (L., 1855), App. xv–xx. Five times Mayor of Doncaster, Ellis was a substantial citizen, being of the third generation of a prominent merchant family. He also bestowed land valued at £21 for a grammar school (*vide post*, 315), gave £20 10s for marriage stipends, £2 10s for the mending of ways, and an estimated £5 for the repair of a well for common use.

[2] PCY 18/19 1568; Jackson, *Doncaster charities*, 120–121; *PP* 1828, XX, 612–613. Heirs of Fullwood seem to have possessed trustee powers as late as 1612. The almshouses were closed in the early nineteenth century.

[3] PCY 19/392 1572; *PP* 1823, IX, 806; Symons, *Kingstoniana*, 108; Tickell, *Hull*, 770; Gent, *Hull*, 82; Hadley, *Hull*, II, 749; Sheahan, *Hull*, 606.

large house next 'White Horse Inn', the premises being valued at £100, and left an endowment of about £87 for the lodging, apparel and, one would suppose, partial support of twelve poor and respectable widows of Hull.[1]

In 1563 the town of Hedon, lying near Hull, was provided with a small almshouse for three impotent men or women under the will of George Paynter, a clergyman of Hull. Three cottages were conveyed to the mayor and commonalty to serve for the lodging of the poor, as well as other properties with a capital value of £74, the endowment being designed to provide each almsman with the small and certainly insufficient annuity of 13s for his support, with a small stipend for coal and peat.[2] A few years later, in 1568, John Hamerton, a gentleman of Featherstone, left lands and a house, then worth approximately £54, as endowment for a hospital which he had built during his lifetime for the succour of four poor women of the parish.[3]

A substantial almshouse was provided at Wakefield in the Elizabethan period by Henry Savile, a member of a younger branch of the great Yorkshire family of his name. Savile in 1569 bequeathed to his executors, as trustees, they including his stepfather, Leonard Bate, £40 for the building of a fit and convenient almshouse for six poor persons on land already in hand. Former chantry lands, of which he and Bate had been large purchasers, were also bequeathed to his trustees to form the endowment of the projected establishment, 'in suche order as the said M^r of the Rolles shal devise, in the names of me and Dorothie my wife, the said Leonard Bate and Anne his wife, being my naturall mother, who I trust will augment the same according to their promyse unto me for six pore people . . . the which hospitall I will shall be erected within thre yeres after my death'.[4] Bate's will, proved in 1581,

---

[1] PCY adm. Sept. 1584; Hadley, *Hull*, II, 749; Tickell, *Hull*, 771–772. The hospital was razed in 1659 for uncertain reasons, but probably because the endowment was inadequate for the uses indicated.

[2] PCY 17/315 1563; Park, G. R., *The history of Hedon* (Hull, 1895), 232–234; *PP* 1823, IX, 761; Tickell, *Hull*, 698. Paynter likewise left £2 to the use of Hedon church, £2 for the repair of roads, £1 for harbour repairs, and £1 p.a. for twelve years, as well as one-third of the residue of his estate (this being of uncertain value), for the relief of the poor of the parish.

[3] *PP* 1896, LXIII, ii, Featherstone, 5–6.

[4] PCY 18/11 1569, PCC 11 Sheffelde 1569; *PP* 1898, LXVIII, Wakefield, 71; *Yorks. Arch. Journal*, XXV (1920), 16–22; *Alum. oxon.*, III, 1319. Savile was the son of John Savile of Lupset and a great grandson of Sir John Savile of Thornhill. His mother was the daughter and heiress of William Wyatt, who on the death of her husband in 1547 married Bate. Savile was Surveyor of the Crown for the Northern Provinces, was a Member of Parliament for Yorkshire in 1558, High Sheriff in 1567, and also served for some time as a member of the Council of the North. He left extensive landholdings to his son, George, who was in 1611 created a baronet. This son in 1603 succeeded to the great estates of the senior branch of the family on the death of his cousin, Edward Savile.

suggests that he had built the almshouse, assuming all the credit for it, and that he endowed it with at least a fraction of the intended properties. Endowment then worth £104 was provided for the support of five poor, while small annuities with an additional capital value of £8 seem also to have been vested. Each of the almsmen was to receive £1 p.a. for his full support, the remainder of the income being charged with the maintenance of the property.[1]

A far more generous foundation was made in Halsham in 1579 by Sir John Constable, whose family had been settled in the parish as lords of the manor since the second year of Richard II. Constable not only founded and endowed a school,[2] but likewise erected a commodious building with apartments for eight almsmen and for two almswomen, a common room being provided on the ground floor. A rent-charge of £36 p.a. was to be paid from certain lands in Keyingham and Paull for the term of a thousand years to provide stipends of £4 p.a. for each almsman and £2 p.a. for each almswoman, the charge for maintaining the premises being laid on his heirs.[3] A rent-charge of £4 p.a. was left by a yeoman, Christopher Fletcher, in 1591 for the augmentation of the capital of the three surviving medieval almshouses of Beverley, the donor also leaving £1 outright to the poor of that city and an annuity of £1 for the general uses of the poor of Sproatley in the East Riding.[4]

In 1592 John Frieston of Altofts, a member of an old and gentle family, began the building of an almshouse at Kirkthorpe which had not been completed at the time of his death in 1594. His will settled extensive properties on trustees for the endowment of a school and for university scholarships,[5] while providing as well for the completion of the hospital and its support. The hospital was finished in 1595 at a cost of about £100, comprising seven rooms with a central hall and an adjacent cottage for the master. The foundation provided for the care of seven almsmen and vested capital then worth £416 for its support, with the addition of charges for the free delivery of coal laid against several of Frieston's nearby properties. The endowment for this and his other charities consisted in large part of Pontefract chantry lands, worth £63 7s p.a. at the time of Frieston's death.[6]

[1] PCY 22/140 1581; *Yorks. Arch. Journal*, XXIV (1917), 30; Walker, *Wakefield*, I, 213, 222, 224, 241–243, 328–329; *S.P.Dom.*, 1566 [?], XLI, 81; *PP* 1826–1827, X, 701–702. The career of this grasping and successful man would well be worth a special study. He was collector of the revenues of the chantry lands and, with Silvester Leigh of Pontefract, a successful speculator in these properties. Together, the patent rolls suggest, the two men purchased chantry lands with a total value of £2247 14s 6d.   [2] *Vide post*, 319.

[3] PCY 23/539, 1000 1587; *PP* 1824, XIII, 661; Lawton, *Collectio*, 382.

[4] PCY 24/647 1591; Poulson, *Beverlac*, 799; *PP* 1823, IX, 776; *PP* 1824, XIII, 688.   [5] *Vide post*, 322, 353.

[6] *PP* 1826–1827, IX, 409, 412–413, X, 687; *PP* 1897, LXVII, iv, Normanton, 4–21; *Yorks. Arch. Journal*, VIII (1884), 3; Boothroyd, *Pontefract*, 410; Walker,

These were the principal of the almshouse foundations made in Yorkshire during the course of the Elizabethan period. But there were likewise a considerable number of smaller houses founded, either with most modest endowments or with incomes so small that they offered no more than rent-free lodging unless, as was often the case, voluntary gifts from the community provided at least a measure of support for the occupants. Among these we may mention three cottages, in which he had supported almsmen during his lifetime, left by William Parote, a Hull merchant, to remain as 'dwellings for three pore people'.[1] A yeoman of Fishlake, Thomas Parkin, in 1574 left land valued at about £30 as endowment for the maintenance of a small almshouse in that parish.[2] In 1576 William Burton, of the lesser gentry of Ingerthorpe, bequeathed £7 and forty feet of timber towards building a small almshouse for three poor persons, together with 'a fire house, a common bed, and a place fit for prayers', while endowing the inmates with £1 p.a. for sixty years and with a wagon load of timber each year.[3] A gentleman at Brompton, James Westropp, had evidently maintained an almshouse at Sheriff Hutton during his later life, since he left his almsmen 5s outright without, however, any provision for placing the property on trust or securing its endowment.[4] Finally, we may mention the foundation in 1593 of a small almshouse at Woodkirk (Ardsley) by Richard Greenwood, a yeoman of that community. The founder provided the house and land, valued at £30, as well as a small endowment with a capital of £20 for the support of three poor women.[5]

Yorkshiremen could in 1600 contemplate with satisfaction the achievement of the preceding 120 years in establishing a system of care for the hopelessly poor in almshouses now scattered over the whole of the county. They had inherited from the medieval past twenty-three functioning institutions which had not only survived the Reformation but which, in terms of their secular purposes, had been strengthened as they came into the hands of lay trustees and received additional support from sixteenth-century benefactors. Moreover, a great addition to these resources had been made by donors of our period, who had in all

---

Wakefield, II, 425; Peacock, *Wakefield Grammar School*, 176; Skelton, *Pietas oxon.*, 11; Cooper, *Memorials of Cambridge*, II, 361. Frieston (1512–1594) was descended from an ancient family, the lords of Mendham in Suffolk. He was trained in the law at Gray's Inn, but did not practise. Through his kinsman, Sir Martin Frobisher, he contracted for duchy leases and farmed duchy fines in the North.

[1] PCY 17/537 1566.   [2] *PP* 1899, LXXIII, 184.
[3] PCY 20/113 1576. Burton also left £2 towards digging a common well and 1s each to the poor of Ingerthorpe and two neighbouring villages.
[4] PCY 22/58 1581.
[5] *PP* 1826–1827, IX, 406; *PP* 1898, LXVIII, West Ardsley, 2–3. The house was still standing, though decayed, at the close of the nineteenth century.

given nearly £10,000 (£9642 17s) towards the founding and endowing of new establishments for the care of the poor. In total, twenty-four endowed and well-vested institutions had been established in all parts of the county, offering lodging and sustenance to 199 almsmen, a considerably greater number than the 162 who were sheltered by the medieval institutions at the opening of our era. But this was by no means the full measure of the resources which kindly and socially sensitive men had provided. They had likewise established at least sixteen small houses, normally unendowed, in which forty-six indigents were lodged, with some care afforded by the founder, his heirs, or by the community.

But this achievement, considerable though it was, was only the beginning of the great movement for the founding of almshouses in the county. There is most abundant and persuasive evidence in the historical materials of the period that in about 1600 all Englishmen agreed that an endowed almshouse provided more of social good and of humaneness than any other single institution with which a community might be blessed. Above all, it relieved the social conscience of a parish and finally resolved the age-old problem of the care of the derelict. There was consequently a flood of giving for the creation of almshouses during the early Stuart period, the great sum of £16,736 2s being disposed in a little more than a generation for these foundations. Some measure of this notable and noble achievement of private men may be gained when it is suggested that in these four decades considerably more capital was provided than during the whole of the preceding 120 years together with the capital worth of all the almshouse foundations, properly defined, that had survived from the Middle Ages.

We may mention first among the early seventeenth century almshouses, the founding of the Trinity House at Scarborough in 1602. This foundation was made by the mariners of this port town, who contributed £100 to build the institution for the care of poor seamen's widows. An agreement was also formally concluded by upwards of sixty shipowners and master mariners of the town under which every vessel clearing Scarborough was to contribute 4d a voyage, every mariner an equal amount, and every seaman earning above 15s a composition of 2d to ensure the support of the almshouse, which was placed under the management of four wardens.[1] In the following year, 1603, still another almshouse in Hull was endowed under the will of William Gee, whose substantial benefactions to the poor of his city have already been noted. This successful merchant had during his lifetime built alms quarters for ten poor women, valued at upwards of £100, which his will con-

---

[1] VCH, Yorks., NR, II, 539; Baker, J. B., Scarborough (L., 1882), 294. There was apparently little if any connection, save in name, with an earlier Trinity House, an almshouse founded in 1408 for six men and six women.

veyed to 'the town's chamber of Kingston-upon-Hull' for perpetual use. He likewise gave permanent endowment to the institution by vesting properties then worth £185, the income of which was to be paid weekly for the maintenance of the almswomen. Gee also left outright £1 10s for distribution to his almspeople, as well as adding £20 to the endowment of the Trinity House of Hull and £1 to two other almshouses in his city.[1] A lesser foundation was provided in Wakefield in the same year by a local chapman, Thomas Cave, who left two cottages valued at £40 to trustees, two of the poor of the town to be lodged in one, and the rents of the other house to maintain the two almsmen.[2]

A large and most substantial foundation was made in Heslington shortly after the death of Sir Thomas Hesketh in 1605. Hesketh had in his later years contemplated building an almshouse in the parish, but it was left for his widow, Dame Julia, to carry forward his intentions. The hospital was built to accommodate nine poor, one being designated master, and each of the almspeople was to have a stipend of £5, with £6 13s 4d for the master. The poor were to be aged and impotent persons, while the master was to be competent to read prayers each morning and evening. The executors of the estate conveyed rentals from five watermills in the suburbs of York with a value of £50 p.a. and a rent-charge of £5 p.a. from an estate at Hutton Rudby, representing in all a capital worth of £1100, for the support of this notable institution situated just outside the city of York.[3]

Another lawyer, John Clapham, in 1608 founded an almshouse, to be known as Christ's Hospital, in the rural village of Firby (Bedale). The

[1] *Vide ante*, 236, and *post*, 306.

[2] PCC 51 Bolein 1603; *PP* 1826, XIII, 681–682; *PP* 1826–1827, X, 687, 692; *PP* 1898, LXVIII, Wakefield, 69–70; *Surtees Soc. Pub.*, CXXI (1912), 193–197; Walker, *Wakefield*, II, 368; *Yorks. Arch. Journal*, XXVII (1924), 409; *VCH, Yorks.*, I, 481; Cooper, *Memorials of Cambridge*, I, 37; Wardale, *Clare College*, 100. *Vide post*, 328. Cave also left £82 for the support of the poor in several Yorkshire communities and an estimated £20 for highways.

[3] PCY 30/141 1606; Cooper, T. P., *History of the Castle of York* (L., 1911), 127, and app.; *PP* 1825, X, 650–652; *Alum. cantab.*, I, ii, 359; Cooper, *Athenae cantab.*, II, 412. A Lancastrian, Hesketh (1548–1605) was educated at Cambridge and Gray's Inn. He acquired a great reputation and a considerable fortune as a barrister. He served in Parliament for Preston in 1586, for Lancaster in 1587, 1604, and for the county of Lancashire in 1601. He was appointed Attorney for the Court of Wards and Liveries in 1589 and was in the same year named Recorder of Lancaster. He was appointed one of the Council of the North in 1603, when he was also knighted and received a grant of crown lands in Essex and in the city of York. Hesketh settled in Heslington in his later years and purchased considerable property in and near York. He also left £50 outright to the poor of Heslington, £20 to the poor of Preston (Lancashire), and a gown of Yorkshire cloth worth one mark to as many poor men of Preston as were the years of his age (57) at the time of his death. His wife was the daughter of Edward Fusey of London, and in 1607 she became the second wife of Sir Ranulf Crewe.

hospital was built at an uncertain cost for a master and six almsmen. The master should be aged forty or upwards and must be able to read English and write legibly, while the almsmen should be single men aged about sixty who had lived for at least seven years in Bedale parish or in neighbouring communities. The almsmen were to be chosen by the parson and twenty-four substantial men of the parish from such of 'the poorer sort' who were least able, though willing, to work for their own support. The hospital was endowed with a rent-charge, on Middlesex property, with a capital worth of £600, from the income of which the master should receive £4 p.a. and raiment 'of some sad colour' worth £1 2s p.a., while each of the almsmen was to have £3 p.a. and clothing to the value of 16s. The almshouse, containing a chapel, an apartment for the master, and accommodations for the almsmen, was built in a garden of about one acre. The master, in addition to his responsibility for the care of the almsmen, was to provide free instruction for six poor boys of the community and might take as many as twenty-five additional students paying proper fees.[1]

At the close of this remarkable decade, in which six large almshouses were founded in Yorkshire, two sisters of a merchant family established a notable almshouse in Halifax for poor widows. In 1610 Jane Crowther, the widow of a clothier, and Ellen Hopkinson, also a clothier's widow, gave approximately £140 for the erection of a suitable structure for eighteen almswomen, all of whom should be widows and natives of Halifax. The institution was large, containing twenty rooms for the inmates and an apartment for a school, also founded by the sisters. The foundation was endowed with only £100, aside from the capital supplied for the school, but each widow was to take one poor child, a student in the school, to live with her and was paid a supplementary fee for this service. Shortly afterwards, it may be noted, the stipends paid by this most worthy institution were augmented by local rates.[2]

---

[1] VCH, Yorks., NR, I, 300; PP 1822, X, 676; Foster, Joseph, ed., Register of admissions to Gray's Inn (L., 1889), 103; Yorks. Arch. Soc. Rec., LIII (1915), 91; S. P. Dom., 1605, XII, 30; S. P. Dom., 1610, LV, 51. Clapham, a native of Firby, was for some time a servant to Lord Burghley. Educated at Gray's Inn, he became Comptroller and Clerk of the Hanaper and one of the Six Clerks in Chancery. Vide post, 340.

[2] PP 1828, XX, 572; PP 1899, LXXI, 233, 433–434; Yorks. Arch. Soc.., XXXIV (1904), 44; Halifax Antiq. Soc. Papers, 1908, 364, 1914, 167, 1917, 96, 103; Turner, Biographia Halifaxiensis, 50–52; Watson, Halifax, 583; Walker, Halifax registers, 67. Ellen Hopkinson, who died in 1610 (PCY 31/552), was the daughter of Richard Hemingway and the widow of John Hopkinson (PCY 29/676 1605), a clothier of Sowerby. In addition to her bequests and gifts for the almshouse and school, she left £20 to that notable pastor, John Favour (vide post, 323 ff.). She is characterized in the parish registers of her church as 'Foemina pia, quae medietatem Xenodochii aedificavit, ut viduarum domicilium esset in perpetuum'. Jane Crowther, the sister, died in 1614 (PCY 33/211),

The great movement for the founding of almshouses in Yorkshire reached its climax in the next decade, when £9559 was vested in endowments by a variety of donors in every part of the county. Sir Hugh Bethell under the terms of his will proved in 1611 endowed an almshouse at Ellerton (E. R.) for six of 'the eldest and poorest sort of people' in the community. Bethell provided rent-charges with a capital worth of £320 for its support and in addition laid on his heirs the responsibility for delivering twelve loads of peat to be 'yearly graven, dried, and carried' to the establishment, which consisted of three cottages with appropriate gardens.¹ In the following year, 1612, generous provision was made by a merchant of the city of York, Sir Robert Watter, for an additional almshouse in that community. Watter's will, drawn in 1609, recited the fact that he had purchased seven small and adjoining houses, in which he was then maintaining twelve almspeople. It was his intention, never realized, to raze these structures and to erect a new and more appropriate hospital in which he would provide perpetual care for ten almspeople. His will did, however, establish an endowment of £420 with which, after his death, the existing almshouse was to be supported. The master of the hospital, with a stipend of £3 p.a., was to be chosen from the almspeople, the remaining nine to have for their support £2 p.a. each.²

Sir Thomas Bland, a justice of the peace in the West Riding, in 1613 founded an almshouse in the parish of Kippax. A dwelling was built for four poor old men of the community, for whose maintenance Bland conveyed property with a capital worth of £267.³ The village of Long

---

being the widow of Brian Crowther, a clothier (vide ante, 236). She left £10 to John Boyes, a nonconformist minister who had been harried out of Kent, £10 to be lent to the poor, £30 to three poor preachers, and £20 to be given to ten poor children. Vide post, 340.

¹ PCY 31/608 1611; PP 1824, XIV, 727–728; Drake, Eboracum, 354; VCH, Yorks., NR, II, 87. Bethell, High Sheriff of Yorkshire in 1608, had no sons. He settled the manor of the rectory of Alne and Tollerton on his nephew, Walter Bethell, in 1603. His heir was his only daughter Grizell, the wife of Sir John Wray (1586–1655).

² PCY 32/72 1612; PP 1823, VIII, 690–691; PP 1825, X, 611; Morrell, J. B., York monuments (L., 1942?), 10; Hargrove, William, History of York (York, 1818, 3 vols.), II, 301, 304–308; Whitaker, Richmondshire, II, 196; Auden, G. A., ed., Survey of York (York, 1906), 251; [Widdrington, Thomas], (Caesar Caine, ed.), Analecta eboracensia (L., 1897), 297; Drake, Eboracum, 221–222, 298, 309, 365. Watter likewise left substantial sums for municipal improvements (vide post, 295) and to the clergy (post, 377), as well as £50 for loans to poor citizens. He was a haberdasher by trade and was twice mayor; his charitable bequests totalled £990.

³ PCY 32/409 1612; Yorks. Arch. Soc. Rec., XVIII (1895), 77–78, LIII (1915), 46, 138, 168, 175; Lawton, Collectio, 64; S. P. Dom., 1609, XLIX, 27. Bland held the manor of Fairburn and scattered lands and numerous cottages in two other parishes. His grandson, Sir Thomas Bland, when as a Royalist in difficulties

Preston derived rich benefits in 1615 under the will of James Knowles, the son of a poor man of that parish, who had accumulated a considerable fortune in the woollen trade in London, being in fact a famous 'Blackwell Hall man'. The principal of these benefactions was the foundation of an almshouse which he settled on the vicar and five other substantial men of the parish as trustees. It appears that £100 was spent in building the hospital on an acre of ground and that the estate yielded £860 additionally as endowment, rather than the £600 contemplated by Knowles. The almspeople were to be ten poor old men or women, not beggars, and of good demeanour, who were natives of the town. Each almsperson should receive £2 p.a. for maintenance as well as a garden plot, while a reader, who should say prayers twice daily at the nearby chapel in which pews should be provided for the almspeople, was to enjoy a stipend of £5 p.a.[1] In the same year a gentleman of Bishop Burton, Ralph Hansby, built in that parish an almshouse at a charge of £35 for two poor and unmarried men and one poor woman. Hansby then conveyed to twelve trustees, they being honest, able, and substantial parishioners, property with a capital worth of more than £267, the income of which should be employed to pay each almsperson £4 p.a. for complete care, and to increase the stipend of the vicar of the parish by £1 6s 8d p.a., with the remainder assigned for the maintenance of the almshouse.[2]

In 1616 four almshouses were founded in Yorkshire, two being richly endowed institutions vested by members of the nobility, one by a tanner of Hedon, and the last by the son of a London tradesman. The Dowager Countess of Cumberland, Margaret Clifford, had in 1593 established an almshouse for thirteen poor women at Beamsley, near Skipton. By subsequent gifts and bequests at the time of her death in 1616 the endowment was settled with lands then possessing a capital worth of £1800. The power of nominating the original inmates was vested in the Earl and Countess of Cumberland, but thereafter vacancies should be filled by election by the almswomen, the right of audit and visitation

with his estates, deposed that his lands in Kippax were forever charged under his grandfather's will with an annuity of £13 6s 8d for the maintenance of four poor persons.

[1] PCC 33 Rudd 1615; *Yorks. Arch. Soc. Rec.*, XXXIV (1904), 38; Whitaker, *Craven*, 149; *PP* 1826, XIII, 686–688; *PP* 1896, LXIII, ii, Long Preston, 1–10; *S. P. Dom.*, 1616, LXXXVI, 113. *Vide post*, 286, for Knowles' other benefactions to the town, the total being £1300. The church, which he repaired, bears a plaintive inscription on one of the stalls provided by Knowles: 'Though I be dead in name, I hope to live in fame. K.' The income in 1896 on the capital provided by Knowles was £229 3s p.a.

[2] PCY 35/432 1619; Foster, *Gray's Inn admissions*, 101; *PP* 1823, IX, 740; Lawton, *Collectio*, 327. Hansby was educated at Gray's Inn, where he was admitted in 1601. He was apparently residing at the Inn at the time of his death in 1619. It is probable that his daughter, and co-heir, married Sir William Hildyard of Bishop Wilton.

remaining in the family of the donor.[1] In the same year Gilbert Talbot, seventh Earl of Shrewsbury, required his executors and trustees to found an almshouse in Sheffield for the perpetual maintenance of twenty poor persons of that community and to endow the institution 'with such revenues and possessions as my executors shall thincke fitt, not being under two hundred pounds a yeare'. As was so often the case with great landed estates, the settlement of the properties and the carrying out of the instructions of the donor proceeded only slowly, though £200 p.a. was apparently paid to the overseers of the poor of Sheffield for their use until the hospital could be completed. It was, in fact, almost a half-century before building was begun in 1665, the erection of the hospital, finished in 1673, being carried forward by Talbot's great grandson, Henry, Earl of Norwich (later Duke of Norfolk), who enlarged it and further endowed it in 1680, when it supported thirty-six almspeople.[2]

But these great foundations of the nobility were very few even in Yorkshire. The burden of social responsibility in England had been undertaken by humbler classes, by men certain of their aspirations and prepared to dedicate their substance to attain them. Hence the other two foundations made in 1616 may be regarded as more typical. Thomas Kirkeby, a tanner of Hedon who had been thrice mayor of the town, left urban properties then worth £100 for the maintenance and further support of almshouses founded there in 1563.[3] In the same year, 1616, a London merchant's son, turned country gentleman, endowed with lands and tithes worth approximately £140 an almshouse for four poor people in Ganton, which he had 'now lately founded and erected and builded'.[4]

In or about 1617 Nicholas Waller 'of Sykehouses', began preparation for his foundation of an almshouse and school for the parish of Snaith.

[1] PCY 34/353 1617; *PP* 1820, IV, 507-508; Dawson, *Skipton*, 328; *Complete peerage*, II, 439. A daughter of Francis, second Earl of Bedford, the donor was the widow of George Clifford, third Earl of Cumberland. She left as her heir Anne, the wife of Richard Sackville, Earl of Dorset, later Countess of Pembroke (*vide post*, 399.)

[2] PCC 51 Cope 1616; *Surtees Soc. Pub.*, CXXI (1912), 208-209; *PP* 1897, LXVII, iii, Sheffield, 8, 141-172; *Complete peerage*, VII, 141; White, William, *History of Sheffield* (Sheffield, 1833), 28; Hunter, Joseph, *Hallamshire* (L., 1819), 76; Drury, *Essays*, 53-56; *S. P. Dom.*, 1635 [?], CCCX, 31; DNB.

[3] PCY 34/63 1616; *PP* 1823, IX, 761; Poulson, *Holderness*, II, 147. For the foundation of the almshouse, *vide ante*, 262.

[4] Legard, J. D., *The Legards of Anlaby and Ganton* (L., 1926), 93-94. The donor was John Legard, son of a London haberdasher who had in 1583 purchased an estate at Ganton, near Anlaby, his birthplace. John Legard (1576-1643) married Elizabeth, a daughter of William Mallory of Studley. He held a commission as captain from the Crown in 1630, but was denounced as a traitor in 1642 because of his support of Parliament.

In that year he and his son conveyed to trustees tithes in six parishes as well as extensive lands in Snaith. The school and almshouse were built between that date and the time of Waller's death in 1624. The almshouse, designed for the housing of six charges, was endowed with an annuity of £20 which was to be employed for the full and perpetual maintenance of poor and aged men, being widowers, of the town.[1] An almshouse was also founded at Richmond, on Anchorage Hill, in 1618 by Eleanor Bowes, the wife of Robert Bowes of Aske. The hospital was endowed with property, then having a capital value of £200, for the support of two poor widows from Richmond and one to be chosen from Easby. Town officials, with the rector and the schoolmaster, were named trustees of her foundation.[2] In the closing year of the decade, 1620, Richard Thwaites, a merchant and former mayor of Pontefract, founded an almshouse in that town for four 'ancient poor single women'. Two cottages, worth approximately £40, were provided, together with gardens for their use, while an endowment of £64 was established to secure for each sister the certainly insufficient stipend of 10s annually and to defray the costs of twelve 'horseloads of coals for their fire'.[3]

The date for the re-foundation and settled endowment of the Trinity House in Hull can hardly be exactly determined. The guild of the Holy Trinity of Hull, open to members of any trade, was established in 1369. In 1456 an agreement was reached by shipmasters of the port to lay stated impositions on shipping, with which an almshouse belonging to the guild should be supported, while the fraternity itself was to be reconstituted as a seamen's guild. In 1521 a royal ordinance confirmed the foundation and empowered it to hold property to the value of £10 p.a. for the support of thirteen poor and decayed seamen. The charter was further confirmed by Edward VI and Elizabeth, but it is evident that somewhat before 1613 the hospital had decayed, while shippers were no longer required to pay the prescribed fees. The institution seems in effect to have been re-founded by the generosity of Thomas Ferres, certain of whose great benefactions to Hull have already been noted.[4] During his term as mayor, in 1621, Ferres gave to the Trinity House, of which he was thrice warden, an endowment valued at £1000, thus ensuring 'the reparation of the chapel of the guild or fraternity of the Trinity House and the support and relief of poor infirm mariners, seamen, and other persons to be relieved'. In 1625 he built a hospital on adjoining land for ten poor widows, at an estimated cost of £400. At

[1] PCY 38/353 1624; *VCH,Yorks.*, I, 480; *PP* 1825, X, 658; *PP* 1898, LXVIII, Snaith, 16–19. *Vide post*, 331–332, for a notice of his educational foundation.

[2] *VCH,Yorks.*, NR, I, 21, 33; Clarkson, *Richmond*, 228–230.

[3] *PP* 1826–1827, IX, 427–428; Boothroyd, *Pontefract*, 393–394, 454. Thwaites was mayor of his city on four occasions.

[4] *Vide ante*, 240, and *post*, 288, 296.

his death in 1630 it was absorbed by the Trinity House foundation, to which he left an additional endowment of £100, as well as 6s 8d and a black gown to each of the poor widows and 10d to each of the almsmen. Ferres' great gift and his administrative skill in reorganizing and enlarging the hospital not only restored and secured its usefulness to the city, but so established its prestige that it became the beneficiary of many later and more modest bequests.[1]

It is likewise difficult to give a precise date for the charitable foundation of Robert Nettleton, a member of the lower gentry seated at Almondbury. In 1614 he conveyed to trustees certain valuable properties with which they were to build an almshouse and administer a fund for general charitable purposes in his parish. Nettleton died in 1621, providing also in his will for the endowment of a school recently founded in the parish, and it seems likely that the deed of gift became effective shortly afterwards. Eight trustees were vested with property totalling £694 in value, of which £100 was designated for the support of the school, £134 for the relief of the poor, and presumably in approximately equal shares £460 for the almshouse and general charitable uses, such as the repair of roads and bridges, marriage portions, and the assistance of poor scholars.[2]

In 1631 Thomas Agar, a tanner who had once been Mayor of York, by will endowed a hospital for six poor widows, which he had purchased and furnished at a cost of about £70 during his lifetime. The almshouse was comprised of three cottages, for which Agar also provided three garths. The donor by will vested the property on trustees, while his wife, Beatrix, in 1634 bequeathed a rent-charge with a capital value of £400 for the support of the sisters and the maintenance of the property.[3] An older almshouse, Trinity Hospital, which since the fifteenth century had been administered by the Merchant Adventurers of York, was also greatly strengthened at about this same date. William Hart, who had for many years served as pastor of the Merchant Adventurers' church at Stade, in addition to bequeathing a large sum to be lent without interest to young merchants, left capital of £300 'to be lent to the fellowship of merchants', the income to be employed for the support of

[1] *Yorks. Arch. Soc. Rec.*, CV (1942), i-xxxii, CXVI (1951), i-xxix; Hadley, *Hull*, II, 714 ff., 805 ff.; Tickell, *Hull*, 700 ff.; *PP* 1823, IX, 784-790; Sheahan, *Hull*, 591-594.

[2] PCY 36/424 1621; *PP* 1828, XX, 545-549; *PP* 1899, LXXI, 715-723. *Vide post*, 319.

[3] (Thomas Agar) PCY 41/447 1631; (Beatrix Agar) PCY 42/315 1634; Drake, *Eboracum*, 181, 222, 365; *PP* 1820, V, 374; *Yorks. Arch. Soc. Rec.*, L (1914), 213-214. Agar was sheriff in 1612 and mayor in 1618. His wife was the daughter of Edward Hansby, a fellow of St John's College, Cambridge, and widow of Herbert Davy, a York mercer. While mayor, Agar was seriously wounded by a drunken tailor, who was held in fetters for seven years. Agar also left capital to set the poor at work (*vide post*, 287).

ten poor widows in Trinity almshouse.[1] A modest but most useful alms-house was established in Beverley a few years later, 1636, by Thwaytes Fox, a baker of that city. Fox conveyed to trustees three cottages with garths for perpetual use as an almshouse for four poor widows who must be natives of Beverley, who had lived within the city for a term of at least twenty years, and who had been recipients of parish relief for at least two years. He conveyed, as well, a rent-charge of £10 p.a. for the endowment of the institution, the income to be divided equally among the almswomen.[2] At the close of the early Stuart period, Sir Richard Scott, a friend of the Earl of Strafford, by will established and most adequately endowed an almshouse for six poor men in Ecclesfield, where his estates lay. The almshouse, comprising five apartments, was built in 1639 at an approximate cost of £85 and was endowed with a rent-charge of £30 p.a., representing a capital worth of £600.[3]

We should mention as well at least a few of the numerous benefactions made during the early Stuart period for the augmentation of existing endowments, for the founding of small and unendowed almshouses, and for the establishment of worthy but most inadequately endowed institutions. Thus in 1611 a merchant, Isaac Waterhouse of Halifax, left £10 for the repair of the almshouse in that town, as well as £10 for the endowment of the school there and a small sum for the relief of the poor.[4] A citizen of Doncaster, John Stockes, at an uncertain date, but probably *ca.* 1621, founded an almshouse in that town, conveying three tenements, of an estimated worth of £30, to be occupied by as many poor widows, for whose partial support he gave a rent-charge of £2 p.a.[5] In 1627 a Scarborough tradesman, John Farrar, devised to the Corporation two adjoining cottages to be used by the town as an alms-

---

[1] PCY 42/215 1633; Drake, *Eboracum*, 222, 302; Auden, *Survey of York*, 226; *Surtees Soc. Pub.*, CXXIX (1917), 207n., 288; *PP* 1825, X, 641; Lawton, *Collectio*, 43. *Vide post*, 293.

[2] PCY July 1636; *PP* 1824, XIII, 680; Poulson, *Beverlac*, 399, 403, 796; Oliver, *Beverley*, 195. Fox was one of the first to sit on the bench of justices of the peace for Beverley, and was mayor of the town in 1630.

[3] PCC 125 Lee 1638; Eastwood, *Ecclesfield*, 237, 297–298, 413–414; *PP* 1894, LXIV, Ecclesfield, 2, 24–25. The estate, Barnes Hall, had been purchased by the great prelate, Archbishop Rotherham, who left it to his cousin, John Scott. Sir Richard was descended collaterally in this line. He was once, while travelling, brought before the Spanish Inquisition, 'but was not to be shaken in his faith, either by promises or threats'. He died in Ireland in 1638 while serving Strafford as a member of his Council. Twice married, Scott left no children, his estate passing to a half-brother, Richard Watts, chaplain to the Earl of Strafford and a fellow of Trinity College, Cambridge.

[4] PCY 31/713 1611. *Vide post*, 325.

[5] Jackson, *Doncaster charities*, 72–76. There were two Doncaster contemporaries of the same name, one being a tradesman who was twice mayor of the town and the other the clerk of the Doncaster Court of Pleas. The slight evidence available does not permit a certain attribution for the gift.

house for poor widows, but with no provision for endowment.[1] A York merchant's widow, Ursula Calam, in 1640 left rent-charges with a capital value of £10 for the augmentation of the income of three almshouses in that city.[2] These are but typical of a great variety of benefactions, made by men and women principally of the urban classes, who by modest contributions sought to afford for the hopelessly poor of the county some measure of permanent sanctuary and decency of life.

The achievement in Yorkshire during the early Stuart period was indeed most remarkable. The county during this generation was experiencing a new prosperity and a quite new sense of full participation in the life and aspirations of the realm. Yorkshire had long lagged a full half-century behind in its institutions, and in this one generation it almost seemed as if a herculean effort was being made to come abreast with the more prosperous and mature counties of the South. In the course of this relatively brief interval twenty-two new and substantial almshouses were established and endowed in every part of the county, offering shelter and sustenance to 198 almspeople, while substantial augmentations had been made to the capital of older institutions. In addition, we have noted the founding, principally in rural parishes, of seven small almshouses, accommodating twenty-one almsmen, most of which were supported during the lifetime of the donor but which remained unendowed and which offered no more than free lodging in the next generation unless they were taken over by the communities which they sought to serve. In all, then, some provision had been made for 219 almspeople during this generation when in Yorkshire the floodgates of charity had been truly opened.

But notable as were the accomplishments of men in the early Stuart period in providing a system of almshouse support for the indigent, the amazing gains made in the revolutionary era were even more impressive. In this short interval, in a county sorely tried by war and political unsettlement, the movement for the founding and endowing of almshouses was to proceed at a markedly accelerated rate, especially after the tolerable security of the Commonwealth and Protectorate was attained. During these two decades the most generous total of £12,457 18s was provided for the building and endowment of almshouses in the county. Some measure of the greatness of this achievement may be sensed when it is noted that this capital sum exceeds substantially the total given for the founding of almshouses from the beginning of our period through the first decade of the seventeenth century, a span of 130 years. We should now speak of at least the principal of these foundations.

---

[1] Baker, *Scarborough*, 283.

[2] PCY December 1640; *Yorks. Arch. Soc. Rec.*, L (1914), 211–213. She was the widow of William Calam, a draper, who had been Sheriff of York in 1590. She also left 10s for named needy persons and £7 15s outright to the poor.

A great merchant and civic leader of Hull, Sir John Lister, by the terms of his will proved in 1641, arranged for the building of an alms-house for twelve poor. He left land in the city, which he settled on fourteen trustees, including the mayor and aldermen, with instructions to tear down the structures then on the property and with the sum of £200, or more, if needed, to build a suitable dwelling for six men and six women, as well as a small house nearby as the residence for the assistant minister of Trinity Church. The executors expended £360 in preparing the site and raising the buildings. Lister's will further pro-vided cash and lands with a capital value of £580, with which the institution was to be endowed, all of the income to be employed for the care of his almspeople, save for an annuity of £2 for the assistant clergyman and £1 for a dinner.[1]

At about the same date Sir Arthur Ingram, who, having made a for-tune in trade as a mercer in London, had settled in the city of York, founded a richly endowed almshouse in that community. Ingram had in 1640 built a large house in the suburbs of York for ten poor widows, at a cost of about £200, which he maintained by outright gifts during the remainder of his lifetime. By his will, proved in 1642, Ingram charged his estate with a stipend of £62 13s annually, from which £5 p.a. should be disbursed for the support of each of his almswomen, a gown costing £1 4s provided for each in alternate years, and £6 13s 4d paid to a man, generally in charge of the inmates, who should likewise read prayers in the chapel.[2] In the next year (1643) Josias Jenkinson by will conveyed to trustees eight cottages which he had earlier erected as almshouses for poor and impotent persons from the town of Leeds. At the same time he devised lands then possessing a capital value of £200, the income of which was to be employed for the relief of the poor of the city and which was, presumably, used by the trustees as an endowment for the almshouse.[3]

[1] PCY February 1641; Denny, Henry, *Memorials of the family of Lister* (Edinburgh, 1913), 272; *PP* 1823, IX, 792–794; Symons, *Hullinia*, 69, 71, 92, *Kingstonia*, 105; Tickell, *Hull*, 331, 748–750; Sheahan, *Hull*, 394. Lister (1587–1640) was born at Southowram, the son of John Lister, a successful merchant. He was Mayor of Hull in 1618 and 1629. He entertained Charles I on his visit to Hull in 1639 and was knighted at that time. He was a Member of Parliament in 1620 and, with Henry Vane, was elected to Parliament in 1640 but died before taking his seat. He married Elizabeth, daughter and heir of Hugh Armin of Hull, who bore him nine sons and six daughters. The value of the endowment of Lister's almshouse increased enormously with the growth of Hull. In 1888, after a portion of the land had been sold for £30,000, the remainder was valued at £81,000.

[2] PCC 107 Cambell 1642; PCY December 1642; Hailstone, Edward, ed., *Portraits of Yorkshire Worthies* (L., 1869, 2 vols.), I, 70; *Surtees Soc. Pub.*, CXXIV (1915), 4; *PP* 1826–1827, IX, 401; Drake, *Eboracum*, 147, 258, 354, 357, 524; DNB. [3] *Vide ante*, 245.

One of the greatest of all of Yorkshire's many benefactors, and certainly one of the wisest, was Nathaniel Waterhouse, a salter, of Halifax. Waterhouse gave in all £3304 9s towards the creation of the social, educational, and religious institutions in his community and, with the great Favour, should be regarded as one of the true founders of the city.[1] During his lifetime, and probably in 1632, he had built at an approximate charge of £180 an almshouse in which he had lodged and supported twelve poor. By the terms of his will, drafted in 1642 and proved in 1645, Waterhouse conveyed property constituting a great charitable trust to the then vicar of Halifax and fifteen other prominent citizens, charged, among other and larger uses, with paying £18 p.a. for the maintenance of his twelve aged almspeople, with the addition of £6 p.a. for their clothing, these two payments together representing a capital endowment of £480 for the support of the institution. His trustees were instructed to choose three of the almspeople from Halifax and the remaining nine from as many designated villages in the large and sprawling parish. The lecturer, whose stipend he had also ensured, was to visit the almshouse regularly, while timberland was vested on the trustees in the expectation that it would be carefully ordered to provide 'strong timbers' for the repair of the almshouse, the workhouse, and the other buildings which together constituted a portion of the endowment of his charitable trust.[2] A more modest foundation was provided for Wakefield shortly afterwards (1646) by Cotton Horne, an attorney of that place. Horne conveyed to trustees an almshouse which he had built at a cost of upwards of £90 for ten poor and aged women of the town. At the same time, Horne placed on trust lands and other properties then valued at approximately £250, the income of which should be used for the support of the sisters lodged in the institution.[3]

[1] *Vide post*, 290, 380, for a discussion of his other charities.
[2] *PP* 1828, XX, 560–568; *PP* 1899, LXXI, 225–230, 369–397; Crossley, *Monumental inscriptions*, 51–52; *Halifax Antiq. Soc. Papers, 1914*, 1–12, *1919*, 73 ff., *1921*, 80–96; Midgley, *Halifax*, 163, 601 ff.; Watson, *Halifax*, 609 ff.; Kennett, White, *The case of impropriations* (L., 1704), 209 (MS. notes in Kennett's own copy, in the Bodleian Library). Waterhouse (1586–1645) was the son of Michael Waterhouse of Skircoat. He made his fortune as a salter and oil-drawer. Interesting excerpts from some of his letters and papers may be found in *Halifax Antiq. Soc. Papers*, 1919, 75 ff.
[3] Walker, *Wakefield*, II, 427, 441, 569; *Yorks. Arch. Journal*, XIX (1907), 419–420; *PP* 1826, XIII, 702; *PP* 1826–1827, X, 702–703. One of the trustees was Horne's son, William, who in 1669 gave a house in Wakefield as an addition to the endowment, as well as enlarging the facilities left by his father. Horne was the son of Cotton Horne of Hemsworth, the bailiff of Sir Cotton Gargrave. An attorney with a lucrative practice in Wakefield, Horne purchased the Mexborough estate and later in life the manor of Cold Hiendley upon the break-up of the Gargrave family. He was fined £40 in 1625 in commutation for knighthood. Horne was a Royalist, having supplied two men and horses to the royal army, and was adjudged worth £600 p.a. by the Parliamentary officials.

In 1652 Francis Layton, a gentleman of Rawdon by indenture settled an annuity of £5 4s, charged on the manor of Horsforth, as an additional endowment for Oglethorpe's hospital at Tadcaster,[1] and for the support of two almsmen in the institution.[2] In the next year John Harrison of Leeds, a great merchant and in a true sense the founder of the basic social institutions of his city, formally constituted a large almshouse which he had been building and supporting there for some years past. Harrison, who according to his own account expended at least £6000 for public and charitable uses in Leeds, was principally occupied following the death of his wife in 1631 with the founding of his almshouse, a grammar school, and the better support of the church in the city. In order soundly to endow these great enterprises and to free the growing town, Harrison was likewise long occupied in the purchase of the manor and lordship of Leeds, which he conveyed to trustees for local charitable uses. He began the building of a great hospital for forty poor of Leeds at an uncertain date, but probably after 1631, while continuing to lend private support to a large number of almspeople until the undertaking could be completed in 1653. The almshouses were built next the churchyard around a quadrangular court, one side being devoted to a chapel where prayers were to be read for the inmates. The cost of the building amounted to something like £450. In 1653 Harrison conveyed the premises to trustees, together with an endowment then valued at £1600. His will, proved in 1658, likewise provided an additional endowment of £30 p.a. for the hospital in the event his sister's children should die without issue, but since this contingency did not occur, the bequest failed. None the less, the hospital was well and carefully endowed, well constituted, and prudently administered, with the result that its gross income had by the end of the nineteenth century risen to more than £1000 p.a.[3]

[1] *Vide ante*, 259.

[2] PP 1826, XIII, 653–655; PP 1894, LXIV, 2–4, 15–18; *Bradford Antiquary*, N.S., II (1905), 142–144; *VCH, Yorks.*, I, 492; *S. P. Dom.*, 1631, CCII, 48; *vide post*, 290, 381, 399, for an account of Layton's larger charities. Francis Layton (1577–1661) was one of the Masters of the Jewel House to Charles I. A devoted royalist, his estates were compounded for in 1645 for £3670. Layton began the building of the chapel at Rawdon *ca.* 1647, though the work was not completed until long afterwards in 1684. His son and heir, Thomas, built a schoolhouse for Rawdon in *ca.* 1710, which was in 1746 endowed with £200 of surplus income accumulated from the apprenticeship fund.

[3] PCC 142 Wootton 1658; *PP* 1826, XIII, 662–665; *PP* 1899, LXXII, Leeds, 368–373; *Thoresby Soc. Pub.*, XXIV (1919), 190, XXXIII (1935), 106–147; *VCH, Yorks.*, I, 458–459, III, 58; Parsons, *Leeds*, II, 168–170; Whitaker, T. D., *Loidis and Elmete* (Leeds, 1816), 62, App., 1–19; Thoresby, *Ducatus*, 30, 34, 55. *Vide post*, 298, 314, 382, 401–402 for a discussion of Harrison's other charitable foundations. The son of a Leeds merchant, Harrison (1579–1656) in 1603 married a daughter of Henry Marton, also a Leeds merchant, to whom he was evidently deeply devoted. The couple had no children. Thrice mayor of the town, Harri-

A third almshouse foundation was made in this same year, 1653, under the terms of the will of a Royalist peer, Thomas, Lord Fauconberg. Fauconberg devised to trustees an almshouse and garth, which he had recently built at an estimated charge of £80, to serve the parish of Coxwold as a sanctuary for ten respectable but poor widows. He conveyed, as well, a rent-charge on property in Kepwick of £22 p.a., in order to ensure the complete maintenance of the sisters admitted to the institution.[1] Just a year later Luke Bagwith, a mariner and probably a merchant of Whitby, by his will set aside a portion of a house for the lodging of two poor widows and charged his estate with an annuity of £15 for the support of the almswomen and the maintenance of the premises.[2] The township of Monk Bretton, in Royston parish, at the same date was benefited by Mary Armyne, the daughter of Henry, Lord Talbot, who provided six cottages to serve as a hospital for as many poor women, while endowing the foundation with capital valued at £300 in order to distribute to each of the sisters £2 p.a. for maintenance and 10s a year for clothing.[3]

There were three other notable almshouse foundations made in Yorkshire by women during the period of the Protectorate. All of them, like Mary Armyne, were strong minded, independent, and thoughtful women who had managed considerable estates and who vested their large charities with prudence and careful forethought. The first of these

son had made his considerable fortune by 1628 and was thereafter principally concerned with his charities. He kept two large rooms in his house filled with food, clothing, and other necessaries which were constantly distributed to the needy. He was a staunch Anglican and a quiet but firm Royalist, his composition in 1651 being £464 18s.

[1] PCC 68 Brent 1653; *Complete peerage*, III, 322; *PP* 1822, IX, 595; *Yorks. Arch. Soc. Rec.*, IX (1890), 54–55, XVIII (1895), 167–170. This donor was the son of Sir Henry Belasye and Ursula, a daughter of Sir Thomas Fairfax. Born in 1577, he was knighted in 1603 and succeeded his father in 1624. He was made Baron Fauconberg in 1627 and viscount in 1643. He was a zealous supporter of the Crown, fleeing abroad for a season after the battle of Marston Moor. His composition fine was £5012. An almshouse for men, endowed with a rent-charge of £59 p.a., was founded in Coxwold in 1696 by Thomas, Earl of Fauconberg, a grandson of this donor, and, it might be mentioned, a son-in-law of Oliver Cromwell.

[2] PCC 459 Alchin 1654.

[3] *PP* 1826–1827, X, 758; Hunter, *South Yorkshire*, II, 277; Walker, J. W., *Monk Bretton Priory* (Leeds, 1926), 59; Wilkinson, Joseph, *Worthies of Barnsley* (L., 1883), 252–267. Henry Talbot, son of the Earl of Shrewsbury, left an estate in Monk Bretton to Mary, his daughter. She lived in the community for some years, but married Sir William Armyne (d. 1651) who was created a baronet in 1619 and who was a zealous Parliamentarian. Dame Mary was a firm Puritan, contributing annually to missionary work among the Indians in New England, assisting Puritan clergy who were in difficulties, and in 1662 placing in Edmund Calamy's hands £500 for the relief of ejected clergy. She died in 1675, aged 80.

was Elizabeth, Viscountess Lumley, whose benefactions for alms-houses and schools in London and in Thornton Dale, where she resided, reached the huge total of £5750. In 1657 by deed poll she vested properties on trustees for a school and almshouse in Thornton Dale, both to be built within six years after her death and apparently to share equally in the endowment, which was then valued at about £2500. The almshouse, with apartments of two rooms for each of twelve poor men and women of Thornton, Sinnington, and vicinity, was built at a cost of £150 and enjoyed for its support approximately half the income of the foundation.[1]

An almost equally large charitable estate was disposed for the same general purposes by the widow of a Yorkshire merchant, Anne Middleton, who in 1658 settled capital totalling £4071 18s principally for an almshouse in the city of York and for a grammar school at Shipton.[2] The hospital was built in the parish of St Mary Bishophill, for twenty widows, each to be the relict of a freeman of the city. The founder conveyed to trustees as well the sum of £2000 as endowment for the institution, with the provision that each sister should have an annual stipend of £4 for her complete maintenance.[3] The fourth of this notable group of women, Dame Mary Bolles of Heath, whose principal benefaction, made in 1660, was for a school and for apprenticeships at Warmfield,[4]

---

[1] PCC 356 Pell 1659; *Complete peerage*, V, 179; *PP* 1822, X, 771; *PP* 1843, XVII, 722–723; *VCH, Yorks., NR*, II, 475–476, 492, 497; Jeffery, R. W., *Thornton-le-Dale* (Wakefield, 1931), 131–132, 212–214; Gilbert, *Liber scholasticus*, 310. *Vide post*, 345, 356. In addition to the almshouse and school, Lady Lumley left an endowment for scholarships and £10 p.a. for the relief of prisoners in York Castle.

Lady Lumley was a granddaughter of John Nevill, fourth baron Latimer, who died in 1577. She married first Sir William Sandys of Montisfont, Hampshire, and in 1630 Richard Lumley, who had been created Viscount Lumley in 1628. Lumley was an ardent Royalist, who took part in the siege of Bristol and who paid £1925 to compound for his estates. Lady Lumley, who died in 1658, lived principally in Yorkshire, but was buried in Westminster Abbey. For her London charities, *vide* Jordan, *Charities of London*, 164.

[2] *Vide post*, 291, 345, for a discussion of her other charities.

[3] PCC 131 Wootton 1658; *VCH, Yorks.*, I, 484; *PP* 1823, VIII, 717; *PP* 1825, XI, 608; Torr, James, *Antiquities of York* (York, 1719), 114. Anne Middleton was the widow of a tanner, Peter Middleton, who, himself the son of a tanner, was admitted to the freedom of the city by patrimony in 1565 and later became sheriff. His widow was evidently a most skilful business woman, greatly increasing her inheritance, so managing her affairs that her will disposed £4900 in personal bequests and £4071 18s in charities, as well as lands in four parishes. None the less, she was apparently illiterate, her will being signed by mark.

[4] *PP* 1826–1827, IX, 414, X, 678, 707, 757; *Complete baronetage*, II, 414; *VCH, Yorks.*, I, 485. *Vide post*, 291, 346.

Mary Bolles (1579–1662) was born Mary Wytham, being the daughter of William Wytham of Ledsham, Yorkshire. She first married Thomas Jopson of Cudworth (Royston) and secondly Thomas Bolles of Osberton, Nottingham-

also provided capital valued at £113 as an augmentation for the alms-house at Kirkthorpe, founded two generations earlier by John Frieston.[1]

In 1658 the then vicar of Catterick bequeathed to trustees the sum of £500 for the founding of a school and an almshouse on the death of his mother and of his wife. Lands and rents were added which brought the total endowment to approximately £800, the income of which was to be about evenly divided between the two institutions. The almshouse was designed for six poor widows of the parish, including all its townships, each of whom should have for her support £3 6s 8d p.a., with any residue of income to be employed for the purchase of clothing and of fuel.[2] Matthew Francke, a merchant of Pontefract, whose bequest for the poor of that community has already been noted, in 1659 endowed with property then valued at £40 a small almshouse for two widows which he had built at an earlier date and had supported during his lifetime.[3] Finally, we should note the substantial foundation vested in the last year of our period by Brian Cooke, the son of a Doncaster merchant. Cooke, who died in 1660 at the age of 41, left in total £3820 for charities in Yorkshire, including funds for a grammar school and a most generous augmentation of the stipend of the vicar of Arksey. He transferred to five trustees the entire *corpus* of this charitable fund, instructing them to build an almshouse in Arksey for twelve poor persons at a cost of £60. The almspeople were each to have an annual stipend of £5 for complete maintenance, rents of £60 p.a. having been left as the endowment for this, still another useful and carefully administered almshouse foundation in Yorkshire.[4]

shire. He died early in 1635 and his widow was created a baronetess (Scottish) later in the same year, this being the only instance in which a woman was so elevated in her own right. She resided in her late life at Heath Hall near Wake-field. Her only son Thomas having died in 1653, she was succeeded by her grandson, William Jopson, in 1662.   [1] *Vide ante*, 263.

[2] M'Call, H. B., *Family of Wandesforde* (L., 1904), 86, 138, 289; *VCH, Yorks.*, I, 484; *PP* 1822, IX, 618–620. *Vide post* 345. This donor, Michael Sydall, was youngest son of Thomas Sydall of York. He was presented to the rectory of Kirklington in 1643, the presentation being long disputed, while somewhat later he became Vicar of Catterick. He was aged only forty-five at the time of his death in 1658. The school and almshouse were not built until 1688, presumably because of the survivorship provisions in Sydall's will.

[3] *Vide ante*, 250, and *post*, 296.

[4] *PP* 1828, XX, 600; *PP* 1897, LXVII, iii, Arksey, I, 7–8; Wainwright, John, *Yorkshire, Wapentake of Strafford* (Sheffield, 1829), 121; Hunter, *South York-shire*, I, 56, 327; *VCH, Yorks.*, I, 484; *Complete baronetage*, III, 191; *Cal. Comm. for Compounding*, II, 945. There is considerable confusion in several accounts between this donor and his father of the same name. The elder Cooke, whose father was likewise named Brian, had been an alderman and a mayor of Don-caster. He died in 1653, aged 83. The son, then at the Inner Temple, appeared for the father in 1645 in connection with charges of delinquency and begged to be included in his father's composition. In the proceedings it was made clear that

We have commented on sixty endowed almshouses which were founded in Yorkshire during the course of our period. When these institutions are taken with the twenty-three older houses, most of which were refurbished and augmented as well in the years after the Reformation, we may conclude that there were in 1660 something like eighty-three functioning and endowed almshouses lending care and shelter to the hopelessly poor in many parts of the shire. We have in addition noticed twenty-nine unendowed, or scantily supported, foundations, many of which were not to serve for more than a generation or two, but which added substantially to the social resources which had been created in the county during this period of amazing generosity and social sensitivity. The great total of £38,836 17s had been poured into these foundations by donors drawn from all classes, but principally by the gentry, the clergy, and the merchants, who were determined to rid their county of the evil of unrequited poverty which for ages past had left every community, rural and urban, cursed with something of bestiality.

The life afforded in these institutions must, save for about a score of exceptions, have been hard and meagre, since the average stipend provided for maintenance was considerably lower than we have found in most of the southern counties. But subsistence, some care, and the blessed benefits of association with others of a similar background and age was provided for 727 derelict human beings in endowed institutions by the close of our period, as well as at least 86 in unendowed houses. In all, then, 813 men and women, all old, all hopelessly poor, and all to some degree deserving, were being maintained as the consequence of the aspirations of men and women of our era to build a society in which no man might be wholly outcast. Nor was this the full measure of the contribution of private donors to the building of a better and certainly an infinitely more humane England on the foundations which medieval piety had supplied. As we have also seen, at least 829 households, embracing perhaps 4200 persons, were being in whole or in part supported constantly during times of ill fortune so that they might be tided over and held together, thereby preventing the social wastage which the many almshouse foundations were designed to relieve. Household relief, then, was the first line of defence thrown up against poverty; the almshouse foundations, the last.

It should also be said that these foundations were remarkably well spread over the great county, if density of population is borne in mind.

father and son were already contemplating the charitable dispositions later to be made. Successive fines of £172 10s, £587, and £200 1s 10d were paid by the Cookes. The younger Cooke, who was both a barrister and a country gentleman, died unmarried in 1660 and was buried at Doncaster. His estate succeeded to his brother, George Cooke, of Wheatley (Yorks.), who was created a baronet in 1661. *Vide post*, 346, 383, for a discussion of Cooke's other charities.

In average terms, which are unfortunately almost meaningless, there was an almshouse, endowed or unendowed, for every fifty-four square miles of the county. There were eleven in the city of York or its suburbs, forty-nine in the West Riding, thirty-seven in the East Riding, and fifteen in the North Riding, this, it would seem probable, bore a reasonably close relation not only to the population but also to the weight of need in these several areas. There were, without doubt, too many foundations in the old and decaying communities of York and Pontefract, while Hull also seems most lavishly endowed. But the only areas, all thinly populated, more than twenty miles distant from the shelter or at least the example of an almshouse foundation were to be found at the centre of the moors to the north of Kirby Moorside, in an area which may be described as the extreme northwestern neck of the West Riding, and in the western neck of the North Riding. The donors of Yorkshire had left a splendid inheritance to their county and to their age.

2. *Social rehabilitation*

The principal concern of Yorkshire benefactors was with the direct relief of poverty. This was, in fact, for all of England the first and the most pressing of social responsibilities, though prescient men, particularly among the powerful and venturesome mercantile aristocracy, were coming to believe that poverty must be more boldly assailed by raising up institutions for its prevention. Yorkshire donors lent but scant support to the various experimental efforts being made to secure the rehabilitation of the poor, measures which would prevent poverty by arming men more adequately for the harsher competitive requirements of sixteenth-century life. In all, £11,805 17s was given for such purposes from 1480 to 1660, this representing 4·85 per cent of the whole of the charitable funds of the county. This amount, being about average for a rural county, was sufficient to establish a number of interesting and helpful endowed undertakings for the cure of poverty in a fair number of communities, undertakings demonstrably effective in their accomplishments before our period came to a close. It is also important to observe that there was a steady and a most pronounced rise in the curve of interest in these experimental ventures if the whole of our period is taken in view. During the decades prior to the Reformation slightly less than half of one per cent (0·49 per cent) of all charitable benefactions were given for purposes of social rehabilitation, while in the Reformation period proper the proportion rose to 1·23 per cent of the whole. In the Elizabethan era there was a pronounced increase of interest in these experiments, £1356 1s being given for their organization, or 5·7 per cent of the total of all charitable benefactions, this being a proportion, be it noted, only slightly less than that (6·48 per cent) bestowed for all religious uses. A much larger sum, £5234 16s, was provided for these purposes during the early Stuart period, though in percentage terms this represented but a slight increase of support for these ventures in the prevention of poverty. There was a considerable rise in the proportion of all charitable funds devoted to experiments in social rehabilitation during the revolutionary era, when 7·64 per cent of all gifts were dedicated to these purposes and when the £4755 11s so given, of which well over half was for apprenticeship foundations, was quite sufficient for bold and effective efforts in the assault being made on the sources of poverty.

Certain of the charitable heads which we have regarded as falling within the broad ambit of social rehabilitation enjoyed but slight support in Yorkshire. Thus no more than £396 7s, or 0·16 per cent of the whole, was provided expressly for the care of the sick or for the maintenance of hospitals in the modern meaning of that term. Most of the gifts for this purpose prior to 1560 were small in amount and were designated for the numerous leper hospitals which had, of course, happily very nearly fulfilled their purpose by the early sixteenth century. The later benefactions for this purpose were scattered and were principally endowments for the care of the sick, with one quite substantial bequest of £200 being made by a Yorkshire donor for the needs of a London hospital. Nor was much more provided for marriage subsidies for poor but deserving young women, a favourite form of charity for the gentry in the later Tudor period in several of the counties we have studied. In all, £507 13s was given for this purpose in Yorkshire, this amounting to only 0·21 per cent of all charitable funds. This charitable instrumentality was particularly popular during the first half of our period, something being provided for it in every decade down to 1570, while it enjoyed merely casual and somewhat eccentric support thereafter. It is noteworthy too that almost all the gifts for this purpose were small and that only slightly more than a third (38·02 per cent) of the amount so given was in the enduring form of a capital foundation. By far the largest sum provided was a capital bequest of £100 made in 1612 by Marmaduke Langdale, of Dowthorpe, the income of which was to be distributed towards the marriages of poor servants and labourerers in four village communities lying about Skirlaugh in the East Riding.[1]

There was a considerable interest in Yorkshire in the relief of

[1] PCY 32/216 1612; *PP* 1823, IX, 780; *PP* 1824, XIV, 742; *Alum. cantab.*, I, iii, 42; *VCH, Yorks.*, I, 481; [Poole, G. A.], *Churches of Yorkshire* (Leeds, 1844), 36–37; Poulson, *Holderness*, II, 207. *Vide post*, 329–330. Langdale was born at Sancton, being the third son of Anthony Langdale, who died at Rome in 1577. He attended Caius College, Cambridge. His connection with Marmaduke Langdale, first Lord Langdale, an ardent Catholic and an officer in the Royalist army has not been clearly established; he was probably Lord Langdale's uncle.

prisoners, prompted not only by the normal concern of men of our period with the plight of prisoners for debt but by the needs of the considerable number of Roman Catholic prisoners detained in York prisons at intervals during certain decades of this era. In all, £1232 4s was given for the relief of prisoners, amounting to 0·51 per cent of the whole of the charitable funds of the county, of which a remarkably high proportion (64·76 per cent) was in the form of endowments. The concern of the county with this charitable cause was also persistent, something being given in every decade to relieve the distress of poor men who found themselves in prison. There were a few substantial benefactions made for this purpose. In 1552 a priest-lawyer, Anthony Belasis, who had profited greatly from the dissolution of the monasteries, left £50 for the care of prisoners, including £30 to those in the various London prisons, £10 to those at Durham, and £10 to those detained in York Castle.[1] John Burley, a London tradesman or merchant, in 1601 left £100 to the municipal government of York as an endowment to serve a double charitable function. The funds were to be lent at 6 per cent interest to young and needy freemen of the city, while the income was to be distributed for the relief of 'the poore prysoners in the lower pryson of the castell of Yorcke'.[2] Shortly afterwards a Roman Catholic gentleman of Kirkby Wharfe, Thomas Leedes, left an annual rent-charge of £3 6s 8d 'unto the Catholic prisoners which shall remaine . . . in the Castle of York for the Catholic faith and for their conscience', with the nostalgic provision that 'if it shall please God to restore the Catholic faith to his church', the income should instead be divided between priests in two Yorkshire parishes.[3] By far the largest bequest for the benefit of prisoners was that made in 1634 by Phineas Hodgson, Chancellor of York Cathedral, who vested rent-charges, representing a capital worth of £600, in trustees for this purpose. A stipend of £25 p.a. was established for the employment of a clergyman to lecture weekly to all prisoners in York Castle, save during times of plague and in assize weeks, with an additional £5 p.a. to provide bread in weekly distributions for their sustenance.[4]

[1] PCC 24 Powell 1552; *Surtees Soc. Pub.*, LXXVIII (1884), 209–210, CXVI (1908), 220–225; Cooper, *Athenae cantab.*, I, 543; DNB. Belasis also left a total of £52 for the poor of various counties, £12 to hospitals, £20 to the clergy, £6 13s 4d for the repair of roads, and £6 13s 4d for marriage subsidies in the bishopric of Durham.

[2] PCC 21 Woodhall 1601; *Surtees Soc. Pub.*, CXXI (1912), 214; Drake, *Eboracum*, 221; *PP* 1825, XI, 603.

[3] PCY 28/681 1602; Lawton, *Collectio*, 67.

[4] PCC 231 Fines 1647; Drake, *Eboracum*, 288, 370; Lawton, *Collectio*, 43; Burton, Thomas (James Raine, ed.), *History of Hemingbrough* (York, 1888), 225; *Alum. cantab.*, I, ii, 386. The son of William Hodgson, of Newcastle-upon-Tyne, Hodgson was educated at Jesus College, Cambridge, from which he was graduated in 1594. He was successively Rector of Elvington, Etton, and Sig-

Most of the resources given by Yorkshire donors for experimentation in social rehabilitation were designated for still more useful and more abiding purposes. Thus there was growing interest after 1586, when the first gift for the use was made, in establishing workhouses and stocks of goods to be fabricated in an effort to provide gainful employment for the poor.[1] A total of £2788 16s was given during our period for such purposes, this being 1·14 per cent of all charitable funds for the county, the whole of the amount, it may be noted, having been established in the form of endowments. The experiments with this form of social rehabilitation were most cautious in the later Elizabethan period, only £120 having been provided between 1581 and 1600, but interest became much more substantial in the early Stuart era, when the considerable capital of £1601 was afforded. Giving for this purpose was relatively even more generous during the revolutionary era, when a total of £1067 16s was designated to establish such experimental ventures.

The earliest of these endowments was ordered under the will of one of the lower gentry of the county, Thomas Basfurth of Thormanby in the North Riding. Basfurth in 1586 conveyed to the municipal authorities of York certain real property, subject to the annual payment of £5 to the churchwardens of Thormanby, with which they should buy wool, flax, or hemp on which the poor of the parish might be put at useful work. From the proceeds gained by the sale of the cloth thus made, one-twentieth was to be retained by those thus employed and the remainder distributed for the general relief of the poor of the community.[2] In 1595 George Savile the younger, a merchant of Wakefield, by will provided £20 for building a house of correction there 'for the setting of the poore on worke or towardes a stocke for the keepinge of them in worke'.[3]

The first considerable workhouse foundation to be made in Yorkshire

glesthorne, and he was from 1611 until his death in 1646 Chancellor of York Cathedral. He was named a member of the Council of the North in 1629, was one of the King's chaplains, and during the Civil War was a fearless and devoted Royalist.

[1] In the City of York, whose economy was adversely affected by the expropriation of the monasteries and by the expanding competition of the West Riding in the cloth trade, ambitious and sustained municipal effort had to be undertaken to deal with the problem of unemployment from 1569 to the close of our period. Successive work schemes were tried, which since they were supported by taxation do not directly concern us. This whole development is admirably discussed by Herbert Heaton, *Yorkshire woollen industries* (Oxford, 1920), 64–67.

[2] PCY 23/280 1586; *PP* 1821, XII, 645; *VCH, Yorks., NR*, II, 208. The capital messuage of Thormanby, with the manor of Raskelf, was leased from the Crown by Thomas Basfurth in 1544. He was succeeded by his brother Ralph (d. 1559), whose son this donor was.

[3] PCC 2 Scott 1595; Walker, *Wakefield*, II, 425–426, 584; Turner, J. H., *Wakefield House of Correction* (Bingley, 1904), 34–35; *VCH, Yorks.*, I, 441; *Surtees Soc. Pub.*, CXXI (1912), 164–165. *Vide post*, 320.

was that vested by deed in 1605 by Thomas Cecil, Earl of Exeter, and Dorothy (Nevill), his wife and a native of the county. The couple gave on trust property valued at £600 for the support, under the management of a master and mistress, of twelve poor girls of Well who should be set at useful work and who should be given instruction in sewing, knitting, and spinning.[1] A few years later, in 1615, the village of Long Preston was endowed with a workhouse by James Knowles, a London cloth merchant, whose notable almshouse foundation has already been noted. Knowles bequeathed £200 to be employed for the setting up of a house of correction and towards provision of a stock of flax or wool on which the needy poor might profitably and usefully be employed.[2] Similar provision was made for the poor of Hull under the will of John Lister, a merchant and former mayor, who in 1617 left £100 as an endowment, the income to be employed for the maintenance of poor children who were to be kept fruitfully at work under supervision in a workhouse recently provided by the city.[3] At about the same date in Leeds, Richard Sykes and other principal merchants and tradesmen built a workhouse and provided a stock of materials, at a personal charge of about £170, with which the poor might be gainfully employed.[4]

It will be noted that endowments were being provided for workhouses and supervised work programmes especially in the various cloth towns of the county, where seasonal unemployment was a persistently serious social problem. These foundations were made, principally by merchant donors who sensed the measure of their own responsibility not only for the prosperity but for the new social difficulties which their

[1] PCC 23 Swann 1623; PP 1821, XII, 368, 651–653; VCH, Yorks., NR, I, 348, 354; Complete peerage, III, 299; DNB; Wardale, Clare College, 99. In 1788 the workhouse was converted into four free schools, two at Well and two at Snape, one for boys and one for girls in either place. These donors had earlier (1600) founded a richly endowed almshouse, the annual income being £116, at Lyddington in Rutland. Thomas Cecil (1542–1623) was the eldest and the undistinguished son of Lord Burghley and Mary Cheke. He was created Earl of Exeter in 1605. His last years were embittered by the scandalous lawsuits of his grandson, Lord Roos.   [2] Vide ante, 269.

[3] PCY 34/411 1617; Yorks. Arch. Soc. Rec., IX (1890), 165 n.; Denny, Lister family, 271; PP 1823, IX, 794; Tickell, Hull, 772; Gent, Hull, 35. The building then used was in 1695 replaced by a new workhouse, built on the same site, which was authorized by Act of Parliament. Lister also left £40 to the poor of Halifax, his birthplace, to be used at Dr Favour's discretion, £10 to the poor of Hull, £20 for the general uses of Trinity church, Hull, and a substantial sum for the construction of a hall to be used by merchants in Hull (vide post, 295). A son of John Lister of Halifax, Lister made a fortune in Hull as a cloth merchant. He married Anne, a daughter of Robert Geyton of Hull. He represented Hull in Parliament in 1601 and was mayor of the city in 1595 and again in 1612. He was the father of Sir John Lister (vide ante, 275).

[4] Old Leeds charities, 41–42; Gent, Thomas, 'A journey into some parts of Yorkshire', in The antient and modern history of Ripon (York, 1733), iv, 24.

energy and creative skill had engendered. In 1631 Thomas Agar, a merchant and former mayor of York, by will established an endowment of £100, the income to be used by the municipal authorities for setting the poor at work.[1] Similar provision was made for Doncaster in 1645 when Edward Rennick, a London merchant tailor who was a native of Doncaster, left £100 for the endowment of some useful project which would give employment to the deserving poor. The Corporation in 1657 hit upon the ingenious, and successful, plan of using this endowment, together with £60 more 'which the town oweth to the poor upon another account', for establishing a fishery and a fowling decoy in a marsh area just to the south of the town (Potteric Carr), with the town providing additional funds to secure the necessary gear.[2] Finally, we may mention the bequest in 1648 by Thomas Armitage of £200 to trustees who should employ the income for providing work for the needy of Huddersfield. Armitage was a merchant residing in Spain, where his will was drawn and where he died. The bequest was shrewdly invested by the trustees, with the result that £271 was shortly placed in lands, the rents being 'distributed and parted by the vicar and other persons . . . to buy wool and deliver the same to the poor to work that they have wherewithal to sustain themselves'. It is happy to relate that the investments made by successive feoffees were sufficient in their yield to permit, in another age when conditions had changed, the foundation of the Armitage Technical School in Huddersfield, which carried forward in new form the aspirations of the donor to establish effective means for the social rehabilitation of the poor.[3]

An even greater interest was displayed by Yorkshire donors in the foundation of endowments which would secure to worthy and ambitious poor youths the priceless benefits afforded by apprenticeships in the several crafts and trades of the times. In total, the useful sum of £4079 3s was given for this purpose, almost the whole being capital, which amounted to 1·67 per cent of the charitable funds provided during our entire period. Save for very small and outright gifts in earlier decades, these undertakings were not instituted in Yorkshire until the comparatively late date of 1591, there being in fact only one gift, in the amount of £133, in the whole of the Elizabethan age. In the course of the early Stuart period, however, sustained interest was aroused in this most effective instrumentality for social rehabilitation and the cure of

[1] *Vide ante*, 272, for a biographical notice and a comment on Agar's almshouse foundation.

[2] PCC 135 Rivers 1645; Jackson, *Doncaster charities*, 127–130. The Carr was so used profitably until it was drained late in the eighteenth century. Rennick likewise left £100 to the Merchant Taylors' Company of London for loans to two young men. His father-in-law, William Marshall, was a mayor of Doncaster.

[3] PCC 149 Essex 1648; *PP* 1899, LXXI, 664; *PP* 1828, XX, 553. Armitage was the son of a Huddersfield clothier.

poverty, with the result that £1251 10s of endowments were provided during the first four decades of the seventeenth century. But the great burst of giving for this purpose came very late in Yorkshire. During the brief and economically troubled time of political upheaval (1641–1660), the impressive total of £2691 was given for apprenticeship endowments, a considerably larger sum than had been provided for this purpose in all the preceding years of our period and substantially more than was given during the revolutionary era for all other experiments in social rehabilitation.

We may mention only a representative group of the numerous apprenticeship foundations that were established in Yorkshire. Thus in 1601 a yeoman of Bishopthorpe left a rent-charge of £10 p.a. for the apprenticing of poor children of the parish of Darrington, as well as £3 7s p.a. for the relief of the poor of that community.[1] John Dunne, a draper of Howden, in 1628 left an endowment of £140, the income of £7 p.a. to be employed for the payment of apprenticeship fees for children born in Howden, Laxton, and Saltmarshe, while also providing an annuity of £1 for an anniversary sermon.[2] In 1631 Samuel Harsnett, Archbishop of York, not only left £100 to complete a workhouse which he had begun building in Cawood but arranged for the apprenticing of poor children of that parish and of Wistow with a rent-charge of £5 5s.[3]

As one would expect, Thomas Ferres, Hull's great benefactor, whose generous foundations for the poor have already been noted, was much interested in the experimentation then proceeding in England in various schemes for social rehabilitation. By his will proved in 1630, Ferres left lands then possessing a capital worth of £400 on trust to the Corporation of the town, the income to be employed towards putting forth poor and fatherless children of the town in the several trades. He also provided a capital sum of £200 as a stock to set the poor at work in the Charity Hall workhouse organized and endowed a few years earlier by a fellow merchant, John Lister. Moreover, Ferres set aside the sum of £50 to be employed as a loan fund, loans of £10 to be made interest free to responsible and needy persons of Hull upon the presentation of adequate security.[4] In the same year Anthony Sawdrie, a clergyman of Harewood, by deed conveyed to trustees real property valued at approximately £60

---

[1] PCY 28/495 1601.   [2] PCY 40/259 1628; PP 1824, XIV, 757.

[3] PCC 78 St John 1631; PP 1824, XIII, 743; PP 1898, LXVIII, Cawood, 7–9; VCH, Yorks., I, 491–492; DNB. Vide post, 335. Harsnett's nephew paid £197 as executor to Archbishop Neile to carry out his uncle's intentions. Neile disposed of £79 only, retaining the balance, to which he proposed to add £100 in order to carry forward the apprenticeship plan. Neile died before the inhabitants of the two towns could agree to a proposed plan. In 1640 suit was brought to enforce payment, the court ordering Sir Paul Neile, the executor, to pay £120 as from Harsnett's estate and the £100 promised by Archbishop Neile.

[4] Vide ante, 240, 271.

for the endowment of apprenticeships for eight communities in that large parish, the village of Harewood having the privilege of placing one child every third year. The twelve trustees were instructed to bind out girls as well as boys, the only restriction imposed being that the child must have been born in wedlock to parents who were inhabitants of the parish. At the same time, Sawdrie created a similar endowment with a capital of £53 for the parish of Wath-upon-Dearne, lying some thirty miles to the south of Harewood, for the benefit of the town of Wath and five other communities within that parish. The donor further stipulated that in both charities should no child apply or be eligible in a given year, the income should be expended for gray cloth for the benefit of the poor.[1]

The town of Ripon was vested with a small apprenticeship endowment in or about 1637 by Hugh Ripley, a mercer of that place. Ripley, who also left an endowment valued at £50 for the benefit of the poor of the community, established under the control of feoffees, they being three recent mayors, the sum of £50 to be lent on good security to five poor tradesmen, the interest, £2 10s p.a., to be employed to bind out one child annually on the nomination of the mayor.[2] At about the same date (1638) Abraham Wall, a native of Heptonstall (Halifax) and a London glazier, ordered most useful bequests for his native community. In addition to establishing a small school endowment,[3] he bequeathed £3 p.a. for sending one of the scholars in the school to London each year for his apprenticeship, evidently reflecting the difficulties which he had himself encountered when as a child he was endeavouring to learn his trade.[4] Two parishes in the North Riding, Catterick and Kirklington, were similarly strengthened in their social institutions in 1641 under the will of Christopher Wandesford, Lord Deputy of Ireland, and a native of Bishop Burton. Wandesford left £100 to the churchwardens of Catterick as an endowment to be used by them for binding children as apprentices from several communities in this large parish, while £50 was left under the same general terms for the parish of Kirklington, where the donor also held lands.[5]

The largest of the benefactions made in Yorkshire for experimentation

[1] PP 1826, XIII, 658; PP 1828, XX, 639; VCH, Yorks., I, 483; Jones, John, History of Harewood (L., 1859), 130–137. Sawdrie also provided an educational charity for Wath, which will be considered later (vide post, 342–343).

[2] PP 1820, IV, 484; PP 1898, LXVIII, Ripon, 4; Ripon millenary record (Ripon, 1892), 44; Yorks. Arch. Soc. Rec., XXXIV (1904), 213. Ripley was the last wakeman of the town in 1604 and personally defrayed most of the costs involved in securing a charter of incorporation. He was nominated by the Crown as Ripon's first mayor, serving again in 1616 and in 1630.

[3] Vide post, 338.

[4] Turner, Biographia Halifaxiensis, 310; PP 1820, XXVIII, 587; PP 1822, IX, 264; PP 1899, LXXI, 611–614; Halifax Antiq. Soc. Papers, 1908, 170.

[5] M'Call, Wandesforde family, 65–84, 282–287; Whitaker, Richmondshire, II, 160–161. A son of Sir George Wandesford, Wandesford was educated at Clare

in social rehabilitation was that left in 1642 by Nathaniel Waterhouse, a merchant of Halifax. As we have seen, Waterhouse had earlier established a well-endowed almshouse in his native city, and his will suggests that he had for some time contemplated a serious effort to attack poverty at its very roots. In 1635 Waterhouse had also given a large house, valued at £60, to be employed as a workhouse and house of correction in the town. A board of governors was designated, a master appointed, and vagrants and other able-bodied poor were put at work on these premises, such severity being used that about seventy unruly persons were whipped during the first three years. Until Waterhouse's death, when £200 of endowment was bequeathed, the house was maintained by rates with a stock of materials for employment. By his will in 1645 Waterhouse provided still another institution, which he endowed with capital amounting to £1000, for the reception of ten poor boys and as many needy girls, all being orphans, who should be maintained from the age of six to about fourteen years, and who should be taught some honourable trade at which they might earn their own living. When their early training and care had been provided, the children should then be apprenticed under the direction of the trustees until such time as their preparation for adult life had been completed. The children benefiting from the trust were to be drawn from the town of Halifax, which should nominate five, and from nine other towns and villages lying in this large parish.[1]

Lord Craven, whose munificent bequest to the poor of Yorkshire has already been discussed, in 1648 by will established an apprenticeship fund in the amount of £500 for the binding of boys in London or elsewhere, without, it should be said, any specific preference for youths from Yorkshire.[2] In 1652 Francis Layton settled the residue of a substantial rent-charge of £40 p.a., placed upon trust for Oglethorpe's almshouse

College, Cambridge, and at Gray's Inn. He married a daughter of Sir Hewit Osborne. Wandesford sat as a Member of Parliament for Aldbrough in 1621, for Richmond in 1625 and 1626, and for Thirsk in 1628. He was deputy bailiff for Richmondshire in 1630 and later declined the ambassadorship to Spain because of his zealous devotion to the reformed faith. He accompanied Wentworth to Ireland as Master of the Rolls and was made Lord Deputy in 1640, dying shortly afterwards.

His Irish experiments in social rehabilitation, while not included in this study, were intelligently planned and costly to execute. In 1637 he purchased a great estate at Castlecomer, where he built a parish church and endowed the living. He opened a cloth factory and built a pottery in the town, and, finding seams of coal and iron nearby, opened a coal mine and built an iron forge.

[1] Vide ante, 276.

[2] Vide ante, 246, for an account of Craven's great endowment for the poor and for a biographical notice. Craven also left £200 to the endowment of Christ's Hospital, £320 to London hospitals, including a bequest of £200 to Bethlehem, and £80 to London prisons. Vide post, 356, for his scholarship foundation.

at Tadcaster and the augmentation of the stipend of the curate of Raw-don, for the foundation of an apprenticeship plan in Rawdon. This income, representing a capital worth of £256, was to be employed by his feoffees for binding out both boys and girls of the town who should be deserving but without means.[1] An endowment for apprenticeships was likewise founded in Whitby in 1658 by the generosity of William Cleaveland, a Westminster lawyer, who left a rent-charge of £5 p.a. to secure the training each year of two poor children from his native town.[2] In this same year (1658) Anne Middleton, whose great almshouse foundation for the city of York has already been mentioned, left a number of well-conceived bequests for the social rehabilitation of the poor of her city. Her will provided £100 as an endowment, the income of which should be employed for binding poor freemen's sons as apprentices, while she gave as well £40 as a stock for setting the poor of York on useful work. The sum of £50 was left to provide loans without interest for poor men, £10 was given to place a clock in Brafferton church, and £66 13s 4d was left to provide suitable silver for the use of the mayor and aldermen of the city of York.[3]

We may conclude our brief notice of the apprenticeship endowments instituted in these years with mention of two founded in the last days of the Protectorate. In 1660 John Bathurst, Cromwell's principal physician, established apprenticeship funds in three parishes, as well as creating educational facilities in these communities, all being in the neighbourhood of Richmond. Messuages and lands were given to trustees in Richmond to pay £12 p.a. to the burgesses, of which £4 p.a. should be employed each year for the apprenticing of a poor boy from that community. The wild and remote manor of Arkengarthdale, which he had purchased in 1656, was laid under a charge of £20 p.a. for charitable purposes, of which £4 p.a. should be employed for sending a poor boy from the parish of Arkengarthdale to carry forward his apprenticeship in London or in York. Other lands to the north of Richmond, at Kirby Hill, were charged with the payment of £4 p.a. for a similar use for a boy to be drawn from the New Forest region.[4] In 1660 Dame Mary Bolles, of Heath, by deed began the creation of most substantial charities for four Yorkshire parishes which were not, however, completed until the time of her death in 1662. In 1660 she established a school at Warmfield in which ten poor boys should be educated until ready for apprenticing; each year the trustees were to bind out one of them in some suitable trade, at £4 p.a., while filling the place thus vacated in order to keep the number at ten. She gave to the clergyman at Sandal Magna and to three other principal inhabitants, as feoffees, the capital sum of £200 to be invested in lands, the income to be

<hr>

[1] *Vide ante,* 277, and *post,* 381, 399.   [2] PCC 141 Wootton 1658.
[3] *Vide ante,* 279, and *post,* 345.   [4] *Vide ante,* 250, and *post,* 346, 356.

employed for putting forth poor children of the parish, in as great numbers as possible, in trades that they might fit themselves to gain an honest livelihood. A similar foundation was established, with the same endowment, for apprenticing poor children from Royston and Cudworth, while an endowment of £500 was provided for the binding of poor children drawn from the town of Wakefield.[1]

Loan endowments for poor young men who had recently completed their training were almost corollary to the apprenticeship endowments created during this period. There was, however, only a moderate interest in this extremely effective instrumentality of social rehabilitation in Yorkshire. In all, £2801 14s was given for loan funds, this being 1·15 per cent of all the charitable funds of the county. No such endowments were available prior to 1577, but thereafter they were vested in at least some amount in every decade. During the later Elizabethan period (1571–1600) a total of £780 was given for loan funds, while in the early Stuart decades the more substantial sum of £1451 10s was provided. There was a marked decline in giving for this use during the Cromwellian era when only £570 4s was provided by donors.

The earliest of the loan funds established for the use of deserving young men in the county was actually the beneficial interest of the city of York in the revolving loan fund established in 1554 by Sir Thomas White, the great London benefactor.[2] York received its first grant of £100 under the trust in 1577, and thereafter every twenty-third year, to be set out in loans to four poor young clothiers of the city. Some years later George Talbot, sixth Earl of Shrewsbury, created substantial loan funds in Sheffield, Rotherham, and Pontefract. The first of these endowments was established in Sheffield in 1588 when the Earl by deed conveyed £200 to four feoffees, being minded that the town was 'fraught with a great number of poore artificers and also with a multitude of aged poore persones'. The fund was to be lent at 5 per cent, in amounts not exceeding £10 each, to poor artificers and tradesmen, while the income was to be distributed to the poor and needy of the community. Similar provisions were contained in his will in 1590 for funds of equal value for the towns of Rotherham and Pontefract, these amounts to 'be employed yearlie unto the benfytt of the poorest artificers . . . and for the increase of trades', though the loans were apparently intended to be restricted to artificers and were not to be made in amounts exceeding £5.[3] At about the same date (1591), Lady Catherine Constable, of

---

[1] We have not included the Wakefield and Royston sums in our totals. *Vide ante*, 279, and *post*, 346.

[2] *Vide* Jordan, *Charities of London*, 174, 215, 257–258, 356, 370, 400.

[3] PCC 86 Drury 1590; *Surtees Soc. Pub.*, CXXI (1912), 148–150; *PP* 1895, LXXV, Rotherham, 17; *Yorks. Arch. Soc. Rec.*, XXXIV (1904), 113–115; *Hunter Archaeological Society Transactions*, IV (1937), 252–257; DNB.

Kirby Knowle, gave a modest loan fund to the city of York to be employed there for the benefit of poor and deserving young men,[1] while some years later, in 1599, William Wooler, a York merchant, left £100 as a loan fund to assist two young merchant adventurers of that city who might be in need of capital as they began their mercantile careers.[2]

The city of York received further augmentation of its loan funds in the later years of our period. A wool merchant and a former mayor, William Robinson, in 1616 bequeathed £40 to the Company of Merchant Adventurers to be lent without interest to poor young freemen of the company, as well as leaving £80 and a silver bowl for the uses of the municipality.[3] A substantial additional loan fund for the Merchant Adventurers of York was given in 1633 by William Hart, who had for many years served the company abroad as their preacher. Hart left £600 upon trust with the company, £100 of which was to be lent without interest to twenty poor men, in amounts of not more than £5 and for a term of not more than two years, while the remainder should be lent to young merchants for a period of two years without interest charge.[4] In 1637 William Breary, a merchant and a former mayor, left an additional £25 to the loan stock of the Merchant Adventurers' Company, with the stipulation that interest be charged and distributed to the poor of the company's hospital, as well as having left, very probably, an additional £150 to the city of York for loans to its poor.[5]

A London chapman, John Lowden, who had trade connections in Wakefield, in 1618 left £10 outright to the poor of that town and provided as well £100 to be lent to poor clothiers and carriers of the community, with whom, it was said, he had dealt harshly during his life-

[1] PCC 47 Sainberbe 1591; *PP* 1824, XIII, 662; Skelton, *Pietas oxon.*, 81; Drake, *Eboracum*, 221; Lawton, *Collectio*, 382; Poulson, *Holderness*, II, 233; Blakiston, *Trinity College*, 87. *Vide post*, 353. She was a daughter of Henry, Earl of Westmorland. Her husband, who died before her, was Sir John Constable, whose family had held the manor of Kirby Knowle since 1330. Sir John had founded the almshouse and the school at Halsham (*vide ante*, 263, and *post*, 319).

[2] PCY 27/541 1599; *PP* 1825, X, 641; *PP* 1826–1827, X, 736–740; *VCH, Yorks.*, I, 477; Dodd, E. E., *Bingley Grammar School* (Bradford, 1929), 13–16. Wooler was born in Bingley, of yeoman stock. He was a trader in wool in York, admitted as a freeman of the city in 1587, made Chamberlain of York in 1593. For his school foundation at Bingley, *vide post*, 310.

[3] Hailstone, *Yorkshire worthies*, I, xl; *Ripon millenary record*, 266; *PP* 1825, X, 641. Robinson resided as a merchant for many years in various Hanse towns. He was made free of the city of York in 1558, was sheriff in 1568, and on two occasions was mayor. He sat for York in Parliament in 1584 and 1588.

[4] *Vide ante*, 272–273.

[5] PCY 42/711, 42/713 1637; *Surtees Soc. Pub.*, CXXIX (1918), 289; Drake, *Eboracum*, 222, 302; *PP* 1825, X, 641.

time.[1] A merchant and a former mayor of Hull, Thomas Thackray, in 1630 left an endowment of £100 to be lent to poor and worthy tradesmen of that community at an interest charge of 5 per cent,[2] while in 1641 an aggrieved and apparently irascible York merchant, Henry Atkinson, pointedly cut York from his will and left £100 as a loan fund for poor artisans of Ripon, the upper limit of the loans being £5 and none to run for a term of more than three years.[3]

In 1643 Samuel Casson, probably a Leeds tradesman, by will established a loan fund with a capital of £100 to be lent to as many as twenty poor tradesmen of the city, they being such 'as have charge of wife and children and want stock and such as are religious people', without the requirement of any interest.[4] Finally, we may note the useful bequest of Charles Greenwood, Rector of Thornhill, of £100 to be employed by his feoffees for loans to the poor of Heptonstall, to be lent from year to year without interest the better to enable them 'to live by their labours in their honest vocations'.[5]

3. Municipal betterments

Relatively meagre as were the benefactions made in Yorkshire for experiments in social rehabilitation, they were generous indeed when compared with the gifts made for the various municipal betterments in which private donors were interested. In total only £6121 11s was provided during the course of our period for such purposes, this amounting to but 2·51 per cent of the charitable funds for the county and being slightly less than half the total given for purposes of social rehabilitation. There were few counties in England in which so slight a proportion of charitable gifts was made for these uses.[6] There were scattered gifts totalling £286 6s vested in companies, with the income designated for municipal uses, while only a trifling sum was provided for public parks and recreation.

We should take somewhat fuller notice of the fairly substantial amounts left by donors of the county for general municipal purposes

[1] PCC 118 Meade 1618; *Yorks. Arch. Soc. Rec.*, XXXIV (1904), 51; *PP* 1898, LXVIII, Wakefield, 70. Lowden, a native of Kendal, was reputed to control at Blackwell Hall the sale of cloth from Wakefield, the clothiers having 'so much imployment from him that they durst [not] contrad . . . so that he paid them at his pleasure . . .'

[2] PCY 41/239 1630; Gent, *Hull*, 61; Tickell, *Hull*, 677. A merchant adventurer, Thackray was sheriff in 1601 and mayor in 1604 and 1624.

[3] *Vide ante*, 244.   [4] *Vide ante*, 244.

[5] *Vide ante*, 244, and *post*, 338, 341, 355.

[6] The proportions given for this use in the several counties studied are as follows: Bristol, 9·10 per cent; Buckinghamshire, 8·80 per cent; Hampshire, 10·92 per cent; Kent, 4·59 per cent; Lancashire, 1·22 per cent; Middlesex (London), 4·95 per cent; Norfolk, 10·58 per cent; Somerset, 0·78 per cent; Worcestershire, 5·44 per cent.

and for the great charitable head which we have defined as *Public Works*. In total, £2322 12s was given for municipal purposes, including provisions for tax relief, during the course of our entire period. There was a considerable number of small gifts and bequests for this purpose prior to the Reformation, when £160 11s was provided, while a somewhat larger total of £176 7s was given during the Reformation period proper. There were relatively few such benefactions in the Elizabethan era, only £273 6s having been so designated during that long generation. From 1601 to the close of our period, however, there was a pronounced awakening of civic pride and interest, rather more than £160 being given for these uses in every decade and a total of £1228 19s in the early Stuart period and of £483 9s during the revolutionary era.

The benefactions made for municipal uses were of course of many kinds and for many purposes, but all had in common the desire to bring about a betterment in the physical character and in the amenities of a community. Brief mention of a representative group of these gifts will suggest both their nature and the aspirations of the donors. A merchant adventurer's widow in York, Mary Gale, in 1558 bequeathed to the mayor for general municipal purposes her interest in the fishing of the Foss and a leasehold, together valued at £80.[1] During the later years of his lifetime and then by bequest, Sir Robert Watter, a merchant and a former mayor of York, whose almshouse foundation has already been mentioned,[2] made most substantial and useful gifts for the improvement of his city. Watter, who was himself a haberdasher, erected a hall for his company at an estimated charge of £100, repaired the common hall of the city at a personal cost of £200, repaired and extended a causeway over Marston Moor, just to the west of the city, at a probable charge of £60, and on his death in 1612 bequeathed to the city the mayor's gold chain at a cost to his estate of £40.[3]

The city of Hull enjoyed similar benefits from its own merchant aristocracy, who had also contributed so heavily towards the relief of the poor of the community and to experiments for their rehabilitation. Thus in 1617 John Lister, a merchant and a former mayor, whose substantial endowment for a stock for the poor has just been discussed, left £100 to defray the costs of building a 'decent meeting place for the merchants and others' of Hull 'which thing I much desired might have been done in my lifetime'. Lister had also, while mayor, secured the building of Charity Hall, in which the public works programme which he largely

[1] PCY 15/2/124 1558. She left, in addition, £40 for charity general, £40 for poor relief, £80 (estimated) for prayers, £20 for marriages, and lesser amounts for church general, church repairs, and prisoners.

[2] *Vide ante*, 268, and *post*, 377.

[3] Watter also left £50 as a loan fund for the poor, fifteen poor citizens to be eligible at any given time for loans not to exceed 5 marks in each instance and with an indicated preference for haberdashers and fishmongers.

financed was carried forward.[1] The city found an even more generous benefactor in Thomas Ferres, whose total gifts to the charitable institutions of Hull amounted to nearly £4300 and the principal of which have already been discussed. Long before his death, Ferres had built a stone bridge over the Esk at Glaisdale in the North Riding, where tradition has it he had very nearly lost his life while fording the stream. A few years earlier, in 1617, he built a wall around the western portion of Trinity churchyard at a cost of £50 and some years later constructed the Hanse House for the use and enjoyment of the Merchant Adventurers' Company. By the terms of his will, proved in 1630, Ferres bequeathed £200 to the Corporation of Hull for the repair of 'the North Bridge, the Castle, and the Blockhouses', as well as providing several smaller benefactions for various useful municipal purposes.[2]

A merchant's widow, Alice Lodge, in 1639 left to the municipality of Leeds the capital sum of £100, the income to be used 'for the good of the town'.[3] A woollen draper of Hedon, William Sagge, in ca. 1650 bequeathed £100 for the general municipal needs of that town as well as leaving three cottages, worth about £30, for the lodging of poor persons who had in any case to be supported by the parish.[4] We may conclude this brief review of benefactions for general municipal betterments with mention of the bequest of Matthew Francke, a merchant and former mayor of Pontefract, who in 1659 left to the town for its uses lands valued at upwards of £200 on condition of the payment of £10 p.a. to a named beneficiary.[5]

A considerably larger total was provided by Yorkshire donors for the improvement of communications in the county, under which we have grouped the repair of roads and streets, the building and care of bridges, the improvement of harbours and causeways, and other public works of this general type. Yorkshire roads in this period were notoriously bad and the wonder really is that relatively so little was given for their improvement. In all £3512 11s was provided for the betterment of communications during the course of our period, this representing 1·44 per cent of the whole of the charitable funds of the county. There was a persistent interest on the part of donors in this great need, into which, save for the improvement of harbours, public funds scarcely intruded during our whole period. Fairly substantial totals are recorded in every decade of our entire era, mostly from scores of small gifts or

---

[1] Vide ante, 286.　　　　　　　　[2] Vide ante, 240, 271, 288.

[3] PCY October 1639; PP 1826, XIII, 661. The income was in fact for many years applied to the needs of the charity school in the town, though in 1816, on advice of counsel, it was determined that use for the maintenance of highways more nearly met the intentions of the donor.

[4] Park, Hedon, 86, 236. Sagge was bailiff of Hedon in 1639 and in 1648.

[5] Vide ante, 250, 280, for an account of Francke's endowment for the relief of the poor and for his almshouse foundation.

bequests for the patching and mending of especially foul ways in a particular parish, though when the cheapness of labour is considered these were by no means inconsiderable totals in each decade. There were, however, also a fair number of larger gifts for the purpose.

In 1530(?) Thomas Ward, a Leeds merchant, drew his will bequeathing, on the death or remarriage of his wife, property in the town then valued at about £160 for the repair and maintenance in perpetuity of the various highways radiating from the town.[1] Some years later the first Earl of Cumberland by his will, proved in 1543, in addition to leaving £24 for funeral alms and £190 of capital for prayers, bequeathed 100 marks for the repair of highways in Yorkshire at the discretion of his executors and an equal amount for the repair of the even more wretched roads of Westmorland.[2] Richard Pymond, a merchant tailor of London and Wakefield, in 1546 vested £100 in the executors of his estate with the instruction to expend the amount in equal instalments over a period of twenty years for the building and mending of roads in and about Wakefield.[3] The widow of a prominent York merchant, Jane Hall, in 1566 gave £100 towards the rebuilding of the bridge over the Ouse, which had been badly damaged by a great flood two years earlier.[4] A gentleman of Selby, Roger Beckwith, in 1574 conveyed lands two generations later possessing a capital worth of £147, the income to be employed by the churchwardens for the repair of the roads of the parish and for needed work on the parish church and its steeple.[5] In 1598 Reginald Harrison, a mercer of Stamford, Lincolnshire, but a native of Sedbergh, in addition to carefully devised bequests for the poor and the school of the latter community, bequeathed a capital sum of £80 for the repairs required on the bridge just to the east of Sedbergh.[6]

There was a quickening of interest in the improvement of roads and public works during the early Stuart decades, when a total of £834 15s was provided for these uses by a considerable number of donors. Among

[1] Whitaker, *Loidis*, 50; Thoresby, *Ducatus*, App., 119; *PP* 1899, LXXII, 350.

[2] PCY 12/664 1543; *Complete peerage*, II, 438; *Surtees Soc. Pub.*, XCII (1893), 403, CVI (1902), 127–130; Dawson, *Skipton*, 36–41; *Yorks. Arch. Journal*, XVIII (1905), 375–379; DNB.

[3] *Vide ante*, 231, for mention of Pymond's large bequest for the relief of the poor of Wakefield.

[4] Torr, *Antiquities of York*, 79; Davies, Robert, *The Fawkes's of York* (Westminster, 1850), 20n. Jane Hall was the daughter of a respected York merchant, William Haryngton, who had served as sheriff in 1531 and mayor in 1536. Her husband, Robert Hall, served his city as an alderman.

[5] *PP* 1824, XIII, 745; Morrell, W. W., *The history and antiquities of Selby* (Selby, 1867), 134, 180. Beckwith was the son of Sir Leonard Beckwith, a goldssmith and merchant of York who had married Elizabeth, the daughter and co-heir of the Lord Chief Justice, Sir Roger Cholmley. In 1568 Sir Leonard conferred the manor of Selby on his son, who maintained his residence there as a county gentleman.   [6] *Vide ante*, 235, and *post*, 309.

the principal of these was the building or repairing at an uncertain cost of four bridges in Yorkshire, including a very beautiful one at Burnsall, by Sir William Craven, a native of the village of Appletreewick, just to the southeast of that town. Craven by deed in 1605 and by will in 1618 provided most generous charities for the Burnsall community, including a well-endowed school,[1] £50 outright to the poor, £80 capital for church repairs, and £10 outright for the two parsons at Burnsall. His will also gave capital of £160 to pay £8 p.a. for the repair and general maintenance of bridges and highways in the parish.[2] Robert Rollinson, a Sheffield mercer, in 1631 provided fire protection for Sheffield by enlarging and walling in a pool lying above the town and opening channels into the town, while giving as well thirty fire buckets which were hung on hooks in the parish church for use in an emergency.[3] In 1637 William Smithson, a gentleman of Kirby Misperton in the North Riding, among other substantial charities for the parish, provided a rent-charge of £5 p.a. for the repair of the church way leading from Great Habton, for three miles across the low moors, to Kirby Misperton, and an even longer road from the latter town to Amotherby where Smithson had lodged while attending school as a boy.[4]

An even greater total of £1025 13s was provided for municipal uses during the Cromwellian period by a considerable number of donors. But this substantial sum is principally to be accounted for by two large benefactions. The first was the charity of the great Leeds merchant, John Harrison, who during his lifetime expended upwards of £300 for various municipal improvements, including the market cross, of which he was particularly proud.[5] In the same general period Sir Hugh Cholmley, who held the manor of Aslaby in Whitby, laid out large amounts for the improvement of that town. In 1632 he was instrumental in persuading the Crown to permit a collection throughout England for the building of a pier to protect the town and to keep the harbour open, to which he made a substantial personal contribution. Two years later he built a new bridge and a pier near St Ninian's Chapel, reclaiming a considerable area of swamp land, while in 1640 he built the town hall in Whitby and gave the land for a new and less crowded market place, at the same time throwing a drawbridge across the Esk to accommodate

---

[1] *Vide ante*, 239, and *post*, 328–329, 400.

[2] PCC 75 Meade 1618; *PP* 1825, XI, 621; Lewis, C., *Wharfedale* (Bradford, [1937]), 73–74. *Vide post*, 328, and *vide* Jordan, *Charities of London*, 110–111, 237–238, 258, 286, 295, 339, 341, for a biographical notice and an account of Craven's great charities.

[3] Hunter, *Hallamshire*, 188; *PP* 1897, LXVII, iii, Sheffield, 305; Fletcher, J. S., *Picturesque history of Yorkshire* (L., 1899, 6 vols.), II, 63. *Vide post*, 330.

[4] *Vide ante*, 242, and *post*, 337.

[5] *Vide ante*, 277, and *post*, 314, 382, 401–402.

the increasing traffic coming into the town. In 1652 he laid out extensive 'new gardens' to supply fruit and food for Whitby, planting orchards and inscribing on the wall the sentiment: 'Our handy worke like to ye frutefull tree / Blesse thou O Lord let it not blasted bee.' In all, Cholmley laid out at least £720 on these considerable municipal improvements, which all but remade the town, while, though by no means a charitable venture, the alum works which he opened just outside Whitby in 1648 accounted principally for its recovery from the long decay into which it had fallen.[1]

Despite a considerable number of substantial and interesting benefactions for municipal betterments, the total provided by Yorkshire donors was relatively small in terms of the size and certainly in terms of the needs of the county. In part this may well have been the consequence of the comparative poverty and backwardness of the county during much of our period and the very immensity of the municipal tasks which lay ahead. But more importantly, it would seem that the comparative neglect of not only the pressing needs for municipal improvements but the opportunities for experimentation in social rehabilitation was occasioned by the intensity with which the county devoted itself to the basic needs of the poor and to the pertinacity with which benefactors of the county addressed themselves to the building of a system of education in this huge and sprawling shire. First things received first attention in Yorkshire.

4. Education

(a) *Founding of the Grammar Schools.* Yorkshire donors displayed a persistent and a most devoted interest in strengthening the meagre educational institutions which they had inherited from the Middle Ages. In the course of our period they gave the great total of £75,812 8s for various educational purposes, this representing 31·12 per cent of all the charitable funds of the county and being only slightly less than the sum given for the relief of the poor (33·46 per cent) and, most surprisingly, somewhat more than that given (28·07 per cent) for the various religious uses. The relative concern of benefactors with this great spectrum of social and cultural need mounted steadily during the course of the decades under study. Even in the interval prior to the Reformation exactly one-fifth of all charitable benefactions were for educational purposes, while in the Reformation interval proper the proportion rose

[1] PCC 206 Nabbs 1660; *Yorks. Arch. Soc. Rec.*, IX (1890), 163–164; *Bradford Antiquary*, n.s., II (1905), 418; Young, George, *History of Whitby* (Whitby, 1817, 2 vols.), II, 531, 573; Robinson, F. K., *Whitby* (Whitby, 1860), 109; Jeffrey, P. S., *Whitby lore* (Whitby, 1952), 74–79; *VCH, Yorks., NR*, II, 510–511; *Complete baronetage*, II, 128; *Cal. Comm. for Compounding*, III, 2062; DNB.

to slightly more than 30 per cent. The substantial sum of £8925 1s was given for the several educational uses during the Elizabethan age, this being about 37 per cent of all benefactions made in the period and nearly six times as much as was designated for religious purposes. The great flood of these endowments came in the early Stuart period, when in four decades the great sum of £32,768 5s, representing 36·70 per cent of all benefactions, was vested for the strengthening of the educational institutions of the county, an amount twice as large as that given for religion and only slightly less than the total given in this period for the care of the poor. There was, relatively speaking, no slackening of giving for these uses during the revolutionary era, £18,702 6s having been provided, though there was some lessening of relative interest, since this amount represents only 30·04 per cent of all charitable gifts made in the interval. Some measure of the devotion of Yorkshire donors to the educational needs of their county may be suggested when it is considered that only in Lancashire, of all the counties studied, do we find so great an intensity of aspirations for the building of educational institutions to provide the cure of ignorance, of which the sixteenth century was so sensitively aware.[1]

The educational aspirations of the benefactors of our period were particularly concentrated on the foundation of schools in all parts of the county for youths who were literally without any hope of gaining even the rudiments of knowledge. In the course of our period the great total of £48,572 16s was dedicated to the founding and endowment of schools, this representing 19·94 per cent of all charitable funds accumulated in Yorkshire and substantially exceeding the amount given for any other single charitable purpose, including even the household relief of the poor. London aside—and London, as we have seen, was engaged in financing the school system of a nation—no county in England provided nearly so large a sum for this worthy and ultimately perhaps the most important of all the cultural institutions being founded by private donors. Practically the whole of this total was in the enduring form of capital endowments, and with very few exceptions the institutions thus created were to endure, transforming the communities in which they were seated into areas of opportunity in the early modern world. Men were addressing themselves devotedly to this great social purpose even during the first decades of our period, when £4531 was given for such foundations, an amount, it may be added, far in excess of the resources— if unendowed medieval income may for a moment be translated into a capital sum—which the medieval period had slowly gathered for the support of schools in the county. There was an immediate and a most pronounced heightening of interest and of giving with the advent of the

[1] The proportion of all benefactions devoted to educational uses ranges from 21·26 per cent for Buckinghamshire to 41·79 per cent for Lancashire.

Reformation, somewhat more (£4978 17s) having been provided during this very brief interval of two decades than in the preceding six. It is notable that thereafter in only one decade did the amount designated by donors for grammar-school endowments ever fall under the sum of £1300, an amazing record for so relatively poor and thinly populated a county. During the Elizabethan age the total provided for school endowments was £6569 9s, about a third of which was given in the last decade of the reign. Indeed, from 1591 onwards to the close of our period there was no decade in which less than £2100 was given for foundations in various parts of the county. The great outpouring came in the early Stuart decades, when £20,677 10s was accumulated by many gifts and bequests for the founding of new or the strengthening of older institutions. This intensity of aspiration was well continued even during the revolutionary decades, when the large total of £11,816 was provided for numerous foundations.

Men of the later fifteenth century began their building of educational resources upon most limited foundations left from the ruin of the medieval world. There were at the most seven schools functioning in Yorkshire in 1480, more probably no more than six, none of which can be described as a really strong or well-administered institution. The oldest and most important of all these was St Peter's School in York. The great antiquity often ascribed to the school seems wholly conjectural, but its useful existence is well documented at least as early as the middle of the twelfth century when the then Archbishop of York vested it with an endowment of £5 p.a. The school was evidently housed within the Cathedral, the Chancellor acting as master until 1343 when reference was made to a recently instituted 'grammar schoolmaster'. The school taught at least sixty students later in the fourteenth century and in 1426 and again in 1486 its position was protected by a prohibition by the Cathedral chapter against the opening of any other school within a radius of ten miles around York City. The institution was a direct responsibility of the monastery of St Mary's, which was obligated to maintain free instruction for fifty scholars; in 1535 a draft of £61 7s p.a. was made on the monastery's funds for its support. The school was unmolested during the Reformation, though, since it possessed no independent endowment, the work of the institution proceeded without great vigour or direction until it was reorganized in 1557 by the Crown. The derelict Bootham Hospital was then conveyed to the school, which continued to be a direct responsibility of the Cathedral chapter, it being chartered to furnish free tuition to fifty boys. Strangely, we have found no record of a gift or bequest of more than £80 to the institution during the entire period under review and but the scantiest of references are made to it in the contemporary sources. We can only conclude that it was in these years a useful but an undistinguished institution, evidently

not too highly regarded by the benefactors of the era, who were after
1540 animated by a deeply secular bias.[1]

There was likewise an early school at Beverley, closely identified with
Beverley Minster and probably dating from the thirteenth century.
The school was particularly vigorous during the early fourteenth century, when there is ample documentary evidence of its functioning, but
it seems to have declined steadily in the early fifteenth century and
references to it are not to be found for almost three generations, from
1456 forward to the Reformation. The school was saved, if not re-
founded, by the Chantry Commissioners in 1548 on the petition of
local citizens who reported Beverley to be the largest town in the East
Riding, 'having a grate nombre of youthe within the same and 5,000
persons and above . . . some of them be apte and mete to be brought up
in learning', and who asked for a grant of £60 p.a. from the minister's
fabric endowments for the support of the school. This grant was not
directly made, but the school was placed within the charge of the town
governors, who evidently assumed responsibility for its maintenance
and £11 9s 11d p.a. was settled for life payments to its two school-
masters. The school remained unendowed during the sixteenth century,
but the master was paid an adequate salary by direct municipal appro-
priations, rising in 1575 to £21 p.a. In 1606 a new schoolhouse was
built, principally by subscriptions from unknown donors, at a total cost
of £155 14s.[2] A graduate of the school, Robert Metcalf, who had himself
received £2 p.a. from the town for his exhibition at Cambridge, in 1652
endowed the school and provided it with scholarship resources. Metcalf settled on the Corporation of Beverley lands then possessing a
capital value of £940, from the income of which £10 p.a. should be paid
towards the stipend of the minister or lecturer of the parish, £10 p.a.
for the augmentation of the schoolmaster's salary, and £20 p.a. to three
poor scholars from the school for their education at the university. The
appointment to the exhibitions should be in the hands of the municipal
authorities, the schoolmaster, and the lecturer, the choice being limited
to the sons of poor men who could not otherwise continue their education.[3]

Pontefract School was founded some time before 1267, when the
Hospital of St Nicholas in that place was distributing forty loaves of
bread weekly to its scholars, though the inference in later documents
makes it decidedly uncertain that the school offered any extra-mural,
or non-clerical, educational facilities. It is certain, however, that by the
beginning of our period the chantry priest, who acted as master,
received no more than £4 p.a. as his stipend and that the school as such

[1] We have followed for this brief review of the history of St Peter's School
A. F. Leach's very full historical notice in *VCH, Yorks.*, I, 416–423.
    [2] *Ibid.*, I, 424–429.   [3] *Vide ante*, 247, and *post*, 360, 385.

possessed no endowment. In 1548 the Chantry Commissioners found that the priest's stipend, which they ordered continued, had declined to £2 19s 2d p.a. and that in addition to his teaching, and attendance on masses, the cleric acted as highway surveyor for the town. We evidently have here a struggling school, without real resources, until in 1583 the Chancery Court of the Duchy of Lancaster appropriated funds from remaining chantry lands to the total value of £25 7s 2d p.a. for its maintenance, of which the master should have £20 p.a. and the usher the remainder. At the same time, principal inhabitants of the community undertook to build a new schoolhouse, at an estimated cost to them of £100. The school thus endowed was continued throughout our period, eliciting but little local support and being weakened in later years by the absorption of a portion of the endowment by Royston and Cawthorne, which appealed successfully for the restoration to them of old chantry income for the support of schools in those two parishes.[1]

There was likewise a suriviving medieval school at Ripon, the first certain reference to which is found in 1348, when the master was charged with a felony. The master was a cleric on the staff of this collegiate church, who in 1548 was receiving, in addition to an emolument as a chantry priest, a total of £10 7s 2d for his services as schoolmaster. On the recommendation of the Commissioners the school was vested in the principal inhabitants of the community and the income for its support was endowed with appropriate chantry lands.[2] A charter was secured from the Crown in 1555, vesting as endowment Ripon chantry lands with a then capital value of £335 for the support of the foundation.[3] The institution was maintained throughout our period, sending numerous graduates to Cambridge, though the only substantial addition to its endowment which we have found was a bequest in 1650 made by Richard Palmes, Esq., of Ripon, of land then valued at about £20 for the use of the schoolmaster.[4]

A medieval school also survived at Northallerton, probably founded in the early fourteenth century by the Prior of Durham. Though there is no certain documentary evidence for a period of a century, the Chantry Commissioners in 1548 thought the school had remained in continuous and useful existence, awarding property valued at £8 8s from guild lands as endowment for its support. The school enjoyed a considerable reputation in the late sixteenth and the early seventeenth

---

[1] We again follow Leach's account in *VCH, Yorks.*, I, 436–438.

[2] There was long litigation regarding these lands, which were 'concealed' guild lands.

[3] *VCH, Yorks.*, I, 430–435; *PP* 1820, IV, 481–484.

[4] PCC 34 Grey 1650; *Yorks. Arch. Soc. Rec.*, IX (1890), 20–22. Palmes also left £14 to the poor of several parishes in this region.

centuries, enrolling about sixty boys, principally the sons of the lesser gentry and the more prosperous yeomanry of the region.[1]

There was likewise a functioning school at Tickhill in 1480, which had been founded rather more than a century earlier (1349) by the wife of Adam Hertehill, a gentleman of the parish. The school was supported by a chantry endowment, with a stipend of £4 13s 11d for the priest-master, which was ordered continued as a grammar-school endowment by the Chantry Commissioners.[2] There were a number of gifts and bequests to the school, almost wholly from yeomen, in the period 1587 to 1611, which increased the meagre endowment by a total of not more than £17 of capital.[3] Finally, there was a school at Howden, controlled by the Prior of Durham, founded some time before 1393, which was, however, declining, if it was functioning at all, during the generation just prior to the Reformation. The school possessed no endowment and gained none with the Reformation, but it was then revived by the community, which supported it with direct subventions to supplement the tuition fees charged by the master. An unavailing effort was made in 1619 by Robert Nelson to secure its endowment as a free school, he having left a bequest of £30 to be used as endowment when such a school could be founded, the income in the meantime to be paid to the poor of the parish.[4]

These, then, were the educational resources with which Yorkshire was endowed at the opening of our period in 1480. There were seven schools, though possibly only six offering instruction to lay youths, together possessing endowments that cannot be valued at more than £1984. There had been several additional medieval foundations, usually in connection with chantry establishments, which had, however, lapsed or decayed well before the close of the fifteenth century. It was upon such slight foundations that men of the early modern age began to build. The earliest of these endowments were of course made within the tradition of clerical control and administration, but it is significant that well before the Reformation donors were vesting their foundations in a secular institutional form which was to persist.

The first of these foundations was the most ambitious creation of a college in the parish of Rotherham by Thomas Rotherham, a native of the parish, who in 1480 was made Archbishop of York. Rotherham in 1481-1483 settled endowments totalling £2457 for the building and support of a college, the foundation to consist of a provost and three fellows who would offer instruction in grammar, music, and writing.

---

[1] Ingledew, *North Allerton*, 281-284; *VCH, Yorks.*, I, 445-446.
[2] *Ibid.*, I, 476.
[3] As, for example, the bequest in 1611 of a rent-charge of 2s p.a. made by Robert Slater, a yeoman of the parish (PCY 31/681 1611).
[4] *PP* 1824, XIV, 756; *VCH, Yorks.*, I, 439-440.

Scholars were to be admitted from all parts of the realm, and the provost was to have a stipend of £13 7s, the grammarian £10 p.a., the singing master £6 13s p.a., and the teacher of writing and ciphering £5 p.a. The students, at first limited to six boys to be selected by the provost, were to receive full maintenance until they were eighteen years of age. By the terms of his will, proved in 1500, the Archbishop bequeathed as well numerous items of plate, several vestments, and 105 books for the school's library. With the Reformation, the choristers' instruction was discontinued and the institution was reorganized as a grammar school, the endowment at the same time being reduced to the capital equivalent of £215 of crown lands in Yorkshire. The school grew in strength and reputation in the course of the sixteenth century, despite the inexplicable expropriation of such a large portion of an endowment, the main purpose of which was so patently educational.[1] There were numerous, though small, bequests made for its support in the last century of our period, of which the largest was a capital gift of £33 made in 1608 by Robert Okes, a yeoman of the parish, for the augmentation of its resources.[2]

At about the same time another prince of the church, Robert Stillington, Bishop of Bath and Wells, a native of York, founded a more modestly endowed college at Acaster Selby, some six miles to the south of the city of York. Stillington provided an endowment of £704, the income of which was designed to support three masters, or fellows, who should offer instruction in grammar and writing quite free of all tuition charges 'to all manner of persons of whatsoever cuntre they be within the realm of England'. The Chantry Commissioners in 1548, at Acaster as at Rotherham, were suspicious of the function of everyone but the grammar master, ordering the endowment confiscated, as being in fact a chantry, save for £8 p.a. to be paid to the schoolmaster. The school continued to flourish throughout our period despite the niggardly endowment with which it was left.[3]

Finally, to deal with the last foundation of the late medieval prelates, John Alcock, Bishop of Ely, in 1484 completed the establishment of a grammar school in his native town of Hull, it being part of the chantry which he had settled there some five years earlier. The school was founded on the earnest representations of the Bishop's merchant

[1] PCY 2/23 1500; *Surtees Soc. Pub.*, LIII (1868), 138–148; Gray, Arthur, *Jesus College, Cambridge* (L., 1902), 31; *PP* 1895, LXXV, Rotherham, 28; Bennett, H. L., *Archbishop Rotherham* (Lincoln, 1901), *passim*; Guest, John, *Historic notices of Rotherham* (Worksop, 1879), 106 ff., 343–344; Fuller, *Worthies*, III, 437–438; Cooper, *Memorials of Cambridge*, I, 212, II, 67; Skelton, *Pietas oxon.*, 43; *VCH, Yorks.*, I, 454–457; DNB. *Vide post*, 357, 369.

[2] *PP* 1895, LXXV, Rotherham, 29.

[3] *VCH, Yorks.*, I, 453–454; *PP* 1898, LXVIII, Stillingfleet, 2–3. Leach believed that the foundation was made before 1480, perhaps in the interval 1467–1475 when Stillington was Lord Chancellor.

brother-in-law, Alderman Dalton, who pointed out the grave need for an institution in which the youth of the city might be trained. The foundation was endowed with lands possessing a capital value of £400, from the income of which the chantry priest, who was also the school-master, received £13 2s and the curate of Trinity Church £2 p.a. for teaching singing to the boys. No tuition was to be charged to scholars and the residue of the income was to be employed as a scholarship fund to pay 6s 8d p.a. to poor boys, to the number of ten, who might be enrolled. The Chantry Commissioners found that the income had declined to £12 p.a., the payments to the clerk and to the scholars having been discontinued,[1] though the decree of the Commissioners made in 1547 endowed the school with a revenue of £13 2s p.a. The school passed into the hands of the municipality and was so heavily attended that in 1578 an usher was also appointed, each scholar being assessed 4d annually towards his stipend. Late in the Elizabethan period a new school was built at a cost of about £150 by public subscription, the principal donor being William Gee, a Hull merchant, whose considerable benefactions to the poor have previously been noted, who gave £80 and 20,000 bricks towards this community undertaking. Gee also left in 1603 urban properties then valued at £120 for the augmentation of the school's endowment and more particularly for increasing the stipend of the master of the institution. In 1647 the master's salary was set at £26 p.a. plus light charges to be collected from boys attending the school from outside the city precincts.[2]

Giggleswick School was founded at the very beginning of the sixteenth century by James Carr, a member of a local family and a clerk turned schoolmaster. It seems probable that he opened a school in the parish as a private venture as early as 1499. In 1507 the school was more elaborately vested when the Prior of Durham conveyed to it a half-acre of land on leasehold, Carr undertaking to build a schoolhouse and gaining the right to nominate his successor as master. The schoolhouse was built by Carr in 1512 'at hys owne propyr charges and costs' and upon his death in 1518 was endowed, in the legal form of a chantry, with capital then worth £120. Thomas Husteler, with another local donor, added £24 13s 4d to the capital of the institution, which well before 1548 was taking boarders from a considerable area in the West Riding. In this year the Chantry Commissioners reported that Richard Carr, a nephew of the founder, was master, describing him as "xxxij yeres of age [and] well learned'. The school was ordered continued by the Commissioners with the support of the £5 6s 8d p.a. then represent-

---

[1] Leach, A. F., *English schools at the Reformation* (L., 1896), 290.

[2] *VCH, Yorks.,* I, 449–452; *Surtees Soc. Pub.,* XCII (1893), 340; Symons, *Hullinia,* 81–82; Hadley, *Hull,* II, 777; *PP* 1833, XVIII, 605–606; DNB; *Vide ante,* 236, 265.

ing the income on its endowment. In point of fact, the institution gained most substantially from the chantry confiscations, since in 1553, upon the petition of leading inhabitants of the parish, additional chantry lands valued at £23 3s p.a. were settled on the foundation, which was then placed in the charge of a board of eight local governors. The school was most admirably administered through the whole of our period, with excellent masters and with a growing reputation which attracted promising boys from several northern counties. In 1603 William Clapham, a clerk of Runcton, Norfolk, left the institution properties which then yielded £4 p.a. for maintaining one of its graduates in the universities, 4s p.a. to the school for a potation, and 5s p.a. to the poor of the parish, while in 1616 a descendant of the founder, Richard Carr, established in Christ's College, Cambridge, a scholarship endowment with a capital of £800 for the benefit of scholars from this now eminent school.[1]

At about the same time another school was founded in the West Riding at Royston by John Forman, for more than a half-century the priest in that parish. Forman in 1502 by will endowed a fellowship in Magdalen College, Oxford, with a capital worth of about £80 and settled on local trustees lands probably worth £4 6s 11d p.a. for the support of a schoolmaster in the parish. These, being chantry properties, were in 1583 added to the endowment of Pontefract School,[2] only to be restored to Royston's most inadequately endowed school upon the indignant representations of the community and the friendly offices of the Archbishop of York.[3] Still another clerical foundation was made about a decade later (1514) at Pocklington by John Dowman, whose father was lord of the manor. Dowman vested the school in the legal form of a guild, to which he conveyed property with a capital worth of £267 for the support of a schoolmaster, while greatly strengthening the school shortly before his death by endowing five scholarships in St John's, Cambridge, for its graduates.[4] The school was to offer free instruction by a master 'sufficiently learned in grammatical science' to boys from any part of England. The foundation was untouched by the Chantry Commissioners and by an Act of Parliament (1551) was legally vested in St John's College and the Archbishop of York, with power to appoint the master. The school suffered from the neglect of distant governors and visitors until the mid-seventeenth century, when under the administration of two successive masters of excellent capabilities

[1] Bell, E. A., *Giggleswick School* (Leeds, 1912); *VCH, Yorks.*, I, 460–462; Fletcher, *Picturesque history*, V, 161; Brayshaw, Thomas, and R. M. Robinson, *Giggleswick* (L., 1932), 239; *PP* 1825, XI, 646–649; *PP* 1895, LXV, Giggleswick, 1–26; Gilbert, *Liber scholasticus*, 285; *Yorks. Arch. Soc. Rec.*, XXXIII (1903), xxxix–xli; *Surtees Soc. Pub.*, XCII (1893), 254, 409.

[2] *Vide ante*, 302–303.

[3] PCY 6/40 1502; Smith, *Old Yorkshire*, I, 92, n.s., I, 161; Hunter, *South Yorkshire*, II, 381–383; *PP* 1826–1827, X, 755.   [4] *Vide post*, 351–352.

the number of its students rose to 118, most of whom were boarding scholars from all parts of the county.[1]

The ill-starred Lord Darcy, whose almshouse foundation at Whitkirk has already been mentioned, in *ca.* 1520 established in conjunction with the hospital there a free grammar school with an endowment of £227, if, as the evidence suggests, the capital was shared equally by the two institutions. The master of the school and the hospital was to have an annual stipend of £16 13s 4d for his services. Darcy shortly after the foundation was completed gave a number of books to constitute its library. It seems certain that much of the endowment fell with the founder's attainder, though the school certainly survived for a considerable period.[2] In 1602, however, the will of a local yeoman, Michael Clough, suggests that there was no longer a master, for he charged lands with £1 p.a. 'towards the maintenance of a schoolmaster . . . and if there be no schoolmaster hyred . . . to dispose unto some of the poore'.[3]

In *ca.* 1525 a more enduring foundation was made in his native town of Sedbergh by Roger Lupton, still another of the swarm of lawyer-clerics which Yorkshire produced towards the close of the fifteenth century. Lupton built a schoolhouse with his own funds and in 1528 established the institution as a chantry with a capital value of approximately £248, the priest to be sufficiently learned and capable to teach the grammar school and to administer its affairs under appointment by St John's College, Cambridge. He was to levy no fees and was to organize the curriculum after the manner of 'some laudably notable and famous school of England'. Lupton bound his foundation inextricably with St John's College by gifts totalling £1000 for fellowships and scholarships, the eight scholars to be selected from among the graduates of the school and with a reversionary clause transferring the assets to the college in the event they should be threatened by wrongful dealing or decay.[4] In 1548 the school was ordered continued and its then income to be paid from crown lands, though the lands consituting the endowment were listed for sale. St John's most vehemently protested the order, arguing that the school was 'remarkable' and served 'a rough people and

---

[1] PCC 14 Porch 1526; *Yorks. Arch. Journal,* XIV (1898), 133–146; *VCH, Yorks.,* I, 463–465; Baker, *St. John's College,* I, 353; Howard, *Finances of St. John's,* 8; Smith, *Old Yorkshire,* n.s., I, 150; *PP* 1828, XI, 541, 619; *Alum. cantab.,* I, ii, 60; Cooper, *Athenae cantab.,* I, 33.

Dowman was trained at Cambridge as a civil lawyer. He was successively appointed Rector of All Saints, Fulbourn (Cambridgeshire), Pocklington (Yorkshire), and St Nicholas Acon (London). He was made Archdeacon of Suffolk in 1507, Prebend of St Paul's in 1507, and of Lichfield in 1509. He served Wolsey as his Auditor of Causes. In addition to his substantial educational gifts, Dowman by will left £40 for church repairs, £21 for prayers, £30 for general church uses, and £2 for prisoners.   [2] *Vide ante,* 255–256.

[3] PCY 28/815 1602; Kirk, *St. Mary, Whitkirk,* 248.   [4] *Vide post,* 352.

a wild country, with no other school within forty or fifty miles of it'. In a later appeal it was most persuasively stated that if the sale should take place 'reformation in religion will be discredited and charity will grow cold, for what rich and charitable men will found schools if they see the schools founded by their charitable predecessors are not allowed to stand'. None the less, the sale took place, only to be denounced in acid terms by Thomas Lever, the Master of St John's, in sermons before the King and at Paul's Cross. Lever's efforts were successful, lands valued at £20 13s 10d p.a. being transferred to the school in 1552. The school, into whose foundation and preservation so much devotion had gone, prospered from that date forward.[1] In 1587 Henry Hebblethwaite, a London draper, founded additional scholarships for its graduates at St John's[2] and a decade later Reginald Harrison, a native of Sedbergh, by bequest gave 10s outright to the schoolmaster and £20 to the school 'to be disposed and bestowed by the discretion of the schoolmaster and feoffees . . . so long as it will last and continue towards the relief of two poor scholars learning in the said school'.[3] There were numerous supporting gifts and bequests to the institution in the first half of the seventeenth century, of which the bequest in 1613 of £2 13s made by Laurence Stanton, a clergyman, for the repair of the school building and £1 outright to the master may be regarded as quite typical.[4]

A school was also certainly founded in Bingley some years before the Reformation, very probably in 1529 when land and a number of closes, which some years later possessed a capital value of £80, were conveyed to trustees for the support of a schoolmaster. The foundation was untouched and in fact went unnoticed by the Chantry Commissioners, strongly suggesting that it may well have been secular from the outset.[5] The school was to enjoy steady support from the community which it served, the small endowment gradually being increased by numerous and principally very modest bequests and gifts. Thus in 1571 Edmund Eltofts of Bingley conveyed a rent-charge of 13s p.a. for the support of the master, which was matched by an annuity of the same amount provided by Francis Paslow and his son and further augmented by the

---

[1] We have followed Leach's excellent historical survey in *VCH, Yorks.*, I, 466–471, for most of this account. *Vide* also *PP* 1826–1827, X, 773–777; *Yorks. Arch. Soc. Rec.*, XXXIII (1903), xli–lxiii, 286–437; Clarke, H. L., and W. N. Weech, *Sedbergh School* (Sedbergh, 1925); and the DNB account of Lupton.

[2] PCC 43 Spencer 1587; *PP* 1897, LXVII, iv, Sedbergh, 44; *Surtees Soc. Pub.*, CXXI (1912), 132–133; Howard, *Finances of St. John's*, 46; Wilson, *Sedbergh School register*, 12. *Vide post*, 353. *Vide* Jordan, *Charities of London*, 262. Hebblethwaite also left £20 to the poor of his native town, £10 for sermons there, and an uncertain amount for the repair of roads and bridges. Hebblethwaite's cousin, Robert, was master of the school, having been first appointed in 1544.   [3] *Vide ante*, 235, 297.

[4] *Yorks. Arch. Soc. Rec.*, XXXIII (1903), 384.

[5] *PP* 1826–1827, X, 735–736; *VCH, Yorks.*, I, 477.

gift of a rent of 7s made by Thomas Mowde and his son.[1] The endowment was greatly strengthened in 1599 under the terms of the will of William Wooler, a merchant of York and a native of the town, who left property, valued in 1616 at £400, half of which under a decree in Chancery was designated for the support of the school and the remainder for the care of the poor.[2] Michael Broadley, probably a clothier, in 1613 left £40 to Thomas Howgill, then the schoolmaster,[3] while in 1637 one of the school's governors, John Rawson, bequeathed £10 of capital towards the maintenance of an usher.[4] We should mention, too, the gift in 1642 made by John Bynnes, a grand-nephew of William Wooler, of £20 towards the building of a new schoolhouse for an institution which for more than a century had served well the community which so evidently regarded it with great pride and affection.[5]

These were the nine foundations certainly made in the two generations just prior to the advent of the Reformation.[6] Some measure of this accomplishment may be gained when we reflect that in this really brief historical interval far more strength had been added to the educational resources of the county than had existed at the outset of our period. In all, endowments of slightly more than £4500 had been provided for these institutions, to which Yorkshire donors in the course of our period were to add £1260 13s after 1541. It should likewise be stressed that these foundations were little damaged by the policy or action of the Chantry Commissioners, who seem in Yorkshire as in England at large to have drawn the line of definition and of confiscation most generously where educational responsibility was clearly and specifically part of the duty of a chantry priest. The principal harm done was actually inadvertent, since the settled income normally conveyed for the support of a school was in later decades to seem slight indeed when compared to the value of the lands with which the foundation had once been endowed. The foundations made from 1480 to 1540 were, it will have been observed, principally the creation of great prelates and of the breed of cleric-lawyers, spawned in such great numbers in the county until the advent of the Reformation. Many were also conjoined with chantries, which must have seemed even at this late date the most secure form of trusteeship to serve in perpetuity the primarily educational purposes which these donors had in mind. These expectations were rudely and irrevocably overthrown not many years later in a great revolution which none the less carefully preserved, more sharply defined, and more

[1] Dodd, *Bingley Grammar School*, 3.   [2] *Vide ante*, 293.
[3] PCY 32/392 1613.   [4] Dodd, *Bingley Grammar School*, 31.   [5] *Ibid.*, 32.
[6] Mention should also be made of Robert Marshall's foundation of a chantry and school at Darlington, Durham, with a capital of £105; the school was continued by the Chantry Commissioners. Marshall was from 1515 until his death in 1531 provost of the collegiate church at Hemingbrough. (Burton, *Hemingbrough*, 73; *VCH, Durham*, I, 387-389; *VCH, Yorks.*, III, 360.)

securely vested these resources to accomplish the secular ends which
society now held in view.

During the brief interval of the Reformation, the movement for the
extension of educational opportunities in Yorkshire was noticeably
accelerated. In the course of these two decades a total of nearly £5000
(£4978 17s) was provided for grammar-school foundations, a substantially larger amount than had been bestowed in the preceding six
decades. The earliest of these foundations, made in 1543, partook somewhat of the nature of numerous earlier Yorkshire educational endowments, having been established in conjunction with a chantry. Sir John
Nevill, Lord Latimer, whose widow was to marry Henry VIII, not only
endowed prayers at Well for a term of forty years, but conveyed in
addition rents of £6 13s 4d p.a. 'to fynde a scole maister at Well for
kepinge of a scole and techinge of gramer ther', with only incidental
obligations of prayers for the founder. The school, which was undisturbed, had been founded and a master was in charge when the Chantry
Commissioners visited the place.[1] A few years later, probably in 1545
or 1546, a priest, George Goldsmith, established and endowed a free
school at Kippax, settling on trustees real property with an estimated
worth of £120 for the support of the master.[2]

The most notable of all the foundations made in the period of the
Reformation was that of Archbishop Holgate in conjunction with his
establishment of the great almshouse at his birthplace, Hemsworth.
Holgate in 1547 received permission under letters patent to found
grammar schools at York, Old Malton, and Hemsworth. The school at
York was first established with an endowment then valued at £240.
The master, who might be a layman, was appointed by the Archbishop
and was to have a stipend of £12 p.a., from which, however, he was
required to pay an usher £2 p.a. to teach the simpler subjects. The curriculum of the York school, like the others in the foundation, was
designed to provide 'good education and instruction of children and
boys of the realm of England in good manners and the art of grammar and
other liberal learning'. It was accordingly required that the master
should possess a competent knowledge of the Latin, Greek, and Hebrew
languages. The master and usher were to confine their instruction to
children who could read, older pupils being appointed to teach those
who were deficient in this basic skill. The endowment provided for the
school at Old Malton, also founded in 1547, was of the value of £400,

[1] PCY 11/672 1543; *Surtees Soc. Pub.*, XCII (1893), 496, CVI (1902), 159–
163; *Complete peerage*, V, 25; *VCH, Yorks.*, I, 478; Nicolas, *Testamenta vetusta*,
II, 704; Jeffery, *Thornton-le-Dale*, 211–212; Whitaker, *Richmondshire*, II, 84,
III, 334; DNB. *Vide post*, 376, 395. Lord Latimer was the great-grandfather of
Elizabeth Lumley, whose many benefactions to Yorkshire have been noted.

[2] *PP* 1826, XIII, 659; *PP* 1898, LXVIII, Kippax, 9; *VCH, Yorks.*, I, 478.

the master to receive a stipend of £10 p.a. and the remaining income to be employed for the salaries of an usher and an organist. An even larger endowment, then valued at £480, was conveyed for Hemsworth in 1548, from the income of which £10 p.a. was to be set aside for scholarships for six poor children, sons of 'husbandmen or men of occupacions', while the remainder was to be employed for the salaries of the master and usher. The statutes defining the government and the curriculum of the three schools were identical and they were further joined by a provision for a common stock for the repair of their buildings, the cost of which had been borne by the Archbishop.[1]

No precise date can be given for the foundation of the grammar school at Bradford. It does appear, however, that in 1548 the Chantry Commissioners were uncertain regarding trusts for lands with an annual value of £2 8s 8d which responsible inhabitants of the town most vigorously insisted had been given for the support of a school in the parish. This claim was allowed in 1552 by the Duchy Chamber with the provision that the income should be employed for the sustenance of a schoolmaster for the town. Feoffees were appointed and the slow process of accumulating endowment by small benefactions began. In 1593 the surviving trustees transferred to others property with an approximate capital worth of about £90, suggesting that most of the support must have come from fees. The school enjoyed a considerable reputation in the mid-seventeenth century, when boarding as well as day students were enrolled, despite the fact that its endowment remained meagre through the whole of our period.[2] The Chantry Commissioners in 1548 also assigned, without any clear authority in the foundation deed of the chantry, an endowment of £5 p.a. for a grammar school at Topcliffe in the North Riding. The early masters were assistant curates, but in ca. 1588, when the endowment was increased by about £30 by local subscriptions,[3] a lay master with no other duties was appointed. The school was well maintained and provided excellent benefits for this small community, despite its inadequate endowment.[4] In 1635, however, a native son of Topcliffe, William Robinson, a rich London mercer, most generously provided for the school when he left on trust with the Grocers' Company £400, from the income of which £16 p.a. should be paid for the maintenance of a schoolmaster to teach the Latin and English tongues in the school where he had himself received his early education.[5]

---

[1] *Vide ante*, 258.

[2] *Bradford Antiquary*, n.s. IV (1921), 65 ff.; *VCH, Yorks.*, I, 471–472.

[3] The principal gift was that of John Hartforth, who subscribed £10 to the stock of the foundation.

[4] *PP* 1820, V, 400; *VCH, Yorks.*, I, 478.

[5] PCC 2 Sadler 1635; *PP* 1820, V, 400; *PP* 1822, IX, 273. *Vide* Jordan, *Charities of London*, 241.

Leeds Grammar School was founded in 1553 under the terms of the will of William Sheffield, late a chantry priest there, though inferences have been drawn that certain chantry endowments may earlier have been used in part for educational purposes. Sheffield's will makes it clear that the endowment was to bear the stipend of a schoolmaster to be appointed to teach in 'a school house' to be 'founded erected and buylded by the paryshioners . . . of Leeds', there being a reversionary clause that the property then being vested should be used for the support of the poor if the conditions were not met. Sheffield's will supplied endowment of about £93, which within three years was increased to a value of £200, or £10 p.a., by local gifts, a schoolhouse also being provided.[1] In addition, Thomas Sheffield, a brother and an executor of the founder, gave several houses, with a very roughly estimated value of £80, towards the strengthening of an endowment which evidently had quickly gained the support of the entire community.[2] The rapidly growing accumulation of endowments for the school was further increased in 1558 under the terms of the will of William Armistead, Vicar of Birstall, who conveyed to the trustees priory lands which he had purchased in 1554 at a cost of £133 6s 8d, as well as the reversion of other properties with a capital value of £10 'to the finding' of a master sufficiently learned to teach in the school.[3] It would seem, therefore, that within five years after the founder's death the conditions imposed by the will had been most generously met and that the capital of the foundation was of the order of £423 6s 8d. There were numerous small additions to the endow-

[1] VCH, Yorks., I, 457–459; Old Leeds charities, 11; Price, A. C., Leeds Grammar School (Leeds, 1919), passim, Leeds and its neighbourhood (Oxford, 1909), 161–162; PP 1826, XIII, 662; Surtees Soc. Pub., XCII (1893), 216; Thoresby, Ducatus, 38. Sheffield was a member of a family of clothiers. A number of the gifts made to complete the endowment were very small indeed, as for example the bequest of 3s left by Agnes Wade for the schoolhouse. (Thoresby Soc. Pub., XIX [1913], 329). The largest of these sustaining gifts was that of Richard Bank and his wife, who gave properties valued at £70 in ca. 1555. (PP 1826, XIII, 662; Old Leeds charities, 10.)

[2] Leach (VCH, Yorks., I, 458) describes him as the uncle of William Sheffield, but the latter's will seems to make it certain that he was in fact a brother (Thoresby Soc. Pub., XIV [1906], xxvii, XXVII [1930], 270).

[3] PCC 52 Welles 1558; Price, Leeds Grammar School, 77; PP 1826–1827, X, 719, 778–780; PP 1894, LXIV, Skipton, 8–10, 17–28; Smith, Old Yorkshire, III, 26; Cradock, H. C., Birstall (L., 1933), 140–142, 236–243; Dawson, Skipton, 228–230; VCH, Yorks., I, 458, 479.

Armistead was educated at Oxford, where he was graduated B.D. in 1527. He held numerous livings in Yorkshire and Northamptonshire, as well as the vicarage of Birstall. He was Master of the Temple, 1539–1558, a Master in Chancery, 1534–1558, and Canon of Windsor, 1554–1558. He was an excellent civil lawyer and stood high in Queen Mary's favour. Armistead devoted more than £600 to educational gifts, very nearly exhausting his estate, the residue of which was left for maintaining poor scholars at Oxford.

ment during the Elizabethan period, when the school was sending its graduates on, principally to Cambridge, as well as more substantial gifts made by Christopher Hopton in 1585, with an estimated capital worth of £35, and by Lawrence Rawson in 1602, who conveyed a cottage and other property valued in all at £80 for the augmentation of the endowment.[1] A new school building was provided for the foundation, at a probable cost of £300, by John Harrison, Leeds' most munificent benefactor, in 1624. Harrison likewise gave generously towards the support of the institution which he and the trustees in 1653 hoped might be able to provide the substantial stipend of £50 p.a. for the headmaster, £25 p.a. for the usher, and smaller emoluments for under masters to teach boys who could not be accommodated in the already overflowing schoolhouse of this rapidly growing town.[2]

We have seen that William Armistead had been a most generous contributor towards the development of the Leeds grammar school at a critical moment in its history. This gift was by no means the full measure of this renowned clergyman's almost fanatical support of the extension of educational opportunity within his native county, and more particularly in the West Riding. In 1548 his intervention helped in securing grants totalling £9 p.a., for the support of a school at Skipton where he had received his own early education. Later in the same year Armistead conveyed to trustees lands then worth £200 as further endowment for the institution, a grammar school with two masters and an enrolment of 120 scholars about the time of its refoundation. Some years later, in 1555, he built as well a small schoolhouse on an adjoining tract to be used as an elementary school in which poor children could be taught reading and writing, endowing it with rents having a capital worth of £160. Meanwhile, he had been husbanding his not considerable estate for the foundation of a grammar school in his own parish of Birstall, which he had served as vicar since 1537. As early as 1546 he had begun negotiations to secure an agreement for the enclosure of 32 acres of common land, the total rent of £4 being hypothecated in 1551 towards the payment of the salary of a schoolmaster. In 1556 Armistead came forward with a gift of £100 made to trustees for the building of a schoolhouse as well as providing land in Birstall and Leeds with an estimated value of £200 to serve as the endowment of the foundation.[3]

We have previously dealt with Bishop William Knight's substantial almshouse foundation at Kirkby Ravensworth made in 1556, with which

---

[1] *PP* 1826, XIII, 732; *Old Leeds charities*, 9-10.

[2] *Vide ante*, 277, 298, and *post*, 382, 401-402.

[3] Though Armistead was a capable lawyer, the Birstall foundation was poorly conceived. One of the trustees diverted the funds to his own use, much of the property was permanently lost, and an angry order of a Commission to enquire into pious uses, in 1601, was required to secure a restoration of a portion of the gift, £100 plus a rent-charge of £5 p.a.

was incorporated a school for that parish. The schoolroom was situated in the hospital, but an endowment of £240 was provided for the maintenance of the master who should offer free instruction in grammar, rhetoric, and verse to boys of the parish. The master was carefully enjoined not to read with the boys any corrupt or heretical books and to bring them up in good manners and pious wisdom.[1] There were occasional later bequests to this foundation, such as £1 to the almshouse and £3 to the grammar school left in 1658 by Thomas Layton, a gentleman of the parish,[2] but the rapid increase in value of the properties underlying the trust ensured the strength of the institution, serving as it did a largely rural parish. A similar foundation was provided at Tadcaster in 1555 for a grammar school and an almshouse by Bishop Owen Oglethorpe. The school was endowed with half the capital, this amounting to at least £400, for the support of a master well learned in grammar, having at least a baccalaureate degree, and being prepared to teach the children of the parish a curriculum meeting the approval of the Archbishop of York.[3]

Though there were efforts made to found a school in Doncaster early in the sixteenth century, it seems certain that none was in existence on the occasion of the careful survey of the Chantry Commissioners. In 1559, however, Thomas Symkinson, a merchant, a former mayor, and an original feoffee of Ellis's hospital, by will left lands with an estimated capital worth of £80 'towardes the foundacion of a scole in Doncaster, if it go forward'.[4] It is evident that the establishment of a school for this thriving town was under discussion by the mercantile aristocracy of the community, for in 1562 Symkinson's friend, Thomas Ellis, left additional property worth £21 'towards the making of one free grammar school in Doncaster . . . for the virtuous education and bringing up of children in learning.'[5] With this rather slender endowment in hand, a school was begun under the direct supervision of the municipal authorities, who seem as well to have supplemented the income available by direct grants from town funds in order to make up the master's salary, which was in 1582 fixed at £10 p.a.[6] In 1606 a yeoman of the parish, James Biningley, left an additional £10 to the stock of the school.[7] A thorough review of the status of the school was made in 1654, when it was stated that for many years past town funds had been required to complete the pay of the master, the school being free, and it was then resolved to increase his stipend to £35 p.a.[8]

During the brief period of the Reformation fourteen additional schools had been founded in Yorkshire, as well as one in Newark-

---

[1] *Vide ante*, 258.   [2] PCC 182 Wootton 1658.   [3] *Vide ante*, 259.
[4] Jackson, *Doncaster charities*, 5, 28n.; *VCH, Yorks.*, I, 447.
[5] *Vide ante*, 261.   [6] *VCH, Yorks.*, I, 447.   [7] PCY 30/33 1606.
[8] Jackson, *Doncaster charities*, 3–4.

upon-Trent, Nottinghamshire, this last having been established with an endowment of £766 by Thomas Magnus, Rector of Sessay and Archdeacon of the East Riding.[1] These Yorkshire schools had been endowed with £3425 7s of capital, all being relatively modest in constitution, and all were to endure with profoundly important social and cultural consequences through the whole of our period. A surprising number of these institutions were founded by clerical donors, principally prelates and priest-lawyers of a type which, as we have seen, also assumed a dominant role in the earlier period of this study. But merchant wealth was now beginning decisively to intervene. This vigorous wealth, with that supplied by the new gentry, was to undertake the responsibility for the extension of the educational system so rapidly framed during the next interval. In addition to the new foundations, and Magnus's notable creation of a school in Nottinghamshire, donors gave a total of £787 10s either for the augmentation of older endowments or for the support of a number of useful, but usually short-lived, unendowed schools instituted during this lively and hopeful period.

The strong interest of benefactors of the county in the foundation of new schools continued unabated during the Elizabethan period, though there was a noticeable slackening of such giving during the troubled decade of the Armada, when only £880 19s was provided. Of these foundations we may mention first that made in 1561 at Guisborough by Robert Pursglove, Bishop of Hull, in conjunction with an almshouse in the town which we have previously discussed. The school, sharing jointly with the hospital a generous endowment, possessed a stock then valued at £407, from the income of which the master was to have an annual stipend of £10 p.a. and to teach without charge, save for an entrance fee of 4d, all properly qualified scholars who presented themselves.[2] A few years later, in 1570, the endowment of the institution was further enhanced by a bequest of property with an estimated worth of £67.[3] Pursglove likewise founded a similar institution with a less substantial endowment in his native parish of Tideswell, Derbyshire.

This period, too, marks the effective organization and endowment of the free grammar school at Bedale. A school was kept in the parish in conjunction with a chantry earlier in the century and was ordered continued by the Chantry Commissioners with a stipend of £7 11s 4d p.a. for the master. This income, in the form of a new endowment, was confirmed under Elizabeth, when the school began to prosper and

[1] VCH, Notts., II, 199–209; Brown, Cornelius, Newark-on-Trent (Newark, 1907, 2 vols.), II, 185; PP 1829, VIII, 323; Yorks. Arch. Journal, XIV (1898), 410; DNB. The school was founded in 1532 and fully endowed under the donor's will, proved in 1551.

[2] Vide ante, 260.

[3] PP 1823, VIII, 806; Yorks. Arch. Soc. Rec., XXXIX (1907), 208–209.

to grow in size, much straining its quite limited resources.[1] In 1628 these difficulties were remedied by a gift from Frances, Countess of Warwick, whose father was a native of the town, representing a capital value of £267. The deed of gift provided that children should be taught in some convenient place in the parish and was inspired by the fact that the town was far in the north and remote from both universities.[2] At about the same time (1563) a school was founded at Burton Agnes in the East Riding. The Archbishop's visitation for 1564 reported that in the preceding years 'Hen. Cowston curatum de Agnes Burton ac ludimagistrum ibidem . . . quem dominus examinavit et inveniens eum idoneum admisit eundem dnm. Henricum ad catechisandum pueros et prime grammatices rudimenta docendum per diocesim Ebor.'[3] In the same year, Richard Green, a resident of the parish, remedied the needs of this rudimentary school by a bequest of £200 for general parish uses, of which £8 p.a. should be made available for the stipend of a competent schoolmaster. He placed the capital upon trust with the provision that the master should be chosen by the vicar, the churchwardens, and four more 'of the ancient men of the parish', it being further provided that no scholar from the town or parish should be liable for fees exceeding 8d in each quarter.[4] More than a generation later, in 1621, the endowment of the institution was further increased by a modest bequest of £5 from Simon Kitchingman, a yeoman of the parish.[5]

The grammar school at Richmond was founded in 1567 by the common effort of the burghers of the town, who in that year gained a charter for its establishment under the direction of the four bailiffs as trustees and governors. The endowment was constituted in part by old chantry and guild revenues totalling £6 3s 4d p.a., which had in 1548 been assigned for the maintenance of a school but which had in fact been lodged in the hands of the Corporation. In part, too, the necessary stock was raised by a general community effort, with the result that a generation later (in 1604) the capital worth of the funds of the school was only slightly less than £500.[6] Typical of these benefactions were a

[1] M'Call, H. B., *The early history of Bedale* (L., 1907), 17; *VCH, Yorks.*, I, 477–478.

[2] *Ibid.*, I, 477; M'Call, *Bedale*, 17; *Complete peerage*, VIII, 65. The benefactor was the daughter of Sir Christopher Wray, successively Queen's Serjeant, Speaker of the House, Justice of the Queen's Bench, and Chief Justice (1574). She first married Sir George St Paul, who was created a baronet in 1611 and died in 1613, and secondly Robert Rich, created Earl of Warwick in 1618.

[3] Quoted in Purvis, J. S., ed., *Tudor parish documents of the diocese of York* (Cambridge, 1948), 105.   [4] *PP* 1824, XIV, 718.

[5] PCY 36/528 1621. Kitchingman (*alias* Sippardson) also left £5 for apprenticing poor children of the parish, £2 to the poor at his burial, and 5s for a funeral sermon.

[6] Clarkson, *Richmond*, 186 ff.; Smith, *Old Yorkshire*, n.s. I, 160; Leach, *English schools at the Reformation*, 287; *VCH, Yorks.*, I, 475.

bequest of land valued at £20 made by Ralph Gower, a burgess, in 1567;[1] a rent-charge of £1 3s p.a. for the endowment left in the next year by a lorimer, Thomas Cooke;[2] an annuity of 7s left by John Crosby in the same year;[3] a Cowper's *Dictionary* left to the school and 'to be kept for ye publick proffitt of ye schollers' by the schoolmaster, John Clarkson, in 1599;[4] and lands valued at approximately £50 bequeathed by a clergyman, Thomas Parkinson, at an uncertain date in the early seventeenth century.[5]

In 1572 Sir Nicholas Fairfax, who held the castle and manor of Gilling, by will charged his son and heir to build and endow a free school for poor scholars in that parish. He instructed his executors to endow the institution with rent-charges on lands at Grimston representing a capital value of £200.[6] A family of the lesser gentry of the county, the Kayes of Almondbury, were likewise responsible for the founding of a grammar school in their parish. John Kaye was cited in a manuscript memorandum no longer extant as having reported that he and his father Arthur, who died in 1578, some time during the reign of Edward VI moved and renovated an old chapel built by their ancestors, converting the building into a schoolhouse with the approbation of the parish.[7] A master was procured by the Kayes, doubtless at their personal charge, and it is certain that an unendowed school was being maintained in the parish at the time of the Archbishop's visitation in 1563.[8] Still another member of the family, Robert Kaye, on his death in 1576 provided the school with its first endowment in the amount of one hundred marks.[9] The school played an important role in the life of the parish during the next two generations, becoming the favourite charity for substantial men of the community. In 1611 its endowment was enhanced

---

[1] *Surtees Soc. Pub.*, XXVI (1853), 194–198. Gower had built a large estate from monastic lands. He was the father of John Gower, attainted for high treason in 1569.

[2] *Ibid.*, 226–227.   [3] Clarkson, *Richmond*, 189.

[4] *Surtees Soc. Pub.*, XXVI (1853), 267n.–268n.

[5] Clarkson, *Richmond*, 189–190.

[6] PCY 19/469 1572; *Yorks. Arch. Journal*, XIX (1907), 188–192. Fairfax was implicated in the Pilgrimage of Grace, but was pardoned. He sat in Parliament for Scarborough and for York and was for a season sheriff of the county. His son, also Nicholas, was involved in the Rising in the North of 1569.

[7] Fletcher, *Picturesque history*, III, 39; Hulbert, C. A., *Almondbury* (L., 1882), 194; *VCH, Yorks.*, I, 479.

[8] The visitation report speaks of 'Ric. Hurstus ludimagister apud Almondbury distincte legit et latinum tum callet tum scribit ac dictat mediocriter grammaticen ad unguem callet, unde examinatus et inventus idoneus et habilis Mag. R. Barnes admisit eum ad docendum et cathechisandum puerulos lingua materna et vulgari ac etiam ad prima grammatices rudimenta tradenda et eundem Ricardum decet super articulis synodi Londonensis examinavit quos omnes et singulos lubenti animo confessus est et subscripsit eisdem' (Purvis, *Tudor parish documents*, 106).   [9] *PP* 1899, LXXI, 702.

by a gift representing a capital value of £20 from William Ramsden, a gentleman of 'Longley', who also gave £1 outright to the needs of Halifax Grammar School.[1] The Kaye family added £40 to the funds of the institution in 1621, while in the same year Robert Nettleton, whose substantial benefactions for the parish have already been noted, increased the capital by the generous gift of £100.[2] Just two years later, the vicar of the parish, George Crosland, gave a rent-charge of £1 p.a. for the augmentation of the stipend of the master, and in the same year a local yeoman gave £4, in capital value, to the governors of the institution. Other gifts, all save one small one being in capital, were received from time to time, with the result that by 1635 the endowment of the school, slowly built by persistent local effort, amounted to the respectable total of £292 13s.[3]

Halsham, in the East Riding, gained a substantially endowed school in 1579 through the generosity of Sir John Constable of Kirby Knowle. The school was connected in government and design with Constable's almshouse foundation in the parish, the master being given an apartment 'above the common hall'. The foundation was endowed with capital in the amount of £880, the master being assured the then generous stipend of £20 p.a. Eight of the boys admitted were to be chosen by the trustees from a list submitted by the parish officers on the advice of the parishioners and were to receive not only free instruction but stipends of £3 p.a. each for full maintenance in their homes. The curriculum was to cover English grammar, writing, and arithmetic, students being accepted between the ages of six and fourteen.[4] Still another member of the gentry of the county, Thomas Conyers of Yarm and of Egglescliffe, Durham,[5] by his will proved in 1590 founded a carefully ordered school in the parish of Yarm. Six of the principal inhabitants were constituted trustees and were empowered to name the master. Lands and other properties then possessing a capital worth of £180 were vested, with the provision that the salary of the schoolmaster should be fixed at £7 p.a. and the remainder of the income devoted to the general needs of the foundation. The school was to offer free instruction to all properly qualified youths of the parish.[6] In the following year, the endowment was modestly increased by the bequest of Henry Parke, a husbandman of the parish, who left a rent-charge of 2s for the support of the new institution.[7]

The founding of Wakefield Grammar School in 1591 was a remarkable example of the immense social power and energy which a merchant

[1] *Ibid.*, 711; Midgley, *Halifax*, 487.

[2] *Vide ante*, 272, for a more detailed account of Nettleton's charities for Almondbury, which totalled £694.   [3] *PP* 1899, LXXI, 711.

[4] *Vide ante*, 263, 293.   [5] Just across the river from Yarm.

[6] *PP* 1823, VIII, 750–751; Graves, *Cleveland*, 79; *VCH, Yorks.*, I, 480.

[7] PCY 24/773 1591.

community possessed and could muster once enlightened leadership was supplied. There had, it is true, been an earlier chantry school in Wakefield, endowed in 1480 under the will of Thurstan Banaster with a stock of £4 3s p.a. for a stipendiary priest, part of whose duties was the holding of a school in the church.[1] There were small later bequests which make it certain that instruction of some kind was offered until the time of the Reformation, though it is doubtful that it was more than a modest singing school. In any event, there was no school in the town in 1564 when Francis Graunt, a Wakefield mercer, drew his will, proved in 1566, bequeathing a cottage with a capital value of £10 'to the use of a fre schole, yf any such fortune to be within the towne of Wakefeild'.[2] Not quite a generation was to pass before the challenge implicit in Graunt's bequest was met by the citizenry, for it was in 1590 that public subscriptions were first solicited when Edward Mawde, a fellow of St John's, Cambridge, and formerly a teacher at Halifax, presented himself as a potential master. Leadership in the undertaking was assumed by George Savile, the elder, a woollen merchant of the town, who probably gave the land on which the school was built and who in 1593 bequeathed lands with a capital worth of £80 for the use of the school.[3] His son, also named George, who died in 1595, gave £100 for the endowment of the institution, as well as bequeathing £20 for the establishment of a workhouse and an endowment to increase by £3 7s p.a. the stipend of the preacher at Otley.[4] A board of governors of fourteen substantial men of the community, a judicious and certainly an effective mixture of local gentry, woollen merchants, and tradesmen, was formed to solicit subscriptions and in 1591 secured the charter founding the school. The foundation was wholly secular, the governors having complete legal authority for the administration of its affairs, save that their nomination of a new master must, as required by law, be laid before the Archbishop of York for his approval. The school building

[1] *Surtees Soc. Pub.*, XCII (1893), 309; Walker, *Wakefield*, I, 209–211, II, 365–366. Banaster, of the lesser gentry of the region, was the son of Roger Banaster of Stanley. He was summoned for debt in 1471 under circumstances which would suggest that he may have been engaged in the wool trade.

[2] PCY 17/564 1566; Walker, *Wakefield*, II, 367.

[3] *Yorks. Arch. Soc. Rec.*, XXXIV (1904), 51; *VCH, Yorks.*, I, 440–441; *PP 1826–1827*, X, 686–687; *Yorks. Arch. Journal*, XXV (1920), 42–44; Walker, *Wakefield*, II, 584. George Savile was the son of Thomas Savile of Lupset. He describes himself as a gentleman in his will. He was a large wool merchant with standing and credit at Blackwell Hall. His estate was large, including 1010 acres of land, 50 messuages, 40 cottages, 40 tofts, and 30 barns.

[4] *Vide ante*, 285. The son is often confused with the father and both with the great gentle family of the same name, two of whom, Sir George and John, were first governors of the school. The younger Savile died in London in January, 1595. He was likewise a merchant who, his will makes clear, was in process of becoming a landed gentleman.

was begun, being fully financed by local gifts, in 1596 and was described by Dodsworth as 'a very beautyfull house and pleasantly situated on a piece of ground distant a bow shoot of the north from the church'.[1]

Almost continuous effort was carried forward by the governors, most of whom were themselves men of modest fortune, to secure the endowment of the school from 1590 to 1620. In the first year funds possessing a capital value of £305 had been secured from numerous donors, while the total given from the outset until 1620 reached the impressive sum of £1383 3s, not including certain scholarship foundations which we have reserved for separate treatment. The achievement is the more remarkable because there was no single great donor, the largest benefaction being that left in 1614 by Elizabeth Savile, the widow of George Savile, senior, who added £150 to the stock of the school.[2] We have recorded in all 109 gifts or bequests to the school during the first generation of its history, of which the median was of the value of £3 8s, and of which twenty-two were in amounts of £1 or less.[3] The entire community was involved and rose to the need, the merchant and tradesman group, comprising fifty-one of the subscribers, assuming the principal responsibility, but with the generous support of nearby gentry and yeomanry. An eminent and from the outset an excellent school could with justifiable pride be regarded by a prosperous and lusty industrial community as a creation meeting the designs and the aspirations of the age.

A grammar school was also founded at Ilkley in 1592, under the terms of the will of George Marshall, probably a yeoman of that parish. Marshall left £100 to charitable uses to be determined by his two executors, the proposal to employ the capital for the support of a grammar school, since an unendowed school was already being kept in the parish, having won widespread approval.[4] There was, however, a dispute between the executors, and two arbitration awards were necessary before it was finally determined in 1607 so to employ the funds. The school was kept in the local church until 1635, when, by general consent of the parish, a voluntary rate was levied, which, with bequests left earlier for the purpose,[5] was employed to build a proper structure.

---

[1] VCH, Yorks., I, 440–444; Peacock, Wakefield School, passim; Yorks. Arch. Soc. Rec., XXXIV (1904), 51.

[2] PCY 33/229 1614; Peacock, Wakefield School, 7; Yorks. Arch. Journal, XXV (1920), 45; PP 1826–1827, X, 687. She was the daughter of a Wakefield tradesman and the second wife of Savile.

[3] We have depended heavily on the list in Peacock, Wakefield School, 34–49, adding a fair number of benefactions noted in the wills of the period.

[4] PCY 24/782 1592; PP 1894, LXIV, Ilkley, 1, 4–6; Collyer, Robert, and J. H. Turner, Ilkley (Otley, 1885), 175–178; Smith, Old Yorkshire, n.s. I, 159; VCH, Yorks., I, 469, 480. Marshall's total estate was valued at £466 13s 4d.

[5] As, for example, £2 left for this purpose before 1631 by Richard Middleton (Collyer, Ilkley, 187) and 10s bequeathed for the same use by Thomas Rogers, a yeoman, in 1636 (PCY March 1636).

A few years later a gentleman of Altofts, John Frieston, whose almshouse foundation has been mentioned, by will provided for the foundation at Normanton of a school which would serve that community and the adjacent village of Warmfield. Frieston bequeathed, in 1594, £133 6s 8d for the purchase of a site and for the construction of a school building suitable for thirty poor scholars, who should be taught without fees by a master enjoying £10 p.a. as a stipend from lands previously (1592) deeded to University College, Oxford. Frieston likewise gave £80 for the endowment of Wakefield Grammar School, while, as we shall note later, he also provided a fund for scholarships at Emmanuel College, Cambridge, for men from Yorkshire, as well as lands for the support of one fellow and two scholars at University College, Oxford. In all, Frieston's educational endowments reached the substantial total of almost £1500.[1]

A school was likewise founded at Thornton in the West Riding, usually known as Easby Grammar School, by Robert Windle, a clergyman whose bequest to the poor of that parish has been noted. Windle, whose will was proved in 1592, had for some years been planning the building and the endowment of a school for the parish. After certain extremely technical legal problems were resolved with the good-natured approval of the testator's nephew, Henry Mitchell, it was agreed in 1599 that Windle's heirs would lay out approximately £100 for the site and the building, while a rent-charge of £20 p.a. was settled on the school for the payment of the salary of a competent master who should offer free instruction to deserving poor boys of the community.[2] The school was popular from the outset, enjoying substantial local support, as is suggested by a bequest in 1623 of William Mitchell of £10 capital towards endowing the stipend of a much-needed usher as well as 6d to every student then enrolled.[3]

In 1598 a grammar school was founded at Kirkby Malham under the terms of the will of Benjamin Lambert, a member of a gentle family seated in the neighbourhood. Lambert vested manorial rents then possessing a capital worth of £204 for the 'erecting of a free schole within the town of Kirkby . . . and for the maintenance of a school master for the teaching of all mannor of schollers in learneing there for ever'. The bequest was declared void in law, since there was a co-owner of the rents, but this person, John Topham, a clerk of Threapland, 'for the good will he bare to Benjamin Lambert', in his turn conveyed his rights to the feoffees named under Lambert's will.[4] The school was pre-

[1] *Vide ante,* 263, and *post,* 353.   [2] *Vide ante,* 238, and *post,* 337.

[3] PCY 37/463 1623; *Bradford Antiquary,* n.s. VII (1952), 269.

[4] Morkill, J. W., *Kirkby Malhamdale* (Gloucester, 1934), 107, 153–154, 255–256; *VCH, Yorks.,* I, 481; *PP* 1826, XIII, 701; *PP* 1894, LXIV, Kirkby in Malham Dale, 2. There had been a chantry school in the parish some years

sumably functioning shortly after 1606, though a bequest by William Preston, a local gentleman, in 1636 of £6 towards erecting a building would suggest that suitable quarters had not yet been provided at that date.[1]

The foundation of the Heath Grammar School at Halifax, and, for that matter, the foundation of the whole cultural and social structure of that rapidly growing community, stands as a kind of memorial to the greatness of a clergyman of sternly Calvinistic persuasion, John Favour. A native of Southampton, where he was born in 1556, Favour was educated in the local grammar school and then at Winchester. Favour was chosen a fellow of New College, Oxford, in 1577 and in 1593, a year after taking his degree as Doctor of Laws, at the age of thirty-seven began his long ministry in the huge and, it must be said, rude, parish of Halifax. He was later appointed Master of the Hospital of St Mary Magdalen at Ripon, made Sub-Dean of Ripon, and Precentor of York, as well as chaplain to the Archbishop. But his whole life and devotion were caught up in his ministry. Favour trusted and loved his people, and they came to hold him in a respectful affection which still keeps fresh the memory of this great man as the student examines the documents of the sprawling parish which Favour held in his charge. A man of precisely his talents was required. One of his predecessors had been murdered and another had sold much of the parish property before resigning his living to his son. Favour preached weekly and lectured every day in the week, administered justice, practised medicine, and led his people. His parish came gradually to form itself in the image of Favour's ranging aspirations. He called his parishioners, in the inscription which he placed on Heath Grammar School, a holy people, who had produced so noble a work in so bad and barren a land, though this is really a perfect memorial to Favour's own career.

Favour was mindful of the whole pattern of development in this flourishing and rapidly growing town, being determined that it should possess greatness of institutions as well as of numbers. He encouraged the development of the cloth industry and was the confidant and often the executor of the clothiers of the parish; he subdued the roistering and the criminal with the breath of fire in his sermons; his influence was predominant with the magistrates, to whom he spoke with the certain convictions of an Old Testament prophet; he consoled the dying and drafted their wills; and in the course of his ministry literally transformed his parish. Favour likewise gave effective refuge, for he could

---

before the Reformation, which was ordered continued 'for the good educacon of the abboundaunt yought in those rewde parties', but, there being no endowment, this school had evidently not survived.

[1] PCY July 1636. Preston also left £6 towards building a bridge, £1 to the poor of the parish, and £8 to the parish church for a silver cup.

bristle, to two Puritan lecturers who helped him. He held dubiously legal meetings each month at which neighbouring clergy preached, and he maintained the highest standards of scholarship in his own sermons and in his writings. In 1619 his *Antiquitie triumphing over noveltie* was published, a ringing defence of Protestant antiquity 'against the spurious claims of Rome', the author excusing the long delays in preparation because of the requirements of a ministry which, one must say, has rarely been equalled. This great and useful man died in 1623 full of honours and surely conscious of the metamorphosis he had wrought in Halifax.[1]

One of the most remarkable aspects of Favour's ministry, which appears to be unique, was the amazing number of bequests left to him to be used at his discretion for charitable purposes. He preached charity to his congregation, he practised it himself, and he literally raised up a generation of clothiers and tradesmen in the full understanding of social and cultural responsibility. We have counted in all more than sixty such bequests left to him, not only from Halifax, but from many other communities in the West Riding and two from distant London. Consequently, when Favour determined that a grammar school should be built, as he had that the needs of the poor should be endowed, and that an almshouse should be founded,[2] the question was only one of time. When Favour arrived in Halifax in 1593, he found that some years earlier (1585) a charter had been procured for the establishment of a grammar school in the town, with a board of governors named, few of whom were residents. No funds had been raised and no plan had been advanced. Favour at once took charge and in 1593 Robert Saltonstall of Halifax gave a rent-charge of £20 capital value for the intended school,[3] while in 1594 Robert Wade, a gentleman of Sowerby, provided £100 for the school's stock.[4] In 1597 two acres of land for the site were given by local gentry, and an appeal, signed by Favour and Sir John Savile, was sent to possible donors in the county, while Favour addressed personal letters to every township in the parish, made earnest personal solicitations, and entered into a contract with a builder for the erection of the school at a cost of £120. The school was opened in 1600, still without much endowment, while Favour exhorted the curates of the twelve chapels in the parish to solicit the aid of the 'richest and best able persons' in their charge. By 1601 Favour had raised funds totalling £266 17s for the building and the support of the school from a goodly number of representative members of the community, including, as well, a gift of £3 7s from Sir Richard Saltonstall, Lord Mayor of

[1] DNB; Walker, *Halifax church registers*, 1-130; Watson, *Halifax*, 466-467; Rowse, *England of Elizabeth*, 431-432; Surtees Soc. Pub., LXXVIII (1884), 277-279. A biography of this man and an account of his ministry are much needed.   [2] *Vide ante*, 236-237 for an example.

[3] *PP* 1828, XX, 570; *VCH, Yorks.*, I, 479.

[4] *Vide ante*, 234, for a notice of Wade's other benefactions.

London, who also by will gave £100 for the support of the poor of the town.[1] Numerous bequests by this date began to fall in to Favour, certain of which were used for the annual support of the still meagerly endowed school, such as that of John Hogge, in 1602, who left £6 13s 4d 'to be ymployed to suche good and godlie uses wth the p'ish of Hallifaxe as by my good freindes Dr. ffavour and myne overseers ... shalbe thought fitt'.[2] A substantial addition to the endowment came in 1608 when Brian Crowther, a clothier and churchwarden and a close friend of Favour, died at the age of seventy, leaving rents with a capital worth of £400 'for the use and behofe' of the grammar school.[3] Other gifts and bequests now began to accrue to the governors and to the indefatigable Favour. Thus Thomas Gledhill in 1607 left £5 to the school;[4] Sir John Savile, who had had little more to do with the founding than to grace Favour's leaters of solicitation with his name, gave the inconsiderable amount of £5;[5] and John Waterhouse in 1610 bequeathed the sum of £10 towards the endowment of the institution.[6]

In all, the resources of the school were in 1610 of the order of £692 10s. The master and usher were together receiving annual stipends somewhat in excess of £20, in part from annual gifts which included £3 p.a. for several years from Dr Favour. The prestige of the school was well established locally and under Favour's insistent tuition gifts and bequests continued to come to hand. Thus in 1608 John Maud, who made Favour co-executor of his will, bequeathed £20 to the uses of the governors,[7] while in 1611 a local merchant, Isaac Waterhouse, left £10 to the stock of the school.[8] In 1613 bequests were received from John Brigg, a London merchant but a former governor, who left £6,[9] and from a clothier, Robert Hemingway, who bequeathed £10 to the capital of the grammar school.[10] In 1618 William Harrison, a clothier, who named Favour an

[1] The bequest for the poor was withheld by Saltonstall's heirs (vide ante, 235).

[2] Walker, Halifax church registers, 5.

[3] Vide ante, 236, for Crowther's endowment for the relief of the poor. His widow, Jane, and her sister also founded an almshouse in Halifax (vide ante, 267).   [4] Halijax Antiq. Soc. Papers, 1922, 116.

[5] Ibid., 1919, 23; Midgley, Halifax, 488; Thoresby Soc. Pub., XXXV (1934), 22–23; Yorks. Arch. Journal, XV (1900), 420–427. A brother of the famous Sir Henry, Savile was a judge of assize and Baron of the Exchequer. He built two chapels in Halifax parish during his lifetime (vide post, 395).

[6] Halifax Antiq. Soc. Trans., 1930, 22.

[7] Halifax Antiq. Soc. Papers, 1924, 202–203; Walker, Halifax church registers, 46–47. Maud also left £20 for highway repairs, £40 for the relief of the poor of Halifax and Skircoat, £40 to poor tradesmen of the two towns, and £1 4s outright to twelve poor.

[8] Vide ante, 273.   [9] Walker, Halifax church registers, 88.

[10] Halifax Antiq. Soc. Papers, 1917, 95–105, Trans., 1930, 36; PP 1899, LXXI, 466. Hemingway likewise left £10 for loans to decayed tradesmen and £40 for the maintenance of a preacher at Coley chapel. He was a brother of Jane Crowther and Ellen Hopkinson (q.v.).

executor of his will, left £100 to his pastor and provided £10 for the school, among charities totalling £250.[1] By the time of Favour's death in 1623 the total that had been provided for the uses of the school had reached £768 10s and the institution was well and soundly established, offering educational opportunities to all the youth of the community and sending on able and more ambitious boys to the universities. The traditions of charitable giving so well established by Favour persisted in the parish, with the result that under the pastorate of his successor, Henry Ramsden, the school was steadily and adequately supported, numerous small augmentations totalling £186 7s having been made to its endowment by the close of his ministry in 1638.[2] Hence, after a long generation of persistent and certainly devoted effort, a notable school had been founded by community endeavour, whose resources had attained nearly £1000. The institution was all the more securely placed because, Crowther's bequest aside, there had been no single large benefaction. The school stood as the achievement of a whole community of clothiers, tradesmen, and nearby gentry and yeomanry, and as an enduring memorial to a great minister of God's Word.

A school was founded in Askrigg, in the North Riding parish of Aysgarth, in 1600 by a London lawyer, Anthony Besson, whose family held lands in the parish but who was himself a native of York. It appears from the deed of gift that a schoolhouse had recently been built 'near Owre's Bridge End' by unnamed persons, which Besson most adequately endowed as a free grammar school with property in the city of York possessing a capital value of £400.[3]

In the course of the Elizabethan period, then, sixteen endowed grammar schools had been added by private donors to the educational resources of the county. These foundations were on the whole more substantial and more carefully constituted than earlier establishments of the kind and they were with few exceptions wholly secular in their organization and administration. The Elizabethan foundations tended to be concentrated in the newer industrial towns and in remote rural parishes standing, as charitably disposed donors realized, in grave need of the educational facilities so rapidly being opened for the county at large. In all, these foundations were endowed with funds totalling £7014 17s in the course of our period. Seven of these institutions pos-

---

[1] PCY 35/115 1618; *Halifax Antiq. Soc. Trans.*, 1931, 12; Walker, *Halifax church registers*, 95–98. Harrison also left £40 to the poor of Halifax, £10 for bringing water into Halifax, £30 for roads and bridges, £20 for poor scholars in Sedbergh Grammar School, and a total of £140 for the maintenance of clergy of a Puritan persuasion.

[2] *Halifax Antiq. Soc. Papers*, 1924, 194, suggests a somewhat larger total.

[3] PCY 32/496 1613; Lawton, *Collectio*, 560; *VCH, Yorks.*, I, 480; *PP* 1822, X, 684; Foster, *Gray's Inn admissions*, 86. Besson was an attorney to the Star Chamber.

sessed capital of more than £400, which was most adequate for a strong and efficient grammar school in a relatively small country town in this period.

But in the Elizabethan period, as in the earlier generation, the founding of the endowed schools, with which we are principally concerned, by no means reflects the full strength of the remarkable educational accomplishments wrought in Yorkshire by private donors. We might, therefore, at least mention certain of the lesser schools, usually unendowed and supported by fees, and occasionally not long-lived, which came into being in this period. Thus a school was ordered maintained at Romaldkirk by the Chantry Commissioners in 1548, with a stipend from chantry lands of £3 6s 8d p.a., which enjoyed local support during the Elizabethan period.[1] Similarly, a school was in effect founded by the Commissioners at Wragby with an endowment of £6 16s 4d p.a., for which in 1573 a suitable building was provided by the parish.[2] The Archbishop's visitation in 1563 reveals the existence of struggling schools at Norton in the East Riding,[3] at Coley in Halifax parish,[4] at Dewsbury,[5] and at Raskelf.[6] Elementary instruction was being offered in an unendowed school at Huddersfield[7] and notes in the churchwardens' accounts for 1573 make it clear that there was also a school at Ecclesfield at that date.[8] A London merchant, Robert Vavasour, in 1575 left £10 to assist poor children in a school at Kirkby Overblow.[9] Still another London bequest suggests that there must have been a school at Kildwick in 1587,[10] while two years later a yeoman of Methley, Robert Hagger, left 6s for aid in building a school there if it could be accomplished within a period of five years.[11] And, finally, in 1600 John Burley of London left £20, Anthony Besson being his trustee, towards the erection of a school in Wensleydale, as well as £100 for loans to young tradesmen of York, the interest to be employed for the relief of poor prisoners in that city.[12]

The spread of small but aspiring schools across the face of the county, as well as the schools for which donors provided permanent endowments, suggests the almost feverish interest of Yorkshiremen by the close of the Elizabethan period in the founding of a system of popular education which would offer opportunity to all aspiring youths and which would tend to cure that poverty which is bred in ignorance. The

---

[1] *Surtees Soc. Pub.*, XCII (1893), 492; *VCH, Yorks., NR.*, I, 119.

[2] *VCH, Yorks.*, I, 476.   [3] Purvis, *Tudor parish documents*, 105.

[4] *Ibid.*, 106.   [5] *Ibid.*, 105.   [6] *Ibid.*, 108.

[7] *Ibid.*, 107.   [8] Eastwood, *Ecclesfield*, 326.

[9] PCC 29 Pyckering 1575; *Surtees Soc. Pub.*, CXXI (1912), 72–74.

[10] William Garforthe left £10 to this school (PCC 9 Rutland 1587).

[11] *Thoresby Soc. Pub.*, XII (1902), 62.

[12] PCC 21 Woodhall 1601; *Surtees Soc. Pub.*, CXXI (1912), 214. *Vide ante*, 326.

achievements of these donors, notable as they were prior to 1600, were, however, but a prelude to the immense outpouring of wealth for the founding of new schools and the augmentation of older institutions during the four decades that comprise the early Stuart period. In this relatively brief interval £20,667 10s was provided for the support of grammar schools in the county, an amount considerably greater than that given for the purpose in the twelve preceding decades. We should now deal, at least briefly, with the principal of these endowments.

Thomas Cave, a Wakefield chapman and one of the first governors and supporters of the grammar school there, on his death in 1603 left £250 on trust for the foundation of a grammar school at Otley, on condition that the inhabitants should within four years raise by private gifts an equal amount for its endowment. The school was to have a master and an usher, and was to offer instruction in a classical curriculum to the sons of persons resident in the parish.[1] Cave's generous bequest was matched by local subscriptions in 1607 and a charter establishing the school was obtained from the Crown, while in 1611 the inhabitants entered into a bond of £140 to ensure the erection of a suitable building in which instruction 'in the feare of God and good learnynge' should be offered.[2] The endowment of this school was further increased in 1643 under the terms of the will of William Vavasour, who left it property valued at £80, as well as gifts of £10 to the school at Guiseley and £5 for the free school at Ilkley.[3] In the year in which Otley Grammar School was founded (1603), a yeoman, John Knowles, of Acaster Malbis, by will endowed an elementary school for that parish with a bequest of £100. Knowles settled the endowment on four trustees of the parish who were to find a single man to teach the children freely, the master not to be paid one 'penny or pennyworth' by the parishioners.[4]

Sir William Craven, the London merchant whose great generosity to his native parish of Burnsall has already been mentioned, by deed in 1605 conveyed to trustees land and a school building, valued at £120, which he had built shortly before this date (1602). Craven presumably supported the master of the school during the next decade, arranging, however, in his will for the Merchant Taylors' Company, as feoffees,

[1] *Vide ante*, 266. Cave also left property valued at £240 to Clare Hall, Cambridge, for the support of 'two of the poorest schollers' from Wakefield Grammar School and gave to the grammar school a rent-charge of £1 p.a. value.

[2] *VCH, Yorks.*, I, 481; *Yorks. Arch. Journal*, XXVII (1924), 409; *PP* 1826, XIII, 681.

[3] PCY October 1643; *Bradford Antiquary*, n.s. VII (1952), 100–104; Baildon, *Baildon*, I, 541; *PP* 1826, XIII, 685; *PP* 1894, LXIV, Otley, 21, 38, 42. Vavasour also left a total of £32 for the benefit of the poor and a very substantial bequest for the support of the clergy. (*Vide post*, 379–380.)

[4] PCY 29/316 1604; *PP* 1824, XIII, 714; *PP* 1895, LXXV, Acaster, 2; *VCH, Yorks.*, I, 491. Knowles also left £30 to be lent at interest to the poor tenants of the parish, the income to be distributed among the poor.

to pay annually the sum of £20 as the stipend of the master, as well as including the repair of the school as one of the objects of a general fund created by will for the municipal needs of the parish.[1] These endowments were further supported by a charitable fund of £200 left in 1624 by Dame Elizabeth Craven for the further maintenance of her late husband's charities in Burnsall.[2]

The first of the Jacobean foundations was made by Matthew Hutton, Archbishop of York, in his native parish of Warton, Lancashire, the school being endowed with a capital of at least £533.[3] A substantial school was founded in 1604 at Coxwold, near his village birthplace at Kilburn, by Sir John Harte, a London merchant and a former lord mayor. Harte devised to trustees property valued at upwards of £733, the income to be used to support a grammar school with a master, an usher, and a schoolmaster to teach English to the children of the parish. A pleasant house and garden were provided for the school, which flourished through the seventeenth century, offering free and excellent instruction to youths who otherwise would have been distant from any grammar school.[4] At about the same time a grammar school was founded at Dent, a chapelry in Sedbergh parish. In 1598 a London vintner, Ralph Lynsey, bequeathed £30 towards the endowment of a free school in this, his native village, on condition that one be established within a reasonable time. The school was founded by royal charter in 1604 with an initial endowment of £102.[5] A school was built at Sancton, where he had received his own early education from an itinerant schoolmaster, by Marmaduke Langdale. The school was established some time before 1609, being maintained by the donor until his death by an annual stipend of £10 for the master. By the terms of his will Langdale endowed the school with lands then having a capital worth of £400, in order to provide a salary of £20 p.a. for a 'godly, learned, and virtuous man, to teach and instruct in learning and virtuous exercises' without fee all scholars from this and other parishes who might present

[1] Vide ante, 239, 298, and post 400. An interesting account of this school, with an excellent photograph, may be found in Country Life, CXXVII (June 9, 1960), 1323–1324.

[2] Lady Craven also left £100 as a stock for the poor of Burnsall. Vide ante, 239.

[3] Surtees Soc. Pub., XVII (1843), 178–183; Cooper, Memorials of Cambridge, II, 263; DNB. Vide post, 359.

[4] PCC 1 Harte 1604; Beaven, Aldermen of London, II, 41; PP 1822, IX, 593; Yorks. Arch. Soc. Rec., XXXIV (1904), 173; VCH, Yorks., I, 480, NR, II, 24. The school was closed in 1894, the population of the community having become sparse. Vide Jordan, Charities of London, 234, 265, 393, for a biographical note on Harte and for his other benefactions, which totalled £1158 6s.

[5] PCC 46 Lewyn 1598; PP 1825, XI, 660; VCH, Yorks., I, 481; Country Life, CXXVIII (July 21, 1960), 138, where a photograph is to be found. Adam Sedgwick (1785–1873), the famous geologist, was a graduate of the school, which continued to serve this remote community until 1897.

themselves. The master should hold a degree from either university and should likewise be an ordained minister prepared to preach weekly. Langdale also founded and endowed a school at South Skirlaugh with a bequest of £400, the prescription again being that the master should be a clergyman who would be responsible for 'teachinge of poore children' of the chapelry, as well as preaching weekly. Langdale laid down remarkably precise and certainly chaste requirements for the mastership at South Skirlaugh, it being 'such a bare and barren place'.[1]

The grammar school at Sheffield came into existence in such gradual stages that no precise date for its founding can be suggested, though it may be said that a school was maintained there as early as 1564 by the burghers of the town, who supplied suitable quarters at a nominal rental and who also defrayed at least a portion of the stipend of the master, he as late as 1595 being an assistant minister of the parish church. The school possessed no endowment for more than a generation or, for that matter, any corporate being until in 1604 a charter was obtained from the Crown at a cost of £46 1s 8d.[2] The school likewise gained its first important financial support in these years, when Thomas Smith, a Lincolnshire lawyer, though a native of Sheffield, left to the town £30 p.a. 'so long as the world should endure, for the finding of two sufficient learned men to teach and bring up the young children there in godliness and learning'. The school thus competently endowed did not possess a building, and in 1606 an assessment was laid on the parish to secure the sum of £103 18s 1d to pay the costs of a schoolhouse, which was to be used until 1648.[3] Some years later, in 1631, a mercer, Robert Rollinson, whose other benefactions to Sheffield have been noted, left property worth about £60 for an augmentation of the endowment,[4] while in 1637 a local citizen, John Hill, gave £100 to the now flourishing school.[5] By 1644 the original school was not only overcrowded but was in disrepair; we have recorded numerous bequests and gifts towards the construction of a new building, which was completed in 1648.

---

[1] *Vide ante*, 283, for Langdale's additional benefactions. The master was 'to be such a teacher, as is an honest, virtuous, godly man, to leade a single life, neither to be a married man, nor to take or marry a wife for his own use or company, neither to be a whoremonger, fornicator, or drunkard, nor a great company keeper, but a civil, honest man in livinge, to all mens judgements; and to behave himself according to God's holie lawes ... and not to run a fleshinge and eating flesh of forbidden dayes, contrary to the injunctions of the holy church, and the king's majesties wholesome and godlie lawes, for I do thinke that a dutiful minister, a painful preacher, and a diligent teacher of children in that place at Skerly chapel, shall have little occasion to have the use or company of any woman ...'

[2] *VCH, Yorks.*, I, 479; *Hunter Arch. Soc. Trans.*, III (1929), 336–343.

[3] *Ibid.*, IV (1937), 283–296; White, *Sheffield*, 97–98; Hunter, *Hallamshire*, 172–173; *PP* 1897, LXVII, iii, Sheffield, 1–2, 57.

[4] *Vide ante*, 298.   [5] Hunter, *Hallamshire*, 173.

A school had been built and furnished at Batley early in the Jacobean period by unknown donors and a master employed who derived his income from tuition fees. This school was endowed by the gift in 1612 of lands purchased in the preceding year by William Lee, a Cambridge-shire rector, who was a native of the parish. Lee vested on trustees lands for which he had paid £250 'out of love he bore . . . to his country from whence he had his beginning', for the support of a master who should teach a free school. The schoolmaster should be competent to offer a classical curriculum to his scholars and the school should undertake to prepare apt students for the universities. By his will proved in 1617 Lee further enhanced the endowment by a bequest of £80, the income of which was to be used to augment the master's stipend, subject to an annual distribution of 10s to the poor and 7s for a sermon.[1] Still another clergyman, Robert Chaloner, Rector of Amersham, Buckinghamshire, founded a well-conceived grammar school in Knaresborough in 1616 with the aid of Peter Benson, a substantial yeoman of the parish. Chaloner conveyed to sixteen trustees property worth £400 to establish a free school for 'as well poor as rich'. No tuition fee should be imposed on any student from the parishes of Knaresborough and Goldsborough, though the trustees were encouraged to admit as well acceptable distant students on the payment of a reasonable fee. The school was divided into five forms for instruction in Greek and Latin authors, and no student should use the English language in class or play after having completed the first form.[2] Peter Benson, a few months later, conveyed to the trustees property then valued at £80 to secure the augmentation of the already substantial endowment.[3]

In the same year (1617) a most generous foundation was made at Snaith by Nicholas Waller, who, as we have seen, also provided an almshouse for this and nearby parishes. It seems certain that for a generation instruction had been offered in the church at Snaith by the curate of the parish, doubtless on the payment of fees.[4] Waller in 1616, or 1617, built an appropriate schoolhouse at an approximate cost of £60, which he most adequately endowed in 1617 with £600, the income of

[1] *PP* 1826–1827, X, 716; Parsons, *Leeds*, II, 94; Sheard, *Batley*, 148–152, 165–166, 182–185. Lee was born in 1550 at Waddersome (Batley), the son of a small farmer. He was educated at Peterhouse, and was for many years Vicar of Stapleford, Cambridgeshire.

[2] *PP* 1820, IV, 463–465; *PP* 1833, XVIII, 8; PCC 69 Dale 1621; *vide ante*, 55.

Chaloner was educated at Oxford, being a student at Christ Church. He was graduated B.A. in 1566, B.D. in 1576, and D.D. in 1584. He was made Rector of Fleet Marston (Buckinghamshire) in 1566 and of Amersham in 1576.

[3] *PP* 1820, IV, 464; *Yorks. Arch. Journal*, XXXIV (1939), 217. Benson was a yeoman and the collector of borough rents. He compounded rather than accept knighthood in 1630.   [4] *VCH, Yorks.*, I, 480.

which was to be employed for the payment of the stipends of a master and an usher on his foundation, the former to have £22 p.a. and the latter £8 p.a.[1] A grammar school was established in Rawmarsh in the following year (1618), the endowments in this case being slowly accumulated by successive small benefactions. The initial gift was made by Alice Darley, who provided £30 for the support of the school.[2] Some years later Thomas Wilson conveyed to nine substantial citizens of the parish as trustees land and other property valued at about £40 for the continued support of the schoolmaster, instruction to be offered especially to the children of poor men in reading, writing, and grammar.[3] In 1653 this donor's son, a London clothworker of the same name, conveyed a house valued at £60 to be employed as a schoolhouse and other property of an estimated worth of £30 for the augmentation of the endowment. On his death in 1659 Wilson left additionally a rent-charge of £3 6s 8d p.a., as well as 6d to each scholar and £2 p.a. to be distributed to such of the poor of Rawmarsh as might attend church regularly. The school thus endowed was well filled and evidently most carefully and prudently administered until the close of our period. A modest endowment was also provided in 1619 for a school at Halton Gill by a native of that place, Henry Fawcett, who had prospered as a merchant in Norwich. This benefactor devised a rent-charge of £10 p.a. as a stipend for the clergyman of the chapel, who should offer free elementary instruction and the 'rudiments of grammar' to poor children of the parish.[4] His brother, William, a London merchant, rebuilt the chapel in 1626 and at the same time erected a small structure to serve as the schoolhouse. William Fawcett also settled on trustees rents of £13 7s p.a. as an augmentation of the schoolmaster's salary, while providing in addition an annual stipend of £4 for the poor of the community and £1 for two sermons on November fifth 'in remembrance of their deliverance from the popish conspiracy'.[5]

---

[1] Vide ante, 270–271.   [2] PP 1828, XX, 626; VCH, Yorks., I, 482.
[3] Idem.   [4] Vide ante, 109, 118, 132, 161–162.
[5] PP 1826, XIII, 692; PP 1894, LXIV, Arncliffe, 1, 6; Shuffrey, W. A., The churches of the Deanery of North Craven (Leeds, 1914), 20–21; Lewis, Wharfedale, 26. Fawcett's generosity was extolled by Edmund Layfielde in his funeral sermon, published in 1633, under the title of The soules solace. We are told that Fawcett resided both in Norwich, where his brother was a leading merchant, and in London. His own children having died, Fawcett's 'care was doubled to provide for Gods-heyres, and poore children on earth, that stood in neede of the uttermost extent of his goodnesse. Unto whom hee lent such a helping hand both in life and death, out of his moderate estate . . .' Thus Fawcett watered 'his native barren soyle' with the benefactions noted above. But during his lifetime, as well, he had supported scholars in both universities, assisted indigent clergy, and had carried forward many other commendable acts of charity. 'Though mammon came thorow his fingers, yet hee washt his heart from the love of it. . . . For the space of this ten yeeres last past, his custome was at

Still another West Riding school was founded in 1619 by the concerted, if somewhat ineffectual, efforts of the substantial men of Laughton-en-le-Morthen. Edmund Laughton, a yeoman of the parish, and Anthony Eyre, a gentleman of Rampton, Nottinghamshire, in that year conveyed to trustees land and a decayed cottage, together comprising a worth of about £30, for the founding of a school. The donors had in view an elementary school for poor children of the parish. The trust was not fully, much less properly, carried forward, though a schoolmaster was employed who was apparently supported by private and somewhat casual local contributions until 1659, when John West, a gentleman of nearby Firbeck, left property valued at £60 for the support of the master, this shortly being augmented by a rent-charge of £3 7s made by Sir Francis Fane.[1]

There were also patient and persistent community efforts to secure the founding of a grammar school at Hatfield (W. R.), which came to fruition in 1619 when in all four grammar schools were to be established in various parts of the county. As early as 1592 John Myrfin, a yeoman of the parish, had left £6 13s of capital for the somewhat ambiguous purpose of teaching a poor child,[2] and a school was certainly being maintained by local contributors when in 1619 John Spivey, a local yeoman, by will left capital valued at £40, the income to be used for the employment of a 'fit schoolmaster' to teach children at Hatfield.[3] At about the same date, a London tradesman, and a native of the parish, Robert Forster, left a rent-charge of 10s p.a. to provide a gown for the master every second year, as well as more substantial benefactions for other charitable uses.[4] The endowment of the school was completed in 1627 when a local gentleman, Thomas Wormeley, conveyed to trustees lands with a capital value of £200, to be used to bring to the grammar school as master an able graduate of one of the universities, who should offer free instruction to all qualified children of the parish.[5]

A large and interesting foundation was also established in 1619 in the

the yeeres end to take a survey of his temporall estate, which hee having briefly sum'md up in a sheete of paper; he made a godly prayer, and thanksgiving, which he annexed unto his account.'

[1] *PP* 1828, XI, 374; *PP* 1896, LXIII, ii, Laughton, 4–5; Hunter, *South Yorkshire*, II, 287–288.

[2] *PP* 1828, XX, 616.

[3] PCY 35/584 1619; *PP* 1828, XX, 616, 621; *VCH, Yorks.*, I, 483. Spivey had also by deed in 1609 created an endowment yielding £2 p.a. for the benefit of the poor of the parish and by bequest augmented the stipend of the parson by £2 p.a.

[4] *PP* 1828, XX, 619–620; *Yorks. Arch. Journal*, XVI (1902), 63. Forster gave £10 for a bell for the parish church, bequeathed £4 p.a. for clothing the poor of the parish, and left 13s p.a. for clerical uses.

[5] PCY 40/168 1627; *PP* 1828, XX, 616–619; *VCH, Yorks.*, I, 483; Hunter, *South Yorkshire*, I, 175.

rural parish of Sherburn by Robert Hungate, a lawyer, which he wished
to model as closely as possible on Christ's Hospital, London. The donor
by will conveyed to trustees endowments with a capital value of almost
£5000 for founding a school and hospital in Sherburn for twenty-four
legitimate orphan children of the towns of Sherburn and Saxton who
were aged between seven and fifteen years. Suitable quarters were provided and a schoolmaster appointed, with a stipend of £30 p.a., and
an usher, with £13 7s p.a., to instruct and prepare the children in
grammar and other subjects in order to fit them for the university if
they were apt, or to prepare them for apprenticeships. The endowment
was likewise to provide £26 13s to be employed as a scholarship fund
to send four able graduates to St John's College, Cambridge. Those
students not qualified for the university were to be placed in apprenticeships, with a stipend of £2 10s p.a., or else set in some other honourable
and useful calling. In addition, complete maintenance was to be afforded
all children on the foundation.[1]

Two much humbler foundations were made in Yorkshire, in 1622,
both probably being elementary schools. Some little time before that
date Robert Moore, Rector of Guiseley, had built a schoolhouse for the
children of his parish at a cost of perhaps £50, endowing his foundation
by will with property having a capital worth of £100. The master was in
perpetuity to be appointed by the rector and was to have his lodging
and diet in the parsonage.[2] In the same year, Ralph Ellis, a gentleman of
York, endowed a school at Bolsterstone (Ecclesfield) with a capital
bequest of £200, the income to be used for the free instruction of all
children of the town. The school was soon afterwards built, but was
weakened during the Civil War when £50 of the endowment was lost.
None the less, the institution was continued, offering instruction in

---

[1] PCY 36/255 1620; *Alum. cantab.*, I, ii, 431; *VCH, Yorks.*, I, 482; *Yorks.
Arch. Journal*, XVIII (1905), 47–48; *PP* 1826–1827, IX, 417–418; *PP* 1898,
LXVIII, Sherburn, 1–9; Morrell, J. B., *Biography of common man of York* (L.,
1927), 19; Wheater, W., *History of Sherburn and Cawood* (L., 1882), 57–60.
Vide post, 377. *Vide* Jordan, *Charities of London*, 262. Hungate was the son of
William Hungate, Esq., of Saxton. He was educated at St John's College and
at Lincoln's Inn, becoming a barrister in 1579. He married Catharine, the widow
of Sir William Bamburgh. Unhappily, Hungate's great design was never fully
realized. The great charitable estate was in 1655 involved in the delinquency of a
descendant, Sir Philip Hungate (*S. P. Dom.*, 1655, CI, 112). Moreover,
the capital was not well invested, the income of £250 available in 1628 having
declined in 1898 to £205.

[2] CCY October 7, 1644; *VCH, Yorks.*, I, 491; *PP* 1826, XIII, 651; Slater,
Philemon, *History of Guiseley* (L., 1880), 136. Moore, a graduate of Cambridge,
was presented with this living in 1581 and served it for sixty-three years. It is
said that he baptized one parishioner and buried him when he had reached the
age of sixty. Moore's will was drafted in 1622, and he apparently maintained
the school until it came into effect.

English, arithmetic, and elementary subjects until in the eighteenth century it gained a great benefactor.[1]

In a brief interval of about five years a number of lesser schools were established and endowed in small and rural communities throughout the West Riding. In 1626 Alexander Stocke, since 1588 the rector of the parish, bequeathed a small endowment of £10 for the support of a school 'lately builded . . . by me and others' in the parish of Kirkheaton.[2] Another clergyman, Robert Wood, of Kirk Sandall, in the same year devised to the churchwardens of that parish, as feoffees, property valued at about £160 for the support of a schoolmaster who should conduct a free grammar school for the benefit of the parish.[3] Gyles Moore, a yeoman resident in the remote hamlet of Eldroth (Clapham), seems to have been the prime mover in securing the founding of a school and chapel to serve that community and two adjacent hamlets. By the terms of his will, proved in 1627, he gave lands with a then value of £30 to secure 'some reeder or schoolmaister that shall reede prayers or teach schollers in the chapell or schoolhouse . . . for the love and zeale I beare to have prayers redd and children taught there being far from any other place of common prayer or schoole for teaching of children'. Moore had also contributed an uncertain sum before his death, to which other men of the community added, to secure a stock of about £90, with which the school and chapel were built shortly before 1630. In that year an interesting covenant was entered into by twenty-five yeomen of the neighbourhood subscribing a total of about £60 additionally for the maintenance of the chapel service and 'for the comfortte and ease of us and many others of our poore neighbours and for the better educatinge and bringing uppe of our children in learninge'. With these slender resources of capital, but with such evident enthusiastic support from an entire community, this elementary school was begun in 1630.[4] In the same year, the then Archbishop of York, Samuel Harsnett, by deed gave rents representing a capital worth of £100 for the founding of a school at Cawood in connection with the elaborate

---

[1] PCY 36/601 1622; Hunter, *South Yorkshire*, II, 197; Eastwood, *Ecclesfield*, 481. The school was served for fifty-six years by Henry Hodgkinson as master. The chapel in which it was taught was unheated, the children having to go out to neighbouring houses on occasion to warm themselves. Hodgkinson persuaded the town to build a school building in 1687. His own son, John, left £100 for the repair of the building and an endowment of £1366 13s 4d.

[2] CCY 25/31/253 1626; *PP* 1829, VIII, 596; *PP* 1897 LXVII, iv, Kirkheaton, I, 5–6; *VCH, Yorks.*, I, 482; Lawton, *Collectio*, 143; Midgley, *Halifax*, 139.

[3] CCY 29/31/251 1626; *PP* 1826–1827, X, 795; *PP* 1897, LXVII, iv, Kirk Sandall, 2–4; *Alum. cantab.*, I, iv, 454; Smith, *Old Yorkshire*, n.s. I, 160; Lawton, *Collectio*, 219. Wood was a native of Little Sandal, Yorkshire. He was educated at Cambridge.

[4] PCY 39/252 1627; *PP* 1825, XI, 631; *PP* 1895, LXXV, Clapham, 16–19. *Vide post*, 397.

institution for social rehabilitation which he sought to found there, unfortunately with insufficient capital.[1] A London merchant, John Rainey, a native of Worsborough (Darfield) who by will provided a substantial stock for the poor of that community and a richly endowed and decidedly Puritan lectureship for the chapel there, completed his charitable gift for the village by the endowment of a school. During his lifetime he had laid out approximately £50 on the repair of an older and unendowed school in the town, as well as providing the whole printed works of the redoubtable William Perkins for the edification of the community. By bequest in 1633 Rainey vested in the Drapers' Company an endowment of £267 value for the proper maintenance of an 'honest, learned, religious, and sufficient schoolmaster' for his foundation. The will further stipulated that if the lecturer should ever be ejected, which did occur promptly after the Restoration, an additional £16 13s 4d p.a. should be bestowed on the grammar-school foundation.[2]

Just a year before his death in 1635 John, Lord Darcy, most adequately endowed with rents representing a capital of £600 a grammar school at Kilham, which he had built some time earlier at his own charge.[3] A small school, designed to afford elementary instruction for poor children in the remote village of Garsdale, where he had been born, was founded in 1634 by a London tradesman, Thomas Dawson, who built a schoolhouse on land he had purchased and who endowed the institution with property valued at about £70. The institution was designed to afford elementary instruction for poor children in this poor and remote chapelry.[4] Still another elementary school was founded at Felkirk by a doctor's wife, Prudence Berry, in 1637 by the terms of her will implementing a conveyance previously made by deed. The endowment, settled unfortunately on a private person, was £100, the estimated income of £6 13s 4d to be paid to a master who would freely provide instruction in the basic disciplines to children of Felkirk and Havercroft.[5]

A most substantial foundation was made at Bridlington in the East

---

[1] *Vide ante*, 288.   [2] *Vide ante*, 246, and *post*, 384.

[3] PCY August 1636; *Complete peerage*, III, 21; *PP* 1823, VIII, 735; Hunter, *South Yorkshire*, II, 163; *VCH, Yorks.*, I, 483. Darcy, known as 'the good lord Darcy', enjoyed his estate for a period of thirty-two years, living quietly and taking little part in public affairs. He was much influenced by one of his four wives, Isabel, the daughter of Sir Christopher Wray, who was a pronounced Puritan and a supporter of the Puritan clergy thereabouts.

[4] *VCH, Yorks.*, I, 492; *PP* 1825, XI, 664.

[5] Hunter, *South Yorkshire*, II, 410-412; *PP* 1826-1827, X, 749. The annual rental of £6 13s 4d was paid for a generation by the founder's heirs, but was ultimately discontinued. The Commissioners of Charitable Uses in 1687 ordered restitution of £174 of interest withheld as well as £145 additionally, the school being in effect re-founded.

This benefactor was a daughter of a gentleman, Thomas Gargrave, the son of Sir Cotton Gargrave, a rich Yorkshire landowner, whose mother was a Fair-

Riding by William Hustler in 1637. Hustler, who had purchased two manors in the neighbourhood during his lifetime, settled on trustees a rent-charge of £40 p.a. out of the manor of Broughton (near New Malton), representing a capital value of £800, for the endowment of a school which he had recently erected at his own charge. The income was to be employed for the full maintenance of a master and one usher, the former to enjoy a salary of forty marks p.a., for the free instruction of the youth of the community 'in the art of grammar'. The trust was vested on seven substantial members of the community, of gentle and yeoman status, for the benefit of this coastal parish.[1] An elementary school was adequately endowed in the same year for the betterment of the sprawling rural parish of Kirby Misperton, in the North Riding, by a local gentleman, William Smithson, who was a perceptive and responsible benefactor to his community. Smithson devised to trustees property with a value of £200, the income of which should be employed as a stipend for 'some poor graduate scholar of Cambridge' who should without charge teach all applying children until they could read and write perfectly and had been 'fitted for the free grammar school near thereunto'.[2]

Haworth Grammar School was formally founded in 1637 under the deed of gift of Christopher Scott, a native of Yorkshire who had succeeded Robert Windle as Rector of Chastleton in Oxfordshire.[3] Scott conveyed to eighteen trustees, they being 'chief men of Haworth', land and a school building, which he had provided at a charge of about £70 shortly before this date. The founder presumably maintained the institution until his death in 1640, when by will he settled an endowment of £360 on the trustees of the school. A stipend of £18 was to be paid annually to a competent master to offer instruction in Greek and Latin of sufficient quality to fit graduates for the universities.[4]

fax and who married the aunt of the first Earl of Strafford. In 1594 he was tried for the murder of a servant boy under particularly gruesome circumstances and was executed for the crime. Prudence Gargrave was the only child, the vast landed estate going to a half-brother of Thomas, Sir Richard Gargrave, who squandered them. The mother and daughter gained only fragments of the personal estate. In about 1637, when she was forty-four, Prudence married Dr Richard Berry, a London physician trained at Padua, who in 1623 had purchased the manor of Havercroft from the wastrel, Sir Richard. Prudence Berry died, without issue, soon after her belated marriage.

[1] PCY October 1646; *PP* 1823, IX, 721; *VCH, Yorks., NR,* I, 467; Prickett, M., *Priory church of Bridlington* (Cambridge, 1831), App., 105. It should be noted that competent instruction was being offered in Bridlington as early as 1564 (Purvis, *Tudor parish documents*, 107–108). But in the absence of endowment the school had lapsed long before Hustler's foundation.

[2] *Vide ante,* 242, 298.

[3] *Vide ante,* 234, 322, for some account of Windle's benefactions.

[4] PCC 64 Coventry 1640; *PP* 1826–1827, X, 726; *PP* 1897, LXVII, iii, Bradford, 59–64; *Bradford Antiquary,* n.s. VII (1952), 264. The school was discontinued in 1895, the endowment being thereafter used for exhibitions.

There was a school of some kind at Heptonstall on the occasion of the Archbishop's visitation in 1564,[1] taught then by an Oxford-trained schoolmaster, two of whose relations about a decade later conveyed a cottage used as the schoolhouse and certain other property towards the support of the school.[2] Whether the school was continued on a fee basis or not is quite uncertain, but it remained in any event unendowed until 1638 when a London glazier, Abraham Wall, a native of the town, who likewise founded an apprenticeship scheme for its benefit, provided a helpful initial stock. Wall left to the churchwardens as trustees £1 p.a. for the distribution of Bibles for the use of poor men's children who could read them, as well as £4 p.a. for the hire of a schoolmaster who would offer free instruction to poor children. In addition, his apprenticeship scheme yielded £3 p.a., which was to be employed each year for sending one of the scholars to London for training.[3] As so frequently happened, this was designed as a 'priming' gift. Charles Greenwood, the clergyman whose generosity created important social institutions in three West Riding towns, shortly afterwards built the schoolhouse at a cost of about £100 and by bequest in 1643 left an endowment of £410 for the support of the institution. The school was thereupon properly and carefully vested in trustees charged with its administration as well as that of an endowment of £100 which Greenwood left to the poor of Heptonstall.[4]

Finally, in our review of the schools endowed during this generation of amazing support for education, we should mention the foundation made at Newby (Seamer), in the North Riding, in 1640. A native of this village, Christopher Coulson, a successful London dyer, built a schoolhouse at an outlay of perhaps £60 which he bequeathed to trustees chosen from the principal inhabitants. To the feoffees he likewise left endowments to the value of £160, the income of which should be used for teaching poor children of the townships of Newby and Seamer, as well as providing clothing for ten of them.[5]

We have dealt, necessarily scantily, with a cultural and social accomplishment of the greatest possible importance. In the relatively

Scott (1568-1640) was graduated from Oxford in 1592 and was presented at Chastleton in that same year. Windle bequeathed him, 'then scholar at Oxford', his best gown and £10. Scott also left £2 p.a. to the poor of Haworth.

[1] The visitation speaks of 'Ric. Michill scolarem Oxoniensem ex contubernio aule beate Marie ludimagistrum apud Heptonstall . . . inveniens eum latinum callere, distincte legere, et in trivialibus artibus bene multum versatum juvenem bone indolis admisit eum ad cathechisandum pueros et ad docendum artem grammatices' (Purvis, *Tudor parish documents*, 106).

[2] *Halifax Antiq. Soc. Papers*, 1917, 141.

[3] *Vide ante*, 289.

[4] *Vide ante*, 244, 294, and *post*, 341, 355.

[5] VCH, *Yorks.*, NR, II, 293; Lawton, *Collectio*, 500; Graves, *Cleveland*, 186-189. *Vide post*, 379.

short period of forty years Yorkshire donors had founded or had endowed thirty-two schools in their county, as well as one in Lancashire.[1] These donors had vested capital in the impressive total of £16,126 to extend into every nook and cranny of this huge county the educational facilities required by a new and more exacting age. Most of these foundations were relatively small, the median having an endowment of £317, but it is notable that all save four, or possibly five, of the establishments were made in communities scarcely larger than small villages. But great as was the accomplishment of these donors, men and women drawn from all social classes, it by no means represents the full measure of the generosity of the county in creating a widely dispersed and a well-secured system of education. They gave as well the substantial total of £4551 10s for the augmentation of the resources of older endowed schools, created by their forbears, or for the founding and support of a considerable number of additional grammar and elementary schools which were not to be so securely founded as the thirty-three with which we have just been concerned. Some little attention should be lent to these often transitory but none the less significant schools, which played no unimportant role in the heroic effort being made in Yorkshire to root out the social evils of ignorance and illiteracy.

In all, Yorkshire donors of the early Stuart period gave £3840 towards the strengthening of school endowments created in the past, leaving something over £700 which was expended on a considerable number of small, recent, and scantily financed schools in all parts of the county. Some of these schools were fee- or tax-supported and are hence not properly within our preview at all; others were hopefully founded with very small gifts and simply failed to elicit the support of their communities; while others served for a generation and then disappeared. But it is important to note that we have counted, in addition to the major foundations already described, twenty-three more schools which were established during the period 1601–1640 to which at least some small charitable gift was made, a large proportion being in the West Riding, where a particularly feverish interest in education is manifest throughout the period.

Among these small foundations were Penistone Grammar School;[2] Thomas Cecil's workhouse foundation at Well which offered educational opportunities for girls;[3] a school probably founded at Mirfield in

---

[1] We have not mentioned specifically the re-founding of Cawthorne School by a decree of the Court of Revenue of the Duchy of Lancaster in 1639. The Court ordered revenues in the amount of £5 4s p.a. to be paid to this foundation from the resources of Pontefract School, which in 1583 had been endowed by the consolidation of parcels of chantry lands in five Yorkshire communities, including lands of this value in Cawthorne. (*VCH, Yorks.*, I, 477; *PP* 1826–1827, X, 744; *PP* 1895, LXXV, Cawthorne, 2–3; *Country Life*, CXXVII (June 9, 1960), 1324, where a photograph of the schoolhouse, used until 1906, may be found.) [2] *VCH, Yorks.*, I, 481. [3] *Vide ante*, 286.

1605; and the almshouse foundation at Firby, established by John Clapham in 1608, whose master was bound to teach six boys without fee.[1] Thomas Remington, a husbandman of Clapham, left land as the site for a schoolhouse there in 1611,[2] while in the next year William Laycock, probably a London grocer, established a trust with an endowment of £67 for the founding of a school at Silsden which would serve that township and nearby Steeton.[3] An elementary school was established in Halifax in *ca.* 1610 by those two remarkable sisters, Ellen Hopkinson and Jane Crowther, as part of their almshouse foundation, and by will in 1614 Jane Crowther, provided an endowment of £160 to support a schoolmaster 'who shall teach the children of the poorest people . . . to know their duties towards God and enable them the better unto several services in the church or commonwealth',[4] to which Isabel Maud added a bequest of £10 in the same year.[5] There is clear evidence that a school was being kept at Bolton-by-Bowland in 1616 when a local husbandman left £1 for the support of the master,[6] and similarly that a school was being built in Ripponden (Halifax) in 1621 when Gilbert Rayner bequeathed £2 towards its completion.[7] John Hanson, a lawyer related to the Saviles, in 1621 established a small endowment of £20 value to secure the founding of an elementary school at Rastrick,[8] while a clergyman's bequest of his Cowper's *Dictionary* and a standing desk to the free school at Gisburn offers proof that it was in 1626 well established.[9] There seems to have been a school at Long Riston in 1636 when John Bankes, a tanner, left 1d to each of the scholars enrolled there, and also at Kirkby Malzeard where in 1640 Timothy [or Gilbert] Horseman bequeathed £100 to maintain in perpetuity five poor scholars, half the income to be employed for their instruction and half for their clothing.[10] In the same year a clergyman of Ilkley, Richard Hodgshon, left lands with a capital worth of upwards of £80 to his wife for life and then to trustees for the foundation of a free school in the hamlet of Flaxby (Goldsborough).[11] These examples are but suggestive of the immense

---

[1] *Vide ante*, 267.   [2] PCY 31/687 1611.

[3] Lawton, *Collectio*, 260; *PP* 1825, XI, 637.   [4] *Vide ante*, 267.

[5] *Halifax Antiq. Soc. Papers*, 1921, 161, 1924, 202; Walker, *Halifax parish registers*, 5. She was the wife of John Maud, who was a supporter of the grammar school in Halifax. She also left £8 for loans to tradesmen, £20 to Coley chapel, and £40 to Dr Favour.   [6] PCY 34/23 1616 (William Ellill).

[7] *Halifax Antiq. Soc. Trans.*, 1931, 121–122.

[8] *VCH, Yorks.*, I, 482; Turner, *Biographia Halifaxiensis*, 338; Midgley, *Halifax*, 488. There had earlier been a chantry school in the town. Hanson, a cousin to Sir John Savile, also gave £1 5s to Halifax School and left a fund of £16 to 'set poor and honest workmen in labour' at clothmaking in Rastrick.

[9] PCY 39/517 1626 (Henry Man).

[10] PCY March 1642; *VCH, Yorks.*, I, 492; *PP* 1820, V, 424.

[11] CCY February 3, 1640; *PP* 1897, LXVII, iv, Goldsborough, 5–7; *Alum. cantab.*, I, ii, 386; *VCH, Yorks.*, I, 492.

thrust of aspiration which was in two generations to create a system of widely dispersed and effective popular education in this once backward county.

So powerful were the forces which were persuading substantial men of the pressing need for the completion of the educational system of the county that there was no diminution in giving to schools during the period of grave unsettlement stretching from 1641 to the Restoration. In the course of these two troubled decades, a total of £11,816 was designated by donors for school endowments, a rate of giving somewhat greater even than that we have observed in the early Stuart period. These foundations were continued without any visible interruption during the tense years of the Civil War, there being, however, a marked pause from the time of the execution of the King until the establishment of the Protectorate signalled even for Yorkshire the restoration of political and social stability. Towards the close of our period, therefore, and particularly during the last four years, there was an almost explosive interval in which numerous and large foundations were made by donors in every part of the county. Some measure of the strength and significance of aspirations during the closing years of our period may be gained when we observe that in the final decade the enormous total of £9398 was poured into grammar-school foundations and that nearly the whole of this (£9005) was given during the last four years of the interval.

The earliest of the foundations made during the revolutionary period was, fittingly enough, that of Richard Rands, a Puritan clergyman, who in 1641 founded a free grammar school at Fishlake, the village of his birth in the West Riding. The donor conveyed to four trustees the sum of £300 as the endowment for his school which should offer instruction without fees of any sort to all the eligible children of the parish. The master should be a university graduate and should enroll no students not prepared to enter upon the study of Latin or who had not 'entered into the accidence'.[1] Shortly afterwards, in 1643, another clergyman, Charles Greenwood, a principal benefactor of the county and the founder of the school at Heptonstall, by will stipulated that the sum of £500 owed to him by his friend Sir William Savile should be employed by Savile, Sir George Radcliffe,[2] and Thomas Nettleton as feoffees to establish a free grammar school at Thornhill. The trustees expended £100 of the *corpus* of the trust for the purchase of a suitable schoolhouse and disposed the remaining £400 as endowment with which a competent schoolmaster was employed with a stipend of £20 p.a.[3] A more modest foundation was made at about the same time at Hepworth (in the chapelry of Holmfirth) by Richard Charlesworth, a husbandman

---

[1] *Vide ante*, 244. [2] Greenwood's first cousin.
[3] *Vide ante*, 244, 294, 338, and *post*, 355.

of the village, who devised lands with an estimated worth of £80 for the use of a free school to be built in that community.[1]

A rich merchant of York, James Hutchinson, who had been mayor in 1634, in *ca*. 1642 built a schoolhouse and a master's lodging at Fremington (Grinton), his birthplace in the North Riding. Hutchinson by will dated 1643 endowed the school with lands then worth about £400 for the support of a qualified master. The foundation was conveyed to local trustees, with the provision that the school should be open to all qualified students of Grinton parish, sons of poor men to pay no fee, and others to pay no more than a 1s entrance fee, a tuition of no more than 2s p.a., and 8d p.a. for fuel for the master.[2] At about the same date, 1642, that remarkable woman, Mary Ward, returned after a lifetime spent abroad to establish first at Hutton Rudby and then at Haworth (near York) a Catholic community of women. The Institute of Mary, which at least until the death of the founder offered instruction to girls of northern Catholic families, was left unendowed and then withered in the blast of revolution already at hand.[3]

A school was built at Barnsley in 1646 with a bequest of £50 left for that purpose by Edmund Rogers, a considerable yeoman of the community, though there is no evidence that it was endowed during our period.[4] In the following year, Anthony Sawdrie, the parson at Harewood, who endowed an apprenticeship scheme for Wath-upon-Dearne and nearby communities, likewise by will bestowed a rent-charge of £2 13s 4d p.a. to trustees to serve as the stipend for a schoolmaster

---

[1] *PP* 1828, XX, 559; *VCH, Yorks.*, I, 492.

[2] PCY July 1648; *VCH, Yorks., NR*, I, 245; *PP* 1822, X, 698; *Surtees Soc. Pub.*, CII (1899), 55; Torr, *Antiquities of York*, 98–99; Drake, *Eboracum*, 222; Auden, *Survey of York*, 252. Hutchinson also left £10 to the poor and a silver basin and ewer valued at about £10 to the City of York.

[3] Coleridge, H. J., ed., *St. Mary's Covent, York* (L., 1887), 1–8; DNB (Supplement); Morrell, *Biography of common man of York*, 163; *VCH, Yorks., NR*, II, 165. One wishes that more were known about this community. Mary Ward was born near Ripon in 1585. She was educated at the convent of the Colettines in St Omer, leaving it in 1607 determined to found a female order expressly for English women. Obtaining land near Gravelines, she established a convent in a temporary dwelling in St Omer, with five nuns transferred thence; in 1609 she endowed the convent with most of her property, leaving it to found still another community in St Omer, dedicated to the teaching of young girls. In 1611 she decided to adopt the canons of the Jesuits for her order, and in that year an affiliated house was established in London. A second subordinate house was founded at Liege in 1617, while others followed in Cologne, Trier, and Rome (1622). She was befriended by the Emperor Ferdinand, who provided a foundation for her in Vienna in 1627. She returned to London in 1639, founding a house in the Strand about which little is known. With a Civil War at hand, she retired to Yorkshire in 1642 where she died in 1645, being buried by a conniving Anglican clergyman in Osbaldwick churchyard.

[4] *Vide ante*, 245, for a biographical notice and for further discussion of Rogers' well-considered charities for his county.

there who should teach poor children of Wath, Brampton Bierlow, and Swinton.[1] A gifted and testy Puritan gentleman, George Abbot, in 1647 established an elementary school in York, devising to trustees £130 in capital, the income of which was to be used to employ a schoolmaster or mistress to teach small children 'to read perfectly'. The endowment supplied a stipend of £5 p.a. for the teacher, while £1 10s p.a. should be employed to furnish the children with needed books and catechisms, and the remainder (£1 10s) was 'to be bestowed in Bibles to such poor people as will not imbezel them'.[2] A Puritan clergyman, William Plaxton, in 1650 founded a school at Rossington, where he served as rector for nearly forty years. The donor by deed conveyed to five trustees landed property then valued at about £133 as an endowment to ensure a stipend of at least £6 13s 4d p.a. for a 'sufficient and painful' schoolmaster to teach the children of the community, 'as well the poor as the rich'. Plaxton's educational scheme, despite the meagre endowment, was ambitious, since the school was to provide instruction not only in reading and writing but in the classical curriculum as well.[3]

These foundations, made during the first decade of the revolutionary period, were all small institutions, save for Fishlake, Thornhill, and Fremington, and were designed to assist remote rural communities too distant from existing schools to benefit from the now rich and widespread educational facilities of the county. This was the case, as well, with the foundation made at Stannington (Ecclesfield) in 1653 by Richard Spoone, a devout and substantial yeoman of that community. Spoone, who in 1652 had built a chapel for Stannington, by his will not only provided an endowment for a minister in the village, but left as well a stock with a value of about £80, the income to serve as the stipend for a schoolmaster who should teach the poor children of the neighbourhood 'whose parents were willing, but not able to keep them

[1] Vide ante, 289.

[2] PCC 54 Fairfax 1649; Hargrove, History of York, III, 654; Lawton, Collectio, 27; PP 1825, XI, 612; DNB; Alum. cantab., I, i, 1. Abbot (1603–1649) was the son of Sir Thomas Abbot of Easington, Yorkshire. He was graduated from Cambridge in 1622 and was made a fellow of Merton College in the same year. He was a learned layman, his Whole book of Job (1640) being a work of ripe and acute scholarship and his Vindiciae Sabbathi (1641) having a significant effect on the Sabbatarian controversy. Abbot married a daughter of Col. Purefoy of Caldecote, Warwickshire, where he resided. He defended the manor house against Prince Rupert and was elected to Parliament for Tamworth in 1645, serving until his death in 1649.

[3] PCC 5 Aylett 1655; Alum. cantab., I, iii, 371; PP 1826–1827, X, 796; Lawton, Collectio, 549. Plaxton was graduated from Cambridge (St John's) in 1603 and was incorporated at Oxford in 1606. Licensed to preach in 1608, he was preferred as Rector of Rossington in 1614, serving there until 1652. He left £2 to the poor of his parish, £10 7s to the poor of Pocklington, and £4 to the poor of Doncaster.

to school'.[1] A London merchant, Matthew Broadley, in 1651 made most generous provision for the founding of a grammar school in Hipperholme, then a small village just to the northeast of Halifax. Broadley, a native of the place, had, as we have seen, also created a substantial endowment for the care of the poor of the community. The donor by will allocated £40 for the building of the schoolhouse, while his nephew and executor, who was given considerable discretionary powers, settled on trustees £500 for the purchase of lands and a rent-charge of £5 p.a., which, subject to an allotment of £2 12s p.a. for bread for the poor, should be used for the support of a graduate schoolmaster to 'educate and instruct in grammar and other literature' the children of the township without any charge whatsoever.[2] A chapel and school were also built and endowed in 1653 by Stephen Cawood, a yeoman of East Hardwick. Cawood by deed settled on trustees lands worth upwards of £260, which were charged with the payment of £12 to a schoolmaster, being also the minister, who should maintain a free school for all children who desired to improve themselves in learning.[3] An elementary school was founded in Hemingbrough in 1654 with the modest endowment of £40,[4] while in 1657 William Hide, the minister at Market Weighton, whose substantial charities for his parish have in part been noted, founded a school for the township of Shipton with an endowment of £120.[5] Two other small foundations were made in that remarkable year, 1657, when in all six schools were established in various parts of the county. A London grocer, William Underwood, who had established an endowment of £100 for the relief of poor widows of Ripon, likewise left a capital bequest of £60 value for the founding of an elementary school in the parish, where the children of poor parents might be taught to read and write,[6] while John Crook, a Sheffield donor of uncertain social status, provided an endowment with which a schoolmistress should be employed to hold a petty school in which poor children might be taught to read.[7]

As we have previously noted, Elizabeth, Viscountess Lumley in 1657

[1] PCC 90 Brent 1653; Dale, Bryan (T. G. Crippen, ed.), *Yorkshire Puritanism* (Bradford, 1909), 48; *PP* 1828, XI, 565; *PP* 1894, LXIV, Ecclesfield, 7–10, 77–83. *Vide post*, 381, 399.   [2] *Vide ante*, 249.

[3] Saywell, J. L., *Parochial history of Ackworth* (Pontefract, 1894), 195–196; *PP* 1826, XIII, 646; *PP*, 1898, LXVIII, Pontefract, 11–12, 61–64; Lawton, *Collectio*, 151. *Vide post*, 381, 399. Cawood also left £1 10s p.a. to the poor and endowed the clergyman's stipend with £6 10s p.a.

[4] Burton, *Hemingbrough*, 141–142, 352.

[5] *Vide ante*, 249, and *post*, 382.   [6] *Vide ante*, 249.

[7] Hunter, *Hallamshire*, 188, 202; *PP* 1897, LXVII, iii, Sheffield, 305; Leader, R. E., *Company of Cutlers* (Sheffield, 1905–1906, 2 vols.), I, 265. This donor was either the John Crook who was curate of Ecclesall, in Sheffield parish, from 1656 to 1659, or a cutler of the same name, master of his company in 1637, and Town Collector, who died in 1669.

created a great charitable trust for the benefit of the parishes of Thornton Dale, Pickering, and Sinnington, in which an almshouse foundation was combined with schools. Approximately half the capital vested, or £1250, was disposed by the trustees 'for the schooling, instructing and teaching of the said parishes and reading of prayers, morning and evening', while about £125 was expended for the erection of suitable quarters to serve the educational objectives of the trust. Grammar schools were erected at Thornton Dale and Pickering, while an elementary school at Sinnington eventually gained its support from the foundation. In addition, Lady Lumley's arrangement provided a scholarship fund of £40 p.a. for the support at Oxford or Cambridge of scholars from the three favoured parishes.[1] In the next year, 1658, another woman donor, Anne Middleton, a merchant's widow of York, whose great almshouse foundation has been discussed, bequeathed £1000 for the building and endowment of a free grammar school at Shipton in the North Riding, the school to be built in the form of a chapel. The executors applied £360 of the legacy towards the construction of the building, devoting the remainder, with accumulations of income, for the purchase of lands as endowment, which at the outset produced a most generous income of £40 p.a. for the support of the work of the institution.[2] Another North Riding school was established in the same year (1658) under the terms of the will of Michael Sydall, the vicar of Catterick, who left £500 to trustees for the building and endowment of a small almshouse and a free grammar school. The donor stipulated that £400 of the *corpus* of the trust should be employed for the maintenance of the school, whose master was to have £20 p.a. as a stipend. The master should be a graduate of a university, must be well versed in Greek and Latin, and should be prepared to teach those tongues and their literatures to qualified students of the region without any charge.[3]

A school at Calverley which had been maintained in the churchyard on a fee basis for some years past was in 1658 more permanently constituted under the terms of the will of Joseph Hillary, a clothworker and a former mayor of Leeds, who on his death made extremely generous and well-considered bequests for the support of the basic institutions of Calverley. Among these, Hillary left properties valued at £160 for the maintenance of the schoolmaster and for the purchase of books and other needs of poor scholars in the school.[4] In the same year Sarah Gledhill, the spinster daughter of a gentle family seated at Barkisland and with substantial interests in the wool trade, bequeathed to trustees the sum of £200 for the founding of a school in the town for the education of poor children whose parents could not afford to send them away

---

[1] *Vide ante,* 279, and *post,* 356.   [2] *Vide ante,* 279, 291.
[3] *Vide ante,* 280. Because of a provision in favour of Sydall's wife and mother, the school and almshouse were not built until 1688.   [4] *Vide ante,* 250.

for their instruction. The endowment was to be invested in lands and the whole profit paid for a qualified schoolmaster who should teach the children the elementary subjects and provide more advanced educational opportunities if the feoffees were so disposed and if the income would permit.[1]

Cromwell's physician, John Bathurst, who had made generous provision for the poor and for apprenticeships in the general region of Richmond, where he had once been schoolmaster, by his will proved in 1660 founded three schools in small and somewhat remote communities in the North Riding, which he endowed with a total of £580. He charged his manor of Clint with £1 p.a. to pay a master to teach reading and writing at Marske, while at Helwith (New Forest) he founded a grammar school in which both the elementary disciplines and Latin should be taught by a competent master who was to have an annual stipend of £12. The third foundation was made in the then remote parish of Arkengarthdale, the lordship of which he had purchased in 1656 and with whose tenants he had quarrelled violently, in which he endowed a grammar school with a most adequate annual income of £16 for the support of the schoolmaster.[2]

That astute and generous lady, Dame Mary Bolles, in the closing years of our period founded a carefully devised grammar school at Warmfield in conjunction with her apprenticeship endowment there. She conveyed to feoffees a building valued at £80 to serve as a schoolhouse and by deed endowed the institution with lands then possessing a capital worth of £400. A schoolmaster was to be appointed with an annual salary of £12, who should offer instruction in grammar to ten poor boys on her foundation, of whom one each year should be suitably apprenticed by the trustees. In addition, the master might take up to twenty other youths, presumably paying a suitable tuition, to bring the school to its full enrolment. From the income on the trust £4 p.a. was to be employed for fitting poor and deserving children elsewhere in the elementary subjects, since no one was to be admitted to the school until prepared for the classical curriculum contemplated.[3] In the same year, Brian Cooke, whose great almshouse foundation at Arksey has been mentioned, by will established a grammar school foundation for that community with the generous endowment of £800, from the income

---

[1] PCC 51 Wootton 1658; *PP* 1828, XX, 591; *PP* 1899, LXXI, 590–595; Ormerod, H., ed., *Parish registers of Elland* (Oxford, 1917), 199; *Yorks. Arch. Soc. Rec.*, IX (1890), 121–122; Turner, *Biographia Halifaxiensis*, 10–11; Thoresby, *Ducatus*, 14; *VCH, Yorks.*, I, 484. This young woman was aged only twenty at the time of her death; she was sister to Thomas Gledhill (*vide post*, 382), and John Harrison, the great benefactor of Leeds, was her great-uncle (*vide ante*, 277). Her family had established itself amongst the lower gentry by the purchase of the manor in 1612.

[2] *Vide ante*, 250, 291, and *post*, 356.   [3] *Vide ante*, 279, 291.

of which the master was to have the considerable salary of £40 p.a. The terms of the bequest were administered by the testator's brother and heir, George Cooke, who some time after our period (1683) provided a bequest of £200 for the erection of a more suitable building for the school.[1] We may conclude with the foundation made by Thomas Keresforth at Barnsley by deed in June, 1660, of a well-endowed and thoughtfully constituted grammar school. Keresforth, of a family of lesser gentry long seated at Keresforth Hill, conveyed to ten trustees a schoolhouse which he had recently built. He devised as well lands with a then capital value of slightly less than £400, they yielding a clear rental of £19 12s 2d p.a., for the support of the foundation. The master, who must be a university graduate, should admit and teach without charge all children, natives of Barnsley, Dodworth, and Keresforth Hill, whose parents were not accounted worth £200 in lands and goods, until such students were prepared for the universities or had been settled in some useful occupations. All other students admitted, they too being natives of the three favoured communities, were to be taught for fees not more than half those prevailing in other schools in that part of the county. The trustees were likewise most carefully enjoined to make certain that the charity students received precisely the instruction gained by those drawn from more substantial families.[2]

There were, in addition to these endowed institutions, a number of attempts made to institute new schools without endowment or foundations made with most meagre resources which left them exposed to the hazards of eighteenth-century neglect. Thus a school was evidently being built at Eastfield-Silkstone (in Thurgoland) in 1658 when Richard Cudworth, a gentleman of the parish, left £5 towards its construction.[3] A yeoman, Robert Slinger, in 1658 apparently gave something like £60 for the founding of an elementary school in the hamlet of Beckermonds (Hubberholme), the school being maintained for some time in a single room in the town.[4] There was likewise a school of some sort at Bolton in 1659, to which John Walker, a yeoman, left £5 for support.[5] Other instances could be cited to suggest that even at the close of our period

[1] Vide ante, 280, and post, 383.

[2] PCY 55/269 1674; PP 1826–1827, X, 764–765; PP 1896, LXIII, ii, Silkstone, 3–4, 17; Smith, Old Yorkshire, n.s., I, 154; Yorks. Arch. Soc. Rec., XX (1896), 55–56. The donor was the son of Gabriel Keresforth of Keresforth Hill. Keresforth pleaded before the Committee on Compounding that he had taken no active part in the Civil War, though he had been forced to assume the post of collector for the King. His own presentation of the facts would suggest that he tried desperately to remain neutral. None the less he was fined £160 in December, 1645 and £54 15s a year later.

[3] PCC 272 Wootton 1658; Yorks. Arch. Soc. Rec., IX (1890), 129.

[4] PCC 66 Nabbs 1660; Pontefract, Ella, Wharfedale (L., 1938), 30.

[5] PCC 455 Pell 1659.

men and women of the county were still not content with the magnificent accomplishment whose annal we have so briefly recited.

The great effort by which private benefactions had created an educational system in Yorkshire closed, therefore, in 1660 with a most impressive velocity. In the last twenty years of our period twenty-nine endowed institutions had been founded, bringing to a climax a century and more of devoted concern of donors for the needs, cultural and social, of their county. As will be recalled, there were at the outset of our period only six functioning grammar schools in Yorkshire, none of which was either well or securely endowed. It is therefore not too much to say that the whole of the great achievement we have recorded must be credited to prescient and socially sensitive men of the early modern era. These donors had vested what was for this age the vast sum of £48,572 16s to secure the founding of exactly one hundred grammar or elementary schools spread across the length and breadth of the county, as well as three in other counties. Yorkshire had, then, at the close of our period 106 endowed schools, of which roughly half possessed at least comfortably adequate funds for the period. In addition, we have at least some record of giving to 38 unendowed or scantily endowed institutions, most of which were not to be generously strengthened.[1] This means that benefactors had vested Yorkshire with an endowed school for every 57 square miles of the huge area of this great and partially mountainous county, as compared, for example, with a school for every 50 square miles of area in the older and more settled county of Kent or one for every 73 square miles in the proud and rich county of Norfolk. More pertinently, it may be said that save for two mountainous and thinly populated stretches of the county no boy in 1660 could have lived more than 12 miles from an endowed school with all the opportunities that were opened to youth by its beneficent presence. It is probably not too much to suggest that in 1660 Yorkshire enjoyed a more widespread and competent system of secondary education, wholly the achievement of private charity, than it was to have again until the full intervention of the state occurred in the later nineteenth century.

Few of these schools were richly endowed, for relatively few were the creations of rich donors. Their resources were measured out most frugally, and their needs stood as a constant invitation to later benefactors to add strength to strength as the inroads of the inflationary process and the requirements of an expanding population laid further demands on already limited endowments. Still, by the close of our period, forty-six of these grammar schools possessed liquid resources of £400 or more,

---

[1] These figures may be compared with those supplied by Professor Dickens, whose comments on the lively interest of Yorkshire in education are of great value. (Dickens, *Lollards and Protestants*, 4–6.) We are, of course, concerned only with those schools founded as charitable endowments.

which may be regarded as roughly the minimum of suitable resources for a small and free grammar school at this date.

The schools of Yorkshire had been founded by many men of many classes, but on the whole with a complexion of social support separating the county rather markedly from the others we have studied. As is to be expected in the earlier decades, down to the coming of the Reformation, a large proportion had been founded by churchmen, of which the county bred so many. But in Yorkshire this clerical support was continued for a full generation longer than in most of England, one would suppose because the county produced so many clerk-lawyers, who very often carved out considerable fortunes, and because younger sons of the gentry still found a career in the church in this somewhat old-fashioned county. Thirty-five schools, spread remarkably evenly over the whole of our long period, were founded by churchmen, eleven of these by prelates and twenty-four by members of the lower clergy. The county differs from most, too, in the relatively important role played by its nobility in the assumption of some measure of social and cultural responsibility, for six school foundations were made by members of that social class. An equal number were endowed by the upper gentry of the county, while sixteen were founded by members of the lower gentry, a fair proportion of whom disposed fortunes actually made in trade in York or in London. It seems remarkable that, in a county in which the yeomanry was economically weak, eight schools were founded by members of this class and that one was the contribution of a husband-man, though it may be mentioned that four of the yeomen had clearly combined farming with some specialized and presumably profitable activity in the cloth industry.

The schools of Yorkshire were, then, largely the contribution of two social groups, roughly a third having been founded by the clergy and a somewhat larger proportion by the various landed classes.[1] In all, twenty-eight, or somewhat more than a fourth of the schools of the county, were the gift of the several urban classes, these donors assuming a dominant responsibility at about the opening of the seventeenth century. It is particularly interesting to observe that ten of the 103 endowed foundations were the gifts of London merchants and tradesmen, all of whom were natives of the county and all of whom made particularly carefully considered foundations to secure the opening of opportunity in the town or village of their birth. The total of the endowments provided by this group of donors was £3082, suggesting of course a substantial average founding benefaction. Local merchants of York, Hull, and Halifax founded five schools in the county, while Yorkshire's tradesmen were responsible for three. There were four more which can most accurately

---

[1] It should be said that one school was founded by judicial decree and that two were established by persons of unknown social status.

be described as the handiwork of burgher effort, they being schools built in vigorous and growing West Riding towns in which the burgher aristocracy simply decided that a school was needed and then by community effort provided the required resources. Lawyers, and we here mean common lawyers, endowed three of Yorkshire's schools, while three were the gift of a physician, Dr Bathurst, whose fortune was made in London but most carefully invested, and ultimately disposed, in his native county. Many men of many classes had joined together to raise up in Yorkshire the most effective of all the instrumentalities with which poverty may be combated and with which hope and opportunity may be diffused through the whole complex structure of that society which is the modern community.

(b.) *Scholarships and Fellowships.* The interest of Yorkshire donors in education was, however, by no means limited to the founding and endowment of schools. The county is notable too for its strong and persistent effort to provide scholarship and fellowship resources wherewith poor youths might gain full opportunity for the use of the educational facilities which the age had created. During the course of our period donors provided the impressive total of £14,096. 14s for scholarship purposes, this being 5·78 per cent of the charitable funds of the shire, a proportion exceeded, and that but slightly, only in the county of Norfolk among all those treated in this study.[1] Since almost the whole of this total (99·54 per cent) was vested in capital form, something more than £700 of income must have been available for the support of aspiring scholars by the close of our period, an amount sufficient to maintain nearly a hundred scholars in the grammar schools of the county and in the universities.

It is noteworthy that the accumulation of these most valuable resources proceeded steadily through the whole course of our period, adding vastly to the cultural inheritance of the whole Yorkshire community. Many of these foundations were inextricably connected with grammar-school trusts and have been more appropriately mentioned in our discussion of the schools, but there remain a number of these benefactions which should be at least briefly treated.

In 1502 John Forman, for many years Vicar of Royston and the founder of the school in that parish, established a fellowship at Oxford with a capital of about £80 for the benefit of his blood kin or, that failing, a deserving applicant from his birthplace, Rothwell, or from Royston.[2] In the next year another priest, Hugh Trotter, Precentor of York, by will founded a fellowship at Queens' College, Cambridge, with a capital

---

[1] The proportion of total charitable funds dedicated to scholarship programmes in the several counties ranges from 0·51 per cent for Bristol to 5·95 per cent for Norfolk.   [2] *Vide ante,* 307.

worth of £253. 7s,[1] while shortly afterwards Martin Collins, his successor as Treasurer of York Cathedral, endowed an exhibition in each university with a total stock of £56.[2] The Rector of Long Marston, William Ackroyd, in 1518 bequeathed an exhibition in either university, with a preference for founder's kin but with residual benefits for the parishes of Marston and Hutton, it having been originally endowed with lands possessing a capital value of £87, which by the close of the nineteenth century were worth nearly £27,000.[3] A pious and kindly layman, Sir Marmaduke Constable, high sheriff of the county, by gift and bequest provided a total of £360 for a fellowship and four scholarships at Cambridge, the fellowship to be in the tenure of a priest who should pray for the soul of the donor.[4]

The principal support lent to scholarship and fellowship resources prior to the Reformation came in Yorkshire almost wholly from the clergy. Thus in 1521 Robert Duckett, a native of Yorkshire but at his death the Rector of Chevening, Kent, founded two scholarships with a capital value of £98 in St John's College, Cambridge, with indicated parochial preferences, but otherwise for any candidate from Yorkshire.[5] A Bedfordshire clergyman, Robert Halitreholm, who was a native of Beverley, in 1525 founded a fellowship, also in St John's College, with an endowment of £120 for a fellow 'born within the towne of Beverley', or, that failing, from the county at large.[6] John Dowman, Archdeacon of

---

[1] PCY 6/83 1503; *Surtees Soc. Pub.*, LIII (1868), 219–221; Cooper, *Memorials of Cambridge*, I, 300; Gray, J. H., *Queens' College* (L., 1899), 39; *Alum. cantab.*, I, iv, 268; Drake, *Eboracum*, 568. Trotter also left seven books to Cambridge, £1 for church general, £2 for church repairs, and £24 13s for prayers. He was graduated B.A. from Cambridge in 1470 and was made a fellow of Queens' in 1490. He held numerous livings and several important administrative appointments at York.   [2] *Vide ante*, 229.

[3] PCY 27/146 1518; *Surtees Soc. Pub.*, LXXIX (1884), 96–98; *PP* 1896, LXIII, ii, Batley, 14–15, 18; Gilbert, *Liber scholasticus*, 467–470; *Halifax Antiq. Soc. Papers*, 1911, 199; Sheard, *Batley*, 192. Ackroyd was a son of Richard Ackroyd, a rich landholder of Hebden Bridge. He was ordained a sub-deacon of York in 1463 and was made Rector of Marston in 1477.

[4] PCY 9/95 1520; *VCH, Yorks.*, III, 276; *Surtees Soc. Pub.*, LXXIX (1884), 88–93; *PP* 1825, XI, 615; Cooper, *Memorials of Cambridge*, II, 91; Baker, *St. John's College*, II, 96; Howard, *Finances of St. John's*, 293; DNB. The head of the house of Constable (at Flamborough) 'Little Sir Marmaduke', as he was known, was a capable soldier and a trusted servant of several kings. At 70 years he with Sir Edward Howard in 1513 commanded a wing at Flodden. His will ordered that there should be no funeral doles disbursed, but rather alms given in eight parishes, in the amount of about £80, according to particulars laid out in memoranda. His epitaph, in Flamborough church, is famous.

[5] Mayor, *Early statutes of St. John's College*, 400–404; Baker, *St. John's College*, I, 481, 547; Smith, *Old Yorkshire*, n.s., I, 150; *Alum. cantab.*, I, ii, 71.

[6] PCY 9/366 1527; *Surtees Soc. Pub.*, LXXIX (1884), 202–203; *VCH, Yorks.*, I, 426; *Alum. cantab.*, I, ii, 284; Cooper, *Memorials of Cambridge*, II, 92. He was Rector of Biddenham, Bedfordshire.

Suffolk, but a native of Pocklington where he had founded a grammar school, in 1525 established five scholarships at St John's College, Cambridge, with an endowment of at least £140 for scholars educated in his free grammar school and on the nomination of the master, the vicar, and the churchwardens,[1] while a few years later, in 1528 and by a second conveyance in 1535, Roger Lupton, the founder of Sedbergh Grammar School, vested the munificent endowment of £1000 in St John's College, with which Yorkshire had such close connections, for the maintenance of two fellows and eight scholars 'who have issued from my grammar school at Sedbergh', with a preference for men from Sedbergh, Dent, and Garsdale.[2] Still another fellowship endowment was vested in St John's College by Dame Joan Rokeby in 1525, with a stock of £170 and with an indicated preference for a scholar from Beverley.[3] William Clifton, Subdean of York, in 1538 established a fellowship at Brasenose College, Oxford, for a fellow from Yorkshire or Lincolnshire, with an estimated endowment of £100,[4] while by this will proved in 1540 Brian Higden, Dean of York, completed the pre-Reformation foundations with a bequest of £110 for a fellow, also at Brasenose, to be chosen alternately from Yorkshire and Lincolnshire.[5]

The Reformation undoubtedly had a most damaging immediate effect on the founding of scholarship endowments in the county, in part because it so seriously weakened the resources of the clerical group who had been the principal donors and in part because new classes of benefactors were not yet prepared to undertake a responsibility which in its very nature implied intimate contacts with the needs and life of the universities. From 1541 to 1580 we have recorded a total of no more than £62 16s given for scholarship needs, almost the whole of this amount having been dedicated to scholarships in local grammar schools.

[1] Vide ante, 307.   [2] Vide ante, 308.

[3] VCH, Yorks., I, 427; Baker, St. John's College, I, 354, 360; Oliver, Beverley, 179; Cooper, Memorials of Cambridge, II, 92; Smith, Old Yorkshire, n.s., II, 145. She was the widow of Sir Richard Rokeby of London and Beverley. (Vide post, 401).

[4] Skelton, Pietas oxon., 65; Alum. oxon., I, 292; Wood, Anthony (Philip Bliss, ed.), Fasti oxonienses (L., 1815, 1820, 2 vols.), I, 45; Brasenose College quartercentenary monographs (Oxford, 1909, 3 vols.), I, iv, 12, v, 13. A canon lawyer, Clifton was appointed succentor at York in 1522 and subdean in 1529, serving in that capacity until his death in 1548.

[5] PCC 19 Crumwell 1540; Brasenose monographs, I, iv, 14 (where the gift is dated 1549); Alum. oxon., II, 706; Surtees Soc. Pub., CXVI (1908), 162–163; Skelton, Pietas oxon., 65; Drake, Eboracum, 496. Higden also left £7 13s to the poor of various parishes, £9 for general church uses, £5 to clergy, £18 1s for church repairs, and £40 for prayers. A graduate of Oxford, he was successively appointed Rector of Buckenham, Norfolk (1508), of Kirkby (1511) and Nettleton (1513) in Lincolnshire, and Canon of Lincoln, in 1508. He was made Archdeacon of the West Riding in 1515, Prebendary of York in 1516, and Dean in 1516.

It was not until 1587 that another really substantial foundation was made, and this was the gift of a London merchant who was Yorkshire bred. Henry Hebblethwaite, a draper, settled on St John's College, Cambridge, the generous capital of £500 to secure the support there of one fellow and two scholars, graduates of Sedbergh Grammar School being preferred in the appointments.[1] Shortly afterwards, in 1592, the then Vicar of Methley left an endowment of £5 p.a. for the support of two scholars at University College, Oxford, with a preference for men from Swinton, Wath, Methley, and Kirkburton, but otherwise from the county at large.[2] Just a year later, in 1591, Lady Catherine Constable of Kirby Knowle bequeathed £200 of endowment for the maintenance at Trinity College, Oxford, of a scholar from Halsham Grammar School, the capital being vested, unfortunately, in private trustees. She likewise created an endowment sufficient to provide an annual stipend of £6 13s to apprentice some worthy but less able boy who had received his education in the same school.[3]

The largest of the Elizabethan scholarship foundations was that created in 1592 by John Frieston, a member of the lesser gentry of the West Riding who likewise was the founder of an almshouse and of a well-endowed school in his native county.[4] Frieston conveyed to trustees lands which he had purchased in 1588 for £532 for the benefit of Emmanuel College, Cambridge, for the support there of scholars to be appointed from Yorkshire. He also conveyed to University College, Oxford, lands in Pontefract for a fellowship, with a stipend of £10, and for two scholarships, each to yield £5 p.a., suggesting a total capital worth of £400, while the college was to have as well £5 p.a. from the endowment for its own uses.[5] At about the same date (1594) a more modest endowment was bequeathed to St John's College, Cambridge, by James Sedgwick, a gentleman of Sedbergh, for a scholarship 'in the same manner that Doctor Luptons ar', for a scholar to be chosen from Sedbergh Grammar School,[6] while two years later a merchant and for-

---

[1] *Vide ante*, 308–309.

[2] CCY, date of probate unknown, will dated 1592; Skelton, *Pietas oxon.*, 11; *Thoresby Soc. Pub.*, XXXV (1934), 51–52; Morehouse, H. J., *History of Kirkburton* (Huddersfield, 1861), 65; *Alum. oxon.*, II, 771. This donor, Otho Hunt, was a native of Swinton. He was graduated from Oxford in 1559 and was presented to the vicarage of Kirkburton in 1562. He was made Rector of Methley in 1567 and was also a fellow of University College.

[3] *Vide ante*, 292–293. The will looks valid, but it appears that no scholar was ever appointed on the foundation. The lands underlying the bequest had by 1674 come into the hands of private owners.   [4] *Vide ante*, 263, 322.

[5] The lands conveyed to University College were in time to become extremely valuable, yielding in 1897 a total of £1688 12s p.a., distributed according to an elaborate schedule.

[6] *Vide ante*, 234, for an account of this donor's endowment for the poor. His charitable bequests totalled £284 18s and were for a variety of purposes.

mer mayor of Hull, John Gregory, left lands of an estimated capital worth of £100 for the maintenance of two poor scholars at 'St. John's or some other Cambridge college'.[1] Towards the close of the Elizabethan age, during which a total of £2250 12s was dedicated to scholarship endowments, Thomas Cartwright of Brodsworth vested in private trustees an endowment with a capital worth of £200 for a scholar in either university, with a preference for his own kin, the scholar to be named by the Dean and Chapter of York.[2]

There was slowly increasing support for the scholarship needs of the county during the early Stuart decades, when a total of £2548 3s of capital was provided for numerous endowments. The earliest of these foundations was made in 1604 by a gentleman of Giggleswick parish who was the last survivor of the original group of governors of the school there. Henry Tenant conveyed by deed £100 to the school governors to buy lands to be 'emploied first for . . . the better mantaynance of Josias Shute . . . in Cambridge . . . and from yeare to yeare for ever for . . . mantayninge of such schollers within the Universitie of Cambridge . . . as shall be naturallie borne within the said parish of Giggleswick and . . . brought upp . . . at the said free grammer schoole'. Tenant, who died a fortnight after this conveyance was concluded, by will left property worth £40 for a second exhibition at Cambridge for a poor scholar from Giggleswick, the candidate to be nominated by the master and governors of the school.[3] Some years later (1616) the school and parish were jointly favoured by the bequest of a cleric, Richard Carr, of Hockley, Essex, a great-grandson of the brother of James Carr, the founder of Giggleswick School. Carr established an endowment of £1334 in Christ's College, Cambridge, contemplating two fellowships each yielding £13 6s 8d p.a. and eight scholarships with a value of £5 each annually, for boys chosen from Giggleswick School and parish.[4]

A grateful scholar on an earlier foundation, Anthony Higgin, Dean of Ripon, by his will proved in 1624 left £130 to St John's College, Cambridge, 'to augment five schollershippes that they may be equall with the foundraces [sic] . . . whereof foure were founded by docter Ashton[5]

---

[1] Vide ante, 234.

[2] Vide ante, 235, for mention of his very large endowment for poor relief.

[3] PCY 29/342 1604; Bell, Giggleswick School, 52–54; PP 1825, XI, 649; Brayshaw, Giggleswick, 239; Gilbert, Liber scholasticus, 286.

[4] Bell, Giggleswick School, 55; Atkinson, H. B., ed., Giggleswick School register (Newcastle-upon-Tyne, 1921), xvii, 1; VCH, Yorks., I, 462; Yorks. Arch. Soc. Rec., XXXIII (1903), 271–277. Vide ante, 306–307. The property was apparently over-valued by the donor and, furthermore, the number of scholarships stipulated exceeded the number of qualified candidates. In 1858 the provisions of the will were altered, two exhibitions of £50 p.a. each being settled on scholars from Giggleswick parish.

[5] For Hugh Ashton, vide post, 358.

for Lancashire, [Durham] Bushopbricke, and Yorkshire. And by Mr. Gregson one for Lancashire'.[1] In 1627 a Hull scrivener, Thomas Bury, bequeathed to his town an estate valued at about £150, the income of which was to be employed for the exhibition at Cambridge of some poor scholar from that community or from Beverley, to be nominated by the mayor and burgesses of Hull,[2] while two years later (1629) Frances Matthew, the widow of Tobias Matthew, bequeathed £200 to Peterhouse, Cambridge, for two scholarships there.[3]

There was a marked increase in the funds provided for scholarships during the revolutionary decades, the most substantial total of £5100 having been given. Among these benefactions was still another exhibition for Giggleswick School. This endowment of £100 was left in 1643 by Josias Shute, a clergyman who was himself the first scholar at Cambridge on Henry Tenant's foundation.[4] At about the same date (1643), Charles Greenwood, whose great charities for his native county have already been described in some detail, left a large endowment of £2000 to University College, Oxford, for the support of two fellowships and two scholarships, though the perversity of one of his executors and the long litigation in which the College was obliged to engage seem to have

---

[1] PCY 38/321 1624; *Surtees Soc. Pub.*, LXIV (1874), 362–364, LXXVIII (1884), 260; Cooper, *Memorials of Cambridge*, II, 96; *Yorks. Arch. Journal*, II (1873), 372–373; *Ripon millenary record*, 54. This donor was the second son of Thomas Higgin, 'occupier', of Manchester. He was educated at St John's, where he was in 1574 appointed a fellow of the college, being the tutor of Thomas Morton, later Bishop of Durham. He served as Rector of Kirk Deighton 1583–1624, as Master of St Michael's Hospital, Well, from 1605–1624, and was after 1608 Dean of Ripon. He also left four marks to the sixteen inmates in Well hospital, five marks to the poor of Kirk Deighton parish, £10 to the poor of Ripon, and £6 to the prisoners at York, Durham, and Lancaster.

[2] Tickell, *Hull*, 697; Hadley, *Hull*, II, 757; Gilbert, *Liber scholasticus*, 293; PP 1823, IX, 791.

[3] Walker, T. A., *Peterhouse* (L., 1906), 120; Drake, *Eboracum*, 512; Morrell, *Biography of common man of York*, 26. Probably no woman has ever been as fully episcopalian: she was the daughter of William Barlow, Bishop of Chichester; Matthew Parker was the father of her first husband; her second husband was Archbishop of York, and four of her sisters married men who became bishops: Wickham (Winchester); Overton (Coventry and Lichfield); Westphaling (Hereford); and Day (Winchester).

[4] Brayshaw, *Giggleswick*, 242; Bell, *Giggleswick School*, 52, 54, 58–60; Gilbert, *Liber scholasticus*, 286; PP 1825, XI, 651; PP 1895, LXXV, Giggleswick, 1, 25; Fuller, *Worthies*, III, 433. *Vide ante*, 354. Shute also left the residue of the income of certain properties, with a then value of £80, for the relief of the poor of Giggleswick parish. He was the son of Christopher Shute, the Vicar of Giggleswick, and was a graduate of the grammar school there and of Cambridge. He was appointed chaplain to the East India Company, was instituted as Rector of St Mary Woolnoth in 1611, and was chosen by Parliament as a member of the Westminster Assembly, though he died before the first session met. Fuller knew him well and declared him to be 'the most precious jewel that was ever shewn or seen in Lombard Street'.

reduced this important benefaction to about £1500 of capital.[1] In the year of the greatest political and constitutional unsettlement, 1648, John, Lord Craven, certain of whose benefactions have already been described, bequeathed the very large sum of £100 p.a., representing a capital worth of £2000, for the support of four poor scholars, two at Oxford and two at Cambridge, who should be appointed by the Vice-Chancellor, the Regius Professor, and the Orator in each university. The scholarships might run for as long as fourteen years or until a holder gained preferment with a value double the stipend. This great endowment was supported by extensive properties in Sussex, the residue of the income from which was to be employed by the Lord Mayor of London, the Recorder of that city, and the Master of Sutton's Hospital for the redemption of prisoners being held for ransom by the Turks. Legal proceedings instituted in 1651 revealed that at that date £100 p.a. was available for this residual use.[2]

There were likewise more modest endowments for needy scholars during these remarkable years. In 1654 Isabel Leighton of London by will confirmed a conveyance made two years earlier 'out of zeal to the glory of God and for the good of the poor', wherewith feoffees were vested with an endowment having a then capital value of £130 for 'the maintenance of poor boys that were most towardly for learning for their teaching and instruction in the school of Leeds'.[3] Ralph Lodge, a husbandman of Hemingbrough, in the same year left a rent-charge with a capital worth of £40 for the education of poor children in that parish and in Barlby,[4] while in 1657, as we have noted, Lady Lumley established an exhibition fund with a value of £40 p.a. for scholars in either university, from those Yorkshire parishes with whose needs she had dealt so generously.[5] Finally, we may note that Dr John Bathurst, the founder of schools in the North Riding, provided an endowment of £160 for the support in Cambridge of two deserving scholars from the town of Richmond where he had once been schoolmaster.[6]

[1] *Vide ante*, 244, 294, 338, 341.

[2] *Vide ante*, 246, 290. The estate was sequestered by Parliament soon after Craven's death. Students in Oxford and Cambridge in 1651 petitioned for its restoration as a charitable trust. The land forming the endowment of the trust increased greatly in value, the number of the scholarships in each university being increased to six and the stipends from £25 p.a. to £80 p.a. in 1860. Further and considerable increase in value occurred, with the result that there was an income surplus of £590 p.a. in 1885, most of which was in 1886 assigned by Chancery to student uses.

[3] PCC 328 Alchin 1654; *Thoresby Soc. Pub.*, XXXVII (1942), 356; *Old Leeds charities*, 30–32; *PP* 1826, XIII, 670. The donor was the widow of Alexander Leighton, a physician and a most formidable Puritan controversialist and incendiary.

[4] Burton, *Hemingbrough*, 141–142, 352.

[5] *Vide ante*, 279, 345.   [6] *Vide ante*, 250, 291, 346.

(c) *Support of the Universities*. It will have been observed that most of the scholarship endowments created by Yorkshire donors, as well as assisting the universities, directly benefited the county in which the aspirations of these generous men and women were principally centred. But this was by no means the full measure of the contribution made directly to the universities by benefactors of this county who, while endowing and building *de novo* a system of education within their own shire, found means as well to assist most substantially in the strengthening of the fabric of university education. In the course of our period the large total of £12,393 19s was given to the universities, this representing 5·09 per cent of all charitable funds for the county. Though there was a fairly steady interest in this great philanthropic need throughout our period, the larger gifts were on the whole concentrated most heavily in the era prior to the Reformation and in the generation extending roughly from 1621 to 1650. It may be observed, as well, that in Yorkshire a high proportion of all benefactions to the universities was made by the clergy of the county, with the notable exception of Savile's great benefactions. We may now comment on at least a few of these endowments.

Lawrence Booth, Archbishop of York, at the outset of our period bequeathed to Pembroke College, Cambridge, properties near Peterborough then worth upwards of £530 for the general uses of the college and for the augmentation of two scholars of the institution.[1] His successor at York, the great Rotherham, whose munificent school foundation has already been described, who was for some years Chancellor of Cambridge, from his own funds gave an estimated £150 towards the completion of King's Chapel, to which work he also bequeathed £100. To the university library, Rotherham left his own collection of two hundred volumes and contributed at least £200, over a period of years, to the completion of the building of Lincoln College, Oxford. Rotherham likewise gave an estimated £200 for the strengthening of the fellowship resources of Lincoln College, whose needs had engaged his attention from 1474 onwards.[2]

A great fifteenth-century lawyer, Richard Pygot, in 1484 left, among many other charitable bequests, £150 for the support over a term of years of three 'vertuous . . . lerners of the law of God' at Oxford or Cambridge.[3] Some years later, in 1503, Richard Nelson, a priest of

---

[1] *Patent rolls*, 20 Edw. IV, Part 2 (1481), Memb. 14; 21 Edw. IV, Part 1 (1482), Memb. 9; Attwater, Aubrey, *Pembroke College* (Cambridge, 1936), 23; Dickinson, William, *History of Southwell* (L., 1819), 226; *VCH, Hunts.*, III, 199, 202; *VCH, Surrey*, IV, 12; *Surtees Soc. Pub.*, XLV (1864), 248–250; DNB. Booth likewise left £267 for the founding of a chantry, £20 for church repairs, and an estimated £100 for church building.

[2] *Vide ante*, 305, and *post*, 369.

[3] PCY 5/231 1484; *Surtees Soc. Pub.*, XLV (1864), 285–286. Pygot stated in his will, 'for that I have been occupied in the worlde, and taken men's money,

Sawston, Cambridgeshire, but a native of Yorkshire, by deed of gift vested £100 in St Catharine's College, Cambridge, for the support of a fellow on the foundation who should by preference be from Lonsdale or from neighbouring parts, the appointment to be made from Yorkshire, Lancashire, or Westmorland if this preference could not be honoured.[1] Still another Archbishop of York, Christopher Bainbridge, by his will in 1514 vested in Queen's College, Oxford, which he had served as provost, properties then valued at approximately £200 for the support of scholars there, but subject to a rent-charge of £5 6s 8d p.a. for the celebration of masses at Appleby, Westmorland.[2] St John's College, Cambridge, which enjoyed the special loyalty of Yorkshire donors throughout our period, received a large and an early endowment in 1523 under the will of Hugh Ashton, Archdeacon of York, who left it £800 for the support of four fellowships and as many scholarships, with the provision that one of the fellows should be a native of Yorkshire.[3] Finally, in dealing with the benefactions made for the support of the universities prior to the Reformation, we should note the gift of Thomas Thompson, who on his death in 1540 was a rich pluralist. Thompson left to Christ's College, Cambridge, lands and other property which we have most uncertainly estimated as having had a then capital worth of £80, as well as vesting an endowment of £107 for fellowships in St John's College, at least one of which must always be held by a native of Yorkshire.[4]

and not done so effectually for it as I ought to have done, for their soules', he therefore left a considerable portion of his estate to be disposed for charity. In all, £384 was designated for charitable uses, of which, in addition to the university bequest, £13 7s was for the relief of the poor and £20 for alms, £20 for the succouring of prisoners, £66 13s for general charitable purposes, £15 7s for church repairs, £66 13s for the general uses of St Mary's Abbey, York, and £12 for the clergy. A native of Yorkshire, Pygot was a noted lawyer in the reigns of Henry VI and Edward IV. In 1463 he became a serjeant-at-law. He lived much in London in his later years.

[1] Browne, *St. Catharine's College*, 37; Jones, *St. Catharine's College*, 63, 208; *Alum. cantab.*, I, iii, 241; Cooper, *Athenae cantab.*, I, 11. Nelson was ordained a priest in 1469, a year after he was graduated from Cambridge. He was presented to the vicarage of Sawston, Cambridgeshire, in 1476.

[2] Magrath, J. R., *The Queen's College* (Oxford, 1921, 2 vols.), I, 155–157, *Obituary book of Queen's College* (Oxford, 1910), 54–55; Hodgkin, R. H., *Six centuries of an Oxford college* (Oxford, 1949), 52; Skelton, *Pietas oxon.*, 29. Elected provost of Queens in 1496, Bainbridge was successively Dean of York and of Windsor, Bishop of Durham, and Archbishop of York. He was a nephew to Bishop Langton. He died in Rome in 1514, it is said of poisoning, while taking part, as an ambassador of Henry VIII, in the papal election of that year (Leo X).

[3] *Surtees Soc. Pub.*, LXXVIII (1884), 221–223; Smith, *Old Yorkshire*, n.s., I, 150; *Alum. cantab.*, I, i, 46; Cooper, *Athenae cantab.*, I, 26; DNB. *Vide ante*, 354.

[4] PCC 23 Alenger 1540; Cooper, *Athenae cantab.*, I, 76; *Surtees Soc. Pub.*, CXVI (1908), 286–287; *Alum. cantab.*, I, iv, 237; Peile, John, *Christ's College*

In large part, no doubt, because the age of the great pluralist as well as the great prelate ended with the Reformation, there was for an extended period after 1540 a marked diminution in benefactions from the county for the support of the universities. In the two generations from 1541 to 1600 the total of such gifts was only £226 13s, all being very modest save for the bequest in 1595 by a Richmond merchant of £100 for the endowment of 'the newly erected college of Dublin' (Trinity College), which had been opened only two years earlier.[1]

Though there was a revival of clerical giving to the universities after 1601, the benefactions of the whole of the remainder of our period are dominated by the famous generosity of Sir Henry Savile towards Oxford, which he served in so many ways as to make him all but the founder of the modern university. Merton College gained greatly in strength and reputation under his wardenship. He assisted Sir Thomas Bodley in the founding of his library, and the university press was steadily encouraged by his interest and his gifts. Savile's generosity was redoubled after the death of his only son, and the many benefactions he made for building, the support of scholarships, and other university uses simply cannot be estimated, it being reported, for example, that he expended £8000 on the great edition of St Chrysostom. By the terms of his deeds of gift and by his testamentary benefactions it may be fairly accurately reckoned, however, that in his late years he vested the university with £7220 in endowments, chiefly from Yorkshire properties, the principal of which were for the foundation of the Savilian professorships of geometry and astronomy with an original capital of £6400, an endowment of £100 for a mathematical 'chest', of £100 for loans to needy students, a gift of £40 p.a. for general university purposes, as well as the great gift in 1620 of his own library of Greek folios and classical manuscripts.[2]

We may mention among the clerical gifts during this same general period the benefaction of £66 13s 4d which Archbishop Matthew Hutton vested in Trinity College, Cambridge, in about 1600.[3] In 1628 Richard

(L., 1900), 41–42, *Biographical register of Christ's College*, I, 6–7. Thompson was an astute dealer in land, and his benefactions to the colleges are difficult to separate from his sales to them. He was Master of Christ's, 1510–1517, and Vice-Chancellor, 1510–1512. He held livings in Middlesex, Norfolk, and Hertfordshire.

[1] PCY 26/165 1595; Clarkson, *Richmond*, App., xix; *Yorks. Arch. Journal*, XVIII (1905), 26–27; Drake, *Eboracum*, 498; *PP* 1825, X, 635. *Vide post*, 377. A native of Dublin, this donor, James Cottrell, appears first in England in the service of the Earl of Sussex. He married a Richmond widow and for twenty years served the Council of the North, 'testes examinando'. He was successfully engaged in trade in his later years and was in 1576 an alderman of Richmond.

[2] PCC 44 Savile 1622; *S. P. Dom.*, 1620, CXV, 52; Brodrick, G. C., *Merton College* (Oxford, 1885), 73, 166–167; *Alum. oxon.*, IV, 1319; DNB.

[3] *Vide ante*, 329, for comment on Hutton's grammar-school foundation in his native Lancashire.

Whittington, Rector of Wheldrake (E. R.), 'a pious and prudent man, who enforced his doctrine by his deeds', left the considerable fortune of £1400 for the purchase of impropriations to be settled on St John's College, Cambridge.[1] Merton College was bequeathed £100 in the same year by Robert Clay, a successor to Favour as vicar of Halifax, the income being designated for two sermons to be preached annually by a Yorkshireman, if any of the fellows or chaplains on the foundation were natives of that shire.[2] Almost a generation later Robert Metcalf, whose benefactions for the poor and for the school at Beverley were of such moment, left to his own St John's College, Cambridge, 'gratitudinis ergo', the sum of £100, as well as £20 for the needs of the university library.[3] These were but the largest of numerous benefactions made by Yorkshiremen, themselves not always university graduates. Many of the benefactions made to the universities, and more of the scholarship endowments, it will have been noted, were linked with the school foundations of the county in various and certainly in fruitful ways. Yorkshire donors were endeavouring to provide a clear channel of opportunity for any poor and able boy that might carry him from the elementary school through the university. This great aspiration had received substantial fulfilment by the close of this remarkable period of social and cultural progress in Yorkshire and in England.

5. Religion

(a) *General Comment.* The religous institutions of Yorkshire had developed in the course of the Middle Ages in a curiously uneven fashion. The seat of an archbishopric as well as the home of numerous great collegiate churches, the county contained as well several of the oldest and richest of the monastic foundations in the entire realm. But great and renowned as these institutions were, they seem extraordinarily detached from the parochial life of this vast county, and to a degree their very eminence and wealth drained away resources needed for bringing to maturity the religious institutions which served more directly and effectively ordinary men and women in the valleys and on the moors of this county.

It is, in fact, all too painfully evident that to the time of the Reformation and for some decades afterwards the county possessed insufficient parishes and that those who ministered to the everyday spiritual needs of the people were inadequate for their task, in large part because a high

[1] CCY April 1628; Cooper, *Memorials of Cambridge*, II, 97; *Alum. cantab.*, I, iv, 397; Baker, *St. John's College*, I, 206; Morrell, *Biography of common man of York*, 20. Whittington was graduated from Cambridge (St John's) in 1601. He was made rector first of St Mary Bishophill, York, in 1607 and of Wheldrake in 1612.

[2] CCY December 1628; Turner, *Biographia Halifaxiensis*, 148-149.

[3] *Vide ante*, 247, 303, and *post* 385.

proportion of wealth formerly given to the church had been absorbed by the monastic establishments and the collegiate churches. The Domesday Survey mentions 169 churches in the county, remarkably evenly distributed with regard to size of area and very possibly in relation to density of population. There was considerable building of new churches in the mid-thirteenth century and a great deal in the first half of the fifteenth century, with the consequence that an estimate of from 475 to 525 churches serving the needs of the county may be hazarded as the count of the physical resources in hand at the outset of our period. This appears to have been a roughly sufficient number for the Yorkshire of this date, though at least a third of these religious centres were chapels. The profoundly important shifts in the density of population of the county were still almost a century away. But these medieval assets, as we may term them, were most shockingly organized with reference to the spiritual and social needs of a still rude and backward area. At least three-fourths of all these livings were impropriated, with almost 250 belonging to the various monasteries and about 100 to the several collegiate bodies of the county. The clergy in such parishes were usually curates or ill-prepared men eking out their living by an incredible variety of ways in order to supplement the miserable stipends left by the impropriators. Archbishop Lee, no favourer of the violence of Henry VIII, was constrained to say that in the Diocese of York there were only twelve parochial clergy either able or willing to preach, and in 1535 he confessed to Cromwell that 'we have very few preachers, as the benefices are so small that no learned man will take them'.[1]

Nor may it be said that improvement in the structure of parochial life showed any marked advance for a full generation after the coming of the Reformation, particularly because of the immense shock and the evident discouragement which pervaded the county for two decades after that strange and spontaneous rising, not so much against the Tudors as against the sixteenth century, which we call the Pilgrimage of Grace. Despite the deserved reputation of the county for religious conservatism, only seventeen of the parochial clergy, or not more than 3 per cent of the whole number, found it impossible to accept the Elizabethan Settlement,[2] which one suspects a great many of them simply did not understand. The first indication of improvement came in the too-brief stay of Grindal at York, for he was deeply concerned with the miserable stipends of his clergy and undertook as rapidly as possible to bring in new and educated clergy from the south, mostly of at least a mild Puritan persuasion, who were charged with a missionary

[1] *L. & P. Henry VIII*, IX, 704.
[2] There were deprived as well Archbishop Heath, two archdeacons, and six prebendaries of York. Nine more of the parochial clergy were deprived for various reasons after 1563.

zeal for the great task in hand. These efforts were renewed in the early seventeenth century, when a considerable number of chapels were built and when, as we shall observe, impressive local attempts were made to better clerical stipends. The population of the county increased rapidly during the last eighty years of our period and there was real need for an extensive and planned campaign of church and chapel building, which, however, never took place. And there was need above all for the fragmenting of many of the huge West Riding parishes which were ill served by chapelries. The first well-considered plan for the improvement and effective support of the parochial institutions of the county was in fact that so carefully framed by the Parliamentary Commissioners during the Commonwealth and Protectorate, with recommendations which, somewhat ironically, were gradually carried out piecemeal over a period of a century and a half after the Restoration. This survey, with several other supplementary sources, suggests that there were by the close of our period 550 churches in the county which may be regarded as properly parochial (with three more that may possibly be so described), 161 churches which were certainly chapels, as well as 14 more probably so constituted. For our purposes, therefore, we shall assume that there were something like 725 settled places of worship, with at least occasional attendance of divine services, which comprised the religious establishment of the county.[1]

This dour sketch of the development of religious institutions in Yorkshire is all the more sad because of the considerable evidence of the deep piety of the county and the generous and persistent effort of the laity to improve parochial life, largely ignored when it was not opposed by the great prelates of York and the many mitred abbots of the county. In the whole course of our period benefactors of the county gave £68,397 5s for various religious purposes, this constituting 28·07 per cent of all charitable funds and being a proportion larger than that for any other county in England save Lancashire, where Puritan wealth was to pour in to lift the county out of recusancy. Great as was this sum, it was far less than the total to be devoted to the needs of the poor and it was, quite surprisingly, also considerably less than the endowments provided for the educational needs of the shire.

The fact is that the great bulk of the wealth amassed by the county for religious needs was late medieval in form, as was the structure of aspirations which men and women were seeking to implement. In the two generations prior to the Reformation, the great total of £35,814 2s

---

[1] We are troubled by the fact that charitable bequests have been recorded for all these 'parishes' as well as sixty-seven other communities which must have possessed some corporate existence. Many of these were townships not served by chapels, while in a number of cases there were chapels in the earlier decades of our period which had vanished well before its close.

was given for religious uses, this comprising about 70 per cent of all charitable funds for the interval and well over half of the total to be given for the needs of the church during the whole of our long period. The chilling impact of the Reformation is evident indeed, for in these two decades the total given fell away to £4261 5s, or a scant quarter (25·16 per cent) of all charitable funds, and an amount considerably less than that provided for the care of the poor or for the schools of the county. This withering of concern for the religious needs of the Yorkshire community was dramatically accelerated during that most secular of ages, the Elizabethan, when Yorkshire proved itself at last fully acclimated to the mood and the direction of Tudor rule. During this long period the incredibly tiny sum of £1543 9s was provided for the whole complex of religious uses, this amounting to no more than 6·48 per cent of all benefactions of the period; indeed, it was not much more than an eighth of what was given for poor relief or a sixth of that supplied for the education of the youth of the county. There was a marked revival of interest in the spiritual needs of the county in the early Stuart period, supported by the direct concern of James I and his queen with the plight of Yorkshire churches and clergy and later by the somewhat frenzied efforts of the Laudian party to secure some repair of the damage wrought by Elizabethan secularism. But these efforts are impressive only against the Elizabethan background. During the interval 1601–1640 a total of £15,942 18s was given for religious needs, amounting to not quite 18 per cent of the whole of the charitable funds of the period, but this represents an intensity of concern roughly only half as great as that felt for the care of the poor or for the educational needs of the youth of the county. Indeed, the contributions made during the revolutionary period were even more significant. In this brief interval £10,835 11s, this being 17·41 per cent of the whole, was given for religious uses. Of this total, nearly all, £9431 8s, was concentrated on the most pressing, the basic, need, the improvement of the scandalously low clerical stipends of the county which yet remained to be restored after the ravages of medieval monasticism and prelatism and of Elizabethen secularism.

(b) *The General Uses of the Church.* It seems evident that benefactions made for the general use of the church provide the most sensitive measure of the devotion of a people to its needs and mission. We have incorporated a wide variety of benefactions under this head, including undesignated gifts for the general support of parochial life, gifts for lights and altars, and bequests for the maintenance of various aspects of the service. In Yorkshire, as in all English counties, by 1480 an almost inflexible tradition had been established that all men included at least a token contribution within this general spectrum of need in their wills, very possibly because the parish priest ordinarily witnessed, if he had not drawn, the will. Most of these gifts were very small, but the church-wardens' accounts prior to the Reformation make it clear that in the mass they were of great importance in maintaining and gradually improving the services which bound men so securely to the life and sacraments of their church.

During the whole course of our period the contributions for these general purposes were slender in Yorkshire, amounting to no more than £2983 1s, or 1.22 per cent of all charitable benefactions, a lower proportion than that found in any other English county save Buckinghamshire (0·61 per cent) and the always secular community of London (0·89 per cent). It is likewise noteworthy that in this county an unusually high proportion (69·97 per cent) of all such benefactions were in the form of gifts for immediate use, only £895 17s having been left as endowments. The explanation for this most pronounced neglect seems to lie in the slowness with which Yorkshiremen accommodated themselves to the revolutionary changes in the services of their churches rather than in any want of piety. This is clearly the case since in the decades prior to the Reformation the respectable total of £1768 19s, almost the whole being accounted for by a mass of small benefactions, was provided for the support of the traditional services of the church. In other words, approximately 60 per cent of all wealth given in the county for general church uses was given in the era prior to the Reformation, though it would seem quite evident that even in these years this was a wholly insufficient total if the size and population of the county are regarded. In these early years such contributions were relatively stable, ranging from £202 14s per decade to £532 11s, while the devastating impact of the Reformation is perfectly documented, since the total provided in the decade 1541-1550 fell catastrophically to £71 14s, or not much more than 2s in average terms for each of the churches of the county.

There was a marked revival of interest and confidence in the next decade, concentrated in the Marian years, when total contributions of £398 11s were made for general church uses, or at a rate somewhat greater than that prevailing in the years prior to the Reformation. In point of fact, rather more was given for parochial uses in this single decade than in the whole of the long period of indifference, 1561-1610, when the amount furnished for church needs was a slender £343 18s. There was no real interest in giving for this purpose during the whole of the remainder of our period, the historical ineffectiveness of the Laudian era being suggested by the fact that from 1621 to 1640 only £106 10s was given by Yorkshire benefactors for general church uses. One might well say that the stunning effect of the Reformation on the traditional piety of Yorkshire was within a generation replaced by an inflexible secular indifference as the tuition of the great Queen began to have its pervasive effect.

This profoundly significant shift in men's aspirations can perhaps be elucidated by at least a brief analysis of the structure of gifts for the general uses of the church in two selected decades. In the interval 1501–1510 a total of £321 6s was given for general church purposes by 241 donors, which means that 93.7 per cent of all charitable donors during these years left at least a token contribution for this purpose. Of this amount, only £22 was in the form of capital gifts, all the remainder being designated for various immediate uses. The great mass of these benefactions were tiny, not more than thirty-four being in amounts of £1 or over and the largest, the bequest of £80 left in 1506 by John Vavasour, the Recorder of York, being for the general uses of monasteries in Yorkshire and Bedfordshire.[1] Far more representative, to select only one, was the bequest of a yeoman of Burton Agnes, Walter Cawood, who in 1507 left £1 to the general uses of his parish church with a particularly poignant testimony of his faith.[2]

Standing in stark contrast is the Elizabethan decade, 1571–1580, when the total given or bequeathed for the general uses of the churches of the county was £19 7s, the lowest, save for one similar interval, in the whole annal of our period. This pitiful amount was given by thirty donors, the average benefaction being very small, and the largest single bequest being £3 7s. Most revealing is the fact that only 7 per cent of all the donors of this decade made any contribution for this purpose and that the amount so provided bears only a trifling relation to the £4614 given for all charitable uses in this generally uncharitable decade. Most of these gifts, in fact all save four, were made by humble men and women who were not as yet fully caught up in the strong and now pervasive secular aspirations which had captured the mind and imagination of men who were transforming the social and cultural institutions of the realm.

(c.) *Prayers for the Dead.* The conservative character of Yorkshire piety at the outset of our period is well illustrated by the extraordinary concern of substantial donors there with the founding of chantries and lesser

[1] *Vide ante,* 229, and *post,* 372.

[2] 'In the name of the moste blessede and holy Trynite, ye Fader, the Sone, and the Holy Goste, oon Gode Almyghty and everlastyng, of whom is all, by Whom is all, and in whom is all; I Walter Cawode, inwardly remembryng that all men lyvyng have here no cite abydyng, bot be as pilgrames passyng towarde ye promysede citie of heven by yis temporall and wrechede lyve, not sure of houre ne tyme when ye Lord of ye hous shall come, laite at mydnyghte, or erly; lest yt dethe, as a thefe, unwares mowghte throw adown yis house of my erthly lyving, yt at ye comyng of ye gret spouse, when His pleasor shalbe to calle me, I be not fownde slepyng, wyllyng yr for to dispose me through the gracyus assistence of Allmyghty God in all thinges to His pleasor' (*Surtees Soc. Pub.,* LIII, 1868, 265–266).

endowments to secure prayers for the repose of their souls. In most of England by 1480 there was a prevailing distrust of these foundations, either because pious men had observed that such endowments rarely survived their trust purposes for more than two or three generations or because they had come to doubt the very efficacy of the prayers being offered. In Yorkshire, however, the county as our period opened was in the midst of a second great movement for the founding of chantries, the first having occurred in the fourteenth century, which was to persist and, if anything, to gain in strength well into the period of the Reformation. These foundations, popular among several of the substantial social classes of the county, were added to already numerous endowments for stipendiary priests. There were certainly as many as 322 endowed chantries in the county at the beginning of our era, about half of which had probably been founded in the fourteenth century.[1] We have counted the amazing total of 94 additional foundations made in the period 1480 to 1557, of which 71 were really considerable endowments with a capital of £80 or more, or an amount sufficient to provide for a stipendiary priest, who in Yorkshire usually could be had very cheaply indeed.[2] No other county in England exhibited anything like this degree of pious concern with what was undoubtedly a decayed medieval institution, suspect throughout western Europe. Moreover, almost all these foundations were chantries in a full sense, only a few making even modest provision for almsgiving, while, as we have already seen, even fewer added teaching functions to the duties of the priest in charge. In all, there were something like 416 endowed chantries in Yorkshire when the order for expropriation went out from Westminster, supporting at least 500 stipendiary priests, since there were numerous large foundations with two or more priests. In average terms, then, there was a chantry in very nearly every parish in Yorkshire.

These endowments absorbed a considerable fraction of the charitable wealth of the county. In total, Yorkshire benefactors gave the considerable sum of £25,568 10s for prayers, whether for the endowment of chantries or lesser amounts for obits or a limited number of masses. This great wealth amounted to something more than a tenth (10·49 per cent) of the whole of charitable benefactions for all purposes during our

[1] We here follow, with some amendments, the particulars as set out by the Chantry Commissioners (*Certificates of chantries, passim*). At the time of the survey there remained 11 foundations which may well have dated from before 1300, 106 which were fourteenth century in institution, and 56 founded in the fifteenth century, but prior to 1480. There were in addition 149 chantries of uncertain date, probably all of which had been endowed at some time prior to 1480 and most of which, internal evidence would suggest, were in fact fifteenth century in date.

[2] Only two of some hundreds were reported by the Commissioners as having university degrees.

entire period, a proportion quite unmatched in any other county in the realm.[1] The intensity of preoccupation with these foundations is suggested by the fact that for the decades prior to the Reformation these gifts amounted to nearly 45 per cent of all charities in the shire and to almost two-thirds of the total provided for all religious uses. In fact, in this period the sum designated for prayers exceeded by far the total provided for all the non-religious charitable needs, suggesting an absorption amounting to obsession and explaining in part the bitterness with which Yorkshire viewed the rapid course of the Reformation. Yorkshire was wholly unprepared for the immense revolution wrought by Henry VIII and his parliament; had there been many Yorkshires in the realm that revolution would have been politically impossible. One must reflect, as well, that of the great wealth devoted to prayers for the dead, more than two-thirds was in the form of capital and that these endowments, totalling £17,301 7s, were substantially larger than the amount provided for the support of the secular clergy throughout our entire period. Perhaps the cure of souls in the county would have been better served and the whole tone and quality of religious life elevated had this generous endowment been provided for the augmentation of the miserable stipends of the parochial clergy. But we must deal with aspirations as they were, not as a later age would have them.

We should devote some comment to the larger of the chantry foundations made in our period, while bearing in mind that these purchases of perpetual spiritual insurance by men of great substance reflect in exaggerated form an almost universal disposition of benefactors in Yorkshire to make some provision for the safety of their souls. Hence it is important to note that by a consecutive count of the first 100 donors whose total charitable contributions were £1 or less in 1501, 76 left some amount for an obit or special prayers, and, it may be pertinent to add, of these 100 donors, 93 made a religious benefaction of some kind. Three of the founders of chantries with endowments of £80 or more were members of the nobility, while twelve were of the upper gentry of the county. The largest single number of these substantial foundations, twenty-three in all, were established by the lower gentry or their widows, and two were endowed by rich yeomen. Two were created by great prelates and thirteen by the lesser clergy of the shire, including a fair number who were in fact rather more devoted to the practice of civil law than to the cure of souls. Quite surprisingly, there were thirteen such foundations made by prosperous merchants from various urban centres in the county, while four were instituted by lawyers.

In the first decade of our period the considerable total of £3036 8s was provided by pious donors for prayers. The larger chantry endow-

[1] The proportion ranges from 0·80 per cent in Buckinghamshire to 9·28 per cent in Somerset.

ments created in these years were founded almost wholly by two classes of men, the clergy and the gentry. Thus in 1481 John Gysburgh, Precentor of York and chaplain to Archbishop Booth, endowed a chapel at St Mary Magdalen, York, with a capital of £187 to secure the maintenance of two stipendiary priests, as well as bequeathing £26 13s in doles for the poor.[1] The venerable Thomas Witham, who had served his country honourably in many capacities, on his death in 1481 endowed with lands valued at about £124 a chantry chapel at Sheriff Hutton, which he had begun building in 1465.[2] In the next year, 1482, Thomas Fitzwilliam, Rector of Sprotbrough, by his will ordered all his goods to be sold and with the proceeds lands to be purchased to the value of £6 13s 4d p.a. 'si fieri potest' in order to maintain a stipendiary priest in his parish church.[3] Sir Richard Conyers, probably in 1483, endowed a chantry chapel at South Cowton with £100,[4] while in the same year Henry Savile commanded his executors to found a chantry at Sandal Magna with an annual value of £5 5s, of which the 5s should be for alms.[5] Sir Hugh Hastings, High Sheriff of Yorkshire in 1480, by his will proved in 1489 ordered substantial sums to be allocated under the watchful eye of his heirs for prayers for a term of years, leaving for the purpose £28 for masses at Campsall, £40 for prayers at Norton Chapel, £66 13s 4d for similar purposes at Gressenhall, Norfolk, and £11 and four quarters of wheat for three years to friars at Doncaster and Pontefract for their prayers for the repose of his soul.[6] A lawyer of gentle

---

[1] PCY 1/350 1481; Surtees Soc. Pub., LIII (1868), 84n–85n.; Auden, Survey of York, 197; Burton, Hemingbrough, 76–77. Gysburgh was Rector of Nunburnholme, 1452–1475, of Eakring (Nottinghamshire), 1454, of Brompton, 1460, and of Spofforth, 1474–1481. He was receiver of the Exchequer to the Archbishop and Canon Residentiary of York.

[2] PCY 5/102 1481; Surtees Soc. Pub., XLV (1864), 264–268, XCI (1892), 93–94; VCH, Yorks., NR, II, 186–187. Witham was the founder of his family fortunes. He was early connected with the powerful Nevile family and was executor for the Earl of Salisbury. From 1471 to 1473 he was concerned with diplomatic relations with Scotland. He was three times Chancellor of the Exchequer, twice under Henry VI and once under Edward IV. His seat was at Sheriff Hutton. Witham also left £1 for alms, 14s for church general, £11 for church repairs, and 3s to the clergy.

[3] PCY 5/70 1482; Surtees Soc. Pub., XLV (1864), 271–272.

[4] Ibid., XLV (1864), 291n., XCI (1892), 145.

[5] PCY 5/214 1483; Surtees Soc. Pub., XLV (1864), 294–295; Yorks. Arch. Journal, XXIV (1917), 27–28; Walker, Wakefield, I, 327. The instruction was not carried out until the death of his brother, Thomas, occurred in 1490. Savile also left 13s to monasteries in London, 15s for general uses of three Yorkshire churches, £1 outright for prayers, 15s for Yorkshire poor, and £1 for bridge repairs.

[6] PCY 5/337 1489; Surtees Soc. Pub., XLV (1864), 273–278; VCH, Yorks., III, 266, 268, 272, 281; Hunter, South Yorkshire, II, 471. Vide post, 389–390. Hastings was the senior member of a rich family, possessing great influence and large landholdings in Yorkshire and Norfolk. His will was drafted in 1482

extraction, William Copley, in 1490 provided an endowment of £90 for the support of a stipendiary priest at Doncaster, as well as outright sums of £30 for prayers at Cambridge for three years, £3 7s for masses at Doncaster, and £4 for prayers at Batley,[1] while Thomas Pearson, an important clerical official, by his will dated in the same year bequeathed £100 towards the endowment of a chantry in York Minster, as well as £93 7s for prayers over a term of years,[2] the chantry being founded jointly with Archbishop Rotherham, who in 1500 left approximately £120 towards its endowment as well as £100 for other prayers.[3]

Substantial chantry foundations such as these might be almost indefinitely listed in the succeeding decades prior to the Reformation. The social and spiritual forces impelling these endowments were evidently gaining somewhat in strength down to the very convention of the Reformation Parliament, it being important to note that by far the largest amount was contributed for prayers in the decade 1521–1530. In this single interval the great sum of £5402 3s was provided for these purposes, which, really incredibly, amounted to nearly 39 per cent of all charitable bequests made in these years. A few examples from this decade may be cited, including, it will be observed, donors from all the classes disposing substantial wealth.

Thus in 1521 Henry Pudsay, a gentleman with enclosures on his conscience, by will founded a chantry in Bolton-by-Bowland church with an endowment of £80,[4] while in the same year two of the lesser gentry of the county, John Radcliffe and Ralph Batty, provided an endowment of £107 for a chantry at Ripon which they proposed to adorn with a statute for which they contracted to pay £20.[5] John Lake, a gentleman of Normanton, by deed in 1522 established a chantry in

when 'intending and purposing, under the proteccion and grace of Almighty God, to passe towardes the Scottis the kingis enmyes'. His brother, Sir Edmund, was on four occasions High Sheriff of Yorkshire, and another, Sir Roger, was in the service of the Earl of Northumberland.

[1] ARY, 23/341 1490; *Surtees Soc. Pub.*, LIII (1868), 46–50. Copley also left £5 10s to the poor of four parishes.

[2] PCY 5/415 1492 [?]; *Surtees Soc. Pub.*, LIII (1868), 51–56. Pearson, Subdean of York, Vicar-General of Richmond, Rector of Bolton Percy, also left £11 outright to the poor, £1 for alms, £4 for roads, £1 for prisons, £6 for church general, £20 for church repairs, and £35 to the monastic clergy.

[3] *Vide ante*, 305, 357.

[4] *Surtees Soc. Pub.*, XCII (1893), 246; *Yorks. Arch. Soc. Rec.*, LVI (1916), 43–45; *VCH, Yorks.*, III, 475. Pudsay married a daughter of Sir Christopher Conyers of Hornby. He was for many years King's Steward and Forester for Barnoldswick. Some time before 1517 he converted 100 acres of arable land into pasture, evicting twelve tenants and demolishing houses in which an additional thirty persons lived.

[5] *Surtees Soc. Pub.*, LXXIV (1881), 181–184, LXXXI (1886), 15–32, CXV (1908), 294–296. It is by no means certain these intentions were ever fully carried out.

that church with an endowment of £145, with a charge 'to gyve every Sonday in the yere to iij poore people, iijd.; that is by the yere xiijs.'[1] A Hull merchant, Geoffrey Threscrosse, in the same year (1522) prudently sought to ensure perpetuity as well as good administration of his chantry by leaving £200 and a house of uncertain value to the civic authorities to secure the services of a stipendiary priest, as well as bequeathing £25 for church repairs, and £2 to the friars of Thetford in Norfolk,[2] while Thomas Wentworth, a gentleman of North Elmsall, in 1524 vested lands valued at £112 for the establishment of a chantry in his parish church, as well as providing £5 for the poor, £15 for Yorkshire monasteries, and leaving £6 13s 4d outright for prayers.[3] Nicholas Bosville [Boswell], a member of the lower gentry of the county, endowed a chantry at Conisbrough with capital of £93 value in 1523,[4] and Thomas Legh of Middleton, also of the gentry, in that year bequeathed £6 13s 4d for an ornament and £16 to the poor 'to pray for my saull daylye duryng an hoole yere' in a chantry which he had somewhat earlier endowed at Rothwell with a capital of £101 13s.[5] The vicar of Leeds, William Evers, by will established a chantry with an endowment of £112 in the parish church which he had served,[6] while at about the same time William Nelson, a leading merchant in York, endowed a chantry in Trinity Church with approximately £100 of capital, leaving at the time of his death in 1525 an additional £10 for special prayers.[7] Still another York merchant and a former mayor, Thomas Drawswerde, in 1529 endowed a chantry in his parish church with an estimated capital of £80, the priest to undertake without charge the teaching of seven poor children of the parish.[8] Thomas Stapleton, a younger son of Sir Brian Stapleton, in 1526 founded a chantry, with lay trustees, in the parish church of Huddersfield with an endowment of £108,[9] while at about the same date John West, a clergyman of Hemingbrough who died in 1529, endowed a stipendiary priest with lands at the time worth

[1] *Surtees Soc. Pub.*, XCII (1893), 322.

[2] PCY 9/240 1522; *Surtees Soc. Pub.*, LXXIX (1884), 117–118, XCII (1893), 346; Tickell, *Hull*, 810.

[3] PCY 9/297 1524; *Surtees Soc. Pub.*, LXXIX (1884), 144–146.

[4] PCY 9/263 1523; Hunter, *South Yorkshire*, I, 121; *Surtees Soc. Pub.*, CVI (1902), 4–6.

[5] PCY 9/267 1523; *Surtees Soc. Pub.*, LXXIX (1884), 164, XCII (1893), 291.

[6] *Ibid.*, XCII (1893), 215–216; Rusby, James, *St. Peter's at Leeds* (Leeds, 1896), 26; Thoresby, Ralph, *Vicaria leodiensis* (L., 1724), 21. Thoresby believed that this endowment was made in 1470 by an earlier vicar of the same name.

[7] PCY 9/305 1525; *Surtees Soc. Pub.*, LXXIX (1884), 198–201.

[8] PCY 9/448 1529; *Surtees Soc. Pub.*, LXXIX (1884), 267–269. Drawswerde was mayor in 1515 and again in 1523, having sat in Parliament for the city in 1511.

[9] PCY 9/340 1526; *Surtees Soc. Pub.*, XCII (1893), 282; CVI (1902), 11–13.

£7 6s 8d p.a.[1] On the very eve of the Reformation, and after the parliament which was to effect the breach with Rome had been convened, these endowments continued without any indication of slackening. Thus in 1530 Walter Bradford, a rich landholder of Glass Houghton, left an estimated £101 for prayers at Pontefract,[2] and Nicolas Richard, a gentleman of Kirk Sandall, bequeathed properties valued at £95 for the support of a stipendiary priest in that parish.[3] In the same closing year of the decade under review Richard Toune, the priest at Cottingham, bequeathed properties with a capital worth of £106 for the support of a chantry priest who should offer prayers for the repose of his soul.[4]

We have dealt briefly with representative chantry foundations at selected intervals during the period prior to the Reformation. There were as well a number of large foundations made during these years, a few of which should be mentioned. Henry Soothill, a landed gentleman of considerable wealth, in 1495 vested the rents of the manor of Wrenthorpe, which in 1548 possessed a capital value of £558 14s 2d, for the creation of a chantry in Wakefield church, to be staffed by four priests who should in addition to their specific chantry duties sing in the choir and assist in the celebration of high mass.[5] Some years later (1505) Lady Jane Hastings, who had survived the misfortune that had engulfed her family during the War of the Roses and who possessed considerable North Riding property in her own right, by her will ordered lands to be sold sufficient to endow six chantry priests with £20 p.a. to sing for assorted husbands and relations in Yorkshire and in London.[6] At about

---

[1] Burton, *Hemingbrough*, 93–94; *VCH, Yorks.*, III, 359–360; *Alum. cantab.*, I, iv, 369.

[2] PCY 10/17 1530; *VCH, Yorks.*, III, 273; *Surtees Soc. Pub.*, LXXIX (1884), 283–287.

[3] PCY 9/461 1530; *Surtees Soc. Pub.*, LXXIX (1884), 280–283, XCI (1892), 173. Richard, who also left £13 6s 8d for church repairs, was a nephew of William Rokeby, Archbishop of Dublin.

[4] PCY 11/470 1530; *Yorks. Arch. Journal*, XXIV (1917), 74n.

[5] Walker, *Wakefield*, I, 211–212; Gray, F. S., and J. W. Walker, *Wakefield Cathedral* (Wakefield, 1905), 23; *Surtees Soc. Pub.*, XCII (1893), 307. Soothill, of Soothill Hall, Batley, was the son of a gentleman of this same name who was a confidant of Richard, Duke of York. In 1548 Soothill's heirs petitioned for the restoration to them of the manor, but this plea was disallowed and the lands were sold to Thomas Gargrave of North Elmsall.

[6] PCC 28 Holgrave 1505; *Surtees Soc. Pub.*, CXVI (1908), 73–75; *VCH, Yorks.*, NR, I, 425; *Complete peerage*, VIII, 78. This lady was the daughter of Sir Richard Welles, Lord Willougby, and a sister of Sir Robert Welles, both of whom were executed for treason by Edward IV. She was first married to Richard Pygot, a rich and successful lawyer who had considerable North Riding property and who died in 1484 (*vide ante*, 357). She then married Richard Hastings, whose brother (Lord Hastings) was executed for treason by Richard III. Hastings petitioned successfully for the restoration to him of lands which his wife would

the same time John Vavasour, the judge who also ordered the distribution of £200 in alms in his will proved in 1507, founded a chantry at
Spaldington with an endowment of £200, as well as endowing prayers
in the parish in which he was buried for a term of thirty years with
eight marks yearly to the priest.[1] Sir John Gilliot, a great York merchant
and a former mayor of that city, in 1488 founded an obit in the church
of St Leonard's Hospital and by the terms of his will proved in 1509
ordered a chapel built in St Saviour's which he richly endowed as a
chantry with a bequest of £400. In addition, Gilliot vested an endowment of £53, or £2 13s p.a., for a chantry priest to pray for his soul at
All Saints' church and provided £18 outright to friars for their prayers.
The total outlay of this particularly pious merchant for prayers may conservatively be reckoned at £491.[2]

During the decade in which the breach with Rome was being accomplished, the almost obsessive devotion of Yorkshiremen to prayers for
the dead is most abundantly demonstrated, well after the time when
this form of religious observance was being arranged in most parts of
England only occasionally by eccentric or stubborn donors of means,
or plaintively by humbler men in remote parishes. During these years,
when such foundations were in imminent danger of seizure and when
they were being subjected to withering attacks by men close to the King,
the incredibly large total of £2093 4s was provided by donors of this
county for prayers for the repose of their souls. Some suggestion of the
religious, and, for that matter, the political, significance of the intense
conservatism of the county is gained when we reflect that this is a larger
total than was provided for prayers in Hampshire and Buckinghamshire
during the whole course of the period 1480–1540. Most of this sum is the
accumulation of many small bequests by simple rural people for an
anniversary obit or for a trental of masses, but by no means was this
wholly the case. In this decade chantry foundations with endowments
of £100 or more were made by nine donors, including a nobleman, two
members of the upper gentry, two of the lower gentry, three merchants,
two being of Hull and one of York, and a yeoman of Farnham in the
West Riding. It is no wonder that this stubborn and intensely conservative county was for so long the despair of the Tudors.

Even more incredible is the annal of the next decade (1541–1550)
when the expropriation of chantry properties was actually begun and
towards the close of which prayers for the dead became at the very least
extra-legal. But the flow of these benefactions in Yorkshire continued,
albeit at a slightly diminished rate. A total of £1801 18s was left for

have inherited save for attainder and in 1483 was summoned to Parliament as
Lord Welles, though he seems to have styled himself variously as Lord Willoughby or Lord Hastings.
[1] *Vide ante*, 229, 365.   [2] *Vide ante*, 230.

prayers of one or another form in the course of this decade. In these years six donors established chantries with endowments of £100 or more, all before 1546; as to the social status of these intrepidly pious men, the group included one nobleman, one of the upper gentry, two of the lower gentry, one chantry priest, and one merchant. But more interesting and significant is the fact that the flow of smaller bequests for this purpose in the rural parishes of the county shows almost no sign of diminution during the decade. There were in all 188 such bequests, in amounts ranging from a few pence to £49, designed to secure prayers, usually by the local priest, in one of the traditionally accepted forms.

The slow but final withering of the solace of prayers for the repose of one's soul was to come in the tumultuous decade 1551–1560 when no more than £744 13s was provided for this purpose by Yorkshire donors. It is interesting and profoundly meaningful that the feverish Catholicism of Queen Mary did little to affect this process of religious and social change one way or the other. The significant fact is that the powerful and articulate men of the county, those who in an ultimate sense were the moulders of action as well as of tradition, doubtless for a variety of reasons, and very probably with extreme reluctance, simply ceased to provide endowments or to support prayers for the dead even with outright stipends. In the course of this decade there was only one substantial capital bequest for prayers. It means, of course, that this religious practice was doomed even though outright bequests for prayers, usually made by humble men and women in rural parishes, continued with a gathering diminution even during the Edwardian years. The amazing fact is that Mary's best effort failed even in Yorkshire, as it had in the rest of England, to revive this pious practice abandoned with such evident and pathetic reluctance in Yorkshire over the two preceding decades. The structure of Catholic worship was in ruins even in Yorkshire well before the accession of Mary Tudor, and her best and hurried ministrations could not secure its reconstitution. And the reign of a great and a ruthlessly secular sovereign was now at hand.

(d) *Support of Monasticism.* There can be no doubt that the dissolution of its old and rich monastic foundations was a severe spiritual and social shock to Yorkshire, having consequences to be found in comparable gravity in no other region in the realm. In large part this was true because these foundations held so high a proportion of the landed wealth of the county that expropriation necessarily meant a social and economic dislocation of the severest kind. It also seems to be true that on the whole the larger foundations of this county were better and more faithfully administered than those in the realm at large; they were old-fashioned houses in an old-fashioned county. All this is quite so, but it is likewise a fact that during the two generations of our period preceding the Reformation the foundations of the county did not command notably enthusiastic or widespread support from donors who were, as we have seen, uncommonly devoted to pious causes. In total, Yorkshiremen gave to their monasteries £3525 1s for various uses in the interval 1480–1540, this being 9·84 per cent of all religious benefactions made in this period and 6·86 per cent of the total of all charitable gifts in the same interval.[1] With respect to this particular religious need, then, the support of the county was by no means generous and was not markedly greater than that lent in a number of southern counties to the establishments in those areas.[2] We must, in fact, conclude that even in Yorkshire the age of monasticism was approaching its close, the very real and certainly intense spiritual aspirations of the county being fastened upon other religious needs. The amount provided for monasticism in Yorkshire was little more than trivial in relation to its historical significance in the life and institutions of the county. The monasteries of Yorkshire, of which there were 120 establishments of various kinds, ranked first in all the realm in wealth at the time of the Dissolution, possessing clear revenues of £11,934 8s, which may be taken as representing capital wealth of the enormous total of £238,688, an amount, it should be noted, almost equal to the great accumulation of charitable wealth (£243,650 14s) gathered in the county during the course of the period with which this study is concerned. Some understanding of the comparative neglect of the monasteries by donors during the first two generations of our period may be gained in the fact that these foundations in relation to their great wealth were distributing only a most

[1] It should be remarked that in Yorkshire as in other counties, only gifts made to Yorkshire monasteries are included in our totals. This is necessary because the support of monasteries was less parochial than any other form of charity, save of course the universities, and only by this treatment could confusing duplications be avoided. It should also be noted that we have included no head for monastic contributions, which were relatively very small in most counties and which were in any case often simply a way of accomplishing another purpose. These 'gathered gifts' to monasteries are treated as an entity in the present discussion, but for other purposes are distributed to the four great heads: *church general*, *clergy*, *church building and repair*, and *prayers*.

[2] For the whole group of counties studied, the total of benefactions made to the monasteries bears the following percentage relation to the whole of charitable funds provided during the period, 1480–1540:

	Per cent		Per cent
Bristol	6·77	London	16·75
Buckinghamshire	2·04	Norfolk	4·60
Hampshire	1·35	Somerset	5·80
Kent	6·42	Worcestershire	3·25
Lancashire	3·57	Yorkshire	6·86

modest proportion of their income in alms for the social betterment of the county. Just prior to the Dissolution these distributions from trusts amounted to £332 5s p.a. on the part of thirty of the larger houses of the county, these holding nearly 80 per cent of all monastic assets. This simply means that the monastic establishments were disposing under trusts somewhat less than 0·14 per cent of the capital value of their assets in the alms which they claimed as one of their great responsibilities and glories. Any donor deeply concerned with the poor and their needs would accordingly find a monastic gift a most unsatisfactory instrument for the attainment of his aspirations. It is pure sentimentality to bewail too much, even in Yorkshire, the loss of alms occasioned by the Dissolution. The fact is that the loss sustained in the county by the cessation of monastic alms had been recovered and more as early as 1560 by private endowments constituted for poor relief.

It must also be observed that the gifts of £3525 1s made to Yorkshire monasteries in these two full generations represent an increase in the capital funds of these great establishments of not more than 1·5 per cent, which is one of the lowest for all the counties of the realm. If in sixty years the rate of augmentation of the funds of any charitable instrumentality, or for that matter any spiritual instrumentality, is this modest, a predictable end is in sight whether a Henry VIII or slow erosion be the moving force. This rate of accumulation was simply inadequate to supply any element of growth and must in fact have fallen far short of meeting the debits inevitably arising by fire, decay, and monastic maladministration.

(e) *Maintenance of the Clergy.* The dissolution of the monasteries, with so many serious consequences for Yorkshire, threw heavy additional burdens on the secular clergy, who were among the most miserably endowed and surely among the most poorly educated in all the realm. We have made frequent comment on their plight and on the slow and painful measures which had to be taken to equip them for the great charge which was theirs. The fact was that parochial revenues in the county had largely been legally looted by monastic and collegiate impropriators and that these revenues passed into lay hands with the Reformation, though it must be observed that the parochial clergy were no worse off after the Reformation than before. Taking the whole course of our period in view, one is happy to record that substantial improvement was made in the revenues of the parish clergy by private benefactors concerned with the quality of a clergy ill-equipped to meet the problems of a rapidly moving age. In all, these benefactors gave the large total of £15,661 9s for the maintenance of the clergy, or 6·43 per cent of the whole of charitable endowments in the county. No other county in England had nearly so proud a record of achievement in this respect,[1] and by the close of our era the quality and the social status of the clergyman, save in much of the rural area, had been considerably ameliorated.

It must at the same time be emphasized that almost the whole of this great social and religious gain was made after 1610. Until 1589 there was, in fact, only one capital endowment of more than £60 for the increase of clerical stipends, and almost all the small amount given was in the quite unsatisfactory form of outright bequests to designated clergy. Thus during our first interval only £1078 1s was given for clerical needs, of which approximately one-third was for the regular clergy, as compared, for example, with the huge total of £22,933 5s provided for prayers. Relatively speaking, there was a considerable improvement in the two decades of the Reformation, when £513 7s was provided, but nearly the whole of this sum was in the dubious form of outright gifts or bequests. During the first two Elizabethan decades almost all support was withdrawn, contributions falling to the incredibly low sum of £30 19s in this age of unrelieved secularism. Slow gains began to be made in the later Elizabethan era, £787 19s having been provided in the course of the whole reign, but it was not until the early Stuart period that the great burst of generosity is to be discerned. In these four decades the substantial total of £7051 14s was given by private donors for the augmentation of clerical stipends, almost the whole amount being in the form of capital funds. This movement, owing little to Laud's efforts, was continued at a decidedly accelerated rate during the unsettled years of revolution, when the generous sum of £6230 8s was provided for augmentations. In all, therefore, nearly 85 per cent of the whole amount vested (and upwards of 90 per cent of the capital) for the betterment of the condition of the clergy of the county was given during the last third of the period under study.

Some few at least of these benefactions deserve comment. The first, and, indeed, the only substantial capital endowment for clerical support made before the late Elizabethan period was that founded in 1543 by Sir John Nevill, Lord Latimer, whose benefactions were as well disposed as they were generous. In addition to providing £240 for the support of a stipendiary priest, this donor left approximately £140 for the augmentation of clerical income in Well parish in the North Riding.[2] More than a generation later, in 1589, Leonard Dent, a merchant adventurer of York, endowed with £20 p.a. the service in Eastrington parish, of which he was a native, requiring four sermons to be preached

---

[1] The amounts provided for clerical maintenance in the other counties studied range from 0·48 per cent in Worcestershire to 3·46 per cent in Kent.

[2] *Vide ante*, 311, for an account of his grammar-school foundation. *Vide post*, 395.

quarterly.[1] Another merchant, James Cottrell, in 1595 vested £200 in the municipal authorities of York and of Richmond for the augmentation of clerical stipends in those communities.[2] These, as we have already indicated, were the only really substantial capital sums provided for the support of the clergy prior to 1611.

In 1611 William Gee, a rich and learned man, who had served as Secretary to the Council of the North, by will vested a rent-charge with a capital value of £533 for the purpose of maintaining a preacher at Bishop Burton in the East Riding, with the prudent provision that he should receive £26 13s p.a. 'so long as the religion now established continue', but with only £10 p.a. in the event a change should occur.[3] Sir Robert Watter, the great merchant benefactor of York, in the next year (1612) provided an endowment of £120, the income to be employed for the augmentation of the salary of the minister of St Crux parish.[4] A few years later, in 1615, Edmund Robinson, of uncertain social status, settled on lay feoffees property with a then capital value of upwards of £200 with which to pay £10 p.a. for the maintenance of a preaching clergyman in the chapelry of Dean Head in Huddersfield parish.[5] Later in the same decade Robert Hungate, the London lawyer of Puritan persuasion who had provided a notable benefaction for the erection and endowment of a hospital and school at Sherburn on the model of London's Christ Hospital,[6] likewise bequeathed the equivalent of £1050 towards the augmentation of clerical salaries, the sum of £30 p.a. to be paid for thirty-five years for the better support of a 'preaching minister, to preach once every Saboth, and to catechise once in ye weekeday' in St Cuthbert's parish, York, in Sand Hutton, and in Saxton, each place having the £30 every third year.[7]

[1] Hall, J. G., *South Cave* (Hull, 1892), 155; *Surtees Soc. Pub.*, CXXIX (1917), 201–202, 243–244. Dent was a merchant trading from both York and Boston, Lincolnshire.

[2] *Vide ante*, 359, for mention of Cottrell's other charities and a biographical note.

[3] PCY 31/760 1611; Morrell, *Biography of common man of York*, 37–38, 170–171; Drake, *Eboracum*, 370, 508–509. His monumental inscription, to translate freely, declares him to have been 'a man illustrious for piety, integrity, and charity, especially to the ministers of God's Word. He was eminent . . . in the Latin, Hebrew, and Greek languages . . . for his knowledge of ecclesiastical and civil law; and especially for his acquaintance with theology'. His first wife was Thomasine, daughter of Matthew Hutton, Archbishop of York. Gee also left lands worth £50 to St John's College, Cambridge, and £20 to the poor of York.   [4] *Vide ante*, 268, 295.

[5] *Halifax Antiq. Soc. Papers*, 1915, 215; Lawton, *Collectio*, 139; Archbishop Sharp's MSS. (York), I, 200. The Parliamentary Survey disclosed that a generation later the clerical income was still £10 p.a., the roads were bad, there were fifty families, and there was still no minister.   [6] *Vide ante*, 334.

[7] Saxton (Hungate's birthplace) lay within the parish of Sherburn, where his school was founded. Sand Hutton was a chapel in the parish of Bossall, which

Thomas Moseley, a York merchant and a former mayor, by the terms of his will in 1624 augmented the salary of the clergyman of St Michael's parish in that city so long 'as he contineweth preaching minister'.[1] In the same decade two gentlemen of Attercliffe, near Sheffield, were principal contributors towards the building of a chapel for their community. Stephen Bright, who seems to have been the prime mover, gave an endowment of £5 p.a., while William Spencer added property worth £40, and other inhabitants subscribed smaller emoluments, in order to establish a stipend of £10 p.a. for a preaching minister.[2]

In the closing decade of the early Stuart period, the generous total of £3620 9s, of which almost the entire amount was capital, was provided by Yorkshire benefactors for the better maintenance of the clergy of the county. Thus in 1631 Sir Timothy Hutton, who had inherited a considerable estate from his father, the Archbishop, not only left outright £10 p.a. for a term of five years to designated clergy, but provided a rent-charge of £20 p.a. for 'a preacheinge minister' at Marrick, the manor of which he had held since 1592, 'soe longe as it shall continue in my poore posterity'.[3] In the same year, a York merchant, John Vaux, settled endowments valued at £180 to secure an augmentation of £6 p.a. for the minister of one York parish and £3 p.a. for the clergyman of another, as well as leaving £3 p.a. to the poor who should be present at the sermons he had endowed.[4] The rectory of Sandal Magna was most adequately endowed by the will of Sir Richard Beaumont in 1632 when its ownership was bequeathed by him to his three nephews subject to

Hungate also remembered with an annuity of £1 for the relief of the poor of the place from any taxes that might be levied.

[1] PCY 38/238 1624; PP 1825, X, 635; Yorks. Arch. Soc. Rec., L (1913), 132–134. A native of Cawthorne, Moseley was admitted a freeman in 1572 and was chosen mayor in 1590 and again in 1602. He represented York in Parliament in 1596. At his death, at the age of eighty-five, his estate was valued at upwards of £1600.

[2] Lawton, Collectio, 223; Hunter Arch. Soc. Trans., IV (1937), 80; Hunter, Hallamshire, 240–241, 248–250. Vide post, 396–397. Bright, the son of a yeoman of Carbrook, made his considerable fortune in the service of the Earl of Arundel. He was granted arms in 1642, the year of his death. His son, Sir John, was Governor of York and an officer of Parliament.

[3] PCY 41/569 1631; Yorks. Arch. Journal, VI (1881), 247–248; Surtees Soc. Pub., XVII (1843), 33–39, 248–253. Born about 1569, Hutton in 1592 married a daughter of Sir George Bowes and with a gift of £1900 from his father established himself as a country gentleman. In 1598 he purchased Marske, which became his principal residence. He was knighted in 1605 and was on two occasions chosen to be chief magistrate of Richmond. His rent rolls at the time of his death ran to more than £1000 p.a., including £250 p.a. from Marrick Abbey and the tithes. (Vide ante, 329, 359.)

[4] Drake, Eboracum, 222–223; PP 1826, XIII, 629.

an annual payment of £20 for the maintenance of divine services in the church.[1]

The stipend of the vicarage of Bishop Wilton was increased by £6 p.a. in 1632 by the bequest of the lord of the manor, Sir William Hildyard, who provided that 10s should be given monthly for a sermon in the church, while £2 13s p.a. was also settled on the trustees for a monthly dole of bread for the poor.[2] A few years later William Rooks, a gentleman of Rodes Hall, in Bradford, assumed the principal responsibility for building a chapel at Wibsey, just to the south of Bradford, at an estimated charge of £80, which he and other inhabitants of the community, including the hamlet of Bierley, endowed with capital to the worth of £410 in order to ensure the conservation of the edifice and the salary of a settled curate or preacher.[3] In the last year of the decade a London tradesman, Christopher Coulson, a native of Seamer, by will settled an endowment worth upwards of £130 to secure the preaching of thirteen sermons annually in Seamer church, with the provision that the income beyond £6 10s should be distributed to the poor of Newby township in that parish.[4]

There was inevitably some diminution of giving for the augmentation of clerical stipends during the decade of Civil War, though one is amazed to note that the substantial total of £1785 was in fact provided. Among the earliest of these benefactions was an interesting one made in 1643 by a gentleman of the region of Otley, William Vavasour, who, as we have seen, likewise assisted with the foundation of grammar

---

[1] PCY 41/803–804 1632; *Yorks. Arch. Journal*, XXIV (1917), 6–7; *Complete baronetage*, II, 51; Lawton, *Collectio*, 152; *PP* 1899, LXXI, 711. Beaumont was the son and heir of Edward Beaumont of Whitley Beaumont. He succeeded to his considerable inheritance in 1575. He was knighted in 1603 and in 1609 purchased Sandal Magna from Sir Henry Savile for the sum of £2400. He represented Pontefract in Parliament in 1625 and was created a baronet in 1628. He died unmarried in October, 1631, bequeathing his principal estates to a distant cousin, Sir Thomas Beaumont. Beaumont had in 1621 given a rent-charge with £27 capital value for the augmentation of the stipend of the schoolmaster at Almondbury.

[2] PCY 42/19 1632; Burton, *Hemingbrough*, 223–224; *Alum. cantab.*, I, ii, 369; *PP* 1824, XIV, 749. Hildyard was the son of William Hildyard, a successful lawyer and the Recorder of York. Born in 1577, he was educated at Cambridge (Trinity College) and at the Inner Temple. He married Isabel, a co-heir of Ralph Hansby, esq., who brought Bishop Wilton to the union. He was knighted in 1603.

[3] Archbishop Sharp's MSS. (York), I, 173; *VCH, Yorks.*, III, 58; *Bradford Antiquary*, n.s., I (1900), 102; Lawton, *Collectio*, 116; Turner, *Biographia Halifaxiensis*, 241. *Vide post*, 398. Rooks was a member of a large family of lesser gentry settled in the general region of Bradford. A brother, Jonas, was a fellow of University College, Oxford.

[4] *Vide ante*, 338, for a discussion of Coulson's grammar-school foundation at Newby.

schools at Otley and Guiseley.[1] Vavasour bequeathed £10 p.a. towards
the proper maintenance 'of an honest and able preacher' at Otley on
condition that the inhabitants of the parish should within the three
years next following ensure an additional £40 p.a. for the minister's
stipend and with the further provision that the whole of his bequest be
employed for the benefit of preaching ministers in five chapels within
the parish if the condition were not met.[2] This donor likewise bequeathed a rent-charge of £4 p.a. for the augmentation of the clergyman's salary at Burley chapel (in Otley parish), or more accurately, for
its endowment, on condition that the inhabitants should within three
years secure an additional £16 p.a. in order to gain the services of a
settled and preaching minister in that community.[3] Vavasour's sister,
Mary Pullein, by indenture in 1647 conveyed by gift £100 for the
additional endowment of the stipend of the clergyman at Otley and £16
for the endowment of the curate of Burley chapel, as well as a gift of
£13 for the general uses of the church at Burley.[4]

A generous and a most carefully considered endowment was created
for the benefit of the large and scattered parish of Halifax in 1645 by
the great benefactor of that town, Nathaniel Waterhouse. This merchant
donor conveyed to trustees an endowment of about £200 to secure the
services of a lecturer in the parish church of Halifax whose special duty
it would be to catechize the children and to pray with the poor in his
almshouse and workhouse, with the prudently added stipulation that
during periods when there should be no such lecturer the income
should be distributed to the poor of Halifax and the other towns within
the parish. Waterhouse further vested an endowment of upwards of
£800, with a then income of £40 to be distributed in amounts ranging
from £2 p.a. to £5 p.a. to the clergy in the twelve chapels within Halifax
parish, while further welding the parish together with the provision
that each of these clergymen should preach a sermon in Halifax parish
church in rotation on the first Wednesday in the month. Since these
funds were invested in properties which increased rapidly in value, this
great bequest did much to relieve the condition created by a steady
increase in population within this already industrialized area and to
provide competent clergy for villages that had long since become
towns.[5]

In the final decade of our period, 1651–1660, there was an amazing
acceleration in the rate of giving for this laudable and greatly needed

---

[1] *Vide ante*, 328.

[2] It appears that the condition was not met, since the Parliamentary Survey
reported a stipend of £10 p.a. paid by the impropriator (*PP* 1894, LXIV,
Otley, 21–22).

[3] This condition was evidently met (*Ibid.*, LXIV, Otley, 42).

[4] *Ibid.*, LXIV, Otley, 22–23, 36, 40.   [5] *Vide ante*, 276, 290.

purpose. In this brief interval the great total of £4445 8s was provided as endowment for the augmentation of clerical stipends, more by far, it may be mentioned, than was given for this purpose in the county from 1480 to 1610. All classes of men participated in this effort, with, however, a predominant contribution by the lower gentry and the yeomanry. Thus in 1652 John Haigh, a yeoman of Midhope, augmented the endowment for the clergyman of that chapelry, leaving lands with a capital value of £133 for the maintenance of a settled preacher in the community; the earliest mention of the chapel is in the will of Ralph Wood, proved in 1626, who left the residue of his small estate to be applied to maintain services at Bradfield and Midhope.[1] In the same year, Francis Layton, a gentleman of Rawdon, whose almshouse foundation and apprenticeship fund have already been noted,[2] provided for the completion of a chapel at Rawdon 'all which and more had not now been to do if the Lord Archbishop Doctor Neale had not denied me the power of presenting of a minister or curate to the said chappel when it was finished and endowed', and endowed it with £400 for the support of a resident clergyman, with powers of presentation reserved to his own family.[3] Another yeoman, Stephen Cawood, whose school foundation at East Hardwick has been discussed, in 1653 endowed with £6 10s p.a. the stipend of a clergyman for the chapel he had built in that village, with the additional provision that he should have £12 p.a. for his services as schoolmaster.[4] In the same year Richard Spoone, also a yeoman, who had built a chapel in Stannington, endowed the minister, who must be known for 'soundness of doctrine, and diligence in preaching', with lands then worth upwards of £160 of capital value.[5] Still another yeoman, Henry Wilson, of Elland, in this year bequeathed considerable property, probably valued at about £400, 'to the use of him, who . . . shall be stipendiary preacher or minister of God's Word' in that place, together with £50 for building a house for the minister.[6] An even larger foundation was made, also in 1653, by Sir Miles Stapleton and other freeholders of Armley to provide an adequate stipend for a curate who would preach in their chapel, common land belonging to

[1] (Wood) PCY 39/17 1626; (Haigh) PCC 213 Bowyer 1652; Lawton, *Collectio*, 190; Hunter, *Hallamshire*, II, 197.

[2] *Vide ante*, 277, 290–291, and *post*, 399.

[3] The then rector of Guiseley, in giving his consent to the foundation, commented that the parish was three miles long with the church in the west end, a chapel in the east end, and Rawdon in the middle. Layton's gift he declared to be a 'convenient and needful woorke both of piety towards God and charyty towards the neighboors of that towne ship . . . where the wayes alsoe are very ill and crooked' (*S. P. Dom.*, 1631, CCII, 48).

[4] *Vide ante*, 344, and *post*, 399.

[5] *Vide ante*, 343, and *post*, 399. In this case, too, a school bequest is mixed with an endowment for clerical support.

[6] PCC 56 Brent 1653; Turner, *Biographia Halifaxiensis*, 21–23.

these proprietors having by agreement been constituted as the endowment with a value of about £540.[1]

The endowment of clerical stipends, particularly to secure settled
clergy in the chaprelries of the county, continued at an accelerated rate
during the more stable years of the Protectorate. In 1657 Thomas
Gledhill of the lesser gentry and the brother of Sarah Gledhill, a
notable benefactor,[2] established an endowment of £120 for the support
of 'a lawfull preaching minister of the word of God at Riponden Chappell' (Halifax), as well as giving £10 outright to a clergyman and £54
of endowment for the 'most needful poor' of Barkisland.[3] Another
landed gentleman, Richard Parkins, who also had trading connections
in Hull, in 1656 left an endowment of £120 for the support of a preacher
in 'Waldby' [Wauldby in Elloughton parish], with an additional £3 p.a.
for the remainder of the life of the incumbent and £4 outright as a token
of his esteem.[4] In the same year a merchant who had translated himself
into the lower gentry of the county, Henry Westby, endowed with lands
then valued at £5 p.a. the stipend of an 'assistant preaching minister'
at Rotherham, as well as providing £2 10s towards the support of a
settled preacher at Greasbrough chapel in that parish.[5] These very
evidently Puritan benefactions for the clergy of the county were further
enhanced in 1657 by the bequest of William Hide, the minister at
Market Weighton, whose most generous charities for the poor and for
education there have already been noted. Hide left his house, valued at
about £80, for the use of the clergyman of the parish and for meetings
of godly parishioners 'for their mutual edification', while also augmenting the stipend of the parish with a rental of £2 p.a.[6] John Harrison, the
merchant who was Leeds' great benefactor, and who had at his own
charge in 1634 built St John's church at a cost of at least £600, confirmed
by his will in 1658 endowments for the support of the minister there
with a capital worth of at least £1600.[7] Finally, we may record the great

[1] *Old Leeds charities*, 20–22; Lawton, *Collectio*, 93; Thoresby, *Ducatus*, 187;
Yorks. Arch. Journal, VIII (1884), 433–440. Stapleton was knighted in 1661 or
1662. The son of Robert Stapleton, Esq., he married Mary, the daughter of Sir
Ingram Hopton. He was fined £500 in 1664 for 'being disordered with liquor
and striking the Lord Mayor of York with his cane'.   [2] *Vide ante*, 346.

[3] PCC 334 Ruthen 1657; *Yorks. Arch. Soc. Rec.*, IX (1890), 108–109; *PP*
1828, XX, 592; *PP* 1899, LXXI, Halifax, 595–596; Turner, *Biographia Halifaxiensis*, 8–9.   [4] PCC 303 Berkley 1656.

[5] PCC 427 Ruthen 1657; *Yorks. Arch. Soc. Rec.*, IX (1890), 113; *PP* 1895,
LXXV, Rotherham, 51. This land, because of underlying minerals, was later
to increase greatly in value. Westby also left £40 as a stock for the poor of
Rotherham and £10 for outright distribution; £20 as a stock for the poor of
Greasbrough and £3 8s outright; and £2 to the poor of Kimberworth, also in
Rotherham parish.   [6] *Vide ante*, 249, 344.

[7] *Vide ante*, 277, 298, 314, and *post*, 401–402, for an account of the great charities,
for the bibliographical references, and for a notice of the career of this remarkable

benefaction of Brian Cooke, the founder of a school and of an almshouse at Arksey, who in 1660 conveyed to five trustees the rectory and parsonage of Arksey, with other properties of an amount sufficient to increase the stipend of the incumbent from £12 p.a. to £100 p.a., thereby creating a living with an income adequate to command a 'preaching minister' of the highest competence.[1]

(f) *Endowment of Lectureships.* We have seen that a substantial number of the benefactions made for the support of the parochial clergy of Yorkshire were from men of Puritan leanings, ranging from mild interest to a fervent zeal for the building in the county of a learned and a preaching clergy which would differ radically from the pathetically inadequate priesthood of the early Tudor period and the ill-provided and neglected ministry of the Elizabethan era. Surely most of these donors must have been moved by the hope that more men like Favour, whose ministry stood like a beacon light, could be established in parishes across the county. Clearly these were the motives of the benefactors who sought by the endowment of lectureships to claim the county for Geneva; to overwhelm the slowly yielding Catholicism of many regions of Yorkshire with God's Word zealously and diligently preached. These endowments, which we have occasionally and quite arbitrarily reckoned as lectureships rather than as augmentations, were in Yorkshire to reach the large total of £6361, all having been given in a concentrated period of two generations extending from 1601 to 1660. This sum, the whole being capital, accounted for 2·61 per cent of all charitable funds provided in the county and, quite surprisingly, represents a proportion of total benefactions exceeded only in Lancashire, where London Puritanism was making an heroic and on the whole a successful effort to gain the county for Geneva before it had ever quite been won by Lambeth. In Yorkshire, too, a considerable fraction of these endowments was provided by Londoners of Yorkshire antecedents, while an even larger proportion was given by merchants with Puritan leanings, whether they were of London or York. At least a few of these foundations should be briefly noted.

In 1616 John Fourness, a Halifax clothier, in addition to providing for an unendowed almshouse with the gift of two cottages then worth an estimated £30, left lands and other property with an approximate capital value of £110 for the support of a preaching minister in Sowerby chapel (Halifax), who must be sufficiently well trained as to hold a master's degree.[2] A stoutly Puritan gentleman of Silkstone, the son

and infinitely generous man. Harrison's religious charities are fully described by White Kennett in the manuscript additions to his *Case of impropriations* (preserved in the Bodleian), I, 200, 210, 222.   [1] *Vide ante*, 280, 346.

[2] *Halifax Antiq. Soc. Papers*, 1910, 204; *PP* 1828, XX, 583; *PP* 1899, LXXI, Halifax, 242, 507–508.

of a London lawyer, Thomas Cutler, in 1622 provided an endowment of £300 towards 'the maintenance of a zealous preacher of God's Word for ever' at Stainborough, as well as leaving £40 as a stock for the relief of the poor of Silkstone.[1] This donor's widow, Ellen, a sister of John Rainey, also a considerable benefactor,[2] at her death in 1636 further endowed the chapel with real property then valued at £420, while providing an endowment for poor relief of approximately £100.[3]

A merchant's widow of York, Elizabeth Moseley, before her death in 1640, richly augmented the living of St John's with an endowment of £800 capital value in order to secure a 'painful and preaching' minister for the parish.[4] In 1633 John Rainey, whose sister's endowment has been mentioned above, generously endowed Worsborough chapel in Darfield parish. A successful London draper, Rainey, as we have seen, lent generous and intelligent support to the principal social needs of the village of his birth—the school, the poor, and now the church—with most carefully devised endowments. In his lifetime he had placed the solid works of William Perkins in three volumes in Worsborough chapel for the edification of the people, while by his will he settled on the Drapers' Company as trustees funds then yielding £30 p.a. to endow the stipend of a 'learned and religious preacher' to preach twice on each Sunday as well as endowing a lectureship in London under the care of the Drapers' Company.[5] It was London wealth, too, which established at Wakefield one of the richest of all lectureships in England, some years after the death in 1643 of Elizabeth Hicks, the widow of Baptist Hicks, who had been elevated to a peerage in 1628 as Viscount Campden. This woman, whose charities are more fully described in another place, bequeathed to the Mercers' Company the great sum of £3100 to purchase impropriate rectories in Yorkshire, Lincolnshire, and Durham. The trustees instead founded two lectureships at Wakefield and at Grantham, Lincolnshire. The Wakefield lectureship was endowed with an annual stipend of £100, to which the first incumbent, Joshua Kirby, a London-bred Oxford graduate, was appointed in 1650.[6]

A quietly determined Puritan gentleman, Robert Dyneley, who was lord of the manor of Bramhope, in Otley, sometime before 1649 endowed a carefully constituted chapelry for a Puritan divine. The chapel was built at Bramhope in 1654 at a charge of about £100. Dyneley controlled most of the common land of the manor and persuaded all the other freeholders to join him in vesting land to the extent of 130 acres, thereby creating a stipend of £40 p.a. The power of

[1] Vide ante, 238.   [2] Vide ante, 241, 336.   [3] Vide ante, 238–239.

[4] PCY April 1640; Drake, Eboracum, 278; Lawton, Collectio, 19; Yorks. Arch. Soc. Rec., L (1914), 132–133. This donor's husband was the only son of Thomas Moseley (vide ante, 378).   [5] Vide ante, 241, 336.

[6] Vide Jordan, Charities of London, 170, 175, 290, 343, 368–369, for a discussion of this donor's charities and for a biographical notice.

nominating the incumbent was reserved to private trustees, subject to approval by the ministers of four solidly Puritan parishes in the West Riding.[1] And finally, we have to note the bequest of £10 p.a. made in 1652 by Robert Metcalf, whose many benefactions for Beverley have already been discussed, for the support of the lecturer in that community.[2]

(g) *Care of the Fabric*. The profoundly important shift in men's aspirations from a deep and moving concern with the whole range of religious needs to the secular preoccupations which mark the structure of life and thought after the middle of the sixteenth century is most pointedly documented, even in Yorkshire, when we consider the care which men assumed for the fabric of the many churches of the county. We have gathered under the broad head of 'church repair' a great variety of donations for ornamentation, the decoration of fabric, the utensils of the service, and the vestments of priests, as well as the care so persistently required by Gothic architecture for its own survival. During our entire period pious Yorkshire donors lent their support to the maintenance and embellishment of the fabric with benefactions totalling £6774. This represents no more than 2·78 per cent of the total of charitable gifts for all causes, and one is perplexed to observe that it is relatively the lowest percentage devoted to this purpose in any of the ten counties we have studied, save for the two great urban communities. This is true despite the fact that Yorkshire gave so freely for religious uses generally.[3] It should, indeed, be noted that the amount provided

---

[1] Dale, *Yorkshire Puritanism*, 46; *Bradford Antiquary*, n.s., I (1900), 325–334; *PP* 1894, LXIV, Otley, 31–34. The first incumbent was Zechariah Crossley, a Presbyterian, who was protected by Dyneley after the Restoration. The ecclesiastical authorities at that time sought to gain control of the endowment, but Dyneley successfully maintained that the chapel was on private property and that the endowment was privately constituted. Crossley died in 1665 and was succeeded by another nonconformist minister, Robert Pickering. Dyneley was indicted for holding a conventicle in 1666, but continued until his death in 1689 to hold services in his house, the chapel having by that date at last come into the hands of the Established Church.

Dyneley was the son of Sir Robert, who had married a daughter of Sir Robert Stapleton of Wighill. Dyneley married Margaret, daughter of Sir John Stanhope of Melford, Kent. Dyneley was without political interests, took no active part in the Civil War, and was respected by all groups in the West Riding, but he was simply, quietly, and most obdurately, a nonconformist.

[2] *Vide ante*, 247, 302, 360.   [3] These proportions are as follows:

	Per cent		Per cent
Bristol	0·95	London	1·78
Buckinghamshire	3·35	Norfolk	7·31
Hampshire	3·41	Somerset	3·66
Kent	7·60	Worcestershire	3·43
Lancashire	5·59	Yorkshire	2·78

for the care of the church fabric of the county constituted slightly less than a tenth of the sum provided for the generality of religious uses.

It should likewise be observed that well over half of all these gifts for the maintenance of the fabric of perhaps 700 churches were given during the decades prior to the storms of reformation. In these two generations £3724 16s was provided, most of this probably scantily adequate total being a gathering of many small bequests. Nor was there a particularly serious falling away of generosity for church repair and decoration during the brief period of the Reformation, when £427 1s was given, again largely by small donors. But what can only be described as disaster was to visit the fabric of Yorkshire's many churches during the long Elizabethan period, when no more than the trifling total of £157 19s was disposed to meet the demands that were mounting steadily as the fabric of most churches fell into a disrepair approaching decay.[1] Matters were at least somewhat bettered in the first three decades of the seventeenth century and were very considerably improved in the Laudian decade, when £1403 14s was contributed for the repair of the parochial churches, though this could not have meant in average terms more than about £2 for each church in the county. This brief and somewhat artificially induced revival of concern was followed during the period of the Puritan Revolution by a neglect of church repairs equalling even the bleak secularism of the Elizabethan era, the total given for this purpose amounting during these years to no more than £69 8s.

We shall not comment on individual benefactions for church repairs in Yorkshire, of which there were in fact relatively few of consequence after 1540, but some further analysis of the structure of gifts for this purpose may be useful. It is significant, in the first place, that a large proportion (69·85 per cent) of all benefactions for this use were in the form of outright gifts for immediate use, the sum of the endowments constituted for the care of particular churches amounting to only £2042 13s in the whole course of our period.

The decade 1521–1530 may perhaps be taken as typical of the attitude of Yorkshire donors towards the architectural inheritance which they enjoyed from the medieval past in the parochial church structure of the county. In this interval benefactions were accumulated totalling £630 1s, or probably something over £1 for every church then serving a parish or chapelry, an amount even then certainly inadequate in relation to the need. Of this total, only one benefaction in the amount

---

[1] We have not included the outlays made, principally from earlier endowments, on York Minster. But these too betray the cold touch of Elizabethan secularism. From 1482 to the accession of Elizabeth, something like £5600 was spent on the fabric of the great church; from that time forward through 1587, something like £1375 was laid out for the purpose.

of £20 was an endowment, the whole of the remainder having been given for immediate uses. There were in all 221 individual gifts and bequests for immediate use, ranging from a penny or so to one relatively large bequest in the amount of £81 13s. Substantially more than half of all the gifts in this decade were amounts of less than 10s, while the median gifts for the entire group of donors was a bequest by a member of the lower gentry of 17s 6d for repairs on his parish church. This structure of giving reveals a rather general sense of responsibility and of participation by all classes of the society, though even in this relatively early period there are neither so many nor as generous donors as the undoubted piety of the county would suggest. The reason for the steady relative indifference of Yorkshiremen to the fabric of their parish churches may almost certainly be found in the fact that so large a proportion of parishes had long before been impropriated by the monasteries and the collegiate churches, this being but another instance of the ill effects flowing from this historical circumstance, which we have on several earlier occasions discussed.

But sufficient as this explanation may be for the comparative uninterest of donors in the proper maintenance of the church fabric of this vast shire, it will certainly not suffice to account for the stark secularism of Elizabethan neglect, a neglect which was complete and all but catastrophic. Thus in the decade 1581–1590 the total of benefactions made by men and women of the county for the support of its churches came to no more than £36 14s. There was not a single capital gift or bequest made for this purpose, wh'le the largest contribution was by a gentlewoman in the amount of £13 7s. The habit of leaving at least some small sum for the repair of a roof, the decoration of a chapel, or the purchase of a bell—for an intricate variety of needs and improvements —had largely disappeared. There were but fifty-seven contributions made for church repairs in this decade, almost the whole number having been made by humble and traditionally pious men and women of the husbandmen and yeomen of the county. Only five benefactions were in amounts of £1 or more, while the median gift for this decade was only 7s. The record of these years, and, for that matter, of a full half-century of Elizabethan rule, suggests an all but complete want of concern for the care of the great heritage of the county, just as in other aspects of religious life and activity the cool dominance of secularism had snuffed out giving for religious uses.

(h) *Church Building*. The donors of the county were relatively much more generous in voluntary contributions for church building than they were in giving for the repair and maintenance of the existing church fabric. None the less, when we take into account the size of the county, the important shifts in population that occurred during our long period, and the quite immature parochial organization of the county in 1480, it seems apparent that Yorkshire was one of the few counties in the realm that was probably 'under-churched' at the outset of our period, most decidedly so at its end. Once again, the large number of impropriations to monasteries and to collegiate churches seem to have deterred and discouraged local efforts at church building, while after the Reformation there are many evidences that impropriators steadfastly resisted attempts occasionally made to carve out new parishes from a number of very large parochial units, especially in the West Riding where a rapid increase in population further aggravated the difficulties for residents of now thriving towns lying quite distant from the parochial church.

During the course of our period Yorkshire benefactors gave an estimated total of £11,049 5s.[1] for new building or major renovations, this amounting to 4·53 per cent of all charitable benefactions and being a quite low proportion when measured by the amounts provided in other counties.[2] This sum was far less than half that given by the pious donors of the county for prayers, substantially less than was gathered for the improvement of the lot of the clergy and, to make a secular comparison, considerably less than a third the capital provided for almshouse foundations. Further, it should be emphasized that in Yorkshire, as in all other counties, interest in church building was principally concentrated in the decades prior to the Reformation. In these six decades such contributions were well sustained and were designated for a considerable variety of building purposes. The total given for this use during these two generations was £6309 1s, this being the heavy proportion of 57·1 per cent of the whole amount provided for the enlargement of the church facilities of the county during the long period with which we are concerned. Very little was given during the unsettled decades of the Reformation, much of the £304 1s that was furnished having been left for the completion of work already in progress. Even so, it is almost staggering to realize that the total for the years of the Reformation substantially exceeded the tiny sum of £240 9s left for church building and major rehabilitation of fabric during the long, prosperous, and stable Elizabethan era. In fact, the whole amount given for church building plus that provided for normal maintenance of the existing fabric was only £398 8s for this entire interval, which in Yorkshire as in the rest of the realm was one of invincible secularism of aspirations. There were slow, though on the

---

[1] It should be emphasized that this total is an aggregate of amounts which are frequently estimates and occasionally not much more than guesses bearing some relation to known costs for roughly comparable construction in roughly the same period. *Vide* Jordan, *Philanthropy*, I, 52, for a discussion of this matter.

[2] The range extends from 2·67 per cent in Bristol to 11·55 per cent in Lancashire.

whole unimpressive, gains in the first two of the early Stuart decades, while from 1621 to 1640 a lively and an important effort was made by private donors to provide chapels, usually, as we have seen, with clerical endowments which sought to relieve the needs of distant communicants in the large and now heavily populated parishes of the West Riding. In all, £3007 14s was given for church building in the early Stuart era, while the by no means inconsiderable sum of £1188 was given during the revolutionary years, almost wholly for the foundation of still more chapels.

We have already had occasion to note a number of chapels added by donors to existing church structures in connection with chantry foundations. Beyond these, we have recorded sixteen additional chapels, most of them for chantry purposes, which were built by private donors during the course of our period at an estimated total cost of £1020, all save two of which had been completed prior to 1540. These benefactions need not be mentioned in detail, though it should be observed that with one exception all the donors were drawn from the ranks of the nobility, the gentry, and the clergy.

Yorkshire was by no means immune from the 'plague of towers' visited upon older churches all over England by fifteenth century taste and carrying over in most counties until Elizabethan parsimony, if not a change in architectural tastes, brought the fad to an end. There were, however, relatively few towers and steeples built in Yorkshire in our period, at least with voluntary funds. In all, we have noted such church works in twenty parishes of the county, of which fifteen were completed prior to 1541, on which a quite tightly estimated outlay of £964 11s was made by voluntary subscriptions. Once more space does not permit the recital of the details, but it may be mentioned that donors drawn from all the substantial classes lent some measure of contribution to this decorative addition to the church fabric of the county.

Slightly less than a third of the total amount provided during our period for church building was employed for the substantial enlargement of existing church structures or for major works of rehabilitation. In view of the size of the county and the significant shifts in population that occurred within it in the course of our period, it is surprising that work of this kind was undertaken, at least with voluntary funds, in no more than thirty-five parishes. We have noted gifts and bequests totalling £3490 7s for such purposes, which in several parishes were evidently supplemented with amounts derived from non-charitable sources. Twenty of these undertakings, it is interesting to observe, were completed prior to the Reformation, the bulk of the funds provided (£2164) having been recorded in this relatively brief interval.

Early in our period Sir Hugh Hastings charged his estate with the building of the north aisle of the parish church of Campsall, the work

being completed shortly after 1489 at an estimated cost of £100.[1]
Extensive improvements and enlargements as well as the admission of
more light were carried out at Doncaster a few years later (*ca.* 1493)
at a charge of perhaps £150,[2] while at Thornhill from 1493 to
about 1500 the choir was enlarged and clerestories added by William
Savile and by Robert Frost, the rector.[3] Bequests or gifts totalling £84
have been noted for the building of the north aisle at Beverley at about
the turn of the century, among which was a legacy received in 1498
from Robert Dacres, a weaver, in the amount of £16, to which in 1502
his widow added a bequest of £4 for the same use.[4] Sir Richard York,
the great York merchant whose almshouse and chantry foundations
have previously been discussed, not only built a chapel in the church of
St John Evangelist but some little time before his death in 1498 rebuilt
the north aisle of the church, repaired the roof, and provided numerous
ornaments, all at a charge to his generosity of about £180.[5] The abbot
of St Mary's, York, William Sever, at about the same date and apparently
from his own purse, rebuilt the abbot's residence,[6] while from 1482 until
about 1520 approximately £800 was contributed towards the extensive
repair of the fabric and general rehabilitation of the church at Ripon,
which was in a state of serious decay.[7] Probably extensive improvements
were undertaken at Hedon in *ca.* 1504, for which, however, we have
found only one bequest of £10 left by a local merchant, John Crofts,
who had also been mayor of the town.[8] Far more elaborate improvements
and enlargements were carried out at Wighill at about the same date by
Sir William Stapleton, who at a fairly certain charge of £140 added a
chapel to the church, inserted a number of much-needed windows,
probably rebuilt the north wall, and repaired, if he did not rebuild, the
roof of the whole structure.[9] We have likewise counted bequests totalling

[1] *Vide ante*, 368, for an account of his other benefactions and for a biographical notice. Hastings also endowed prayers at Campsall.
[2] Jackson, *St. George's church*, 19.
[3] *Yorks. Arch. Journal*, I (1870), 71, 109, XXIV (1917), 37–38, XXV (1920),
8; *Surtees Soc. Pub.*, LIII (1868), 187n.–188n.   [4] *Ibid.*, LIII (1868), 137.
[5] *Vide ante*, 255, for a biographical sketch and for an account of his charities.
We may note here as well the bequest of Thomas Spicer, a merchant, who in
1505 left five timbers and stone 'to fulfill the space of two roomes' towards the
building of the north aisle (*Surtees Soc. Pub.*, LIII, 1868, 135n.).
[6] Davies, Robert, *The King's mannour house at York* (York, 1883), 1.
[7] Smith, Lucius, *Ripon Minster* (Leeds, 1914), 1–144, *passim*, as well as a large
number of legacies noted for this work.
[8] PCY 6/121 1505; *Surtees Soc. Pub.*, LIII (1868), 230. Crofts was a shipowner
and merchant. He had been bailiff of Hedon and the town's mayor from 1500
to 1504. His will also provided an estimated £3 for church general and £31 10s
for prayers.
[9] PCY 6/96 1503; *Yorks. Arch. Journal*, XXIII (1915), 112–113; *Surtees
Soc. Pub.*, LIII (1868), 221–222. Stapleton was a great-grandson of Sir Brian,
also of Wighill, a fourteenth-century soldier; his father was Sir John. Sir William

£28 4s towards apparently extensive rehabilitation being carried forward at Ottringham in this period of about a decade at the turn of the century when a great deal of major work was being done on the fabric of the parochial churches of the county.

Considerable work was also undertaken in the two following decades, 1511–1530, particularly in the West Riding. Thus the choir at Waddington was built about 1511 by Richard Tempest at a roughly estimated charge of £60.[1] Extensive renovations and enlargements were completed at Stillingfleet in *ca*. 1520, for which bequests totalling not quite £50 have been recorded. At Selby, at about the same time, the church was considerably extended.[2] The north aisle at Woolley was built somewhat before 1522 by Sir Richard Woodrove at a cost of £47, this donor also providing the church with a bell,[3] while a few years later Alvered Comyn built the choir in the monastery church of St Oswald's (Nostell Priory), of which he was prior.[4]

Improvements and enlargements of this kind were continued, though at a rapidly declining rate, during the two decades of the Reformation. Among these undertakings may be mentioned the building of the south aisle of Osmotherley church by the executors of Sir James Strangwayes shortly after 1544,[5] and the similar work carried out at Easby (near Richmond) somewhat more than a decade later, to which Matthew Phillip left a bequest of £2.[6] In the middle of the century the church of St Martin's in York was far gone with decay and demolition when John Beane, a merchant and mayor, intervened to save the structure, with the aid of other parishioners, and to which in 1580 he was to leave a bequest of one hundred marks for a ring of three bells.[7] Sir William Gascoigne

married first a daughter of Sir James Pickering of Oswaldkirk and secondly Joan, a daughter of Sir Thomas Tunstall and the widow of Sir Roger Warde. He also left £23 for prayers, £1 to the clergy, £3 for church repairs, £1 for church general, £1 to the sick, and 3s to the poor.

[1] PCY 11/296 1537; *Bradford Antiquary*, n.s., I (1900), 491–502; James, John, *Bradford* (L., 1891), 203–204. Tempest likewise built a chapel in Bradford church at about the same date. He was Squire of the Body to Henry VII and was knighted at Tournai in 1513. Tempest was High Sheriff of Yorkshire in 1516 and held the posts of Bailiff of Wakefield and Master Forester of Bowland. He died in 1537.　　　　　　　　[2] Morrell, *Selby*, 117.

[3] *Yorks. Arch. Journal*, XXVII (1924), 295, 311.

[4] Hunter, *South Yorkshire*, II, 209; VCH, *Yorks.*, III, 235.

[5] PCY 11/557 1541; Surtees Soc. Pub., CVI (1902), 125–126. The charge of £40 was borne by the estate. The son of Sir Thomas Strangwayes had been High Sheriff of Yorkshire in 1538. He also left £45 to prayers and £20 to the poor of several parishes.

[6] *Ibid.*, XXVI (1853), 103–104. The will, dated 18 November 1557, was proved at Richmond Commissary Court, probably in 1558. This donor, who was a member of the lower gentry, also left £5 p.a. for prayers.

[7] PCY 21/414 1580; Torr, *Antiquities of York*, 79; Davies, Robert, *Walks through the city of York* (Westminster, 1880), 182; Auden, *Survey of York*, 109.

in 1551 by will provided £40 for the building of the choir at Harewood church, while bequeathing as well £27 for prayers for the repose of his soul.[1]

As we have indicated, there was practically no private support for church building, or for that matter for repairs, during the whole of the Elizabethan period, such small undertakings as there were dating from the closing years of the reign. In 1592 the 'great loft' of Wakefield church was built at an estimated charge of £20, while in 1607 the long gallery was provided for this church.[2] Similarly, a first gallery, the so-called 'merchants' loft', was erected at a cost of perhaps £40 in Trinity Church, Hull, while the remaining two galleries were built early in the seventeenth century, the most substantial bequest being one for £10 left by Robert Ambler, a shipowner, in 1606 for the building of the loft 'for better hearing of God's word'.[3] The building of these galleries completes the short annal of major improvements and enlargements undertaken over a period of forty years which was marked by an almost complete secularization of aspirations in Yorkshire as in England.

Nor was there any widespread interest among private donors in major renovations during the early decades of the seventeenth century. At an uncertain date, but possibly in 1612, Sir Christopher Hildyard built the small transept on the south side of Winestead church in the East Riding,[4] while donations were being made at about the same date to secure the enlargement of Cross Stone chapel, in Halifax parish, towards which, however, we have found no more than four contributions, totalling £5 10s, of which the largest was made by Anthony Sutcliffe in 1613 in the amount of £2.[5] Rather more than a decade later Miles Moodie, a merchant and mayor of Ripon, rebuilt the deanery there at an estimated personal charge of £90.[6] Extensive work was carried out at Halifax from 1632 to 1638, including a wholly new roof, a complete redecoration, a bell frame and bells, on which a total of £175 15s was expended.[7] The price of long neglect began to be exacted when, as for example, the chancel at Eastrington fell early in the seventeenth century, the structure being rebuilt in 1632 by Sir Michael Wharton.[8]

---

[1] PCY 13/839 1551; *Thoresby Soc. Pub.*, XIX (1913), 307.

[2] Walker, *Wakefield*, I, 253; Waters, S. H., *Wakefield* (Wakefield, 1933), 90.

[3] Tickell, *Hull*, 795-797; (Ambler) PCY 3/136 1606.

[4] Miller, N. J., *Winestead* (Hull, 1933), 139-140, 195. Hildyard, who was knighted in 1603 and who was Sheriff of Yorkshire in 1612, sat in almost every parliament from 1588 until his death in 1634.

[5] *Halifax Antiq. Soc. Papers*, 1909, 48.

[6] *Surtees Soc. Pub.*, LXXVIII (1884), 262. This rebuilding was done between 1625 and 1635.

[7] *Halifax Antiq. Soc. Papers*, 1909, 309-313.

[8] Hall, *South Cave*, 156; Lawton, *Collectio*, 335; Poulson, *Beverlac*, 333, 392; Oliver, *Beverley*, 226, 515; *Yorks. Arch. Soc. Rec.*, XVIII (1895), 55-57. Wharton was involved for years in suits and countersuits against the Corpora-

Similarly, the church in Howden had been reported to the Queen's Surveyor as decayed as early as 1591, but no measure was taken to remedy the increasing faults until in 1630 it was declared unsafe for use. The parishioners thereupon undertook painfully to repair the nave and to replace the roof, the work being completed in 1635 at a total charge of perhaps £180.[1] During the revolutionary era the Parliamentary Army took measures in Trinity Church, Hull, which were tolerant rather than charitable and hence have not been included,[2] while at the very close of our period, in 1659, the parishioners of St Mary Bishophill Senior in York, roofed a portion of that church and built a stone and brick steeple at the west end of the structure.[3]

When any interest was shown in new church building during our period, the principal concern of donors was with the construction of chapels to serve the needs of isolated villages distant from the parochial centre, and, as our period developed, to minister to the needs of growing urban communities which could not well be served by the existing parochial churches. The movement for chapel building falls into two distinct periods. In the first, extending from 1484 to 1543, most of these foundations were conjoined with chantries, provision being made for a stipendiary priest who would minister to an isolated community as well as perform the prescribed services for the donor. In all, nineteen such chapels were built by private benefactors, all save four being in the West Riding. There followed two generations, the Elizabethan period with its all but complete secularization of aspirations, in which, so far as our records reveal, not a single chapel was built in the entire county by voluntary subscriptions or private gift. The long-interrupted movement for the extension of more adequate religious facilities for the county was almost abruptly resumed in 1602, a total of twenty-eight chapels having been built between that date and the end of our period by private donors, all save one, it should be noted, in the now populous West Riding with its still archaic parochial system. In total, we have found benefactions amounting to £2776 provided towards the building

tion of Beverley of which he claimed the stewardship, a post held by his father, of the same name, before him. He was returned to Parliament in 1640 from Beverley, with Sir John Hotham. Wharton supported the King, and his eldest son was killed in the King's service, but he sought after the royal defeat to make his peace with Parliament, and to preserve his huge landed estate. He represented before the Parliamentary Commissioners that at the outbreak of the war his estate had been worth about £2600 p.a., but had been despoiled in the course of the war to the extent of £30,000 of capital worth. He was none the less fined £2920. Wharton died in 1655, aged 82.

[1] Smith, *Old Yorkshire*, III, 107–108.

[2] The army laid up a wall dividing the church so the Independents might hold services in the building simultaneously with their Presbyterian brethren.

[3] Knight, C. B., *A history of York* (York, 1944), 460; Torr, *Antiquities of York*, 114.

of these forty-seven chapels, almost all of which were very simple buildings and some of which were scarcely more than *ad hoc* structures.

In the first two decades of our period chapels were built at Middlesmoor, Wentworth, and Hook, the latter serving as well the townships of Armin and Goole, at a cost of perhaps £90, the small building at Wentworth being enlarged in 1546 by a bequest of Thomas Wentworth, Esq., who added an aisle at a charge of about £40.[1] The inhabitants of Luddenden in 1496 built a chapel at their own expense which was licensed for the celebration of mass and other divine offices for the benefit of this and three nearby hamlets, all lying from three to four miles to the west of the mother church at Halifax.[2] In the same year, the lord of the manor of Wombwell, Roger Wombwell, built at his own charge a commodious chantry chapel in his village, which also served the inhabitants who were three miles distant from the parish church at Darfield over roads often subject to flooding.[3] Sir Thomas Tempest in 1507 bequeathed £13 6s 8d for building a small chapel in the parish of Bracewell,[4] while in 1511 a larger chapel, seating about seventy, was built at Murton (Osbaldwick) at an estimated charge of £35.[5] At a somewhat uncertain date, but most probably in 1518, a chapel was built at Coley in Halifax parish by William Rooks and other principal inhabitants, the building being considerably enlarged in 1631 at a quite uncertain charge, but again by private subscription.[6] At about the same date Henry Vavasour, a gentleman of Hazlewood, by will required his executors to build a chapel at Eastburn at an approximate cost of £40.[7] In 1523 Thomas Boynton, also of the lower gentry, built a chapel at Roxby in the North Riding of considerable size and merit, in which he was buried.[8]

A chapel was erected at Sowerby Bridge (Halifax) in 1526 by contributions totalling about £60, and was renovated and enlarged a century later (1622–1632) at a charge of £67 8s.[9] A commodious chapel was erected at Lightcliffe (Eastfield), just to the east of Halifax, in 1529 at

---

[1] Lawton, *Collectio*, 158, 241, 569; *VCH, Yorks.*, III, 44.

[2] *Halifax Antiq. Soc. Papers*, 1909, 33–34. *Vide post*, 396.

[3] Lawton, *Collectio*, 182; *Surtees Soc. Pub.*, XCII (1892), 192.

[4] PCY 6/229 1507; *Surtees Soc. Pub.*, LIII (1868), 249–252. Tempest also left by will £2 10s for church repairs, £1 10s for church general, 13s for highway betterment, and an endowment of £94 10s for prayers.

[5] Lawton, *Collectio*, 451.

[6] *Halifax Antiq. Soc. Papers*, 1903, 'Brief notes on Coley Church', no folios, 1904, 246–247; (Rooks) PCY 9/74 1518.

[7] PCY 9/27 1515; *Surtees Soc. Pub.*, LXXIX (1884), 8–9. Vavasour also left £33 to the poor at his burial and 5s to the general uses of the church.

[8] PCY 9/251 1523; *Yorks. Arch. Journal*, XVII (1903), 307–308; *VCH, Yorks., NR*, II, 370–371.

[9] Watson, *Halifax*, 447–448; Whitaker, *Loidis and Elmete*, 391; *Halifax Antiq. Soc. Papers*, 1915, 85–112.

the charge of the principal families, Richard Rooks giving the site and the largest contribution, while the subscribers also raised an endowment for the support of a priest to serve the village.[1] A member of a powerful gentle family, Sir William Bulmer, in *ca.* 1528 built a chantry chapel to serve the village of Wilton in the North Riding.[2] A small chapel was built in *ca.* 1542 at Kneton, in the parish of Harthill, by a member of the lesser gentry at a charge of not more than £20,[3] while in the same year Sir John Nevill bequeathed £3 7s for the building of the chapel at Glaisdale, an amount which suggests that the work had been well begun during his lifetime.[4]

This brief survey has enumerated at least the principal of the chapels built for public worship during the period prior to the Reformation. Exactly sixty years were to elapse before private donors again began the slow and arduous task of extending even further, and especially in the West Riding, the facilities required for convenient and general worship. Thus in 1602 the inhabitants of Rastrick demolished an old and long since disused chapel in their village, in Halifax parish, and rebuilt it at a cost of £20 4s, including a bell, men of the community contributing their own labour for the rougher carpentry and masonry.[5] Sir John Savile had been influential in persuading the local magnate at Rastrick, Henry Ramsden, that he enjoyed no property rights in the old chapel premises there, while he displayed his own interest in the needs of the region by building a chapel in the village of Bradley and still another in Methley, where his family had for many years been the principal land-owners.[6] Nor was this the extent of the ubiquitous Savile family's contribution to the needs of their county. In 1622 quite another Sir John, with Sir Thomas Savile, gave the site and contributed towards the erection of a large chapel at Headingley (Leeds), completed before 1636 at an estimated cost of £100 to the numerous subscribers.[7] In the same year, largely through the exertions of Thomas Toller, for forty-six years Vicar of Sheffield, the residents of Ecclesall built a large chapel for

[1] *Ibid.,* 1908, 289–295; *Halifax Antiq. Soc. Trans.,* 1943, 87; Lawton, *Collectio,* 133. The founders of the chapel thought it threatened by the royal commissioners, the Rooks family thereupon assuming private possession of the premises and of the endowment, until in 1557 Anthony Rooks, Richard's son, conveyed it back to trustees representing the township.

[2] *Vide ante,* 256.

[3] *Surtees Soc. Pub.,* XCI (1892), 187–188; Lawton, *Collectio,* 196.

[4] *Vide ante,* 311, 376.

[5] *Halifax Antiq. Soc. Papers, 1904,* 289–300, *1928,* 257. Dr Favour encouraged the building of chapelries in his too-large parish and was delighted with the service and attention when he preached at Rastrick in May, 1605.

[6] *Vide ante,* 325, for Savile's help in founding Halifax Grammar School.

[7] *PP* 1826, XIII, 734; Sprittles, J., *A survey of the plate of Leeds parish church* (Leeds, 1951), 17; *Old Leeds charities,* 13; Lawton, *Collectio,* 95. *Vide post,* 398.

the conduct of services in their community.[1] The parochial chapel at Luddenden was rebuilt in about 1624 at a charge of upwards of £50, a considerable number of gifts and bequests from men engaged in the wool trade as well as from yeomen having been left for this purpose.[2] In 1626 William Fawcett, the London merchant who with his brother, a Norwich merchant, had greatly bettered the life and institutions of their native village of Halton Gill, built a small chapel with a gallery at a charge of about £140.[3] Another West Riding chapel was built in the following year (1627) at Denby, for that community with Gunthwaite, at a fairly certainly estimated cost of £65, the principal contributor being a gentleman of the locality, Godfrey Bosville, who promptly placed in the pulpit an extremely zealous Puritan divine.[4]

The strong interest in chapel building, as well as the endowment of clerical stipends for these churches, reached its climax in the decade 1629-1638, when a total of thirteen chapels were built in Yorkshire, in whole or in part by private donors. To some degree this interesting and important development was a consequence of Archbishop Laud's strenuous exertions, reflected in the Archdiocese of York by the ministrations of his faithful followers Harsnett and Neile. But there were extremely complex counter-currents of influence at work, for five, possibly six, of these chapel foundations were made by Puritan donors for the express purpose of combating the now spreading Laudian domination of the service and administration of the sacraments in the parochial churches of the realm. In any case, however, the Church and Yorkshire were well served in this decade.

A chapel was built and later endowed at Armley (Leeds) in ca. 1629 under the leadership of Sir Ingram Hopton, and his son-in-law, Sir Miles Stapleton, but with the assistance of numerous yeomanry of the community. It may be reckoned that the building and site cost approximately £60,[5] while, as we have earlier seen, the living was in 1653 most adequately endowed by the enclosure of the common land of the manor.[6] In 1629 also work was begun on a chapel at Attercliffe (Sheffield) under the guidance of Stephen Bright and William Spencer, leading

---

[1] Odom, W., *Memorials of Sheffield* (Sheffield, 1922), 74; Hunter, *Hallamshire*, 201-202; Lawton, *Collectio*, 224. There were remains of an old chapel at Ecclesall which had not been used for almost a century. The first curate was Edward Hunt, Toller's son-in-law.

[2] *Vide ante*, 394.   [3] *Vide ante*, 109, 118, 132, 161-162, 332.

[4] Lawton, *Collectio*, 210-211; Hunter, *South Yorkshire*, II, 352. Bosville, a member of the Long Parliament and a colonel in the Parliamentary Army, persuaded the Committee for Compounding to settle on the chapel as endowment for the support of the minister £1000 received from the estate of Sir Edward Osborne, who had been adjudged a delinquent.

[5] Thoresby, *Ducatus*, 193.   [6] *Vide ante*, 381-382.

landowners in the community, to which a large number of local residents made contribution to defray the charge of £104 11s for this substantial structure serving a community of 250 families.[1] The inhabitants of Hunslet, then a village of about 200 families, probably in 1630 built a plain but substantial chapel for their worship. Most of the contributors, the chief of whom was, however, a lesser gentleman, Richard Sykes, were clothiers and yeomen in this growing industrial village, lying about a mile from the parochial church at Leeds.[2] We have in another connection dealt rather fully with still another chapel, and school, built and endowed in this same year (1630) by local effort in the remote hamlet of Eldroth, in Clapham parish.[3] The fifth chapel to be built in this remarkable period of two years when the religious facilities of the West Riding were so greatly improved was in the village of Idle, where the inhabitants, most of the donors being yeomen, erected a small but convenient structure for worship, the mother church at Calverley being some three miles distant.[4]

A small chapel was built with local subscriptions totalling somewhat more than £40 at Bramley in the now populous parish of Leeds in 1631, replacing a dilapidated structure dating from the early thirteenth century. Just a year later an equally decayed chantry chapel at Holbeck, in the same parish, was replaced by a new, though depressingly severe, building at the charge of local subscribers.[5] A chapel was built in 1632 at Holmfirth, in the sprawling parish of Kirkburton, which contained upwards of 25 square miles, at a cost of at least £100 by local subscriptions, in a region which took a considerable pride in the support of what was evidently a decidedly Puritan worship.[6] A large and most pleasant chapel was built at Harwood Dale, some five miles to the north of the mother church at Hackness, in 1634 by that pious and amiable gentleman, Sir Thomas Posthumous Hoby. Hoby explained in an inscription affixed to the east wall that when he and 'the lady Margarett his wife were united together in this world they both resolved to have a chappell erected for devine service for ye good of ye soules & bodys of ye inhabitantes dwelling w^{th}in Harewooddale & in very fewe monthes next after

---

[1] *Vide ante*, 378, for the details of the endowment of this living, in which Bright and Spencer also took the lead.

[2] Sprittles, *Plate of Leeds church, passim*; Lawton, *Collectio*, 96.

[3] *Vide ante*, 335, for the particulars of this school-chapel foundation.

[4] *Bradford Antiquary*, n.s., II (1905), 364; Lawton, *Collectio*, 117–118. The living for many years remained unendowed save for a rent-charge of £1 p.a. left in 1650 for the support of a minister. It was to be adequately endowed by gifts in the eighteenth century.

[5] Sprittles, *Plate of Leeds church, passim*; Lawton, *Collectio*, 94, 96.

[6] Morehouse, *Kirkburton*, 156–157; Lawton, *Collectio*, 142. The minister was supported by local subscriptions and by pew rents, there being no endowment until well into the eighteenth century.

his said wives decease he did erect this chappell'.[1] Archbishop Neile's prickly sensibilities thwarted an effort to provide a chapel in or near Hatfield at about the same time for the French and Dutch Protestants engaged as workmen in Vermuyden's great drainage project at Hatfield Chase, though protection and permission were gained from Bishop Williams to erect the structure at Sandtoft just across the border of the county and diocese.[2] In 1636 James Cotes, probably of yeoman status, was a principal contributor to the erection of a chapel at Headingley, the whole cost of which we have reckoned at £100, to which he gave as well £28 as an initial endowment for the support of the curate, who was appointed by the Vicar of Leeds.[3] And, finally, in reviewing the principal chapels erected in Yorkshire during this decade, just before the political and religious explosion of 1640, we must mention a large and well-appointed edifice built at Wibsey, in Bradford parish, in 1636, which, we have already noted, was provided at a charge of about £80 and suitably endowed by William Rooks, the local squire, with the help of other freeholders of the neighbourhood.[4]

The two decades of religious unsettlement with which our period closed dampened but by no means quenched the pertinacious interest of Yorkshire donors in the further extension of the facilities for worship in the county. Seven chapels were founded in the period, all, it so happens, in the brief interval 1646–1653, the principal of which we shall at least note.[5] One of the most substantial of these was the chapel built at Great Houghton (Darfield) in 1650 by Sir Edward Rodes, in which he established and maintained a clergyman of undiluted Presbyterian zeal.[6] We have already had occasion to mention the building and endow-

---

[1] *Yorks. Arch. Journal*, XVII (1903), 77–86; *VCH, Yorks., NR*, II, 531–532; Lawton, *Collectio*, 302. Hoby in 1636 endowed the chapelry with the tithes of Harwood Dale, Harwood, and Hingles in order to secure the services of a settled curate.

[2] Sir Philibert Vernatti at first gave them a barn for their worship. Archbishop Neile placed the congregation under an interdict, but could not prevent the building of the Lincolnshire chapel, to which a minister was appointed and in which Dutch services were held in the morning and French in the afternoon. (Smith, *Old Yorkshire*, IV, 64; Hunter, *South Yorkshire*, I, 165–166; *VCH, Yorks.*, III, 58–59.)

[3] Smith, *Old Yorkshire*, I, 99; Parsons, *Leeds*, II, 149; Thoresby, *Ducatus*, 55. *Vide ante*, 395.   [4] *Vide ante*, 379.

[5] We have not included the Friends' Meeting House in Scarborough, built in about 1651, about which we have gleaned few particulars as to cost or financing, or the place of worship which may have been erected in *ca.* 1653 by a Calvinistic Baptist congregation in Stokesley.

[6] Hunter, *South Yorkshire*, II, 130–132; Dale, *Yorkshire Puritanism*, 88. The eldest son of Sir Godfrey Rodes, Sir Edward was a parliamentary supporter, his manor house being plundered by Royalist troops in 1642. He served as knight of the shire for Perth in the Parliament of 1656, was High Sheriff of Yorkshire, and was a member of Cromwell's Council. He died in 1666.

ment of another chapel in 1654 at Bramhope by an equally stalwart
Calvinist, Robert Dyneley.[1] At about the same time, 1651, the inhabitants of Meltham in Almondbury parish completed the erection of a
small but graceful chapel, for which subscriptions of upwards of £80
were taken, which was actually consecrated by an Anglican bishop,
Henry Tilson, Bishop of Elphin, Ireland, who likewise ordained the
first curate to hold the living.[2] A chapel was built in Stannington in
1652 by Richard Spoone, a yeoman, who, as we have seen, not only
endowed this Presbyterian living but likewise founded a school for this
rural township.[3] We have commented, as well, on the foundation of a
school and chapel in East Hardwick in 1653 by another rich yeoman,
Stephen Cawood,[4] while Francis Layton, who had carried on a private
feud with Archbishop Neile, was also in 1652 at last able to endow what
he trusted would remain for all time a Presbyterian chapel at Rawdon
in the parish of Guiseley.[5] Finally, we should mention the chapel at
Barden, in the West Riding, which was rebuilt in 1657 at a charge of
£100 by the remarkable and completely generous woman, Anne,
Countess of Pembroke, who could 'not dwell in a ceiled house and let
the House of God lie waste', whose great work in the restoration of
churches was carried forward principally in Westmorland and Cumberland.[6]

   While there was considerable activity in Yorkshire in the building of
small chapels to serve isolated as well as newly populous communities,
there was but little building or rebuilding of parish churches in the
county through the whole of our period. In all, it is our estimate that
not more than £2798 7s was given by private donors for this purpose.
And, it may be added, there was not much more expended from monastic
funds or by taxes laid upon parochial areas. The years prior to the
Reformation saw such church building as there was, when ten churches
were erected, as well as one substantial benefaction made for a church
being constructed in another county and one uncertain instance of
church building. This almost completes the annal of church building
for this huge county, since only one church was built in the century and
more of our period after the full impact of the Reformation had touched
Yorkshire. Eleven new churches were doubtless but a tithe of the whole
number that decayed or were destroyed by time and nature in the course
of the long and increasingly secular age under study; the number of new
churches built was in point of fact fewer than the number of parish
churches in the city of York in ruins and ready for demolition by the
close of our period.

---

[1] *Vide ante*, 384.
[2] Hughes, Joseph, *History of Meltham* (Huddersfield, 1866), 12–25; Lawton,
Collectio, 107.   [3] *Vide ante*, 343, 381.   [4] *Vide ante*, 344, 381.
[5] *Vide ante*, 277, 290–291, 381.   [6] Lewis, *Wharfedale*, 62–67, 78.

The earliest of the churches rebuilt was at Withernsea, a town persistently ravaged by the wash of the sea, which as early as 1409 had apparently lost its church and burying ground to this relentless erosion. A decision was reached to rebuild the church about the middle of the fifteenth century, the principal outlay being made very early in our period and the work completed in 1488 at an estimated charge of £150.[1] One of the ablest of the many priest-lawyers spawned by Yorkshire in the later Middle Ages, Thomas Barowe, in 1499 bequeathed the substantial sum of £240 towards the building of Great St Mary's Church in Cambridge,[2] while the ancient parish church at Ecclesfield was all but rebuilt about 1500 at an estimated cost of £180.[3] The church at Old Malton was rebuilt, apparently from his personal funds, by Prior Roger Bolton shortly after 1500,[4] while St Peter's Church in Huddersfield was completed in 1503.[5] The church serving Birstall was all but rebuilt between 1490 and 1520, with many small bequests for the work, on which there seems to have been a total outlay of something like £170,[6] while a small church at Honley, also in the West Riding, was completed in ca. 1507 at a cost of perhaps not more than £100.[7] The church at Arncliffe, which was in a state of decay, was demolished late in the reign of Henry VII and a new structure built on the site at a most uncertainly estimated charge of £200,[8] while at Darton, still another West Riding parish, repairs and restorations were undertaken in ca. 1517 amounting to a rebuilding of the structure.[9] The church at Burnsall was also rebuilt in 1520, with the addition of a tower, and was extensively repaired and enlarged not quite a century later (1612) by Sir William Craven, the great London merchant who dealt so generously with this his native parish.[10] Shortly afterwards, ca. 1522, All Saints' Church in Almondbury was rebuilt and considerably enlarged with a spacious nave and a tower.[11]

The large church of St Mary in Beverley was seriously damaged in 1520 when the tower collapsed with irreparable injury to the nave. A complete rebuilding and enlargement was immediately undertaken, the

---

[1] Lawton, *Collectio*, 384–385; Sheppard, Thomas, *The lost towns of the Yorkshire coast* (L., 1912), 137. The Parliamentary Survey, in the middle of the seventeenth century, reported that the church had been again all but destroyed and that at least £300 would be required to rebuild it. The parish was ultimately joined with Hollym.

[2] PCC 37 Horne 1499; *Surtees Soc. Pub.*, LIII (1868), 117n., CXVI (1908), 266; DNB.

[3] Eastwood, *Ecclesfield*, 152.   [4] *VCH, Yorks., NR*, I, 538.

[5] Lawton, *Collectio*, 137; *VCH, Yorks.*, III, 44.

[6] Cradock, *Birstall*, 38.   [7] Hughes, *Meltham*, 13n.

[8] Shuffrey, *North Craven churches*, 2; Graves, *Cleveland*, 135.

[9] Hunter, *South Yorkshire*, II, 371.

[10] Lewis, *Wharfedale*, 71, 73–74; Lawton, *Collectio*, 250–251. *Vide ante*, 239, 298, 328–329.   [11] Hulbert, *Almondbury*, 70–71.

western piers being given by John Crosley and his wife, the next two piers by the women of the city, and the easternmost pier by the minstrels.[1] The work thus begun was greatly assisted when in 1521, William Rokeby, Archbishop of Dublin, died leaving an outright sum of £200 towards the construction.[2] In 1523 Rokeby's brother, Sir Richard, comptroller of Wolsey's household and treasurer of Ireland, also died, bequeathing in his turn £200 for the completion of the work, on which at least £680 was expended.[3] While technically a chapel, the place of worship erected at Illingworth (Halifax) in 1525 at a probable charge of about £120 to the subscribers, including Henry Savile, may for our purposes be better regarded as another example of mid-Henrician church building.[4] The church at Marton cum Moxby, in a remote region of the North Riding, was largely rebuilt about 1540, materials from the recently dissolved priory almost certainly being used.[5]

This would seem to complete the roster of churches built either wholly or in large part by private donors in Yorkshire during our entire period, save one which was undertaken a full century after the construction of Marton church had been finished.[6] As we have seen, during two full generations of this century even chapel building was at a complete standstill in Yorkshire as the aspirations of substantial men of the county turned to almost completely secular concerns. It was not until 1634 that another church was built by a private donor, this being St John's at Leeds, which was constructed and richly endowed by John Harrison, the merchant who was the founder of most of the basic social institutions of a city which he fathered with a singular devotion. And even the consecration of this church, on whose building Harrison had laid out about £600, symbolized the disunity and the eroding religious

[1] *Yorks. Arch. Journal*, XXV (1920), 414–419.

[2] ARY 27/165 1521; *Surtees Soc. Pub.*, LXXIX (1884), 140–144; *Halifax Antiq. Soc. Papers*, 1918, 141–163. He built chapels during his lifetime at Kirk Sandall, where he also endowed a chantry, and at Halifax. He left £40 (Irish) for prayers in Dublin, £10 for a D.D. to preach for a year at Halifax, Beverley, and Kirkby, £3 8s for sermons at Fakenham, Norfolk, £23 8s to clergy, about £200 for general church uses in Ireland, and a total of £81 6s for church repairs. *Vide* DNB for biographical particulars.

[3] PCC 7 Bodfelde 1523; *Surtees Soc. Pub.*, CXVI (1908), 110–111. Rokeby also left £146 14s for prayers. A native of Kirk Sandall, Rokeby was a successful and able administrator and civil servant. For his widow, *vide ante*, 352.

[4] *Halifax Antiq. Soc. Trans.*, 1942, 19.

[5] *VCH, Yorks., NR*, II, 156; Lawton, *Collectio*, 448–449.

[6] We have not included the rebuilding (*ca.* 1540) of St Michael-le-Belfrey in York, the charge for which was almost entirely borne by the Minster endowments. A yeoman's will (*ca.* 1542), leaving all save twenty of his sheep for the building of Featherstone church in the West Riding would seem to refer to church repairs rather than to extensive rebuilding, as would the will of George Hogge (PCY 20/75 1576), leaving one gimmer lamb for the 'building' of the parish church at Kettlewell.

frictions of the age. Archbishop Neile had resisted the founder's firm decision to vest the patronage in the municipal authorities of Leeds and had feared that St John's pulpit might refute that which St Peter's taught. John Cosin, then Archdeacon of the East Riding, preached the consecration sermon on the ominously Laudian text, 'Let all things be done decently and in order', while the newly appointed incumbent, Robert Todd, a clergyman of decidedly Puritan persuasion, answered in the afternoon with the words of the catechism, 'Yea, verily, and by God's help so I will', mustering language of refutation which the Archbishop could not brook. Todd found himself suspended for a year on the very day of the consecration of his church.[1] Harrison, the donor, was the perfect exemplar of a class which had not only attained great liquid wealth in England but which had in large measure assumed the burden for founding and maintaining the necessary institutions of the society of which they were such a vigorous and articulate part. Neither the cold indifference of Elizabeth nor the sectarian zeal of Laud and Neile, masked though it was in a fuzzy conception of the church catholic, aroused in such men the wish to build churches or to endow them. These merchants, whether of Leeds, or London, or Bristol, founded institutions which they could control through carefully vested deeds of trust which lent steady support in perpetuity to the aspirations they held for a whole society. Increasingly, and for a complex variety of reasons, these aspirations were assuming severely secular shape and substance.

D. THE STRUCTURE OF CHARITIES IN THE PARISHES

Yorkshire was not only by far the largest county in the realm, but likewise an exceedingly diverse and complex social and economic community, with an old and prosperous rural society in most of the East Riding, an agricultural economy in the North Riding ranging from some of the most fertile to some of the most marginal in the whole of England, and a rapidly expanding industrial and commerical revolution which was urbanizing the relatively backward West Riding during the course of our period. The charitable interests of almost all donors were centred on a particular parish among the many in this sprawling county and on the building of more fitting and adequate institutions in the tiny area in which the benefactor had lived and to which he was bound by the strongest ties of sentiment. As a consequence, the transformation of the county from what was at the outset of our period a rude and backward region was not accomplished uniformly, and in many parts of the shire it was not accomplished at all. The great changes of which we have spoken and which we have been tracing out in detail came in

[1] *Vide ante*, 277, 298, 314, 382, for a discussion of this great donor's benefactions for Leeds and for a biographical notice.

parish after parish as institutions of social and cultural strength, fully competent to introduce swift and mensurable transformation in a whole community, were founded by prescient donors who possessed the means to give reality to their aspirations for a particular parish or township. Much, therefore, depended upon the whim of fate and upon genetic accident: on the quality and the place of residence of the local squire, the industry and vision of a rich yeoman, the singular good fortune of possessing a clergyman with even a tithe of the vision and energy of a Favour, or that complex chain of events which could send a yeoman's son to London where quick and viable wealth might be gained by the able and the resolute. The translation of the county into modernity was accordingly slow and it was most uneven, there being, as it were, a patchwork of change and of gain as parish after parish was provided by private benefactors with the substance and the institutions to make opportunity and a better life possible. In many areas there was to be little change indeed: in parishes possessing no man of means with the vision and the daring required by the age, in communities never blessed with the leadership required for the slow building by humbler men of the school or the almshouse which in so many parishes were founded by groupings of yeomen and of husbandmen who with many very small gifts and bequests set the cleaving wedge of opportunity in the stony social soil of their parish.

As we take our whole period in view, the men and women of Yorkshire must be credited with a great and beneficent achievement. We have reckoned that there were approximately 550 fully organized parishes in the county by the time of the convention of the Long Parliament and that there were 728 settled places of worship, all chapelries being included, which afforded nuclei around which charities and social institutions could be formed. It is amazing indeed that in this relatively poor and backward county at least some charitable benefaction has been found in all these communities, as well as in 77 other rural townships or tiny hamlets which did not even possess the benefit of a chapel.[1] Of these 805 communities in which some charity has been noted, and for rough convenience we will describe them all henceforward as parishes, 248, or 30·8 per cent of the whole, were to be found in the East Riding; 333, or 41·4 per cent, in the burgeoning West Riding; 223, or 27·7 per cent in the North Riding, with the city of York being counted as one despite the multiplicity of parishes within its walls.

We are concerned, then, with the structure of the distribution of the great sum of £243,650 14s over the terrain of this large and unevenly

---

[1] It should be said that for purposes of this analysis each community, including the city of York, is counted as one parish. That is, we are concerned with the structure of charitable funds in 805 separate communities in the county, a few of which were sufficiently large to have more than one parish.

developed county and with the social and cultural transformation that resulted when large and well-disposed aggregates of this wealth were vested in a variety of institutions in scores of particularly favoured parishes. It must be observed at the outset, however, that the whole of this great sum was not disposed for the benefit of particular parishes. Substantial amounts were given by a number of donors for the benefit of other counties,[1] while an even larger total was given, often by the most generous and wisest of donors, for the benefit of the county as a whole or for large areas, such as a Riding, rather than for the needs of specific communities. But there remains the great sum of £219,565 6s which was designated for the needs and benefit of particular parishes held by donors in special and sentimental regard. It is with the distribution of this charitable wealth among upwards of 800 Yorkshire communities that we are now concerned.[2]

It is our view, after considering with some care the structure of life and institutions in many communities, that any parish in our period blessed with charitable endowments of £400 or more was girded with social and institutional resources setting it apart as a highly favoured centre. Such funds, yielding as they did about £20 p.a., were sufficient for a great variety of most useful and beneficent purposes, which could create an environment of hope for the youth of a village or relieve a parish of the degrading spectacle of stark poverty. Such capital was sufficient to found an almshouse, to endow a grammar school, to finance an ambitious apprenticeship scheme, or to regenerate and inspire a town or a rural parish in any one of several socially efficacious ways. These were the 'areas of opportunity' in the county created by the generosity and wisdom, and often by the daring, of men who were moved by mature aspirations which they translated into enduring institutions which could and did change and better the quality of life in an entire parish. We should now analyze in some detail the topography of these communities in which such a large proportion of all the charitable wealth of the county came for a variety of reasons to be concentrated.[3]

[1] Vide post, 415–418.
[2] The totals under the large charitable heads may be compared for the county as a whole and for parishes in the following table:

	County total £ s.	Parish total £ s.
Poor	81,513 13 (33·46%)	74,660 7 (34·00%)
Social rehabilitation	11,805 17 (4·85%)	10,640 18 (4·85%)
Municipal betterments	6,121 11 (2·51%)	5,855 2 (2·67%)
Education	75,812 8 (31·12%)	63,423 4 (28·89%)
Religion	68,397 5 (28·07%)	64,985 15 (29·60%)
	243,650 14	219,565 6

[3] These communities, with appropriate data, are listed in Table D, *Appendix*.

There were in all ninety-six of these highly favoured communities, and there was disposed among them £186,402 5s of charitable endowments dedicated to a great variety of uses. But several of these parochial entities included as well sizable and dependent towns and villages, particularly in the West Riding where the parishes tended to be large and the increase of population great, which were normally included within the benefits of charities left for the entire parish. More accurately, therefore, there were 138 favoured localities in Yorkshire, of which 20 were in the East Riding, 91 in the West Riding, 26 in the North Riding, with the city of York being counted as one. It will at once be observed that the building of modern social and cultural institutions was heavily concentrated in the West Riding, where a recent but a highly responsible burgher aristocracy, working in close unison with the landed gentry of Tudor creation, was disposing large sums for the betterment of numerous communities which were rapidly becoming important urban centres. Almost two-thirds of the favoured communities were to be found in the West Riding, though considerably less than two-thirds (56·7 per cent) of the whole of the charitable funds held by the communities under study had been vested in these towns. It is also pertinent to observe that during the last two generations of our period the rate of giving to and within the West Riding was rising very rapidly indeed, with more than a suggestion of the future cultural and institutional dominance of the area in the life and affairs of the entire county. The East Riding fared much less well, 20 of its communities having amassed a total of £31,355 17s of charitable funds, with a particularly heavy concentration of interest in the needs of the poor. There were in all 26 favoured towns in the North Riding, which by the close of our period possessed a total of £23,290 13s of charitable wealth; about half this sum (£10,599), it is interesting to observe, was devoted to the advancement of education in this thinly populated region. The slowly declining city of York must have been to a considerable degree buoyed up by the substantial total of £26,067 9s given for the support of its institutions and for the staying of the evil effects of the chronic poverty with which it had to contend.

But these comments on the distribution of the particularly favoured communities among the Ridings of the county must not distract us from our discussion of the county as a whole.[1] These 138 most favoured

[1] Some further analysis of the distribution of charitable funds by Ridings may be of use. The total of the benefactions for the East Riding was £39,314 13s, this amounting to only 17·9 per cent of the funds for the entire county, though the Riding included 248, or 30·8 per cent, of all the communities of the shire. This sum was provided by a total of 2305 donors, these constituting 26·11 per cent of the whole number. In the analysis in this note the donor count is regarded as 8828 rather than 8632. The discrepancy is due to the fact that numerous 'parish donors' gave in more than one parish. It is interesting to observe that

only a tiny proportion (4·79 per cent) of all the benefactions for this Riding were derived from London sources. The gifts for this area were distributed to the following charitable heads in the proportions indicated, a comparison also being afforded with the county at large:

	£	s		
Poor	15,080	15	(38·36%)—county at large:	(33·46%)
Social rehabilitation	1,538	15	(3·91%)	(4·85%)
Municipal betterments	1,380	16	(3·51%)	(2·51%)
Education	9,795	10	(24·92%)	(31·12%)
Religion	11,518	17	(29·30%)	(28·07%)
	39,314	13		

There were only 1269 donors for the North Riding, these being 14·37 per cent of the whole number, while the £33,001 18s of charitable gifts for this area amounted to nearly the same proportion (15·03 per cent) of the benefactions for the entire county. In this region 223 communities were counted, or 27·6 per cent of the whole number for the shire. There was considerable emigration of youth from the North Riding to London, which doubtless explains the very heavy proportion (25·66 per cent) of the region's benefactions which were given by men from that city, and of this total of £8467 6s, nearly half (46·24 per cent) was for the improvement of education in the Riding. The charities of this Riding were distributed as follows:

	£	s		
Poor	11,401	7	(34·55%)—county at large:	(33·46%)
Social rehabilitation	1,658	3	(5·02%)	(4·85%)
Municipal betterments	883	4	(2·68%)	(2·51%)
Education	12,034	6	(36·47%)	(31·12%)
Religion	7,024	18	(21·29%)	(28·07%)
	33,001	18		

The £26,067 9s given for the charitable uses of York City amounts to not quite 12 per cent (11·87 per cent) of the whole of the funds for the county and was given by 509 donors, or 5·77 per cent of the total number. London donors gave £2404 5s to the city, that being not quite 10 per cent (9·22 per cent) of the whole sum. The division of charities for the city was:

	£	s		
Poor	8,613	17	(33·04%)—county at large:	(33·46%)
Social rehabilitation	2,607	12	(10·00%)	(4·85%)
Municipal betterments	1,125	7	(4·32%)	(2·51%)
Education	4,126	2	(15·83%)	(31·12%)
Religion	9,594	11	(36·81%)	(28·07%)
	26,067	9		

We have frequently stressed the strength of the dominant classes in the West Riding, which in a relatively short time provided the region with institutions comparable to those in the oldest areas of England. A total of £121,181 6s was given for the various charitable uses in this Riding, this amounting to 55·19 per cent of the whole for the county at large. There were 4745 donors in the West Riding, these accounting for 53·75 per cent of the whole number of the county, while the 333 communities counted, including a great many chapelries and rural townships, amount to 41·4 per cent of the total for the county. The closeness of the commercial connections of the region with London is suggested by the fact

towns included only a relatively small proportion (17·1 per cent) of the many parishes and dependent communities of this great and on the whole sparsely populated shire, yet there had been concentrated in them a total of £186,402 5s, representing more than three-fourths (76·5 per cent) of the charitable endowments of the county. All the principal towns were of course included in this group of favoured communities, with, however, a particularly heavy concentration of charitable wealth in York, Hull (which in relation to its size held huge endowments), Leeds, Halifax, Wakefield, Sheffield, and Beverley, these as a group possessing nearly a third (£78,144 14s) of the whole of the charitable wealth of the entire county. There were as well among these especially favoured communities as many as sixty small market towns or villages lying in typical rural reaches of the shire. These had gained their charitable wealth through the generosity of a local benefactor, or, more commonly, of a native son who had found his fortune in London but who had kept alive his remembrance of the needs of the region from which he had sprung.

These most highly favoured communities likewise possessed an advantage in that so many of their resources had been vested by large benefactors who not only gave carefully constituted gifts but dedicated them to uses which were socially and historically most effective. In a qualitative sense, therefore, an important and a powerful historical leverage had been applied, further favouring these parishes in relation to the county at large. Thus these 138 towns possessed something over 80 per cent of all the funds left for experimentation in social rehabilitation, far more than their due share of the almshouse endowments of the shire, and slightly more than 78 per cent of all its educational endowments. These Yorkshire communities were well fitted by thoughtful and certainly generous donors to meet the exacting social and cultural problems of the modern world.

We have likewise concluded that a simple rural community—a village with its surrounding and well-knit rural area—and there were hundreds of them in Yorkshire—which possessed charitable endowments of from £100 to £400 was well armed on the whole for the needs of its youth and that 13·78 per cent (£16,704 2s) of all its charitable wealth was given by men and women from that city, of which almost exactly half (49·13 per cent) was for educational uses. The distribution of the charitable funds for the Riding was as follows:

	£	s		
Poor	39,564	8	(32·65%)—county at large:	(33·46%)
Social rehabilitation	4,836	8	(3·99%)	(4·85%)
Municipal betterments	2,465	15	(2·03%)	(2·51%)
Education	37,467	6	(30·92%)	(31·12%)
Religion	36,847	9	(30·41%)	(28·07%)
	121,181	6		

of its poor. These were uncomplicated parishes which might have an almshouse, a substantial endowment for home relief, or a grammar school of quite respectable stature. Such an agricultural village might in fact be rather better fitted to meet the needs of its people than a textile town with much larger charitable funds at its disposal, standing as it did at the peril of seasonal or cyclical unemployment.

There were in total 109 of these parishes, all save Scarborough having been rural parishes or rural communities possessing a small urban complex, the largest of which could not have been more than populous villages about to become towns. The charitable funds of these 'comfortably-off' parishes, in almost all of which the traditions of charitable giving were well established by the close of our period, amounted in total to £21,930 17s, or an average for the entire group of £201 4s.[1] These endowments ranged in amount from the £101 8s accumulated over the years as the gift of fourteen donors in Kirby Moorside, a thinly populated community of about 21 square miles in the North Riding,[2] to the £395 15s provided by twenty-six separate donors for the needs of Bradfield, which was a rural chapelry, described by the Parliamentary Survey as possessing about 300 families, in the West Riding parish of Ecclesfield.[3] The median parish in this large group was Hornby, in the North Riding, dominated through much of our period by the Conyers

---

[1] Here again we find the social and cultural dominance of the West Riding to be well defined. Of these communities, 52, with charitable resources of £10,578 5s, were in the West Riding, 35 with £6768 4s were in the North Riding, and 22 with £4584 8s were in the East Riding.

[2] Its charities were vested: £68 for the care of the poor, £13 in social rehabilitation, and £20 8s for the uses of the church. Of the fourteen donors, two were London tradesmen, both being natives, who had given £19 13s to the charitable needs of the poor. The parish was largely moorland, save for two confined but fertile valleys. It possessed no resident or responsible lord of the manor at any time during our period. In the earlier years it was a possession of the Nevill's, being forfeited to the Crown in 1569 as a result of Westmorland's share in the rebellion of that year. It was held by the Crown under lease to a local farmer until 1616, when it was one of the many crown properties granted by James I to his favourite, George Villiers. The charitable accumulations were the fruit of a slowly developing local tradition of responsibility, yeomen and husbandmen being the principal donors, fortified by the not very substantial assistance of London.

[3] Bradfield, lying to the northwest of Sheffield some seven or eight miles, had made considerable progress, again as the consequence of the efforts of quite humble men, assisted, however, by the leadership of a curate, in establishing sound and impressive community resources. There was no dominant benefactor among the twenty-four who had made contributions, but there was a quite impressively steady flow of gifts from yeomen, husbandmen, weavers, and clothiers from 1564 onwards. The accumulation at the close of our era was distributed: £149 4s for poor relief, 1s for municipal uses (this of course being an outright gift), £80 for educational needs, and £166 10s for the support of the chapel.

family, and with charitable endowments totalling £184 17s at the time of the Restoration.

Through the growth of traditions of responsible giving spreading by degrees, certain of these rural and contiguous regions and occasionally whole wapentakes, particularly in the West Riding, had raised themselves by slow but persistent effort into a position of comfortable institutional strength. We may take the wapentake of Staincross, an almost wholly rural region in the West Riding, lying to the north of Sheffield and to the west of Doncaster, and comprising approximately 135 square miles, as exemplifying this most interesting and significant cultural development. The wapentake included twenty-three communities in all, the market town of Barnsley being the most considerable urban complex in the district. At the close of our period the total of the charitable resources of the wapentake was £5425 15s, distributed in such wise that £1670 14s was vested for the relief of the poor, £42 14s for experimentation with social rehabilitation, £95 5s for municipal uses, the very substantial total of £2138 had been provided for the foundation of three schools within the area, and £1479 2s for the support of the churches and chapels of the wapentake. These funds had been given during the course of our period by 188 different donors, most of whom were yeomen, gentry, clothiers, and husbandmen, and almost all of whom were firmly rooted in the neighbourhood. It is noteworthy that this considerable accomplishment had been attained without the leadership or intervention of any Maecenas, there having been only one London benefaction for the entire wapentake and that amounting to no more than £7. As we have noted,[1] of the twenty-three communities composing the area four possessed charitable resources of £400 or more at the time of the Restoration; a second group of nine were comfortably endowed, in relation to their population and needs, with funds ranging from £100 to £400; while another six had charitable resources ranging from the £26 15s for the rural township of Ardsley to the £99 12s for Woolley. Only four communities, all being rural chapelries or townships, held less than £25 of charitable funds, and all these had been direct beneficiaries of at least some charitable gift of their own as well as participating in the benefits of endowments for schools, almshouses, and poor relief which extended to the whole of the wapentake.

In total, then, we have found 247 Yorkshire communities in which the charitable accumulations amounted to more than £100 and in which, the circumstances of size, population, and relative need being taken into account, we may be reasonably confident that youth possessed some considerable measure of opportunity and that the poor were protected at least against the disastrous effects of abject and eroding poverty. These communities were the truly favoured areas of this large county,

[1] *Vide Appendix*, Table D.

for they comprised not quite a third (30·69) of all its recognizable settled entities, whether parochial or not, while disposing the enormous total of £208,333 2s, or 85·5 per cent, of its charitable resources.

Yet perhaps the most notable fact about Yorkshire was the spread of philanthropy over all the communities comprising this large shire, even including remote and very poor mountain and moor townships which could have supported but a tiny rural population under the agrarian conditions of the seventeenth century. There were in all 258 parishes and lesser rural communities, none being larger than a small village, with its dependent agricultural region, in which we find benefactions ranging from £10 to £100, most of which was in capital gifts, albeit of modest proportions. These places possessed in all charitable wealth totalling £9346 17s, or a respectable average of £36 4s 7d for the group, the largest number being found in the West Riding and the largest total of funds in the North Riding. These were by no means blighted communities, all possessing in relation to need some measure of strength, and many having been vested with institutions which lent dignity and a degree of opportunity to the lives of the almost wholly humble people who resided in them. These parishes comprised almost a third of all the communities in the county. In most of these villages and rural townships, too, habits of giving and of local responsibility had by the close of our era been well and securely established. These communities were not without resources to meet the complex and pressing demands of a new age.

There were, then, a total of 505 parishes and other communities, York City being included, in which was vested an overwhelming proportion of the charitable funds of the county and which included not quite two-thirds (62·73 per cent) of all the communities counted, though it should be added that by a certainly conservative estimate these 'areas of opportunity' must have included fully 90 per cent of the population of the shire.

There remain 300 rural communities in which the total of charitable benefactions amassed during the course of our period ranged from a few pence to £10. These were the areas of social blight in Yorkshire, concentrated principally in the decaying agricultural areas of the East Riding and in the back reaches of the moors and mountains of the county where men possessed no leadership, no helpful institutions, and only a most limited measure of opportunity. Very few of these communities were parishes and a fair number have long since disappeared as settled entities. They were the marginal reaches, yet it is important to record that so strong and pervasive was the charitable instinct of this remarkable county that in no known community did men fail to grace life with at least some recorded gift for the betterment of an emerging society.

E. THE IMPACT OF LONDON ON THE COUNTY

Yorkshire lay at what seemed to men of our period a vast distance from London. Scores of the wills we have read were drawn by men about to undertake what was for them a hazardous and certainly formidable journey to the capital, whether because of private or public emergency. Perhaps half the county was upwards of 200 miles from London by the tortuous roads of the period, roads which were notoriously evil within the confines of Yorkshire itself. This factor of distance, complicated by poor communications, was one with which all the Tudors struggled in dealing with the county and accounts principally for the relative backwardness of the area when viewed from the more settled perspective of the Home Counties. This also accounts for the economic isolation of Yorkshire from London during the first century of our era, which was, however, greatly lessened as the industrial development in the West Riding began to gather momentum. Nor was there any considerable calculated investment made by London merchants in Yorkshire lands unless they were themselves rooted there by ties of birth, nor any effective linking of the county to the city by merchants who retired there as landed gentlemen. The county simply lay outside the great orbit of the metropolis, save for one most important exception. One of the principal exports of Yorkshire has always been men, and throughout our period there is constant evidence of the drifting down of ambitious younger sons who sought and very frequently made substantial commercial fortunes in the city in the course of their lifetimes. These were the London donors, imbued with the aggressive energy and the well-formulated aspirations of the burgher aristocracy. These were men who were to play an important part in the social and cultural transformation of their native county with the immense leverage supplied by their benefactions.

The influence of London wealth and of London aspirations on the shaping of Yorkshire institutions was of course inevitably less pervasive than in counties nearer to London, but it was none the less very great indeed.[1] It is also important to observe that these London benefactions usually possessed great qualitative strength, since they were well and most carefully disposed and since they were sufficiently large to accomplish the foundation on a secure basis of an institution which could

[1] The proportion of total charitable funds derived from London sources is as follows for the counties studied:

	Per cent		Per cent
Bristol	19·73	Norfolk	13·21
Buckinghamshire	17·04	Somerset	26·05
Hampshire	29·23	Worcestershire	23·01
Kent	40·74	Yorkshire	12·09
Lancashire	28·03		

transform the quality of life in a whole area of the county. In all, London donors supplied the considerable total of £29,457 14s for charitable uses in Yorkshire, this amounting to 12·09 per cent of all the charitable wealth amassed in the course of our period. These gifts were especially effective since almost the whole (94·67 per cent) of them were in the form of endowments.

This formidable contribution to the social and cultural development of Yorkshire was made by 171 donors distributed surprisingly evenly over the whole span of our period, but with a particularly heavy concentration of the large benefactions in the generation extending from 1600 to 1630. On the average, then, London benefactors gave the substantial total of £172 5s 4d each, which we have seen to be a sufficient amount for an almshouse foundation or a small grammar school on the modest scale to which this county was accustomed. The qualitative strength of these benefactions is suggested when we reflect that while Londoners constituted less than 2 per cent of all donors for the county, their gifts comprised somewhat more than 12 per cent of the aggregate of charitable funds. These men were bound to Yorkshire by the closest of ties, since of the whole number 104 were native sons, 16 more were almost certainly born in the county, and of the remaining 51 benefactors it can be said that no more than 15 were without doubt natives of other counties.

Very nearly half of all London donors to Yorkshire's charitable needs were members of the great London livery companies. These eighty-three merchants gave £15,639 5s to Yorkshire institutions, with a heavy proportion being designated for school foundations and for almshouse endowments. Rather more than half (forty-four) of these men, or their widows, belong to the period 1480–1600, though the total of the contributions of these early donors reached only the modest sum of £1520 5s. The thirty-nine merchants whose wills were proved or who made their foundations by deeds of gift from 1601 to 1660 gave as a group the substantial total of £14,119, of which eleven made contributions exceeding £400 each.

The next most important group were sixteen professional men, all lawyers or doctors, who had found good fortune in London and who gave £9276 2s to various charitable uses in their native county. There were as well twenty-five tradesmen who gave the surprisingly modest total of £1159 11s, while a slightly smaller group of nineteen who can be identified no more accurately than as 'other burghers', most of whom were also probably tradesmen, bequeathed £1108 13s to the charitable uses of the county. The remaining total of £2274 3s was given by three of the upper gentry, by ten more donors who at least described themselves as of the gentry, by two of the upper clergy and six of their humbler colleagues, and by two artisans who gave £10 and £1 8s each in their wills to the needs of the West Riding parishes in which they had been born. There remain five whose social status cannot be determined, who gave a total of £504 10s for various charitable purposes.[1]

It is revealing to compare the spectrum of London aspirations with those of Yorkshire. If the proportions given for the several great charitable heads are compared, it will at once be noted that London donors were far more consistently secular in their interests than were the generality of Yorkshiremen, while this contrast is in a sense heightened when it is observed that almost 40 per cent of the sum given for religious uses was designated either to found Puritan lectureships or to endow chapelries with at least some assurance of the power of presentation. A brief table will perhaps best set out these qualitative differences:

	Poor	Social rehabilitation	Municipal betterments	Education	Religion
	£ s	£ s	£ s	£ s	£ s
County at large	81,513 13	11,805 17	6,121 11	75,812 8	68,397 5
	(33·46%)	(4·85%)	(2·51%)	(31·12%)	(28·07%)
London gifts to County	8,735 2	1,190 9	596 13	12,833 7	6,102 3
	(29·65%)	(4·04%)	(2·03%)	(43·57%)	(20·71%)

It is immediately evident that Londoners fastened with a most impressive pertinacity on the educational needs of Yorkshire. Rather more than 43 per cent of all their benefactions were designated for this purpose, accounting for substantially more than a fourth of the capital with which donors of our period created a system of secondary education in the county. In no other charitable head was London's interest proportionately so great as that of the county as a whole, while, as we have said, in the sphere of religious need it was not only markedly less but it was likewise markedly different.

We have seen in county after county that London's great generosity, which pervaded the entire realm, was extraordinarily effective in remoulding the social and cultural institutions of the nation because it possessed such amazing qualitative strength. This great store of capital was not frittered away in sentimental doles for the poor or in conspicuous acts of piety. It was, on the whole, carefully and fruitfully concentrated on almshouse foundations or endowments for poor relief, on grammar-school creations or on scholarship resources, on apprenticeship plans, and on the building and endowment of sorely needed chapels which the donors were usually able to cast in a Genevan mould. The impressive and selective power of these benefactions can perhaps be best observed by noting first a group of communities possessing substantial charitable resources of £400 or more that were relatively unaffected by the aggressive and articulate aspirations of London and then a similar group in which the whole institutional framework was, so to speak, fabricated in London.

[1] The size and nature of these last gifts would suggest that at least three of these donors were in fact merchants.

In one large group of communities, numbering sixty-seven and including old towns as well as several of the new industrial towns of the West Riding, London's assistance in the founding of local institutions was insubstantial.[1] These were parishes together holding nearly 45 per cent of the whole of the charitable wealth of the county, of which less than 2 per cent was provided by London donors. They were self-reliant communities which had slowly built up substantial indigenous charitable resources. It is particularly striking that the East Riding, taking in view all its parishes as well as these most-favoured communities, profited only modestly from London generosity. Of the whole of the charitable wealth of this region (£39,314 13s), somewhat less than 5 per cent was provided by London benefactors. Relatively few East Riding boys found their way to the capital to enter upon apprenticeships there, and there were in the ordinary course of life in this predominantly agricultural region few direct contacts of any kind with the immensely stimulating currents of thought and activity for which the city was so justly renowned.

There was, at the same time, a considerable group of communities, including both towns and rural parishes, in which the intervention of London was of decisive importance.[2] In most cases these parishes were lifted from medievalism to modernity by the great and compelling generosity of a native son, who, having made his fortune in trade or in the law in London, remembered the place of his birth with carefully devised institutions on which so evidently years of thought and preparation had been spent. In a few cases, notably Halifax and Wakefield, the fame of a local preacher or some commercial affinity drew gifts from Londoners having no apparent personal connection with the favoured towns, and there were a substantial number of benefactions made for reasons of sentiment to the birthplace of a donor's wife or parents.

This smaller group of cities, towns, and rural parishes was spread over the whole of Yorkshire in a curious pattern which, as we have observed, was principally the result of genetic accident. These twenty-eight communities possessed slightly less than a third (30·32 per cent) of all the charitable wealth of Yorkshire, and the development of the institutional resources with which they might meet the harsh requirements of the modern age was greatly assisted, when not framed, by the outpouring of London generosity. In all, nearly a third (30·52 per cent) of their charitable funds had been given by London donors. It should be noted, too, that London giving to the entire county was heavily concentrated in these favoured communities, something more than three-fourths (76·54 per cent) of the generous total of London benefactions having been settled for the endowment of social and cultural needs in these twenty-eight towns.

[1] *Vide* Table E, *Appendix*, for the particulars.
[2] These are listed in Table F, *Appendix*.

We have observed that London interest in the pressing needs of the East Riding was scant indeed. Nor was it particularly impressive in its impact on the West Riding, save for aid to fifteen favoured communities, including Halifax and Wakefield. The West Riding possessed both the leadership and the wealth required to build its own institutions, the £16,704 2s which Londoners contributed to the region amounting to not more than 13·78 per cent of the whole of the great charitable resources that were to be accumulated there in the course of our period. It is interesting to note, however, that almost half (49·13 per cent) of the substantial total given by London was concentrated on the educational needs of this rapidly growing area.

It was in the North Riding that London's aid was to be of such very great importance, clearly because this then poor and on the whole backward region sent so many of its sons to find their fortunes in the great city which lay so far to the south. Somewhat more than a quarter (25·66 per cent) of the charitable resources of this region were provided by London benefactors, who alone were to give a full third of all the funds disposed to education in this region which so acutely needed opportunity and a release from the iron grip of ignorance. The export of men from the North Riding, and indeed from the whole of this vast county, was to bring abundant fruits, for old and frail men, rich and famous in London, did not as they prepared the final balance sheets of their careers forget the county that had bred and nurtured them.

F. THE IMPACT OF THE COUNTY ON THE NATION

Yorkshire was not only a large and a remarkably self-contained county, but it was likewise quite severely parochial in its charitable interests. Excluding gifts to the universities and for university scholarships, Yorkshire benefactors gave a total of £6350 7s for the social and cultural needs of sister counties. This sum was provided by 157 separate benefactors, or about 1·82 per cent of all the donors, and represents no more than 2·61 per cent of the whole of the great charitable wealth given in the course of our period. This establishes Yorkshire as among the more parochial of the counties we have examined; the explanation seems to lie in the crying need for the amelioration of social and cultural institutions in Yorkshire itself and in the intense loyalty which even men of substantial affairs maintained for their own little corner of their great county.[1]

[1] The proportion of total charitable wealth provided for extra-county needs in the other counties comprised in our study is as follows:

	Per cent		Per cent		Per cent
Bristol	0·79	Kent	4·20	Norfolk	2·40
Buckinghamshire	4·85	Lancashire	2·18	Somerset	0·87
Hampshire	8·54	London	30·95	Worcestershire	3·11

An extraordinarily high proportion of benefactions made by York-shiremen outside their own county was vested in the nearby or adjoining counties of Derbyshire, Lancashire, Northamptonshire, and Notting-hamshire, with the addition, most surprisingly, of London, the needs of whose poor and prisoners evidently pricked the Yorkshire con-science. Well over two-thirds of all the extra-territorial benefactions were made in these five counties, in amounts ranging from £385, given

Extra-Yorkshire benefactions:

County or country	Number of donors	Total benefactions	
		£	s
Bedfordshire	2	41	0
Berkshire	1	6	14
Buckinghamshire	3	186	3
Cambridgeshire	5	263	15
Cheshire	1	6	13
Cumberland	4	31	13
Derbyshire	3	1,037	10
Durham	8	130	18
Essex	2	43	7
Hampshire	1	26	13
Herefordshire	1	20	0
Hertfordshire	1	10	0
Huntingdonshire	3	5	0
Kent	6	107	1
Lancashire	8	768	18
Leicestershire	2	41	13
Lincolnshire	19	218	13
London	28	1,746	5
Norfolk	6	93	14
Northamptonshire	2	403	0
Northumberland	7	43	0
Nottinghamshire	12	385	0
Oxfordshire	4	41	18
Shropshire	1	5	0
Staffordshire	3	12	3
Suffolk	2	4	0
Surrey	2	9	0
Warwickshire	2	103	0
Westmorland	4	97	13
Worcestershire	4	32	0
Ireland	2	340	0
Scotland	1	0	3
New England	4	62	0
France	2	26	0
Rome	1	1	0
	——	———	
	157	6,350	7

by twelve donors to Nottinghamshire, to £1746 5s, given by twenty-eight benefactors to London's needs. One is particularly struck, in the preceding table, by the indifference displayed for the needs of neighbouring counties such as Cumberland, Northumberland, Lincolnshire, and Westmorland. But at least nominal gifts were made to thirty counties, as well as rather substantial amounts to Ireland and New England.

These 'realm-minded' donors displayed a markedly different complexion of interests in their gifts to other counties from that we have observed in Yorkshire itself. Considerably more than a third (37·53 per cent) of the whole amount was given for various religious uses, these being chiefly early gifts and bequests for monasteries and for prayers in distant parts of England. The quite amazing total of £1805 14s was provided for sundry plans of social rehabilitation, particularly in London, by donors in a county almost shockingly careless about the endowment of sorely needed schemes for this purpose within its own borders. As we should expect, save for sentimental gifts to London, the needs of the poor did not weigh heavily on the Yorkshire conscience, while distant educational foundations, the universities always aside, commanded only a little less than 14 per cent of the total of the benefactions made to other counties.[1]

A large proportion (42·72 per cent) of the total of these benefactions beyond the Yorkshire borders were made by nineteen members of the upper gentry who held lands in other parts of England or who were perhaps in any event not so parochial in their concerns as most of their contemporaries. Somewhat surprisingly, only £265 11s was given by members of the lower gentry for such uses, this amounting to but 4·18 per cent of the whole amount of extra-county gifts. These benefactions of the lower gentry were likewise heavily concentrated in the period prior to 1560, a large proportion being for prayers and for monastic purposes. The total given by the yeomanry and husbandmen of the county was nominal (£17 10s), all, save £1 given in 1558 for the poor of London, having been disposed for parishes lying just across the border in other counties. Something like a fourth (23·77 per cent) of the total was given by divers bishops and abbots, who, interestingly enough, displayed greater concern with the needs of other counties for education and social rehabilitation than with expressly religious uses. A relatively

---

[1] The amounts and proportions given under the large charitable heads were as follows:

	£	s	
Poor	1,144	14	(18·02%)
Social rehabilitation	1,805	14	(28·43%)
Municipal betterments	135	0	(2·13%)
Education	881	13	(13·88%)
Religion	2,383	6	(37·53%)

large number of these donors, thirty-nine in all, were members of the lower clergy, who as a group gave £1007 3s for extra-county needs, or 15·86 per cent of the whole, with a heavy concentration of interest on the religious needs of distant parishes in which they had once served or which they still held as pluralists. A small group of merchants provided £434 8s for the charitable uses of other counties, with a predominant interest in the plight of the poor and the needs of religion in distant places, the mere recital of whose names—London, Norwich, Dublin, Bordeaux, Calais, Chipping Campden, and New England—suggests the nature of the ties that ran from them across the Yorkshire borders. All the other social classes made but slight contribution outside the county in which their interests were so deeply and firmly rooted.

G. THE STRUCTURE OF CLASS ASPIRATIONS

We have observed that Yorkshire was a predominantly rural county throughout our period, invigorated during the last third of this long era by an impressive and relatively swift urban growth concentrated in the West Riding. It was a county in which older and once firmly seated local magnates may be seen losing their grip on the economy and the leadership of the county: nobility and gentry who had grudgingly accepted the Tudors but who could not accept the revolutionary implications of Tudor religious policy. This older landed aristocracy was rapidly being replaced during the last century of our period by a new gentry whose fortunes were based on grazing or upon monastic spoils and who were more firmly committed not only to Tudor order but to the founding and nourishing of the secular institutions of a new age. This is a county, too, in which a strong and numerous yeomanry emerges rather late, but which was to undertake a considerable measure of social responsibility in many areas. These yeomen were often sustained quite as much by wool as by farming, with the frequent result that a man in his will might in one phrase describe himself as yeoman and in another as clothier. We have seen, too, that the old and once powerful city of York was slowly declining in fortune and population, though there remained a merchant class with considerable wealth who sought to nurture their beautiful city with their generosity. Hull, too, had lost the vigour of its fourteenth-century development, though it was fortunate in possessing a small but extraordinarily responsible and lavishly generous mercantile aristocracy who vested it with most impressive institutions during the course of our period. But the most interesting, the most spontaneously generous, and perhaps the most important merchant groups were to be found in the new and raw urban centres of the West Riding, for these were men who simply created *de novo* the institutions which they so quickly saw were necessary if civilized life were to be possible at all in Halifax, Wakefield, and Leeds. We are dealing, then, with the way in which various classes of men assumed responsibility in a singularly interesting and complex county.

As we have noted, there were 8632 identified individual donors to the charitable funds of Yorkshire during the course of our period. We have seen that these men and women gave in all £243,650 14s to the several charitable uses of the county, or an average of £28 4s 6d for each donor. This is the lowest average benefaction for the group of counties studied, and is probably accounted for not only by the comparative poverty of the shire but likewise by the remarkable extent to which the humbler agricultural classes participated in framing the structure of its charities.[1] We have found it possible to establish the social identity of a considerable number (7694) of these benefactors, amounting to nearly 90 per cent (89·13 per cent) of the entire group. There remain 938 unidentified individuals, a large proportion of whom are forever cloaked in the social anonymity of the term 'widow'. We may say, however, that the places of residence and the terms of the wills establish the fact that 741 of these donors were country dwellers, while the size and nature of their bequests suggest that they were in average terms of yeoman status with some admixture from the lesser gentry. There were also 197 unidentified donors who were town dwellers, and who, again in average terms, were probably mostly tradesmen with a slight seasoning of artisans.

If we may somewhat arbitrarily reckon all the parish clergy as rural dwellers, we may then say that 6823 of our donors were country men, or not quite 80 per cent (79·04 per cent) of the whole number. Since it seems probable that the urban population of the county even at the close of our period did not constitute more than 10 per cent to 13 per cent of the whole, we see at once that there was a much heavier proportionate participation of the urban classes in mustering the charitable resources of the county, which were further and most vigorously strengthened by the generosity, not to mention the wisdom, of their giving. Excluding from our consideration the benefactions of the Crown and of the unidentified group of donors, we find that though the great mass of the donors of our period were rural, they gave not quite 56 per cent of the whole of the charitable resources of the county, whereas in this overwhelmingly rural county the relatively small group

---

[1] The average benefaction in the several counties was as follows:

	£	s	d		£	s	d
Bristol	173	6	9	London	255	12	2
Buckinghamshire	51	3	10	Norfolk	65	10	10
Hampshire	44	10	2	Somerset	32	2	3
Kent	37	15	10	Worcestershire	66	17	10
Lancashire	110	9	10	Yorkshire	28	4	6

of urban donors were to provide the amazing proportion of 37·10 per cent of the whole of its charitable wealth.[1]

In every county in England in our period the heavy burden of social and historical responsibility was assumed by two small social groups, the gentry and their newer urban counterparts, the merchants. And as it was in the realm at large so it most decidedly was in Yorkshire. The gentry, who probably could not have numbered more than 2 per cent of the population of the county, constituted nearly 14 per cent of all its donors, while they bore not much less than a third (31·12 per cent) of the formidable social and cultural load which private donors undertook during our long period. Even more remarkable was the role of the merchant aristocracy, who, far less numerous and without the traditional as well as the quasi-legal weight of social responsibility upon them, were to over-match an older aristocracy in the quality of their generosity and to draw near to it in the extent of their liberality. For this tiny merchant class, numbering no more than 3·87 per cent of all donors in the county, was to give almost 21 per cent of the total of its charitable wealth. These two classes together, while numbering rather less than 18 per cent of all donors, were to provide somewhat more than half (52·07 per cent) of the whole of the great wealth poured into the charitable and institutional needs of Yorkshire during the course of our long era.

It is evident in all counties in England that the various classes of men

[1] Analysis of the social status of Yorkshire benefactors:

No. of donors in the class	Social status	Percentage of all county gifts	Percentage of all county persons	Totals for class	
4	Crown	1·12	0·05	2,740	7
25	Nobility	5·94	0·29	14,484	12
185	Upper gentry	14·65	2·14	35,685	5
1017	Lower gentry	16·47	11·78	40,139	15
1616	Yeomen	5·22	18·72	12,707	2
2616	Husbandmen	0·46	30·31	1,120	6
192	Agricultural labourers	0·03	2·22	74	3
22	Upper clergy	5·90	0·25	14,382	2
431	Lower clergy	12·71	4·99	30,977	4
334	Merchants	20·95	3·87	51,037	6
525	Tradesmen	3·14	6·08	7,659	17
169	Burghers	0·97	1·96	2,356	3
450	Artisans	0·28	5·21	681	0
98	Professional	5·39	1·14	13,139	14
10	Public officials	0·47	0·12	1,155	12
938	Unidentified	6·28	10·87	15,310	6
8632				243,650	14

did not assume a proportionate responsibility for the needs of their age and that they responded in quite different ways to the aspirations which were becoming dominant in the society. We see, in fact, a momentous shift in responsibility from a great landholding aristocracy, whose social consciousness had been blunted by the decay of feudalism and the almost abusive distrust of the Tudors, to a new aristocracy of humbler and very often most recent antecedents, which was prepared to supply leadership and resources to found a startlingly different society in England. The nobility and the older families among the upper gentry in all England, but in Yorkshire particularly, tended not only to distrust the new directions on which the national course had been set but to find themselves without the fluid, the disposable, wealth wherewith to lend sanction to whatever aspirations they may have had for their age. The lesser and the newer gentry, on the contrary, with their urban counterparts, were aggressively and most vigorously dedicated to the support of a monarchy which had given them status, had given them confidence as well as favour, and whose fortunes were as one with their own. These were men with keen and historically relevant aspirations, who likewise had the disposable, the exploitable, wealth with which the institutions of a new and an intensely secular England might be created. The price of leadership in the sixteenth century was responsibility, and the fee demanded by the Tudors for responsibility was generosity. This the merchants and the gentry supplied with an ardour and a sense of dedication rare indeed in human history. These men possessed the fluid means, and these means they were prepared to use to attain the aspirations which moved them. This will be abundantly clear in our discussion of the degree of responsibility undertaken by the various social classes in Yorkshire.[1]

It may be said first of all that the Crown, particularly in Tudor days, undertook little direct responsibility for the institutions of the county. There were four separate royal gifts to Yorkshire, made by as many sovereigns, which totalled £2740 7s and which constituted only 1·12 per cent of the whole of the charitable funds of the county.

The nobility of this huge county were relatively numerous, rich, and socially tenacious in their claims on the loyalty and esteem of the shire. But their importance in framing the social and cultural institutions of their county may perhaps be most accurately stated by suggesting that the weight of their influence and contribution was approximately that of the yeomanry or of the tiny professional class of the county. In total, twenty-five members of the great landed aristocracy gave £14,484 12s to the charitable needs of their county, or a relatively high average of

---

[1] *Vide* Jordan, *Philanthropy*, I, 330–342, *Appendix*, Tables VII and VIII for a discussion of the disposable wealth held by the several social classes in our period.

£579 7s 8d for the inconsiderable number of the class who gave anything at all. This represents 5·94 per cent of the total of the wealth vested for philanthropic uses during the course of our period. It must be said, however, that three great benefactions by members of the Clifford and Talbot families established a high qualitative value to the philanthropy of the nobility, since almost two-thirds of all the gifts of the class were designated for almshouse foundations.

The numerous and powerful upper gentry of the county, on the other hand, assumed a steadily increasing degree of social and cultural responsibility for its developing needs. Though the 185 donors of this class numbered only 2·14 per cent of all benefactors, they gave the generous total of £35,685 5s for various charitable uses, this constituting 14·65 per cent of the whole of the charitable resources to be amassed during our long period. Taking the whole period into account, men of this class were especially interested in the building of the educational system of the county, to which they gave more than 40 per cent of all their charitable funds. The needs of the poor commanded not quite a third of their charitable wealth, with a particular interest being shown in almshouse foundations, to which they gave £6719 8s. They displayed a relatively modest concern for the religious needs of the county, to which less than a fourth (24·11 per cent) of all their benefactions were dedicated, with however a heavy outlay of £3786 11s, constituting 10·61 per cent of all their contributions, for the endowment of chantries and prayers. The exciting and commanding opportunities for social rehabilitation in their county received only limited support from these men, 3·42 per cent of all their gifts having been made for this purpose, while the various possibilities for municipal improvement were ignored by the class, save for a total of £628 (1·76 per cent), which they disposed for the improvement of roads and bridges.

The pattern of giving of the upper gentry of the county in the decades prior to the Reformation is especially interesting in that it suggests almost predictably the cataclysm that was in the late Henrician period to overwhelm so many of the powerful and firmly seated families in this group. During these years members of the class gave the substantial total of £5741 17s for various charitable causes, this amounting to 16·09 per cent of all the contributions of the class. A heavy proportion (81·82 per cent) of this large total was dedicated to various religious uses with, most significantly, the incredibly high proportion of almost 60 per cent of all their benefactions having been made for the endowment of prayers. This almost obsessive concern with religious needs left little for other charitable uses, the relief of the poor, for example, absorbing in all only 11·58 per cent of the charitable wealth disposed by the upper gentry during these years. The improvement of educational opportunities commanded slightly more than 6 per cent of all their benefactions, while only trivial amounts were given for purposes of social rehabilitation or municipal improvements.

This class was clearly both gravely weakened and socially confused during the two decades of reformation. In these years donors of the class, of families many of which were rightly suspected by the Tudors, gave only £1420 8s for all charitable purposes, this being but 3·98 per cent of the total of benefactions made by the class during our whole period. They remained as stubbornly devoted to the religious needs of their communities as they dared, since somewhat more than half (51·59 per cent) of all their gifts were for this general purpose, with, it should be noted, well over a quarter of all their gifts still being left to endow prayers. There was, however, a considerable increase in giving for poor relief, to which about 23 per cent of all their gifts were made, while educational needs in these years absorbed a quarter of their charitable bequests.

But, relatively speaking, the nadir of the upper gentry in terms of social responsibility and cultural leadership was to occur in the Elizabethan era. In this long and prosperous period the total of their benefactions was only £2676 7s, or 7·5 per cent of the whole amount to be given by the class. It was evident that the Elizabethan Reformation was permanent and hence could not command the support of the older and dominant families of the class. The proportion of charitable funds left for religious purposes fell precipitously to 4·24 per cent of the almost insignificant total of all charitable dispositions made by the great gentry in this period. More than half (51·58 per cent) of the total of their charitable wealth was vested in educational undertakings, with the £1180 given to grammar schools alone constituting 44·09 per cent of all benefactions made in this long generation. There was likewise a rising interest in the plight of the poor, to whose relief somewhat more than a third (37·71 per cent) of all gifts were dedicated, while upwards of 6 per cent was designated for various plans of social rehabilitation.

Even a casual study of the names of benefactors drawn from the upper gentry makes it clear that a veritable metamorphosis in the structure of the class occurred during the interval 1575–1610. New families drawn from the lesser gentry, from the law, from trade, and even from the yeomanry had risen during the Elizabethan period to replace an old and obdurate gentry which had lost its historical if not its genealogical importance. These new men were to transform the class and were in the early Stuart period to restore its leadership in the vital affairs of the county. In this interval the impressive sum of £14,062, this being 39·41 per cent of the whole contribution of the class, was given for charitable purposes. By far the greatest concern was now with the extension and strengthening of the educational resources available to the youth of the county, towards which nearly

60 per cent of the great sum given in this one generation was disposed. Approximately a fourth of the whole (23·00 per cent) was designated for poor relief. The needs of the church again began to receive at least modest support, something like 17 per cent of the charitable funds of the period being disposed for these uses, with the particularly heavy concentration of £1503 in endowments for the support of the clergy and £400 for Puritan lectureships.

The period of Civil War and profound political unsettlement, which so divided the upper gentry of the county, seemed if anything to accelerate the rate of giving by members of this class and to confirm the now thoroughly secular aspirations of the men who composed it. In this short interval of two decades the generous total of £11,784 13s was devised for charitable uses, this being almost a third of the contributions of the class during our entire period. Members of the class, and there are few new names, were in these years devotedly concerned with remedying the condition of the poor, to whom they gave almost half of their charity. In all, the upper gentry poured £3075 into almshouse foundations and £2571 13s into endowments for household relief, while various schemes for social rehabilitation attracted 7·65 per cent of their charitable funds. Almost exactly a third of the total charitable outlay was for educational endowments, while the needs of the church were once more all but ignored, not quite 6 per cent of all charitable gifts having been made for religious purposes, or only slightly more than the total designated for the repair of roads and bridges.

The lower gentry of Yorkshire exhibit many characteristics similar to those we have been tracing out in their more powerful and certainly much richer contemporaries. This was in Yorkshire a large and an extraordinarily fluid class which would offer to the social historian a rich field for detailed study. In the course of our period there were 1017 benefactors drawn from this class, numbering 11·78 per cent of the county's donors, who gave the very large total of £40,139 15s towards the support of its charitable institutions, this constituting 16·47 per cent of the whole of the charitable wealth of the county from all sources during the entire period; a larger proportion, it might be added, than that contributed by the class in any other English county save Somerset.

Taking our entire era in view, the lower gentry was to bear an important and in many areas of the county a dominant role in framing the social institutions of Yorkshire. Their total contribution was exceeded only by that of the merchants, while among other social classes it was rivalled only by the great gentry and the lower clergy. One is struck by the essential conservatism of the group, which remained far more steadily devoted to the needs of the church than any other social class, bestowing the remarkably high proportion of 42·29 per cent of all their benefactions on religious uses as compared with about 28 per cent for the county at large. They gave not quite a third (31·96 per cent) of all their charitable resources for the relief of the poor, with a special emphasis on endowments to secure household relief, to which may be added a modest 2·31 per cent which they devoted to experimentation in social rehabilitation. Their support of education was relatively cautious, 22·26 per cent of all their gifts being designated for this great use, with a particular concern for the endowment of schools, to which members of the class gave £6736 5s, this amounting to about a sixth of all their benefactions. Their concern with municipal improvements was limited indeed, only slightly more than 1 per cent of all their charitable wealth being disposed for the several uses that comprise this head.

When we examine the structure of the contributions of this great and important class, we discover that it underwent stresses and strains not dissimilar from those we have noted among the great gentry. Moreover, there are persuasive indications suggesting that the gentry of, say, 1640 bore but a most limited genetic relation to the gentry of 1540, just as the aspirations of the class were so profoundly modified in this historically brief interval. The old gentry (with reasonable accuracy one might say the medieval gentry) were relatively rich and were almost obsessively concerned with the claims of faith on their lives and fortunes. In the decades prior to the Reformation members of this class gave £11,654 2s for charitable purposes, which accounts for the amazing proportion of 29·03 per cent of the whole contribution of the group for our entire period. Further, the very high proportion of 83·54 per cent of all their benefactions during these years was disposed for one or another religious purpose, including £7832 19s for prayers, this one item absorbing somewhat more than two-thirds of the whole of their charitable dispositions. The relief of the poor commanded less than a tenth of their charities, education received slightly more than 5 per cent of the whole, while relatively trifling amounts were left for municipal betterments or for experiments in social rehabilitation. Then the all but paralyzing wave of the Reformation swept over this pious, stubborn, and unresilient class. The total of their giving from 1541 to 1560 fell to £1897 8s, or 4·73 per cent of the whole for the class, of which considerably more than half (57·03 per cent) was still dedicated to the needs of faith. Indeed, even at this late date more than 40 per cent of all their charitable bequests were for prayers, far more than double any other single charitable head and a pathetic testimony to the resolute piety of a class which was about to undergo a ruthless metamorphosis as scores of new families holding very different aspirations emerged from the wreckage of ancient institutions.

During the long Elizabethan era, the lesser gentry, whose ranks were studded with many new names, especially in the West Riding and the

North Riding, made a slow recovery in wealth, in influence, and in responsibility. In these years its members gave £5830 3s, this being 14·52 per cent of the whole for the class, to various charitable causes, among which religion had all but withered away within the structure of their aspirations. Religious undertakings commanded only the unbelievably small proportion of 2·44 per cent of all their gifts in this generation of almost frightening secularism, less even than the amounts devoted to municipal improvement (2·77 per cent) or to social rehabilitation (3·84 per cent). The dominant concern of the gentry in these years was with the needs of the poor, on which they lavished more than 46 per cent of all their benefactions, and with the advancement of education, to which they devoted nearly as much (44·38 per cent).

What can perhaps be described as the 'new gentry' attained its full measure of social strength and clarification of its aspirations during the early Stuart period, when £10,250 12s, constituting a fourth (25·54 per cent) of the whole contribution of the class, was left for charitable employment. Large and well-disposed sums were vested in various endowments for poor relief, absorbing close to half of all the charities of the group in these years, while almost a third was concentrated on the educational needs of the shire, with particularly heavy support being lent to grammar schools. More was also given to religious needs, on which 18·45 per cent of all charities were vested, with a marked and persistent attention to strengthening clerical incomes and to founding Puritan lectureships.

The generosity of the lesser gentry attained its climax during the brief closing interval of our period, when the great total of £10,507 10s, representing a velocity of contribution double that even in the early Stuart period, was provided for an interesting spectrum of social needs. Most, though by no means all, of these benefactions were made by a now rich and powerful Puritan wing of the gentry whose principal concern was in strengthening the long neglected religious institutions of the county. Almost 40 per cent of all their gifts were designated for religious uses, with a particularly concentrated concern for the bettering of clerical incomes, on which £3182 8s, or 30·29 per cent of the whole, was laid out. There was a sharp decline during this interval in giving by this class for the needs of the poor, something less than a third of all their charities being for this purpose, while approximately a fourth of their endowments were designated for the further strengthening of the educational resources of the county. All in all men of this class had done well for their county and their country.

The yeomanry of Yorkshire, while emerging relatively late, constitute a numerous, an important, and a most interesting segment of the society. There were 1616 individual donors who may certainly be reckoned as in this class, comprising 18·72 per cent of all benefactors, who gave the impressive total of £12,707 2s for the charitable needs of their county. The total of their charities constituted 5·22 per cent of the whole for Yorkshire, establishing the yeomanry of this county as decidedly the most influential and responsible among all the counties examined, and that includes the vaunted yeomanry of Kent. The aggregate of their contributions, which averaged approximately £7 17s 3d for each donor, compares favourably with the totals contributed in Yorkshire by such social groups as the nobility, the professional classes, and the upper clergy. Taking in view the span of our period, one is impressed by their steady preoccupation with the needs of the poor, to which they devoted about 61 per cent of all their considerable charities, as compared with 33·46 per cent for the county as a whole. The moderate support which they lent to the church, 20·73 per cent of the whole of their gifts, is of course to a degree explained by the late emergence of the group in numbers and in wealth. They gave £1483 9s to the grammar-school foundations of the county, while 3·61 per cent of all their benefactions were made for municipal betterments and a frugal 2·88 per cent was risked on social experimentation.

The relatively few members of this class reckoned among donors in the county during the early decades of our period were profoundly pious, the huge proportion of almost 91 per cent of their benefactions having been given for religious uses. The total of their benefactions increased markedly in the period of the Reformation, when £930 11s was given for various charitable uses, while the proportion bequeathed or given for religious uses was exactly halved. In the Elizabethan era, when their benefactions for all purposes rose to £1488 13s, the yeomanry of Yorkshire were, save for the 'additional burghers', the most profoundly secular of all social classes, no more than 2·87 per cent of this considerable sum having been left for religious uses. The great period of their prosperity and dedication to the social needs of the county came with the early Stuarts, when members of the class contributed £5314 2s for charitable causes over a broad spectrum of mature interests. By far the largest amount, this being 68·61 per cent of the whole, was devoted to the needs of the poor, while an additional 6 per cent (5·96 per cent) was vested by benefactors of the class in various schemes of social rehabilitation. Substantial sums were devoted to the extension of educational facilities in the county, accounting for 13·67 per cent of all their benefactions, while the needs of the church commanded about 9 per cent of all their charitable wealth.

A far more profound economic and social gulf seems to have separated the yeomen and husbandmen in Yorkshire than that setting off the yeomanry from the lesser gentry. We have recorded the charitable contributions of 2616 certainly identified husbandmen, who constitute nearly a third (30·31 per cent) of all benefactors in the county. But these

were very poor and very humble men whose average benefaction
amounted to only 8s 7d and the aggregate of which accounts for no
more than 0·46 per cent of the charitable wealth of Yorkshire. Taking
the whole period in view, one may venture the suggestion that this was
a curiously conservative and slowly changing social class, lagging at
least a half-century behind other rural classes in the inexorable shifting
of aspirations which was occurring even in the remote fastnesses of
Yorkshire. But when change came it was complete. This may perhaps
best be exemplified by a brief plotting of the curve of giving for religious purposes. In the period prior to the Reformation practically the
whole (91·41 per cent) of all the many customary gifts and bequests of
men of this class were for religious uses. Even during the years of violent
religious change the proportion held at the very high level of 60·03
per cent and remained by far the highest for any class in the county
during the chilly secularism of the Elizabethan era, when almost 17
per cent (16·92 per cent) of their benefactions were made for the needs
of the church. Then, as the proportion of benefactions for religious
uses began to rise sharply for all other classes, that of the husbandmen
continued to fall to 3·54 per cent in the early Stuart era and all but
disappeared during the decades of civil commotion when only 1·34
per cent of their gifts were made for religious purposes. There was,
then, a slow but impressively steady shifting of interests and aspirations
from the religious life which had once been the absorbing object of
their concern to the needs of the very poor from which they were
separated by the thinnest of economic margins.[1]

We have found bequests for charitable uses made by only 192 men
who may certainly be counted among the vast class of agricultural
labourers and landless rural poor who comprised such a large proportion of the rural population in the period under study. This is a class
which we know existed, which on occasion could erupt violently, but
which by and large simply lived, bred, worked, hungered, and died
without an historical trace. The total of the bequests of this class was
very small indeed, amounting to £74 3s, and is distributed rather
evenly over the several intervals of our period. Aside from an unusually
large bequest of 9s for the improvement of roads, all these tiny benefactions were either for doles for the poor or for religious purposes. One
is struck by the fact that even in the decades prior to the Reformation
this class was in proportionate terms only moderately interested in the
support of the church, while for the whole period only 16·85 per cent
of all their benefactions were designated for this purpose. The preoccupation of these men and women was steadily with the plight of the poor,

---

[1] Curve of giving for religious uses (by solid line) by husbandmen,
1480–1660, compared with curve of giving for relief of poor (by broken line)
in same period.

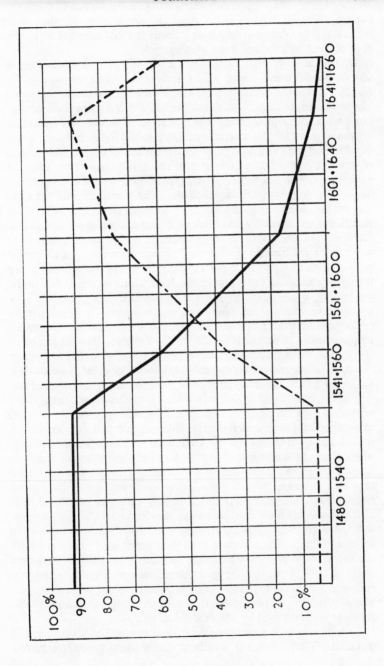

among whom in times of agricultural disaster or adversity they were inevitably numbered and to whose immediate relief they left 82·54 per cent of their pathetic and hard-won legacies.

We should expect that Yorkshire, the seat of a great see and of many famous monasteries, would gain greatly from the generosity of its bishops, its abbots, and its priors. There were twenty-two of the upper clergy who made charitable benefactions to the county in the course of our period, these men giving in all £14,382 2s for various charitable purposes, or a quite high average of £653 14s 8d for each donor. Their benefactions constituted 5·9 per cent of the whole of the charitable funds of the county, which suggests that the great churchmen assumed approximately the same degree of responsibility as did the yeomanry of the county or its professional classes. The contribution of the class was on the whole well and carefully devised, though in relation to traditional responsibility and leadership it was throughout our period unimpressive. Inevitably, of course, their gifts were most heavily concentrated in the decades prior to the Reformation when the archbishops retained something of their medieval power and substance and before the disappearance of the great abbots. In this interval nearly half of the total contribution of the group is represented in the £7022 16s they provided for various charitable uses in the county. It is noteworthy that in this interval the proportion given by these great churchmen for religious uses (28·84 per cent) was markedly lower than for any other social class, while the modest proportion (11·93 per cent) left for prayers was particularly and most conspicuously lower. The great preoccupation of the prelates in this early period was with the advancement of education in the county and in the universities, something more than 70 per cent of all their benefactions having been for this purpose. The pattern established by these pre-Reformation churchmen was in fact consistently maintained by their successors. Taking the whole period in view, the upper clergy gave upwards of 60 per cent of all their charitable funds to the extension of educational opportunities, a proportion unrivalled save by the benefactions of their lesser colleagues and by the professional classes. It is most revealing that only 14·49 per cent of all their charities were disposed for the uses of the church which they administered, the great clergy being the most secular of all social classes in terms of their aspirations. Nor were they particularly concerned with the needs of the poor, to which they gave less than a fourth (22·83 per cent) of their charities. The great churchmen as a group were conspicuous neither for the extent of their charity nor for particularly persuasive evidence of deep piety in the distribution of such charitable funds as they disposed by will or deed of gift.

Certainly no such strictures may be laid against the lower clergy of Yorkshire. There were 431 members of this social group, comprising

4·99 per cent of all donors, who gave the large total of £30,977 4s for charitable uses. This comprises 12·71 per cent of all the charitable funds of the county and approaches the contributions of a class as important in Yorkshire affairs as the upper gentry. One gains some clue to the persisting influence and prestige enjoyed by the secular clergy of Yorkshire when it is suggested that in no other county in England did the lower clergy bear so heavy and continuous a burden of social responsibility.[1] The singular importance of the lower clergy in the moulding of social institutions in the county seems to be the consequence of three factors. In the period ending roughly in 1560, Yorkshire produced an amazing number of priest-lawyers who were to hold important and extremely lucrative administrative posts all over England and who tended to remember the needs of their native county, often in a most secular fashion, when the time came to draft their last wills. It is also clear that an uncommonly large proportion of the lower clergy of Yorkshire were drawn, throughout our period, from the gentle families of the shire and that these men possessed at once the means and a sense of responsibility which caused them to become substantial donors. Finally, it seems evident that the rank and file of the clergy of the county, whether before or after the Reformation, were simply more sensitive to the needs of their people and of their charge than were their colleagues in any other county examined. The impressive amount given by the clergy of the county, as well as the extraordinary structure of their gifts, was of course largely determined by the relatively small group of priest-lawyers and those of the clergy who as sons of gentle families were possessed of independent means. Thus in the period prior to 1560 there were twenty-eight clerical donors who gave amounts ranging from £100 to £1000 and two who gave large benefactions of £1000 or more. Similarly, in the next century (1561–1660) there were nineteen clerical donors giving sums of from £100 to £1000 and six who gave endowments for charitable purposes of £1000 or more. This small group of fifty-five donors, wholly constituted of the two groups just mentioned, while comprising only 12·76 per cent of the clergy as a whole must be credited with the amazing proportion of 83·40 per cent of all the charities of this social class. The lower clergy of Yorkshire were well led and well inspired, not by the great prelates at York or Fountains but by those of their own number who had gained wealth by inheritance or by administrative skills.

When we consider the charitable interests of the lower clergy over

---

[1] The proportion of gifts made by the lower clergy in relation to the total of charitable funds in the various counties is: Bristol, 8·69 per cent; Buckinghamshire, 2·64 per cent; Hampshire, 0·94 per cent; Kent, 5·30 per cent; Lancashire, 4·25 per cent; London, 3·59 per cent; Norfolk, 3·23 per cent; Somerset, 5·77 per cent; Worcestershire, 1·87 per cent.

our whole period, we are impressed at once by the great generosity of the class and quite as much by its essentially secular quality. The needs of the church were nurtured by only 20·58 per cent of the total benefactions of this group, as compared with 28·07 per cent for the county at large. The charitable interests of the class, like those of their great brethren, were heavily and continuously focussed on the development of the educational resources of the county and of the universities, to which they gave substantially more than half (57·32 per cent) of all their charitable wealth. The pressing needs of the poor were summarily dealt with, the several uses devoted to this good cause receiving no more than 16·82 per cent of all their gifts, a lower proportion, incidentally, than was provided by any other social class save the lawyers (15·85 per cent). This left only modest amounts for social rehabilitation (4·72 per cent) and a really trivial sum (0·58 per cent) for various municipal needs.

Though, as we have so persistently stressed, Yorkshire was a predominantly rural county with no more than a few commercial and industrial centres through the whole course of our period, a little band of merchants were in fact to bear the heaviest social burden of any class in the county and to lay down by their remarkable generosity the broad foundations for its institutional development. This was accomplished because a typical merchant felt so strongly and so certainly about his aspirations for his town or his county that he left approximately a quarter of his entire fortune to implement the vision he held of the future of Yorkshire. There were only 334 of these men, representing less than 4 per cent (3·87 per cent) of all donors, yet they gave the great sum of £51,037 6s for the charitable needs of their county. This amounted to more than a fifth (20·95 per cent) of all the charitable wealth provided during our entire period and over-matched by almost £11,000 the total provided by the next most responsible class of men, the lower gentry. It is true that the merchants of Hull, York, Halifax, and Leeds were inspired by the support and example of men with precisely defined ideals who, while Yorkshire-born, were Londoners. We have seen that a fourth (24·85 per cent) of these merchant benefactors were members of London livery companies, who gave on a slightly more lavish scale than did their Yorkshire contemporaries, since the £15,639 5s provided by them represents about 30 per cent of the enormous total given by the class. These gifts, whether from London or Leeds, were likely to be well and most securely vested. Many of them were very large, and there is to be discovered in the whole range of these benefactions little of waste or feckless sentimentality.

These merchant benefactions were so important not only because they were in the aggregate so large, but because they were so carefully and skilfully concentrated to attain clearly defined aspirations. The dominant concern of these men was with the care of the poor, to which they gave 37·54 per cent of all their benefactions, as compared with 33·46 per cent for the county at large. Thus they vested £10,794 14s in the institutional form of almshouse endowments, an amount far exceeding that devoted to this purpose by any other social group and amounting to 21·15 per cent of their own great total. They gave almost twice as much proportionately (9·90 per cent) to experiments in social rehabilitation as did the county at large, their contribution for apprenticeship schemes (£1944) and endowed work programmes (£1614 9s), for example, accounting for about half that given by all classes in Yorkshire for these fresh and forward-looking ventures. They gave, as well, nearly thrice as generously proportionately (6·86 per cent) as the county at large to various undertakings to secure municipal improvements. On the other hand, their concern with the advancement of education was relatively much less pronounced than that of a number of other important social classes, since only 19·47 per cent of all their benefactions were for this use. But this in effect means that they had but slight interest in the universities or in scholarship and fellowship endowments, since their large aggregate contribution of £9128 17s for grammar-school foundations was considerably larger than the amount so given (£6736 5s) by the lower gentry, whose benefactions for this purpose ranked next. The support given by the merchant aristocracy to the needs of the church was surprisingly liberal considering the universally secular bias of the class, it having amounted to 26·23 per cent of the whole of their gifts as compared with 28·07 per cent for the county at large. But this statement is quite misleading unless one observes that their gifts were heavily concentrated on the endowment of clerical incomes, particularly in the chapels which they were also helping to build, and on the creation of lectureships with a normally Puritan bias. Thus the merchant aristocracy provided well over a quarter (26·50 per cent) of all the funds given for the maintenance of the clergy and more than half (58·17 per cent) the amount given by all classes for the establishment of lectureships, these two charitable uses together accounting for 15·38 per cent of their total gifts.

There were 525 Yorkshire donors, constituting 6·08 per cent of all benefactors in the county, who may certainly be identified as shopkeepers and tradesmen, whose aggregate contribution of £7659 17s, however, amounted to only 3·14 per cent of the charitable wealth of the county. One is somewhat puzzled by the extraordinarily low average contribution of £14 11s 9d made by members of this class, particularly since, as we have noted, a fair number of really substantial benefactions were made by London tradesmen. In Yorkshire, as elsewhere, the pattern of giving by these men differed markedly from that of the merchants, from whom they were separated by a social and economic gulf quite as broad as that dividing the lower gentry from the yeomanry. Thus, through the whole of our period, they devoted a substantially greater proportion (44·45 per cent) of their charitable gifts to the care of the poor than did their merchant colleagues, markedly less to schemes for social rehabilitation (5·72 per cent) and municipal improvements (2·73 per cent). At the same time, it is remarkable that they devoted a slightly larger proportion (21·72 per cent) of their philanthropy to the strengthening of education than did the merchants, while, though the proportion of their gifts made for religious purposes (25·36 per cent) was nearly identical with that of the merchants, it was well spread over the whole spectrum of need rather than sharply concentrated.

We have to mention as well a relatively small group of 169 urban dwellers, comprising 1·96 per cent of all donors, who are most accurately described as 'additional burghers'. These were men whose occupations are unknown but who held some civic dignity or who were freemen in the various towns of the county. As a group these donors gave £2356 3s to charitable needs, this constituting not quite 1 per cent of the whole of Yorkshire's charitable wealth. Both the average size of their benefactions (£13 18s 10d) and the structure of their aspirations as revealed by their gifts would suggest that nearly all these men were in fact small shopkeepers and tradesmen. These burghers, if we take into account the whole period, were principally interested in the care of the poor, to whom they gave almost half (48·16 per cent) of all their benefactions, and with the needs of the church to which 29·94 per cent of all their gifts were made. They exhibited, as well, considerable interest in education, which absorbed not quite 17 per cent of the whole of their charities, while the opportunities for social rehabilitation and municipal betterment together commanded the remaining 5·14 per cent of their charitable dispositions.

There were likewise 450 benefactors who were artisans and urban poor, who gave a total of £681 towards the betterment of their own communities. These men, numbering 5·21 per cent of all identified donors, belonged to an amazing variety of trades, though about two-thirds of them can be roughly grouped in order within the cloth-making industry, building, fishing, mining, and metal working. On the average they gave the surprisingly high figure of £1 10s 3d for charitable institutions of the county, amounting to no more than 0·28 per cent of the whole, yet the structure of their aspirations throws considerable light on the sentiments of these urban dwellers, particularly when contrasted with that of their rural counterparts, the husbandmen and agricultural labourers. This class was from the early days of our period principally concerned with the needs of the poor, to whom, over all, they disposed about three-fourths (74·28 per cent) of their contributions. After the Reformation particularly they constituted one of the most secular of all classes, during the whole of our period having provided only 17·79 per cent of all their gifts for religious purposes and during the closing interval (1641–1660) bestowing the incredibly low proportion of 1·83 per cent for these uses. They displayed a persistent, though of course limited, interest in the various schemes for social rehabilitation, on which they bestowed 5·50 per cent of their slender charities, while 2·27 per cent of their gifts were for purposes of municipal betterment, particularly the improvement of streets and bridges. In Yorkshire, as elsewhere, their interest in the great task being undertaken for the education of their children excited almost no support at all, the whole of their contributions for this use being 4s given by three donors as outright scholarship awards.

There were as well 108 substantial donors who were members of the professional classes, if ten public officials may be included. In total, this social class, numbering 1·26 per cent of all donors, gave £14,295 6s for community needs, this constituting 5·86 per cent of the whole of the charitable resources of the county. By far the largest and most generous group within this broad classification were the fifty-two lawyers whose total contributions came to £10,830 15s, the structure of whose aspirations is quite typical of the whole class.[1] The prime concern of the lawyers was with the development of the educational resources of the county, to which they gave 54·76 per cent of all their charitable funds. They disposed in all not quite a fourth (24·50 per cent) of all their gifts for the uses of the church, slightly more than half of this total being for the improvement of clerical stipends, particularly in new chapelries. A relatively small proportion (15·85 per cent) of their benefactions were designated for the betterment of the state of the poor, though it may be mentioned that the professional classes as a whole gave £1610 for almshouse endowments.[2] Small proportions were also given for schemes of social rehabilitation (3·66 per cent) and municipal improvements (1·25 per cent).

[1] The contributions of the 'professional classes' were as follows:

Number	Occupation	Total of charitable gifts	
		£	s
52	Lawyers	10,830	15
8	Notaries	97	2
8	Bailiffs	101	10
10	Physicians	1,225	1
1	Apothecaries	13	7
2	Scriveners	150	3
12	Teachers	685	16
5	Scholars, artists, musicians	36	0
10	Public officials (not being lawyers)	1,155	12

[2] The lawyers alone gave £1084 for this purpose.

There remains a group of 938 donors, representing 10·87 per cent of all benefactors, whose social status cannot be ascertained. These donors gave in all £15,310 6s, or 6·28 per cent of the whole of the charitable funds of the county, slightly more than did the professional classes or the yeomanry. We have observed that most of these men and women were rural dwellers with a probable 'average status' of yeoman and that the urban dwellers among them seem in average terms to be of the quality of lesser tradesmen. This presumption is likewise confirmed by an analysis of their charitable interests, which very closely resemble those we have noted for the yeomanry, with the remarkable difference, reflecting the contributions principally of townsmen, that nearly 20 per cent of all the charitable benefactions of these socially anonymous donors were disposed for the strengthening of school resources in many urban communities of the shire. These men and women, too, played their important role in making Yorkshire a better community in which to live and work and in bringing it level with a kingdom which in the course of our period had found and had secured new aspirations which were the harbingers of a new, a very different, and just possibly a better civilization.

The institutional shape and the moral content of the world in which we live were largely fashioned by the actions of men and women in the period with which we have been concerned. They came to possess a vision of a society which bore little relation to the world which medieval man had inhabited for so long, and this society they created with their own substance as they found means to implement the aspirations which they held so tenaciously and which they defined so clearly. Men of the sixteenth and the seventeenth centuries were able by their charities, by their private actions, to build so mightily, because during this relatively long and this critical historical era they came to possess a consensus of aspirations. They were creating and they were ordering a world for themselves and for their children which fitted more comfortably and exactly the grand design which their ethical sentiments delineated with such remarkable clarity. This new world and the institutions which framed it was intensely secular, even though there was much of piety, much of the fear of God, and much of evangelical fervour implicit in the complex of aspirations which moved them to noble and effective historical action. It has been rare indeed in the long and often tragic history of mankind that the good men, the historically effective men, of a society have been moved by such a strongly entertained moral consensus. It becomes clear in such brilliant and happy historical moments that man does order his own destiny, that his actions can be freighted with immense moral power, and that the hope which must at all times sustain any society may brighten into that effulgence which makes an age famous in the memory of mankind.

Appendix

NOTE REGARDING THE COMPOSITION OF
TABLE I, TABLE II, AND *TABLE III*

Difficulties of tabular representation make it inconvenient to present in full the data included in the first three tables. In our discussion in the text, however, full treatment is given to the data under each of the sub-heads as well as for the great charitable heads. There are in all twenty-four categories (sub-heads) under which we have listed charities, these being in turn gathered under the five great heads which are presented in the tables following. The full classification is as follows:

POOR

Outright relief
Almshouses
Charity General
Aged

EDUCATION

Schools
Colleges and Universities
Libraries (non-university)
Scholarships and fellowships

SOCIAL REHABILITATION

Prisons
Loans
Workhouses and stocks
Apprenticeship schemes
Sick and hospitals
Marriage subsidies

RELIGION

Church general
Prayers
Church repairs
Maintenance of the clergy
Puritan lectureships
Church building (estimated)

MUNICIPAL BETTERMENTS

General uses
Companies for public benefit
Parks and recreation
Public Works (Roads, etc.)

For a full discussion of the categories employed and a synthesis of the statistical evidence for the whole group of ten counties, *Vide*, Jordan, *Philanthropy in England*, I, 40–53, 369–375.

TABLE I

BUCKINGHAMSHIRE

	Poor (£ s)	Social Rehabilitation (£ s)	Municipal Betterments (£ s)	Education (£ s)	Religion (£ s)	Totals (£ s)	
1480–1490					765 7	765 10	
1491–1500	1,127 0		948 13		1,316 15	3,392 8	
1501–1510	681 13		48 10		1,066 4	1,796 7	
1511–1520			106 0		295 16	401 16	
1521–1530	189 3	10 0	93 0		360 5	652 8	
1531–1540	5 15		26 0	208 0	1,656 14	1,896 9	
Sub-total	2,003 11	10 0	1,222 6	208 0	5,461 1	8,904 18	
%	(22·50%)	(0·11%)	(13·73%)	(2·34%)	(61·33%)		(10·10%)
1541–1550	130 5	2 2	627 4	160 0	162 12	1,082 3	
1551–1560	2,171 7	55 0	85 4	523 0	1,224 13	4,059 4	
Sub-total	2,301 12	57 2	712 8	683 0	1,387 5	5,141 7	
%	(44·77%)	(1·11%)	(13·86%)	(13·28%)	(26·98%)		(5·83%)
1561–1570	3,923 2		83 13		352 8	4,275 10	
1571–1580	3,125 19		2 0		498 14	3,708 6	
1581–1590	1,086 1			720 0	92 19	1,901 0	
1591–1600	2,376 15	2 7	2,004 10	200 0	316 10	4,900 2	
Sub-total	10,511 17	2 7	2,090 3	920 0	1,260 11	14,784 18	
%	(71·10%)	(0·01%)	(14·14%)	(6·22%)	(8·53%)		(16·77%)
1601–1610	3,818 7	18 13	103 3	240 7	989 3	5,169 13	
1611–1620	3,426 7	220 0	120 2	227 15	488 8	4,482 12	
1621–1630	9,621 13	814 0	198 10	1,640 0	442 16	12,716 19	
1631–1640	7,999 3	2,290 0	1,000 7	12,417 0	916 4	24,622 14	
Sub-total	24,865 10	3,342 13	1,422 2	14,525 2	2,836 11	46,991 18	
%	(52·91%)	(7·11%)	(3·03%)	(30·91%)	(6·04%)		(53·31%)
1641–1650	4,281 14	245 0	2,055 0	1,200 0	211 5	7,992 19	
1651–1660	1,908 9	263 0	256 0	1,205 0	303 17	3,936 6	
No Date					400 0	400 0	
Sub-total	6,190 3	508 0	2,311 0	2,405 0	915 2	12,329 5	
%	(50·21%)	(4·12%)	(18·74%)	(19·51%)	(7·42%)		(13·99%)
TOTALS	45,872 13	3,920 2	7,757 19	18,741 2	11,860 10	88,152 6	
%	(52·04%)	(4·45%)	(8·80%)	(21·26%)	(13·45%)		

TABLE II
NORFOLK

	Poor	Social Rehabilitation	Municipal Betterments	Education	Religion	Totals	
	£ s	£ s	£ s	£ s	£ s	£ s	
1480–1490	705 0	81 2	420 8	1,847 6	2,917 13	4,124 3	
1491–1500	1,009 0	111 15	1,287 9	1,346 6	3,568 19	7,824 18	
1500–1510	1,218 9	153 13	1,396 6	253 0	9,693 7	13,808 1	
1511–1520	1,092 10	26 8	604 18	516 13	2,878 8	4,855 4	
1521–1530	521 7	215 10	683 12	829 0	5,601 13	7,538 15	
1531–1540	801 14	12 1	2,176 4		1,715 1	5,534 0	
Pre-Reformation	5,348 9 (12·24%)	600 9 (1·37%)	6,568 17 (15·04%)	4,792 5 (10·97%)	26,375 1 (60·38%)	43,685 1	(24·56%)
1541–1550	2,973 7	299 14	1,903 0	1,383 0	582 11	7,141 12	
1551–1560	1,788 2	640 17	1,763 16	69 0	946 3	5,207 18	
Reformation	4,761 9 (38·56%)	940 11 (7·62%)	3,666 16 (29·69%)	1,452 0 (11·76%)	1,528 14 (12·38%)	12,349 10	(6·94%)
1561–1570	2,514 15	554 4	718 13	1,739 0	327 9	5,854 1	
1571–1580	2,860 15	277 9	437 1	410 0	242 1	4,227 6	
1581–1590	2,122 11	400 6	285 19	5,010 0	1,313 17	9,132 13	
1591–1600	6,477 17	901 12	2,546 6	2,047 6	616 8	12,589 9	
Elizabethan	13,975 18 (43·94%)	2,133 11 (6·71%)	3,987 19 (12·54%)	9,206 6 (28·95%)	2,499 15 (7·86%)	31,803 9	(17·88%)
1601–1610	7,862 9	195 0	95 10	3,593 13	1,877 19	13,624 11	
1611–1620	6,247 1	2,427 14	1,709 15	6,355 0	1,663 8	18,402 19	
1621–1630	5,994 6	1,951 16	1,071 11	3,553 0	1,503 13	14,204 0	
1631–1640	4,836 14	2,685 16	955 5	4,970 0	4,090 5	17,538 10	
Early Stuart	24,940 10 (39·11%)	7,260 5 (11·39%)	3,832 1 (6·01%)	18,471 13 (28·97%)	9,265 10 (14·53%)	63,769 10	(35·85%)
1641–1650	7,151 12	3,547 7	225 2	3,298 0	815 9	15,037 10	
1651–1660	3,390 8	2,625 13	540 0	3,660 0	177 9	10,393 10	
No Date	507 0	20 0		40 0	278 1	845 1	
Civil War	11,049 0 (42·05%)	6,193 0 (23·57%)	765 2 (2·91%)	6,998 0 (26·63%)	1,270 19 (4·84%)	26,276 1	(14·77%)
TOTALS	60,075 6 (33·77%)	17,127 16 (9·63%)	18,820 15 (10·58%)	40,920 4 (23·00%)	40,939 10 (23·01%)	177,883 11	

TABLE III
YORKSHIRE

	Poor £ s	Social Rehabilitation £ s	Municipal Betterments £ s	Education £ s	Religion £ s	Totals £ s	
1480–1490	559 16	72 0	50 8	4,634 0	4,607 17	9,924 1	
1491–1500	558 9	20 15	38 18	263 14	7,467 3	8,348 19	
1501–1510	779 11	46 11	160 7	760 7	7,116 4	8,863 0	
1511–1520	779 19	8 0	227 17	388 9	5,015 14	6,010 19	
1521–1530	1,568 5	53 14	277 6	3,823 17	8,337 8	14,060 0	
1531–1540	372 12	49 8	59 1	403 15	3,269 16	4,154 17	
Pre-Reformation	4,209 12 (8·20%)	250 8 (0·49%)	814 1 (1·58%)	10,274 2 (20·00%)	35,814 2 (69·73%)	51,362 5	(21·08%)
1541–1550	1,828 4	21 9	346 19	875 6	2,490 9	5,562 7	
1551–1560	4,740 9	187 12	406 18	4,267 8	1,770 16	11,373 3	
Reformation	6,568 13 (38·79%)	209 1 (1·23%)	753 17 (4·45%)	5,142 14 (30·37%)	4,261 5 (25·16%)	16,935 10	(6·95%)
1561–1570	2,607 8	119 7	279 16	2,259 12	258 19	5,525 2	
1571–1580	2,891 16	104 7	243 10	1,320 13	54 7	4,614 0	
1581–1590	2,382 16	613 5	30 6	1,520 19	658 0	5,205 6	
1591–1600	3,394 4	519 2	154 0	3,823 17	572 3	8,463 6	
Elizabethan	11,275 11 (47·36%)	1,356 1 (5·70%)	707 12 (2·97%)	8,925 1 (37·49%)	1,543 9 (6·48%)	23,807 14	(9·77%)
1601–1610	4,002 16	1,033 0	302 12	6,121 13	1,175 7	12,635 8	
1611–1620	13,511 18	933 13	811 6	9,179 6	3,724 7	28,160 10	
1621–1630	8,494 9	1,454 1	841 17	12,963 3	2,733 11	26,487 1	
1631–1640	7,058 0	1,814 2	321 4	4,504 5	8,309 13	22,007 2	
Early Stuart	33,067 3 (37·03%)	5,234 16 (5·86%)	2,276 19 (2·55%)	32,768 5 (36·70%)	15,942 18 (17·86%)	89,290 1	(36·65%)
1641–1650	8,742 14	3,408 19	227 13	8,210 2	5,192 18	25,782 6	
1651–1660	17,650 0	1,346 12	1,341 9	10,492 4	5,642 13	36,472 18	
Civil War	26,392 14 (42·39%)	4,755 11 (7·64%)	1,569 2 (2·52%)	18,702 6 (30·04%)	10,835 11 (17·41%)	62,255 4	(25·55%)
TOTALS	81,513 13 (33·46%)	11,805 17 (4·85%)	6,121 11 (2·51%)	75,812 8 (31·12%)	68,397 5 (28·07%)	243,650 14	

TABLE A
BUCKINGHAMSHIRE PARISHES WITH CHARITABLE ENDOWMENTS EXCEEDING £400

	Poor (£ s)	Social Rehabilitation (£ s)	Municipal Betterments (£ s)	Education (£ s)	Religion (£ s)	Totals (£ s)
Amersham–Coleshill	717 7	502 0		2,670 0	181 15	4,071 2
Aston Clinton	33 19		945 0		2 9	981 8
Aylesbury borough	1,652 16	13 0	1,560 10	400 7	224 12	3,850 15
Beachampton	2,877 10	1,100 0	771 0	9,100 0 (6000 for Oxford)	108 18	13,957 8
Bradenham	653 0				267 0	920 0
Brickhill (Bow, Great, Little)	625 3	100 0		100 0	94 2	919 2
Brill	1,533 3			200 0	1 0	1,734 3
Buckingham borough	1,085 10	25 0	500 0	588 0	101 18	2,300 8
Burnham	603 3				53 7	656 10
Chenies	1,101 9				133 11	1,234 16
Chesham	1,030 19				955 18	1,987 17
Chilton	1,578 2	312 0		27 0	7 17	1,924 19
Colnbrook	575 0	600 0			310 0	1,485 0
Datchet		10 0	1,210 7		1 13	1,237 0
Drayton Beauchamp	360 4			140 0	51 0	551 0
Eton	47 4	1 0	2,005 0	1,240 0	1 11	3,294 15
Fulmer	325 15				400 0	725 5
Great Marlow	1,928 15	200 0	140 0	1,160 0	410 0	3,838 15
Great Missenden	85 0	330 0	186 0	5 0	71 1	677 1
Halton	421 0				1 8	422 8
Hambleden	159 0			300 10	81 14	541 4
Hanslope	604 1		4 0		100 1	708 2
Hillesden					400 0	400 0
Ivinghoe	507 12				0 16	508 8
Langley Marish	733 15			60 0	140 1	933 16
Lathbury				480 0		480 0
Loughton	352 5				300 0	652 10
Newport Pagnell	551 13	300 0	405 5		298 8	1,554 12
Olney	217 13		81 13		114 10	413 16
Princes Risborough	346 0	35 0	2 10		25 1	408 11
Quainton	556 0		1 0	20 0	28 4	605 4
Shabbington	303 3		2 0		42 10	347 13
Shenley	604 13				100 0	704 0
Simpson	800 13				1 10	802 3
Stoke Poges	1,614 10	200 0		60 0	326 10	2,201 0
Stony Stratford	122 10		696 0	600 0	212 12	1,631 2
Waddesdon	1,048 15		2 7		156 15	1,207 7
Wendover	649 0				1 18	651 8
Wing	1,000 0		37 7		813 0	1,850 7
Wooburn	464 0				7 10	471 10
Wycombe (Great, High, West)	3,950 12		700 0	260 0	201 5	5,111 17

TABLE B

NORFOLK PARISHES WITH CHARITABLE ENDOWMENTS EXCEEDING £400

Parish	Poor (£ s)	Social (£ s)	Municipal (£ s)	Education (£ s)	Religion (£ s)	Total (£ s)
Alburgh			580 0			580 0
Attleborough	463 10		250 0		669 8	1,383 4
Aylsham	697 6	20 6	320 0	302 0	221 17	1,561 11
Bawburgh					431 7	431 7
Bergh Apton	25 0		580 0			605 0
Blickling	167 0			1,333 0	571 14	2,071 14
Brancaster	141 0			900 0		1,041 0
Bressingham	40 0				404 5	444 5
Brooke	102 0		450 0			552 6
Burnham Thorpe	49 13			240 0	300 13	590 6
Caister	125 13			100 0	670 15	896 8
Castle Acre	125 0				315 0	440 11
Castle Rising	2,551 14				2 0	2,553 14
Colveston					645 0	645 10
Costessey	190 0	820 6			100 0	1,110 6
Dickleburgh	95 10		300 0		35 10	433 0
Diss	1,184 0	60 0	992 8		122 19	2,359 7
East Dereham	526 15	545 13	150 10	268 0	66 4	1,557 2
East Harling	157 11		530 0		11 5	698 16
Felbrigg				200 0	1,908 0	2,108 0
Feltwell	412 0			800 0		1,218 5
Garboldisham	19 10		475 0		186 8	680 18
Grimston	17 4		180 0	322 0	5 17	525 1
Harpley	38 17			4,520 0		4,558 17
Hedenham	6 12		730 0			736 12
Heydon	80 0			500 0	30 0	610 0
Holt	11 0			2,560 0	1 0	2,572 5
Hunstanton	155 0		20 0	80 0	1,125 5	1,380 0
King's Lynn borough (4 parishes)	5,036 0	2,568 0	462 8	1,941 0	2,573 5	12,580 18
Kirby Cane	500 0				19 4	519 4
Little Walsingham	128 10	794 4		1,905 0	69 2	2,896 16
Lynn (N., W., S.)	43 0		8 0		340 8	391 13
Needham	12 0		461 13			473 13
North Creake	602 0			5 13	242 10	850 3

TABLE B—cont.

	Poor £ s	Social £ s	Municipal £ s	Education £ s	Religion £ s	Total £ s
North Elmham	735 4		4 11		10 5	750 0
North Lopham	30 8		80 0		302 0	412 0
North Walsham	142 8				2,007 10	2,150 12
Northwold	16 0		610 12			632 0
Norwich (38 parishes)	24,633 13	7,748 19	2,616 4	7,093 19	10,925 10	53,018 5
Ormesby (St Margaret) (St Michael)	297 16	10 0	66 13	533 6	114 11	1,022 6
Outwell	484 10				103 3	587 13
Oxborough	421 0				267 15	688 15
Oxnead	432 0	32 0			41 0	505 6
Pulham	611 10				52 16	664 6
Redenhall	54 0		300 0		487 12	841 12
Rushford	300 0			1,314 0	348 12	1,962 12
Saham Toney	263 0	8 8	40 0	355 0	41 0	707 8
Saxlingham	412 0		380 0		80 0	872 0
Scarning	11 13			800 0	24 4	835 17
Shipdham	831 0	20 0				851 0
South Lopham	2 0		400 0			402 0
Sprowston	220 17	260 0			1 0	481 17
Stow Bardolph	40 0	512 0		1,300 0	50 0	1,902 0
Stratton	84 6		200 0		107 0	391 6
Swaffham	136 2		10 0		1,364 6	1,510 8
Tacolneston					400 0	400 0
Thetford (7 parishes)	824 7	100 0	114 0	1,700 0	633 12	3,371 19
Tilney	78 15	10 0	25 10	200 0	94 0	407 10
Walpole (St Andrew, St Peter)	534 15		32 10		380 16	948 1
Watton	269 13			155 0	1 12	426 5
Wighton	420 10				1 11	421 1
Winfarthing	73 1		20 0		203 7	813 7
Worstead	173 17			1,098 0	352 8	1,543 9
Wymondham	1,763 17	53 13	2 10		435 12	2,365 12
Yarmouth, Great (borough)		2,909 2	610 0	2,761 0	274 5	10,139 9
	48,000 9	16,475 1	14,434 9	34,986 18	30,185 19	144,082 16

TABLE C

NORFOLK PARISHES WITH SUBSTANTIAL CHARITIES RELATIVELY
UNAFFECTED BY LONDON GIFTS

	Charities from local and county sources		Charities from London sources		Total	
	£	s	£	s	£	s
Alburgh	580	0			580	0
Attleborough	1,383	4			1,383	4
Bawburgh	431	7			431	7
Bergh Apton	605	0			605	0
Blickling	2,061	14	10	0	2,071	14
Brancaster	1,041	0			1,041	0
Bressingham	424	5	20	0	444	5
Brooke	552	0			552	0
Burnham Thorpe	590	6			590	6
Caister	896	8			896	8
Castle Acre	440	11			440	11
Colveston	645	10			645	10
Costessey	1,070	6	40	0	1,110	6
Dickleburgh	433	0			433	0
Diss	2,208	7	151	0	2,359	7
East Harling	688	16	10	0	698	16
Felbrigg	2,108	0			2,108	0
Feltwell	1,218	5			1,218	5
Garboldisham	680	18			680	18
Grimston	498	1	27	0	525	1
Heydon	610	0			610	0
Hunstanton	1,380	0			1,380	0
Kirby Cane	519	4			519	4
Little Walsingham	2,896	16			2,896	16
Needham	473	13			473	13
North Creake	850	3			850	3
North Elmham	750	0			750	0
North Lopham	412	0			412	0
North Walsham	2,150	12			2,150	12
Northwold	632	0			632	0
Norwich	51,291	5	1,727	0	53,018	5
Ormesby (Saint Margaret and Saint Michael)	1,022	6			1,022	6
Outwell	587	13			587	13
Oxborough	688	15			688	15
Oxnead	505	0			505	0
Pulham	664	6			664	6
Redenhall	841	12			841	12
Saham Toney	707	8			707	8
Saxlingham	872	0			872	0
Scarning	835	17			835	17
Shipdham	851	0			851	0
South Lopham	402	0			402	0
Sporle	621	7			621	7
Sprowston	481	17			481	17
Stow Bardolph	1,902	0			1,902	0
Swaffham	1,402	8	108	0	1,510	8

TABLE C *contd.*

	Charities from local and county sources	Charities from London sources	Total
Tacolneston	400 0		400 0
Thetford	3,121 19	250 0	3,371 19
Tilney	402 10	5 0	407 10
Walpole (St Peter and St Andrew)	948 1		948 1
Watton	426 5		426 5
Winfarthing	793 7	20 0	813 7
Worstead	1,534 9	9 0	1,543 9
Yarmouth, Great	9,689 9	450 0	10,139 9
	110,224 0	2,827 0 (2·5%)	113,051 0

TABLE D • YORKSHIRE PARISHES (OR BOROUGHS) WITH CHARITABLE ENDOWMENTS EXCEEDING £400

	Poor	Social	Municipal	Education	Religion	Total
	£ s	£ s	£ s	£ s	£ s	£ s
EAST RIDING						
Acaster Selby		4 13		704 0		704 13
Beverley	1,706 13		89 3	1,431 0	3,048 12	6,279 18
Bishop Burton	328 9			50 0	558 0	937 13
Bridlington	31 17			1,280 0	4 4	1,315 15
Bubwith	110 8	5 0			452 7	563 14
Burton Agnes	57 8			205 0	337 18	610 6
Eastrington	3 0				573 7	576 7
Halsham	736 19			880 0	8 12	1,625 11
Hemingbrough	37 7		1 0	155 0	234 0	427 7
Heslington	1,260 0					1,260 0
Howden	357 3	211 0		30 0	200 7	799 0
Hull (borough)	6,656 11	966 3	1,095 16	1,479 0	2,020 0	12,218 0
Kilham	38 11	2 0		700 10	53 7	791 8
Pocklington	261 13		6 13	417 0	2 4	689 10
Sancton	11 3			500 0	34 10	545 13
Swine	62 0	100 0	1 10		425 19	589 9
Wheldrake	13 10			1,400 0	8 3	1,421 13
	11,672 10	1,288 19	1,201 7	9,231 11	7,961 10	31,355 17
WEST RIDING						
Almondbury	612 2			343 8	245 6	1,200 16
Altofts	519 0			1,000 0		1,519 0
Arksey	1,294 16		4 19	800 0	1,779 9	3,879 4
Arncliffe	354 10		3 11	507 0	426 6	1,291 7
Barkisland	75 4			200 0	142 2	417 6
Barnsley	464 0		10 0	1,125 0	140 1	1,739 1
Batley	36 0			426 13	15 13	478 6
Bingley	70 15		1 0	353 0	37 2	461 17
Birstall	27 9			280 0	484 2	791 14
Bradford	101 15			509 0	601 16	1,212 1
Brodsworth	400 13			200 0	18 16	619 12
Burnsall	198 5		163 0	500 8	169 5	1,030 18
Calverley	117 1			160 0	117 9	394 10
Cawood	157 1	285 0		100 0	49 8	591 18
Darfield	355 2		6 13	317 0	869 4	1,548 3
Doncaster	630 10	233 15	67 14	133 0	602 9	1,667 8
Ecclesfield	1,169 1	3 0	1 5	260 10	344 16	1,778 12

TABLE D—contd.

	Poor £	s	Social £	s	Municipal £	s	Education £	s	Religion £	s	Total £	s
Fishlake	1,067	5			2	17	300	0	168	5	1,538	11
Gargrave	143	8					360	0	2	0	505	16
Giggleswick	31	8	5	1			2,153	0	2	17	2,192	10
Great and Little Preston	963	7	200	0	20	4			135	2	1,318	9
Guiseley			256	0		7	150	0	524	0	930	12
Halifax¹ (incl. 11 of the dependent villages in the parish)	2,655	1	1,916	13	157	7	1,735	1	3,170	2	9,634	4
Hatfield	346	4		1			256	13	64	18	667	16
Hemsworth	124	16					570	0	46	13	741	9
Heptonstall	49	19			3	7	410	0	129	0	592	6
Huddersfield	137	11	200	0		15	40	0	516	14	895	0
Kildwick	355	0					77	0	58	7	490	7
Kippax	364	13	2	10	1	4	100	0	73	17	539	14
Knaresborough	886	17			1	14	520	0	158	13	1,369	4
Leeds	3,102	14	262	19	659	17	2,053	9	3,697	10	9,776	1
Methley	264	6			10	17	105	6	211	10	591	19
Normanton	46	13	7	13	5	9	333	7	285	1	678	3
Otley	137	8			10	1	580	0	1,939	1	2,666	10
Pontefract	872	14	66	0	212	2	700	0	795	1	2,646	5
Ripley	385	11	30	0	5	10			47	7	468	8
Ripon	1,357	15	175	13	57	3	1,600	0	2,012	1	5,001	17
Rotherham	739	15	534	2	106	6	2,504	0	819	0	4,703	1
Rothwell	691	1			2	15			339	0	1,034	16
Royston	393	12			1	0	234	0	1	13	630	7
Ryther	576	8	7	0	5	0	533	17	305	6	1,428	1
Sandal Magna	130	15	200	0	5	0			1,073	16	1,405	8
Saxton	10	10			7	16			427	10	445	16
Sedbergh	378	3			108	2	2,250	3	77	10	2,813	18
Selby	266	6			149	11			289	11	705	8
Sheffield	4,404	18	12	0	87	11	937	10	1,261	8	6,703	3
Sherburn	21	18					5,000	0	318	4	5,340	13
Skipton	2,510	1			68	13	200	0	157	6	2,936	0
Snaith	539	17			2	0	660	0	6	19	1,207	10
Sprotborough	19	0							441	0	462	2
Stainborough	100	0							720	0	820	0
Tadcaster	305	8			6	9	400	0	158	8	870	5
Thornhill	167	0					500	0	151	17	818	18
Thornton	161	11					511	18			672	18
Wakefield	2,161	11	179	13	210	15	1,794	11	3,119	9	7,465	19
Warmfield	394	0					480	0	82	9	956	2
Whitkirk	307	7			5	12	20	0	68	1	401	8
	33,753	9	4,579	2	2,171	13	35,285	1	29,899	1	105,688	6

¹ Sir Henry Savile's university gifts of £7,220 are not included.

TABLE D—contd.

	Poor		Social		Municipal		Education		Religion		Total	
	£	s	£	s	£	s	£	s	£	s	£	s
NORTH RIDING												
Bedale	652	0				7	418	0	250	0	1,320	0
Catterick	410	7	100	0			400	0	156	14	1,067	8
Coxwold	691	3					733	0	26	3	1,450	6
Grinton	4	18			2	11	406	0	1	10	414	19
Guisborough	1,033	17	6	13	1	0	844	0	32	0	1,917	10
Kirby Misperton	119	15			100	0	200	0	23	7	443	2
Kirby Ravensworth	515	7					463	0	6	8	984	7
Marske	248	16					453	0	488	8	1,190	4
Northallerton	199	13							433	8	633	1
Old Malton	9	15					400	0	176	9	586	4
Overton	1	10					1,800	0	6	14	1,807	14
Richmond	683	3	293	0	6	7	1,349	0	128	14	2,460	4
Sand Hutton	4	15							401	8	406	3
Sessay	90	18					768	0	103	7	962	5
Snape	60	0					240	0	383	7	683	7
Thornton Dale	1,382	17					1,575	0	3	7	2,961	5
Topcliffe	98	13					430	0	138	10	667	4
Well	113	9	600	0	13	1			86	5	813	12
Whitby	496	19	104	7	678	0			188	6	1,467	12
Wilton	320	8							83	4	403	12
Witton	401	0	30	0			120	0	100	5	651	5
	7,538	13	1,134	0	801	14	10,599	0	3,217	6	23,290	13
York City	8,613	17	2,607	12	1,125	7	4,126	2	9,594	11	26,067	9
TOTALS, all Yorkshire	61,578	9	9,609	13	5,300	1	59,241	14	50,672	8	186,402	5

TABLE E

YORKSHIRE PARISHES WITH SUBSTANTIAL CHARITIES RELATIVELY UNAFFECTED BY LONDON GIFTS

	Charities from local and county sources		Charities from London sources		Total	
	£	s	£	s	£	s
EAST RIDING						
Acaster Selby	704	13			704	13
Beverley	5,795	10	484	8	6,279	18
Bishop Burton	931	0	6	13	937	13
Bridlington	1,315	15			1,315	15
Bubwith	563	14			563	14
Burton Agnes	610	6			610	6
Eastrington	553	0	23	7	576	7
Halsham	1,625	11			1,625	11
Hemingbrough	424	7	3	0	427	7
Heslington	1,260	0			1,260	0
Hull	11,830	10	387	10	12,218	0
Kilham	791	8			791	8
Sancton	545	13			545	13
Swine	589	9			589	9
Wheldrake	1,402	9	19	4	1,421	13
	28,943	5	924	2	29,867	7
WEST RIDING						
Almondbury	1,200	16			1,200	16
Altofts	1,519	0			1,519	0
Arksey	3,875	17	3	7	3,879	4
Barnsley	1,739	1			1,739	1
Batley	478	6			478	6
Bingley	461	17			461	17
Birstall	791	14			791	14
Bradford	1,212	1			1,212	1
Brodsworth	619	12			619	12
Doncaster	1,544	1	123	7	1,667	8
Ecclesfield	1,778	12			1,778	12
Fishlake	1,537	3	1	8	1,538	11
Gargrave	505	16			505	16
Giggleswick	2,092	10	100	0	2,192	10
Guiseley	930	12			930	12
Hemsworth	740	9	1	0	741	9
Heptonstall	559	6	33	0	592	6
Huddersfield	813	0	82	0	895	0
Kildwick	480	7	10	0	490	7
Kippax	539	14			539	14
Leeds	9,726	1	50	0	9,776	1
Normanton	678	3			678	3
Otley	2,636	10	30	0	2,666	10
Pontefract	2,416	5	230	0	2,646	5
Ripley	468	8			468	8
Ripon	4,744	17	257	0	5,001	17
Rotherham	4,643	1	60	0	4,703	1

TABLE E *contd.*

	Charities from local and county sources		Charities from London sources		Total	
Rothwell	1,034	16			1,034	16
Royston	630	7			630	7
Ryther	1,428	1			1,428	1
Sandal Magna	1,405	8			1,405	8
Selby	700	8	5	0	705	8
Sheffield	6,621	3	82	0	6,703	3
Skipton	2,934	0	2	0	2,936	0
Snaith	1,207	10			1,207	10
Sprotbrough	462	2			462	2
Stainborough	820	0			820	0
Thornhill	818	17			818	17
Thornton	672	18			672	18
Warmfield	956	2			956	2
Whitkirk	391	8	10	0	401	8
	68,815	19	1,080	2	69,896	1
NORTH RIDING						
Catterick	1,067	8			1,067	8
Grinton	414	19			414	19
Guisborough	1,898	7	19	3	1,917	10
Kirby Misperton	443	2			443	2
Old Malton	586	4			586	4
Overton	1,807	14			1,807	14
Sessay	962	5			962	5
Snape	683	7			683	7
Well	812	8		13	813	1
Wilton	393	12	10	0	403	12
Witton	651	5			651	5
	9,720	11	29	16	9,750	7
TOTALS FOR COUNTY	107,479	15	2,034 0 (1·86%)		109,513	15

TABLE F

YORKSHIRE PARISHES WITH SUBSTANTIAL CHARITIES DECISIVELY
AFFECTED BY LONDON GIFTS

	Charities from local and county sources		Charities from London sources		Total	
	£	s	£	s	£	s
EAST RIDING						
Howden	527	13	271	7	799	0
Pocklington	269	0	420	10	689	10
WEST RIDING						
Arncliffe	734	7	557	0	1,291	7
Barkisland	202	6	215	0	417	6
Burnsall	120	18	910	0	1,030	18
Cawood	411	18	180	0	591	18
Darfield	498	3	1,050	0	1,548	3
Great and Little Preston	18	9	1,300	0	1,318	9
Halifax	8,687	4	947	0	9,634	4
Hatfield	554	16	113	0	667	16
Knaresborough	1,049	4	320	0	1,369	4
Methley	506	19	85	0	591	19
Saxton	45	16	400	0	445	16
Sedbergh	2,148	18	665	0	2,813	18
Sherburn	340	13	5,000	0	5,340	13
Tadcaster	270	5	600	0	870	5
Wakefield	4,709	9	2,756	10	7,465	19
NORTH RIDING						
Bedale	720	0	600	0	1,320	0
Coxwold	697	6	753	0	1,450	6
Kirkby Ravensworth	784	7	200	0	984	7
Marske	1,090	4	100	0	1,190	4
New Malton	163	8	187	0	350	8
Northallerton	204	16	428	5	633	1
Richmond	1,341	11	1,118	13	2,460	4
Sand Hutton	6	3	400	0	406	3
Topcliffe	347	4	320	0	667	4
Whitby	1,222	2	245	10	1,467	12
YORK CITY	23,663	4	2,404	5	26,067	9
	51,336	3	22,547 (30·52%)	0	73,883	3

General Index

(An asterisk denotes a benefiting parish or institution)

Abbot, Sir Thomas, 343
*Abbotside (Yorks), 248
*Acaster Malbis (Yorks), 328
*Acaster Selby (Yorks), 305, 446, 449
Act of Parliament (1551), 307
Act of Parliament (1593), 34
Act of Parliament (1610), 157
*Addington (Bucks), 69
Agricultural labourers, 81, 203, 420, 428–429
Agriculture, importance of, 89, 214, 215, 225–226
Aire River, 216
*Alburgh (Norfolk), 442, 444
Aldbrough (Yorks), 290
*Alderford (Norfolk), 188
*Aldfield (Yorks), 243
Aldwark (Yorks), 238
*All Saints' Church, York (Yorks), 372
*All Souls College, Oxford, 116, 178
*Almondbury (Yorks), 272, 318–319, 379, 399, 400, 446, 449
Almshouses, 21–22, 41–49, 252–253, 264–265, 281–282; London gifts for, 433; total endowments for, 98, 99, 100, 114–115, 218, 222, 226–227, 228, 252
Alne (Yorks), 268
*Altofts (Yorks), 263, 322, 446, 449
Alum, mining of, 216
*Amersham (Bucks), 23, 36, 41, 45, 46, 55, 70, 331, 441
*Amotherby (Yorks), 298
Anlaby (Yorks), 270

*Appleby (Westmorland), 358
Appletreewick (Yorks), 298
Apprenticeship schemes, 50, 60, 130–131, 287–288, 433
Ardsley (Yorks), 264, 409
*Arkengarthdale (Yorks), 291, 346
*Arksey (Yorks), 241, 280, 346–347, 383, 446, 449
Armin, Hugh, 275
*Armin (Yorks), 394
*Armley (Yorks), 243, 248, 381–382, 396
Armyne, Sir William, 278
*Arncliffe (Yorks), 247–248, 400, 446, 451
Artisans, 28, 81, 98, 198, 203, 208, 211–212, 225, 412–413, 420, 434–435
Aske, Robert, 256
Aske (Yorks), 271
*Askham Richard (Yorks), 232
*Askrigg (Yorks), 326
Aslaby manor (Yorks), 298
Aspall's manor (Norfolk), 147, 177
Asterby manor (Lincs), 242
Aston (Bucks), 35
Aston Abbots (Bucks), 69
*Aston Clinton (Bucks), 32, 67, 441
*Attercliffe (Yorks), 378, 396
*Attleborough (Norfolk), 162–163, 442, 444
*Aylesbury (Bucks), 17, 23, 24, 32, 34, 36, 37, 38, 41, 42–43, 44, 51, 53, 61, 62, 65, 67, 73, 75, 441
*Aylsham (Norfolk), 101, 107, 119, 137, 153, 169, 183, 199, 442
*Aysgarth (Yorks), 326

Bacon, Sir Nathaniel, 111
Bacon, Sir Nicholas, 162
*Badsworth (Yorks), 245–246, 254
Balliol College (Oxford), 30
Bamburgh, Sir William, 334
*Barden (Yorks), 399
Bardsey (Yorks), 254
*Barkisland (Yorks), 251, 345, 382, 446, 451
*Barlby (Yorks), 356
Barlow, William, Bishop of Chichester, 355
*Barnham Broom (Norfolk), 184
Barnoldswick (Yorks), 369
*Barnsley (Yorks), 245, 246, 254, 342, 347, 409, 446, 449
Barsham, North (Norfolk), 171
*Barton Bendish (Norfolk), 101
*Barton Turf (Norfolk), 183, 189
Barwick in Elmet (Yorks), 216
Bate, Leonard, 262–263
*Bath, 160
*Batley (Yorks), 331, 369, 371, 446, 449
Battlesden (Beds), 35
*Bawburgh (Norfolk), 442, 444
*Beachampton (Bucks), 39, 40, 51, 57, 74, 75, 76, 441
*Beaconsfield (Bucks), 31
*Beamsley (Yorks), 369
Beaumont, Sir Thomas, 379
Beccles (Suffolk), 232
*Beckermonds (Yorks), 347
Beckwith, Sir Leonard, 297
*Bedale (Yorks), 266–267, 316–317, 448, 451
Bedford chapel, Chenies (Bucks), 70
*Bedfordshire, charities for, 38, 44, 55, 80, 201, 365, 416; donor from, 351
Bedingfield, Sir Henry, 105
Beeston priory (Norfolk), 156
*Beeston-next-Mileham (Norfolk), 128
Belasye, Sir Henry, 278
Bennett, Sir Thomas, 59

*Bergh Apton (Norfolk), 148, 442, 444
*Berkshire, charities for, 80, 81, 416; compared, 23
Berry, Dr. Richard, 337
Berwick-upon-Tweed (Northumberland), 255
*Bethlehem Hospital (London), 290
*Beverley (Yorks), 231, 237, 242, 247, 253, 263, 273, 302, 351, 352, 355, 360, 385, 390, 393, 400–401, 407, 446, 449
Biddenham (Beds), 351
Bierley (Yorks), 379
*Bierton (Bucks), 71
Bigod, Sir Francis, 256
*Bingley (Yorks), 293, 309–310, 446, 449
*Binham (Norfolk), 177
*Binley (Warwickshire), 246
*Birkin (Yorks), 259
*Birstall (Yorks), 313, 314, 400, 446, 449
*Bishop Burton (Yorks), 269, 289, 377, 446, 449
*Bishopthorpe (Yorks), 288
Bishop Wilton (Yorks), 269, 379
Bix (Oxon), 56
Bixley (Norfolk), 132, 133
Blackwell Hall, London, 269, 294, 320
*Bletchley (Bucks), 69
*Blickling (Norfolk), 153, 179, 442, 444
*Boarstall (Bucks), 41, 67
Bodley, Sir Thomas, 359
Boleyn, Anne, 179
Boleyn, Sir Geoffrey, 179
Boleyn, Thomas, 179
*Bolsterstone (Yorks), 334
*Bolton (Yorks), 347
*Bolton-by-Bowland (Yorks), 340, 369
Bolton Percy (Yorks), 369
Bond, William, 239
Bookham Magna (Surrey), 59
Bootham Hospital, York (Yorks), 301

Bordeaux (France), 418
*Boroughbridge (Yorks), 246
*Borston (Bucks), 53
*Bossall (Yorks), 377
*Boston (Lincs), 245, 377
Bourton (Bucks), 39
Bowes, Sir George, 378
Bowes, Robert, 271
Bowland (Yorks), 391
Boys' Hospital, Norwich, *vide* Children's Hospital
*Bracewell (Yorks), 394
*Bradenham (Bucks), 43, 69, 75, 441
*Bradenham, East (Norfolk), 121
*Bradfield (Yorks), 228, 381, 408
*Bradford (Yorks), 312, 379, 391, 398, 446, 449
*Bradley (Yorks), 395
Bradshaw, Henry, 30
*Bradwell (Bucks), 69
*Brafferton (Yorks), 291
*Bramham (Yorks), 254, 259
*Bramhope (Yorks), 384, 399
*Bramley (Yorks), 397
*Brampton Bierlow (Yorks), 343
*Brancaster (Norfolk), 123, 158, 442, 444
*Brasenose College, Oxford, 352
*Bressingham (Norfolk), 190, 442, 444
Brettenham (Norfolk), 151
*Brickhill (Bow, Great, Little), 36, 57, 71, 75, 79, 441
Brick-making, 24
*Bridlington (Yorks), 336–337, 446, 449
*Brill (Bucks), 32, 38, 44, 57, 75, 76, 79, 441
Bristol, 17, 96; compared, 33, 52, 60, 95, 141, 168, 173, 194, 197, 215, 223, 224, 294, 350, 374, 385, 388, 411, 415, 431
Briston (Norfolk), 104
*Brodsworth (Yorks), 235, 354, 446, 449
*Bromholm (Norfolk), 113
*Brompton (Yorks), 239, 264, 368

Brooke, Robert, 240
Brooke (Norfolk), 128, 442, 444
Broughton (Yorks), 337
*Bubwith (Yorks), 446, 449
*Buckenham, New (Norfolk), 164, 188
*Buckenham, Old (Norfolk), 113, 159, 352
*Buckingham Borough (Bucks), 23, 29, 31, 35, 39, 44, 53, 55, 58, 66, 73, 75, 441
Buckinghamshire, average benefaction in, 25; charities for, 201, 416; compared, 141, 150, 176, 197, 204, 218, 223, 224, 294, 300, 364, 367, 372, 374, 385, 411, 415, 431; description of, 18, 21, 23–24; donors, 96, 331; general discussion of, 23–88; total charities for, 20, 24, 27, 438, 441
*Buckland (Bucks), 41
*Bukenfield (Bucks), 36
*Bunwell (Norfolk), 187
*Burgh-next-Aylesham (Norfolk), 185
Burghers, 81, 98, 200, 202, 203, 211, 225, 236–237, 349–350, 405, 412, 420, 434
*Burley (Yorks), 245, 380
*Burlingham, North (Norfolk), 184
*Burnham (Bucks), 36, 70, 75, 441
*Burnham Deepdale (Norfolk), 123, 158
Burnham Overy (Norfolk), 123
*Burnham Thorpe (Norfolk), 159, 442, 444
*Burnsall (Yorks), 239, 298, 328–329, 400, 446, 451
Burston (Bucks), 72
*Burton Agnes (Yorks), 317, 365, 446, 449
*Bury St. Edmunds (Suffolk), 161, 171
Butler, Thomas, 124

*Caister St. Edmund (Norfolk), 160, 442, 444

Caius, John, 168
Calamy, Edmund, 278
*Caldecote (Norfolk), 183
Caldecote (Warwickshire), 343
*Calverley (Yorks), 250, 345, 397, 446
*Calverton (Bucks), 39, 40, 51
*Cambridge (Cambs), 161, 167, 178, 179, 369, 400
*Cambridgeshire, benefactions for, 113, 161, 200, 201, 416; donors from, 331, 358
*Cambridge University, 36, 43, 106, 116, 117, 126, 166, 170, 200, 212, 234, 251, 256, 302, 337, 345, 351, 354, 356, 357; *et vide sub* College names
Camden, Richard, 31
*Campsall (Yorks), 368, 389, 390
*Canterbury, 169, 194
Capital gifts, 50, 58, 66, 94, 98, 99, 113–114, 141, 144, 150, 175, 197, 212, 223, 226, 228, 257, 284, 285, 286, 339, 350, 365, 367, 376; *et vide* Endowments
Carbrook (Yorks), 378
*Carleton-Rode (Norfolk), 187
Carr, Richard, 306
Carter, George sr., 32
*Castle Acre (Norfolk), 184, 442, 444
Castlecomer (Ireland), 290
*Castle Rising (Norfolk), 125, 199, 442
Caston (Norfolk), 126
Catesby, Anthony, 44
Catholicism, 342, 373, 383
*Catterick (Yorks), 280, 289, 345, 448, 450
*Cawood (Yorks), 288, 335–336, 446, 451
Cawthorne (Yorks), 303, 339, 378
Cecil, William, Lord Burghley, 29, 267
Chamberlain, Sir William, 152
Chantry Commissioners (1548), 302, 303, 305, 306, 307, 309, 310, 311, 312, 315, 316, 327

Charitable wealth, totals of, 20, 217
Charity Hall, Hull (Yorks), 288, 295–296
*Chart (Kent), 116
Chastleton (Oxon), 234, 338
*Cheddington (Bucks), 38
Cheke, Mary, 286
*Chenies (Bucks), 28–29, 45, 64, 70, 75, 79, 441
*Chesham (Bucks), 36, 37, 39, 46, 47, 71, 75, 79, 441
*Chesham Bois (Bucks), 36
Chesham Leicester (Bucks), 39
Chesham Woburn (Bucks), 39
*Cheshire, 80, 416
Chevening (Kent), 351
Chicheley (Bucks), 54, 68–69
*Children's Hospital, Norwich (Norfolk), 118, 127, 131–136 *passim*, 155
*Chilton (Bucks), 38, 75, 76, 79, 441
Chipping Campden (Glos.), 418
*Cholesbury (Bucks), 36
Cholmley, Sir Roger, 297
*Christ Church, Oxford, 54, 55, 331
*Christ's College, Cambridge, 307, 354, 358, 359
Christ's Hospital, Buckingham, *vide* Queen Elizabeth's Hospital
*Christ's Hospital, Firby (Yorks), 266–267
*Christ's Hospital, London, 290, 334, 377
Church: building, 25, 67–71, 82, 185–187, 361, 388, 399; general uses of, 174–175, 364; repair, 65–67, 174, 182, 385
*Clackclose (Norfolk), 127
*Clapham (Yorks), 335, 340, 397
*Clare College, Cambridge, 170, 171, 289–290, 328
Claydon (Bucks), 24
Claydon, Middle (Bucks), 47, 62, 70

Claydon, Steeple (Bucks), 58
Clere, Edward, 158
Clergy, donors from, 349, 367,
    373; maintenance of, 65, 222,
    361–362, 363, 375–376, 424,
    433
Clergy, lower, 28, 81, 85, 86, 202,
    203, 205, 208–209, 412, 418,
    420, 431–432
Clergy, upper, 81, 85, 200, 202,
    203, 208, 412, 417, 420,
    430
Clint, manor of (Yorks), 346
Cloth industry, 23, 89–90, 211,
    215, 216, 285, 323, 434
*Clun (Salop), 125
Coal mining, 216
*Cockley Cley (Norfolk), 179
*Cockthorpe (Norfolk), 185
*Coley (Yorks), 325, 327, 340, 394
*Colnbrook (Bucks), 23, 41, 47,
    71, 75, 79, 441
*Colveston (Norfolk), 107, 108,
    442, 444
Commissioners for Charitable
    Uses (1616), 228; (1687),
    336
Commission of Pious Uses (1681),
    244
Coney, William, 127
*Conisbrough (Yorks), 370
Conyers, Sir Christopher, 369
Cooke, George, 281
Cooke, George (1683), 347
Cooper, Thomas, vide Cowper's
    Dictionary
Corbett, John, 125
Corbett, Miles, 125
Corbett, Sir Thomas, 125
*Corpus Christi College, Cam-
    bridge, 169, 171
Cosin, John, 402
*Costessey (Norfolk), 122, 442, 444
*Cottingham (Yorks), 371
Council of the North, 359, 377
Coventry, 17
Coventry, Thomas, Baron
    Coventry, 239

Cowper's [Cooper's] Dictionary,
    318, 340
Cowston, Henry, 317
*Cowton, South (Yorks), 368
*Coxwold (Yorks), 243, 278, 329,
    448, 451
Crabhouse Nunnery, Wiggenhall
    (Norfolk), 122
Craven, William, first Earl of,
    239
*Creake Abbey (Norfolk), 188–189
Creech St Michael (Somerset),
    43
*Crendon (Bucks), 37
Crewe, Sir Ranulf, 266
Cringleford (Norfolk), 117
Crome, Nicholas, 120
*Cromer (Norfolk), 152, 166, 199
Cromwell, Oliver, 278, 291, 346
Crossley, Zechariah, 385
*Cross Stone Chapel, Halifax
    (Yorks), 392
Crown, benefactions of, 81, 165,
    202, 203, 204, 225, 420, 421
*Cuddington (Bucks), 38, 79
Cudworth (Yorks), 279, 292
Cumberland, benefactions for,
    399, 416, 417
Cutler, Sir Gervase, 238
Cutler, John, 238

Dakin, John, 258
*Danby (Yorks), 240, 241–242
*Darfield (Yorks), 336, 384, 394,
    398, 446, 451
*Darlington (Durham), 310
Darrell, Sir Marmaduke, 70
*Darrington (Yorks), 288
*Darton (Yorks), 400
*Datchet (Bucks), 51, 441
Day, William, Bishop of
    Winchester, 355
*Dean Head (Yorks), 377
Delafield, William, 62
*Denby (Yorks), 396
*Denham (Bucks), 76
*Dent (Yorks), 234, 242, 329, 352

*Derbyshire, benefactions for, 201, 416

Dethick, Sir John, 134

*Devonshire, benefactions for, 80, 201

Dewsbury (Yorks), 327

*Dickleburgh (Norfolk), 442, 444

*Didlington (Norfolk), 107, 108

*Diss (Norfolk), 113, 124, 442, 444

*Doddershall (Bucks), 35

*Dodington (Bucks), 65

*Dodworth (Yorks), 347

*Doncaster (Yorks), 254, 261, 273, 280, 287, 315, 343, 368, 369, 390, 446, 449

Dormer, Sir William (d.1575), 44

*Dormer's Hospital, Wing (Bucks), 44

*Dorney (Bucks), 69

Dowthorpe (Yorks), 283

Drapers' Company, trustee, 241, 336, 384

*Drayton (Norfolk), 167

*Drayton Beauchamp (Bucks), 36, 37, 69, 79, 441

*Dublin, Ireland, 359, 371, 401, 418

*Durham, 234, 239, 284, 355

Durham, Bishopric of, 284, 355

Durham, County of, 384, 416

Dutch refugees, 29, 398

Dynham, John, Lord, 64

*Eakring (Notts), 368

"Early Stuart Period" (1601–1640), vide "Stuart Period, Early"

*Easby (Yorks), 271, 322, 391

*Easington (Bucks), 38, 48

Easington (Yorks), 343

*Eastburn (Yorks), 394

*East Dereham (Norfolk), 106, 107, 110, 127–128, 135, 163, 184, 187, 199, 442

*Eastfield-Silkstone, Thurgoland (Yorks), 347, 394

East Ham (Essex), 30

*East Hardwick (Yorks), 344, 381, 399

*East Harling (Norfolk), 144, 442, 444

East India Company, 355

East Riding (Yorks), 214, 258, 282, 402, 403, 405–406, 408, 410, 414, 446, 449, 451

*Eastrington (Yorks), 376–377, 392, 446, 449

East Smithfield (London), 107

*Ecclesall (Yorks), 344, 395–396

*Ecclesfield (Yorks), 238, 241, 244, 246, 273, 327, 334, 343, 400, 408, 446, 449

*Edgefield (Norfolk), 159

Education, 151, 301–304, 437; benefactions by classes for, 84, 85, 87, 204–213 passim, 422–427 passim, 430–436 passim; benefactions of women for, 28, 225; totals for, 25, 26, 52–53, 78, 92, 94, 150–151, 193, 198, 218–222 passim, 299–301, 404, 406, 407, 409, 413, 417, 438–443, 446–448

Edward VI, 29, 116, 118

Egglescliffe (Durham), 319

*Eldroth (Yorks), 335, 397

"Elizabeth, Age of" (1561–1600), 25–26, 93, 97, 221, 438–440; charities for:

education, 150, 169, 300, 301, 316, 326–327

municipal uses, 147, 295

poor, 34, 99, 114, 227, 232, 252, 260

religion, 60, 66, 68, 173–174, 175, 181, 182, 185, 186, 232, 282–283, 363, 364, 376, 386, 388

social rehabilitation, 282, 285, 287

total benefactions by classes, 86, 205, 206, 208, 210, 211, 423, 425–426, 427, 428

*Elland (Yorks), 251, 381
*Ellerton (Yorks), 268
*Ellingham (Norfolk), 112
Ellis's Hospital, Doncaster, 315
Ellough (Suffolk), 145
*Elloughton (Yorks), 382
Elm (Cambs), 111
Elmsall (Yorks), 250, 251
Elvington (Yorks), 284
*Emmanuel College, Cambridge,
170, 171, 322, 353
*Emneth (Norfolk), 121
Endowments, 27, 49, 73, 94–95,
129, 130–131, 145, 230–231,
251, 252, 300, 375, 380, 412
Erpingham, Hundred of (Norfolk),
129
*Erpingham, North, Hundred of
(Norfolk), 160
Esk River, 296, 298
*Essex, County of, 30, 80, 182,
201, 354, 416
Estates, value of, 36, 38, 57, 108,
135, 168, 248, 251, 279, 321,
393
*Eton (Bucks), 53, 58, 441
Etton (Yorks), 284
Exeter, 167
Expropriation, 180, 226, 258,
366, 372–373
Extra-Buckinghamshire benefac-
tions, 80–81
Extra-Norfolk benefactions,
200–201
Extra-Yorkshire benefactions,
415, 416, 417
*Eye (Suffolk), 165
Eythrope (Bucks), 64

Fairfax, Sir Thomas, 278
*Fakenham (Norfolk), 401
Farnham (Yorks), 372
Fauconberg, Thomas, Earl of,
278
*Featherstone (Yorks), 262, 401
*Felbrigg (Norfolk), 442, 444
*Felkirk (Yorks), 336
Fellowships, vide Scholarships

*Feltwell (Norfolk), 112, 164, 442,
444
*Fersfield (Norfolk), 144, 187
Firbeck (Yorks), 333
*Firby (Yorks), 266–267, 340
Fishing industry, 89
*Fishlake (Yorks), 245, 264, 341,
343, 447, 449
Fishmongers' Company, 156
Flamborough (Yorks), 351
*Flaxby (Yorks), 340
Fleet Marston (Bucks), 331
*Flegg, East and West, Hundreds
of (Norfolk), 160
Fleming, Barbara, 247
Fortescue, Sir Francis, 50
Foss River, 295
Fotheringhay College, 64
*Foulby (Yorks), 247
Foxcroft, Anthony, 245
France, 416
*Fremington (Yorks), 342, 343
Frobisher, Sir Martin, 264
Fulbourn (Cambs), 308
*Fulmer (Bucks), 70, 79, 441
Fyebridge ward, Norwich, 118

*Ganton (Yorks), 270
*Garboldisham (Norfolk), 145,
442, 444
Gargrave, Sir Cotton, 276, 336
Gargrave, Sir Richard, 337
Gargrave, Thomas, 336–337, 371
*Gargrave (Yorks), 447, 449
*Garsdale (Yorks), 336, 352
Garway, Sir Henry, 251
*Gayton (Norfolk), 107
Gedding (Suffolk), 152
Gentry, 81, 179, 200, 237–239,
349, 372–373; lower, 21, 28,
31, 81, 84, 98, 165, 203, 205,
206–207, 225, 367, 381, 417,
420, 421, 424–426, 433;
upper, 21, 28, 29–31, 81–83,
97, 165, 204–205, 225, 367,
412, 417, 420, 422–424
*Giggleswick (Yorks), 306–307,
354, 355, 447, 449

*Gilling (Yorks), 318
*Gillingham (Norfolk), 147–148
*Girls' Hospital, Norwich, 135, 136–137
*Gisburn (Yorks), 340
*Glaisdale (Yorks), 240, 296, 395
Glass Houghton (Yorks), 371
Gloucester, 17
*Gloucestershire, 29, 201
God's House, Norwich, vide St Giles' Hospital
*Goldsborough (Yorks), 55, 331, 340
*Goldsmiths' Company, 106, 152
Gonville, Edmund, 151
*Gonville and Caius College, Cambridge, 91, 151, 160, 161, 163, 166–167, 168, 169, 170–171, 172, 283
Goodrick, Sir Henry, 250
*Goole (Yorks), 232, 394
Gower, John, 318
Grammar schools, 22, 58, 150, 165, 300–301, 348–349; et vide Education
*Grandborough (Bucks), 69
*Grantham (Lincs), 384
*Greasbrough (Yorks), 382
*Great and Little Preston (Yorks), 447, 451
Great Fen (Norfolk), 112
*Great Habton (Yorks), 298
Great Hospital, Norwich, vide St Giles' Hospital
*Great Houghton (Yorks), 398
*Great Marlow (Bucks), 23, 32, 45, 51–52, 56, 75, 441
*Great Missenden (Bucks), 31, 38–39, 47, 70, 79, 441
*Greenwich, 43, 125
Greenwood, James, 245
*Grendon Underwood (Bucks), 51, 70
Gresham, William, 155
*Gresham's grammar school, Holt (Norfolk), 155, 156, 197–198
*Gressenhall (Norfolk), 368
*Grimston (Norfolk), 163, 442, 444

Grimston (Yorks), 318
Grindal, Edmund, Archbishop of Canterbury, 361
*Grinton (Yorks), 342, 448, 450
Grocers' Company, 312
*Guisborough (Yorks), 260–261, 316, 448, 450
*Guiseley (Yorks), 328, 334, 380, 381, 399, 447, 449
*Gunthwaite (Yorks), 396

*Hackford (Norfolk), 190
Hackness (Yorks), 397
*Halifax (Yorks), charities for:
    education, 234, 237, 245, 273, 276, 319, 323–326, 340, 395
    municipal uses, 326
    poor, 234, 235, 236–237, 239, 254, 267, 273, 276, 286, 290, 324–326
    religious uses, 237, 254, 268, 276, 380, 382, 392, 401
    social rehabilitation, 268, 290, 325, 340
    et vide 216, 349, 360, 395, 407, 414, 415, 419, 432, 447, 451; Heptonstall, Hipperholme, Sowerby
"Hall, Mr", of Norwich, 155
*Halsham (Yorks), 263, 293, 319, 353, 446, 449
*Halton (Bucks), 30, 75, 79, 441
*Halton (Yorks), 245
*Halton Gill (Yorks), 162, 332, 396
*Hambleden (Bucks), 30, 441
Hampden, John, 31
*Hampden, Little (Bucks), 69
*Hampshire, benefaction for, 416; compared, 27, 64, 96, 141, 197, 218, 224, 294, 372, 374, 385, 411, 415, 419, 431
*Hampstead (Middlesex), 57
Hanley Park, 59
Hansby, Edward, 272
Hanse House, Hull (Yorks), 296
*Hanslope (Bucks), 69, 75, 441

Happing, Hundred of (Norfolk), 160
*Hardmead (Bucks), 69
*Harewood (Yorks), 288–289, 342, 392
Harling, Sir Robert, 152
Harling, Middle (Norfolk), 190
*Harpley (Norfolk), 199, 442
*Hartfield (Sussex), 244
*Harthill (Yorks), 237, 395
*Harwood Dale (Yorks), 397
Haryngton, William, 297
Hastings, Richard, 371–372
*Hatfield (Yorks), 237, 333, 398, 447, 451
Hatfield Chase (Yorks), 398
*Havercroft (Yorks), 336, 337
*Haworth (Yorks), 337, 338, 342
Hazlewood (Yorks), 216, 394
Headingley (Yorks), 395, 398
Heath, Nicholas, Archbishop of York, 361
Heath, Thomas, 163
*Heath (Yorks), 247, 279, 280, 291
*Heath Grammar School, Halifax, 234, 235, 323–326
Hebden Bridge (Yorks), 351
*Hedenham (Norfolk), 145, 199, 442
*Hedon (Yorks), 262, 269, 270, 296, 390
*Hedsor (Bucks), 71
Heighington (Durham), 239
*Helhoughton (Norfolk), 108
*Helwith (Yorks), 346
*Hemingbrough (Yorks), 310, 344, 356, 370, 446, 449
*Hemsby (Norfolk), 105
*Hemsworth (Yorks), 258, 276, 311–312, 447, 449
*Henley (Oxon), 30, 59, 162
*Heptonstall (Yorks), 245, 289, 294, 338, 341, 447, 449
*Hepworth (Yorks), 341
*Herefordshire, 201, 416
Hertehill, Adam, 304
*Hertfordshire, 29, 80, 81, 201, 359, 416

Hesketh, Dame Julia, 266
*Heslington (Yorks), 266, 446, 449
Heydon, Sir Henry, 179
*Heydon (Norfolk), 162, 442, 444
Hicks, Baptist, Viscount Campden, 384
Higgin, Thomas, 355
*Hilborough (Norfolk), 184
*Hillesden (Bucks), 68, 441
*Hillington (Norfolk), 145
Hinde, Augustine, 181
*Hindringham (Norfolk), 123
*Hingham (Norfolk), 120
Hingles (Yorks), 398
*Hipperholme (Yorks), 249, 344
*Hitcham (Bucks), 70
Hoby, Lady Margaret, 397
Hockley (Essex), 354
Hodgkinson, Henry, 335
Hodgkinson, John, 335
*Hoe (Norfolk), 127–128
*Holbeck (Yorks), 243, 248, 254, 397
Holderness, 259
Hollym (Yorks), 400
*Holmfirth (Yorks), 341, 397
*Holt (Norfolk), 155–156, 166, 199, 442
Honley (Yorks), 400
*Hook (Yorks), 232, 394
Hooton, Elizabeth, 248
Hooton Pagnell (Yorks), 233
*Horbury, Wakefield (Yorks), 248
*Hornby (Yorks), 231, 369, 408–409
Horncastle (Lincs), 242
Horne, William, 276
*Hornsea (Yorks), 237
*Horton (Bucks), 38, 41, 70
Hospitals, vide Guisborough, St. John (High Wycombe), St. Mary Magdalen (Ripon), St. Nicholas (Pontefract)
Hotham, Sir John, 393
*Hoveton St. Peter (Norfolk), 191
Howard, Sir Edward, 351
*Howden (Yorks), 234, 240, 242, 288, 304, 393, 446, 451

Howgill, Thomas, 310
*Hubberholme (Yorks), 347
*Huddersfield (Yorks), 287, 327, 370, 377, 400, 447, 449
*Hulcott (Bucks), 69
*Hull (Yorks), charities for:
    education, 235, 240, 305–306, 355
    municipal uses, 231, 236, 255, 286, 295–296
    poor, 231, 232, 234, 235, 236, 240, 248, 253, 254, 255, 257–258, 259–260, 261–262, 264, 265–266, 271–272, 275, 282, 286
    religion, 231, 235, 236, 286, 370, 393
    social rehabilitation, 231, 235, 236, 286, 288, 294
    et vide 262, 349, 354, 372, 407, 418, 432, 446, 449; Trinity House
Humphrey, Thomas, 240
Hungate, Sir Philip, 334
Hunsdon, John, Baron, 113
*Hunslet (Yorks), 397
*Hunstanton (Norfolk), 179, 442, 444
Hunt, Edward, 396
Hunt, John, 30
*Huntingdonshire, 416
Hurst, Richard, 318
Husbandmen, 28, 81, 85, 98, 203, 207–208, 225, 349, 417, 420, 427–429
*Hutton (Yorks), 351
*Hutton Rudby (Yorks), 266, 342

*Idle (Yorks), 397
*Ilkley (Yorks), 321, 328, 340
*Illingworth (Yorks), 239, 401
Industries, 24, 89, 216, 434
*Ingerthorpe (Yorks), 264
*Ingham (Norfolk), 179, 187
Ingram, Sir Arthur, 245, 275
Institute of Mary, Haworth (Yorks), 342

*Ireland, 401, 416, 417
Iron industry, 216
*Ivinghoe (Bucks), 35, 75, 79, 441

James I, 363
Jenkinson, Grace, 245
Jesus, Hospital of, in Guisburn (Yorks), 260–261
Jesus College, Cambridge, 284

Kendal (Westmorland), 294
*Kenninghall (Norfolk), 144
*Kent, benefactions for, 57, 80, 416; compared, 96, 182, 197, 217, 218, 224, 294, 348, 374, 376, 385, 411, 415, 427, 431; donor from, 351
*Kepwick (Yorks), 278
*Keresforth Hill (Yorks), 347
*Kettlewell (Yorks), 401
Kett's Rebellion, 117, 123–124
Keyingham (Yorks), 263
Kilburn (Yorks), 329
*Kildwick (Yorks), 230, 327, 447, 449
*Kilham (Yorks), 336, 446, 449
*Kilnwick (Yorks), 238
*Kilnwick Percy (Yorks), 233
*Kimberley (Norfolk), 113
*Kimberworth (Yorks), 382
*King's Chapel, Cambridge, 357
*Kingsey (Bucks), 61
*King's Lynn (Norfolk), charities for:
    education, 107, 126, 152–153, 170
    municipal uses, 149, 153
    poor, 105, 123–124, 126, 139, 149, 179
    religion, 105, 149, 153, 170, 178, 179, 184–185, 190
    social rehabilitation, 105, 139, 161, 169
    et vide 192, 193, 199, 201, 202, 208, 209, 442
Kingston-upon-Hull, *vide* Hull
Kingston-upon-Thames (Surrey), 30

*Kippax (Yorks), 268, 269, 311, 447, 449
Kirby, Joshua, 384
*Kirby Cane (Norfolk), 112, 442, 444
Kirby Hill (Yorks), 291
Kirby Knowle (Yorks), 293, 319, 353
*Kirby Misperton (Yorks), 242, 298, 337, 448, 450
*Kirby Moorside (Yorks), 282, 408
*Kirkburton (Yorks), 353, 397
*Kirkby (Yorks), 352, 401
*Kirkby, South (Yorks), 231, 245
*Kirkby Malham (Yorks), 322
*Kirkby Malzeard, 340
*Kirkby Overblow (Yorks), 327
*Kirkby Ravensworth, 258, 314–315, 448, 451
Kirkby Wharfe (Yorks), 284
*Kirk Deighton (Yorks), 355
*Kirkheaton (Yorks), 335
*Kirklington (Yorks), 280, 289
*Kirk Sandall (Yorks), 335, 371, 401
*Kirkthorpe (Yorks), 247, 263, 280
*Knapton (Norfolk), 184, 190
*Knaresborough (Yorks), 55, 242, 246, 331, 446, 451
*Kneton (Yorks), 395
Knevet, Sir John, 188
Knevet, Sir Thomas, 123
*Knottingley (Yorks), 248

Lace-making, 24
Lackford (Suffolk), 171
*Lancashire, benefactions for, 355, 358, 359, 416; compared, 33, 52, 60, 91, 92, 95, 96, 141, 150, 173, 197, 219, 223, 224, 294, 300, 362, 374, 383, 385, 388, 411, 415, 431
*Lancaster (Lancs), 266, 355
Langdale, Lord Marmaduke, 283
*Langley Marish (Bucks), 41, 47, 69, 70, 75, 441

Later values, 35, 38, 46, 47, 55, 104, 107, 112, 133, 140, 142, 145, 159, 239, 269, 275, 334, 353, 356
*Lathbury (Bucks), 54, 58, 441
Latimer, Lord, vide Nevill, Sir John
Laud, William, Archbishop of Canterbury, 30, 60, 66, 185, 363, 376, 396
*Laughton-en-le-Morthen (Yorks), 333
*Lavendon (Bucks), 69
*Laxton (Yorks), 288
Layfielde, Edmund, 332
Layton, Thomas, 277
Ledsham (Yorks), 279
Lee, Edward, Archbishop of York, 361
Lee, Sir Richard, 54
*Leeds (Yorks), charities for:
    education, 277, 313–314, 356
    municipal uses, 296, 297, 298
    poor, 243, 244–245, 248, 250, 275, 277
    religion, 243, 277, 370, 382, 395, 396, 397, 401–402
    social rehabilitation, 287, 294
    et vide 216, 229, 255, 345, 346, 398, 402, 407, 419, 432, 447, 449; Armley, Headingley, Holbeck
*Leicestershire, 201, 242, 416
Leigh, Silvester, 263
Leighton, Alexander, 356
*Leighton Buzzard (Beds), 38, 47
Lever, Thomas, 309
*Lexham, East (Norfolk), 110, 195
Libraries, 47, 140, 169, 170, 357, 359; et vide Education
*Lightcliffe (Yorks), 394
*Lillingstone Lovell (Bucks), 71
Limestone, mining of, 216
*Lincoln, 32, 61, 62, 67, 352
*Lincoln College, Oxford, 357
*Lincolnshire, benefactions for, 184, 201, 242, 352, 416, 417; et vide 214, 256, 330, 384

*Linford, Great (Bucks), 69
*Litcham (Norfolk), 113
*Little Horwood (Bucks), 70
*Little Marlow (Bucks), 32, 56, 57, 59
*Little Missenden (Bucks), 36, 68
Little Sandal (Yorks), 335
*Little Walsingham (Norfolk), 139, 163–164, 166, 442, 444
Livery companies, 143, 294, 412; et vide sub Companies [by name]
Loan funds, 49, 141–143, 292; et vide Social rehabilitation
*Loddon (Norfolk), 148, 189
Lombard Street, London, 355
*London, 77–78, 82, 86, 96, 194, 196–197, 431; benefactions for, 101, 106, 182, 200, 201, 242, 246, 279, 290, 368, 371, 416, 417
    charities of, for:
    education, 57, 82, 152, 155–156, 162, 163, 164, 235, 241, 249, 289, 309, 312, 324–325, 326, 327, 329, 332, 336, 338, 340, 353, 356, 377, 384
    municipal uses, 297
    poor, 30, 36, 38, 46, 75, 103, 106, 107, 123, 231, 233, 235, 237, 239, 241, 242, 248–249, 255, 258, 269, 286, 293–294, 324–325, 332, 336, 338, 379, 384
    religion, 233, 241, 242, 255, 269, 332, 336, 379, 384, 396
    social rehabilitation, 43, 133, 237, 283, 284, 286, 287, 291, 292, 293–294, 327, 338, 356, 377
    compared, 194, 198, 202, 215, 218, 223, 224, 364, 374, 385, 411
    total benefactions from, 20, 75, 76, 77–78, 79, 197, 199, 209, 211, 412, 413, 414, 415, 417, 444–445, 449–450, 451

et vide 18, 24, 72, 89, 166, 195, 216, 349, 350, 383, 406, 408, 409, 415, 418, 431
Long Marston (Yorks), 351
*Long Preston (Yorks), 268–269, 286
*Lonsdale (Yorks), 358
Loughborough (Leics), 29
*Loughton (Bucks), 57, 69, 441
*Luddenden (Yorks), 394, 396
*Ludham (Norfolk), 177
Lumley, Richard, Viscount, 279
Lupset (Yorks), 262, 320
*Lyddington (Rutland), 286
Lyhert, Walter, Bishop of Norwich, 149
Lynn (Norfolk), vide King's Lynn
*Lynn, South (Norfolk), 178, 442

Maccarty, Sir Donald, 223
*Magdalen College, Oxford, 59, 257, 307
*Magdalene College, Cambridge, 170
Mainwaring, William, 30
Mallory, Sir John, 238
Mallory, William, 270
Manchester, 17, 194, 355
Mann, John, 136
Marham (Norfolk), 127
Mariners, almshouse founded by, 265
*Market Weighton (Yorks), 249, 344, 382
Marriage subsidies, 50, 283; et vide Social rehabilitation
*Marrick (Yorks), 379
Marsden (Yorks), 216
Marshall, William, 287
*Marsham (Norfolk), 137
*Marske (Yorks), 246, 248–249, 250, 346, 378, 448, 451
*Marston (Yorks), 351
Marston Moor (Yorks), 278, 295
*Marston, North (Bucks), 61
*Martham (Norfolk), 162
*Marton cum Moxby (Yorks), 401

Mary, Queen, 54, 373
Massingham, Great (Norfolk),
    161
Matthew, Tobias, Archbishop of
    York, 355
*Mattishall (Norfolk), 121, 158,
    186, 195, 199
Mattishall Burgh (Norfolk), 121
*Medmenham (Bucks), 56, 65,
    76
Melford (Kent), 385
*Melford Bridge, 146
Melsonby (Yorks), 246
*Meltham (Yorks), 399
Mendham (Suffolk), 264
*Mentmore (Bucks), 38, 69, 76
Mercers' Company, 384
Merchant Adventurers' Company,
    Hull, 296
Merchant Adventurers' Company,
    York, 272, 293; et vide
    Trinity Hospital
Merchant donors, 28, 81, 87, 98,
    166, 195, 197–198, 202, 203,
    205, 209–210, 225, 349, 367,
    372, 373, 412, 418, 420, 432–
    433
*Merchant Taylors' Company,
    106, 287, 328–329
*Merton College, Oxford, 59, 343,
    359, 360
Metcalf, John, 250
*Metfield (Suffolk), 177
*Methley (Yorks), 239, 251, 327,
    353, 395, 447, 451
Mexborough, 276
Middlesex, 80, 90, 267, 294, 359;
    et vide London
*Middlesmoor (Yorks), 394
Middleton, Peter, 279
*Middleton (Norfolk), 107
*Middleton (Yorks), 370
*Midhope (Yorks), 246, 381
*Mileham (Norfolk), 162
*Mirfield (Yorks), 339–340
Mitchell, Henry, 322
*Mitford, Hundred of (Norfolk),
    107

Monasticism, 62–64, 180, 215,
    226, 361, 373–375
*Monk Bretton (Yorks), 278
Montisfont (Hants), 279
*Morley (Norfolk), 163
Morton, Thomas, Bishop of
    Durham, 355
*Moulton (Norfolk), 185
*Mountnessing (Essex), 182
Municipal uses, benefactions by
    classes, 84, 85, 87, 204, 206,
    207, 209, 210, 211, 422, 424–
    427 passim, 429, 432–435
    passim; benefactions of
    women, 28, 97, 225; endow-
    ments for, 95; total benefac-
    tions for, 25, 26, 50, 78, 92, 93,
    94, 143–144, 145, 198, 218,
    219, 221, 222, 294–299 passim,
    404, 406, 407, 409, 413, 417,
    438–443, 446–448; et vide 60,
    437
*Murton (Yorks), 394

*Nash (Bucks), 40
*Needham (Norfolk), 442, 444
Neile, Richard, Archbishop of
    York, 288, 381, 396, 398,
    399, 402
Neile, Sir Paul, 288
Nerford, Rev. Henry, 163
Nettleton, Thomas, 341
Nettleton (Lincs), 352
Nevile, Sir Thomas, 254
Nevill, John, Fourth Baron
    Latimer, 279
*Newark-upon-Trent (Notts),
    315–316
*Newby (Yorks), 338, 379
Newcastle upon Tyne (Northum-
    berland), 284
New College, Oxford, 323
*New England, 416, 418
*New Forest (Yorks), 291, 346
*"New House for the Poor,"
    King's Lynn, 139
*New Malton (Yorks), 337, 45

Newnham manor (Cambs), 166, 167

*Newport Pagnell (Bucks), 24, 41, 46, 69, 75, 441

*Newton Blossomville (Bucks), 70

*Newton Kyme (Yorks), 259

Nobility, 28, 81, 97, 203, 204, 225, 367, 372, 373, 402, 421–422

*Noke (Oxon), 30

Norfolk, benefactions from other counties for, 80, 416; compared, 223, 224, 294, 348, 350, 374, 385, 411, 415, 431; general discussion of, 89–213; total benefactions for, 20, 91–92, 173, 202, 439, 442–445; *et vide* 18, 21, 172–173, 201–202, 359, 368

*Norland (Yorks), 237

*Norman's Hospital, Norwich, 119–120, 137, 153, 177, 178

*Normanton (Yorks), 322, 369–370, 447, 449

*Northall (Bucks), 29

*Northallerton (Yorks), 239, 253, 303–304, 448, 451

*Northamptonshire, 55, 80, 201, 242, 246, 416

*North Creake (Norfolk), 123, 188, 442, 444

*North Elmham (Norfolk), 128, 443, 444

*North Elmsall (Yorks), 370, 371

*North Lopham (Norfolk), 190, 443, 444

North Riding (Yorks), 282, 402, 403, 405, 406, 408, 410, 415, 426, 448, 450, 451

*Northumberland, 416, 417

*North Walsham (Norfolk), 103, 160, 443, 444

*Northwold (Norfolk), 146, 443, 444

*Norton in Hales (Salop), 162

*Norton (Yorks), 327, 368

*Norwich, 138, 149, 215, 332; charities for:

education, 101, 116, 151, 154–155, 167, 169, 171

municipal uses, 101, 109, 116, 128, 133, 135, 142, 146–147, 148, 177, 183

poor, 101, 102, 103, 104, 105, 107, 108, 109, 111, 112–113, 115, 116, 117, 120, 121, 125–126, 128, 133, 134, 135, 142, 146, 153, 164, 167, 178, 180

religion, 101, 103, 104, 107, 109, 111, 116, 117, 133, 134, 135, 148, 159, 160, 168, 177, 178, 179, 180, 183–190 *passim*

social rehabilitation, 100, 102, 103, 107, 108–109, 121, 124, 125, 131–135 *passim*, 141–143, 145, 161, 178, 180

merchants of, 130, 166, 202, 209; total benefactions for, 193–195, 443, 444; *et vide* 17, 19, 90, 99, 192, 201, 208, 212, 396, 418; Girls' Hospital; Norman's Hospital; St Giles' Hospital

*Nostell Priory (Yorks), 391

*Nottinghamshire, 217, 242, 416, 417

Nunburnholme (Yorks), 369

*Oglethorpe's almshouse, 259, 277, 290–291, 315

*Old Malton (Yorks), 311, 400, 448, 450

*Olney (Bucks), 24, 67, 70, 441

*Ormesby (Norfolk), 100, 168, 443, 444

*Ormesby (Yorks), 249

Osbaldwick (Yorks), 342, 394

Osberton (Notts), 279

Osborne, Sir Edward, 396

*Osmotherley (Yorks), 391

Osney fraternity (Oxon), 64

Oswaldkirk (Yorks), 391

*Otley (Yorks), 245, 320, 328, 379–380, 384, 447, 449
*Ottringham (Yorks), 391
Ouse River, 214, 297
*Outwell (Norfolk and Cambs), 110, 443, 444
*Ovenden (Yorks), 239
Overton, William, Bishop of Coventry and Lichfield, 355
*Overton (Yorks), 448, 450
*Oxborough (Norfolk), 105, 109–110, 443, 444
*Oxfordshire, 30, 31, 38, 48, 80, 81, 416
*Oxford University, 30, 43, 58–59, 64, 256, 313, 345, 350, 351, 354, 356, 357, 359; et vide sub Colleges [by name]
*Oxnead (Norfolk), 124, 160, 443, 444

Pakenham manor (Norfolk), 153
Paper-making, 24
Parishes, structure of, 19, 21, 71–77, 191–200, 361–362, 402–410
Paston, Erasmus, 103, 160
Paston, John, 177
Paull (Yorks), 263
Pelham, Sir William, 44
*Pembroke College, Cambridge, 357
*Pembroke College, Oxford, 59
Penistone (Yorks), 339
Perkins, William, works of, 336, 384
Peterborough (Northants), 357
*Peterhouse College, Cambridge, 331, 355
*Pickering (Yorks), 345
Pickering, Sir James, 391
Pickering, Robert, 385
Pilgrimage of Grace, 256, 258, 318, 361
*Pitchcott (Bucks), 61
*Pitstone (Bucks), 70
*Pocklington (Yorks), 307–308, 343, 352, 446, 451

*Pontefract (Yorks), benefactions for, 238, 250, 259, 271, 280, 282, 292, 296, 302–303, 307, 368, 371, 447, 449; et vide 216, 253, 256, 263, 339, 353
Poor, benefactions by classes, 84, 85, 87, 204–212 passim, 422–427 passim, 430–435 passim; benefactions of women, 28, 97, 224; total benefactions for, 25, 26, 74–77, 78, 91, 93, 94, 98, 193, 198, 218–222 passim, 226–228, 404, 406, 407, 409, 413, 417, 438–443 passim, 446, 447, 448; et vide 33–49, 95, 137–138, 226, 375, 437; Almshouses
Population, estimates of, 19, 24, 90, 201, 214–217, 226, 362
Potteric Carr (Doncaster, Yorks), 287
Prayers, benefactions for, 64, 173, 176, 205, 219, 220, 365, 376; et vide Religious uses
"Pre-Reformation era" (1480–1540), 25, 92–93, 205, 219, 438, 439, 440; charities for: education, 53, 168–169, 299, 300, 310, 351
municipal uses, 295
poor, 34, 99, 114, 119, 227, 252, 253–254, 256
religion, 60, 63, 173, 175, 176, 180–181, 182, 186, 190–191, 362–363, 364, 367, 374, 376, 386, 388, 399
social rehabilitation, 282
total benefactions by classes, 83, 86, 206, 210, 422, 425, 427, 428, 430, 434
*Preston (Lancs), 266
*Princes Risborough (Bucks), 31, 441
Prisoners, relief of, 49, 283–284; et vide Social rehabilitation
Professional classes, 28, 81, 87, 98, 198, 203, 213–214, 225, 350, 367, 412, 420, 431, 435

Public officials, 225, 420, 435; *et vide* Professional classes

*Pulham St Mary Magdalene (Norfolk), 105, 443, 444

Puritanism, evidences of, 36, 65, 81, 87, 91, 172, 175, 181, 201, 231, 240, 249, 278, 324, 326, 336, 341, 343, 356, 361–362, 377, 382, 383, 384–385, 396, 397, 413, 424, 426, 433

*Quainton (Bucks), 61, 75, 95, 441

Quakers, 248, 398

*Quarrendon (Bucks), 53, 61

Quarries, 216

*Queen Anne's Hospital, Newport Pagnell, 46

*Queen Elizabeth's Hospital, Buckingham, 44, 55

*Queens' College, Cambridge, 255, 350–351

*Queen's College, Oxford, 358

Radcliffe, Sir George, 341

*Radnage (Bucks), 70

Rampton (Notts), 333

Ramsden, Henry, 326, 395

Raskelf (Yorks), 285, 327

*Rastrick (Yorks), 340, 395

Ravenspur (Yorks), 254

*Rawdon (Yorks), 259, 277, 291, 381, 399

*Rawmarsh (Yorks), 238, 332

Ray River (Bucks), 51

*Raynham, East (Norfolk), 108, 110–111, 199

*Raynham, South (Norfolk), 108

*Raynham, West (Norfolk), 108

*Redenhall (Norfolk), 188, 190, 443, 444

Redman, George, 117

"Reformation, Age of" (1541–1560), 25, 93, 220–221, 438, 439, 440; charities for:
education, 299–300, 301, 311, 315–316
municipal uses, 295

poor, 34, 99, 114, 227, 252, 257
religion, 60, 69–70, 173, 175, 181, 182, 186, 363, 364, 376, 386, 388
social rehabilitation, 282
total benefactions by classes, 205, 210, 423, 425, 427, 428

Refugees, 29, 90, 398

Religious uses, benefactions by classes, 84–87 *passim*, 204–213 *passim*, 422–436 *passim*; benefactions of women, 28, 225; total benefactions for, 25, 26, 60, 74, 78, 93, 94, 193, 198, 219–222 *passim*, 362, 404, 406, 407, 409, 413, 417, 438–443, 446–448; *et vide*, 360–361, 437

"Revolutionary era" (1641–1660), 26, 94, 195, 222, 438, 439, 440; charities for:
education, 300, 301, 341, 348, 355
municipal uses, 148, 295, 298
poor, 40, 100, 114, 128, 228, 243–244, 252, 274
religion, 60, 174, 175, 182, 363, 376, 386, 389
social rehabilitation, 283, 285, 288

total benefactions by classes, 206, 207, 210, 424, 426, 427, 428

*Richmond (Yorks), 246, 271, 290, 291, 317–318, 346, 356, 359, 369, 377, 448, 451

*Ripley (Yorks), 246, 447, 449

Riplingham, William, 255

*Ripon (Yorks), 244, 246, 247, 249–250, 257, 289, 294, 303, 342, 344, 354, 355, 369, 390, 392, 447, 449

*Ripponden (Yorks), 340, 382

*Riston, Long (Yorks), 340

Roads, repair of, 148, 296–297; *et vide* Municipal uses

*Rochdale (Lancs), 169

Rochester, 194
*Rockland St Peter (Norfolk), 188
Rodes, Sir Godfrey, 398
Rodes Hall, Bradford, 379
Rokeby, William, Archbishop
    of Dublin, 371
*Romaldkirk (Yorks), 327
*Rome, 201, 342, 416
*Rossington (Yorks), 343
*Rotherham (Yorks), 216, 236, 238,
    241, 292, 304–305, 382, 447,
    449
Rotherhithe (Surrey), 39
*Rothley (Leics), 236
*Rothwell (Yorks), 350, 370, 447,
    450
*Roxby (Yorks), 394
Royal Latin School, Buckingham,
    53
*Royston (Yorks), 278, 279, 292,
    303, 307, 350, 447, 450
*Rudham, East (Norfolk), 108
*Runcton, North (Norfolk), 107,
    108, 307
*Rushford (Norfolk), 199, 443
*Rushworth (Norfolk), 151, 166
*Rushworth College, 145, 151
*Rutland, County of, 286
*Ryburgh, Little (Norfolk), 162
*Ryther (Yorks), 251, 256, 447,
    450

*Saham Toney (Norfolk), 126,
    161, 443, 444
*St Andrew's, Norwich, 189
*St Catharine's College, Cam-
    bridge, 167, 358
*St Giles' Hospital, Norwich,
    115–119, 133, 135, 154
*St John, Hospital of, High
    Wycombe, 53, 54
*St John's College, Cambridge,
    127, 170, 249, 255, 272, 307,
    308, 309, 320, 334, 343, 351,
    352, 353, 354, 355, 358, 360,
    377
*St John the Baptist, Hospital of,
    Ripon, 257

*St Leonard's Hospital, York, 253,
    372
St Martin Vintry, London, 255
*St Mary Bishophill Hospital,
    York, 279, 360
St Mary Magdalen, Hospital,
    Ripon, 257
*St Mary Magdalen, York, 368
St Mary's Hospital, Great
    Yarmouth, 155
St Mary's Hospital, King's Lynn,
    123
St Mary's Monastery, York, 301
*St Michael Coslany, Norwich,
    189
St Michael's Hospital, Well, 355
St Nicholas, Hospital of,
    Pontefract, 302
St Nicholas Acon, London, 308
*St Oswald's, Nostell Priory, 391
St Paul, Sir George, 317
St Peter's School, York, 301–302
*St Saviour's, York, 372
*St Stephen, Norwich, 189–190
*Sall (Norfolk), 162, 177
*Saltmarshe (Yorks), 288
Sancton (Yorks), 283, 329, 446,
    449
*Sandal Magna (Yorks), 236, 291–
    292, 368, 378–379, 446, 450
*Sand Hutton (Yorks), 377, 448,
    451
*Sandtoft (Lincs), 398
Sandys, Edwin, Archbishop of
    York, 167
Sandys, Sir William, 279
*Santon (Norfolk), 191
Savile, family of, 239, 251, 262,
    320, 325, 341, 368
*Sawrethaite Bridge (Yorks), 235
Sawston (Cambs), 358
*Saxlingham (Norfolk), 443, 444
*Saxthorpe (Norfolk), 190
*Saxton (Yorks), 334, 377, 447,
    451
*Scarborough (Yorks), 265, 273–
    274, 318, 398, 408
Scargill, Sir Robert, 232

*Scarning (Norfolk), 159, 443, 444
Scholarships, 58–59, 168–172,
    350–360; et vide Education
Schools, vide Education,
    Grammar Schools, etc.
*Scotland, 416
Scottow (Norfolk), 168
Scrope, John, Lord de Bolton, 151
*Seamer (Yorks), 338, 379
Secularism, evidences of, 25–26,
    27, 60, 84–85, 88, 93–94, 97,
    174, 175, 176, 198, 205, 221,
    363, 386–387, 432
*Sedbergh (Yorks), 234, 235, 297,
    308–309, 326, 329, 352, 353,
    447, 451
*Sedgeford (Norfolk), 159
Sedgwick, Adam, 329
*Selby (Yorks), 233, 297, 391, 447,
    450
*Sessay (Yorks), 316, 448, 450
*Shabbington (Bucks), 47, 79, 441
*Sharleston (Yorks), 247
*Sheffield (Yorks), 216, 241, 270,
    292, 298, 330, 344, 378, 395,
    396, 407, 447, 450
*Shenley (Bucks), 46, 69, 75, 441
*Sherburn (Yorks), 334, 377, 447,
    451
*Sheriff Hutton (Yorks), 264, 368
*Sherington (Bucks), 41, 69
*Shipden Chapel (Norfolk), 152
*Shipdham (Norfolk), 443, 444
*Shipton (Yorks), 279, 344, 345
*Shotesham (Norfolk), 188, 199
*Shropham (Norfolk), 102
*Shropshire, 80, 201, 416
Sigglesthorne (Yorks), 284–285
*Silkstone (Yorks), 238, 239, 245,
    347, 383–384
*Silsden (Yorks), 340
*Simpson (Bucks), 35, 75, 441
*Sinnington (Yorks), 279, 345
*Skelton (Yorks), 248
*Skipton (Yorks), 269, 314, 447,
    450
*Skipton in Craven (Yorks), 246
*Skircoat (Yorks), 276, 325

*Skirlaugh (Yorks), 382
*Slapton (Bucks), 47, 76
*Smithley (Yorks), 241
*Snaith (Yorks), 232, 270–271,
    331–332, 447, 450
*Snape (Yorks), 250, 286, 448, 450
Snelshall Priory, Whaddon, 69
*Snetterton (Norfolk), 127
Social rehabilitation, benefactions
    by classes, 84, 207, 210, 211,
    212, 422, 423, 425, 426, 427,
    432–435 passim; benefactions
    of women for, 28, 97, 225;
    definition, 437; total benefac-
    tions for, 25, 26, 49–50, 78,
    91–92, 93, 94, 130, 193, 198,
    218, 219, 221, 222, 282–285,
    404, 406, 407, 409, 413, 417,
    438–443, 446–448
*Somerset, benefactions for, 201;
    compared, 91, 96, 141, 197,
    218, 224, 294, 367, 374, 385,
    411, 415, 424, 431
*Soulbury (Bucks), 64–65, 69
Southampton, 323
*South Lopham (Norfolk), 100,
    443, 444
Southowram (Yorks), 275
*Southrepps (Norfolk), 181, 199
*South Skirlaugh (Yorks), 330
*South Walsham (Norfolk), 187
*Sowerby (Yorks), 234, 267, 324,
    383
*Sowerby Bridge (Yorks), 394
*Spaldington (Yorks), 372
Spofforth (Yorks), 368
*Sporle (Norfolk), 444
*Sproatley (Yorks), 263
*Sprotbrough (Yorks), 241, 368,
    447, 450
*Sprowston (Norfolk), 125, 443,
    444
Stade, Germany, 272
*Staffordshire, 416
*Stainborough (Yorks), 238, 384,
    447, 450
Staincross (Yorks), 409
*Stainland (Yorks), 251

Stamford (Lincs), 234–235, 297
*Stanfield (Norfolk), 188
*Stanhoe (Norfolk), 162
Stanhope, Sir John, 385
Stanhope, Sir Michael, 108
Stanley (Yorks), 320
*Stannington (Yorks), 343, 381, 399
Stapleton, Sir Brian, 370, 390
Stapleton, Sir Robert, 385
Statistical tables:
  General:
    Amounts by decades for municipal purposes and tax relief, 144
    Amounts given in pre-Reformation era, 205
    Average benefactions in the several counties, 419
    Charitable endowments in principal cities, 194
    Percentage of women donors and their total gifts, 96, 224
    Proportions for care of church fabric, 385
    Proportions of total charitable funds derived from London gifts, 197
    Proportions of total charitable wealth provided for other counties, 415
    Total of benefactions made to the monasteries, 374
  Buckinghamshire:
    Analysis of the social status of donors, 81
    Benefactions to other counties, 80
    Parishes decisively affected by London gifts, 79
    Parishes with endowments for poor exceeding £400, 441
    Parishes with endowments of upwards of £400, 75–76
    Proportions provided for the several charitable heads by the county and by London, 78

    Total of benefactions, 438
  Norfolk:
    Analysis of the social status of donors, 203
    Benefactions to other counties, 201
    Parishes decisively affected by London gifts, 199
    Parishes with charitable endowments exceeding £400, 442–443
    Parishes with substantial charities relatively unaffected by London gifts, 444–445
    Proportions provided for the several charitable heads by the county and by London, 198
    Total of benefactions, 439
  Yorkshire:
    Analysis of the social status of donors, 420
    Analysis of the social status of women donors and their relative generosity, 225
    Benefactions to other counties, 416, 417
    Contributions of the professional classes, 435
    Parishes decisively affected by London gifts, 457
    Parishes with charitable endowments exceeding £400, 446–448
    Parishes with substantial charities relatively unaffected by London gifts, 449–450
    Proportions provided for the several charitable heads by the county and by London, 413
    Total of benefactions, 440
    Totals compared for the county as a whole and for parishes, 404

*Steeton (Yorks), 340
*Stewkley (Bucks), 32, 69, 70
*Stiffkey (Norfolk), 162
Stillingfleet (Yorks), 391
*Stoke Goldington (Bucks), 69
*Stokenchurch (Bucks), 70
*Stoke Poges (Bucks), 29, 41, 69, 75, 441
Stokesley (Yorks), 249, 398
Stone (Bucks), 59
*Stony Stratford (Bucks), 35, 39, 45, 51, 55, 68, 441
*Stow Bardolph (Norfolk), 126–127, 187, 443, 444
*Stowe (Bucks), 64, 69
Stratton (Norfolk), 443
"Stuart Period, Early" (1601–1640), 26, 94, 221–222, 438, 439, 440; charities for: education, 52–53, 150, 300, 301, 328, 338–339, 354, municipal uses, 148, 295, 297
poor, 37, 42, 45–46, 99–100, 106, 114, 125–128, 227–228, 235, 243, 252, 265, 274
religion, 60, 174, 175, 182, 185, 186, 363, 376, 386, 389
social rehabilitation, 283, 285, 287–288
total benefactions by classes, 83, 86, 206, 207, 210, 423–424, 426, 427, 428
*Studley (Oxon), 38, 48
Studley (Yorks), 270
*Sturton (Notts), 232
Suffield, Walter, Bishop of Norwich, 115
*Suffolk, County of, benefactions for, 80, 113, 121, 201, 416; et vide 148, 197
*Surrey, County of, 80, 201, 416
Sussex, County of, 356
*Sutton (Yorks), 241
Sutton's Hospital, London, 356
*Swaffham (Norfolk), 115, 147, 177, 183, 443, 444
*Swanbourne (Bucks), 69, 71

*Swannington (Norfolk), 199
*Swanton Morley (Norfolk), 164
*Swine (Yorks), 446, 449
Swinfield, Thomas, 242
*Swinton (Yorks), 343, 353
Sykes, William, 245

Tables, vide Statistical Tables
Tackley (Oxon), 234
*Tacolneston (Norfolk), 189, 443, 445
*Tadcaster (Yorks), 216, 259, 277, 291, 315, 447, 451
Talbot, Henry, Lord, 278
Talman, John, 163
Tamworth (Staffs), 343
*Tankersley (Yorks), 247
*Tattenhoe (Bucks), 46, 69
Taunton (Somerset), 17, 194
Tax-relief, 143–145, 247
*Terrington (Norfolk), 187
*Terrington (Yorks), 234
Thame (Oxon), 38
*Thetford (Norfolk), 110, 113, 121, 122, 135, 146, 157, 193, 370, 443, 445
Thirsk (Yorks), 229, 290
*Thorganby (Yorks), 233
*Thormanby (Yorks), 285
*Thornham (Norfolk), 158
*Thornhill (Yorks), 244, 245, 262, 294, 341, 343, 390, 447, 450
*Thornton (Yorks), 234, 322, 447, 450
*Thornton Dale (Yorks), 279, 345, 448
Thorp Arch (Yorks), 233
*Thorpe Audlin (Yorks), 245
*Thorpe Market (Norfolk), 181
Threapland (Yorks), 322
Threxton (Norfolk), 126, 160–161
Throckmorton, Sir Thomas, 54
Thurgoland (Yorks), 347
*Tibenham (Norfolk), 144–145, 183
*Tickhill (Yorks), 260, 304
*Tideswell (Derbyshire), 260, 316

*Tilney (Norfolk), 158, 187, 443, 445
Tilson, Henry, Bishop of Elphin, Ireland, 399
*Titchwell (Norfolk), 158
Tofts, West (Norfolk), 128
Tollerton (Yorks), 268
*Topcliffe (Yorks), 229, 312, 448, 451
Topcroft (Norfolk), 128
Topham, John, 322
*Tottington (Norfolk), 187
Townshend, Sir John, 111, 162
Tradesmen, 28, 81, 87, 98, 198, 202, 203, 210, 225, 349, 412, 420, 433–434
*Tring (Herts), 31, 36, 65
*Trinity Church, Hull, 255, 275, 296, 392, 393
*Trinity Church, York, 370
*Trinity College, Cambridge, 36, 59, 107, 167, 169, 273, 359, 379
*Trinity College, Dublin, 359
*Trinity College, Oxford, 244, 353
*Trinity Hospital, York, 272–273
*Trinity House, Hull, 240–241, 266, 271–272
*Trinity House, Scarborough, 265
*Trowse Milgate, Norwich, 134
*Tuddenham, East (Norfolk), 146
Tunis, 105
Tunstall, Sir Thomas, 391
*Tunstead, Hundred of (Norfolk), 160
"Turkish" captives, 356
*Turville (Bucks), 67, 69
Tyrewhitt, Sir William, 238

*Universities, support of, 166, 357; et vide Cambridge University, Colleges [by name], Education, Oxford University
*University College, Oxford, 59–60, 245, 322, 353, 355, 379
Unknown status, donors of, 82, 88, 91, 98, 202, 203, 213, 225, 413, 419, 420, 436

*Upton (Norfolk), 185
Urban donors, 202, 419; et vide Burghers

Vane, Henry, 275
Vermuyden, Cornelius, 398
Vernatti, Sir Philibert, 398
Villiers, George, 408

Waddersome (Yorks), 331
*Waddesdon (Bucks), 47, 55, 61, 62, 69, 71, 75, 441
*Waddington (Yorks), 391
*Wakefield (Yorks), charities for:
    education, 319–321, 328
    municipal uses, 297
    poor, 231, 232, 233–234, 239, 248, 257, 262–263, 266, 276, 293, 297
    religion, 248, 371, 384, 392
    social rehabilitation, 285, 293
    total benefactions for, 447, 451
    et vide 216, 233, 280, 292, 321, 391, 407, 414, 415, 419
*Wales (Yorks), 237
*Walkeringham (Notts), 259
*Walkington (Yorks), 230
Walloons, 90; et vide Refugees
*Walpole (St Peter and St Andrew) (Norfolk), 127, 443, 445
*Walsingham (Norfolk), 122, 123, 131
*Walton (Bucks), 55–56, 57
*Walton, East (Norfolk), 107, 108, 145
Wandesford, Sir George, 289
Wandon, vide Wavendon
Warde, Sir Roger, 391
*Warmfield (Yorks), 247, 259, 279, 291, 322, 346, 447, 450
*Warton (Lancs), 329
*Warwickshire, 80, 416
*Wath (Yorks), 289, 353
*Wath-upon-Dearne (Yorks), 289, 342–343
*Watton (Norfolk), 126, 161, 443, 445

Watts, Richard, 273
*Wauldby (Yorks), 382
*Wavendon (Bucks), 55, 57
Waveney River, 148
Wayland, Hundred of (Norfolk), 126
*Well (Yorks), 250, 286, 311, 339, 355, 376, 448, 450
Welles, Sir Richard, Lord Willoughby, 371
Welles, Sir Robert, 371
*Wendover (Bucks), 23, 30, 38, 75, 441
*Wensleydale (Yorks), 327
Wensum River, 147
*Wentbridge (Yorks), 245
Wentworth, Thomas, 250, 251, 290
Wentworth, Thomas, Earl of Strafford, 245, 273, 290
*Wentworth (Yorks), 394
*Westcott (Bucks), 62
Westgate (Yorks), 257
*Westmorland, County of, 201, 297, 358, 399, 416, 417
Westphaling, Herbert, Bishop of Hereford, 355
West Riding (Yorks), 18, 214, 268, 282, 350, 352, 362, 385, 388, 389, 391, 393, 395, 397, 402, 403, 405-410 passim, 414, 415, 418, 425, 446-447, 449-450, 451
*Wexham (Bucks), 69
*Whaddon (Bucks), 40, 69
Whalley, Abbot of, vide York, Thomas
Wheatley (Yorks), 281
*Wheldrake (Yorks), 360, 446, 449
*Whitby (Yorks), 216, 232, 233, 278, 291, 298-299, 448, 451
*White Friars, Hull, 254
*Whitkirk (Yorks), 232, 255, 308, 447, 450
Whitmore, William, 239
*Wibsey (Yorks), 379, 398
Wickham, William, Bishop of Winchester, 355

*Wiggenhall St Mary (Norfolk), 122
*Wighill (Yorks), 385, 390
*Wighton (Norfolk), 123, 199, 443
*Wilby (Norfolk), 128
Williams, John, Bishop of Lincoln, 398
Wills, 223-224, 231-232
*Wilton (Yorks), 256, 395, 448, 450
*Wiltshire, 80, 201
*Winch, East (Norfolk), 107, 118
Winch, West (Norfolk), 108
Winchester, 194, 323
Windsor (Berks), 51, 55, 358
*Winestead (Yorks), 392
*Winfarthing (Norfolk), 147, 443, 445
*Wing (Bucks), 29, 38, 44, 75, 441
Wingfield, Sir Robert, 151
*Wingrave (Bucks), 38
Winston (Norfolk), 112
*Wistow (Yorks), 288
*Withernsea (Yorks), 400
*Withernwick (Yorks), 237
*Witton (Norfolk), 113
*Witton (Yorks), 448, 450
*Wiveton (Norfolk), 103-104, 199
Wolsey, Cardinal Thomas, 308, 401
*Wolverton (Bucks), 32
Wombwell (Yorks), 239, 394
Women donors, 27-33, 96-98, 202, 224-225, 278-279
*Wooburn (Bucks), 75, 441
Wood, Sir Robert, 117
*Wood Dalling (Norfolk), 113
*Woodhall in Holderness (Yorks), 259
*Woodkirk (Yorks), 264
*Woolley (Yorks), 391, 409
Worcester, 194
Worcestershire, benefactions for, 416; compared, 23, 96, 197, 224, 294, 374, 376, 385, 411, 431
Workhouses, 50, 60, 137-140, 285, 433; et vide Social rehabilitation

*Worsborough (Yorks), 241, 336, 384
*Worstead (Norfolk), 90, 177–178, 443, 445
*Worthing (Norfolk), 128
Wortley (Yorks), 247, 248
*Wotton-under-Edge (Glos), 29
*Wragby (Yorks), 327
Wray, Sir Christopher, 317, 336
Wray, Sir John, 268
Wrenthorpe manor (Yorks), 371
Wrotham (Kent), 241
Wroxham manor (Norfolk), 125
Wyatt, William, 262
*Wycombe (Great, High, West), 23, 24, 37, 44, 53, 54, 70, 73, 75, 76, 79, 441; et vide St John, Hospital of
*Wymondham (Norfolk), 133, 156, 169, 199, 225, 443
Wytham, William, 279

*Yarm (Yorks), 319
*Yarmouth, Great (Norfolk), charities for:
education, 140, 155
municipal uses, 149, 170
poor, 100, 125, 160
religion, 122
social rehabilitation, 102, 139, 140
total benefactions for, 193, 443, 445
et vide 90, 108, 109, 146, 149, 166, 201, 209
*Yelverton (Norfolk), 190
Yeomanry, 21, 28, 31, 81, 84–85, 98, 166, 201, 202, 203, 207, 215, 225, 349, 367, 381, 417, 418, 420, 426–427
York, Richard, Duke of, 371
York, Thomas, Abbot of Whalley, 255
York (Yorks), 194, 215, 216, 285, 372, 418; charities for:
education, 251, 279, 311, 343, 370
municipal uses, 230, 233, 268, 291, 293, 295, 297, 342
poor, 229, 230, 233, 237, 240, 244, 248, 253, 255, 268, 272–273, 274, 275, 279, 282, 291, 295, 310, 377
religion, 229, 230, 255, 268, 275, 284, 295, 358, 369, 370, 372, 377, 378, 384, 386, 390, 391, 393, 401
social rehabilitation, 229, 230, 232, 233, 234, 237, 248, 255, 268, 272, 279, 284, 287, 291, 292, 293, 295, 327, 355
total benefactions for, 405, 406, 448, 451; et vide 17, 19, 266, 280, 326, 345, 349, 376, 407, 432; Bootham Hospital; St Leonard's Hospital
Yorkshire, benefactions from other counties for, 58, 80, 81, 113, 201; compared, 64, 96, 114, 168, 176, 197, 202, 204; general discussion of, 214–436; total benefactions for, 20, 440, 446–448, 449–450, 451; et vide 18–19, 21, 217

Index of Donors

(Biographical data appear on pages indicated in bold type)

Abbott, George, **343**
Acham, Anthony, 242
Ackroyd, William, **351**
Adams, Theophilus, 124
Adryanson, Brand, 255
Agar, Beatrix, **272**
Agar, Thomas, **272**, 287
Agard, Katherine, 31, 35
Alcock, John, Bishop of Ely, 305–306
Allee, William, 110
Allen, William, 163
Almond, Nicholas, 38–39
Ambler, Robert, 392
Amies, Christopher, 162
Amies, Robert, 162
Amys, Thomas, 183, 189
Angos, Richard, 188
Anguish, Edmund, **132**
Anguish, John, **132**
Anguish, Thomas, **131**–132, 134
Anguish, William, 132
Anne, Sir William, 41
Annesley, James, 41
Annison, Robert, 113
Ardys, Edmund, 41
Armistead, William, **313**–314
Armitage, Thomas, **287**
Armyne, Mary, **278**
Ashton, Hugh, 354, 358
Aston, Nicholas, 66
Atkinson, Henry, 244, 294
Awnflys, William, 178–179

Bacon, Henry, 120
Bagwith, Luke, 278
Bailey, Richard, 232
Bainbridge, Christopher, **358**
Baker, John, 41
Baldwin, Agnes, 32

Baldwin, Sir John, 65
Baldwin, William, 41
Ball, John, 41, 67
Bampton, Jeffrey, 55–56
Banaster, Thurstan, **320**
Bancroft, Thomas, 191
Bank, Richard, 313
Bankes, John, 340
Barker, John, 100
Barker, Robert, 51
Barnham, William, 135
Baron, Robert, **136**
Barowe, Thomas, 400
Barrett, Christopher, 118
Basfurth, Thomas, **285**
Bate, Leonard, 262–263
Bates, William, 51
Bathurst, Dr John, 250, 291, 346, 350, 356
Batty, Ralph, 369
Bayles, Brian, 232–**233**
Beane, John, 391
Beaumont, Sir Richard, 378–**379**
Beckwith, Roger, **297**
Bedford, John, 34, 51
Bedingfield, Sir Edmond, 183
Bedingfield, Edmund, **105**
Beke, Elizabeth, 32
Belasis, Anthony, 284
Bennett, Agnes, 45
Bennett, Ambrose, 39
Bennett, John, 45
Bennett, Mirabell, 133
Bennett, Sir Simon, 39, 51, 59–60
Benson, Peter, **331**
Benson, Richard, 250
Berkeley, Jane, Lady, **108**, 111
Berry, Prudence, **336**–337
Besson, Anthony, **326**, 327
Bethell, Sir Hugh, 268

Bickley, Thomas, **59**
Biningley, James, 315
Bisby, William, 184
Bishop, Alice, 136
Blake, Joan, 115
Blake, Simon, 115, 147, 177
Blakeney, Dame Joan, 119
Bland, Sir Thomas, **268**
Blomefield, Augustine, 118, 135
Bloss, Prudence, 128, 134
Blythe, Anthony, 233–234
Bokenham, Thomas, **177**
Bole, Thomas, 145
Boleyn, Sir William, **179**
Boller, Thomas, 61
Bolles, Dame Mary, **279**, 291–292, 347
Bolton, Roger, 400
Bond, Richard, 139, 163–164
Bonfellow, Henry, 112
Booth, Lawrence, Archbishop of York, 357, 368
Borage, John, 171
Borlase, Sir William, 56
Bosville, Godfrey, **396**
Bosville [Boswell], Nicholas, 370
Bowes, Eleanor, 271
Boynton, Thomas, 394
Boys, Lady Jane, 31
Bradbury, Edmond, 67
Bradford, Walter, 371
Bradshaw, Dame Joan, 30
Branthwaite, William, **170–171**
Breary, William, 293
Brereton, William, 128
Brigg, John, 325
Briggs, Thomas, 177
Bright, Stephen, **378**, 396–397
Brinkhurst, John, 45
Broadley, Matthew, **249**, 344
Broadley, Michael, 310
Brockhouse, Ellen, 31
Brooke, William, 136–137
Brookhouse, Edmund, 254
Brotherick, Elizabeth, 261–262
Brown, Philip, 122
Brudenell, Joan, 61
Bullock, Robert, 163

Bulmer, Sir William, 256, 395
Bulwer, Edward, **113**
Bunting, Richard, 159
Burley, John, 284, 327
Burton, William, 264
Bury, John, 153
Bury, Thomas, 355
Butler, Robert, **127**
Bynnes, John, 310

Calam, Ursula, 274
Calthorp, James, 185
Calthorp, Sir William, 188
Capel, Richard, 70
Carr, James, 306, 354
Carr, Richard, 307, 354
Carre, John, 228–229
Carter, Alice, 32, 44
Cartwright, Thomas, 235, 354
Casson, Samuel, 244, 294
Caster, John, 119
Cave, Anthony, 54, 58
Cave, Thomas, 266, 328
Cavendish, William, Earl of Devonshire, 39
Cawood, Stephen, 344, 381, 399
Cawood, Walter, 365
Cecil, Thomas, Earl of Exeter, **286**, 339
Chalfount, Christopher, 54
Chaloner, Robert, 55, 58, **331**
Chaloner, Thomas, 58
Charlesworth, Richard, 341–342
Cheyney, Lady Agnes, 64
Cheyney, Sir Francis, 36–37
Cheyney, Sir John, 36, 59, 65
Cheyney, Thomas, 36
Chibnall, Joan, 31
Childe, Jeffrey, 237
Cholmley, Sir Hugh, 298–299
Clapham, John, 266–**267**, 340
Clapham, William, 307
Clarkson, John, 318
Clay, Robert, 360
Cleaveland, William, 291
Clere, Sir Edward, **170**
Clere, Elizabeth, 100, 168

Clifford, Henry, first Earl of Cumberland, 297
Clifford, Henry, last Earl of Cumberland, 245
Clifford, Margaret, Dowager Countess of Cumberland, 269–270
Clifford family, 422
Clifton, Sir Gervase, 248
Clifton, William, 352
Clough, Michael, 308
Cockman, William, 44
Codd, Thomas, 117
Coleman, Edward, 171
Colich, Nicholas, 189
Collins, Daniel, 134
Collins, Martin, 229, 351
Comyn, Alvered, 391
Constable, Lady Catherine, 292–293, 353
Constable, Sir John, 263, 293, 319
Constable, Sir Marmaduke, 351
Conyers, George, 261
Conyers, Sir Richard, 368
Conyers, Thomas, 319
Conyers family, 408–409
Cook, Richard, 67
Cooke, Brian, 280–281, 346–347, 383
Cooke, Thomas, 318
Cooper, Walter, 187
Cootes, James, 183
Copley, William, 369
Corbett, Sir Miles, 125
Cory, Thomas, 117
Cotes, James, 398
Cottrell, James, 359, 377
Coulson, Christopher, 338, 379
Craske, Ann, 134–135
Craske, Robert, 134
Craven, Dame Elizabeth, 239, 329
Craven, John, Lord, 246, 290, 356
Craven, Sir William, 239, 246, 298, 328–329, 400
Cressy, Thomas, 107
Crofts, John, 390
Croke, Sir George, 38; widow of, 48

Croke, John, 37–38
Croke, Sir John (d. 1608), 38
Croke, Sir John (d. 1620), 38
Crokehay, William, 231, 259–260
Crome, Alice, 120
Crook, John, 344
Crosby, John, 318
Crosland, George, 319
Crosley, John, 401
Crowther, Brian, 236–237, 268, 325, 326
Crowther, Jane, 237, 267–268, 325, 340
Cudworth, Richard, 347
Cutler, Ellen, 238–239, 384
Cutler, Thomas, 238, 383–384
Cutting, William, 106

Dacres, Robert, 390
Dakin, John, 258
Damett, Thomas, 125
Darcy, John, Lord, 336
Darcy, Thomas, Lord, 255–256, 308
Darley, Alice, 332
Dawson, Thomas, 336
Day, William, 237
Dayrell, Dorothy, 31, 44
Daywell, Thomas, 183
Deane, Anne, 32
Debney, Robert, 134
Dehem, Tobias, 134
Dent, Leonard, 376–377
Denton, Dame Isabel, 29, 53
Dickinson, William, 244
Disley, Margaret, 32
Dixson, John, 259
Dormer, Lady Elizabeth, 29
Dormer, Sir John, 37
Dormer, Sir Robert (d.1552), 37
Dormer, Sir Robert (d.1616), 29, 37, 50
Dormer, Roger, 69
Dormer, William, 37
Doughty, Richard, 254
Doughty, Thomas, 143
Dowman, John, 307–308, 351–352
Drake, Edmund, 105

Drake, Sir William, 46
Drawswerde, Thomas, **370**
Drew, Thomas, 51
Duckett, Robert, 351
Duncombe, Alice, 35
Duncombe, William (c. 1576), 35
Duncombe, William (c. 1631), 35–36
Dunne, John, 288
Duplake, Richard, 184
Duvall, Percival, 64–65
Dyneley, Robert, **384–385**, 399
Dynham, John, 61
Dynham, Roger, 64

East, Agnes, 189
Elizabeth, Queen, 233
Ellill, William, 340
Ellingham, Jeffrey, 144, 187
Elliott, Thomas, 42–43
Ellis, Ralph, 334
Ellis, Thomas, **261**
Ellvis, John, 260
Elmer, William, 40, 57–58
Elsy, William, 119
Eltofts, Edmund, 309
Elwyn, Allan, 162
Elwyn, John, 120
Everard, Edward, 147
Evers, William, 370
Eyre, Anthony, 333

Fairfax, Sir Nicholas, **318**
Fane, Sir Francis, 333
Farrar, John, 273–274
Fauconberg, Thomas, Lord, **278**
Favour, John, 276, **323–326**; et vide 236, 267, 286, 360, 383, 395
Fawcett, Henry, 108–**109**, 118, 132, 161–162, 332, 396
Fawcett, William, **332**, 396
Feke, William, 123
Ferres [Ferries], Thomas, **240–241**, 271–272, 288, 296
Ferrour, Richard, 178
Fisher, Luke, 111
Fisher, Richard, 124
Fitzwilliam, Thomas, 368

Fletcher, Christopher, 263
Forman, John, 307, 350
Forster, Richard [or John], 243
Forster, Robert, 333
Foster, Robert, 186
Fourness, John, 383
Fox, Thwaytes, 273
Francke, Matthew, **250**, 280, 296
Franke, Thomas, 190
Frieston, John, 263, **264**, 280, 322, 353
Frost, Robert, 390
Fryar, Agnes, 32
Fuller, William, 184
Fullwood, Thomas, 261
Fulmerston, Sir Richard, 121–122, **157**

Gale, Mary, 295
Gardiner, Robert, 189
Garforthe, William, 327
Garratt, William, 105
Garrett, Emanuel, 132
Gascoigne, Margaret, Lady, 232
Gascoigne, Sir William, 391–392
Gee, William, 235–**236**, 265–266, 306, 377
Gilbert, John, 135
Gilliot, Sir John, **230**, 372
Girling, Richmond, 113
Gledhill, Sarah, **345–346**, 382
Gledhill, Thomas (d. 1607), 325
Gledhill, Thomas (d. 1657), 346, 382
Goffe, Edward, **126**, 160–161
Goldsmith, George, 311
Goldwell, James, Bishop of Norwich, 115–116, 178
Golland, Christopher, 260
Gooch, Christian, 127–128
Gooch, Thomas, 127–128, 133–134
Goodwin, Arthur, **47–48**
Goodwyn, Ralph, 184
Gostlin, John, **167–168**, 171
Gower, Ralph, **318**
Graunt, Francis, 320
Grave, Thomas, 105–106

Gray, Robert, 242
Green, Charles, 111–112
Green, Richard, 317
Greenaway, Ralph, 103–**104**
Greenwood, Charles, 244–**245**,
    294, 338, 341, 355–356
Greenwood, Richard, 264
Gregory, John, 234, 354
"Gregson, Mr", 355
Gresham, Edmond, **181**
Gresham, Sir John, **155**–156, 181,
    197–198
Gyfford, Roger, 62, 70
Gysburgh, John, **368**

Hagger, Robert, 327
Haigh, John, 381
Hall, Jane, **297**
Halley, Richard, 64
Hamelyn, John, 184
Hamerton, John, 262
Hampden, William, 65
Hansby, Ralph, **269**, 379
Hanson, John, 340
Hare, Nicholas, 187
Hare, Sir Ralph, 126–**127**
Harleston, Robert, 158
Harleston, Thomas, 121
Harman, Richard, **135**
Harmer, John, 119
Harper, Arthur, 241
Harris, Robert, 44–45
Harrison, John, 257–258, **277**, 298,
    314, 346, 382–383, 401–402
Harrison, Reginald, 234–235, 297,
    309
Harrison, William, 325–326
Harsnett, Samuel, Archbishop of
    York, 288, 335–336, 396
Hart, William, 293
Harte, Sir John, 329
Hastings, Edward, Lord, 29, **43**
Hastings, Sir Hugh, 368–369,
    389–390
Hastings, Lady Jane, 371
Hastings, Sir Thomas, 43
Hatton, Lady Elizabeth, 29
Hawes, Agnes, 32

Hawkesworth, Sir Richard, **250**
Head, Richard, 142
Hebblethwaite, Henry, **309**, 353
Hemingway, Robert, 325
Herring, Thomas, 133
Hesketh, Sir Thomas, **266**
Hewar, Thomas, 109–110
Heydon, Dame Anne, 119, 179–
    180
Heyhow, Richard, 120
Heyward, Edward, 112–113
Hicks, Elizabeth, 384
Hide, William, **249**, 344, 382
Higden, Brian, 352
Higgin, Anthony, 354
Higginson, Margaret, 162
Higginson, Rev. Robert, 45
Hildyard, Sir Christopher, **392**
Hildyard, Sir William, 269, 379
Hill, John, 330
Hillary, Joseph, **250**, 345
Hipwell, Michael, 45, 55
Hirnynge, John, 187
Hobart, Sir James, 119, **148–149**,
    189
Hobart, Dame Margery, 119
Hoby, Sir Thomas Posthumous,
    397–398
Hodgshon, Richard, 341
Hodgson, Phineas, **284**
Hogan, Robert, 121
Hogge, George, 401
Hogge, John, 325
Holgate, Robert, Archbishop of
    York, 258–259, 311–312
Hoot, Thomas, 190
Hopes, Rev. Thomas, **107–108**
Hopkinson, Ellen, 237, **267**, 325,
    340
Hoppay, Edward, 231
Hopton, Christopher, 314
Hopton, Sir Ingram, 382, 396
Horne, Cotton, **276**
Horseman, Timothy [or Gilbert],
    340
Hough, Walter, 177–178
Howard, Henry, Earl of North-
    ampton, 125

Howard, Richard, 183
Hungate, Robert, 334, 377–378
Hunt, Otho, 353
Husteler, Thomas, 306
Hustler, William, 337
Hutchinson, James, 342
Hutchinson, Thomas, 248–249
Hutton, Matthew, Archbishop of
    York, 329, 359, 377, 378
Hutton, Sir Timothy, 378
Hynd, Edmund, 260

Ingham, Nicholas, 187
Ingram, Sir Arthur, 275
Ingram, Joan, 61

Jackson, John, 246
Jannys, Robert, 101, 102, 146,
    147, 153
Jenkinson, Josias, 244–245, 275
Jenkinson, William, 245
Jermy, Sir John, 177
Jermyn, Thomas, 128–129
Jernegan, Sir Henry, 122
Johnson, Ann, 125–126
Jowell, John, 183
Juby, William, 164

Kaye, Arthur, 318
Kaye, Francis, 239
Kaye, John, 318
Kaye, Robert, 318
Kaye family, 319
Keresforth, Thomas, 347
Kiderminster, Sir John, 47
King, Roger, 187
Kirkeby, Thomas, 270
Kitchingman, Simon, 317
Knight, Geoffrey, 166
Knight, William, Bishop of Bath
    and Wells, 258, 314–315
Knowles, James, 269, 286
Knowles, John, 328
Knowles, Thomas, 257
Knyghton, Rev. Thomas, 47

Lake, John, 369–370
Lambert, Benjamin, 322

Langdale, Marmaduke, 283,
    329–330
Large, Thomas, 186
Laughton, Edmund, 333
Laycock, William, 340
Layton, Francis, 277, 290–291,
    381, 399
Layton, Thomas, 315
Lee, Sir Henry, 53–54
Lee, Richard, 61
Lee, Sir Robert, 61–62
Lee, William, 331
Leedes, Thomas, 284
Legard, John, 270
Legge, Thomas, 167
Legh, Thomas, 370
Le Grice, John, 186
Leighton, Isabel, 356
Le Strange, Roger, 179
Levynder, Richard, 66–67
Lewen, Agnes, 30
Lewin, William, 65
Lister, Sir John (d. 1641), 275
Lister, John (d. 1617), 286, 288,
    295–296
Lodge, Alice, 296
Lodge, Ralph, 356
Lonyson, John, 139
Love, Robert, 146
Lovell, Sir Thomas, 101
Lowden, John, 293–294
Lumley, Elizabeth, Viscountess,
    279, 311, 344–345, 356
Lupton, Roger, 308, 352, 353
Lynsey, Ralph, 329
Lynster, William, 144–145, 183

Magnus, Thomas, 316
Malby, Thomas, 147
Mallory, Dame Troth, 237–238
Manseur, Richard, 123
Marshall, George, 321
Marshall, Robert, 310
Marshall, Susanna, 240
Marsham, Joan, 137
Marsham, Robert, 137
Martin, Andrew, 132
Mason, Thomas, 184–185, 190

Matthew, Frances, 355
Maud, Isabel, **340**
Maud, John, 325, 340
Mauleverer, Edmund, 254
Mawde, Edward, 320
Mawdeslay, John, 259
Metcalf, Henry, 243
Metcalf, Robert, 247, 302, 360, 385
Metham, Francis, 234
Middleton, Anne, **279**, 291, 345
Middleton, Richard, 321
Midgeley, John, 254
Mitchell, William, 322
Moodie, Miles, 392
Moore, Gyles, 335
Moore, Robert, **334**
Moseley, Elizabeth, **384**
Moseley, Thomas, **378**, 384
Moulston, John, 228
Moundeford, Sir Edmund, **112**, 164
Mowde, Thomas, 310
Mowfett, Thomas, 233
Mowting, William, 107
Mundes, Roger, 105
Myrfin, John, 333

Nelson, Richard, 357–**358**
Nelson, Robert, 304
Nelson, William, 370
Nettleton, Robert, 272, 319
Nevile, Dame Alice, 254
Nevill, Dorothy, 286
Nevill, Sir John, Lord Latimer, 311, 376, 395
Nevill family, 408
Nicholls, Richard, 158, 187
Nix, Richard, Bishop of Norwich, 91, 169
Norgate, Nicholas, **153**
Norris, John, 178
Nutting, Edward, 128

Oglethorpe, Owen, Bishop of Carlisle, 259, 277, 290–291, 315
Okes, Robert, 305
Owner, Edward, 139–140, 155

Palmer, Henry, 185
Palmes, Richard, 303
Parke, Henry, 319
Parker, Agnes, 183
Parker, Matthew, Archbishop of Canterbury, 121, 158, 169, 355
Parker, Thomas, 117, 120, 169
Parkin, Thomas, 264
Parkins, Richard, 382
Parkinson, Thomas, 318
Parote, William, 264
Parrett, Charles, 57
Paslow, Francis, 309
Paston, Clement, **124**, 160
Paston, William, **103**, 104
Paston, Sir William (d. 1554), 103
Paston, Sir William (d. 1610), **160**
Paynter, George, 262
Pearson, Thomas, **369**
Peart, Henry, 181–182
Peckover, Alexander, 135
Peckover, Matthew, 132
Peirson, John, 126
Pelham, Dame Dorothy, 44
Pelham, Sir Edward, 54
Pembroke, Anne, Countess of, 399
Pennyman, James, 249
Percy, Henry, Earl of Northumberland, **229**
Periam, Lady Elizabeth, 29–30, 58–59, 162
Perrott, John, 61
Perse, Stephen, 161
Peterson, Peter, 107
Pettus, Thomas, **142**
Peyrs, John, 146
Phillip, Matthew, **391**
Pigott, Thomas (d. 1520), 34–35
Pigott, Thomas (d. 1564), 70
Pigott, Thomas (deed 1573), 35
Pilkington, Sir Roger, 190
Pipe, Nicholas, 135
Pitt, Thomas, 41
Plaistowe, Thomas, 67
Plaxton, William, **343**
Potter, William, 179
Pratt, Thomas, 38
Preston, William, 323

Proo, John, 146
Pudsay, Henry, **369**
Pullein, Mary, 380
Pursglove, Robert, Bishop of Hull, 260, 316
Pye, Anne, 126
Pye, Thomas, 126
Pygot, Richard, **357**, 371
Pygott, Robert, 122
Pym, John, 64
Pymond, Richard, 230–231, 297
Pynnes, Alexander, 183–184

Rabanke, Samuel, 241–242
Radcliffe, John, 369
Radcliffe, Robert, Earl of Sussex, 163
Rainey, John, **241**, 336, 384
Ramsden, William, 319
Ramsey, William, 189
Rands, Richard, **244**, 341
Ratcliffe, Robert, 261
Rawson, John, 310
Rawson, Lawrence, 314
Rayner, Gilbert, 340
Rede, Sir Bartholomew, **152**
Rede, Peter, **104–105**
Redman, George, **117**
Reeve, Nicholas, 133
Remington, Nathaniel, 133
Remington, Thomas, 340
Rennick, Edward, **287**
Richard, Nicolas, **371**
Rickman, Robert, 145
Ripley, Hugh, **289**
Riplingham, John, **255**
Roberts, William, **170**
Robinson, Edmund, 377
Robinson, William (d. 1616), **293**
Robinson, William (d. 1635), 312
Rodes, Sir Edward, **398**
Rogers, Edmund, **245–246**, 342
Rogers, Katherine, 102–103
Rogers, Thomas, 321
Rogers, William, 102
Rokeby, Dame Joan, 352
Rokeby, Sir Richard, 352, 401

Rokeby, William, Archbishop of Dublin, 401
Rollinson, Robert, 298, 330
Rookby, Robert, 261
Rooks, Richard, 395
Rooks, William (d. 1518), 394
Rooks, William (c. 1632), 379, 398
Rools [Rooks], Cecilia, 67
Rotherham, John, 52
Rotherham, Thomas, Archbishop of York, 273, 304–305, 357, 369
Rous, Francis, 59
Royd, Richard, 237
Rugge, Francis, **118**
Rugge, William, 132
Rycroft, John, 230
Ryther, Thomas, 256

Sagar, Othoneus, 259
Sagge, William, **296**
St Paul, Thomas, 254
Salter, David [Daniel], 47
Salter, Thomas, 119–120
Saltonstall, Sir Richard, 235, 324–325
Saltonstall, Robert, 324
Savage, Thomas, Archbishop of York, 229
Savile, Elizabeth, **321**
Savile, George (d. 1593), **320**, 321
Savile, George (d. 1595), 285, 320
Savile, Henry (d. 1483), 368
Savile, Henry (c. 1525), 401
Savile, Henry (d. 1569), **262**
Savile, Sir Henry (d. 1622), 359, 379, 447
Savile, Sir John (c. 1597), 324, **325**, 340, 395
Savile, Sir John (c. 1622), 395
Savile, John, of Methley (d. 1659), 250–**251**
Savile, Sir Thomas, 395
Savile, William, 390
Sawdrie, Anthony, 288–289, 342–343
Scales, Christopher, 231
Scott, Christopher, 337–**338**
Scott, John, 69

Scott, Sir Richard, 273
Scrope, Lady Anne, 151-152, 166, 168
Scrope, Lady Philadelphia, 30
Sea, Sir Martin of the, 254
Secker, William, 159
Sedgwick, James, 234, 353
Segrave, Robert, 149
Sever, William, 390
Seymour, John, 51-52
Shaw, John, 241
Sheffield, Thomas, 313
Sheffield, William, 313
Sherwood, William, 230
Shirecliffe, Margaret, 246
Shirecliffe, Thomas, 246
Shute, Josias, 354, 355
Sidney, Sir Henry, 164
Sidney, Thomas, 122
Simpson, Elizabeth, 123, 158
Sippardson, vide Kitchingman
Slater, Robert, 304
Slinger, Robert, 347
Small, William, 164-165
Smallpece, Francis, 134
Smith, George, 243
Smith, Gregory, 123
Smith, Henry, 110
Smith, Joan, 107
Smith, John, 190
Smith, Robert (d. 1506), 179
Smith, Robert (c. 1559), 145
Smith, Robert (d. 1596), 123, 158
Smith, Robert (d. 1634), 134
Smith, Thomas, 330
Smithby, William, 242
Smithson, William, 298, 337
Smyth, William, 184
Somerscales, Richard, 239
Soothill, Henry, 371
Southwell, Sir Richard, 117, 120
Spencer, William, 378, 396-397
Spicer, Thomas, 391
Spivey, John, 333
Spoone, Richard, 343-344, 381, 399
Sprignell, Luke, 236
Sproxton, Dorothy, 239
Spurlynge, Thomas, 121

Stafford, Thomas, 46
Stalon, John, 189
Stalon, Stephen, 189
Stanton, Laurence, 309
Stapleton, Sir Miles, 381-382, 396
Stapleton, Thomas, 370
Stapleton, Sir William, 390-391
Steward, Augustine, 117
Stillington, Robert, Bishop of Bath and Wells, 305
Stocke, Alexander, 335
Stockes, John, 273
Stokes, Matthew, 171
Strangwayes, Sir James, 391
Stringer, Thomas, 247
Strutte, Thomas, 185
Stubb, Edmund, 168
Stubb, Richard, 158-159
Sturdivant, Matthew, 159
Suckling, Sir John, 111
Sugate, Anthony, 190
Sutcliffe, Anthony, 392
Sutton, Thomas, 237
Swinburne, Henry, 239-240
Sydall, Michael, 280, 345
Sykes, Richard, 286, 397
Sykes, William, 248
Symkinson, Thomas, 315

Talbot, Edward, Eighth Earl of Shrewsbury, 238
Talbot, George, Sixth Earl of Shrewsbury, 292
Talbot, Gilbert, Seventh Earl of Shrewsbury, 270
Talbot family, 422
Taylor, Richard, 185
Taylor, William, 187
Teasdale, George, 247
Tempest, Richard, 391
Tempest, Sir Thomas, 394
Tenant, Cicely, 247-248
Tenant, Henry, 354, 355
Tenwinter, Christopher, 148
Terry, John, 141-142, 145
Terry, Richard, 161
Tesmond, Thomas, 132
Thackray, Thomas, 294

Thistlethwaite, Thomas, 242
Thompson, Thomas, **358**
Thoresby, Thomas, 152–**153**, 190
Thornhill, Robert, 259
Threscrosse, Geoffrey, 370
Thurston, Hammond, 132
Thwaites, Richard, 271
Tipping, William, 47
Titley, John, 139, 169–170
Tocketts, Roger, 260
Toller, Thomas, 395–396
Tolye, John, 133, **134**
Toune, Richard, 371
Townshend, Lady Anne, **162**
Townshend, Sir Roger, 108, **110–III**
Tristram, Robert, 261
Trotter, Hugh, **350–351**

Underwood, William, 249–**250**, 344

Valentia, Lord Viscount, 233
Vaux, John, 378
Vavasour, Henry, 394
Vavasour, John, **229**, 365, 372
Vavasour, Richard, 232
Vavasour, Robert, 327
Vavasour, William, 328, 379–380
Verney, Sir Ralph, 24, 47

Wade, Agnes, 313
Wade, Robert, 234, 324
Walker, John, 347
Walker, Miles, 187
Walker, William, 258
Wall, Abraham, 289, 338
Waller, Nicholas, 270–271, 331–332
Walter, William, 147
Wandesford, Christopher, **289**–290
Ward, Mary, **342**
Ward, Thomas, 297
Warwick, Anne, Countess of, 28–29, 45
Warwick, Frances, Countess of, 317
Waterhouse, Isaac, 273, 325
Waterhouse, John, 325
Waterhouse, Nathaniel, 276, 290, 380

Watson, Stephen, **251**
Watter, Sir Robert, 268, 295, 377
Weddall, William, 237
Wedon, Richard, 47
Weedon, Thomas (d. 1561), 47
Weedon, Thomas (d. 1624), **46**–47, 48
Wentworth, Thomas (d. 1524), 370
Wentworth, Thomas (*c.* 1546), **394**
West, John (d. 1529), 370–371
West, John (d. 1659), 333
Westby, Henry, 382
Westropp, James, 264
Wharton, Sir Michael, **392–393**
Whitacre, John, 166–167
White, Bartholomew, 188
White, Sir Thomas, 292
Whittingham, Robert, 136
Whittington, Richard, **359–360**
Williamson, Joan, 119
Wilson, Henry, 381
Wilson, Thomas, 332
Wilton, Henry, 183
Wilton, Richard, 128
Windham, Sir Thomas, 186
Windle, Robert, **234**, 322, 337
Windsor, Edward, Lord, 43, 69
Witham, Thomas, **368**
Withnale, Clare, 189
Wombwell, Roger, 394
Wood, Augustine, 143
Wood, Barney, 238
Wood, Edmund, 116, **155**
Wood, Ralph, 381
Wood, Robert, **335**
Wood, Thomas, **233**, 238
Woodhouse, Sir Thomas, **113**
Woodhouse, Thomas, 236
Woodrove, Sir Richard, 391
Wooler, William, **293**, 310
Wormeley, Margaret, 241
Wormeley, Thomas, 241, 333
Wortley, Sir Francis, **247**
Wright, John, 147
Wymer, Thomas, 119

York, Sir Richard, **255**, 390